Advance Praise for
The Advocate College Guide for LGBT Students

"A wealth of information to help the LGBT high school senior make an intelligent college choice. *The Advocate College Guide for LGBT Students* has provided a much-needed resource that should be on the bookshelves of every high school guidance office."
—*Savannah Pacer, Mother of Kerry Pacer, 17-year-old high school senior and* The Advocate *2005 Person of the Year*

"I hear stories of loneliness and anxiety every day—young people who feel alone and unsupported by their communities, families, and friends. *The Advocate College Guide for LGBT Students* gives hope to thousands of young people who are seeking a supportive educational environment in which they can learn, grow, and form relationships that will allow them to lead happy, healthy lives. I commend this work."
—*Jorge Valencia, President and Executive Director, The Trevor Project—National Suicide Prevention Helpline*

"The only book of its kind, *The Advocate College Guide for LGBT Students* is a must-have for queer students beginning the college search process. As an LGBT high school junior, the guide provides a remarkable resource, giving insight into the climate of colleges and the resources available for LGBT students. While other college guides pay mere lip service to LGBT issues if mentioned at all, this guidebook incorporates quotes from actual members of the LGBT campus community, allowing prospective students to see what LGBT campus life is really all about. Covering all of the topics essential to queer students—from the LGBT-friendly academic courses to the LGBT social calendar to the queer resources available on campus—*The Advocate College Guide for LGBT Students* answers all of the queer-related questions. The guide is just in time for LGBT students like me. Thank you!" —*Charlie Syms, LGBT high school junior, Class of 2007*

"This is an indispensable source of information for college-bound students and their parents. While LGBT college students truly are everywhere and on every campus, *The Advocate College Guide for LGBT Students* delivers an insider's look at the academic climates and the social scenes at schools where LGBT students are allowed to flourish. This is perhaps the most useful—and important—information ever compiled for helping LGBT high school students find a campus that's right for them."
—*Neil G. Giuliano, President, Gay & Lesbian Alliance Against Defamation (GLAAD)*

"How times have changed! *The Advocate College Guide for LGBT Students* provides information on both the academic life and social life for LGBT students . . . a source book for queers, if you will, to assist in choosing an institution of higher education where they can feel safe, valued, and appreciated. The fact that this resource exists is testament to how far we have come in regards to institutionalizing LGBT issues in higher education." —*Susan Rankin, Ph.D., Senior Diversity Planning Analyst and Assistant Professor, Office of the Vice Provost for Educational Equity, Pennsylvania State University*

Also by Shane L. Windmeyer, M.S., Ed.

Brotherhood: Gay Life in College Fraternities

Inspiration for LGBT Students and Their Allies
(co-author)

Secret Sisters: Stories of Being Lesbian and Bisexual in a College Sorority
(with Pamela W. Freeman)

Out on Fraternity Row: Personal Accounts of Being Gay in a College Fraternity
(with Pamela W. Freeman)

the Advocate

COLLEGE GUIDE

FOR LGBT STUDENTS

SHANE L. WINDMEYER, M.S.,Ed.

alyson books
NEW YORK

© 2006 by Shane L. Windmeyer. All rights reserved.

Manufactured in the United States of America.

This trade paperback original is published by Alyson Books,
P.O. Box 1253, Old Chelsea Station, New York, New York 10113-1251.
Distribution in the United Kingdom by Turnaround Publisher Services Ltd.,
Unit 3, Olympia Trading Estate, Coburg Road, Wood Green,
London N22 6TZ England.

First Edition: August 2006

06 07 08 09 00 **a** 10 9 8 7 6 5 4 3 2 1

ISBN 1-55583-857-X
ISBN-13 978-1-55583-857-7

The Library of Congress Cataloging-in-Publishing data is on file.

Illustrations: Thomas A. Feldman, Tyvola Design, Charlotte, NC.

Dedicated to the first generation
of "out" college students: The time is now.

• •

The Time Is Now
by Elizabeth Marie Couch

You pack your cardboard boxes
With assorted memories
And board a plane or hit the road
Or sail the shining seas.
And though you're full of promise—
Of dreams and Great Unknowns,
Your fear, at times, blows cold and hard
And chills you to your bones.

But deep down in your soul there stirs
Those stories you once wrote
When wax crayon on parchment sheets
Were the records of your hopes.
You wrote of your castle with towering walls
That sat on cotton clouds,
You were fearless and brilliant with nothing to lose,
You thought and laughed out loud.
You were a baby of the moonlight
And a child of the sky.
Your only wish? To be a bird
With wings so you could fly.

So here you are with arms outstretched,
Journeying through life.
You've found yourself against the wall,
And known your share of strife.
But regardless of your troubles,
And regardless of the tears,
Regardless of the friends you've met
And lost throughout the years,
You've done your time in purgatory,
So let those old dogs lie.
Make light your feet and close your eyes . . .

It's time for you to fly.

CONTENTS

Vassar College
Washington State University
Wellesley College
Whitman College
Williams College
Yale University

INTRODUCTION

The Advocate College Guide for LGBT Students is the companion to your college search. This valuable resource showcases campuses that have demonstrated an ongoing commitment to lesbian, gay, bisexual, and transgender (LGBT) students and helps you prepare for determining the most progressive and LGBT-friendly campus choices for you.

You and your family may read the guide page by page, starting with "The Top 10 Criteria LGBT Students Look for in a Campus" (which follows the introduction), taking notes about what you like and what stands out about each campus. You might only glance at the Gay Point Average of the colleges and universities in your region of the country. Or you might want to read through the "Buzz Bites" quotes to see what catches your attention. No matter what your approach, the guide was designed with all of this in mind and many more ways to help you find what you want.

This college guide represents the best 100 LGBT campuses "out" there, arranged alphabetically. But remember, progress is relative and there is still much work to be done to achieve LGBT equality on campuses and in society. Depending on the region of the country, some colleges may have a longer way to go and may be confronting different issues. Consider this when you think about what type of campus environment you want and need. Read about the campus LGBT history, services, and annual events as indicators of the campus climate and progress. There is plenty of diversity among the 100 campuses listed to help you choose the one just right for you.

For the campus officials using this guide in program development and recruiting, there is a section titled "Advice for Campus Officials to Improve LGBT Efforts" with contributions from top experts in the field.

The Advocate College Guide for LGBT Students started by asking current LGBT students across the United States, "What campuses do you consider to be LGBT-friendly?"

More than a year of planning and design went into shaping the strategy and criteria for selecting the best four-year LGBT campuses across the United States. LGBT student populations, faculty, staff, and administrators were contacted with the support of the National Consortium of Directors of LGBT Resources in Higher Education through Campus PrideNet, a national online network committed to LGBT and ally student leaders and campus organizations. Without their expert advice, the college guide would not live up to the vision of being a true LGBT voice. Through this extensive network of experts— administrators and LGBT students themselves—the challenge was met head-on.

In January 2005, a national "Call for Nominations from LGBT Students" was issued and the release ran in regional LGBT newspapers, college newspapers, online LGBT community channels and list serves, as well as national media like mtvU. Only current LGBT college students could nominate a campus and 680 individual campuses received at least one nomination that next month. All campuses that received a nomination were required to have at least five current LGBT college students and at least one faculty or staff member take an online interview.

The online interviews were designed differently for students and staff to determine the LGBT friendliness and inclusive practices from each campus. Various questions also probed campus-climate measures such as support and institutional commitment, campus policies, academic life, housing, student life, campus safety, counseling and health, as well as recruitment and retention efforts.

A total of 4,650 online interviews were completed by current LGBT students and 560 online interviews with faculty and staff on campuses across the country. The response rate is significant in light of the fact that there are only 561 known campuses in the United States that have sexual orientation as part of their campus nondiscrimination policies[1] and just over 60 campuses that have the same inclusion policy for gender identity or expression.[2]

A list of 212 colleges and universities made the final cut. Any campus that scored less than a ten out of twenty on the Gay Point Average was immediately eliminated from the pool. Further attention was paid to ensure LGBT progress was represented in a diversity of ways—type of institutions, campus size as well as regional locales. A final evaluation tool was designed to gather more LGBT student perspectives and to choose the top 100 LGBT-friendly campuses presented in this first edition of *The Advocate College Guide for LGBT Students*.

Remember that the college guide is based mainly on LGBT student perspectives and the facts related to current policies and practices listed in the Gay Point Average. Things do change on campus. So on your campus visit, ask plenty of questions. Use the resources at the end of this guide to help determine what questions to ask and how to dig deep to get the answers you want.

Good luck with your search!

by Shane L. Windmeyer, M.S.,Ed.

1 Human Rights Campaign. http://www.hrc.org, accessed May 20, 2006.

2 Transgender Law & Policy Institute. http://www.transgenderlaw.org, accessed May 20, 2006

TOP 10 CRITERIA LGBT STUDENTS LOOK FOR IN A CAMPUS

BEFORE YOU BEGIN reading the 100 best LGBT campus profiles, there is an important question to ask yourself: Do you know what you're looking for? Even more, do you know what exactly you want or need in a college in terms of LGBT issues? Possibly hearing perspectives from other out LGBT high school students can help you to consider all your choices. Following is a top 10 list compiled from feedback of LGBT high school students searching for the best LGBT campus. Keep this list close by as you narrow down your LGBT campus choice. Think about whether any of these LGBT issues matter to you and how much!

1. ACTIVE LGBT STUDENT ORGANIZATION(S) ON CAMPUS   For many campuses, it all started with a queer student organization creating positive change. LGBT students want to find a sense of community with their peers. LGBT student organizations provide social, educational, and leadership opportunities which many students ask for in a college campus.

   Such groups are critical to the well-being of LGBT students as a social network, support system, and outlet for activism. Some students inquire about groups specific to gender identity/expression, students of color, religion, and special interests/activities. What do you want in LGBT student organizations on your future campus?

2. OUT LGBT STUDENTS   "Where are the queers?" That is how one LGBT high school student put it. Prospective LGBT college students look for other LGBT students to be visible and active in all aspects of the academic setting and campus life.

3. OUT LGBT FACULTY AND STAFF   LGBT students have stated their desire for visible role models to identify with and to provide insight into the local community. Out LGBT faculty and staff can serve as advisers and be a common thread of support throughout the college years.

4. LGBT-INCLUSIVE POLICIES   Campus policies demonstrate a commitment and a standard for students to follow. They are a campus promise of sorts. LGBT-supportive campuses have "sexual orientation" in their nondiscrimination policy. Another indicator of LGBT support, although it currently appears in a smaller number of campus policies, are the words "gender identity or expression" in the campus nondiscrimination statement. Also indicators of LGBT-inclusiveness are a campus policy for same-sex domestic partner benefits or trans-inclusive health benefits. Each of these policies expresses an acceptance level of the campus and its commitment to LGBT issues.

5. VISIBLE SIGNS OF PRIDE   Rainbow flags and pink triangles are socio-environmental influences that can create a sense of openness, safety, and inclusion in the campus community toward LGBT issues. Their prominent presence also sends a clear signal that it is "okay to be gay." Other visible signs would include an Ally or Safe Space/Safe Zone program.

6. OUT LGBT ALLIES FROM THE TOP DOWN   Allies are essential to LGBT students, especially those found in LGBT-friendly college administrations. LGBT students listen for top-level administrators such as the president, vice president, or a dean to include LGBT issues in the campus dialogue. Visible allies are also important in the classroom and in student life on campus. Listen for examples of how allies stand up for LGBT students on campus.

7. LGBT-INCLUSIVE HOUSING AND GENDER-NEUTRAL BATHROOMS   The option for LGBT-theme housing and gender-neutral bathrooms are elements that foster an LGBT atmosphere conducive to living and learning.

8. ESTABLISHED LGBT CENTER/OFFICE ON CAMPUS   Many LGBT students check right away to see what committed campus resources are available. One of the most easily recognizable and visible support services is an established LGBT center/office on campus. Such a place allows for queer students and allies to build friendships, find support, and learn about LGBT issues. They also serve as the hub of LGBT campus life. A college that has an LGBT center or office shows a commitment to LGBT students that goes beyond words, especially if the center/office has dedicated paid professional staff. Remember that it may not be realistic for a smaller campus to have a separate center/office, but you can look beyond that for other LGBT commitments and resources.

9. LGBT/QUEER STUDIES ACADEMIC MAJOR OR MINOR   Some LGBT high school students are looking for a campus with outlets to study LGBT issues. Their passion in life is to not only get a degree but also take classes where they can learn about LGBT identity, politics, and history. And for some that means even graduating with an academic major or minor in LGBT/queer studies.

10. LIBERAL ATTITUDE AND VIBRANT LGBT SOCIAL SCENE   These are actually two separate issues, but they are interrelated. LGBT students want to be accepted fully and not merely be tolerated. In addition, a vibrant LGBT social scene not only is a high priority but can also mean different things to each student. Some LGBT students want to live on a campus that offers queer entertainment choices, whereas others prefer relying on the local city where the campus resides, for activities. Whatever your need, take note of the liberalness and the queer life on campus. Then, determine what you desire.

The Format

Each of the colleges and universities listed in the book has a three-page profile. The profile format is designed to be user-friendly, easy to read, and informative. Look at the breakdown below to understand what each profile has to offer and where to find the information that is most useful to you.

NAME AND CONTACT INFORMATION   Along with the name of the college or university, the top of every profile offers the address, telephone, fax, and e-mail for the admissions office and the campus's Website address. If the campus is above and beyond, you may also find the "Best of the Best Top 20" seal of approval.

CAMPUS STATS   The "Campus Stats" section lists the type of institution, founding year, campus undergraduate size, average class size, the popular majors, the cost, and the admission application deadline.

LGBT POLITICS PROGRESSIVE METER   As many of us know, a campus is a product of its location: the state and the local community. Most colleges are much more progressive on LGBT issues than their surrounding locales. Others are only slightly better or the same. The "LGBT Politics Progressive Meter" gives you a quick rundown on where the state, the local community, and the campus fall on being LGBT-progressive in politics. It's a handy tool to put you in the mind-set to gauge for yourself.

OUTSPOKEN: ANSWERS FROM LGBT STUDENTS   Hear from the real college experts on whether or not a campus is LGBT-friendly. This section, comprised entirely of LGBT student perspectives, is divided into three parts: the "Overall Campus Environment," the "Academic Scene," and the "Social Scene."
   Under the "Overall Campus Environment" you can find the top three ways that LGBT students describe the campus along with student answers to the questions "What makes your campus feel welcome and safe for LGBT students?" and "How do you feel about coming out on your campus?" In the "Academic Scene" there are listed the top three supportive academic areas and student answers to the questions: "How LGBT friendly are faculty in the classroom?" And in case you're interested in the Social Scene, the last part details the top three things to do in the LGBT social life as well as answers to the questions "How would you describe the social scene for LGBT students?" and "What annual social event should an LGBT student not miss?"
   Plus, all students quoted detail their age, gender identity/expression, sexual orientation, and class standing in their own words, so you might better relate to the particular individual and view a diversity of responses. This section will answer many of your questions and lend the perspective directly from the minds of LGBT students.

BUZZ BITES   This section samples of the best LGBT offerings, by category, at a glance.

OUTRAGEOUS FACTOID   This section looks at interesting, out-of-the-ordinary facts about the campus. They're a great way to start a chat on your campus visit.

THE RAINBOW RUMOR   This section highlights areas for improvement indicated by LGBT students, faculty, and/or staff on the campus.

"THAT'S SO GAY?!" ANNUAL LGBT EVENT HIGHLIGHTS   A listing of annual LGBT events that take place throughout the year is provided to show the various activities and events available to LGBT students.

THE GAY POINT AVERAGE OFFICIAL CAMPUS CHECKLIST   The Gay Point Average Official Campus Checklist was specifically designed for scoring campus policies, programs, and practices. The checklist targets different aspects of the campus climate to render a score up to 20 possible points. You can quickly see where a campus stands out on LGBT issues by looking at the checked responses. The Gay Point Average checklist provides an excellent quick reference to the most important factors of an LGBT-friendly and progressive it.

CAMPUS QUEER RESOURCES   The "Campus Queer Resource" section provides the names of select LGBT student organizations, the founding dates and numbers of members, as well as contact information. If there is an LGBT resource center/office or an office that is responsible for LGBT issues, you can also find out where to go and how to contact it.

The Terminology

LGBT words and descriptions may have different meanings based on your experience. The following presents an alphabetical listing of a variety of terms that appear in this guidebook along with definitions to better understand and gain insight into what the campus offers LGBT students.

Ally: A person who advocates for and supports members of the LGBT community. More broadly, any person who reaches out across differences to achieve mutual goals on behalf of another community.

Bias Incident Team: A campus method to systematically report incidents of bias or prejudice that do not rise to the level of a bias or hate crime. Other descriptors used might be "Bias Response Team" or "Bias Response Protocol."

Coming Out Week: A week of educational and social events to recognize the importance of coming out and lend support to others making the decision. Usually planned during the National LGBT History Month of October or the observance of National Coming Out Day on October 11.

Domestic Partner Benefits: Domestic partner benefits are a legal method for extending the same workplace benefits of married heterosexual couples to the same-sex partners of employees. Such benefits usually include medical and dental insurance, disability and life insurance, pension benefits, family and bereavement leave, education and tuition assistance, credit union membership, reimbursement of relocation and travel expenses, and inclusion of same-sex partners in events and gatherings.

Drag: The act of dressing in gendered clothing as part of a performance. Drag queens perform in highly feminine attire. Drag kings perform in highly masculine attire. Drag may be performed as a political comment on gender, as parody, or simply as entertainment. Drag performances or the drag performers are not to be confused with indication of sexuality, gender identity, or sex identity.

F-to-M: Female-to-Male Transsexual. A transsexual sometimes undergoes medical treatment to change his/her physical sex to match his/her sex identity through hormone treatments and/or surgery. Not all people who are transgender can have or desire surgery.

Gay Point Average: Refers to the ranking of campus policies, programs, and practices. The score targets different aspects of the campus climate and provides a solid measure of LGBT progress.

Gay-pril: An affectionate term for the many LGBT events and activities that happen during the month of April on many college campuses.

Gender Identity: The gender that a person considers him- or herself to be. This may include refusing to label oneself with a gender. Gender identity should not be fused with sexual orientation. Gender identity is separate and has no causal relationship with sexual orientation. For example, a feminine man is not necessarily gay.

Gender-Neutral Bathrooms: A bathroom where the signage is visibly identified with open, inclusive language: not just male or female. It is evident that these facilities are void of gender identity and have accommodations that are especially sensitive to the needs of transgender individuals.

Genderqueer: A person who redefines or plays with gender, or who refuses gender labels altogether. A label for people who bend or break the rules of gender and blur the boundaries.

Gender-Variant/Gender Nonconforming: Displaying gender traits that are not normatively associated with their biological sex. "Feminine" behavior or appearance in a male is gender-variant, as is "masculine" behavior or appearance in a female. Gender-variant behavior is culturally specific.

Lavender Graduation/Rainbow Graduation: A special ceremony designed to recognize graduating LGBT and ally students on college campuses. Some of these ceremonies may include a guest speaker, a reception, or a formal presentation.

LGBT: The acronym for Lesbian, Gay, Bisexual, Transgender individuals.

LGBT and Ally Student Organization: A campus group of students who have a primary purpose centering on LGBT issues. Many of these groups form coalitions and interest around political issues, social opportunities, gender identities and/or cultural identities.

LGBT Alumni Group: A group of alumni that has formed with the primary purpose of supporting LGBT issues at their alma mater. Many of these groups publish newsletters, plan alumni events, raise scholarship monies, and support the campus in a variety of LGBT-visible ways.

LGBT Housing Options and Themes: A specific method and/or program designed for housing LGBT students. Examples include a residence hall floor for LGBT students and allies, or a living-learning community based on social justice and LGBT issues. Inclusive housing options may also include methods for choosing an LGBT-sensitive roommate or ways to request gender-neutral living spaces.

LGBT Resource Center/Office: A visible space to educate on LGBT issues and respond to the needs of the LGBT campus community. The center/office usually plans a number of LGBT events and activities throughout the year and serves as the main hub of queer activity. Other services offered may include counseling, peer mentoring, a library, lounge spaces, staff offices, computers, and multi-media entertainment. Many center/office spaces operate under different LGBT-identified names like "The Q Center," "LGBT Student Services Office," or "The Stonewall Center." Most have a full-time professional staff or at minimum part-time graduate-level staff.

LGBT Speakers Bureau/Speaker Panels: An educational awareness program consisting of LGBT and possibly straight ally students who participate individually, in pairs, or in a group panel presentation on LGBT concerns. Such a program may be offered anywhere on campus, but is most often largely facilitated in academic classroom settings.

LGBT Studies and Courses: A collection of and/or individual course offerings for academic credit primarily focused on LGBT issues and concerns. Many campuses offer an academic concentration, a minor, or a major in LGBT studies.

LGBT Student Scholarship: An opportunity specifically offered to incoming and/or current students for financial assistance related to a combination of LGBT-focused criteria.

M-to-F: Male-to-Female Transsexual; A transsexual sometimes undergoes medical treatment to change his/her physical sex to match his/her sex identity through hormone treatments and/or surgery. Not all transsexuals can have or desire surgery.

National Coming Out Day: A national event for LGBT people to "come out" to others about their gender identity/expression and sexual orientation. The observance also provides a means of increasing the visibility of LGBT people. The first National Coming Out Day was held on October 11, 1988. This date was chosen to commemorate the 1987 March on Washington for Lesbian and Gay Rights.

National Day of Silence: A national event originally initiated by college students as a day of action, when those who support making anti-LGBT bias unacceptable take a day-long vow of silence to recognize and protest the discrimination and harassment—in effect, the silencing—experienced by LGBT students and their allies. The event takes place traditionally in the month of April and is organized jointly by the Gay, Lesbian and Straight Education Network and the United States Student Association.

National Transgender Day of Remembrance: The observance symbolizes a day set aside to memorialize those who have been killed due to anti-transgender hatred or prejudice. The event is held annually in November to honor Rita Hester, whose murder in 1998 kicked off the "Remembering Our Dead" web project and a San Francisco candlelight vigil in 1999. Rita Hester's murder—like most anti-transgender murder cases—has yet to be solved. The Day of Remembrance gives allies and LGBT individuals a chance to step forward and stand in vigil, memorialize those who have died, and continue the fight for transgender rights for those who are living.

Nondiscrimination Statement: Also sometimes referred to as "antidiscrimination" statements or policies. A policy against the act of discrimination, supporting the belief that decisions involving students and employees be based on individual merit and be free from any prejudice, bias and/or discrimination. Colleges in particular have these statements as a way to show a commitment to fundamental principles of academic freedom, equality of opportunity, and human dignity. Some campuses are required by state law to include them in order to qualify for funding. LGBT-inclusive nondiscrimination statements expressly include the words "sexual orientation" as well as "gender identity or expression."

Out: Refers to varying degrees of being open about one's sexual orientation and/or gender identity or expression.

Pride Week: A week of educational and social events to celebrate being LGBT and acknowledge queer identity in general. Along with guest LGBT speakers, a common form of entertainment to top off the week is a campus-wide drag show. Usually the week is planned during the month of April or the spring term.

Queer: A term used in a number of different ways as an umbrella term for lesbian, gay, bisexual, transgender, intersex, genderqueer and other non-heterosexual identities. Many LGBT members of Generation Y adopted the term as a way to reclaim a once negative term: to remove queer as a term of abuse. "Queer" was first widely used after the Gay Liberation Movement of the 1970s. Some believe the term "queer" also alludes to a fluidity of gender and sexuality and a rejection of socially imposed categories.

Rainbow Flag: A symbol of LGBT pride and celebration, the six bold-colored stripes of the flag (red, orange, yellow, green, blue, and purple) can be seen flown in pride marches and other queer celebrations. Also referred to as the Rainbow Freedom Flag, it was designed in 1978 by Gilbert Baker to reflect the diversity of the LGBT community, and has been recognized by the International Flag Makers Association as the official flag of the LGBT civil rights movement.

Safe Zone/Safe Space or Ally Program: A campus-wide program designed for outreach and training of visible LGBT allies. An important aspect of such a program is a readily identified LGBT symbol, which designates a person as a visible advocate who is comfortable with, willing to listen to, and understand the needs of individuals who have LGBT issues and concerns. The program may be referred to as a "Safe Zone," a "Safe Space," an "Ally Space" or a combination thereof. Some programs include a mandatory training for students, faculty, or staff to become a "Safe Zone/Safe Space Ally" while others do not require training of any kind. Some programs not only include LGBT advocates but also represent other marginalized or oppressed communities.

Sexual Orientation: An internal feeling or direction of one's sexual attraction; referring to the sex, sexes, gender, or genders that form the focus of a person's sexual inclinations and desires. Sexual orientation evolves through a multistage developmental process and is considered to be a born genetic trait by many in the LGBT and scientific communities.

Stonewall: Refers to "Stonewall Inn," the name of a local bar in New York City, which was a hangout for predominantly homosexual men. On July 28, 1969, New York police raided the Mafia-owned bar with a charge of illegal sale of alcohol, in an attempt to arrest the more "deviant" patrons, as they were then referred to (drag queens and butch lesbians, especially those of color). Patrons decided to fight back and rioted in the streets, setting off a weekend of protests and demonstrations. The event is often considered to be a pivotal point in queer history, marking the beginning of the LGBT civil rights movement.

Transgender: An umbrella term for transsexuals, cross-dressers (transvestites), transgenderists, genderqueers, and people who identify as neither female nor male and/or as neither a man nor a woman. Transgender is not a sexual orientation; transgender people may have any sexual orientation. It is important to acknowledge that while some people may fit under this definition of transgender, they may not identify with this umbrella terminology.

World AIDS Day: An international day of action on the issue of HIV and AIDS which takes place every year on December 1. Customary events include a vigil, rally, and/or educational awareness campaigns and activities. Some campuses designate an entire week in December for World AIDS Day.

100 BEST CAMPUSES FOR LGBT STUDENTS

BEST OF THE BEST TOP 20 CAMPUSES

The "BEST OF THE BEST Top 20 Campuses" rise above expectations as pioneering LGBT leaders in higher education. Not only do the campuses rank among the highest on the Gay Point Average but they also boast the most outstanding accomplishments for LGBT progressiveness across the United States. The campuses chosen for the "BEST OF THE BEST" represent a diverse array of demographics such as type of institution, locale, and size.

American University
Duke University
Indiana University
New York University
Oberlin College
Ohio State University
Pennsylvania State University
Princeton University
Stanford University
Tufts University
University of California—Berkeley
University of California—Los Angeles
University of California—Santa Cruz
University of Massachusetts—Amherst
University of Michigan
University of Minnesota—Twin Cities
University of Oregon
University of Pennsylvania
University of Puget Sound
University of Southern California

AMERICAN UNIVERSITY

A LEADER IN LGBT issues in higher education, American University was among the first to include sexual orientation and gender identity/expression in the campus nondiscrimination clause. In addition, the Gay, Lesbian, Bisexual, Transgender and Ally Resource Center takes pride in its advocacy role, showing tremendous dedication to LGBT educational programming and resources.

From the moment you walk on campus, the presence of LGBT people and issues is apparent—whether you notice the Safe Space stickers on office doors or the "queer-tagious" bulletin boards in the residence halls. LGBT issues are addressed throughout the campus community. The Admissions Office even has an outreach program for prospective queer students. Plus, the bonus of being in Washington, DC, means that many American University students have the opportunity to hone their queer leadership skills by interning at organizations like the National Gay and Lesbian Task Force, the Human Rights Campaign, the Mautner Project, and the National Center for Transgender Equality. Some LGBT students have even worked in the offices of queer members of Congress, such as Barney Frank and Tammy Baldwin.

Perhaps the most telling comment comes from a new LGBT student on campus during the opening fall mixer: "I've just never seen so many gay people in one place before. That there are so many out faculty members and staff members on campus! You can't be here and not meet gay people—not only students but also the person teaching your class or your admissions counselor or your resident director. It just makes campus feel like a really safe and welcoming place."

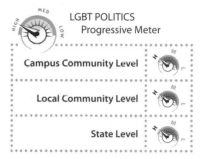

LGBT POLITICS
Progressive Meter

Campus Community Level

Local Community Level

State Level

OUTSPOKEN *Answers from LGBT students:*

Top Three Descriptors of the LGBT Campus Environment:
1. Visible   2. Political   3. Fabulous

What makes your campus feel welcoming and safe for LGBT students?
"The omnipresence of a large out student population influences even straight students to be more tolerant and makes for an overall positive atmosphere."
—23-year-old gay male, senior

"Pretty much as soon as I got here, I discovered I could be completely out and accepted for who I am. The vast majority of students, faculty, and staff are at the very least open to new perspectives, if not already accepting of LGBT people."
—21-year-old genderqueer lesbian, senior

How do you feel about coming out on your campus?
"Coming out isn't an issue here."   *—21-year-old gay male, senior*

"I've been out the entire time I've been at AU, and I have had a considerable number of other students come out to me because they see me as a visible part of the campus LGBT community. It's a fantastic thought that my comfort with my identities can help others develop confidence in their own."   *—21-year-old genderqueer lesbian, senior*

INFO

AMERICAN UNIVERSITY
4400 Massachusetts Avenue, NW
Washington, DC 20016
Phone: 202-885-6000
Fax: 202-885-6014
E-mail: admissions@american.edu
Website: www.american.edu

CAMPUS STATS
Type of Institution: Private university, Methodist religious affiliation
Founding Year: 1893
Size: 5,870
Avg. Class Size: 20 students
Popular Majors: Business Administration/Management, International Relations and Affairs, Mass Communications/Media Studies
Cost: Tuition: $27,552
Admission Application Deadline: January 15

• • • • • • • • • • • • • • • • • • • •

• • • • • • • • • • • • • • • • • • • •

THAT'S SO GAY!

ANNUAL LGBT EVENT HIGHLIGHTS

Fall Mixer and Spring Mixer: Beginning of each semester

LGBT Alumni Reception for Homecoming Week: October

Coming Out Week: Around October 11

Drag Show: National Coming Out Week

Lavender Languages and Linguistics Conference: February

Freedom to Marry Day: Around February 14

National Day of Silence: April

LGBT and Ally Awards/Graduation Ceremony: End of April

LGBT Job Search and Career Workshop : Spring

ACADEMIC SCENE

Top Three Supportive LGBT Academic Areas:
1. Anthropology   2. Literature   3. Sociology

How LGBT-friendly are faculty in the classroom?

"I find the faculty exceptionally friendly because a lot of them are gay themselves! Also, many have incorporated gender/sexual identity into their curriculum." —*18-year-old lesbian, sophomore*

"They are very open to LGBT topics and never seem awkward when an LGBT question is brought up." —*18-year-old gay male, freshman*

SOCIAL SCENE

Top Three Things in the LGBT Social Life:
1. Mixers   2. Queers and Allies   3. Dancing

How would you describe the social scene for LGBT students?

"Never been gayer." —*32-year-old gay male, graduate student*

"Fabulous LGBT social scene—eclectic, from bars and clubs to art and readings. There is something for everyone." —*20-year-old gay male, junior*

"The social scene on campus is fairly constant. There are a lot of groups and activities for LGBT students, and people are always welcome to socialize in the Resource Center." —*19-year-old lesbian, sophomore*

What annual social event should an LGBT student not miss?

"The GLBTA RC Mixer. A good time for all students to meet other members of the community." —*20-year-old gay male, junior*

"The Drag Show in October. The DC Kings, some queens, and Queers and Allies put together an awesome show that fills the Tavern to capacity to raise money for a different local DC charity every year that does work to improve the lives of LGBT people." —*21-year-old genderqueer lesbian, senior*

BUZZ BITES *Fun Queer Stuff to Know*

THE BEST...

Party Locale: Apex *or* Liquid Ladies

Hangout: Sparky's Café *or* Dupont Circle area

Eating Place: Hamburger Mary's

Place to Check Out Guys: Lambda Rising *or* Capitol Hill

Place to Check Out Ladies: Takoma Park

LGBT-Cool Athletic Sport: Men's swimming *and* women's rugby

Non-LGBT-Specific Campus Club: Rude Mechanicals Theater Troupe

LGBT Course Offering: Gay and Lesbian Documentary Film Class

LGBT Educational Involvement Opportunity: Rainbow Speakers Bureau

LGBT-Accepting Religious/Spiritual Organization(s): Methodist Student Association *and* Jewish Student Association

THE GAY POINT AVERAGE
OFFICIAL CAMPUS CHECKLIST

LGBT & ally student organization ✓

LGBT resource center/office ✓

LGBT Pride Week &/or Coming Out Week ✓

Safe Zone/Safe Space or Ally Program ✓

Significant number of LGBT social activities ✓

Significant number of LGBT educational events ✓

Variety of LGBT studies/courses ✓

Nondiscrimination statement inclusive of sexual orientation ✓

Nondiscrimination statement inclusive of gender identity/expression ✓

Extends domestic partner benefits to same-sex couples ✓

Actively recruits LGBT students to enroll on campus ✓

Trains campus police on LGBT sensitivity ✓

Procedure for reporting LGBT bias, harassment & hate crimes ✓

Offers LGBT housing options/themes

Offers LGBT-inclusive health services/testing ✓

Offers LGBT-inclusive counseling/support groups ✓

Offers LGBT student scholarships ✓

Conducts special LGBT graduation ceremony for LGBT & ally Students ✓

Offers support services for process of transitioning from M to F & F to M ✓

Active LGBT alumni group ✓

UNIVERSITY
GAY POINT AVERAGE (19)
(out of 20)

CAMPUS QUEER RESOURCES

Select LGBT Student Organization(s):
Queers and Allies, Lambda Grads, and Lambda Law Society
Founding Date: Queers and Allies (1970s, under several different names); Lambda Grads (1994); Lambda Law Society (1984).
Membership: 50+ on average
Phone(s): 202-885-3347 or 202-274-4410
E-mail: queersandallies@american.edu
Website(s): www.american.edu/ocl/glbta/ groups/campus_clubs.html or www.wcl.american.edu/org/lambda/

LGBT resource center/office:
Gay, Lesbian, Bisexual, Transgender, and Ally Resource Center
American University
201 Mary Graydon Center
4400 Massachusetts Avenue, NW
Washington, DC 20016 8164
Year Established: 1994
Number of Staff: 2 full-time professional, 6–8 student staff members
Phone: 202-885-3347
E-mail: glbta@american.edu
Website: www.american.edu/glbta

ANTIOCH COLLEGE

The official motto of Antioch College is, "*Be ashamed to die until you have won some victory for humanity.*" Well, LGBT students at Antioch College have been forging a fight to create a welcoming LGBT campus and they believe they have done just that. One LGBT student remarks: "At Antioch, acceptance is widespread." The college has been on a winning path since 1969, when an LGBT student organized the Homophile Discussion Group and held the first organized group of lesbians and gays on campus. These efforts gave birth to the current Queer Center for LGBT students and the beginning of necessary "consciousness raising" from coast to coast in the dawn of the LGBT movement. And it was happening in southwestern Ohio. Antioch College ranks among the first in the nation and in the state of Ohio in terms of early LGBT student organizing.

Today the queer progress continues. LGBT students not only have the Queer Center but also have new efforts like the burgeoning LGBT student of color group, called "Queer Colors," and a recently formed transgender support group. Together, these groups plan social and educational experiences on campus and do outreach to area colleges. Plus, the campus hosts annual LGBT events like Queer Take-Over Week, National Coming Out Day and the GenderFuck Dance Party. All the queer events are the rage and are well attended by queers and allies alike. With an edge of humor, one LGBT student admits: "Straight people feel left out here, like I want to be 'one of the cool kids.'"

Antioch College has been LGBT-inclusive for a number of years. Another LGBT student shares: "Being queer is just another facet of diversity, which is the foundation of Antioch. It's kind of what makes Antioch what it is."

LGBT POLITICS
Progressive Meter

Campus Community Level

Local Community Level

State Level

𝟿𝟿 OUTSPOKEN *Answers from LGBT students:*

Top Three Descriptors of the LGBT Campus Environment:
1. Liberal 2. Accepting 3. Diverse

What makes your campus feel welcoming and safe for LGBT students?
"The queer community is a large and ever-present part of the Antioch community. Its focuses are exploring and supporting queer students, faculty and staff's specific issues and needs while representing the queer community as a whole." —*27-year-old femme dyke, junior*

How do you feel about coming out on your campus?
"I was supported through the process of changing my identity while I was here. Antioch allows for changes in identity. … I can attend the Trans Support Group here on campus, which is student-run. There is a doctor in town [who] can write prescriptions for hormones and provide letters in support of having surgery." —*22-year-old queer F-to-M dyke, senior*

INFO

ANTIOCH COLLEGE
795 Livermore Street
Yellow Springs, OH 45387
Phone: 937-769-1100
Fax: 937-769-1111
E-mail: admissions@antioch-college.edu
Website: www.antioch-college.edu

CAMPUS STATS
Type of Institution: Private college
Founding Year: 1852
Size: 488
Avg. Class Size: Less than 10 students
Popular Majors: Ethnic Studies, Liberal Arts, Environmental Science
Cost: Tuition: $25,230
Admission Application Deadline: February 1

⊘ ACADEMIC SCENE

Top Three Supportive LGBT Academic Areas:
1. Women's Studies   2. Psychology   3. Gender and Sexualities

How LGBT-friendly are faculty in the classroom?
"There are queer faculty members here. Those classes are extremely friendly. Sexuality is Antioch's favorite topic, or so it seems. It has been nice to see myself reflected by the teachers here." —*27-year-old femme dyke, junior*

"Professors are extremely inclusive in regards to LGBT students. Most are gender-inclusive and are respectful of community members' decisions and identities." —*22-year-old queer F-to-M dyke, senior*

☺ SOCIAL SCENE

Top Three Things in the LGBT Social Life:
1. Socializing   2. Parties   3. Dancing

How would you describe the social scene for LGBT students?
"Three words: GenderFuck, GenderFuck, GenderFuck. The GLBT Center generally has the best parties, the safest parties, and the most creative and outrageous parties." —*27-year-old femme dyke, junior*

What annual social event should an LGBT student not miss?
"GenderFuck dance by far!" —*21-year-old bisexual female, junior*

OUTRAGEOUS FACTOID Forget about boundaries. People are free to define themselves however they choose and Antioch supports them. The annual GenderFuck dance party, hosted by the Queer Center, is one example. Everyone plays with gender and sexuality. For newbies, there is a drag workshop earlier in the day.

• • • • • • • • • • • • • • • • • • • •

RAINBOW RUMOR LGBT students readily admit that Antioch College is not completely trans-friendly but hope that the newly started Transgender Advocacy Group will help transform the campus. Some positive signs: the addition of gender identity and expression to the campus nondiscrimination statement in 2005, student advocacy for gender-neutral bathrooms, and trans-inclusive resident hall staff trainings.

• • • • • • • • • • • • • • • • • • • •

THAT'S SO GAY!

ANNUAL LGBT EVENT HIGHLIGHTS

Queer Take-Over Week: Fall/Spring

GenderFuck Dance Party: Fall/Spring

National Coming Out Day: October 11

World AIDS Day: December

Day of Silence: First week of April

Div Dance: End of Spring

BUZZ BITES *Fun Queer Stuff to Know*

THE BEST...

Hangout: Oregon District in Dayton

Eating Place: Winds Restaurant and Bakery, Current Cuisine

Place to Check Out Guys: Short North in Columbus

Place to Check Out Ladies: On Main in Dayton

Non-LGBT-Specific Campus Club: By Any Means Necessary Student of Color Group

LGBT Course Offering: Queer Cartographies

LGBT Educational Involvement Opportunity: Queer Center

LGBT-Accepting Religious/Spiritual Organization(s): Unitarian Universalist Church

Select LGBT Student Organization(s):

Queer Center
Founding Date: 1969
Phone: 937-769-1050

Resource Center/Office Responsible for LGBT Issues:

Coretta Scott King Center for Cultural and Intellectual Freedom

795 Livermore Street
Yellow Springs, OH 45387
Year Established: 1995
Number of Staff: 1 full-time professional staff member and many student workers
Phone: 937-769-1154
Website: www.antioch-college.edu/Campus/csk/index.html

THE GAY POINT AVERAGE OFFICIAL CAMPUS CHECKLIST

✓ LGBT & ally student organization

LGBT resource center/office

✓ LGBT Pride Week &/or Coming Out Week

Safe Zone/Safe Space or Ally Program

✓ Significant number of LGBT social activities

✓ Significant number of LGBT educational events

✓ Variety of LGBT studies/courses

✓ Nondiscrimination statement inclusive of sexual orientation

✓ Nondiscrimination statement inclusive of gender identity/expression

✓ Extends domestic partner benefits to same-sex couples

✓ Actively recruits LGBT students to enroll on campus

Trains campus police on LGBT sensitivity

✓ Procedure for reporting LGBT bias, harassment & hate crimes

Offers LGBT housing options/themes

✓ Offers LGBT-inclusive health services/testing

✓ Offers LGBT-inclusive counseling/support groups

Offers LGBT student scholarships

Conducts special LGBT graduation ceremony for LGBT & ally Students

✓ Offers support services for process of transitioning from M to F & F to M

Active LGBT alumni group

13 ANTIOCH COLLEGE GAY POINT AVERAGE
(out of 20)

BOWLING GREEN STATE UNIVERSITY

SITUATED IN NORTHWESTERN Ohio about 20 miles south of Toledo, Bowling Green State University has cultivated LGBT inclusiveness. LGBT students argue that the campus has become more and more LGBT-progressive each year, mostly thanks to the tenacity of LGBT and ally students, faculty and staff. In 1990, the first LGBT student group was formed, called Vision. Currently on campus, it's one of the five largest organizations and plans LGBT annual celebrations like the Welcome Back Dance, Coming Out Week, Transgender Awareness Days and the Vision Prom.

In 2003, an LGBT Task Force convened, which set up an LGBT Advisory Board. The board still deals directly with the administration and has several current queer projects, including an effort to develop gender-neutral restrooms across campus. As recently as 2005, the campus opened the LGBTA-Q Resource Center, which includes a library and educational resources. The center has been a leading advocate for progress on campus, especially in the area of transgender issues.

The Gay Point Average shows noteworthy queer accomplishments for Bowling Green State University. From one LGBT student: "I could not come out in my rural Ohio high school. There was nobody like me. I felt alone. Here the opposite is true. … an openness, acceptance and visibility can be found."

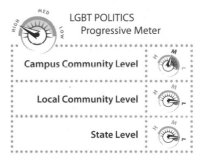

LGBT POLITICS
Progressive Meter

Campus Community Level

Local Community Level

State Level

OUTSPOKEN *Answers from LGBT students:*

Top Three Descriptors of the LGBT Campus Environment:
1. Empowering   2. Friendly   3. Improving

What makes your campus feel welcoming and safe for LGBT students?
"Having Vision and the LGBTA-Q Resource Center on campus is a huge help to making people feel welcome to campus. Also, having services like "Out@BGSU," a coming out counseling service, and the new "Gay and Greek Group" for gays/lesbians in a fraternity/sorority … makes everyone feel better about being here. With all of these programs, you know if you have a problem, there are people that you can turn to." *—20-year-old gay male, junior*

How do you feel about coming out on your campus?
"I am very comfortable with myself, so I don't mind coming out on campus. But I believe that there is way to do it. Some people take it too far." *—18-year-old gay male, freshman*

"My coming out was easy on campus, much more so than high school. Here at Bowling Green there are a lot of people who are very open-minded and accepting of people. I came out to two different roommates, and in both cases the experiences went quite well. I even rushed a fraternity as an openly gay male." *—20-year-old gay male, junior*

INFO

BOWLING GREEN STATE UNIVERSITY
110 McFall Center
Bowling Green, OH 43403
Phone: 419-372-2478
Fax: 419-372-6955
E-mail: choosebgsu@bgsu.edu
Website: www.bgsu.edu

CAMPUS STATS
Type of Institution: Public university
Founding Year: 1910
Size: 17,300
Avg. Class Size: 20–29 students
Popular Majors: Education, Business/Marketing, Early Childhood Education and Teaching, Psychology
Cost: In-state tuition: $6,818
Out-of-state tuition: $14,126
Admission Application Deadline: February 1

OUTRAGEOUS FACTOID COW does not stand for a large dairy animal with spots and a fat wet tongue. It's the gay secret code for Coming Out Week on campus. Every October you will see flyers with cows advertising LGBT events.

• • • • • • • • • • • • • • • • • • • •

RAINBOW RUMOR Be on the queer lookout! It is said that in less than five years, Women's Studies will have an LGBT minor.

• • • • • • • • • • • • • • • • • • • •

THAT'S SO GAY! **ANNUAL LGBT EVENT HIGHLIGHTS**

Welcome Back Dance: Fall

Coming Out Week: October

Vagina Monologues: February

Transgender Awareness Days: November

Day of Silence: March/April

Rainbow Days: April

Vision Prom: April

ACADEMIC SCENE

Top Three Supportive LGBT Academic Areas:
1. Women's Studies   2. American Culture Studies   3. Music, Theater and Film

How LGBT-friendly are faculty in the classroom?
"Most of the faculty at BGSU has been LGBT-friendly but sometimes forget to point things out, such as heterosexual privilege." —*19-year-old lesbian, sophomore*

"I have had many professors ask me to come and present to their class about LGBT issues, especially relating to the climate on BGSU's campus. Most professors themselves are interested in the topic and are willing to help out as much as they can." —*23-year-old gay male, graduate student*

SOCIAL SCENE

Top Three Things in the LGBT Social Life:
1. Vision   2. Hanging out   3. Dancing

How would you describe the social scene for LGBT students?
"Undergrads have Vision. Uptown has drag night, but it is not very interesting if you do not like that sort of scene. I just think LGBT students need to find a wonderful group of friends from all over the campus, not just in the LGBT community of students." —*21-year-old bisexual queer female, junior*

What annual social event should an LGBT student not miss?
"Oh my gosh … queer prom! So fun." —*19-year-old lesbian, sophomore*

BUZZ BITES *Fun Queer Stuff to Know*

THE BEST…

Party Locale: Uptown on Tuesday Gay Night

Hangout: LGBTA-Q Resource Center

Eating Place: The Union *and* Grounds for Thought

Place to Check Out Guys: On the Quad

Place to Check Out Ladies: Local coffee shop

LGBT-Cool Athletic Sport: Cheerleading

Non-LGBT-Specific Campus Club: Honors program

LGBT Educational Involvement Opportunity: Vision speaker panels

THE GAY POINT AVERAGE
OFFICIAL CAMPUS CHECKLIST

LGBT & ally student organization	✓
LGBT resource center/office	✓
LGBT Pride Week &/or Coming Out Week	✓
Safe Zone/Safe Space or Ally Program	✓
Significant number of LGBT social activities	✓
Significant number of LGBT educational events	✓
Variety of LGBT studies/courses	
Nondiscrimination statement inclusive of sexual orientation	✓
Nondiscrimination statement inclusive of gender identity/expression	
Extends domestic partner benefits to same-sex couples	
Actively recruits LGBT students to enroll on campus	
Trains campus police on LGBT sensitivity	✓
Procedure for reporting LGBT bias, harassment & hate crimes	✓
Offers LGBT housing options/themes	
Offers LGBT-inclusive health services/testing	
Offers LGBT-inclusive counseling/support groups	✓
Offers LGBT student scholarships	✓
Conducts special LGBT graduation ceremony for LGBT & ally Students	
Offers support services for process of transitioning from M to F & F to M	
Active LGBT alumni group	

BOWLING GREEN STATE UNIVERSITY GAY POINT AVERAGE

11

(out of 20)

BRYN MAWR COLLEGE

JUST WEST OF Philadelphia, Bryn Mawr College is quite visibly diverse. Students of color and international students make up nearly one-third of the campus community. But what about LGBT students?

For its size, Bryn Mawr has made some stellar progress toward LGBT-inclusive policies and practices. The campus commits to providing a safe space and supportive community for everyone, including queers. From the early 1980s until 2004, the student group Rainbow Alliance was Bryn Mawr's sole organizational network for LGBT students and allies. In 2004, the campus provided support staff from the Office of Intercultural Affairs to also assist with LGBT services, including outreach and educational efforts. Also in 2004, students created a new student coalition called Zami to address the different needs of questioning and queer students of color.

Together the queer entities collaborate on creating campus programs, providing services and connecting the community. Some of the past annual event highlights include National Coming Out Day, Drag Ball and National Day of Silence. According to Bryn Mawr queer students, the academic environment is a "nurturing, expressive one" for LGBT issues. The process of self-discovery and individuality is supported holistically. One student adds: "Even if you aren't questioning your own sexual identity, you are being exposed to changes people are going through. And that in itself is helpful."

Bryn Mawr College has an impressive climate for queer women, and the Gay Point Average highlights notable progress. The campus should be considered a definite choice among private colleges for women. Plus, as one student says: "There is such a spectrum of women here, from the 'super straight woman' to the 'out and proud' gay woman. I didn't feel pressure to be gay. When I had a boyfriend it wasn't a big deal, and now when I'm with my girlfriend, it isn't a big deal either."

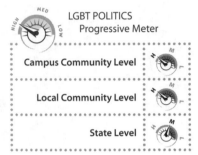

LGBT POLITICS
Progressive Meter

Campus Community Level

Local Community Level

State Level

INFO

BRYN MAWR COLLEGE
101 North Merion Avenue
Bryn Mawr, PA 19010
Phone: 610-526-5152
Fax: 610-526-7471
E-mail: admissions@brynmawr.edu
Website: www.brynmawr.edu

CAMPUS STATS
Type of Institution: Private college for women
Founding Year: 1885
Size: 1,327
Avg. Class Size: 10–19 students
Popular Majors: Biology/Biological Sciences, English Language and Literature, Political Science and Government
Cost: Tuition: $29,570
Admission Application Deadline: January 15

🗩🗩 OUTSPOKEN *Answers from LGBT students:*

Top Three Descriptors of the LGBT Campus Environment:
1. Visible   2. Supportive   3. Dramatic

What makes your campus feel welcoming and safe for LGBT students?
"Support seems all around you. The LGBT students are involved on campus and tend to be very out. I was glad to find acceptance without any problems."
—19-year-old queer female, sophomore

How do you feel about coming out on your campus?
"If you can get past the fact that people will talk about you for about a day, it's no big deal." *—20-year-old lesbian, junior*

⊘ ACADEMIC SCENE

Top Three Supportive LGBT Academic Areas:
1. History   2. Sociology   3. Gender and Sexuality

How LGBT-friendly are faculty in the classroom?
"The campus faculty are open-minded, I find, for the most part. I have brought up queer issues in class, and it is seen as a bonus, really. The faculty have all embraced my queer perspectives in the classroom." —*21-year-old queer bisexual female, senior*

"It depends on the class. I've never had a professor treat me differently. Actually, most of my professors don't limit what I write about—I can write about queer issues if I like." —*20-year-old lesbian, junior*

☺ SOCIAL SCENE

Top Three Things in the LGBT Social Life:
1. Parties   2. Bars   3. Dancing

How would you describe the social scene for LGBT students?
"We're well integrated into the college social scene. It's too small to have many of our own parties, but we're active!" —*20-year-old lesbian, junior*

What annual social event should an LGBT student not miss?
"Drag ball, of course." *22-year-old queer female, senior*

OUTRAGEOUS FACTOID Bryn Mawr students celebrate May Day by dancing around the maypole.

RAINBOW RUMOR Rainbows are bliss at Bryn Mawr College. LGBT students remark that the campus is "so safe" that students do not need to be activists. "They're out, they're comfortable with their queer identity, they have a girlfriend. ..." Other LGBT students think the campus needs to be shaken up, not stirred, once in a while—especially in the area of queer women of color.

THAT'S SO GAY!
ANNUAL LGBT EVENT HIGHLIGHTS

National Coming Out Day: October 11

World AIDS Day: December

Drag Ball: March

National Day of Silence: April

BUZZ BITES *Fun Queer Stuff to Know*

THE BEST...

Place to Check Out Ladies: All over Bryn Mawr

LGBT-Cool Athletic Sport: Rugby

Non-LGBT-Specific Campus Club: Association of Multicultural Organizations

LGBT Educational Involvement Opportunity: Q Forum during orientation

LGBT-Accepting Religious/Spiritual Organization(s): Episcopal Campus Ministry, Jewish Students' Union, Athena's Circle

CAMPUS QUEER RESOURCES

Select LGBT Student Organization(s):

Rainbow Alliance *and*
Zami (for students of color)

Founding Date: Rainbow Alliance (formerly BGALA, early 1980s); Zami (2004)

Membership: 80+

Phone: 610-526-6594

LGBT Resource Center/Office:

LGBT Services: Office of Intercultural Affairs

Bryn Mawr College
101 North Merion Avenue
Bryn Mawr, PA 19010

Year Established: 2004

Number of Staff: 3 full-time professional staff members (varying responsibilities)

Phone: 610-526-6594

Website: www.brynmawr.edu/intercultural/

THE GAY POINT AVERAGE OFFICIAL CAMPUS CHECKLIST

- ✓ LGBT & ally student organization
- ✓ LGBT resource center/office
- LGBT Pride Week &/or Coming Out Week
- Safe Zone/Safe Space or Ally Program
- ✓ Significant number of LGBT social activities
- ✓ Significant number of LGBT educational events
- ✓ Variety of LGBT studies/courses
- ✓ Nondiscrimination statement inclusive of sexual orientation
- Nondiscrimination statement inclusive of gender identity/expression
- ✓ Extends domestic partner benefits to same-sex couples
- ✓ Actively recruits LGBT students to enroll on campus
- Trains campus police on LGBT sensitivity
- ✓ Procedure for reporting LGBT bias, harassment & hate crimes
- Offers LGBT housing options/themes
- Offers LGBT-inclusive health services/testing
- ✓ Offers LGBT-inclusive counseling/support groups
- Offers LGBT student scholarships
- Conducts special LGBT graduation ceremony for LGBT & ally Students
- Offers support services for process of transitioning from M to F & F to M
- ✓ Active LGBT alumni group

11 BRYN MAWR COLLEGE GAY POINT AVERAGE
(out of 20)

CALIFORNIA STATE POLYTECHNIC UNIVERSITY—POMONA

BEGINNING AS A "School for Boys" back in the late 1930s, California State Polytechnic University—Pomona is so much more today. The Southern California university is slightly east of the city of Los Angeles and has a thriving history of LGBT progressiveness.

Since the early 1990s, the campus has included sexual orientation in its nondiscrimination statement, and in 2002 it extended full domestic partner benefits to faculty and staff. The LGBT commitment was most visibly manifested in 1995, when the Pride Center opened its doors on campus. Cal Poly was among the first colleges in the state system to hire a full-time LGBT center director in 1997. Since then, the Pride Center has paved the way for the emergence of other LGBT resource centers within the California state university system.

From its inception, the Pride Center has helped create an inclusive environment for all students. The center reaches out to hundreds of students every year with cutting-edge services such as the LGBTA Speakers Bureau. These educational panels receive over thirty requests per year from academic areas like the College of Science and the College of Letters, Arts and Social Sciences. Additionally, with the support of Associated Students, the Pride Center and the various LGBT student clubs receive annual programming funds to support the main queer events like LGBT History Month, National Coming Out Day, World AIDS Awareness Day and yearly Safe Zone trainings.

Every year, Cal Poly gives out approximately $2,000 in scholarship awards at the annual Celebrating Pride and Excellence Scholarship Dinner. The "caring atmosphere" of the Pride Center is noteworthy. This LGBT student agrees: "The Pride Center provides a welcoming family environment that I'm proud to be a part of today."

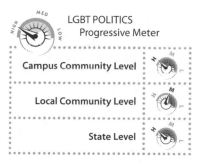

LGBT POLITICS
Progressive Meter

Campus Community Level

Local Community Level

State Level

OUTSPOKEN *Answers from LGBT students:*

Top Three Descriptors of the LGBT Campus Environment:
1. Collaborative   2. Inclusive   3. Diverse

What makes your campus feel welcome and safe for LGBT students?
"I was surprised to find out how open the campus was to LGBT students. Sometimes when walking by teachers' offices, I will see Safe Zone logos. This lets me know that there are people on campus who are supporters of the LGBT student population." *—20-year-old gay male, junior*

How do you feel about coming out on your campus?
"At first, I didn't know. But then when I visited the Pride Center, I felt right at home. It was never an issue." *—19-year-old gay male, sophomore*

INFO

CALIFORNIA STATE POLYTECHNIC UNIVERSITY—POMONA

3801 West Temple Avenue
Pomona, CA 91768

Phone: 909-869-3210

Fax: 909-869-4848

E-mail: admissions@csupomona.edu

Website: www.csupomona.edu

CAMPUS STATS

Type of Institution: Public university

Founding Year: 1938

Size: 16,955

Avg. Class Size: 20–29 students

Popular Majors: Computer and Information Sciences, Electrical, Electronics and Communications Engineering, Mechanical Engineering

Cost: In-state tuition: $3,012
Out-of-state tuition: $13,002

Admission Application Deadline: November 30

Atop the largest hill overlooking campus, you can find three tremendously large letters—CPP—denoting Cal Poly Pomona. Every year a small group of dedicated students, faculty, and staff climb up the treacherous mountain-like terrain and paint the gargantuan letters rainbow for LGBT History Month.

• • • • • • • • • • • • • • • • • • •

Lavender grads can march down the commencement aisle with pride, knowing that the president of the university, the dean of students and the vice president of student affairs actually attend the annual Lavender Graduation Celebration and Celebrating Pride and Excellence Scholarship Dinner.

• • • • • • • • • • • • • • • • • • •

**ANNUAL LGBT
EVENT HIGHLIGHTS**

Safe Zone Trainings: Fall

Welcome Back Picnic: September

LGBT History Month: October

Gay Tour of L.A.: Fall

National Coming Out Day: October

Drag Show: Fall/Spring

**Celebrating Pride and Excellence
Scholarship Dinner:** April

Lavender Graduation: June

Rap (LGBT Discussion) Groups: Fall/Spring

LGBTA Speakers Bureau: Fall/Spring

Hip-Hop Dance Class Fundraiser: Fall/Spring

ACADEMIC SCENE

Top Three Supportive LGBT Academic Areas:
1. Ethnic and Women's Studies   2. Biology   3. History

How LGBT-friendly are faculty in the classroom?
"There hasn't been an issue with any of the faculty on campus regarding my sexual orientation. From what I can tell, I have only had one gay teacher, and he was really cool. He was the same as all my other teachers, but I was able to relate to him on a different level and was able to talk to him about some of my personal issues." —*20-year-old lesbian, junior*

"I have not had an experience where I felt the professor was against the LGBT community. They have done a good job of keeping their professor-student relationships purely academic." —*20-year-old gay male, junior*

SOCIAL SCENE

Top Three Things in the LGBT Social Life:
1. Movies   2. Online chatting   3. Dancing

How would you describe the social scene for LGBT students?
"The social scene is okay on campus; a majority of the time students go off campus to hang out." —*20-year-old lesbian, junior*

What annual social event should an LGBT student not miss?
"This year the Pride Center hosted a drag show on campus. This was a great event that brought together both the LGBT community and allies on campus." —*20-year-old gay male, junior*

BUZZ BITES *Fun Queer Stuff to Know*

THE BEST. . .

Party Locale: West Hollywood

Hangout: Pride Center and Out for Coffee

Eating Place: Cal Poly Market Place

LGBT-Cool Athletic Sport: Women's basketball

Non-LGBT-Specific Campus Club: Barkada

Place for LGBT Students to Live On Campus:
Encinitas Residence Hall

LGBT Course Offering: Diverse Sexual and Gender Identities

LGBT Educational Involvement Opportunity:
LGBTA Speakers Bureau

LGBT-Accepting Religious/Spiritual Organization(s):
Round Earth Society

THE GAY POINT AVERAGE
OFFICIAL CAMPUS CHECKLIST

LGBT & ally student organization ✓

LGBT resource center/office ✓

LGBT Pride Week &/or Coming Out Week ✓

Safe Zone/Safe Space or Ally Program ✓

Significant number of LGBT social activities ✓

Significant number of LGBT educational events ✓

Variety of LGBT studies/courses

Nondiscrimination statement inclusive of sexual orientation ✓

Nondiscrimination statement inclusive of gender identity/expression ✓

Extends domestic partner benefits to same-sex couples ✓

Actively recruits LGBT students to enroll on campus

Trains campus police on LGBT sensitivity ✓

Procedure for reporting LGBT bias, harassment & hate crimes ✓

Offers LGBT housing options/themes

Offers LGBT-inclusive health services/testing ✓

Offers LGBT-inclusive counseling/support groups ✓

Offers LGBT student scholarships ✓

Conducts special LGBT graduation ceremony for LGBT & ally Students ✓

Offers support services for process of transitioning from M to F & F to M ✓

Active LGBT alumni group ✓

CALIFORNIA STATE POLYTECHNIC UNIVERSITY—POMONA GAY POINT AVERAGE (17)

CAMPUS QUEER RESOURCES

Select LGBT Student Organization(s):
Queer Students and Allies for Equality
Founding Date: late 1970s
Membership: 15+
E-mail: cpp_qsafe@yahoo.com
Website: groups.yahoo.com/group/QSAFE1/

LGBT Resource Center/Office:
Pride Center
California State Polytechnic University—Pomona
Building 26, Room 107
3801 West Temple Avenue
Pomona, CA 91768
Year Established: 1995
Number of Staff: 2 full-time professional staff members and 4 student workers
Phone: 909-869-2573
Website: www.dsa.csupomona.edu/pride

CARLETON COLLEGE

"TRULY EXTRAORDINARY" IS how many describe Carleton College. But what about queer issues? It has taken several decades for Carleton to stand out as among the best colleges for LGBT students.

It started in 1970, when a Carleton student published an anonymous message in the campus news bulletin, stating how isolated and awful it felt to be gay on campus. The campus response was immediate, leading to the establishment of the Northfield Gay Liberation Front—one of only a handful of then "radical" gay liberation organizations nationally. The first campus queer voice had been heard, and slowly, incremental positive changes began to take place on and off campus.

Over the next three decades, Carleton College implemented several LGBT-inclusive polices and practices to further demonstrate its commitment to LGBT students. In 1999, the Human Rights Campaign of Minneapolis awarded the campus the Brian Coyle Leadership Award "for outstanding leadership and service to the lesbian and gay community" for its work on same-sex benefits for employees and its continued institutional support for LGBT students. Then in 2001, the campus opened the Gender and Sexuality Center; the most visible symbol of the college's support of LGBT issues.

Today, the campus leads the way as a welcoming place for LGBT students. Just take a look at its Gay Point Average and see how far Carleton has come. As one LGBT student explains: "Carleton is the first place where I feel comfortable identifying as gay in a public arena. People consciously make efforts to welcome LGBT students without isolating them. During New Student Week, the dean of student affairs described Carleton as a school where all imaginable types of people can interact happily and productively. She included students of different sexual orientations among these types. I admired the boldness she exhibited as an administrator. Since then, nobody at Carleton has treated me differently because of my sexuality."

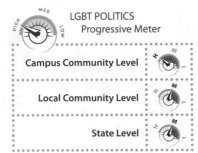

LGBT POLITICS
Progressive Meter

Campus Community Level

Local Community Level

State Level

INFO

CARLETON COLLEGE
One North College Street
Northfield, MN 55057
Phone: 507-646-4190
Fax: 507-646-4526
E-mail: admissions@carleton.edu
Website: www.carleton.edu

CAMPUS STATS
Type of Institution: Private college
Founding Year: 1866
Size: 1,932
Avg. Class Size: 10–19 students
Popular Majors: Biology/Biological Sciences, Economics, Political Science and Government
Cost: Tuition: $30,501
Admission Application Deadline: January 15

OUTSPOKEN *Answers from LGBT students:*

Top Three Descriptors of the LGBT Campus Environment:
1. Close-knit   2. Welcoming   3. Flexible

What makes your campus feel welcoming and safe for LGBT students?
"I have found that my needs are met here at Carleton. I have never once found myself in a situation where I have felt threatened or unsafe because of my sexual orientation. There are always resources available to me and there are always people to talk about LGBT issues. I feel comfortable being out at Carleton."
—19-year-old lesbian, sophomore

How do you feel about coming out on your campus?
"Coming out to my friends here was much easier than I thought—the most difficult part was getting over my own internalized homophobia. I thought my straight friends would react much more dramatically to my 'coming out' than they actually did." *—21-year-old queer female, senior*

ACADEMIC SCENE

Top Three Supportive LGBT Academic Areas:
1. Women's and Gender Studies   2. Sociology/Anthropology   3. Geology

How LGBT-friendly are faculty in the classroom?
"I once wrote a term paper on a gay-related issue, and both my professor and the research librarian who assisted me were extremely positive. There are also a healthy number of LGBT professors on campus." —*20-year-old gay male, junior*

"I can name five profs that I've had in three years who are gay—so I would say that classes are pretty sensitive to LGBT issues, but even straight professors have introduced ways of looking at certain pieces of literature from a 'queer lens,' which is pretty refreshing." —*21-year-old queer female, senior*

SOCIAL SCENE

Top Three Things in the LGBT Social Life:
1. Queers and Allies House Party   2. Socials   3. Hanging out

How would you describe the social scene for LGBT students?
"I think it's easy to be involved in the queer community, even if you're not ready to be out yet. People generally have many different groups of friends, not all queer-centric, which is one of the best things about social life here—we don't interact with just one group of people, but know folks from all walks of life."
—*19-year-old genderqueer dyke, sophomore*

What annual social event should an LGBT student not miss?
"The Glam Jam, which was held during National Coming Out Week. I believe more students learned about Queers and Allies House through the party. As for myself, I danced and laughed more than I had since graduation!" —*18-year-old transgender gay male, freshman*

OUTRAGEOUS FACTOID Carleton College not only has a vibrant LGBT campus population but also an active, giving LGBT alumni group. The campus has repeatedly ranked high in alumni giving, and the LGBT alums help raise the dollars too! The Human Sexuality Endowment Fund, established in 1993, generates money every year for educational and support programs for LGBT issues. The Geology Department even has its own separate LGBT alumni group!

RAINBOW RUMOR Beyond the normal complaints of a "bad dating scene," some students acknowledge that the Carleton College atmosphere does not seemingly allow for students to make mistakes when it comes to diversity issues. One student explains: "Students, especially those who are straight, often feel as though they should already know all there is to know about LGBT life and be unconditionally supportive—yet this does not allow for the legitimization and exploration of their concerns."

THAT'S SO GAY!

ANNUAL LGBT EVENT HIGHLIGHTS

Safe Sex and Sex Toys 101 Workshop: Fall/Spring

LGBTA Speaker Panels: Fall/Spring

LGBT Chapel Service: Fall/Spring

Coming Out Week: October

Rainbow Retreat: November

Drag Ball: February

Pride Month: April

Pride Banquet: May

BUZZ BITES
Fun Queer Stuff to Know

THE BEST...

Party Locale: Queers and Allies House

Hangout: Blue Monday's

LGBT-Cool Athletic Sport: Women's rugby

Place for LGBT Students to Live on Campus: Queers and Allies House

LGBT Course Offering: Amazons, Valkyries, Naiads and Dykes: Women-Identified and Lesbian Artists in Europe

LGBT Educational Involvement Opportunity: LGBTA Speaker Panels

LGBT-Accepting Religious/Spiritual Organization(s): Unitarian Universalists, Progressive Christian Dialogue

CAMPUS QUEER RESOURCES

Select LGBT Student Organization(s):

Carleton In and Out (CIAO) *and* **Sexuality and Gender Activism (SAGA)**

Founding Date: CIAO and SAGA formed in 1999 from an earlier group.

Membership: 20+

Website: orgs.carleton.edu/CIAO/ *or* orgs.carleton.edu/~saga/

LGBT Resource Center/Office:

Gender and Sexuality Center
One North College Street
Northfield MN 55057

Year Established: 2001

Number of Staff: 1 full-time professional staff member, 12 student staff

Phone: 507-646-5222

E-mail: gsc@acs.carleton.edu

Website: apps.carleton.edu/campus/gsc/

- ✓ LGBT & ally student organization
- ✓ LGBT resource center/office
- ✓ LGBT Pride Week &/or Coming Out Week
- Safe Zone/Safe Space or Ally Program
- ✓ Significant number of LGBT social activities
- ✓ Significant number of LGBT educational events
- ✓ Variety of LGBT studies/courses
- ✓ Nondiscrimination statement inclusive of sexual orientation
- Nondiscrimination statement inclusive of gender identity/expression
- ✓ Extends domestic partner benefits to same-sex couples
- ✓ Actively recruits LGBT students to enroll on campus
- Trains campus police on LGBT sensitivity
- ✓ Procedure for reporting LGBT bias, harassment & hate crimes
- ✓ Offers LGBT housing options/themes
- ✓ Offers LGBT-inclusive health services/testing
- ✓ Offers LGBT-inclusive counseling/support groups
- Offers LGBT student scholarships
- ✓ Conducts special LGBT graduation ceremony for LGBT & ally Students
- ✓ Offers support services for process of transitioning from M to F & F to M
- ✓ Active LGBT alumni group

16

CARLETON COLLEGE
GAY POINT AVERAGE
(out of 20)

CARNEGIE MELLON UNIVERSITY

IT'S NOT ALL about computers! The small grassy campus with yellow brick buildings sits in suburban Pittsburgh and has a lot to offer LGBT students looking for a variety of queer programs and social activities. From Pride Month events to bidding on a date at the Valentine's Day Charity Date Auction, students can stay involved and meet that special someone along the way.

LGBT allies are sprinkled across campus. Every year, the Safe Zone program trains 150-plus students, faculty, staff and administrators on how to be an ally. The training is open to everyone, and the level of participation continues to "skyrocket." In addition, Carnegie Mellon should be acknowledged because it is one of a limited number of campuses to include both sexual orientation and gender identity in its campus nondiscrimination clause. As a result, LGBT students are allowed the freedom to be who they are and express themselves without fear. Such an environment of inclusiveness often encourages LGBT students to get involved and build bridges of understanding with other campus organizations.

One active LGBT student states: "Most active students are heavily involved in LGBT organizations, as well as the campus in general. Rarely have I encountered someone who has reacted at all when finding out that I am gay. Usually, I hear 'oh cool,' or 'so what?' Because Carnegie has so many different kinds of people, being gay isn't abnormal, and the community isn't isolated by the rest of the campus."

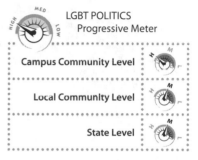

LGBT POLITICS
Progressive Meter

Campus Community Level

Local Community Level

State Level

OUTSPOKEN *Answers from LGBT students:*

Top Three Descriptors of the LGBT Campus Environment:
1. Diverse   2. Inclusive   3. Open-minded

What makes your campus feel welcoming and safe for LGBT students?
"Our campus is full of diversity of all forms, from racial to political to intellectual. There are all kinds of people, and rather than stigmatizing someone, being a member of the GLBT community adds to this diversity." —*21-year-old gay male, senior*

How do you feel about coming out on your campus?
"While I came to campus as an openly gay person, 'coming out' doesn't just stop there. You always end up coming out to new people in your life in some form or another. I'm happy to say that from the Carnegie Mellon community, I've received no negative reactions—only support and acceptance." —*22-year-old gay male, senior*

"My freshman year, a girl on my floor grew up in a very conservative Catholic community from small-town Ohio. When she heard I was gay, she asked me if I was, and I said, 'Yes—does that bother you?' She replied, saying, 'Well, it bothers the Catholic church.' I responded, saying, 'But does it bother you?' She thought for a bit, and replied, 'No, not at all.' A few months later she was dancing with me at the local GLBT club, and had joined the gay/straight alliance on campus."
—*21-year-old gay male, senior*

INFO

CARNEGIE MELLON UNIVERSITY
5000 Forbes Avenue
Pittsburgh, PA 15213
Phone: 412-268-2082
Fax: 412-268-7838
E-mail: undergraduate admissions@andrew.cmu.edu
Website: www.cmu.edu

CAMPUS STATS
Type of Institution: Private university
Founding Year: 1900
Size: 5,389
Avg. Class Size: 20–29 students
Popular Majors: Business Administration/ Management, Computer Engineering, Computer Science
Cost: Tuition: $31,650
Admission Application Deadline: January 1

OUTRAGEOUS FACTOID Carnegie Mellon teases the lines surrounding sexuality. Full of bold choices, the campus learned how to criss-cross the lines from its infamous, modern, pop art alum Andy Warhol, class of 1949.

● ● ● ● ● ● ● ● ● ● ● ● ● ● ● ● ● ● ● ●

RAINBOW RUMOR Put bluntly by one student, "Students need to leave campus and explore the Pittsburgh community to see all the culture." Another area cited for improvement would be "gender-blind housing." Currently, the housing system only acknowledges "male" and "female" gender identities. Supporters on campus are advocating for a campus protocol to allow transgender students to self-identify and find necessary support in campus housing.

● ● ● ● ● ● ● ● ● ● ● ● ● ● ● ● ● ● ● ●

THAT'S SO GAY!

ANNUAL LGBT EVENT HIGHLIGHTS

GLBT Welcome Reception: During orientation for first-year students

GLBT and Friends Welcome Reception: First Friday of classes

Pride Month: October

National Coming Out Day Dance: October

World AIDS Day: December 1

Valentine's Day Charity Date Auction: February

National Freedom to Marry Day: February

Carnival Booth for ALLIES: April

National Day of Silence: April

OUTspoken Discussion Series: Each month

Safe Zone Ally Training: Approximately three times in Fall, two times in Spring

ACADEMIC SCENE

Top Three Supportive LGBT Academic Areas:
1. College of Fine Arts   2. Computer Science   3. English

How LGBT-friendly are faculty in the classroom?
"My faculty members are very accepting of the GLBT community. Rarely does it come up in class that I am gay, and never have I encountered a professor who has had a negative reaction. Several professors are openly gay on campus and serve as role models for students on campus, GLBT and straight alike."
—*21-year-old lesbian, sophomore*

"A student in one of my classes freshman year called another student a 'fag.' My professor heard him, and not only corrected him, but explained to him and the rest of the class where the word came from and why it is so terrible. I think many students learned a lot that day and thought twice before using such awful language."
—*22-year-old gay male, senior*

SOCIAL SCENE

Top Three Activities in the LGBT Social Life:
1. Hang with friends   2. Party   3. Campus social events

How would you describe the social scene for LGBT students?
"The social scene is great for all students. From parties to clubbing to just hanging out with friends—anything and everything is offered. You have to find it." —*21-year-old gay male, senior*

"Unlike most major cities, there is no 'gay district' of Pittsburgh. While some see this as a negative thing, I like the fact that the community isn't sectioned off and that we are integrated with the rest of the city." —*22-year-old gay male, senior*

What annual social event should an LGBT student not miss?
"School of Drama Drag Show and the Gay Pride Month events (especially the keynote!)" —*21-year-old gay male, senior*

BUZZ BITES *Fun Queer Stuff to Know*

THE BEST...

Party Locale: The 5801 *and* house parties

Hangout: SoHo, the LGBT Resource Center

Eating Place: Tuscany Cafe

Place to Check Out Guys: School of Drama

Place to Check Out Ladies: AB Tech Club

LGBT-Cool Athletic Sport: Women's soccer

Place for LGBT Students to Live on Campus: Mudge House

LGBT Course Offering: Who Will Serve? Gays and Blacks in the Military

LGBT Educational Involvement Opportunity: Safe Zone Ally Program

LGBT-Accepting Religious/Spiritual Organization(s): Hillel *and* the majority of Interfaith Groups

THE GAY POINT AVERAGE
OFFICIAL CAMPUS CHECKLIST

LGBT & ally student organization	✓
LGBT resource center/office	✓
LGBT Pride Week &/or Coming Out Week	✓
Safe Zone/Safe Space or Ally Program	✓
Significant number of LGBT social activities	✓
Significant number of LGBT educational events	✓
Variety of LGBT studies/courses	
Nondiscrimination statement inclusive of sexual orientation	✓
Nondiscrimination statement inclusive of gender identity/expression	✓
Extends domestic partner benefits to same-sex couples	✓
Actively recruits LGBT students to enroll on campus	
Trains campus police on LGBT sensitivity	
Procedure for reporting LGBT bias, harassment & hate crimes	
Offers LGBT housing options/themes	
Offers LGBT-inclusive health services/testing	✓
Offers LGBT-inclusive counseling/support groups	✓
Offers LGBT student scholarships	
Conducts special LGBT graduation ceremony for LGBT & ally Students	✓
Offers support services for process of transitioning from M to F & F to M	✓
Active LGBT alumni group	

CARNEGIE MELLON UNIVERSITY
GAY POINT AVERAGE *13*
(out of 20)

CAMPUS QUEER RESOURCES

Select LGBT Student Organization(s):
OUT *and* **ALLIES**
Founding Date: OUT (1986, under a different name); ALLIES (late 1980s/early 1990s)
Membership: 300+
Phone: 412-268-8794
E-mail: out@andrew.cmu.edu; allies@andrew.cmu.edu
Website(s): www.andrew.cmu.edu/user/out/ *or* www.andrew.cmu.edu/user/allies/

LGBT Resource Center/Office:
SoHo
University Center
Box 99
Carnegie Mellon University
Pittsburgh, PA 15213
Year Established: 2000
Number of Staff: 1 full-time professional staff member, 1 student intern
Phone: 412-268-8794
E-mail: soho@andrew.cmu.edu
Website: www.studentaffairs.cmu.edu/soho/

CASE WESTERN RESERVE UNIVERSITY

"A BUTTERFLY FLUTTERING fresh out of its cocoon" might be an apt analogy for Case Western Reserve University. In just a few years, Case Western Reserve University has transformed itself into a more LGBT-inclusive institution. The university has a nondiscrimination policy based on sexual orientation and is currently going through the process of adding gender identity/expression. As early as 2001, the university also adopted domestic partner benefits as part of campus personnel policies.

Case is also undeniably one of the most wired campuses around. A wireless network covers the entire campus. Each dorm room has gigabit networking.

The Gay Point Average makes it clear that Case has some room to improve in years to come. Nevertheless, this tight-knit campus population, including LGBT and ally students, faculty and staff, has accomplished enough to be a campus of queer choice. An LGBT student remarks: "I always feel welcome, encouraged, and supported when I see prominent straight administrators at LGBT-centered events, such as the LGBT grad student pizza party, Drag Ball, and Lavender Ball. They listen, respect us all, and are open to learning about our experiences and our issues."

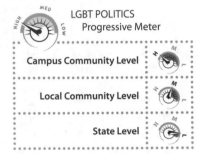

LGBT POLITICS
Progressive Meter

Campus Community Level

Local Community Level

State Level

OUTSPOKEN   *Answers from LGBT students:*

Top Three Descriptors of the LGBT Campus Environment:
1. Conservative   2. Civil   3. Friendly

What makes your campus feel welcoming and safe for LGBT students?
"Case has changed a lot in the past three years with respect to LGBT students. In my time here, I've witnessed the creation of the 'Safe Zone Ally' program, a 'Committee on LGBT Concerns' at the administrative level and an on-campus Human Rights Campaign group. As a freshman I felt isolated and ignored by the powers that be. Since then, I have seen an outpouring of support for LGBT issues." —*21-year-old gay male, senior*

How do you feel about coming out on your campus?
"I was already out when I came to campus, but since I've been here I've seen and helped many people come out. 'Coming Out Stories'—which takes place each year on National Coming Out Day at a local coffee house—is an empowering event where people share their personal coming out stories and provide inspiration for more closeted members to come out to friends and family." —*21-year-old gay male, senior*

"I was very closeted when I came to Case. I feel one of the biggest reasons why I felt comfortable to ultimately come out is the fact that Case offers so many leadership opportunities, that you feel inclined to come out. I became the president of the Gay-Straight Alliance my sophomore year, and I felt totally unprepared, but as time went on, I learned so much about myself and other people, I became empowered to be true to myself and be an example for others. I wanted other closeted students to feel comfortable to come out as well." —*20-year-old lesbian, junior*

⊘ ACADEMIC SCENE

Top Three Supportive LGBT Academic Areas:
1. Mandel School of Applied Social Sciences   2. Gender Studies   3. History

How LGBT-friendly are faculty in the classroom?
"The overall curriculum is generally heterocentric, but there are certain departments where the faculty are gender-friendly and aware…they make an effort to be gender- and sexual-orientation-inclusive." *—19-year-old lesbian, sophomore*

☺ SOCIAL SCENE

Top Three Things in the LGBT Social Life:
1. Casual hanging out   2. Dance clubs/bars   3. Spectrum social events

How would you describe the social scene for LGBT students?
"Spectrum, our undergraduate LGBT social group, is funded by the Undergraduate Student Government and has a lot of social events throughout the year, including Coming Out Week in the fall and Break the Silence week in the spring. In addition to Spectrum, a lot of the LGBT students just hang out in our spare time." *—21-year-old gay male, senior*

"There are definitely more out gay male students than out lesbian students. This doesn't mean that lesbians don't exist on campus but, because of a number of disparities, many of the events are planned by men. Personally, I've enjoyed myself during social events on campus. While I wish there were more out gay women, we have a very large group of allies that make any social event fun." *— 21-year-old lesbian, senior*

What annual social event should an LGBT student not miss?
"Our biggest event of the year is our annual Lavender Ball, a dance party which culminates our 'Break the Silence' week each spring. The event features a professional DJ and finger food from various local restaurants and is our biggest LGBT party of the year. Last year, the president of our university and his wife attended the event, along with students from Case, other local colleges, and several new prospective freshmen. … it's a blast!" *—21-year-old gay male, senior*

OUTRAGEOUS FACTOID Last year the university president not only attended the queer Lavender Ball but also got "jiggy with it" on the dance floor with his wife.

RAINBOW RUMOR LGBT students do not deny the progress made on campus, but all are in agreement that the campus desperately needs an LGBT center to focus on LGBT issues on campus. One LGBT student lays it all out: "We have a center for women, an office of multi-cultural affairs, and it's high time we have a center for LGBT students!"

THAT'S SO GAY!

ANNUAL LGBT EVENT HIGHLIGHTS

Coming Out Week: October

Drag Ball: November

Break the Silence Week: April

Cleveland Human Rights Campaign Dinner: April

Cleveland Pride Weekend: June

BUZZ BITES *Fun Queer Stuff to Know*

THE BEST…

Party Locale: Bounce

Hangout: Starbucks or Truffles Pastry Shop

Eating Place: Union Station

Place to Check Out Guys: Men's soccer *or* The Grid

Place to Check Out Ladies: The Grid on Wednesdays

LGBT-Cool Athletic Sport: Women's softball

Non-LGBT-Specific Campus Club: College Democrats

Place for LGBT Students to Live on Campus: Village at 115

LGBT Educational Involvement Opportunity: Human Rights Campaign

LGBT-Accepting Religious/Spiritual Organization(s): UpCam

CAMPUS QUEER RESOURCES

Select LGBT Student Organization(s):

Case Human Rights Campaign; Spectrum

Founding Date: 2005

Membership: 40+

Resource Center/Office Responsible for LGBT Issues:

Office of the Provost

216 Adelbert Hall
Cleveland, OH 44106-7001

Year Established: 2004

Number of Staff: 1 part-time professional staff

Phone: 216-368-0705

E-mail: vws1@case.edu

Website: www.case.edu/provost/lgbt

THE GAY POINT AVERAGE
OFFICIAL CAMPUS CHECKLIST

- ✔ LGBT & ally student organization
- LGBT resource center/office
- ✔ LGBT Pride Week &/or Coming Out Week
- ✔ Safe Zone/Safe Space or Ally Program
- ✔ Significant number of LGBT social activities
- ✔ Significant number of LGBT educational events
- Variety of LGBT studies/courses
- ✔ Nondiscrimination statement inclusive of sexual orientation
- Nondiscrimination statement inclusive of gender identity/expression
- ✔ Extends domestic partner benefits to same-sex couples
- ✔ Actively recruits LGBT students to enroll on campus
- Trains campus police on LGBT sensitivity
- Procedure for reporting LGBT bias, harassment & hate crimes
- Offers LGBT housing options/themes
- ✔ Offers LGBT-inclusive health services/testing
- ✔ Offers LGBT-inclusive counseling/support groups
- Offers LGBT student scholarships
- Conducts special LGBT graduation ceremony for LGBT & ally Students
- Offers support services for process of transitioning from M to F & F to M
- Active LGBT alumni group

10 CASE WESTERN
RESERVE UNIVERSITY
GAY POINT AVERAGE
(out of 20)

CENTRAL MICHIGAN UNIVERSITY

"YOU'RE NOT ALONE here!" LGBT students at Central Michigan University believe in commitment and a sense of community on campus. The Gay Point Average shows that the campus has a vested interest in being LGBT-inclusive. But just how gay-friendly is it?

The most obvious area of support comes from the Office of Gay and Lesbian Programs. This office opened on campus in 1992 and since then has increased from having no budget and a quarter-time director to having a budget and a half-time director. But, even before there was an office, Central Michigan had already shown signs of progress by adding sexual orientation to its nondiscrimination policy and extending domestic partner benefits to employees with same-sex partners. There is also queer support in various administrative offices and academic departments, such as the Counseling Center, Residence Life, the Office for Institutional Diversity, Women's Studies and Social Work, to name a few.

In addition, the campus offers a plethora of LGBT activities and events to educate and create awareness for all students. Some of the most popular are the Masquerade Ball, National Day of Silence, Straight Ally Week and Coming Out Week. Past events have included guest speakers, comedians, peer panels, rallies, game shows and movies. LGBT students warn that it may be a bit hard to discover other queer students on campus. Queers looking for queers should instead get involved in the Gay/Straight Alliance student group. Regardless, no matter where you go on campus, you will find a "Safe Zone," or someone with an ally button or sticker. As one LGBT student says: "We're awesome! They try really hard to promote diversity. It's incredible how hard they try. They include everybody. No one is left out."

One LGBT student sums it up: "I feel welcome and safe here…my comfort level being out has only grown as I have found more support among friends and staff/faculty on campus. Other students should give Central Michigan a chance."

OUTSPOKEN *Answers from LGBT students:*

Top Three Descriptors of the LGBT Campus Environment:
1. Welcoming   2. Supportive   3. Safe

What makes your campus feel welcoming and safe for LGBT students?
"I felt welcome after I joined the Gay/Straight Alliance. I found that I'm not the only one. It was a good feeling.…I also liked the signs saying that CMU doesn't discriminate. That helps a lot, and so do the Safe Zone stickers…along with the nondiscrimination policy." *—19-year-old lesbian, sophomore*

How do you feel about coming out on your campus?
"I feel acceptance coming out on campus. I've had experiences in classrooms where we talked about LGBT issues and it's always been very comfortable." *—23-year-old bisexual female, senior*

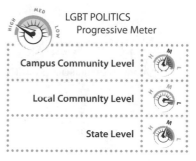

LGBT POLITICS
Progressive Meter

Campus Community Level

Local Community Level

State Level

INFO

CENTRAL MICHIGAN UNIVERSITY
105 Warriner Hall
Mount Pleasant, MI 48859
Phone: 989-774-3076
Fax: 989-774-7267
E-mail: cmuadmit@cmich.edu
Website: www.cmich.edu

CAMPUS STATS
Type of Institution: Public university
Founding Year: 1892
Size: 20,012
Avg. Class Size: 20–29 students
Popular Majors: English Language and Literature, Psychology, History
Cost: In-state tuition: $4,610
Out-of-state tuition: $11,712
Admission Application Deadline: January 15

OUTRAGEOUS FACTOID The queers at Central Michigan are sometimes hidden on campus.

. . . .

RAINBOW RUMOR Demands for LGBT support have grown exponentially over the years, but the Office of Gay and Lesbian Programs struggles to find adequate staffing and funding.

. . . .

THAT'S SO GAY!

ANNUAL LGBT EVENT HIGHLIGHTS

Straight Ally Week: September

Coming Out Week: October

Transgender Remembrance Day: November

World AIDS Day: December

Pride Week: April

National Day of Silence: April

Masquerade Ball: Spring

LGBT Speaker Panels: Fall/Spring

ACADEMIC SCENE

Top Three Supportive LGBT Academic Areas:
1. Education   2. Psychology   3. Sociology/Social Work

How LGBT-friendly are faculty in the classroom?
"Almost every professor I've had is completely an ally. I can't think of a professor [who] wasn't LGBT-friendly to the max. If I heard something in class that offended me, I've approached them and they did everything they could to address it. In all of my major classes (English and Interpersonal Communications), my professors are completely welcoming, and they use gender-neutral language whenever possible. They include LGBT issues in the curriculum without me even mentioning it. They are extremely helpful and supportive if I come out in class." —*22-year-old bisexual male, senior*

"I haven't really noticed one way or another. I've never felt uncomfortable in a class. I'm a theater major, and there seems to be acceptance of everyone. I've never had an issue with it." —*19-year-old bisexual female, sophomore*

SOCIAL SCENE

Top Three Things in the LGBT Social Life:
1. Hanging out with the Gay/Straight Alliance   2. Dancing   3. Drag show

How would you describe the social scene for LGBT students?
"Central has a lot of events that are visibly LGBT-friendly. For example, the Masquerade Ball is cosponsored by the Gay/Straight Alliance, and there are programs like MainStage. LGBT programs are always there." —*22-year-old bisexual male, senior*

What annual social event should an LGBT student not miss?
"Coming Out Week! Especially on a college campus, it's cool to see others who are comfortable being out and being able to help yourself to be out." —*22-year-old bisexual female, senior*

BUZZ BITES *Fun Queer Stuff to Know*

THE BEST...

Hangout: Kava Coffeeshop

Eating Place: Lil' Chef

Place to Check Out Guys: Student Activity Center

Place to Check Out Ladies: Library

LGBT-Cool Athletic Sport: Women's rugby team

Non-LGBT-Specific Campus Club: Program Board

Place for LGBT Students to Live on Campus: The Towers

LGBT Educational Involvement Opportunity: LGBT Speaker Panels

LGBT-Accepting Religious/Spiritual Organization(s): Open Grove Society

THE GAY POINT AVERAGE
OFFICIAL CAMPUS CHECKLIST

LGBT & ally student organization	✓
LGBT resource center/office	✓
LGBT Pride Week &/or Coming Out Week	✓
Safe Zone/Safe Space or Ally Program	✓
Significant number of LGBT social activities	✓
Significant number of LGBT educational events	✓
Variety of LGBT studies/courses	
Nondiscrimination statement inclusive of sexual orientation	✓
Nondiscrimination statement inclusive of gender identity/expression	
Extends domestic partner benefits to same-sex couples	✓
Actively recruits LGBT students to enroll on campus	
Trains campus police on LGBT sensitivity	✓
Procedure for reporting LGBT bias, harassment & hate crimes	✓
Offers LGBT housing options/themes	
Offers LGBT-inclusive health services/testing	✓
Offers LGBT-inclusive counseling/support groups	✓
Offers LGBT student scholarships	
Conducts special LGBT graduation ceremony for LGBT & ally Students	
Offers support services for process of transitioning from M to F & F to M	
Active LGBT alumni group	

CENTRAL MICHIGAN UNIVERSITY
GAY POINT AVERAGE   12
(out of 20)

CAMPUS QUEER RESOURCES

Select LGBT Student Organization(s):

Gay/Straight Alliance
Founding Date: 2003
Membership: 55+
Phone: 989-774-7470
E-mail: info@cmugsa.org
Website: www.cmugsa.org

LGBT Resource Center/Office:

Office of Gay and Lesbian Programs
Sloan Hall 130
Mount Pleasant, MI 48859
Year Established: 1992
Number of Staff: 1 nine-month, half-time director; 1 student assistant
Phone: 989-774-3637
Website: www.diversity.cmich.edu/glp

CENTRAL WASHINGTON UNIVERSITY

CENTRAL WASHINGTON UNIVERSITY is a college town built in the middle of rural bliss. From the lookout point at the top of the hill overlooking campus, you can see the rodeo, the perimeters of campus, and the gorgeous landscape of the state of Washington.

The campus itself is not nearly as western or conservative as the surrounding community. Central Washington University has a longstanding commitment to LGBT issues, as evidenced by its high marks on the Gay Point Average. Recently, the campus joined the ranks of a select number of campuses nationwide to have gender identity and expression as part of their nondiscrimination clauses. And a year ago, the campus created a Bias Response Plan to effectively advocate for and support victims of bias-motivated incidents. The campus also spearheaded the first Power of One LGBT and Ally Leadership Conference. Several hundred LGBT and ally students attended from all over the region.

Central Washington is not only progressive for its area but also proactive in forging ahead on LGBT issues. So much so that Fred Phelps of Westboro Baptist Church in Topeka, Kansas, came to protest the campus LGBT efforts. His group came not once but twice in one year. Nevertheless, the phenomenal community response shows the level of LGBT support on campus. Hundreds of students, faculty and staff staged a silent counterdemonstration with the motto, "Love All, Hate None"! One LGBT student summarizes: "I felt so empowered, like this was 'my' campus!"

OUTSPOKEN   *Answers from LGBT students:*

Top Three Descriptors of the LGBT Campus Environment:
1. Growing   2. Transforming   3. Changing

What makes your campus feel welcoming and safe for LGBT students?
"A Bias Response Plan is the first step in creating a safer environment for LGBT students. Our campus is one of the few universities with a Bias Response Plan. Several faculty and staff members have worked diligently with students to put these policies in place in order to protect GLBT students." —*22-year-old bisexual female, senior*

"It is well known that the campus police force is sensitive to GLBT issues and takes extreme steps to help those students who may be hate crime victims." —*21-year-old gay male, junior*

How do you feel about coming out on your campus?
"College is a great place to define who you are as a person. I came out the first day in my dorm. Everyone was very supportive. After I came out, so did three other people. We were all elected to our hall leadership council the next week. Go, Wildcats!" —*18-year-old gay male, freshman*

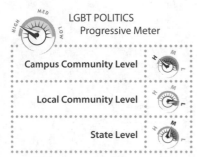

LGBT POLITICS
Progressive Meter

Campus Community Level

Local Community Level

State Level

INFO

CENTRAL WASHINGTON UNIVERSITY
400 East University Way
Ellensburg, WA 98926
Phone: 509-963-1211
Fax: 509-963-3022
E-mail: cwuadmis@cwu.edu
Website: www.cwu.edu

CAMPUS STATS
Type of Institution: Public university
Founding Year: 1891
Size: 9,900
Avg. Class Size: 20–29 students
Popular Majors: Business Administration/ Management, Criminal Justice/Safety Studies, Elementary Education and Teaching
Cost: In-state tuition: $4,278
Out-of-state tuition: $12,477
Admission Application Deadline: May 1

⚡ ACADEMIC SCENE

Top Three Supportive LGBT Academic Areas:
1. Sociology   2. Theater Arts   3. Music

How LGBT-friendly are faculty in the classroom?
"When I first came out, I was worried about how people would react. It was comforting when one of my professors not only talked to me about my lifestyle but also shared with me about her life partner." —*22-year-old lesbian, senior*

"We all sort of look out for each other. I don't think there has been a class that I have had here where I didn't know that someone in the room was gay. As strange as that sounds, it's true!" —*21-year-old gay male, junior*

☺ SOCIAL SCENE

Top Three Things in the LGBT Social Life:
1. Bonfires   2. SUB Pit   3. Str8 D8 Wednesdays

How would you describe the social scene for LGBT students?
"We are like one big family here at Central. Not a day goes by without hanging out with someone from GALA." —*19-year-old lesbian, sophomore*

What annual social event should an LGBT student not miss?
"That would be Central Pride. It is a week-long campaign in the spring that creates awareness, educates the campus and community and allows students to celebrate diversity. The main highlight of the week is the annual student drag show. Even the shyest students in GALA-LGBTSA want to participate."
—*22-year-old bisexual female, senior*

OUTRAGEOUS FACTOID
In 2005, the campus implemented a Bias Response Plan to advocate for students affected by bias-motivated incidents—including LGBT bias. Then in the same year, the campus added transgender protections to the campus nondiscrimination policies for students, faculty, and staff. Whoa!

• •

RAINBOW RUMOR
Central Washington gives new meaning to "flamer." The students love the monthly campus bonfires. Of course, everyone is invited—straight, gay, or in-between.

• •

THAT'S SO GAY!

ANNUAL LGBT EVENT HIGHLIGHTS

National Coming Out Day: October

Transgender Day of Remembrance: November

Freedom to Marry: February

Ally Trainings: Ongoing

Guess the Straight Panels: Ongoing

The Power of One: LGBT Leadership Conference: April

Pride Week: May

BUZZ BITES *Fun Queer Stuff to Know*

THE BEST...

Party Locale: Hippie House

Hangout: SUB Pit or Fishbowl Room in the library

Eating Place: Yellow Church Café

Place to Check Out Guys: Pavilion Gym

Place to Check Out Ladies: The SUB

LGBT-Cool Athletic Sport: Lacrosse

Place for LGBT Students to Live on Campus: Kennedy Hall

CAMPUS QUEER
RESOURCES

Select LGBT Student Organization(s):

GALA-GLBTSA
Student Union Building, M/S 7448
400 East University Way
Ellensburg, WA 98926
Founding Date: Before 1989
Membership: 30–50
Phone: 509-963-1994
Website: www.cwu.edu/~gala

LGBT Resource Center/Office:

Diversity Education Center
LGBT Student Services
400 East University Way
Ellensburg, WA 98926
Year Established: 2002
Number of Staff: 3 full-time professional staff
members
Phone: 509-963-1368
E-mail: webble@cwu.edu
Website: www.cwu.edu/~diversity

THE GAY POINT AVERAGE
OFFICIAL CAMPUS CHECKLIST

- ✓ LGBT & ally student organization
- ✓ LGBT resource center/office
- ✓ LGBT Pride Week &/or Coming Out Week
- ✓ Safe Zone/Safe Space or Ally Program
- ✓ Significant number of LGBT social activities
- ✓ Significant number of LGBT educational events
- Variety of LGBT studies/courses
- ✓ Nondiscrimination statement inclusive of sexual orientation
- ✓ Nondiscrimination statement inclusive of gender identity/expression
- ✓ Extends domestic partner benefits to same-sex couples
- ✓ Actively recruits LGBT students to enroll on campus
- ✓ Trains campus police on LGBT sensitivity
- ✓ Procedure for reporting LGBT bias, harassment & hate crimes
- ✓ Offers LGBT housing options/themes
- ✓ Offers LGBT-inclusive health services/testing
- ✓ Offers LGBT-inclusive counseling/support groups
- ✓ Offers LGBT student scholarships
- Conducts special LGBT graduation ceremony for LGBT & ally Students
- ✓ Offers support services for process of transitioning from M to F & F to M
- Active LGBT alumni group

17 CENTRAL WASHINGTON UNIVERSITY
GAY POINT AVERAGE
(out of 20)

COLBY COLLEGE

JUST AN HOUR north of Portland on a hill sits Colby College—a quintessential campus with elite academic programs, aged red brick buildings, and an adjacent pond surrounded by woods.

Its Gay Point Average reflects a sincere commitment to LGBT issues. Particularly in recent years, the campus has committed itself to LGBT progress and advocacy. In 2002, the president commissioned the Queer Task Force to study the campus climate for the LGBT community. The comprehensive report acknowledged many of the challenges and obstacles for LGBT students and laid out a road map for progress. Recommendations ranged from increased diversity training for coaches and professors to creating a queer studies minor. Throughout the entire report, visibility and enhanced LGBT support seem to be the answer. One student states: "With this report, the ball is now in the administration's court."

The administration has been dribbling ever since. As a result, LGBT students on campus today see the incremental progress of the Queer Task Force. Slowly but surely, much has changed "positively queer" on campus. Another LGBT student says: "I find Colby to be a welcoming campus, a truly progressive place when it wants to be. It takes leadership to change campus environments, and finally we are seeing the results."

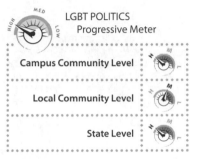

OUTSPOKEN *Answers from LGBT students:*

Top Three Descriptors of the LGBT Campus Environment:
1. Accepting   2. Supportive   3. Safe

What makes your campus feel welcoming and safe for LGBT students?
"When I see out faculty on campus, that means a lot and makes me feel safe. I appreciate the level of openness at Colby." —*20-year-old lesbian, junior*

How do you feel about coming out on your campus?
"I am very queer. I came out without any fear of negativity from my classmates. Colby is a wonderful place for those recently out of the closet or those coming out for the first time." —*22-year-old gay male, senior*

INFO

COLBY COLLEGE
4000 Mayflower Hill
Waterville, ME 04901
Phone: 207-872-3168
Fax: 207-872-3474
E-mail: admissions@colby.edu
Website: www.colby.edu

CAMPUS STATS
Type of Institution: Private college
Founding Year: 1813
Size: 1,820
Avg. Class Size: 10–19 students
Popular Majors: Biology/Biological Sciences, Economics, English Language and Literature
Cost: Tuition: $41,770
Admission Application Deadline: January 1

OUTRAGEOUS FACTOID

Colby students rave about how wonderful it is to have out LGBT faculty and staff involved in campus life. One such faculty member, Jennifer Finney Boylan, is professor of English and co-chair of the English Department. She is also the best-selling author of the memoir *She's Not There: A Life in Two Genders*.

. . . .

RAINBOW RUMOR

Although the campus is located in rural Maine, that does not stop Colby College from pushing the envelope. The recent Queer Task Force underscored the sincere campus interest in establishing a queer studies minor or, at minimum, an academic concentration in LGBT issues.

. . . .

THAT'S SO GAY!

ANNUAL LGBT EVENT HIGHLIGHTS

Film Series: Fall/ Spring

Queer Tea: Fall/Spring

Coming Out Week: Fall

Be Who You Are Dance: Fall

PFLAG Family Homecoming Weekend: Fall

Maine Guys Like Us: Fall

Pride Week: Spring

Annual Drag Show/Dance: Spring

ACADEMIC SCENE

Top Three Supportive LGBT Academic Areas:
1. American Studies 2. Women's Gender and Sexuality Studies 3. English

How LGBT-friendly are faculty in the classroom?
"The bond with faculty at Colby seems unique compared to what I hear at other campuses. It may be that the size of the campus allows for stronger relationships. As such, faculty that I know care about you as an individual. Being LGBT does not seem to matter." —*22-year-old gay male, senior*

"The faculty rock! I feel very open to sharing in the classroom related to LGBT issues." —*19-year-old bisexual female, sophomore*

SOCIAL SCENE

Top Three Things in the LGBT Social Life:
1. The Bridge 2. House parties 3. Hanging out

How would you describe the social scene for LGBT students?
"[The] dating scene is lacking. But, keep in mind we are in rural Maine. So much of what happens socially is due to the Bridge [LGBT campus group]."
—*20 year-old gay male, sophomore*

What annual social event should an LGBT student not miss?
"The drag show … it's the biggest thing of the year! Awesome! Once, the college president even got on stage to do a little dance." —*20-year-old lesbian, junior*

BUZZ BITES *Fun Queer Stuff to Know*

THE BEST...

Party Locale: AMS Party Lounge *and* the Spa

Hangout: Pugh Center

Eating Place: Foss Dining Hall

LGBT-Cool Athletic Sport: Ultimate Frisbee

Non-LGBT-Specific Campus Club: The CIRCLE

Place for LGBT Students to Live on Campus: Mary Low/Coburn *and* Foss/Woodman Residence Halls

LGBT Educational Involvement Opportunity: Annual Drag Ball/Dance

THE GAY POINT AVERAGE
OFFICIAL CAMPUS CHECKLIST

LGBT & ally student organization ✓

LGBT resource center/office

LGBT Pride Week &/or Coming Out Week ✓

Safe Zone/Safe Space or Ally Program ✓

Significant number of LGBT social activities ✓

Significant number of LGBT educational events ✓

Variety of LGBT studies/courses ✓

Nondiscrimination statement inclusive of sexual orientation ✓

Nondiscrimination statement inclusive of gender identity/expression ✓

Extends domestic partner benefits to same-sex couples ✓

Actively recruits LGBT students to enroll on campus ✓

Trains campus police on LGBT sensitivity ✓

Procedure for reporting LGBT bias, harassment & hate crimes ✓

Offers LGBT housing options/themes

Offers LGBT-inclusive health services/testing ✓

Offers LGBT-inclusive counseling/support groups ✓

Offers LGBT student scholarships

Conducts special LGBT graduation ceremony for LGBT & ally Students

Offers support services for process of transitioning from M to F & F to M ✓

Active LGBT alumni group ✓

COLBY COLLEGE
GAY POINT AVERAGE (16)
(out of 20)

**CAMPUS QUEER
RESOURCES**

Select LGBT Student Organization(s):
The Bridge and Project Ally
Founding Date: The Bridge (1974); Project Ally (1998–1999)
Membership: 30+
Phone: 207-872-3635
E-mail: bridge@colby.edu
Website: www.colby.edu/bridge;
www.colby.edu/project_ally

Resource Center/Office Responsible for LGBT Issues:
Office of Multicultural Affairs
Eustis Building
4000 Mayflower Hill
Waterville, ME 04901
Year Established: 2003–2004
Number of Staff: 1 full-time professional staff member
Phone: 207-859-4256
Website: www.colby.edu/administration_cs/dos/multicultural/glbtq/index.cfm

COLGATE UNIVERSITY

LIKE MANY COLLEGES and universities, Colgate University has not always accepted LGBT students, staff or faculty. Nestled in the middle of upstate New York, the campus is an old institution steeped in long-standing tradition—a formula for conservatism and a lack of desire for change.

Although it has been almost 30 years since the first LGBT support group was formed on campus, it is only since the mid-1990s that Colgate has developed into a first-rate queer campus. In fact, the campus has had an LGBT space called the Rainbow Room for quite some time. But only within the last three years has there been a funded staff position for LGBT issues. In addition, the campus has developed a Safe Zone training program open to the entire campus and required of all residential life staff. LGBT activities and events include the LGBTQ Alumni Speaker Series, Drag Ball, film series, and Holi-Gay Party.

The LGBT positive changes show no sign of stopping anytime soon. According to some LGBT campus officials, the number of out LGBT students at Colgate has gone from 10 to over 40 and is growing monthly. Not only does Colgate have more students coming out, but they're also getting involved outside of LGBT activities on campus—fraternities, sports teams, and student government leaders, to name a few. One such LGBT student goes on record: "I was nervous when I was first asked by my boyfriend to be his date at his Theta Chi fraternity formal, but the brothers treated me great. ...actually some of them treated me like a fellow brother. ...it was one of the best experiences I've ever had."

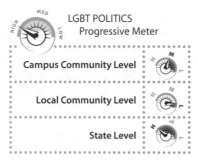

LGBT POLITICS
Progressive Meter

Campus Community Level

Local Community Level

State Level

OUTSPOKEN *Answers from LGBT students:*

Top Three Descriptors of the LGBT Campus Environment:
1. Active   2. Supportive   3. Safe

What makes your campus feel welcoming and safe for LGBT students?
"Talk about a Safe Zone. Colgate has so many visible signs for Safe Zone, and there are many allies. This made me feel welcome from day one."
—21-year-old lesbian, junior

How do you feel about coming out on your campus?
"Be yourself. I did. I was pleasantly surprised at how it was a nonissue. I don't think my experience is unlike many at Colgate. It is a great place to be queer!"
—20-year-old queer male, junior

INFO

COLGATE UNIVERSITY
13 Oak Drive
Hamilton, NY 13346
Phone: 315-228-7401
Fax: 315-228-7544
E-mail: admission@mail.colgate.edu
Website: www.colgate.edu

CAMPUS STATS
Type of Institution: Private university
Founding Year: 1819
Size: 2,800
Avg. Class Size: 10–19 students
Popular Majors: Political Science, English Language and Literature, Economics, History
Cost: Tuition: $32,885
Admission Application Deadline: January 15

ACADEMIC SCENE

Top Three Supportive LGBT Academic Areas:
1 Women's Studies   2. Sociology   3. Psychology

How LGBT-friendly are faculty in the classroom?
"Faculty understanding of LGBT issues in the classroom seems high. Occasionally, I have encountered a lack of awareness by some faculty, but they seemed open to my ideas always." —*19-year-old lesbian, sophomore*

"I have had professors who have come out to me. That makes me feel as though it is okay to be gay. I always contribute openly in class discussions. My friends and other classmates seem to get a kick out of it." —*19-year-old gay male, junior*

SOCIAL SCENE

Top Three Things in the LGBT Social Life:
1 Watching movies   2. Trips to Syracuse   3. Hanging out

How would you describe the social scene for LGBT students?
"Well, you got to get out. Many of my friends and I take trips elsewhere to local bars and clubs. Plus, there are many allies [who] come and party with us." —*20-year-old bisexual male, junior*

What annual social event should an LGBT student not miss?
"Holi-Gay Party. It's festive and sweet holiday fun!" —*20-year-old gay male, junior*

OUTRAGEOUS FACTOID The number of LGBT students has quadrupled in recent years, so much so that one student remarks: "We have a ridiculously high number of gay fraternity dates to formals without even having a gay fraternity."

RAINBOW RUMOR Colgate has come a long way on LGBT issues. However, some LGBT students and faculty acknowledge that there needs to be a greater connection with multiculturalism on campus, believing students who have multiple cultural identities beyond LGBT issues need to be able to find their place and feel comfortable too.

THAT'S SO GAY!

ANNUAL LGBT EVENT HIGHLIGHTS

GLBT Film Series: Fall/Spring

Safe Zone Trainings: Fall/Spring

Sex Week: October

National Coming Out Day: October 11

College Recruitment Fair: October

Holi-Gay Party: December

AIDS Awareness: December 1

Drag Ball: Spring

Pride Speaker Series: Spring

Lavender Graduation: April/May

BUZZ BITES *Fun Queer Stuff to Know*

THE BEST...

Party Locale: Creative Arts House

Hangout: Rainbow Room

Eating Place: Hamilton Whole Foods

Place to Check Out Guys: O'Connor Campus Center

Place to Check Out Ladies: Barge Canal Coffee House

LGBT-Cool Athletic Sport: Swimming *and* diving

Non-LGBT-Specific Campus Club: Latin American Student Organization

Place for LGBT Students to Live on Campus: Creative Arts House

LGBT Course Offering: Gay and Lesbian Identity in the Nineteenth and Twentieth Centuries

LGBT Educational Involvement Opportunity: Safe Zone Training

LGBT-Accepting Religious/Spiritual Organization(s): Colgate Jewish Union

CAMPUS QUEER RESOURCES

Select LGBT Student Organization(s):

Rainbow Alliance and Advocates
Founding Date: 1977
Membership: 150+
Phone: 315-228-7279
E-mail: rainbowalliance@mail.colgate.edu

LGBT Resource Center/Office:

LGBTQ Initiatives Office
115 East Hall
13 Oak Drive
Hamilton, NY 13346
Year Established: 2003
Number of Staff: 1 full-time professional staff member, 3 student workers
Phone: 315-228-7279
E-mail: rainbowalliance@mail.colgate.edu
Website: www.colgate.edu/DesktopDefault 1.aspx?tabid=1255andpgID=96

THE GAY POINT AVERAGE OFFICIAL CAMPUS CHECKLIST

✓ LGBT & ally student organization

✓ LGBT resource center/office

✓ LGBT Pride Week &/or Coming Out Week

✓ Safe Zone/Safe Space or Ally Program

✓ Significant number of LGBT social activities

Significant number of LGBT educational events

Variety of LGBT studies/courses

✓ Nondiscrimination statement inclusive of sexual orientation

Nondiscrimination statement inclusive of gender identity/expression

✓ Extends domestic partner benefits to same-sex couples

✓ Actively recruits LGBT students to enroll on campus

✓ Trains campus police on LGBT sensitivity

✓ Procedure for reporting LGBT bias, harassment & hate crimes

✓ Offers LGBT housing options/themes

✓ Offers LGBT-inclusive health services/testing

✓ Offers LGBT-inclusive counseling/support groups

Offers LGBT student scholarships

✓ Conducts special LGBT graduation ceremony for LGBT & ally Students

✓ Offers support services for process of transitioning from M to F & F to M

✓ Active LGBT alumni group

16 COLGATE UNIVERSITY GAY POINT AVERAGE
(out of 20)

COLORADO STATE UNIVERSITY

COLORADO STATE UNIVERSITY is situated at the base of the Rocky Mountains in the northern part of the state, a mecca for outdoor enthusiasts.

In 1974, LGBT students created their own organization at Colorado State, one of the first in the nation to address the needs of gay and lesbian students. In addition, the campus was the first university in Colorado to add sexual orientation to its nondiscrimination policy, in 1985; gender identity/expression was added in 2004.

In 1998 the campus put policy into practice by establishing GLBT Student Services. It started out as a small office in the basement of the student center but since has grown into a four-room suite with an expansive lounge space averaging 12,000 contacts a year. The office operates a phenomenal Safe Zone program as well as a well-utilized LGBT Speakers Bureau. In addition, GLBT Student Services and the queer student group plan annual events, including hikes, a ski trip, visits to corn mazes, and a drag show twice a year. The queers put the outdoors to use on this campus. According to some LGBT students, the campus tends to be "far more active and into the outdoors than anywhere else."

You may not have thought of the word "progressive" as a description of Colorado State University, but look over their outstanding Gay Point Average in further detail and possibly go on a campus visit to discover for yourself. At least one LGBT student thinks so: "GLBT Student Services make the campus feel like home. While the area is most conservative, the campus takes steps to ensure LGBT students can still feel welcome and safe. I came out when I came here. ... I have never regretted coming out or coming to Colorado State."

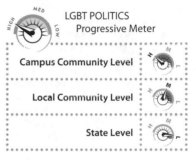

LGBT POLITICS
Progressive Meter

Campus Community Level

Local Community Level

State Level

OUTSPOKEN *Answers from LGBT students:*

Top Three Descriptors of the LGBT Campus Environment:
1 Vibrant   2. Supportive   3. Changing

What makes your campus feel welcoming and safe for LGBT students?
"Given the priceless resource of the GLBTSS office, I feel that this alone was a crucial step in making this campus a safer place for me as an LGBT individual. For instance, when I walk into the office, I know that I will not be looked at as if I am unnatural or wrong for the way I feel. Also, the fact that our office provides Speakers Bureaus to educate numerous classes on campus about the issues facing LGBT individuals contributes to the increased safety on this campus."
—22-year-old bisexual female, junior

How do you feel about coming out on your campus?
"I've never had a problem with it. ... As always, for anyone who may or may not be acquainted with the LGBT community at large, learning that someone they know is gay, LGBT issues can no longer be such a distant thing. Coming out can only make us stronger, and it's never been an issue on campus." *—20-year-old gay male, sophomore*

INFO

COLORADO STATE UNIVERSITY
8020 Campus Delivery
Fort Collins, CO 80523
Phone: 970-491-6909
Fax: 970-491-7799
E-mail: admissions@colostate.edu
Website: www.colostate.edu

CAMPUS STATS
Type of Institution: Public university
Founding Year: 1870
Size: 25,032
Avg. Class Size: 20–29 students
Popular Majors:
Microbiology, Physical Sciences, Psychology
Cost: In-state tuition: $3,790
Out-of-state tuition: $14,377
Admission Application Deadline: July 1

OUTRAGEOUS FACTOID Colorado State is located mere minutes away from the spectacular Rocky Mountains. A typical first date is to go hiking, skiing, rock climbing, or rafting.

• • • • • • • • • • • • • • • • • • •

RAINBOW RUMOR Colorado State and the local community of Fort Collins know how to come together to support LGBT issues. But, as with many campuses, it sometimes takes a tragedy of hate to provoke education and awareness. In 1998, after the hate crime in which Matthew Shepard, a gay University of Wyoming student, was murdered, a fraternity and sorority thought it would be "funny" to have a scarecrow depicting the slain gay student on their Wizard of Oz–themed homecoming float. Antigay graffiti was spray-painted on the face and back of the scarecrow by the fraternity. The homecoming parade took place the same weekend that Matthew was lying on his deathbed in the local Fort Collins hospital. Disciplinary sanctions were immediately imposed on the involved Greek organizations. A month after the scarecrow incident and Shepard's death, over 2,500 members of the campus community, mainly fraternity and sorority members, came out to show their queer support for a campuswide LGBT speaker.

• • • • • • • • • • • • • • • • • • • •

THAT'S SO GAY!

ANNUAL LGBT EVENT HIGHLIGHTS

Fall Night Hike: September

Halloween Pumpkin Carving Party: October

Corn Maze Outing: October

National Coming Out Day Rally: October 11

Harvey Milk Day: November 2

Fall Drag Show: December

Spring Ski Trip: February

Moonlight Snowshoe Hike: March

T'BGLAD: April

Spring Drag Show: April

Lavender Graduation: April

ACADEMIC SCENE

Top Three Supportive LGBT Academic Areas:
1. Social Work   2. Fine Arts   3. English Department

How LGBT-friendly are faculty in the classroom?
"Professors I've had, if they've bothered to mention anything pertaining to LGBT issues, have been supportive. Just like the student body, they're a mixed group, but I feel more confident being around them by knowing that so many have taken part in Safe Zone training and display their Safe Zone stickers prominently on their office doors." —*20-year-old gay male, sophomore*

"I have not experienced many teachers [who] discuss LGBT issues without some sort of prompt. It seems to be a rather taboo topic, but when it is presented, I have yet to experience a teacher that did not discuss the matter further." —*22-year-old lesbian, junior*

SOCIAL SCENE

Top Three Things in the LGBT Social Life:
1. Outdoor activities   2. SOGLBT   3. Clubs

How would you describe the social scene for LGBT students?
"The social scene for LGBT students is a very active one. … Aside from our office, we have a student organization which provides a safe place for members of the community to get together … share experiences and interact on a person-to-person level." —*22-year-old bisexual female, junior*

What annual social event should an LGBT student not miss?
"T'BGLAD is absolutely not to be missed, by anyone, if possible. It's our Transgender, Bisexual, Gay and Lesbian Awareness Days, a week in April chock full of fantastic and fabulous LGBT events. We usually schedule a number of speakers, educational forums, and fun activities in and around campus. I know I would never miss it!" —*20-year-old gay male, sophomore*

BUZZ BITES *Fun Queer Stuff to Know*

THE BEST...

Party Locale: Club Static

Hangout: Alley Cat, GLBTSS Office

Eating Place: Rainbow Café

Place to Check Out Guys: In front of the Clark Building or West Lawn

Place to Check Out Ladies: Rec Center

LGBT-Cool Athletic Sport: Women's rugby *and* men's lacrosse

Non-LGBT-Specific Campus Club: Snowriders

Place for LGBT Students to Live on Campus: Summit Hall

LGBT Course Offering: Twentieth-Century Gay and Lesbian Fiction

LGBT Educational Involvement Opportunity: Safe Zone

LGBT-Accepting Religious/Spiritual Organization(s): Unitarian Church, Plymouth Congregational Church

THE GAY POINT AVERAGE
OFFICIAL CAMPUS CHECKLIST

LGBT & ally student organization ✓

LGBT resource center/office ✓

LGBT Pride Week &/or Coming Out Week ✓

Safe Zone/Safe Space or Ally Program ✓

Significant number of LGBT social activities ✓

Significant number of LGBT educational events ✓

Variety of LGBT studies/courses

Nondiscrimination statement inclusive of sexual orientation ✓

Nondiscrimination statement inclusive of gender identity/expression ✓

Extends domestic partner benefits to same-sex couples

Actively recruits LGBT students to enroll on campus ✓

Trains campus police on LGBT sensitivity ✓

Procedure for reporting LGBT bias, harassment & hate crimes ✓

Offers LGBT housing options/themes

Offers LGBT-inclusive health services/testing ✓

Offers LGBT-inclusive counseling/support groups ✓

Offers LGBT student scholarships ✓

Conducts special LGBT graduation ceremony for LGBT & ally Students ✓

Offers support services for process of transitioning from M to F & F to M ✓

Active LGBT alumni group ✓

COLORADO STATE UNIVERSITY
GAY POINT AVERAGE (17)
(out of 20)

**CAMPUS QUEER
RESOURCES**

Select LGBT Student Organization(s):

**Student Organization for Gays,
Lesbians, Bisexuals and the
Transgendered**

Founding Date: 1974 (under a different name)

Membership: 75+

Phone: 970-491-4342

E-mail: soglbt@yahoo.com

LGBT Resource Center/Office:

**Gay, Lesbian, Bisexual and
Transgendered Student Services**

Lory Student Center, Room 171

Fort Collins, CO 80523

Year Established: 1998

Number of Staff: 1 full-time professional staff member, 11 student staff

Phone: 970-491-4342

E-mail: glbtss@lamar.colostate.edu

Website: www.glbtss.colostate.edu

COLUMBIA COLLEGE— CHICAGO

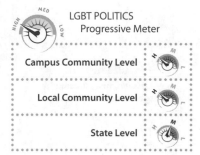

LGBT POLITICS
Progressive Meter

Campus Community Level

Local Community Level

State Level

INFO

COLUMBIA COLLEGE—CHICAGO
600 South Michigan Avenue
Chicago, IL 60605
Phone: 312-344-7131
Fax: 312-344-8024
E-mail: admissions@colum.edu
Website: www.colum.edu

CAMPUS STATS
Type of Institution: Private university
Founding Year: 1890
Size: 9,708
Avg. Class Size: 10–19 students
Popular Majors: Arts Management,
Cinematography and Film/Video
Production, Fine/Studio Arts
Cost: Tuition: $15,580
Admission Application Deadline: January 15

"QUEER FLAIR" IS how one LGBT student describes Columbia College–Chicago. Scattered around the South Loop of downtown Chicago, the college is the nation's largest arts and communications college and offers an urban queer experience like no other. An LGBT student proclaims: "You can be yourself, find yourself, accidentally bump into yourself."

Of course, you might expect LGBT friendliness from a college with a primary mission of "innovation and art," but the commitment goes beyond words. Columbia College has proven itself an ally, providing LGBT administrative support in policy and practice. As early as the 1990s, the campus had enacted a nondiscrimination policy inclusive of sexual orientation and shortly thereafter extended domestic partner benefits to same-sex employees. Then, in 2001, the campus established the Office of GLBT Student Concerns to support the needs and concerns of queer students on campus. As a result, an LGBT student group called Q-Force was founded in 2001 and now plans several LGBT awareness events throughout the year, such as the Queer Forum and the LGBT Health Fair.

One of the biggest event highlights is Gender Fusions. The celebration mixes together queer performance art, burlesque and drag in a single spectacular night. In addition to the LGBT-specific events, Q-Force and the Office of GLBT Student Concerns also actively participate in campuswide annual events like Manifest, the end-of-the-year student artwork exhibit. Queer students even have a parade float in Chicago Pride every year. As a result of experiences like these and the sheer numbers of LGBT students, campus life has been coined "inherently queer." Another student jokingly admits: "Ever since I came to Columbia, I don't have any more straight male friends."

If all of that is not proof, listen to this LGBT student perspective: "Already out, my expectations were high coming to Columbia. I kind of expected there to be queers like me, but I was surprised to find LGBT resources and specific LGBT events. … At other art colleges, I think LGBT students are assumed but not always supported…Here queer students have a collective voice and feel at home."

OUTSPOKEN *Answers from LGBT students:*

Top Three Descriptors of the LGBT Campus Environment:
1. Colorful   2. Flaming   3. Supportive

What makes your campus feel welcoming and safe for LGBT students?
"The fact that there is an office of GLBT Student Concerns to support us."
—20-year-old bisexual female, junior

"The number of LGBT students walking around." *—26-year-old queer, sophomore*

How do you feel about coming out on your campus?
"It's such a nonissue. It's an artistic mecca, so it's all queer! Coming out as straight might be an issue, but not queer." *—20-year-old gay male, junior*

"Every time I have come out, it has been a nonevent. Even coming out to my roommate, all he said was, 'Oh, that's cool.'" *—19-year-old gay male, freshman*

⊘ ACADEMIC SCENE

Top Three Supportive LGBT Academic Areas:
1. English   2. Liberal Education   3. Fiction Writing

How LGBT-friendly are faculty in the classroom?
"The faculty are most definitely queer-inclusive. There are faculty who are LGBT and who come out in classes. It's queer everywhere at Columbia."
—21-year-old lesbian, junior

"Totally gay-friendly. It really is not a big deal at all. Queer people are represented vastly in the arts, so it is not a surprise really that the faculty are LGBT-friendly. The faculty understand queers, their contributions to society…and it is as natural as the world is round." *—22-year-old queer female, senior*

☺ SOCIAL SCENE

Top Three Things in the LGBT Social Life:
1. Q-Force   2. Chicago nightlife   3. Coffee shops

How would you describe the social scene for LGBT students?
"It's too sexy for my…never mind! We do things outside of Columbia."
—18-year-old non-label-conforming female, freshman

What annual social event should an LGBT student not miss?
"The Halloween Party!"   *—26-year-old queer, sophomore*

 OUTRAGEOUS FACTOID A lesbian faculty member who teaches "The History of Rock and Soul" is the late morning show host and the host of "Breakfast with the Beatles" on 93.1 WXRT. Tune in.

 RAINBOW RUMOR Columbia College has some catching up to do in order to institutionalize LGBT policies and practices related to transgender issues.

THAT'S SO GAY!  **ANNUAL LGBT EVENT HIGHLIGHTS**

Queer Forum: Fall

Halloween Party: October

World AIDS Day: December 1

LGBT Health Fair: March

Manifest with Q-Force: Spring

Day of Silence: First week of April

Gender Fusions: April

Queer Burlesque Show: Fall/Spring

LGBT Art and Spoken Word: Fall/Spring

BUZZ BITES *Fun Queer Stuff to Know*

THE BEST…

Party Locale: Hydrate

Hangout: Kit Kat Lounge

Eating Place: PingPong

Place to Check Out Guys: Halstead Area

Place to Check Out Ladies: Andersonville

Non-LGBT-Specific Campus Club: Latino Alliance

Place for LGBT Students to Live on Campus: Plymouth Court Residence Halls

LGBT Educational Involvement Opportunity: Q-Force

LGBT-Accepting Religious/Spiritual Organization(s): Hillel Jewish Organization

CAMPUS QUEER RESOURCES

Select LGBT Student Organization(s):

Q-Force
Founding Date: October 2004
Membership: 120+
E-mail: info@qforcecolumbia.org
Website: www.qforcecolumbia.org

LGBT Resource Center/Office:

Office of GLBT Student Concerns
623 South Wabash Avenue, Suite 301 |
Chicago, IL 60605
Year Established: 2001
Number of Staff: 1 part-time professional
staff; 1 part-time student assistant
Phone: 312-344-8594
Website: www.colum.edu/student-affairs/glbt/

THE GAY POINT AVERAGE
OFFICIAL CAMPUS CHECKLIST

- ✓ LGBT & ally student organization
- ✓ LGBT resource center/office
- LGBT Pride Week &/or Coming Out Week
- Safe Zone/Safe Space or Ally Program
- ✓ Significant number of LGBT social activities
- ✓ Significant number of LGBT educational events
- Variety of LGBT studies/courses
- ✓ Nondiscrimination statement inclusive of sexual orientation
- Nondiscrimination statement inclusive of gender identity/expression
- ✓ Extends domestic partner benefits to same-sex couples
- Actively recruits LGBT students to enroll on campus
- Trains campus police on LGBT sensitivity
- ✓ Procedure for reporting LGBT bias, harassment & hate crimes
- Offers LGBT housing options/themes
- ✓ Offers LGBT-inclusive health services/testing
- ✓ Offers LGBT-inclusive counseling/support groups
- Offers LGBT student scholarships
- Conducts special LGBT graduation ceremony for LGBT & ally Students
- ✓ Offers support services for process of transitioning from M to F & F to M
- Active LGBT alumni group

10 COLUMBIA COLLEGE—CHICAGO
GAY POINT AVERAGE
(out of 20)

CORNELL UNIVERSITY

ONE OF THE first signs new students see at the Cornell University is a massive, centrally located red-and-white banner that reads: LESBIAN, GAY, BISEXUAL, TRANSGENDER RESOURCE CENTER. The huge block letters cannot be missed at the campus information fair, and neither can the visible campus commitment to LGBT students.

Cornell University prides itself on being "absolutely gay"! LGBT inclusiveness is obvious at Cornell from Opening Day on. Orientation week activities include an LGBT new student meeting as well as a welcome reception to meet other LGBT student leaders and staff. And then on the second weekend, it's off to Queer Camp, the official LGBT campuswide community retreat. LGBT students quickly learn about the 15-plus LGBT and ally student groups on campus and the plethora of LGBT activities. These activities are generated by Cornell's LGBT student groups, the LGBT Resource Center, and the Program in Lesbian, Bisexual, Gay Studies.

LGBT students can always stop by the LGBT Resource Center between classes, where they can lounge and discuss politics in giant chairs in the shape of leopard-print stiletto-heeled shoes. Beyond the center, many departments on campus also conscientiously reach out to LGBT students—from the health center staff to residence life staff. The annual National Coming Out Day ad runs a full page and lists hundreds of names of out and proud LGBT and ally members of the Cornell community.

Perhaps the words of a current LGBT student capture Cornell's LGBT progressiveness best: "The LGBT Resource Center is simply amazing! But more importantly, there is a common thread of acceptance and recognition of diversity that permeates … the campus." Sounds queer to me!

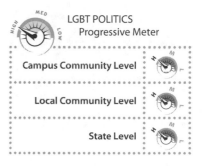

OUTSPOKEN *Answers from LGBT students:*

Top Three Descriptors of the LGBT Campus Environment:
1 Fabulous   2. Outstanding   3. Warm

What makes your campus feel welcoming and safe for LGBT students?
"I believe that it is the extensive outreach and education by veteran members of the LGBT community on campus. We have a very active community of leaders that is directly involved in groups like ZAP! which go into residence halls, classrooms, and the wider community to engage people with queer issues as well as confronting harmful stereotypes and homophobia. My personal joy is when I recognize people from former ZAP! panels and other events showing up more and more often within the sphere of LGBT activities and groups on campus. It's also extremely satisfying to have people contact you afterwards and thank you for your efforts in making the campus climate a little more conducive to being more open for everyone." *—20-year-old bisexual female, sophomore*

How do you feel about coming out on your campus?
"I feel that it is generally very safe to come out on campus. I came out to people in my residence hall within a few weeks of arriving at Cornell, and I not only found positive affirmation coming from these people, but one of them actually came out as well. A very close friend of mine was able to come out to me very recently, despite much fear and anxiety. I was proud of her and was able to hook her up with the right resources on campus." *—21-year-old lesbian, junior*

INFO

CORNELL UNIVERSITY
410 Thurston Avenue
Ithaca, NY 14850
Phone: 607-255-5241
Fax: 607-255-0659
E-mail: admissions@cornell.edu
Website: www.cornell.edu

CAMPUS STATS
Type of Institution: Private university
Founding Year: 1865
Size: 13,625
Avg. Class Size: 10–19 students
Popular Majors: Agriculture, Business/Commerce, Engineering
Cost: Tuition: $31,300
Admission Application Deadline: January 1

OUTRAGEOUS FACTOID

Cornell celebrates a long and proud LGBT history. The first adviser of the Student Homophile League (the LGBT student group) back in 1968 was Father Daniel Berrigan, campus chaplain, who became internationally renowned as a peace activist and was at one time featured on the FBI's Ten Most Wanted Fugitives list. And two of the most prominent leaders of the transgender rights movement are Cornell alumni—Shannon Minter, Law 1993, legal director of the National Center for Lesbian Rights; and Paisley Currah, Ph.D. 1994, professor at Brooklyn College and executive director of the Center for Lesbian and Gay Studies.

RAINBOW RUMOR

More efforts are being taken to put into practice transgender-inclusive actions to support the recent addition of gender identity and expression to the university equal opportunity policy. The campus also recognizes the need to support same-gender-loving students of color and is working to raise awareness and improve support of LGBT students of color across the campus. One LGBT student commends the move, saying: "I would rather be on a campus that works to improve than simply ignores an issue."

THAT'S SO GAY!

ANNUAL LGBT EVENT HIGHLIGHTS

LGBTQ New Students Meeting: August

LGBTQ Welcome Reception: August

Queer Camp LGBTQ Student Retreat: September

HOMOcoming: September/October

Coming Out Rocks!: October/November

GAYpril: April

Queer Prom: April/May

Lavender Graduation: May

ACADEMIC SCENE

Top Three Supportive LGBT Academic Areas:
1. Program in Lesbian, Gay and Bisexual Studies   2. Feminist, Gender and Sexuality Studies   3. English

How LGBT-friendly are faculty in the classroom?
"I have yet to find a faculty member who spews any antiqueer rhetoric…Most have been very receptive to listening to what I have had to say in challenging their assumptions and biases. I have yet to find any faculty that even bats an eyelash at my manner of dress or gender expression. I feel very safe and welcome in expressing myself free from discrimination." —*20-year-old bisexual female, sophomore*

SOCIAL SCENE

Top Three Things in the LGBT Social Life:
1. Flirting   2. Common Ground   3. Queer dances

How would you describe the social scene for LGBT students?
"I think the social scene for LGBT students at Cornell varies a lot depending on your level of 'out-ness.' As someone who is totally out, I enjoy a wide variety of social activities available to me, going to dances and other group functions." —*23-year-old gay male, senior*

What annual social event should an LGBT student not miss?
"DON'T MISS QUEER PROM!!! It's an enormous LGBT dance held once each year, and it's simply fabulous!" —*20-year-old gay male, junior*

BUZZ BITES *Fun Queer Stuff to Know*

THE BEST…

Party Locale: Common Ground

Hangout: Felicia's Atomic Lounge

Eating Place: Juna's Restaurant

Place to Check Out Guys: Facebook and Gay.com

LGBT-Cool Athletic Sport: Women's rugby

Non-LGBT-Specific Campus Club: Student Assembly

Place for LGBT Students to Live on Campus: JAM and Risley Hall

LGBT Educational Involvement Opportunity: ZAP! Sexuality Discussion Panel

THE GAY POINT AVERAGE
OFFICIAL CAMPUS CHECKLIST

LGBT & ally student organization ✓

LGBT resource center/office ✓

LGBT Pride Week &/or Coming Out Week ✓

Safe Zone/Safe Space or Ally Program ✓

Significant number of LGBT social activities ✓

Significant number of LGBT educational events ✓

Variety of LGBT studies/courses ✓

Nondiscrimination statement Inclusive of sexual orientation ✓

Nondiscrimination statement inclusive of gender identity/expression ✓

Extends domestic partner benefits to same-sex couples ✓

Actively recruits LGBT students to enroll on campus ✓

Trains campus police on LGBT sensitivity ✓

Procedure for reporting LGBT bias, harassment & hate crimes ✓

Offers LGBT housing options/themes

Offers LGBT-inclusive health services/testing ✓

Offers LGBT-inclusive counseling/support groups ✓

Offers LGBT student scholarships

Conducts special LGBT graduation ceremony for LGBT & ally Students ✓

Offers support services for process of transitioning from M to F & F to M

Active LGBT alumni group ✓

CORNELL UNIVERSITY
GAY POINT AVERAGE
(out of 20)
17

CAMPUS QUEER RESOURCES

Select LGBT Student Organization(s):

Haven
282 Caldwell Hall
Ithaca, NY 14853
Founding Date: May 1968 (although the name has changed many times)
Membership: 600
Phone: 607-255-3608
Website: www.dos.cornell.edu/haven/

LGBT Resource Center/Office:

Lesbian, Gay, Bisexual, Transgender Resource Center
282 Caldwell Hall
Ithaca, NY 14853
Year Established: 1994
Number of Staff: 2 full-time professional staff members, 4 part-time student staff
Phone: 607-254-4987
E mail: lgbtrc@cornell.edu
Website: www.lgbtrc.cornell.edu/

DARTMOUTH COLLEGE

THOSE LGBT STUDENTS looking for an exemplary liberal arts education on a small campus close to nature have found the perfect match.

Over the last 10 years, Dartmouth College has been actively working to support its LGBT students in policy and in practice. All students have opportunities to learn about sexual orientation and gender identity, beginning with new student orientation and ending with commencement. Even the traditions have been given a queer makeover to be LGBT-inclusive. One such tradition is the Winter Carnival—a full week of skiing, ice sculptures, polar bear swims and other outdoorsy activities, including an LGBT student-initiated Carnival Drag Ball. All the students flock to see the winter drag spectacle. It is now considered to be the "most popular event" of the weeklong tradition.

Dartmouth truly offers a place for LGBT students to thrive and become change agents. The list of past LGBT leaders proves it—from famous LGBT activist and author Keith Boykin to Hillary Smith Goodridge, the lead plaintiff in the historic case that yielded today's same-sex marriage equality in the state of Massachusetts.

Andrew Goldsmith, a recent LGBT student and current alumni, was one of Dartmouth's most respected athletes and, according to ESPN, "the most accomplished male, team-sport athlete in North America to be openly gay during his playing career." He also scored in the NCAA—something no hockey goalie has done in over three decades. I guess it takes a gay goalie to have enough balls to score in the NCAA Tournament." As far as his hockey teammates' responses to his coming out, Andrew stressed the support he felt from everyone. "I felt like there was, there was a hand on my back, pushing me forward and supporting me. There's really no feeling like that." Such LGBT student courage, coupled with strong support for LGBT students, is evidence of what can be a positive coming out experience at Dartmouth College.

𝄞 OUTSPOKEN *Answers from LGBT students:*

Top Three Descriptors of the LGBT Campus Environment:
1. Diverse   2. Responsive   3. Easygoing

What makes your campus feel welcoming and safe for LGBT students?
"Dartmouth feels LGBT-friendly because of the diversity inherent in being a college with prestige. The campus draws applicants from countless numbers of different socioeconomic, racial/ethnic, political and familial backgrounds. I personally come from a welfare-recipient single-parent mixed-race household in fiercely liberal Seattle with a mother who is Deaf. Note that it is not just geography that makes our campus safe; it is our differences that bind us together." —*21-year-old gay male, senior*

"Dartmouth has different LGBT organizations such as the Gay/Straight Alliance and Dartmouth Rainbow Alliance, that ensure the confidentiality of its members, and provide different resources for LGBT students." —*18-year-old gay male, freshman*

How do you feel about coming out on your campus?
"Honestly, I think being out at Dartmouth is way easier (at least for me) than being out at home. There are so many LGBT-positive messages here that I feel aren't nearly as present at other schools." —*20-year-old lesbian, sophomore*

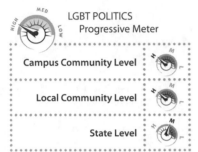

LGBT POLITICS
Progressive Meter

Campus Community Level

Local Community Level

State Level

INFO

DARTMOUTH COLLEGE
6016 McNutt Hall
Hanover, NH 03755

Phone: 603-646-2875

Fax: 603-646-1216

E-mail:
admissions.office@dartmouth.edu

Website: www.dartmouth.edu

CAMPUS STATS

Type of Institution: Private college

Founding Year: 1769

Size: 3,996

Avg. Class Size: 10–19 students

Popular Majors: Social Sciences and History, English, Biological/Life Sciences

Cost: Tuition: $30,279

Admission Application Deadline: January 1

"Initially I was extremely uncomfortable with the idea of being out on campus, only because it was so frustrating at home. After being at Dartmouth for a while, you realize that the community here is so welcoming, and coming out no longer seems so frightening." —*19-year-old bisexual female, sophomore*

ACADEMIC SCENE

Top Three Supportive LGBT Academic Areas:
1. Women and Gender Studies   2. English   3. Psychology

How LGBT-friendly are faculty in the classroom?
"The classroom … that's a difficult topic. I've yet to encounter an actively LGBT-friendly professor. I've encountered a professor or two, however, that laughs every time homosexuality is brought up in literature. I'm not sure why that is, but it's not very comfortable." —*21-year-old queer male, junior*

"Faculty are extremely friendly, at least within the social science and humanities divisions, which is where I spend all of my time. I have had no difficulty talking with my professors about sexuality, or bringing up issues of identity during class discussions. There are classes that are still ostensibly white and male-dominated, which I sometimes struggle to get my voice heard in. More and more professors are becoming comfortable correcting their own heterosexism when they are made aware of it." —*20-year-old lesbian, sophomore*

How would you describe the social scene for LGBT students?
"Well, Dartmouth is a small place, so really any particular scene is also going to be small. That being said, the LGBT social scene for students is actually kind of sprawling, though in many ways [it] maintains a feeling of a close-knit group. I personally feel myself becoming even more connected to the scene on a daily basis. Breaking into the scene initially is just somewhat intimidating because you're still figuring yourself out." —*20-year-old lesbian, sophomore*

What annual social event should an LGBT student not miss?
"The Drag Ball. It is usually held during winter term, and I find it an incredible and radical way for students to question gender norms, push their own limitations with gender performance and just have a good time seeing their friends cross-dress and compete for Drag King/Drag Queen stardom!"
—*21-year-old queer male, junior*

OUTRAGEOUS FACTOID
Dartmouth is well known for the Dartmouth Outing Club, the oldest and largest collegiate club designed for outdoor adventures. It's a tradition that the club has LGBT students who are out and proud!

RAINBOW RUMOR
Don't let the Ivy League mystique fool you. From the outset, you may think the Dartmouth LGBT community (particularly the G) seems to be an elite clique. This campus is all about heart and soul. Students may have to push themselves harder to meet other LGBT students, but there are many "open arms" on the other end. Be warned, though: dancing in the arms of a same-sex date is probably not a good idea at every fraternity house.

THAT'S SO GAY!
ANNUAL LGBT EVENT HIGHLIGHTS

Coming Out Month: October

Homecoming DGALA, an alumni-focused event: Late October

Queer Bar Night: Every quarter

Various LGBT speakers: Throughout the year

Drag Ball Winter Carnival: February

National Day of Silence: April

Dimensions LGBT Open House: May

LGBT Prom: Spring

LGBT Graduation Celebration: May

 BUZZ BITES *Fun Queer Stuff to Know*

THE BEST...

Party Locale: Tabard House

Hangout: Panarchy House *or the* Gay Room

Eating Place: Collis Café

Place to Check Out Guys: Robo *or* West Gym Fitness Center

Place to Check Out Ladies: Fitness Center *or* rugby fields

LGBT-Cool Athletic Sport: Crew

Non-LGBT-Specific Campus Club: Dartmouth Outing Club

Place for LGBT Students to Live on Campus: Tabard House *and* Panarchy House

LGBT Course Offering: Judaism, Sexuality and Queerness

LGBT Educational Involvement Opportunity: Gay-Straight Alliance Education in Greek Houses

CAMPUS QUEER
RESOURCES

Select LGBT Student Organization(s):

Dartmouth Rainbow Alliance and
Gay-Straight Alliance

Founding Date: DRA (1972); GSA (1999)

Membership: 60+

Phone: 603-646-0800

E-mail: Dartmouth.Rainbow.
Alliance@dartmouth.edu;
GSA@dartmouth.edu

Website: www.dartmouth.edu/~dra;
www.dartmouth.edu/~gsa

LGBT Resource Center/Office:

**Office of Pluralism and Leadership
LGBT Programming and Advocacy**

6217 Collis Center
Hanover, NH 03755

Year Established: 1994

Number of Staff: 1 full-time professional staff
member, other part-time volunteers and
interns

Phone: 603-646-3635

E-mail: pam.misener@dartmouth.edu

Website: www.dartmouth.edu/~glbprog *or*
www.dartmouth.edu/~glbtprog

THE GAY POINT AVERAGE
OFFICIAL CAMPUS CHECKLIST

✓ LGBT & ally student organization

✓ LGBT resource center/office

✓ LGBT Pride Week &/or Coming Out Week

✓ Safe Zone/Safe Space or Ally Program

✓ Significant number of LGBT social activities

✓ Significant number of LGBT educational events

✓ Variety of LGBT studies/courses

✓ Nondiscrimination statement inclusive of sexual orientation

Nondiscrimination statement inclusive of gender identity/expression

✓ Extends domestic partner benefits to same-sex couples

✓ Actively recruits LGBT students to enroll on campus

Trains campus police on LGBT sensitivity

✓ Procedure for reporting LGBT bias, harassment & hate crimes

Offers LGBT housing options/themes

✓ Offers LGBT-inclusive health services/testing

✓ Offers LGBT-inclusive counseling/support groups

Offers LGBT student scholarships

✓ Conducts special LGBT graduation ceremony for LGBT & ally Students

✓ Offers support services for process of transitioning from M to F & F to M

✓ Active LGBT alumni group

16 DARTMOUTH COLLEGE
GAY POINT AVERAGE
(out of 20)

DEPAUL UNIVERSITY

DEPAUL UNIVERSITY IS an extremely progressive campus for LGBT issues. It has a stated and ongoing commitment to multiculturalism and service to a diverse student body. As such, its commitment to diversity includes LGBT students. The Gay Point Average rating reflects the campus commitment to positive LGBT policies and practices.

Since 1999, there has been a paradigm shift at DePaul. LGBT issues have become increasingly visible. The campus developed a Safe Zone program to highlight the many LGBT allies across campus. In addition, there are a number of LGBT student groups at DePaul, including Pride, T-Global, and Spectrum. The Counseling Center also has LGBT support groups, and the University Ministry organizes a training for peer ministers on LGBT issues and concerns. There are even LGBT course offerings dating back to the mid to late 1990s. And, as recently as 2005, a core group of faculty developed a minor in LGBT studies. One LGBT student shares poignantly: "I have always been proud to be a Catholic. My gay identity always kept my faith in question and conflicted [with] what I was taught to believe. I have found peace with who I am at DePaul University. It's okay to be gay."

OUTSPOKEN *Answers from LGBT students:*

Top Three Descriptors of the LGBT Campus Environment:
1. Accepting   2. Progressive   3. Safe

What makes your campus feel welcoming and safe for LGBT students?
"The queer population is highly visible—that visibility makes me feel comfortable being out on campus. But, it's a double-edged sword sometimes; with that visibility comes the potential to be a greater target of bias and hate. The campus understands this and sends strong messages condemning such acts." *—21-year-old gay male, senior*

How do you feel about coming out on your campus?
"I did it. I was out when I decided to come to DePaul and it was a nonissue, really. I did not want to be known just for being gay. My fraternity welcomed me as a brother regardless." *—22-year-old gay male, senior*

LGBT POLITICS
Progressive Meter

Campus Community Level

Local Community Level

State Level

INFO

DEPAUL UNIVERSITY
1 East Jackson Boulevard
Chicago, IL 60604
Phone: 312-362-8300
Fax: 312-362-5749
E-mail: admitdpu@depaul.edu
Website: www.depaul.edu

CAMPUS STATS

Type of Institution: Private university, Catholic religious affiliation
Founding Year: 1898
Size: 14,239
Avg. Class Size: 20–29 students
Popular Majors: Accounting, Business Administration/Management
Cost: Tuition: $19,700
Admission Application Deadline: January 1

OUTRAGEOUS FACTOID

DePaul is known for its Vincentian Catholicism and its commitment to serving marginalized and oppressed groups through service to the community. The teachings place an emphasis on the human dignity and value of each individual person's life. So what does that mean for gays on campus? Quite simply, the campus embraces a progressive Catholic ideology that openly accepts LGBT students.

• • • • • • • • • • • • • • • • • • • •

RAINBOW RUMOR

Tragically, in fall 2004 a lesbian student was physically assaulted by a male student in an alley on campus. LGBT and ally students immediately staged a sit-in, rally and march to support her. The president of DePaul University not only attended the rally without being asked but wanted to publicly condemn any act of homophobia on campus. He announced: "All students at DePaul have the right to feel safe." Nonetheless, students say the campus needs to come out publicly more often.

• • • • • • • • • • • • • • • • • • • •

THAT'S SO GAY!

ANNUAL LGBT EVENT HIGHLIGHTS

Coming Out Ball: October

Coming Out Week: October

Spectrum Pride Week: April

National Day of Silence: April

Take Back the Night: April

Drag Fest: April

Night of Colors: Spring Quarter

Spectrum Banquet: May

Sexuality and Diversity Workshop Series: All year

Safe Zone: Winter quarter

ACADEMIC SCENE

Top Three Supportive LGBT Academic Areas:
1 LGQ Studies   2. Women and Gender Studies   3. Sociology

How LGBT-friendly are faculty in the classroom?
"The campus has come a long way for being affiliated with the Catholic Church. After all, we do have an LGBT resource center as well as [an] academic minor available in LGBT studies. I would guess the program is the only one of its kind at a Catholic religiously affiliated campus." —*20-year-old bisexual female, junior*

"You have a mix of allies and those who are rumored not to be supportive of LGBT issues. I have never experienced disparaging words from a faculty member toward LGBT people, though." —*22-year-old gay male, senior*

SOCIAL SCENE

Top Three Things in the LGBT Social Life:
1. Going out to Boystown   2. Shopping   3. Dance clubs

How would you describe the social scene for LGBT students?
"Amazing. Our location is a 'gay mecca.' We have Boystown right around the corner. What more could you want, really?" —*22-year-old gay male, senior*

What annual social event should an LGBT student not miss?
"The drag show, of course. Be prepared to be shocked!"
—*20-year-old gay male, junior*

BUZZ BITES
Fun Queer Stuff to Know

THE BEST...

Party Locale: Boystown

Hangout: Lola's

Eating Place: Kopi Cafe

Place to Check Out Guys: Halstead area

Place to Check Out Ladies: Andersonville area

LGBT-Cool Fraternity for Men:
Sigma Phi Epsilon

LGBT Course Offering: Creating Change: Contemporary LGBT Politics and Deconstructing the Diva

LGBT-Accepting Religious/Spiritual Organization(s): Buddhist/Meditation Services

THE GAY POINT AVERAGE
OFFICIAL CAMPUS CHECKLIST

LGBT & ally student organization	✓
LGBT resource center/office	✓
LGBT Pride Week &/or Coming Out Week	✓
Safe Zone/Safe Space or Ally Program	✓
Significant number of LGBT social activities	✓
Significant number of LGBT educational events	✓
Variety of LGBT studies/courses	✓
Nondiscrimination statement inclusive of sexual orientation	✓
Nondiscrimination statement inclusive of gender identity/expression	
Extends domestic partner benefits to same-sex couples	
Actively recruits LGBT students to enroll on campus	
Trains campus police on LGBT sensitivity	✓
Procedure for reporting LGBT bias, harassment & hate crimes	✓
Offers LGBT housing options/themes	
Offers LGBT-inclusive health services/testing	
Offers LGBT-inclusive counseling/support groups	✓
Offers LGBT student scholarships	
Conducts special LGBT graduation ceremony for LGBT & ally Students	
Offers support services for process of transitioning from M to F & F to M	✓
Active LGBT alumni group	

DEPAUL UNIVERSITY
GAY POINT AVERAGE   (12)
(out of 20)

CAMPUS QUEER
RESOURCES

Select LGBT Student Organization(s):
Spectrum
Founding Date: 2003
Membership: 60+
Phone: 773-325-7361
E-mail: spectrumdepaul@gmail.com
Website: www.spectrumdepaul.org

LGBT Resource Center/Office:
Office of LGBTQA Student Services
2250 North Sheffield Ave, Room 307
Chicago, IL 60614
Year Established: 2004
Number of Staff: 1 graduate assistant
Phone: 773-325-7294
E-mail: nperez@depaul.edu
Website: studentaffairs.depaul.edu/lgbtqa/

DEPAUW UNIVERSITY

DEPAUW UNIVERSITY OFFERS an LGBT-progressive choice in the rural area of Greencastle, Indiana. The religiously affiliated Methodist campus has demonstrated a commitment to LGBT issues that deserves to be noted.

Definitely an Indiana queer pioneer, DePauw is among the first colleges in the state to include both sexual orientation and gender identity/expression as a protected class in campus policies. The Gay Point Average demonstrates that this campus has been out front as a leader with many LGBT-inclusive policies and practices. Nevertheless, the campus is probably best-known for its huge fraternity and sorority population, which easily dominates the majority of campus life. But don't be fooled: not only are there LGBT allies among the Greeks, but also LGBT students themselves have come out and pledged Greek on campus.

The number of out LGBT students at DePauw overall has never been larger than in recent years. Many of these queer students are actively involved with the LGBT and ally student group called United DePauw. In addition, in 1999 the campus succeeded in developing an office for LGBT Services, with a full-time professional coordinator. The office advocates on behalf of queer students and works collaboratively with queer students to plan annual event favorites like National Coming Out Week, Denim Day, the Anti Prom, and a host of educational workshops and trainings across campus.

DePauw University has unquestionably made a commitment to LGBT-inclusiveness. Queer students describe the climate at DePauw as one of general acceptance. Some hail the campus as "lively," "gay-hospitable" and "queer caring." Another LGBT student adds: "I feel safe and have found acceptance for who I am on this campus. ... I did not have that in high school. DePauw represents a 'bubble' of gay-friendliness, unlike the rest of Indiana."

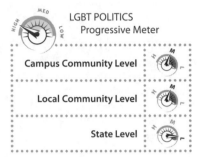

LGBT POLITICS
Progressive Meter

Campus Community Level

Local Community Level

State Level

OUTSPOKEN *Answers from LGBT students:*

Top Three Descriptors of the LGBT Campus Environment:
1. Ever-changing   2. Supportive   3. Welcoming

What makes your campus feel welcoming and safe for LGBT students?
"I was impressed by the support through the LGBT services office. The office is visible to many on campus who are queer-identified as a place to be yourself. I found comfort and solace." —*22-year-old queer male, senior*

How do you feel about coming out on your campus?
"I have never been afraid to come out. But it is a lot easier than high school where I was closeted and worried what my friends would say or do. It's a special place for Indiana." —*19-year-old bisexual female, sophomore*

INFO

DEPAUW UNIVERSITY
101 East Seminary
Greencastle, IN 46135
Phone: 765-658-4006
Fax: 765-658-4007
E-mail: admission@depauw.edu
Website: www.depauw.edu

CAMPUS STATS

Type of Institution: Private university, Methodist religious affiliation

Founding Year: 1837

Size: 2,350

Avg. Class Size: 10–19 students

Popular Majors: Biology, Economics, English Composition, Mass Communications/Media Studies

Cost: Tuition: $32,760

Admission Application Deadline: February 1

⊘ ACADEMIC SCENE

Top Three Supportive LGBT Academic Areas:
1. Sociology/Anthropology   2. Biology   3. Art

How LGBT-friendly are faculty in the classroom?
"Faculty tend to be LGBT-supportive. I don't think they get the 'trans issue' nearly as much … but I think some try to be open and accepting overall. It depends on the discipline, really." —*21-year-old queer female, junior*

"I think it wavers in support, as I am sure many campuses do. I have always felt supported in my classes, but I don't think all faculty are nearly as LGBT-inclusive in their subjects … from what I hear on campus."
—*19-year-old gay male, freshman*

☺ SOCIAL SCENE

Top Three Things in the LGBT Social Life:
1. Hanging out   2. United DePauw   3. House parties

How would you describe the social scene for LGBT students?
"A variety of queerness…thanks to United DePauw and LGBT Services. Thank goodness." —*20-year-old lesbian, sophomore*

What annual social event should an LGBT student not miss?
"Drag Ball … it's a hoot!" —*20-year-old gay male, junior*

OUTRAGEOUS FACTOID The DePauw Queer Center, a student activity space in Senior Hall, is not to be confused with the Q-Center, where students go for tutoring in math-related subjects.

• • • • • • • • • • • • • • • • • • • •

RAINBOW RUMOR Most DePauw residence halls have at least one unisex restroom to be more trans-inclusive of students. However, the university continues to struggle in academic buildings with creating gender-neutral restroom and changing facilities.

• • • • • • • • • • • • • • • • • • • •

THAT'S SO GAY!
ANNUAL LGBT EVENT HIGHLIGHTS

Drag Ball: Fall
Trans-Panel: Fall
LGBT History Month: October
Coming Out Week: October
Denim Day: April
Anti Prom: Spring
Queer Art Exhibit: Spring

BUZZ BITES *Fun Queer Stuff to Know*

• •

THE BEST...

Hangout: LGBT Lounge
Eating Place: Union HUB
Place to Check Out Guys: Lily Athletic Center
Place to Check Out Ladies: West Library
Non-LGBT-Specific Campus Club:
College Democrats
LGBT Educational Involvement Opportunity:
Trans-Panel

CAMPUS QUEER RESOURCES

Select LGBT Student Organization(s):

United DePauw
Founding Date: 1985
Membership: 50
Phone: 765-658-4850
Website: www.depauw.edu/student/orgs/
RECOGNIZED/UnitedDepauw.asp

LGBT Resource Center/Office:

LGBT Services
Office of Multicultural Affairs
Union Building 100A
DePauw University
408 South Locust
Greencastle, IN 46135
Year Established: 1999
Number of Staff: 1 full-time professional staff
member, 2 part-time staff
Phone: 765-658-4026
Website: www.depauw.edu/admin/
multicultural/LGBT_services.asp

THE GAY POINT AVERAGE
OFFICIAL CAMPUS CHECKLIST

- ✓ LGBT & ally student organization
- ✓ LGBT resource center/office
- ✓ LGBT Pride Week &/or Coming Out Week
-   Safe Zone/Safe Space or Ally Program
- ✓ Significant number of LGBT social activities
- ✓ Significant number of LGBT educational events
-   Variety of LGBT studies/courses
- ✓ Nondiscrimination statement inclusive of sexual orientation
- ✓ Nondiscrimination statement inclusive of gender identity/expression
- ✓ Extends domestic partner benefits to same-sex couples
-   Actively recruits LGBT students to enroll on campus
- ✓ Trains campus police on LGBT sensitivity
- ✓ Procedure for reporting LGBT bias, harassment & hate crimes
- ✓ Offers LGBT housing options/themes
- ✓ Offers LGBT-inclusive health services/testing
- ✓ Offers LGBT-inclusive counseling/support groups
-   Offers LGBT student scholarships
- ✓ Conducts special LGBT graduation ceremony for LGBT & ally Students
-   Offers support services for process of transitioning from M to F & F to M
-   Active LGBT alumni group

14 DEPAUW UNIVERSITY
GAY POINT AVERAGE
(out of 20)

DUKE UNIVERSITY

DUKE ADDED SEXUAL orientation to its nondiscrimination policy as early as 1989 and extended benefits to same-sex partners in 1994. Even today, senior administrators are openly supportive and affirming of the LGBT community. Recent examples include the university's decision in 2000 to begin allowing same-sex union ceremonies in Duke Chapel and in the Freeman Center for Jewish Life. In 2003, the Office of Undergraduate Admissions assigned an LGBT liaison to handle admission inquiries from prospective LGBT students.

Also in 2003, Duke became the birthplace of the "Gay? Fine by Me" national t-shirt phenomenon, which spread to hundreds of campuses. In 2004, Duke terminated its relationship with the Durham YMCA because of that organization's discriminatory refusal to offer family benefits to same-sex couples. In 2006, members of the campus LGBT community are currently working to add gender identity and gender expression to the campus nondiscrimination policy.

Duke has an active LGBT student center featuring a cyber-center, as well as several LGBT student groups, including a large gay-straight student alliance.

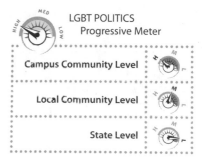

OUTSPOKEN *Answers from LGBT students:*

Top Three Descriptors of the LGBT Campus Environment:
1. Accepting   2. Growing   3. Active

What makes your campus feel welcoming and safe for LGBT students?
"The close-knit gay community on campus, the LGBT Center (through programming and outreach) and the fact that more people are getting involved as allies every year makes it a more reassuring place to be out and gay." —*21-year-old lesbian, junior*

How do you feel about coming out on your campus?
"Fortunately, being out on campus has not been an issue for me since coming to Duke. I have found an open and available LGBT community on campus. In addition, I have been out to my classmates since the first day and still feel as popular and welcomed as other students." —*25-year-old gay male, graduate student*

ACADEMIC SCENE

Top Three Supportive LGBT Academic Areas:
1. Cultural Anthropology   2. Women's Studies   3. English Literature

How LGBT-friendly are faculty in the classroom?
"Good question. The levels vary, depending on the course and faculty member. I think most of my faculty have been 'LGB-inclusive.' I don't know if the 'T' has registered quite as well." —*21-year-old genderqueer female, junior*

"Most of the faculty in general are very open-minded. There are professors here who know I am gay, one I even respected enough that I introduced him to my girlfriend, and he was totally cool with it." —*19-year-old lesbian, sophomore*

INFO

DUKE UNIVERSITY
2138 Campus Drive
Box 90586
Durham, NC 27708
Phone: 919-684-3214
Fax: 919-681-8941
E-mail: undergrad-admissions@duke.edu
Website: www.duke.edu

CAMPUS STATS
Type of Institution: Private university, Methodist religious affiliation
Founding Year: 1838
Size: 6,066
Avg. Class Size: 10–19 students
Popular Majors: Economics, Psychology, Public Policy and Analysis, English, History
Cost: Tuition: $32,655
Admission Application Deadline: January 2

OUTRAGEOUS FACTOID

The Duke Center for LGBT Life has one of the largest dedicated LGBT office spaces of any college in the United States—approximately 2,500 square feet.

• • • • • • • • • • • • • • • • • • •

RAINBOW RUMOR

Duke University recognizes the need to become more active in its support of the transgender community. Major progress in this area is expected within the next couple of years, including inclusion of gender identity and gender expression in the nondiscrimination policy.

• • • • • • • • • • • • • • • • • • •

THAT'S SO GAY!

ANNUAL LGBT EVENT HIGHLIGHTS

NC Pride: September

Coming Out Week: September

National Coming Out Day: October 11

Trans Awareness Week: November

Day of Silence: First week of April

GLBT Film Festival: January

Pride Week: March

Lavender Ball: March

Lavender Graduation: May

☺ SOCIAL SCENE

Top Three Things in the LGBT Social Life:

1. Coffeehouse   2. Freaky Friday   3. Dancing

How would you describe the social scene for LGBT students?

"I have found that the social scene at Duke provides me with what I need. No, I am not out at local bars and clubs every night, but there is a critical mass of students with which I can bond and explore Duke and the Triangle."
—*25-year-old gay male, graduate student*

What annual social event should an LGBT student not miss?

"The annual Lavender Ball in the spring brings together LGBT students and allies from colleges around North Carolina. It is always an evening of fun and dancing, in a completely queer-friendly atmosphere." —*21-year-old lesbian, junior*

BUZZ BITES *Fun Queer Stuff to Know*

THE BEST...

Party Locale: Sirens

Hangout: Jo and Joe's *and* Center for LGBT Life

Eating Place: Blue Corn Café

Place to Check Out Guys: Legends

Place to Check Out Ladies: Visions

LGBT-Cool Athletic Sport: Women's rugby

Non-LGBT-Specific Campus Club: Thread Magazine

Place for LGBT Students to Live on Campus: SHARE Living Group

LGBT Course Offering: Sexuality in Literature

LGBT Educational Involvement Opportunity: SAFE on Campus Training

LGBT-Accepting Religious/Spiritual Organization(s): Episcopal Center

THE GAY POINT AVERAGE
OFFICIAL CAMPUS CHECKLIST

LGBT & ally student organization ✓

LGBT resource center/office ✓

LGBT Pride Week &/or Coming Out Week ✓

Safe Zone/Safe Space or Ally Program ✓

Significant number of LGBT social activities ✓

Significant number of LGBT educational events ✓

Variety of LGBT studies/courses ✓

Nondiscrimination statement inclusive of sexual orientation ✓

Nondiscrimination statement inclusive of gender identity/expression

Extends domestic partner benefits to same-sex couples ✓

Actively recruits LGBT students to enroll on campus ✓

Trains campus police on LGBT sensitivity ✓

Procedure for reporting LGBT bias, harassment & hate crimes ✓

Offers LGBT housing options/themes ✓

Offers LGBT-inclusive health services/testing ✓

Offers LGBT-inclusive counseling/support groups ✓

Offers LGBT student scholarships ✓

Conducts special LGBT graduation ceremony for LGBT & ally Students ✓

Offers support services for process of transitioning from M to F & F to M

Active LGBT alumni group ✓

DUKE UNIVERSITY
GAY POINT AVERAGE (18)
(out of 20)

CAMPUS QUEER RESOURCES

Select LGBT Student Organization(s):

Alliance of Queer Undergraduates Duke (AQUADuke); DukeOUT

Founding Date: AQUADuke (1980s); DukeOUT (2002)

Membership: 50+

Website: www.duke.edu/web/aquaduke/; www.duke.edu/web/gap/DukeOUT/

LGBT Resource Center/Office:

Center for LGBT Life
Duke University
02 West Union Building
Box 90958
Durham, NC 27708

Year Established: 1994

Number of Staff: 3 full-time professional staff members, 3 interns, 5 student workers

Phone: 919-684-6607

E-mail: lgbtcenter@duke.edu

Website: lgbt.studentaffairs.duke.edu/

EASTERN MICHIGAN UNIVERSITY

WITH A HIGH Gay Point Average, Eastern Michigan University deserves to be listed among the best, most LGBT-progressive and friendly colleges and universities.

Much of the queerness radiates from the fully staffed, very active and well-resourced Lesbian, Gay, Bisexual and Transgender Resource Center. Along with several active LGBT student organizations, the center plans a cadre of educational and social activities to support the LGBT community. Such activities include hosting a weekly Coming Out/Being Out Support Group, a Comedy Drag Show, and the Reel Queers Film Festival, as well as planning regular ally trainings across campus. In addition, the LGBT commitment is systemic throughout the campus, with an active LGBT faculty and staff advisory board as well as a thriving LGBT alumni chapter.

So what makes Eastern Michigan University a top LGBT choice? It's the institutional commitment to the values of diversity and inclusion and the fact that students get it. As one LGBT student states: "It's like coming home with a big 'welcome' sign proudly displayed. I am part of a great big queer family." Another LGBT student added: "Eastern is 'my' place to be who I am. I never have felt isolated or fearful. The campus is like a queer world in and of itself."

LGBT POLITICS
Progressive Meter

Campus Community Level

Local Community Level

State Level

OUTSPOKEN *Answers from LGBT students:*

Top Three Descriptors of the LGBT Campus Environment:
1. Diverse   2. Welcoming   3. Friendly

What makes your campus feel welcoming and safe for LGBT students?
"My first experience on EMU's campus was rather eye-opening. As I walked through the Union, I spotted a few newsstands with LGBT newspapers next to the EMU student newspaper. I also noticed a large rainbow flag hanging at the EMU info desk. I immediately felt welcome. I have attended other colleges from around the country, and I had never seen or felt such a presence of the LGBT community anywhere else. It was a great feeling." *—29-year-old lesbian, graduate student*

How do you feel about coming out on your campus?
"I feel very safe coming out on EMU's campus. One of the first things I discovered on campus was the LGBT Resource Center and was able to look at books and talk to a fellow LGBT student about the campus climate." *—22-year-old gay male, senior*

INFO

EASTERN MICHIGAN UNIVERSITY
401 Pierce Hall
Ypsilanti, MI 48197
Phone: 734-487-3060
Fax: 734-487-6559
E-mail: admissions@emich.edu
Website: www.emich.edu

CAMPUS STATS
Type of Institution: Public university
Founding Year: 1849
Size: 18,485
Avg. Class Size: 20–29 students
Popular Majors: Business Administration/ Management, Elementary Education and Teaching, Psychology
Cost: In-state tuition: $4,707
Out-of-state tuition: $14,714
Admission Application Deadline: June 30

ACADEMIC SCENE

Top Three Supportive LGBT Academic Areas:
1. Women's and Gender Studies   2. Communication and Theater Arts   3. Social Work

How LGBT-friendly are faculty in the classroom?
"Faculty are as friendly as can be expected. I'm not treated any differently than anyone else, which is how it should be." —*19-year-old bisexual female, sophomore*

"Faculty are not only friendly but supportive. After hearing some of my classmates laugh upon hearing the title of a gay magazine in class, my African American literature professor made it clear that their behavior in class was unacceptable. She said that we will never truly be free until we all learn to respect each other's differences, including sexual orientation." —*30-year-old gay male, senior*

SOCIAL SCENE

Top Three Things in the LGBT Social Life:
1. QUEST dances   2. Drinks at MJ's Wooden Nickel   3. Free movie nights

How would you describe the social scene for LGBT students?
"The LGBT Resource Center organizes a lot of events. Also, in the Ypsilanti–Ann Arbor area there is the Aut Bar, owned and operated by and for the queer community. There's also MJ's Wooden Nickel, which holds a Pride night every Sunday night. Plenty to do." – *19-year-old bisexual female, sophomore*

What annual social event should an LGBT student not miss?
"The LGBT Luau is my favorite annual event and is the perfect way to start the school year. And there's always a huge crowd!" —*20-year-old gay male, junior*

 OUTRAGEOUS FACTOID Eastern Michigan boasts that it has the "best drag queens in the world."

 RAINBOW RUMOR One student notes: "I feel that there is a need to reach a more diverse LGBT student base. Being a gay black male myself, I have found that I encounter difficulty finding organizations that are tailored to me and cater to my needs, wants and concerns."

THAT'S SO GAY!

ANNUAL LGBT EVENT HIGHLIGHTS

Welcome Back Luau: September

Coming Out Week: October

LGBT Domestic Violence Awareness Week: October

Comedy Drag Show: November

Transgender Day of Remembrance: November

Reel Queers Film Festival: January

Jody "T" Norton Lecture: March

LGBT Awareness Month: April

Lavender Graduation: April

Role Models and Mentors Celebration: April

BUZZ BITES *Fun Queer Stuff to Know*

THE BEST...

Party Locale: Necto Nightclub *and* Stilleto's Nightclub

Hangout: LGBT Resource Center

Eating Place: Aut Bar

Place to Check Out Guys: Necto Nightclub

Place to Check Out Ladies: Halle Library

LGBT-Cool Athletic Sport: Basketball *and* softball

Non-LGBT-Specific Campus Club: Gang Green Spirit Club

Place for LGBT Students to Live on Campus: Buell Residence Hall

LGBT Educational Involvement Opportunity: CloseUP Theatre Troupe

LGBT-Accepting Religious/Spiritual Organization(s): Crossroads, a Catholic LGBT Student Organization *and* Gaygle, a Jewish LGBT Student Organization

CAMPUS QUEER RESOURCES

Select LGBT Student Organization(s):

Queer Unity for Eastern Students (QUEST)
Founding Date: 1995
Membership: 30
Phone: 734-487-4149
E-mail: lgbtrc@emich.edu
Website: www.emich.edu/lgbtrc

LGBT Resource Center/Office:

Lesbian, Gay, Bisexual and Transgender Resource Center
234 King Hall
Ypsilanti, MI 48197
Year Established: 1995
Number of Staff: 5 staff, including student part-time staff
Phone: 734-487-4149
E-mail: lgbtrc@emich.edu
Website: www.emich.edu/lgbtrc

THE GAY POINT AVERAGE OFFICIAL CAMPUS CHECKLIST

- ✓ LGBT & ally student organization
- ✓ LGBT resource center/office
- ✓ LGBT Pride Week &/or Coming Out Week
- ✓ Safe Zone/Safe Space or Ally Program
- ✓ Significant number of LGBT social activities
- ✓ Significant number of LGBT educational events
- ✓ Variety of LGBT studies/courses
- ✓ Nondiscrimination statement inclusive of sexual orientation
- Nondiscrimination statement inclusive of gender identity/expression
- ✓ Extends domestic partner benefits to same-sex couples
- ✓ Actively recruits LGBT students to enroll on campus
- ✓ Trains campus police on LGBT sensitivity
- ✓ Procedure for reporting LGBT bias, harassment & hate crimes
- ✓ Offers LGBT housing options/themes
- ✓ Offers LGBT-inclusive health services/testing
- ✓ Offers LGBT-inclusive counseling/support groups
- ✓ Offers LGBT student scholarships
- ✓ Conducts special LGBT graduation ceremony for LGBT & ally Students
- Offers support services for process of transitioning from M to F & F to M
- ✓ Active LGBT alumni group

18 EASTERN MICHIGAN UNIVERSITY GAY POINT AVERAGE
(out of 20)

EMORY UNIVERSITY

THERE ARE RELATIVELY few places to go in the South that are considered LGBT-progressive or LGBT-friendly. Emory University is one of the exceptions. Just 15 minutes from downtown Atlanta in a tree-lined historic neighborhood, Emory has worked hard over the years to build an LGBT-friendly campus.

Despite the fact that Emory was founded as a Methodist seminary and is still affiliated with the United Methodist Church, the campus was the first school in the Southeast to have an LGBT resource center, to include sexual orientation as a protected category in its equal opportunity policy, and to offer domestic partner benefits to the same-sex partners of both students and employees. James T. Laney, a Methodist minister, was president of Emory University when the Office of Lesbian/Gay/Bisexual Life opened in 1991. Speaking out in defense of the university's action to create the center, he often noted that the Methodist Book of Discipline states that all human beings are beings of "sacred worth." Today, fittingly so, the LGBT student group in Emory's Candler School of Theology is named "Sacred Worth."

The true test for Emory on LGBT friendliness came in 1997. Two gay men planned to hold a commitment ceremony in the chapel on the Oxford campus of Emory University. The dean of Oxford refused to allow the ceremony to take place in the chapel, asserting that all Emory's chapels are Methodist churches and that no same-sex ceremonies are permitted in Methodist churches. The situation led to a confrontation between then President William Chace and Emory's Board of Trustees, which includes several Methodist bishops. Finally a decision was made allowing gays to marry. The caveat was that the ceremonies had to be performed by a campus minister or an ordained member of the clergy from the Department of Religion whose faith or denomination sanctioned such ceremonies.

Emory has solidly stood by LGBT students. Just take a look at their Gay Point Average score to see the LGBT progress today. One LGBT student said: "Emory has been a surprisingly queer place. I find the campus to be extremely gay-friendly, with many LGBT allies who are out and proud. It shows you that to be queer on a religiously affiliated campus in the South is more than possible."

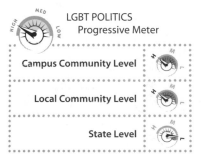

LGBT POLITICS
Progressive Meter

Campus Community Level

Local Community Level

State Level

OUTSPOKEN *Answers from LGBT students:*

Top Three Descriptors of the LGBT Campus Environment:
1. Accepting   2. Laid-back   3. Open-minded

What makes your campus feel welcoming and safe for LGBT students?
"Emory's LGBT office provides a welcome and safe space for LGBT students and allies alike. Students use the space not only for holding LGBT student group meetings and informal discussions on queer concerns, but also for hanging out between classes and even borrowing a book out of the office's library."
—*21-year-old queer female, senior*

How do you feel about coming out on your campus?
"I feel at home. The campus has provided me a safe haven of understanding and acceptance. More than I could have ever imagined. I feel lucky to have come out on such an accepting campus with so many LGBT resources."
—*21-year-old gay male, junior*

INFO

EMORY UNIVERSITY
Boisfeuillet Jones Center
201 Dowman Drive
Atlanta, GA 30322
Phone: 404-727-6036
Fax: 404-727-4303
E-mail: admiss@emory.edu
Website: www.emory.edu

CAMPUS STATS
Type of Institution: Private university, Methodist religious affiliation
Founding Year: 1836
Size: 6,260
Avg. Class Size: 10–19 students
Popular Majors: Economics, Psychology, Political Science and Government
Cost: Tuition: $30,400
Admission Application Deadline: January 15

OUTRAGEOUS FACTOID

Emory is sometimes jokingly called "Coca-Cola U" because in 1979, the university received approximately $105 million from Coca-Cola heirs Robert W. Woodruff and his brother, George W. Woodruff. And the name is fitting when you consider this: in 1992 LGBT students marched across campus in protest over an antigay incident of campus harassment and occupied President James T. Laney's office. What does the president's secretary do? She politely offers drinks to the student protesters: "Now, who wants diet and who wants regular Coca-Cola?" Now that's true "Southern hospitality."

● ● ● ● ● ● ● ● ● ● ● ● ● ● ● ● ●

RAINBOW RUMOR

Emory University is a pocket of liberal thought in a conservative southern region. Word has it that the administration plans on adding gender identity/expression to its nondiscrimination statement in Fall 2006. And don't forget about "Hotlanta," as the city is affectionately termed, the thriving and growing LGBT-friendly metropolis surrounding the campus.

● ● ● ● ● ● ● ● ● ● ● ● ● ● ● ● ●

THAT'S SO GAY!

ANNUAL LGBT EVENT HIGHLIGHTS

Black Gay Pride: September

Sacred Worth Week: Fall

Emory Pride: Fall

LGBT Awareness Week/Coming Out Week: October

Valentine's Day Dance: February

Annual Pride Banquet: March

LGBT Film Festival: March/April

LGBT Alumni Brunch: May

EGALA Law School Panel: Spring

Atlanta Pride: June

ACADEMIC SCENE

Top Three Supportive LGBT Academic Areas:
1. Women's Studies   2. English Department   3. Institute for the Liberal Arts

How LGBT-friendly are faculty in the classroom?
"I have never had a professor who seemed negative about LGBT issues, but most of them don't mention LGBT things unless it relates to the subject of the course." —*18-year-old gay male, freshman*

"In my human sexuality class, I felt awkward being the out gay man with several athletes. But, the entire class seemed curious when I would speak out and shared my opinions. The faculty member encouraged [me to speak] to the extent I felt comfortable. Surprise to me, I saw one of the athletic guys out at a gay bar later that semester." —*22-year-old gay male, senior*

SOCIAL SCENE

Top Three Things in the LGBT Social Life:
1. Midtown area   2. Coffee shops   3. Dancing

How would you describe the social scene for LGBT students?
"Amazing. Emory University has several key LGBT events to socialize and enjoy, but I love HOTLANTA! Something for everyone in the party scene." —*22-year-old queer female, senior*

What annual social event should an LGBT student not miss?
"The Gay Games during LGBT Awareness Week—awesome! Also the Drag Competition, which I won." —*21-year-old gay male, senior*

BUZZ BITES *Fun Queer Stuff to Know*

THE BEST...

Party Locale: Red Chair

Hangout: Blake's

Eating Place: Flying Biscuit

Place to Check Out Guys: Buckhead Bars

Place to Check Out Ladies: My Sister's Room

Place for LGBT Students to Live on Campus: Woodruff Residence Hall

LGBT Course Offering: Sexual Identities and Politics in Twentieth-Century America

LGBT Educational Involvement Opportunity: LGBTA Speakers Bureau

LGBT-Accepting Religious/Spiritual Organization(s): Office of Religious Life

THE GAY POINT AVERAGE
OFFICIAL CAMPUS CHECKLIST

LGBT & ally student organization	✓
LGBT resource center/office	✓
LGBT Pride Week &/or Coming Out Week	✓
Safe Zone/Safe Space or Ally Program	✓
Significant number of LGBT social activities	✓
Significant number of LGBT educational events	✓
Variety of LGBT studies/courses	✓
Nondiscrimination statement inclusive of sexual orientation	✓
Nondiscrimination statement inclusive of gender identity/expression	
Extends domestic partner benefits to same-sex couples	✓
Actively recruits LGBT students to enroll on campus	
Trains campus police on LGBT sensitivity	✓
Procedure for reporting LGBT bias, harassment & hate crimes	✓
Offers LGBT housing options/themes	
Offers LGBT-inclusive health services/testing	✓
Offers LGBT-inclusive counseling/support groups	✓
Offers LGBT student scholarships	
Conducts special LGBT graduation ceremony for LGBT & ally Students	
Offers support services for process of transitioning from M to F & F to M	
Active LGBT alumni group	✓

EMORY UNIVERSITY
GAY POINT AVERAGE
(out of 20)

14

**CAMPUS QUEER
RESOURCES**

Select LGBT Student Organization(s):

Emory Pride
Founding Date: 1987
Membership: 60
Website: userwww.service.emory.edu/
~dkatz3/Pride/default.html

LGBT Resource Center/Office:

**Office of Lesbian/Gay/Bisexual
Transgender Life**
P.O. Box 24075
Dobbs University Center,
Rooms 242–246E
Atlanta, GA 30322
Year Established: 1991
Number of Staff: 2 full-time professional staff
members, plus part-time student workers
Phone: 404-727-0272
Website: www.emory.edu/CAMPUS_LIFE/
LGBTOFFICE/

GEORGE MASON UNIVERSITY

GEORGE MASON, THE namesake of the university, was the driving force behind the U.S. Bill of Rights back in the 1700s. He argued passionately for individual freedoms, ultimately helping ensure that the first 10 amendments to the US constitution were ratified in 1791. Mason would be proud today of his campus. His prophetic protests for freedom still ring true when it comes to an institutional commitment to LGBT issues.

Located in northern Virginia, George Mason University is just 15 miles from the heart of Washington, D.C. The university does a remarkable job as far as LGBT progressiveness in the state of Virginia.

From the president to the provost and all the way down, the university believes strongly in protecting the freedom and human rights of all genders and sexual orientations. Although it does not include gender identity and gender expression in its campus nondiscrimination policy, the university has still advocated successfully for gender-variant students' needs for safe bathroom and changing spaces, housing accommodations, and/or name change. The campus Gay Point Average highlights the many pro-gay initiatives and polices in place on campus, as well as future areas for improvement.

LGBT students are highly visible on campus, participating in a myriad of LGBT and non-LGBT activities and student organizations. LGBT student programming includes events such as Coming Out Week, Transgender Awareness/Remembrance, and Pride Week. But more importantly, LGBT students know that they "belong" on campus. One LGBT student explains: "George Mason allows me to be all of who I am. I do not have to check my race or my sexuality at the door. To be gay is welcomed; I belong here."

LGBT POLITICS
Progressive Meter

Campus Community Level

Local Community Level

State Level

OUTSPOKEN *Answers from LGBT students:*

Top Three Descriptors of the LGBT Campus Environment:
1. Visible   2. Energetic   3. Family

What makes your campus feel welcome and safe for LGBT students?
"The people. I know that whatever happens, my 'family' is there for me in the Pride office." —*20-year-old multigendered, junior*

How do you feel about coming out on your campus?
"I came out in high school, years before I came to Mason, and never really went back 'in the closet,' so I didn't feel the pressure of coming out on this campus. As far as outing myself to fellow students and teachers as I get to know people, I've rarely felt uncomfortable or judged." —*22-year-old genderqueer, senior*

"When I first came to Mason, I thought it was going to be a very conservative university; however, when I saw the 'rainbow bench' in front of SUB I, I knew this was a place where I would be welcomed; thus making coming out a lot easier." —*20-year-old gay male, junior*

INFO

GEORGE MASON UNIVERSITY
4400 University Drive
MSN 3A4
Fairfax, VA 22030
Phone: 703-993-2400
Fax: 703-993-4622
E-mail: admissions@gmu.edu
Website: www.gmu.edu

CAMPUS STATS
Type of Institution: Public university
Founding Year: 1972
Size: 18,000
Avg. Class Size: 10–19 students
Popular Majors: International Relations and Affairs, Political Science and Government, Psychology
Cost: In-state tuition: $5,880
Out-of-state tuition: $17,160
Admission Application Deadline: January 15

ACADEMIC SCENE

Top Three Supportive LGBT Academic Areas:
1. New Century College   2. Visual and Performing Arts
3. Sociology and Anthropology

How LGBT-friendly are faculty in the classroom?
"I've had more teachers than ever who do not speak in hetero-normalized terms and expressions. Most of my teachers do not know that I am gay. I don't make it a point to go up and introduce myself as gay, as most people don't make it a point to introduce themselves as straight. However, I've had more teachers simply not assume that any particular student has any particular preference, which is simply refreshing." —*22-year-old gay male, senior*

SOCIAL SCENE

Top Three Things in the LGBT Social Life:
1. Dancing   2. Pride Alliance   3. Checking out hot students

How would you describe the social scene for LGBT students?
"The social scene on campus is really diverse. There are LGBT-identified students in nearly every group on campus. Regardless of what scene you're into, it's probable that you'll meet someone who is somehow involved in the LGBT community. Because we're close to D.C., there are always ways on any night of the week to get involved and plenty of places to dance on the weekends. The Pride organization has meetings once a week, too, and an informal get-together for dinner after the meeting. TransMason, our transgender/transsexual/gender queer organization, meets once a week, as well. Beyond meetings, though, the LGBT community on-campus is really tightly knit, though inclusive—rather than exclusive or cliquish." —*22-year-old genderqueer, senior*

"The Pride Alliance is a place to be social. There are meetings every Tuesday, and afterwards, the members go out for dinner. Many LGBT students go to clubs in D.C. during the week and weekends." —*21-year-old lesbian, junior*

What annual social event should an LGBT student not miss?
"The drag show!!!!!!! There's nothing like seeing your faculty adviser singing along as a professional drag queen snags a dollar." —*20-year-old multigendered, junior*

OUTRAGEOUS FACTOID With Mason's student population encompassing over 130 countries of origin, all 50 U.S. states, and 27 percent communities of color, the campus embraces diversity.

• • • • • • • • • • • • • • • • • • • •

RAINBOW RUMOR Students tend to agree that the campus needs to build into administrative policy, procedures, and training the full inclusion of trans and gender-variant persons. One M-to-F pre-op transwoman shares: "Transitioning on campus can be a wonderful experience, but it is a lot of work. If you're transitioning and thinking of coming to Mason, you must call ahead to the LGBT coordinator's office. There are so many issues with housing, name changes, bathrooms, etc."

• • • • • • • • • • • • • • • • • • • •

THAT'S SO GAY!

**ANNUAL LGBT
EVENT HIGHLIGHTS**

Coming Out Day/Week: October

Transgender Awareness/Remembrance: November

Pride Week: First week in April

Day of Silence: April

LGBTQ Safe Zone Trainings: Monthly

BUZZ BITES —*Fun Queer Stuff to Know*

THE BEST...

Party Locale: Apex
Hangout: Pride Alliance Office
Eating Place: Ike's
Place to Check Out Guys: Sunbathing on the Quad in front of the Student Union
Place to Check Out Ladies: Johnson Center
LGBT-Cool Athletic Sport: Lacrosse and basketball
Non-LGBT-Specific Campus Club: Student Government

Place for LGBT Students to Live on Campus: Liberty Square
LGBT Course Offering: Cultural Constructions of Sex and Sexuality
LGBT Educational Involvement Opportunity: NCBI Training Workshops
LGBT-Accepting Religious/Spiritual Organization(s): Hillel Jewish Student Center and Unitarian Universalist Church

CAMPUS QUEER RESOURCES

Select LGBT Student Organization(s):

Pride Alliance
Founding Date: Early 1990s
Membership: 300
Phone: 703-993-2895
E-mail: pride@gmu.edu
Website: www.gmu.edu/org/pride/

LGBT Resource Center/Office:

Lesbian, Gay, Bisexual, Transgender and Questioning Student Services
GMU Diversity Programs and Services
4400 University Drive—MS-2F6
Student Union Building I, Room 223
Fairfax, VA 22030
Year Established: 2002
Number of Staff: 1 full-time professional staff member
Phone: 703-993-2700
E-mail: lgbtq@gmu.edu
Website: lgbtq.gmu.edu

THE GAY POINT AVERAGE
OFFICIAL CAMPUS CHECKLIST

- ✓ LGBT & ally student organization
- ✓ LGBT resource center/office
- ✓ LGBT Pride Week &/or Coming Out Week
- ✓ Safe Zone/Safe Space or Ally Program
- ✓ Significant number of LGBT social activities
- ✓ Significant number of LGBT educational events
- Variety of LGBT studies/courses
- ✓ Nondiscrimination statement inclusive of sexual orientation
- Nondiscrimination statement inclusive of gender identity/expression
- Extends domestic partner benefits to same-sex couples
- ✓ Actively recruits LGBT students to enroll on campus
- Trains campus police on LGBT sensitivity
- ✓ Procedure for reporting LGBT bias, harassment & hate crimes
- Offers LGBT housing options/themes
- ✓ Offers LGBT-inclusive health services/testing
- ✓ Offers LGBT-inclusive counseling/support groups
- Offers LGBT student scholarships
- Conducts special LGBT graduation ceremony for LGBT & ally Students
- ✓ Offers support services for process of transitioning from M to F & F to M
- ✓ Active LGBT alumni group

(13) GEORGE MASON UNIVERSITY GAY POINT AVERAGE
(out of 20)

GRINNELL COLLEGE

FROM THE ORIGINAL Gay/Human Resource Center to the current Stonewall Resource Center, Grinnell College has grown from just serving gay men and lesbians to programs covering bisexuals, transgender people, intersex individuals, asexuals, allies and more.

The positive impact of the Stonewall Resource Center has left an indelible queer mark on campus. In fact, administrators are so supportive of LGBT issues that in order to increase visibility and outreach, the Stonewall Resource Center moved this year into a new space almost three times larger. In addition, the LGBT student organization StoneCo has gained support and visibility through its collaborative programming, movies, speakers and social activities, including Coming Out Week, Queer Sex Signals and the "Mary Be James" Cross-Dressing Party.

The Gay Point Average marks Grinnell's commitment to progressive LGBT policies and practices. All over Grinnell, LGBT students are embraced at all levels—from administrators to faculty to non-LGBT students. An LGBT student agrees: "You never have to hide your queerness at Grinnell. We have out LGBT faculty and staff, and the atmosphere reflects a sincerity of real concern for all student needs. I have never felt queerer!"

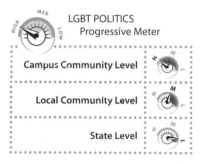

OUTSPOKEN *Answers from LGBT students:*

Top Three Descriptors of the LGBT Campus Environment:
1. Welcoming   2. Quirky   3. Liberal

What makes your campus feel welcoming and safe for LGBT students?
"It's the attitude of the student body that is very accepting and warm that makes the campus seem welcoming and safe for LGBT students. There are a lot of allies on campus." —*20-year-old bisexual female, junior*

How do you feel about coming out on your campus?
"I came out when I came to Grinnell and I have yet to encounter someone who disapproves of me because of my homosexuality. Everyone whom I have talked to is either simply okay with it or actually wants to know more about my experiences as a homosexual. At Grinnell, being gay isn't a social blight. People find you more interesting because of it." —*18-year-old gay male, freshman*

ACADEMIC SCENE

Top Three Supportive LGBT Academic Areas:
1. Sociology   2. Gender and Women's Studies   3. Art

How LGBT-friendly are faculty in the classroom?
"Faculty have always encouraged me to explore issues of sexuality within a course topic if I wished to do so." —*21-year-old gay male, senior*

"In one of my education classes, we discussed heterosexism in schools. The professor is really great about bringing up queer issues and making those of us in her class comfortable who are queer." —*20-year-old bisexual female, junior*

INFO

GRINNELL COLLEGE
1103 Park Street, 2nd Floor
Grinnell, IA 50112
Phone: 641-269-3600
Fax: 641-269-4800
E-mail: askgrin@grinnell.edu
Website: www.grinnell.edu

CAMPUS STATS
Type of Institution: Private college
Founding Year: 1846
Size: 1,518
Avg. Class Size: 10–19 students
Popular Majors: Biology/Biological Sciences, Economics, English Language and Literature
Cost: Tuition: $34,814
Admission Application Deadline: January 20

RAINBOW RUMOR

Star football players can come out gay and still play for the team!

THAT'S SO GAY!

ANNUAL LGBT EVENT HIGHLIGHTS

StoneCo: Every Sunday

Coming Out Group: Once a week, first semester

Lesbian Movie Night Organized Procrastination: Every Monday

All-Boys Cinema: Every Wednesday

Trans Reading Group: Every Tuesday

Queer Sex Signals: October

Coming Out Week: October

Pride Week: April

"Mary Be James" Cross-Dressing Party: March/April

☺ SOCIAL SCENE

Top Three Things in the LGBT Social Life:
1. "Mary Be James" Cross-Dressing Dance   2. All-Boys Cinema
3. Lesbian Movie Night

How would you describe the social scene for LGBT students?
"The social scene is very laid-back. There are a bunch of quirky parties. Though most of my friends are straight, I've never felt uncomfortable. I like that Grinnell doesn't have a gay clique nor feels the need to develop one." —*21-year-old gay male, senior*

What annual social event should an LGBT student not miss?
"Queer Sex Signals! We put on a show that demonstrates the queer side to tough issues like labeling, rape, STDs and sexual situations at parties. In the beginning, it's really funny and entertaining and then toward the end, we bring up more difficult issues that spark a lot of discussion." —*20-year-old bisexual female, junior*

BUZZ BITES *Fun Queer Stuff to Know*

THE BEST...

Party Locale: Harris Party

Hangout: Stonewall Resource Center

Eating Place: Quad Dining

Place to Check Out Guys: Gay cocktail parties

Place to Check Out Ladies: StoneCo meetings

LGBT-Cool Athletic Sport: Soccer *or* women's rugby

Non-LGBT-Specific Campus Club: Grinnell Singers

Place for LGBT Students to Live on Campus: South Campus

LGBT Course Offering: Queer Theory

LGBT-Accepting Religious/Spiritual Organization(s): Christian Fellowship

THE GAY POINT AVERAGE
OFFICIAL CAMPUS CHECKLIST

LGBT & ally student organization ✓

LGBT resource center/office ✓

LGBT Pride Week &/or Coming Out Week ✓

Safe Zone/Safe Space or Ally Program ✓

Significant number of LGBT social activities ✓

Significant number of LGBT educational events ✓

Variety of LGBT studies/courses ✓

Nondiscrimination statement inclusive of sexual orientation ✓

Nondiscrimination statement inclusive of gender identity/expression

Extends domestic partner benefits to same-sex couples ✓

Actively recruits LGBT students to enroll on campus ✓

Trains campus police on LGBT sensitivity ✓

Procedure for reporting LGBT bias, harassment & hate crimes ✓

Offers LGBT housing options/themes

Offers LGBT-inclusive health services/testing ✓

Offers LGBT-inclusive counseling/support groups ✓

Offers LGBT student scholarships

Conducts special LGBT graduation ceremony for LGBT & ally Students

Offers support services for process of transitioning from M to F & F to M ✓

Active LGBT alumni group

GRINNELL COLLEGE
GAY POINT AVERAGE (15)
(out of 20)

CAMPUS QUEER RESOURCES

Select LGBT Student Organization(s):

StoneCo
Founding Date: 1990s
Membership: 100+
Phone: 641-269-3327
E-mail: stoneco@grinnell.edu
Website: web.grinnell.edu/Groups/
Stoneco/

LGBT Resource Center/Office:

Stonewall Resource Center
1210 Park Street, Box B-1
Grinnell, IA 50112
Year Established: 1986 (as the Gay/Human
Resource Center)
Number of Staff: 1 part-time professional
staff; 2 student staff
Phone: 641-269-3327
E-mail: srcenter@grinnell.edu
Website: www.grinnell.edu/offices/
studentaffairs/src/

HAVERFORD COLLEGE

HAVERFORD COLLEGE ESPOUSES the Quaker ideals of trust, concern, respect and egalitarianism. The campus culture that results is open-minded and accepting and encourages all community members to view one another as equals. For LGBT students, Haverford is a progressive place that respects difference and believes strongly in support for LGBT issues.

Whether it's the Out Week, Outtalk forums or even the Pornfest, there is plenty to do queer on the Haverford campus. In addition, the college has a wonderfully supportive academic environment for LGBT students. Students can even develop their own areas of studies. A few years ago, several Haverford students developed a specialized academic program in Gay and Lesbian Studies.

Haverford's LGBT alumni group formally encourages internships with LGBT-affiliated causes. As a result, Haverford students may receive academic credit for summer internships with organizations that focus on causes, concerns or issues important to the LGBT community.

The campus allows students to shape and administer a student-run honor code that informs academic and social policies. As one LGBT student says: "Haverford's long tradition of Quaker heritage attracts students who are open-minded, tolerant, and above all, respectful of others. Our honor code ensures that we live in a community of trust, concern, and respect. ... These values along with our small, close-knit campus make LGBT students feel not only welcome and safe, but respected and loved."

LGBT POLITICS
Progressive Meter

Campus Community Level

Local Community Level

State Level

INFO

HAVERFORD COLLEGE
370 Lancaster Avenue
Haverford, PA 19041
Phone: 610-896-1350
Fax: 610-896-1338
E-mail: admission@haverford.edu
Website: www.haverford.edu

CAMPUS STATS
Type of Institution: Private college
Founding Year: 1833
Size: 1,172
Avg. Class Size: 10–19 students
Popular Majors: Biology/Biological Sciences, Economics, English Language and Literature
Cost: Tuition: $31,466
Admission Application Deadline: January 15

OUTSPOKEN *Answers from LGBT students:*

Top Three Descriptors of the LGBT Campus Environment:
1. Strong community   2. Respectful   3. Open-minded

What makes your campus feel welcoming and safe for LGBT students?
"I remember when I was a senior in high school, I spent the night at Haverford for an admitted-students weekend, and there were chalk messages all over the campus welcoming queer students. I didn't feel that welcome at any other college I visited, and that played a huge part in my decision to enroll."
—19-year-old gay male, sophomore

How do you feel about coming out on your campus?
"It's a liberal campus. Gay students don't get attacked. Lots of classes talk about gay issues, and even conservatives tend to be socially liberal. If you're comfortable with yourself, you will be accepted." *—20-year-old lesbian, junior*

"Haverford is a very safe community to come out in. The vast majority of students tend to be very liberal, so it's often said that it's easier to come out as queer at Haverford than to come out as a Republican!" *—19-year-old gay male, sophomore*

◉ ACADEMIC SCENE

Top Three Supportive LGBT Academic Areas:
1. Gender and Sexuality Studies   2. Spanish   3. Political Science

How LGBT-friendly are faculty in the classroom?
"Most faculty are perfectly friendly to everyone, including queers. Being an institution founded on Quaker principles, Haverford tends to attract a certain scholarly population open to such identities. … Professors are enthusiastic about incorporating queer theory and issues into their curriculum."
—*21-year-old gay male, senior*

"Haverford's honor code and emphasis on community challenges us to push not only ourselves and our peers, but also our faculty, staff and administration to a higher level of awareness and action concerning LGBT issues on, and off, campus."   —*20-year-old queer male, junior*

☺ SOCIAL SCENE

Top Three Things in the LGBT Social Life:
1. Concert series   2. SAGA   3. Outtalk

How would you describe the social scene for LGBT students?
"Gay, straight, whatever; we all just have fun together. However, with downtown Philadelphia's vibrant gay scene 20 minutes away and accessible by public transportation, bars, clubs, dancing—even gay bingo—are never far away."
— *20-year-old queer male, junior*

What annual social event should an LGBT student not miss?
"Drag Ball: lacrosse players in fishnets…need I say more?" —*20-year-old gay male, junior*

"Outtalk: Find out who's gay, who's curious, who's dated people of their own sex, who loves gay people, etc. It's always more people than you think."
—*21-year-old lesbian, senior*

 OUTRAGEOUS FACTOID Haverford College students a few years back felt that there was not enough emphasis within SAGA on "actual sex." So LGBT students organized the first-ever Pornfest, showing films in the college auditorium. The guest speaker was a "real-life" porn star.

 RAINBOW RUMOR Lesbian students are vastly underrepresented on this small campus: students estimate that there are five gay men to every lesbian. The campus plans to do more outreach to correct the shortage of lesbians and bisexual women in the near future.

 **THAT'S SO GAY!** **ANNUAL LGBT EVENT HIGHLIGHTS**

Daylight Drag: Fall
Coming Out Week: Fall
Drag Ball: November
Day of Silence: April
Pride Week: Spring
Pornfest: Late Spring
Outtalk Queer Forum: Twice per year

BUZZ BITES *Fun Queer Stuff to Know*

THE BEST...

Party Locale: Haverford College Apartments
Hangout: SAGA Lounge
Eating Place: Lunt Café
Place to Check Out Guys: Athletic fields
Place to Check Out Ladies: Bryn Mawr College
LGBT-Cool Athletic Sport: Ultimate Frisbee and women's rugby

Non-LGBT-Specific Campus Club: The S-Chords
LGBT Course Offering: Foucault on Sex and Power

CAMPUS QUEER RESOURCES

Select LGBT Student Organization(s):

Sexuality and Gender Alliance (SAGA)

Founding Date: 1970s

Membership: varies

E-mail: saga@go.haverford.edu

Resource Center/Office Responsible for LGBT Issues:

Office of Multicultural Affairs
Haverford College
370 Lancaster Ave
Haverford, PA 19041

Founding Date: 1984

Number of Staff: 3 full-time professional members
staff (varying responsibilities)

Phone: 610-896-1000

THE GAY POINT AVERAGE
OFFICIAL CAMPUS CHECKLIST

- ✓ LGBT & ally student organization
- LGBT resource center/office
- ✓ LGBT Pride Week &/or Coming Out Week
- ✓ Safe Zone/Safe Space or Ally Program
- ✓ Significant number of LGBT social activities
- ✓ Significant number of LGBT educational events
- ✓ Variety of LGBT studies/courses
- ✓ Nondiscrimination statement inclusive of sexual orientation
- Nondiscrimination statement inclusive of gender identity/expression
- ✓ Extends domestic partner benefits to same-sex couples
- ✓ Actively recruits LGBT students to enroll on campus
- ✓ Trains campus police on LGBT sensitivity
- ✓ Procedure for reporting LGBT bias, harassment & hate crimes
- ✓ Offers LGBT housing options/themes
- ✓ Offers LGBT-inclusive health services/testing
- ✓ Offers LGBT-inclusive counseling/support groups
- Offers LGBT student scholarships
- Conducts special LGBT graduation ceremony for LGBT & ally Students
- Offers support services for process of transitioning from M to F & F to M
- ✓ Active LGBT alumni group

15 HAVERFORD COLLEGE
GAY POINT AVERAGE
(out of 20)

INDIANA UNIVERSITY

INDIANA UNIVERSITY MAY seem like an odd pick for an LGBT-progressive campus. Nevertheless, the campus scores high marks from LGBT students, as well as on the Gay Point Average. Back in 1938, when famed researcher and campus professor Alfred C. Kinsey received tremendous pressure to stop his human sexuality research, long-standing chancellor Herman B Wells defended his work every step of the way. Today the Kinsey Human Sexuality Scale validates the natural occurrences of homosexuality and bisexuality.

In 1994, when the campus decided to fund an office to support LGBT students, a state legislator threatened to withdraw all state monies to the campus. The campus responded by finding a private donor through the alumni foundation to foot the bill for infinity. The Hoosiers have made a commitment to LGBT issues, and the campus has something for everyone.

One gay male senior says it the best: "My freshman year on campus, I was going through the process of coming out. I had seen other gay people on campus and felt like it was the right time for me. I was nervous and afraid. Lucky for me, I went to the GLBT support office and found Doug. He comforted me and let me cry. I was emotionally finally able to talk openly about being gay. From that moment on, I felt like the GLBT support office was my home, my family. IU was the place for me!"

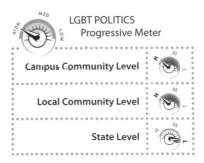

LGBT POLITICS
Progressive Meter

Campus Community Level

Local Community Level

State Level

🗩 OUTSPOKEN *Answers from LGBT students:*

Top Three Descriptors of the LGBT Campus Environment:
1. Accepting   2. Supportive   3. Safe

What makes your campus feel welcoming and safe for LGBT students?
"When I first arrived on campus, I was skeptical about the commitment to LGBT students in rural Indiana. I soon learned that there are many LGBT and ally people in the administration who are there to support me along the way. Plus, to my surprise, there are many 'out' gay students." *—18-year-old lesbian, freshman*

How do you feel about coming out on your campus?
"Just be open about it. If I feel like someone needs to know, I will tell them. To date, I have not had a negative reaction from fellow students."
—21-year-old gay male, junior

🖉 ACADEMIC SCENE

Top Three Supportive LGBT Academic Areas:
1. Social Work   2. Human Sexuality   3. Music

How LGBT-friendly are faculty in the classroom?
"Most faculty seem to be very LGBT-friendly. I openly came out in my English class and the teacher expressed support and was glad that I felt comfortable to come out. If there was a negative LGBT response by faculty, the response by IU administration, namely the LGBT Anti-Harassment team, would be severe."
—19-year-old lesbian, freshman

INFO

INDIANA UNIVERSITY
300 North Jordan Avenue
Bloomington, IN 47405
Phone: 812-855-0661
Fax: 812-855-5102
E-mail: iuadmit@indiana.edu
Website: www.iub.edu

CAMPUS STATS
Type of Institution: Public university
Founding Year: 1820
Size: 29,062
Avg. Class Size: 20–29 students
Popular Majors: Business, Education, Biomedical Science, Music and Communication Technologies
Cost: In-state tuition: $4,946
Out-of-state tuition: $16,739
Admission Application Deadline: February 1

OUTRAGEOUS FACTOID

Alfred C. Kinsey was an acclaimed zoologist at Indiana University—Bloomington when in 1938 he changed his research interest from gall wasps to human sexuality. Kinsey's findings led to the development of the Kinsey Human Sexuality Scale, which looked for the first time at the varying degrees of sexuality—from homosexuality to bisexuality to heterosexuality. The Kinsey Institute for Research in Sex, Gender and Reproduction continues his research at Indiana University, today focusing on contemporary issues.

• • • • • • • • • • • • • • • • • • • •

RAINBOW RUMOR

Indiana University in Bloomington, Indiana, is known as the "gay oasis" of the state of Indiana.

• • • • • • • • • • • • • • • • • • • •

THAT'S SO GAY!

ANNUAL LGBT EVENT HIGHLIGHTS

National Coming Out Day: October 11

GLBT Film Festival: January

Pride Week: Spring

Miss Gay IU Drag Pageant: Spring

Day of Silence: April

Lavender Graduation: April/May

"In my class on understanding diversity in a pluralistic society, the professor actually came out as a lesbian to the class, and she used examples to demonstrate oppression in the United States."
—*22-year-old gay male, senior*

😃 SOCIAL SCENE

Top Three Things in the LGBT Social Life:
1. Parties   2. Bars   3. Dancing

How would you describe the social scene for LGBT students?
"Surprisingly active. I pretty much know everyone, and it is a close-knit community." —*19-year-old gay male, freshman*

What annual social event should an LGBT student not miss?
"Without a doubt, Miss Gay IU! The drag show is outrageous. Everyone attends, even the frat boys. The whole event is like a GAY fest!" —*20-year-old gay male, junior*

BUZZ BITES *Fun Queer Stuff to Know*

THE BEST...

Party Locale: Bullwinkle's Dance Club
Hangout: Starbucks
Eating Place: Laughing Planet
Place to Check Out Guys: Bullwinkle's *or* a swim meet
Place to Check Out Ladies: Willy Joe's *or* a women's basketball game
LGBT-Cool Athletic Sport: Soccer *or* women's basketball
Non-LGBT-Specific Campus Club: College Democrats

Place for LGBT Students to Live on Campus: Collins *or* Read Residence Halls
Place for LGBT Students to Live Off Campus: University Commons
LGBT Course Offering: Homosexuality *and* Religion
LGBT Educational Involvement Opportunity: "Guess Who's Straight" Panels
LGBT-Accepting Religious/Spiritual Organization(s): St. Paul's Catholic Center, Hillel, Beth Shalom Synagogue, and Unitarian Universalist Church

THE GAY POINT AVERAGE
OFFICIAL CAMPUS CHECKLIST

LGBT & ally student organization ✓

LGBT resource center/office ✓

LGBT Pride Week &/or Coming Out Week ✓

Safe Zone/Safe Space or Ally Program ✓

Significant number of LGBT social activities ✓

Significant number of LGBT educational events ✓

Variety of LGBT studies/courses ✓

Nondiscrimination statement inclusive of sexual orientation ✓

Nondiscrimination statement inclusive of gender identity/expression

Extends domestic partner benefits to same-sex couples ✓

Actively recruits LGBT students to enroll on campus ✓

Trains campus police on LGBT sensitivity ✓

Procedure for reporting LGBT bias, harassment & hate crimes ✓

Offers LGBT housing options/themes

Offers LGBT-inclusive health services/testing ✓

Offers LGBT-inclusive counseling/support groups ✓

Offers LGBT student scholarships ✓

Conducts special LGBT graduation ceremony for LGBT & ally Students ✓

Offers support services for process of transitioning from M to F & F to M ✓

Active LGBT alumni group ✓

INDIANA UNIVERSITY
GAY POINT AVERAGE (18)
(out of 20)

CAMPUS QUEER RESOURCES

Select LGBT Student Organization(s):
OUT
Founding Date: 1984
Membership: 300+
Phone: 812-855-5688
E-mail: out@indiana.edu
Website: www.indiana.edu/~out

LGBT Resource Center/Office:
**Gay, Lesbian, Bisexual
and Transgender Student
Support Services**
705 East Seventh Street
Bloomington, IN 47408
Year Established: 1994
Number of Staff: 2 full-time professional staff
Phone: 812-855-4252
E-mail: glbtserv@indiana.edu
Website: www.indiana.edu/~glbt

IOWA STATE UNIVERSITY

RAINBOW FLAGS ARE flying high at Iowa State University, from the director of housing's office to the women's center to the Student Services Building to the LGBT Student Services resource library.

In 1993, Iowa State established LGBT Student Services to support LGBT issues and concerns. The office has since provided advocacy, education and outreach through vital services, including the LGBT Speakers Bureau. In 2005, gender identity was added to the university's antidiscrimination and antiharassment policies, as a result of a student-initiated petition that garnered hundreds of signatures, not only from LGBT students but also from many LGBT allies across campus. In addition, the university recently surveyed the academic and social environment for LGBT students. The President's Committee on Diversity is committed to addressing the issues raised in the survey and continuing progressive efforts to make the university more welcoming to LGBT students, faculty and staff.

Another indication of LGBT visibility is that Iowa State boasts some prominent LGBT and ally faculty, among them Dr. Nancy Evans and Dr. Warren Blumenfeld. Evans has published several articles on LGBT issues in higher education, including her book, *Beyond Tolerance: Working with Gays and Lesbians on College Campuses*. Blumenfeld is best-known for his ground-breaking workshops and his book *Homophobia: How We All Pay the Price*.

Iowa State has a proven record of LGBT friendliness, and the Gay Point Average is proof. That says a lot for a campus situated in the middle of rural Iowa. But perhaps this LGBT student summarizes it best: "Iowa State is more queer-friendly than I ever imagined. LGBT students can find much to do, and there is always a feeling of comfort. Openness and acceptance are words that describe my experience being gay on campus."

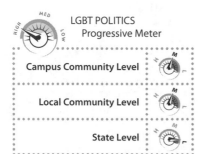

LGBT POLITICS
Progressive Meter

Campus Community Level

Local Community Level

State Level

OUTSPOKEN *Answers from LGBT students:*

Top Three Descriptors of the LGBT Campus Environment:
1. Open   2. Supportive   3. Proud

What makes your campus feel welcoming and safe for LGBT students?
"I think the LGBT Student Services and the Student Alliance make the campus feel very welcoming. Also, we run a Safe Zone program that provides people with stickers to designate LGBT-friendly areas on campus, such as offices, dorm rooms, etc." —*24-year-old bisexual female, sophomore*

How do you feel about coming out on your campus?
"I felt nervous at first, but after visiting the LGBTSS office, I felt comfortable, and I came out to my roommate. I have no problem with people knowing who I am. My roommate said I had a lot of courage for telling him."
—*18-year-old gay male, freshman*

"Although we are from a fairly small Midwestern city, I think our community is more open and accepting than most people would expect."
—*24-year-old bisexual female, sophomore*

INFO

IOWA STATE UNIVERSITY
100 Alumni Hall
Ames, IA 50011
Phone: 515-294-5836
Fax: 515-294-2592
E-mail: admissions@iastate.edu
Website: www.iastate.edu

CAMPUS STATS
Type of Institution: Public university
Founding Year: 1858
Size: 21,354
Avg. Class Size: 20–29 students
Popular Majors: Management Information Systems, Marketing/Marketing Management, Mechanical Engineering
Cost: In-state tuition: $4,702
Out-of-state tuition: $14,404
Admission Application Deadline: January 15

ACADEMIC SCENE

Top Three Supportive LGBT Academic Areas:
1. Art and Design   2. Women's Studies   3. Sociology

How LGBT-friendly are faculty in the classroom?
"There are a lot of supportive faculty and staff. There is even an LGBT faculty/staff group and an ally support group. I think a lot of the LGBT support will depend on what classes you are taking." —*22-year-old lesbian transgender, senior*

"I'm out to a few professors on campus. They are very supportive. I have an English class that has an online forum and I came out on it so I could share my gay experiences and I haven't ever felt unsafe in the class. I'm out in my psych class, and they are supportive. I feel that if I needed to, I could talk to them."
—*18-year-old gay male, freshman*

SOCIAL SCENE

Top Three Things in the LGBT Social Life:
1. Hanging out   2. Drag shows   3. Dancing

How would you describe the social scene for LGBT students?
"There is no current gay bar; however, there is a drag show every week at a bar/restaurant called Bali Satay. Once a month there is a drag show at another bar called the Bohème, which is where many of the art, theater, international and LGBT students hang out. It's kind of the UN-official gay bar. If you want to go out to bars and clubs, you go to Des Moines twenty minutes away or you go to Minneapolis for the weekend." —*22-year-old lesbian, senior*

What annual social event should an LGBT student not miss?
"National Coming Out Week. It makes you feel good to be gay. It lets you know there are others just like you in a much more public fashion."
—*18-year-old gay male, freshman*

 OUTRAGEOUS FACTOID In order to be a true "Iowa-State-er," one must go "campaniling" at least once. That is, one must be kissed at the stroke of midnight under the central tower—the Campanile. Even though "campaniling" can happen any night throughout the year, the LGBT community has its own special "campaniling" night.

• • • • • • • • • • • • • • • • • • •

 RAINBOW RUMOR There are a few student religious organizations that openly oppose the LGBT community. One of those organizations is the largest on campus. An LGBT student warns: "If you come out to some of the members, they will literally try to convert you: 'Place you on the path God intended for you.'"

• • • • • • • • • • • • • • • • • • •

 THAT'S SO GAY!
ANNUAL LGBT EVENT HIGHLIGHTS

Welcome Ice-Cream Social: August

Coming Out Week: October

Coming Out Party: October

Small Victories Celebration: January

LGBT Awareness Days: April

Got Ignorance? Multicultural Rally: April

Lavender Graduation: May

BUZZ BITES
Fun Queer Stuff to Know

THE BEST...

Party Locale: The Bohème
Hangout: Stomping Grounds
Eating Place: Bali Satay
Place to Check Out Guys: Beyer Hall
Place to Check Out Ladies: Women's Studies classes
LGBT-Cool Athletic Sport: Wrestling *and* women's hockey
Non-LGBT-Specific Campus Club: Student Organic Farm

Place for LGBT Students to Live on Campus: Martin Hall
LGBT Course Offering: Introduction to Queer Studies
LGBT Educational Involvement Opportunity: LGBT Speakers Bureau
LGBT-Accepting Religious/Spiritual Organization(s): Lord of Life Lutheran, Unitarian Fellowship, United Church of Christ, Quaker Community

CAMPUS QUEER RESOURCES

Select LGBT Student Organization(s):

The Alliance
Membership: 50+
Phone: 515-294-2104
E-mail: alliance@iastate.edu
Website: www.alliance.stuorg.iastate.edu/homepage.html

LGBT Resource Center/Office:

LGBT Student Services
Dean of Students Office
1034 Student Services Building
Ames, IA 50011-2222
Year Established: 1993
Number of Staff: 3 full-time professional staff (varying levels)
Phone: 515-294-5433
E-mail: lgbtss@iastate.edu
Website: www.dso.iastate.edu/lgbtss/

THE GAY POINT AVERAGE
OFFICIAL CAMPUS CHECKLIST

- ✓ LGBT & ally student organization
- ✓ LGBT resource center/office
- ✓ LGBT Pride Week &/or Coming Out Week
- ✓ Safe Zone/Safe Space or Ally Program
- Significant number of LGBT social activities
- ✓ Significant number of LGBT educational events
- ✓ Variety of LGBT studies/courses
- ✓ Nondiscrimination statement inclusive of sexual orientation
- ✓ Nondiscrimination statement inclusive of gender identity/expression
- ✓ Extends domestic partner benefits to same-sex couples
- Actively recruits LGBT students to enroll on campus
- ✓ Trains campus police on LGBT sensitivity
- ✓ Procedure for reporting LGBT bias, harassment & hate crimes
- Offers LGBT housing options/themes
- ✓ Offers LGBT-inclusive health services/testing
- ✓ Offers LGBT-inclusive counseling/support groups
- ✓ Offers LGBT student scholarships
- ✓ Conducts special LGBT graduation ceremony for LGBT & ally Students
- Offers support services for process of transitioning from M to F & F to M
- Active LGBT alumni group

15 IOWA STATE UNIVERSITY GAY POINT AVERAGE
(out of 20)

ITHACA COLLEGE

NESTLED IN THE heart of New York State's beautiful Finger Lakes region, Ithaca College is located roughly halfway between Manhattan and Toronto. Ithaca was one of the first cities in the nation to adopt a nondiscrimination law inclusive of sexual orientation. There are out LGBT city and county legislators, campus faculty and staff, as well as inclusive LGBT policies and practices from the local community to the college campus.

Without a doubt, LGBT students have a place to call home at Ithaca College. The campus strives to become the standard of excellence for residential comprehensive colleges. This standard includes a long-standing institutional commitment to LGBT students, faculty and staff. As such, the campus nondiscrimination policy is inclusive of sexual orientation, and employees' domestic partners are eligible for all benefits afforded to married spouses. Currently, efforts are being made to add gender identity/expression to campus policies as well. It seems inevitable this year! Most importantly, Ithaca College set up the Center for LGBT Education, Outreach and Services. In 2001, the doors opened to much celebration and applause. Today the center is known for a variety of queer offerings, including ongoing themed film festivals, academic lectures, ally trainings, support groups, study breaks, performers, artists, dances and more.

LGBT students are active on campus, from the academic setting to the social setting, creating the momentum that pushed Ithaca College to the top of the queer charts. The college boasts two LGBTA student organizations, one of which has been continuously operating for more than 25 years. In addition, there are scores of out and proud faculty and staff, not to mention the overwhelming number of straight allies. As one LGBT student states: "There really aren't areas on campus that are not supportive! Some majors are known for having more out faculty and students than others, but almost everyone is friendly and welcoming."

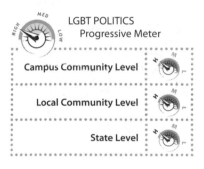

LGBT POLITICS
Progressive Meter

Campus Community Level

Local Community Level

State Level

OUTSPOKEN *Answers from LGBT students:*

Top Three Descriptors of the LGBT Campus Environment:
1. Creative 2. Active 3. Inquisitive

What makes your campus feel welcoming and safe for LGBT students?
"The [number] of people who feel comfortable about their queer identity and the visible support from straight allies." *—18-year-old bisexual female, freshman*

How do you feel about coming out on your campus?
"I had a very easy time coming out on the Ithaca College campus. I don't think it would have been so easy had I been anywhere else. I had a lot of support from friends and from organizations such as Prism and the LGBT resource center. I haven't had a negative experience coming out to anyone on campus the entire time that I've been here." *—20-year-old bisexual female, junior*

"It took me two years to do it, but once I did, I was extremely happy and surprised at the acceptance that I found." *—21-year-old gay male, senior*

INFO

ITHACA COLLEGE
100 Job Hall
Ithaca, NY 14850
Phone: 607-274-3124
Fax: 607-274-1900
E-mail: admission@ithaca.edu
Website: www.ithaca.edu

CAMPUS STATS
Type of Institution: Private college
Founding Year: 1892
Size: 6,159
Avg. Class Size: 10–19 students
Popular Majors: Business Administration/Management, Film/Video and Photographic Arts, Radio and Television
Cost: Tuition: $25,194
Admission Application Deadline: February 1

OUTRAGEOUS FACTOID

Many LGBT alumni now work for key national and regional LGBT organizations such as the Gay, Lesbian and Straight Education Network (GLSEN), Mautner Project, GenderPAC, Victory Fund, National Coalition for Sexual Freedom, Human Rights Campaign, Latino/a Lesbian and Gay Organization (LLEGO) and Callen Lourde. A recent graduate even designed the dress Nicole Kidman wore to the Golden Globe Awards.

RAINBOW RUMOR

The rainbow flag has been stolen 4 out of the 5 times it has flown on the campus flagpole to celebrate gay pride events. But Ithaca queers and allies were determined and put the flag back up! Students organized nightly vigils underneath the flagpole to keep watch over it. Campus police responded seriously, nabbing the perpetrator. Pride colors flew high once again!

THAT'S SO GAY!

ANNUAL LGBT EVENT HIGHLIGHTS

LGBT Center Open House: September

National Coming Out Day: October

Transgender Day of Remembrance: November

International Bisexuality Day: October

"Out of the Closet and Onto the Screen" Film Series: September and April

LGBT Health Awareness Week: March

GAYpril LGBT Awareness Month: April

Rainbow Graduation Reception: April

ACADEMIC SCENE

Top Three Supportive LGBT Academic Areas:
1. Sociology   2. Music   3. Theater

How LGBT-friendly are faculty in the classroom?
"I have never had a problem with being out in the classroom. All of my professors have been great—and because they know I have a lot of information about LGBT topics, they often come to me when they need assistance or information. It's an awesome feeling." —*20-year-old bisexual female, sophomore*

"In my department there are two married [same-sex] couples that are faculty. I've seen pictures of their weddings. I'm very comfortable being out in the classroom." —*21-year-old lesbian, junior*

SOCIAL SCENE

Top Three Things in the LGBT Social Life:
1. Dancing   2. Hanging out with friends   3. Parties

How would you describe the social scene for LGBT students?
"There are a lot of hangouts for gay, lesbian, bisexual and transgender people, both on and off campus. The LGBT Resource room is a good place for people to chill out, eat lunch, and do homework together on campus. If people are interested in hanging out off campus, they can check out Common Ground, the gay bar located just off of campus, or places like Felicia's Atomic Lounge or Juna's Café." —*20-year-old bisexual female, junior*

What annual social event should an LGBT student not miss?
"The Coming Out Day rally! I love getting up in front of people and saying out loud that I'm gay." —*21-year-old lesbian, junior*

BUZZ BITES *Fun Queer Stuff to Know*

THE BEST...

Party Locale: Common Ground

Hangout: LGBT Resource Center

Eating Place: Juna's Café

Place to Check Out Guys: Common Ground

Place to Check Out Ladies: Felicia's Atomic Lounge

LGBT-Cool Athletic Sport: Women's rugby

Non-LGBT-Specific Campus Club: IC Feminists

Place for LGBT Students to Live on Campus: Terrace 2 *and* Music Fraternities

LGBT Course Offering: Sexual Oppression

LGBT Educational Involvement Opportunity: ZAP! Programs

LGBT-Accepting Religious/Spiritual Organization(s): Hillel

THE GAY POINT AVERAGE
OFFICIAL CAMPUS CHECKLIST

LGBT & ally student organization ✓

LGBT resource center/office ✓

LGBT Pride Week &/or Coming Out Week ✓

Safe Zone/Safe Space or Ally Program ✓

Significant number of LGBT social activities ✓

Significant number of LGBT educational events ✓

Variety of LGBT studies/courses ✓

Nondiscrimination statement inclusive of sexual orientation ✓

Nondiscrimination statement inclusive of gender identity/expression

Extends domestic partner benefits to same-sex couples ✓

Actively recruits LGBT students to enroll on campus ✓

Trains campus police on LGBT sensitivity ✓

Procedure for reporting LGBT bias, harassment & hate crimes ✓

Offers LGBT housing options/themes ✓

Offers LGBT-inclusive health services/testing ✓

Offers LGBT-inclusive counseling/support groups ✓

Offers LGBT student scholarships

Conducts special LGBT graduation ceremony for LGBT & ally Students ✓

Offers support services for process of transitioning from M to F & F to M ✓

Active LGBT alumni group ✓

ITHACA COLLEGE
GAY POINT AVERAGE
(out of 20)
18

**CAMPUS QUEER
RESOURCES**

Select LGBT Student Organization(s):
Prism; Created Equal
Founding Date: Prism (before1980);
Created Equal (2000)
Membership: 400+
Website: www.ithaca.edu/prism;
www.ithaca.edu/equal

LGBT Resource Center/Office:
**Center for LGBT Education,
Outreach and Services**
Ithaca College
150 J. David Hammond Center
Ithaca, NY 14850
Year Established: 2001
Number of Staff: 1 full-time professional staff;
2 paid student workers, plus volunteers
Phone: 607-274-7394
Website: www.ithaca.edu/lgbt

KALAMAZOO COLLEGE

LOCATED IN THE SCENIC city of Kalamazoo in southwestern Michigan, LGBT progress on this campus has been incremental over the years, as reflected in the Gay Point Average. Nevertheless, Kalamazoo College has always displayed a commitment to LGBT issues and has a nondiscrimination policy inclusive of both sexual orientation and gender identity/expression.

Most significantly, queer student activism has been fervent over the years, helping to create the positive campus climate seen today. Kaleidoscope, the LGBT and ally student group, is responsible for most everything queer on campus, from LGBT Awareness Week to distributing Safe Zone signs. Membership in the student group, as well as attendance at meetings, has been on the rise.

One of the most anticipated events of the year is the annual Crystal Ball. Gay and straight students alike cross-dress for a "wild, wonderful, and totally accepting night of dancing and gender bending." Kaleidoscope also collaborates with campus departments like residence life and the counseling center to provide LGBT awareness and educational opportunities. This LGBT outreach supplements the annual list of guest speakers and panel discussions already held throughout the year.

LGBT progressive "Gay-K" students are applauded for creating a place that is welcoming and supportive for queers. Even the faculty and staff think so. They often show their queer support by hosting "support dinners" for Kaleidoscope members in their homes. One LGBT student explains: "It's like a family. We work together and live together. … straight allies stand beside us. Gay K is a special place."

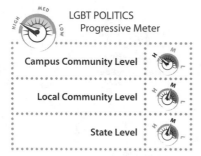

LGBT POLITICS
Progressive Meter

Campus Community Level

Local Community Level

State Level

INFO

KALAMAZOO COLLEGE
1200 Academy Street
Kalamazoo, MI 49006
Phone: 616-337-7166
Fax: 269-337-7390
E-mail: admission@kzoo.edu
Website: www.kzoo.edu

CAMPUS STATS
Type of Institution: Private university
Founding Year: 1833
Size: 1,242
Avg. Class Size: 10–19 students
Popular Majors: Biology/Biological Sciences, Economics, Psychology, Political Science
Cost: Tuition: $32,353
Admission Application Deadline: February 15

OUTSPOKEN *Answers from LGBT students:*

Top Three Descriptors of the LGBT Campus Environment:
1. Accepting 2. Thriving 3. Unique

What makes your campus feel welcoming and safe for LGBT students?
"Gay K lives up to its reputation of being open and accepting of LGBT students. From the first day on campus, the queer visibility was there. … I felt welcome and at home." —*19-year-old lesbian, freshman*

How do you feel about coming out on your campus?
"A no-brainer. I came out without any concern. The response was overwhelmingly positive." —*22-year-old queer male, senior*

⊘ ACADEMIC SCENE

Top Three Supportive LGBT Academic Areas:
1. English   2. Psychology   3. Women's Studies

How LGBT-friendly are faculty in the classroom?
"The number of out faculty seems very high on campus. I have also found my classes to be queer-affirming. I think the level of gay-friendly faculty is way high."
—*20-year-old bisexual female, sophomore*

"LGBT issues are brought up just like any other issue. It is normal to find queer class examples. I have been very surprised. … The reaction is also supportive from classmates on the whole." —*21-year-old bisexual male, senior*

☺ SOCIAL SCENE

Top Three Things in the LGBT Social Life:
1. Socializing with friends   2. Kaleidoscope   3. Local parties

How would you describe the social scene for LGBT students?
"Very gay…and what's fun is that the straights love to come too."
—*19-year-old gay male, freshman*

What annual social event should an LGBT student not miss?
"The Crystal Ball…where you can see straight guys put on a dress and really get into it."—*22-year-old lesbian, junior*

BUZZ BITES
Fun Queer Stuff to Know

THE BEST…

Hangout: Water Street Coffee Joint

Eating Place: Pasta Pasta *and* Safron

Place to Check Out Guys:
Men's diving practice

Place to Check Out Ladies: Athletic Center

LGBT-Cool Athletic Sport: Men's soccer *or* women's softball

Non-LGBT-Specific Campus Club:
Amnesty International

LGBT-Accepting Religious/Spiritual Organization(s): Campus chaplain, Catholic Student Parish

OUTRAGEOUS FACTOID Famous philanthropist Jon Stryker is a longtime resident of Kalamazoo and a graduate of Kalamazoo College. He established the Arcus Foundation, which provides funding to projects and organizations that promote social justice, youth, arts and culture and environmental concerns. Any application to the Arcus Foundation must come from an organization that has a nondiscrimination policy that includes sexual orientation as well as gender identity/expression. That is one of the reasons that Kalamazoo College has specifically included gender identity in its nondiscrimination policy.

RAINBOW RUMOR The student coalition Kaleidoscope oversees all LGBT activities, from the distribution of Safe Zone signs to all LGBT-related events. Some LGBT students think having an LGBT resource center or a staff person responsible for LGBT issues would ensure a long-term approach to queer issues on campus.

THAT'S SO GAY!

ANNUAL LGBT EVENT HIGHLIGHTS

Fall Orientation LGBT Welcome: September

LGBT Awareness Week: October

National Coming Out Day: October 11

Crystal Ball: Spring

Listening Ear Support Group: Fall/Spring

LGBT Speaker Series: Fall/Spring

THE GAY POINT AVERAGE
OFFICIAL CAMPUS CHECKLIST

✓ LGBT & ally student organization

LGBT resource center/office

✓ LGBT Pride Week &/or Coming Out Week

✓ Safe Zone/Safe Space or Ally Program

✓ Significant number of LGBT social activities

✓ Significant number of LGBT educational events

Variety of LGBT studies/courses

✓ Nondiscrimination statement inclusive of sexual orientation

✓ Nondiscrimination statement inclusive of gender identity/expression

Extends domestic partner benefits to same-sex couples

✓ Actively recruits LGBT students to enroll on campus

Trains campus police on LGBT sensitivity

Procedure for reporting LGBT bias, harassment & hate crimes

Offers LGBT housing options/themes

✓ Offers LGBT-inclusive health services/testing

✓ Offers LGBT-inclusive counseling/support groups

Offers LGBT student scholarships

Conducts special LGBT graduation ceremony for LGBT & ally Students

Offers support services for process of transitioning from M to F & F to M

Active LGBT alumni group

10 KALAMAZOO COLLEGE
GAY POINT AVERAGE
(out of 20)

KNOX COLLEGE

"INSTITUTIONAL SELF-CONFIDENCE also means speaking out for what is right. We embrace diversity at Knox. We reject invidious discrimination based on race, sex, national origin, disability and sexual orientation. I realize that speaking out against discrimination based on disability and sexual orientation is still not entirely accepted in our society. Speaking out against discrimination based upon race was not entirely popular on the frontier prairies of Illinois in the 1840s and 50s. But that didn't stop the early leaders of this college from speaking out fiercely against discrimination. And it should not stop us."

These words were spoken by Roger Taylor, president of Knox College, in his installation address. The LGBT commitment expressed in this statement is one of the main reasons why Knox College is among the most progressive colleges for LGBT students. Students frequently cite the openness of the campus as one of the most attractive features of Knox.

Knox has been a leader in the fight for inclusion and opportunity since its founding by abolitionists in 1837. Women have enrolled at the college since the 1850s. The first black student to receive a college degree in Illinois received it from Knox. The first African American U.S. senator went to Knox. So the efforts made by Knox College to embrace LGBT students arise naturally from its history.

Knox was one of the first in Illinois to include sexual orientation in its affirmative action statement and one of a select few to take the additional step of adding both "gender" and "affectional preference." In addition, Knox College provides full domestic partner benefits for faculty, staff and their families. There are over a dozen out LGBT faculty and numerous LGBT-specific courses. One such LGBT course brings in a variety of guest lecturers.

Even former U.S. president Abraham Lincoln would not debate the facts when it comes to Knox College and its propensity for LGBT inclusion in its policies and practices. One LGBT student states: "[U.S. president Abraham Lincoln] may or may not have been gay, but it's interesting to attend the college where Lincoln's role in history was defined by the famous Lincoln-Douglas Debates. The plaques of Lincoln and Douglas adorn the brick exterior of Old Main, the last surviving site of those debates and the location of Lincoln's most vocal statements on the immorality of slavery. Today the fight for equality continues to be made by orators on the steps of Old Main—by LGBT and ally faculty, students and guest speakers alike."

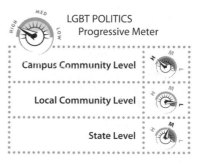

LGBT POLITICS
Progressive Meter

Campus Community Level

Local Community Level

State Level

🗩🗩 OUTSPOKEN *Answers from LGBT students:*

Top Three Descriptors of the LGBT Campus Environment:
1. Safe   2. Accepting   3. Curious

What makes your campus feel welcoming and safe for LGBT students?
"When I visited campus as a prospective student, my boyfriend called me while I was at the snack bar with my student host and some of his friends. When my host asked who had called, I said it was my boyfriend. He just said 'Oh' and went on with the conversation. I was worried that they were uncomfortable. But then I noticed a pride flag on my host's backpack and realized that my revelation was just a nonissue. I realized then that this was the college for me!" —*19-year-old gay male, sophomore*

INFO

KNOX COLLEGE
2 East South Street
Galesburg, IL 61401
Phone: 309-341-7100
Fax: 309-341-7070
E-mail: admission@knox.edu
Website: www.knox.edu

CAMPUS STATS
Type of Institution: Private college
Founding Year: 1837
Size: 1,245
Avg. Class Size: 10–19 students
Popular Majors: Biology, Creative Writing, Psychology
Cost: Tuition: $25,815
Admission Application Deadline: February 1

OUTRAGEOUS FACTOID Lincoln may or may not have been gay, but Knox College is where the debate rages on. The campus is the historical site of the famous Lincoln-Douglas debates. The plaques of Lincoln and Douglas adorn the brick exterior of Old Main, where "Pumphandle," one of the oldest traditions, commemorates the debates every fall. Students, faculty and staff gather on the campus lawn before the first day of classes to shake hands with every other student, faculty member and staff member. The line winds around the campus until everyone's hand has been shaken.

RAINBOW RUMOR The LGBT group Common Ground knows how to plan a party and provides a range of cultural and social activities throughout the year.

THAT'S SO GAY!

ANNUAL LGBT EVENT HIGHLIGHTS

National Coming Out Day/Week: October

Drag Show: October

LGBT Parties at Cherry Street: October, February, May, July

Homecoming LGBT Alumni Reunion: October/November

AIDS Awareness Week: April

Gender Confusion Party: March/April

Pride Week: May

How do you feel about coming out on your campus?

"Coming out on this campus is no big deal. There is always someone who's out already whom you can look to as a role model. That makes it safe and easy

to come out. And I've been able to play a role in the coming out of others, who have felt comfortable talking to me in the same way."
—*21-year-old lesbian, junior*

ACADEMIC SCENE

Top Three Supportive LGBT Academic Areas:
1. Psychology   2. Gender and Women's Studies   3. History

How LGBT-friendly are faculty in the classroom?

"It's a bit strange—I'm used to having to 'speak for my kind' in class. This was especially true in high school. But here, nobody expects me to do that. I almost miss having everyone look to me for insights every time someone brings up a gay topic in class!!! At Knox, I've never been a token gay."
—*22-year-old gay male, senior*

SOCIAL SCENE

Top Three Things in the LGBT Social Life:
1. Gender Confusion Parties 2. Gossip on Gizmo 3. Hanging out with friends

How would you describe the social scene for LGBT students?

"It's fun to hang out in the Human Rights Center after the weekly Common Ground meetings. But everyone knows everyone at Knox; it's a close-knit community. It's easy to have a rich social life." —*18-year-old lesbian, freshman*

"I met one person from Common Ground at the campuswide fair of student clubs at the beginning of the year. After that initial connection, I quickly got to know many of the LGBT people on campus. It's a very friendly campus, accessible, and [an] open-minded group of people." —*20-year-old gay male, sophomore*

What annual social event should an LGBT student not miss?

"National Coming Out Week is a blast!" —*21-year-old gay male, junior*

BUZZ BITES *Fun Queer Stuff to Know*

THE BEST...

Party Locale: Cherry Street LGBT parties

Hangout: Gizmo Snack Bar

Eating Place: Innkeeper's Coffee

Place to Check Out Guys: Facebook.com

Place to Check Out Ladies: Softball games

LGBT-Cool Athletic Sport: Ultimate Frisbee *and* softball

Non-LGBT-Specific Campus Club: Alliance for Peaceful Action

Place for LGBT Students to Live on Campus: Theme Houses

LGBT Course Offering: Social Constructions in Deviance

LGBT Educational Involvement Opportunity: National Coming Out Week Activities

LGBT-Accepting Religious/Spiritual Organization(s): Intervarsity Christian Fellowship

THE GAY POINT AVERAGE
OFFICIAL CAMPUS CHECKLIST

LGBT & ally student organization	✓
LGBT resource center/office	✓
LGBT Pride Week &/or Coming Out Week	✓
Safe Zone/Safe Space or Ally Program	
Significant number of LGBT social activities	✓
Significant number of LGBT educational events	✓
Variety of LGBT studies/courses	✓
Nondiscrimination statement inclusive of sexual orientation	✓
Nondiscrimination statement inclusive of gender identity/expression	✓
Extends domestic partner benefits to same-sex couples	✓
Actively recruits LGBT students to enroll on campus	✓
Trains campus police on LGBT sensitivity	✓
Procedure for reporting LGBT bias, harassment & hate crimes	✓
Offers LGBT housing options/themes	✓
Offers LGBT-inclusive health services/testing	✓
Offers LGBT-inclusive counseling/support groups	✓
Offers LGBT student scholarships	
Conducts special LGBT graduation ceremony for LGBT & ally Students	
Offers support services for process of transitioning from M to F & F to M	
Active LGBT alumni group	

KNOX COLLEGE
GAY POINT AVERAGE
(out of 20)

15

CAMPUS QUEER
RESOURCES

Select LGBT Student Organization(s):
Common Ground
Founding Date: 1988
Membership: 100+
Website: deptorg.knox.edu/
commonground

LGBT Resource Center/Office:
**Center for Intercultural Life and
Human Rights Center**
Box 134, Knox College
2 East South Street
Galesburg, IL 61401
Year Established: 1991
Number of Staff: 2 professional staff (varied
responsibilities)
Phone: 309-341-7230
E-mail: cwalters@knox.edu
Website: www.knox.edu/x976.xml

LAWRENCE UNIVERSITY

LAWRENCE UNIVERSITY is set in a beautiful location in downtown Appleton, Wisconsin, on the Fox River. Not only is the campus LGBT-friendly, but also the city of Appleton shares the commitment to LGBT inclusion efforts.

Lawrence University highlights the fact that it has a progressive community. All groups, LGBT or not, work together on queer projects and events. The health and counseling service is LGBT-sensitive and offers a "transgender" option when completing forms to see a campus nurse or doctor. In addition, every year the LGBT organization, Gay, Lesbian, Other, or Whatever (GLOW), holds a spring conference. Past topics included "Who Are the People in Your Neighborhood? Recognizing the T and B in GLBT," which concentrated on transgender issues and bisexual issues. The conference provides LGBT and ally students an opportunity to discuss relevant and timely LGBT issues. Quite commendable, indeed.

The numbers of LGBT students and their allies are increasing at Lawrence University. The Gay Point Average shows the reasons why. As one LGBT student explains: "I have friends who called themselves straight and then started dating a person of the same gender. ... No one really thought twice about it. This is one aspect of Lawrence that I find to be most comforting; you can be who you are."

LGBT POLITICS
Progressive Meter

Campus Community Level

Local Community Level

State Level

OUTSPOKEN *Answers from LGBT students:*

Top Three Descriptors of the LGBT Campus Environment:
1. Diverse   2. Open   3. Fabulous

What makes your campus feel welcoming and safe for LGBT students?
"I feel like most Lawrence students don't feel the need to label or categorize themselves and can explore their personalities and sexualities more freely because of it." —*20-year-old bisexual female, junior*

How do you feel about coming out on your campus?
"It was scary at first, like all coming out, but eventually I realized that Lawrence and its students were incredibly accepting and willing to help me. Many students hardly made an issue of it." —*19-year-old gender/sexual orientation nonconforming, sophomore*

"I came out to my roommate by telling him I went to the GLBT support group. He was very accepting and it was never an impediment to our relationship as roommates." —*19-year-old gay male, sophomore*

ACADEMIC SCENE

Top Three Supportive LGBT Academic Areas:
1. Gender Studies   2. Art History   3. Anthropology

How LGBT-friendly are faculty in the classroom?
"All of my professors have been very accepting of my gender identification and try their best to accommodate my preferences."
—*22-year-old gay male, senior*

INFO

LAWRENCE UNIVERSITY
PO Box 599
Appleton, WI 54912
Phone: 920-832-7000
Fax: 920-832-6782
E-mail: excel@lawrence.edu
Website: www.lawrence.edu

CAMPUS STATS

Type of Institution: Private university
Founding Year: 1847
Size: 1,344
Avg. Class Size: 10–19 students
Popular Majors: Biology/Biological Sciences, Musical Performance, Psychology
Cost: Tuition: $26,145
Admission Application Deadline: January 15

"Many professors have given lectures at GLOW's annual conference, speaking on GLBT issues in disciplines ranging from music to physics." —*22-year-old gay female, senior*

😊 SOCIAL SCENE

Top Three Things in the LGBT Social Life:
1. Queer Movie Series   2. Socializing   3. Hanging out with friends

How would you describe the social scene for LGBT students?
"Gay couples can dance at parties without there being an issue, usually. It's no big thing." —*19-year-old gay male, sophomore*

"Most people at Lawrence hang out with all kinds: gay, straight, liberal, conservative. We operate on a real individual basis here."
—*19-year-old gay male, freshman*

What annual social event should an LGBT student not miss?
"The drag show. It's hilarious, and all sorts participate, including football players and physics nerds. We really come together for that and have a lot of fun."
—*20-year-old bisexual female, junior*

OUTRAGEOUS FACTOID Students rave about the high level of "outness" by faculty and how labels lose their place on campus. One student says: "Nobody needs to be just gay or straight; we don't define ourselves in order to fit in—we get along across any boundary of difference."

• • • • • • • • • • • • • • • • • • • •

RAINBOW RUMOR Coming your way: Lawrence University has plans for an Alliance House for LGBT housing—particularly to address the needs of transgender students by adding co-ed housing options on campus.

• • • • • • • • • • • • • • • • • • • •

THAT'S SO GAY!

ANNUAL LGBT EVENT HIGHLIGHTS

Welcome Party: September

Coming Out Week and Coming Out Confessionals: October

Queer Movie Series: Twice a month

Safe Sex and Queer Relationships: November

Transgender Week of Remembrance: November

Antihate Week: Spring

GLBT Formal/Dance: April/May

BUZZ BITES *Fun Queer Stuff to Know*

THE BEST...

Hangout: Underground Café

Eating Place: Memorial Grill

Place to Check Out Guys: Steele G. Mudd Library

Place to Check Out Ladies: Conservatory of Music

LGBT-Cool Athletic Sport: Swimming

Non-LGBT-Specific Campus Club: Campus Democrats

LGBT Course Offering: Economy of Family, Sex, Sexuality and Gender

LGBT Educational Involvement Opportunity: Queer Arts Festival

LGBT-Accepting Religious/Spiritual Organization(s): Hillel

CAMPUS QUEER RESOURCES

Select LGBT Student Organization(s):
Gay, Lesbian, Other, or Whatever (GLOW)
Founding Date: Early 1990s (with several name changes)
Membership: 120+
Phone: 920-832-7395
E-mail: lu_glow@yahoo.com
Website: www.lawrence.edu/sorg/glow

Resource Center/Office Responsible for LGBT Issues:
Diversity Center
LGBT Services
Lawrence University
Appleton, WI 54912
Year Established: 1997
Number of Staff: 2 full-time professional staff (varied responsibilities)
Phone: 920-832-7051
Website: www.lawrence.edu/about/tour/diversity.shtml

THE GAY POINT AVERAGE
OFFICIAL CAMPUS CHECKLIST

- ✓ LGBT & ally student organization
- ✓ LGBT resource center/office
- ✓ LGBT Pride Week &/or Coming Out Week
- ✓ Safe Zone/Safe Space or Ally Program
- ✓ Significant number of LGBT social activities
- ✓ Significant number of LGBT educational events
- ✓ Variety of LGBT studies/courses
- ✓ Nondiscrimination statement inclusive of sexual orientation
- Nondiscrimination statement inclusive of gender identity/expression
- ✓ Extends domestic partner benefits to same-sex couples
- Actively recruits LGBT students to enroll on campus
- Trains campus police on LGBT sensitivity
- ✓ Procedure for reporting LGBT bias, harassment & hate crimes
- Offers LGBT housing options/themes
- ✓ Offers LGBT-inclusive health services/testing
- ✓ Offers LGBT-inclusive counseling/support groups
- Offers LGBT student scholarships
- Conducts special LGBT graduation ceremony for LGBT & ally Students
- ✓ Offers support services for process of transitioning from M to F & F to M
- Active LGBT alumni group

(13) LAWRENCE UNIVERSITY GAY POINT AVERAGE
(out of 20)

MACALESTER COLLEGE

MACALESTER COLLEGE IS well known for values of openness, individuality and diversity. Not surprisingly, the campus championed domestic partner benefits and other LGBT-inclusive policies to persuade local businesses to also enact queer positive changes. The urban environment of Macalester College provides opportunities for greater LGBT involvement beyond the campus.

But even on campus, Macalester provides LGBT students much to consider. Queer Union, the campus GLBT student organization, was founded in 1970. It plans such activities as Queer Cabaret, Coming Out Week and Big Hair Mania. In addition, the annual Dyke Out brings women within the community together. And each Valentine's Day, Queer Union sponsors "Crush Notes," to help explore sexuality by writing short notes of affection to others.

The Gay Point Average highlights that Macalester has much to be proud of. The atmosphere is one of LGBT acceptance. Not only are there many LGBT students, but also many leaders within the faculty and staff identify openly as LGBT too. This LGBT student remarks: "What makes Mac unique, in my opinion, is the openness with which the word 'queer' is used, embraced and understood.... It's amazing. It's the type of community where you are expected to have either a fluid sexuality or be 'comfortable' if you are straight. It's just a normal thing to be LGBT here."

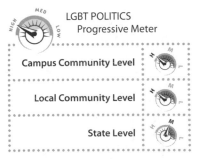

LGBT POLITICS
Progressive Meter

Campus Community Level

Local Community Level

State Level

OUTSPOKEN *Answers from LGBT students:*

Top Three Descriptors of the LGBT Campus Environment:
1. Accepting   2. Phenomenal   3. Safe

What makes your campus feel welcoming and safe for LGBT students?
"The first time I walked onto campus was during my senior year of high school during Coming Out Week. All around me were posters about the week's events and sidewalk chalking. The next day I visited another college and saw nothing LGBT-related. That's when I first felt that Macalester is a welcome and safe environment for LGBT students. Macalester is a place where many different identities collide. I feel that the campus is the perfect fit for anyone who embraces complexity." —*20-year-old gay male, sophomore*

How do you feel about coming out on your campus?
"I would not be the lion-hearted, K. D. Lang–toting sexual justice advocate I am today if it weren't for having come out in this most unique and overwhelmingly positive of campus environments." —*21-year-old lesbian, senior*

ACADEMIC SCENE

Top Three Supportive LGBT Academic Areas:
1. Women, Gender and Sexuality Studies   2. Visual and Performing Arts
3. American Studies

INFO

MACALESTER COLLEGE
1600 Grand Avenue
St. Paul, MN 55105
Phone: 651-696-6357
Fax: 651-696-6724
E-mail: admissions@macalester.edu
Web site: www.macalester.edu

CAMPUS STATS
Type of Institution: Private college, Presbyterian religious affiliation
Founding Year: 1874
Size: 1,841
Avg. Class Size: 10–19 students
Popular Majors: Economics, English Language and Literature, Political Science and Government
Cost: Tuition: $28,642
Admission Application Deadline: January 15

OUTRAGEOUS FACTOID

Macalester College is an extremely sex-positive campus. Tradition calls for anyone who has had his or her first sexual experience to ring the "Bell." The large 12-foot-high cast-iron bell is located in the middle of campus.

• • • • • • • • • • • • • • • • • • •

RAINBOW RUMOR

For upperclass students, accommodations at Macalester College are no longer segregated by sex. Gender-open housing was recently made available for upperclass students in suite-style apartments and residences. Such an improvement signals a commitment for more education on trans-identity and support services.

• • • • • • • • • • • • • • • • • • •

THAT'S SO GAY!

ANNUAL LGBT EVENT HIGHLIGHTS

Queer Cabaret: Fall

Dyke Out: Fall

LGBT Alumni Reunion: Fall

Coming Out Week: Around October 11

Diversity Weekend: October

Big Hair Mania: November

Day of Silence: April

Lavender Graduation: May

Pride Week: July

Queer Union Meetings: Weekly, Fall/Spring

Queers of Color: Monthly, Fall/Spring

How LGBT-friendly are faculty in the classroom?

"I have yet to meet any faculty that are homophobic. It's really cool, because you can connect with your teachers and ask for advice without worrying about them judging you."
—*18-year-old bi-lesbian, sophomore*

"Here at Macalester it is not only encouraged but understood that normative structures, whether they be external institutions of power or internal constructions of opinion, are to be flexibly questioned and challenged. This not only applies to discussions surrounding sexuality, but the intersection of race, class and gender as well." —*21-year-old lesbian, senior*

☺ SOCIAL SCENE

Top Three Things in the LGBT Social Life:
1. Queer Union   2. Kiss-In   3. Cabaret

How would you describe the social scene for LGBT students?

"The social scene at Macalester is not the best it could be. There are great student organizations such as Queer Union, Queer Students of Color, Bisexuality Discussion Group and Identity Collectives, which foster a decent social atmosphere. But the lack of a dating scene at Macalester is still present, nonetheless. The dating scene isn't too hot for anyone, really."
—*20-year-old gay male, sophomore*

What annual social event should an LGBT student not miss?

"The Queer Cabaret is not to be missed. There are drag performances, group choreographed numbers, guitar and saxophone duets, "Manties" (panties for men), catwalk runs, feminist monologues, dental dam beat boxing and so much more. There is something for everyone, really." —*21-year-old lesbian, senior*

BUZZ BITES *Fun Queer Stuff to Know*

THE BEST...

Party Locale: Gay 90s Uptown Minneapolis

Hangout: Vera's *and* Nutella

Eating Place: Acme Deli

Place to Check Out Guys: Saloon

Place to Check Out Ladies: Blue Moon Café

LGBT-Cool Athletic Sport: Soccer *or* women's rugby

Non-LGBT-Specific Campus Club: KAADATT

Place for LGBT Students to Live on Campus: Grand Cambridge *or* Veggie Co-op

LGBT Course Offering: Sexual Margins, Colonial Legacies: Introduction to Lesbian, Gay, Bisexual and Transgender Studies

LGBT Educational Involvement Opportunity: Safe Space Allies Program

LGBT-Accepting Religious/Spiritual Organization(s): Catholic Center, Jewish Organization, Unitarian Universalists, Bahai Faith

THE GAY POINT AVERAGE
OFFICIAL CAMPUS CHECKLIST

LGBT & ally student organization	✓
LGBT resource center/office	
LGBT Pride Week &/or Coming Out Week	✓
Safe Zone/Safe Space or Ally Program	✓
Significant number of LGBT social activities	✓
Significant number of LGBT educational events	✓
Variety of LGBT studies/courses	✓
Nondiscrimination statement inclusive of sexual orientation	✓
Nondiscrimination statement inclusive of gender identity/expression	
Extends domestic partner benefits to same-sex couples	✓
Actively recruits LGBT students to enroll on campus	✓
Trains campus police on LGBT sensitivity	✓
Procedure for reporting LGBT bias, harassment & hate crimes	✓
Offers LGBT housing options/themes	✓
Offers LGBT-inclusive health services/testing	✓
Offers LGBT-inclusive counseling/support groups	✓
Offers LGBT student scholarships	
Conducts special LGBT graduation ceremony for LGBT & ally Students	✓
Offers support services for process of transitioning from M to F & F to M	
Active LGBT alumni group	✓

MACALASTER COLLEGE
GAY POINT AVERAGE **16**
(out of 20)

CAMPUS QUEER RESOURCES

Select LGBT Student Organization(s):
Macalester College Queer Union
Founding Date: 1970
Membership: 25
E-mail: qu@macalester.edu
Website: www.macalester.edu/qu

*Resource Center/Office Responsible
for LGBT Issues:*
Lealtad-Suzuki Multicultural Center
1600 Grand Avenue
St. Paul, MN 55105
Year Established: 2002
Number of Staff: 4 full-time professional
staff (varying responsibilities)
Phone: 651-696-6243
Website: www.macalester.edu/
lealtad-suzuki/

MARLBORO COLLEGE

VERMONT WAS THE first state in the United States to enact a civil union law. In keeping with the climate of the state, Marlboro College welcomes everyone, regardless of their sexual orientation or gender identity. What is most valued is that students are dedicated community members who understand what personal responsibility means and act accordingly.

Located in the foothills of the Green Mountains of southern Vermont, Marlboro College is a small, intimate campus. It is one place where brand names, cell phones and desires to be like everyone else are oddities rather than the norm. The college is dedicated to including all individuals who crave academic rigor and, who have felt disillusioned with mainstream society—drama kids, band kids, science geeks, literature nerds, creative writers and, of course, queers.

Marlboro College considers its entire campus to be a Safe Zone for LGBT students, faculty and staff. The dean of students, the associate dean of students, a professor of political science and theory, an adjunct professor of dance and several other campus support staff are all openly lesbian. In the past, the now-retired religion professor was openly gay too.

The Queer Homecoming and Gender Bender Ball put on by Marlboro Pride, the LGBT campus group, are the most anticipated events of the year by gay and straight alike. In addition, the after-hours emergency staff are trained in LGBT sensitivity, and the Health Center staff provides queer-inclusive literature and information on LGBT health concerns. Recently, the nurse practitioner asked an F-to-M alumnus to help advise any transgender students on current hormone therapies. Last, but not least, the campus attends the LGBT College fair in Boston to recruit prospective LGBT students.

What makes Marlboro College a most unique campus is that it grows and changes with the students' interests and concerns. One LGBT student comments: "More than the average 10 percent are queer here. We have a high degree of individuality at Marlboro. For the first time, I feel not only welcome but also empowered to grow and learn more."

LGBT POLITICS
Progressive Meter

Campus Community Level

Local Community Level

State Level

INFO

MARLBORO COLLEGE
2582 South Road
PO Box A
Marlboro, VT 05344

Phone: 802-257-4333
Fax: 802-257-4154
E-mail: admissions@marlboro.edu
Website: www.marlboro.edu

CAMPUS STATS
Type of Institution: Private college
Founding Year: 1946
Size: 317
Avg. Class Size: Less than 10 students
Popular Majors: Visual and Performing Arts, Social Sciences and History, Biological Life Sciences
Cost: Tuition: $26,940
Admission Application Deadline: February 15

99 OUTSPOKEN *Answers from LGBT students:*

Top Three Descriptors of the LGBT Campus Environment:
1. Inclusive 2. Fun 3. Close-knit

What makes your campus feel welcoming and safe for LGBT students?
"The Marlboro community feels welcoming and safe largely because of its tight-knit nature. The overall atmosphere can be very friendly and accepting for LGBT and non-LGBT students." *—21-year-old bisexual male, junior*

"As a pre-op trans student, I have totally been accepted on campus by administration and students. The school has accommodated me—making my name on my ID my chosen name and changing my gender in the computer system." *—27-year-old queer transgender, freshman*

How do you feel about coming out on your campus?
"I came out my freshman year. All my friends were like, 'duh.'"
—21-year-old lesbian, junior

"Being queer is no big deal here. I ask questions related to it in biology class, anthropology; I talk about my girlfriend with my work-study boss; I hold hands with my sweetie in public. It's great." —*23-year-old lesbian genderqueer, junior*

 ACADEMIC SCENE

Top Three Supportive LGBT Academic Areas:
1. Anthropology   2. Biology   3. Political Science

How LGBT-friendly are faculty in the classroom?
"When I came out, my dance teacher wrote me a note congratulating me on my decision." —*21-year-old lesbian, junior*

"Pretty much all my professors have been very cool when I explained that I'm a transguy. Some of my language teachers haven't 'gotten' it , probably because they weren't from the U.S." —*20-year-old transguy polysexual, sophomore*

 SOCIAL SCENE

Top Three Things in the LGBT Social Life:
1. Movies   2. Pride meals   3. Hanging out with friends

How would you describe the social scene for LGBT students?
"The social scene is open, accepting, friendly and energetic. Sometimes we casually hang out, talk and have a blast. The Pride group also throws the best campuswide parties, and everybody knows it. Our events are the most anticipated parties each semester." —*23-year-old bi-questioning female, senior*

What annual social event should an LGBT student not miss?
"The Gender Bender Ball invites people to dress in a way that plays with gender.… People really get into it and invent characters to go along with their amazing costumes. It looks and sounds like a real club. … We take turns dancing in and around our own Pride cage." —*23-year-old bi-questioning female, senior*

 OUTRAGEOUS FACTOID Marlboro College straight guys know how to party in style. All decked out to the hilt, they always attend the Queer Homecoming and Gender Bender Ball, dressed most fabulously as "gay men."

 RAINBOW RUMOR Next on the "Marlboro Gay Agenda": establishment of an LGBT alumni group and the addition of gender identity/expression to the nondiscrimination policy.

 THAT's SO GAY! **ANNUAL LGBT EVENT HIGHLIGHTS**

Gender IdenitiTEA Workshop Series: Fall/Spring

PeopleTalk: Every week, Fall/Spring

Queer Film Series: Weekly

Queer Homecoming: November

Gender Bender Ball: March

Day of Silence: Spring

BUZZ BITES *Fun Queer Stuff to Know*

THE BEST...

Party Locale: Diva's

Hangout: Campus Library

Eating Place: "Gay Table" at the Dining Hall

Place to Check Out Guys: Theater

Place to Check Out Ladies: Community Workday

LGBT-Cool Athletic Sport: Broomball, the Mighty Dykes Team

Non-LGBT-Specific Campus Club: Outdoor Program

LGBT Educational Involvement Opportunity: PeopleTalk

CAMPUS QUEER RESOURCES

Select LGBT Student Organization(s):

Marlboro PRIDE
Founding Date: 1990
Membership: 25–30
Phone: 802-258-9496
E-mail: pride@mailinglists.marlboro.edu

THE GAY POINT AVERAGE OFFICIAL CAMPUS CHECKLIST

- ✓ LGBT & ally student organization
- LGBT resource center/office
- LGBT Pride Week &/or Coming Out Week
- Safe Zone/Safe Space or Ally Program
- ✓ Significant number of LGBT social activities
- ✓ Significant number of LGBT educational events
- Variety of LGBT studies/courses
- ✓ Nondiscrimination statement inclusive of sexual orientation
- Nondiscrimination statement inclusive of gender identity/expression
- ✓ Extends domestic partner benefits to same-sex couples
- ✓ Actively recruits LGBT students to enroll on campus
- ✓ Trains campus police on LGBT sensitivity
- ✓ Procedure for reporting LGBT bias, harassment & hate crimes
- ✓ Offers LGBT housing options/themes
- ✓ Offers LGBT-inclusive health services/testing
- ✓ Offers LGBT-inclusive counseling/support groups
- Offers LGBT student scholarships
- Conducts special LGBT graduation ceremony for LGBT & ally Students
- ✓ Offers support services for process of transitioning from M to F & F to M
- ✓ Active LGBT alumni group

13 **MARLBORO COLLEGE GAY POINT AVERAGE**
(out of 20)

MASSACHUSETTS INSTITUTE OF TECHNOLOGY

FOR MANY YEARS MIT has been known as a diverse institution—socially, politically and professionally—within the Cambridge, Massachusetts, area. According to LGBT students, it is common to hear student discussions about the fluidity of gender and sexuality that then morph into comments about the latest breakthroughs in astrophysics, biochemistry or mechanical engineering.

Maybe it's not a surprise, but MIT was also one of the first campuses in New England to include both sexual orientation and gender identity in its nondiscrimination policy. In addition, MIT has been home to Gay, Lesbians, Bisexuals, Transgenders and Friends @MIT (GaMIT) since 1969, among the oldest LGBT student groups in the country. When you couple these facts with MIT's outstanding Gay Point Average, you discover a queer tangent of progress going straight up.

MIT is proud to have an active LGBT presence on campus. In 2000, the campus founded the LBGT@MIT office and hired a full-time professional staff person. It also has a student space called the Rainbow Lounge, complete with a living room with couches, computers, a kitchen and a full library of LBGT resources. Including GaMIT, there are five LGBT student groups, an LGBT alumni group and a queer faculty/staff group. All of them work together to plan annual LGBT events like National Coming Out Week, the Queer Women and Ally Brown Bag Lunch Series, Safer Sex Jeopardy and the Steer Roast. One of the most popular events (attendance tops 500) is the Fierce Forever Drag Show.

Numbers count on this campus: MIT estimates that there are over 1,000 students involved annually with LGBT campus life. MIT offers a most progressive and LGBT-friendly place to live and learn. One LGBT student states: "This campus feels queer in every way. Values of open-mindedness, ingenuity and respect are not just words, but truthful actions. LGBT students will find acceptance, not just fit in but feel nurtured…I do."

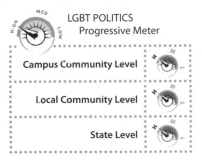

LGBT POLITICS
Progressive Meter

Campus Community Level

Local Community Level

State Level

🗩 OUTSPOKEN *Answers from LGBT students:*

Top Three Descriptors of the LGBT Campus Environment:
1. Innovative   2. Equal   3. Diverse

What makes your campus feel welcoming and safe for LGBT students?
"I was stupefied when I found out that an LBGT community existed here because where I come from, no part of LBG or T is ever brought up. There are 'You are welcome here' signs all around campus; these rainbow-colorful signs shows that the MIT campus is safe for LBGT students."
—19-year-old pansexual male, sophomore

How do you feel about coming out on your campus?
"I decided consciously to be out as soon as I got here. I know that some people in other fraternities end up being closeted their entire time at MIT because they're afraid of the reaction, but East Campus, Senior House, Random, and my

INFO

MASSACHUSETTS INSTITUTE OF TECHNOLOGY
77 Massachusetts Avenue, Room 3-108
Cambridge, MA 02139
Phone: 617-253-4791
Fax: 617-258-8304
E-mail: admissions@mit.edu
Website: www.mit.edu

CAMPUS STATS
Type of Institution: Private college
Founding Year: 1861
Size: 4,136
Avg. Class Size: 10–19 students
Popular Majors: Business Administration/Management, Electrical, Electronics and Communications Engineering, Mechanical Engineering
Cost: Tuition: $32,300
Admission Application Deadline: January 1

OUTRAGEOUS FACTOID
One student notes: "the entire campus is bisexual practically." The main event for the LGBT community is the annual Steer Roast—a 2-day-long party.

• • • • • • • • • • • • • • • •

RAINBOW RUMOR
The LBGT community on campus has grown signficantly over the past 30 years. However, one of the big issues remaining is racism in the queer community and issues of homophobia in communities of color. Several initiatives have been launched to improve race relations, including the new Race and Sexuality Task Force and the Diversity Peer-to-Peer program.

• • • • • • • • • • • • • • • •

ANNUAL LGBT EVENT HIGHLIGHTS

Queer Women and Ally Brown Bag Lunch Series: Weekly, Fall/Spring

Sunday Series—Films and Discussions: Weekly, Fall/Spring

LBGT Orientation: August/September

Coming Out Week: October

Ally Appreciation Party: October

Coming Out Party: October

World AIDS Day: December

Safer Sex Jeopardy: January

TGIF Ice Cream Social: February

Fabulous Friday Fiesta: April

Fierce Forever Drag Show: Spring

Steer Roast: First weekend in May

Lavender Graduation: May

fraternity are wonderful places to come out—people's fears there are always worse than the reality of their open-minded friends."
—*22-year-old gay male, graduate student*

ACADEMIC SCENE

Top Three Supportive LGBT Academic Areas:
1. Women's Studies   2. Humanities, Arts and Social Sciences
3. Music and Theater Arts

How LGBT-friendly are faculty in the classroom?
"I think faculty are extremely LGB friendly, but when it comes to the T, I think it is questionable. There is a need for more education with faculty on how to be respectful of T students." —*19-year-old queer male, sophomore*

"Very. I've never heard a faculty member say anything that could possibly be construed as antigay." —*22-year-old gay male, graduate student*

SOCIAL SCENE

Top Three Things in the LGBT Social Life:
1. Fraternity parties   2. Clubbing   3. Dancing at Axis on Mondays

How would you describe the social scene for LGBT students?
"The LBGT social scene on campus is as lively as any other community at MIT. There are many social activities, parties and outings that are a lot of fun. Quite a few of the parties on campus are not LBGT-unfriendly, so LBGT students go to parties and have nothing to worry about. The dorm that I lived in would throw parties and to not see an LBGT couple would be weird. … This shows how accepting/tolerant the people are." —*19-year-old pansexual male, sophomore*

What annual social event should an LGBT student not miss?
"Coming Out Week is a blast. …My straight friends enjoy [it] too!"
—*20-year-old bisexual male, junior*

BUZZ BITES *Fun Queer Stuff to Know*

THE BEST...

Party Locale: Senior House

Hangout: Rainbow Lounge

Eating Place: Francesca's Coffee Shop *and* Deli Haus

Place to Check Out Guys: Embassy *and* Axis

Place to Check Out Ladies: Toast

LGBT-Cool Athletic Sport: Women's rugby *and* Shotokan karate

Non-LGBT-Specific Campus Club: Ballroom dancing

Place for LGBT Students to Live on Campus: East Campus *or* Senior House

LGBT Educational Involvement Opportunity: Coming Out Week Events

THE GAY POINT AVERAGE
OFFICIAL CAMPUS CHECKLIST

LGBT & ally student organization ✓

LGBT resource center/office ✓

LGBT Pride Week &/or Coming Out Week ✓

Safe Zone/Safe Space or Ally Program ✓

Significant number of LGBT social activities ✓

Significant number of LGBT educational events ✓

Variety of LGBT studies/courses ✓

Nondiscrimination statement inclusive of sexual orientation ✓

Nondiscrimination statement inclusive of gender identity/expression ✓

Extends domestic partner benefits to same-sex couples ✓

Actively recruits LGBT students to enroll on campus ✓

Trains campus police on LGBT sensitivity

Procedure for reporting LGBT bias, harassment & hate crimes ✓

Offers LGBT housing options/themes

Offers LGBT-inclusive health services/testing ✓

Offers LGBT-inclusive counseling/support groups ✓

Offers LGBT student scholarships ✓

Conducts special LGBT graduation ceremony for LGBT & ally Students ✓

Offers support services for process of transitioning from M to F & F to M ✓

Active LGBT alumni group ✓

MASSACHUSETTS INSTITUTE OF TECHNOLOGY GAY POINT AVERAGE

18

(out of 20)

CAMPUS QUEER RESOURCES

Select LGBT Student Organization(s):

Gays, Lesbians, Bisexuals, Transgenders and Friends @ MIT (GaMIT); Undergraduate LGBT Community (ULC)

Founding Date: GaMIT (1969, as Student Homophile League); ULC (2000)

Membership: 60+

E-mail: gamit-admin@mit.edu; ulc_officers@mit.edu

LGBT Resource Center/Office:

LBGT@MIT's Rainbow Lounge

77 Massachusetts Avenue
Building 50-005
Cambridge, MA, 02139

Year Established: 2000

Number of Staff: 1 full-time professional staff; 1 part-time professional staff; 4 student workers

Phone: 617-253-5440

E-mail: lbgt@mit.edu

Website: https://web.mit.edu/lbgt/

METROPOLITAN STATE COLLEGE OF DENVER

LGBT STUDENTS COMMENT that Metropolitan State College of Denver is "a wonderfully diverse and affirming school." One LGBT student remarks: "There are many LGBT students and staff on campus. *We are everywhere*. You just never knew."

Located in downtown Denver, Colorado, the college shares a campus with the University of Colorado at Denver and Community College of Denver, as well as an office of GLBT Student Services that was founded jointly in 1992. The central administration has been not only receptive to LGBT issues throughout the years but also pivotal to LGBT progress. Acting on the recommendations of the 1992 LGBT campus climate study, the Metro State president established a queer resource center that same year. Since then, GLBT Student Services has grown into a full-size office suite with a library, lounge and workstations for several student employees. The impact has been immeasurable: LGBT students, faculty and staff have prospered and become more visible.

The only thing missing is a vibrant LGBT student group. The former group recently folded and is currently being overhauled by new members. Nevertheless, the Metro State LGBT community strives to make its resources available to all people and has particularly found success in outreach to straight allies on campus. Plus, the campus recreation area actively incorporates LGBT workshops and training for athletes.

The campus is constantly striving to improve its already admirable Gay Point Average. One LGBT student sums it up: "The conservative politics of the area has created a queer attitude with a kick. …we all work hard, stand tall and have come out on top!…there is a lot to offer queer students at Metro!"

LGBT POLITICS
Progressive Meter

Campus Community Level

Local Community Level

State Level

INFO

METROPOLITAN STATE COLLEGE OF DENVER
900 Auraria Parkway
Denver, CO 80204
Phone: 303-556-3058
Fax: 303-556-6345
E-mail: askmetro@mscd.edu
Website: www.mscd.edu

CAMPUS STATS
Type of Institution: Public university
Founding Year: 1963
Size: 21,109
Avg. Class Size: 20–29 students
Popular Majors: Behavioral Sciences, Criminal Justice/Safety Studies, Management Information Systems
Cost: In-state tuition: $2,800
Out-of-state tuition: $8,974
Admission Application Deadline: December 15

OUTSPOKEN *Answers from LGBT students:*

Top Three Descriptors of the LGBT Campus Environment:
1. Affirming   2. Explorative   3. Diverse

What makes your campus feel welcoming and safe for LGBT students?
"The LGBT Student Services office is a safe place for students to interact and meet. Also, [it] allows students to come in and share stories of what is going on around campus with one another. I have met many different types of people who were coming out… or are struggling with their sexuality. The GLBTSS was a safe place for many students to express who they were and seek support."
—*40-year-old lesbian, junior*

How do you feel about coming out on your campus?
"Because MSCD is an urban campus, there is a great deal of diversity on campus. In a sense, most of the campus community understands that we are all different.… Coming out, therefore, was not a problem. It should be mentioned that there are various services (through our GLBT office, clubs, counseling centers, etc.) that help students along the process of coming out—especially if it is their first time."
—*26-year-old bisexual male, senior*

⊘ ACADEMIC SCENE

Top Three Supportive LGBT Academic Areas:
1. Social Work   2. Women's Studies   3. Political Science

How LGBT-friendly are faculty in the classroom?
"All the instructors I have had are LGBT-friendly. I believe that the process of coming out never ends—I have given presentations in class regarding LGBT issues, and during the presentations I came out once again. I surprised many people as well as the instructor; however, I opened new doors for conversations."
—*40-year-old lesbian, junior*

"Very friendly. Most of my professors incorporate tolerance of all diverse groups into their curriculum." —*31-year-old lesbian, junior*

☺ SOCIAL SCENE

Top Three Things in the LGBT Social Life:
1. Clubs   2. Pizza night   3. Dancing

How would you describe the social scene for LGBT students?
There is no shortage of ways to find a social network—or simply have a good time with other queers."
—*26-year-old bisexual male, senior*

What annual social event should an LGBT student not miss?
"Coming Out Day. Last year there was a double 'marriage' on our campus. Vows were exchanged, and hugs and kisses were enjoyed by all."
—*31-year-old lesbian, junior*

 OUTRAGEOUS FACTOID Two of the most anticipated events of the year are the Ally of the Year Awards and the annual High Tea for Allies.

 RAINBOW RUMOR Metro State College has a queer strategy and is currently working on three areas of LGBT improvement. The Council for LGBT Concerns plans to target domestic partner benefits, work on developing gender-neutral bathrooms and add gender identity/expression to the campus nondiscrimination policy.

 THAT'S SO GAY!

ANNUAL LGBT EVENT HIGHLIGHTS

LGBT Welcome Back Reception: August

LGBT Awareness Month: October

National Coming Out Day: October 11

High Tea for Allies and Ally of the Year Awards: October

Transgender Day of Remembrance: November

World AIDS Day Event: December 1

Black History Month GLBT Event: February

Queer Prom: April

LGBT Spring Banquet: May

 BUZZ BITES *Fun Queer Stuff to Know*

THE BEST...

Party Locale: Tracks

Hangout: GLBTSS Office

Eating Place: Pete's Kitchen

Non-LGBT-Specific Campus Club: Feminist Alliance

LGBT Educational Involvement Opportunity: National Coming Out Day

LGBT-Accepting Religious/Spiritual Organization(s): King Life Church

CAMPUS QUEER RESOURCES

LGBT Resource Center/Office:

Gay, Lesbian, Bisexual, Transgender Student Services at Auraria

Tivoli Student Union

900 Auraria Parkway, Suite 213

Denver, CO 80204

Year Established: 1992

Number of Staff: 1 full-time professional staff, 4–6 student employees

Phone: 303-556-6333

E-mail: info@glbtss.org

Website: www.glbtss.org

THE GAY POINT AVERAGE
OFFICIAL CAMPUS CHECKLIST

LGBT & ally student organization

✓ LGBT resource center/office

✓ LGBT Pride Week &/or Coming Out Week

✓ Safe Zone/Safe Space or Ally Program

✓ Significant number of LGBT social activities

✓ Significant number of LGBT educational events

Variety of LGBT studies/courses

✓ Nondiscrimination statement inclusive of sexual orientation

Nondiscrimination statement inclusive of gender identity/expression

Extends domestic partner benefits to same-sex couples

✓ Actively recruits LGBT students to enroll on campus

Trains campus police on LGBT sensitivity

✓ Procedure for reporting LGBT bias, harassment & hate crimes

Offers LGBT housing options/themes

✓ Offers LGBT-inclusive health services/testing

✓ Offers LGBT-inclusive counseling/support groups

✓ Offers LGBT student scholarships

✓ Conducts special LGBT graduation ceremony for LGBT & ally Students

✓ Offers support services for process of transitioning from M to F & F to M

Active LGBT alumni group

13 METROPOLITAN STATE COLLEGE OF DENVER GAY POINT AVERAGE (out of 20)

MICHIGAN STATE UNIVERSITY

MICHIGAN STATE OFFERS a taste of "real queer life." That's how some LGBT students would put it. Although Michigan State is a large public university that serves a rural community. it is home to many LGBT communities—not just one. The campus is driven by LGBT student leaders involved in strong coalitions working to create campus change. There are LGBT groups that meet the needs of same-gender-loving students, international students and students of color. The LGBT arts community on campus produces a queer zine that covers art, news and personal queer perspectives. In addition, Michigan State has the first-ever Phi Tau Mu—an advocacy and support fraternity for female-to-male transgender students. Every dorm complex houses an LGBTA social and support group. Also, there has been an LBGT faculty and staff organization since the early 1990s.

As a result of the hard work of earlier LGBT student leaders, Michigan State students today can choose to be out when, where and how they want to be. As an added bonus, the Office of LBGT Concerns provides further support to LGBT students, holds the LGBT student coalitions together and works to enhance the LGBT campus environment. One LGBT student shares: "The LGBT Concerns Office has several opportunities for involvement and supports all of us. I feel welcome and safe because there are so many diverse LGBT groups. ... The sense of community among LGBT students and faculty is impressive."

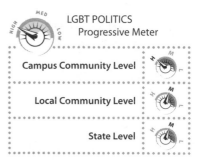

LGBT POLITICS
Progressive Meter

Campus Community Level

Local Community Level

State Level

⁇ OUTSPOKEN   *Answers from LGBT students:*

Top Three Descriptors of the LGBT Campus Environment:
1. Mega fabulous   2. Visible   3. Networking

What makes your campus feel welcoming and safe for LGBT students?
"Knowing that there are people like me that at one point were lost and felt that they could not be who they wanted to be. Then later after getting involved and making a change wherever I could, I felt safe and welcome."
—20-year-old lesbian, junior

How do you feel about coming out on your campus?
"I've always been out on campus. As an incoming student I won the Pride scholarship, which immediately propelled me into activism. I am comfortable talking about LBGT issues in my classes and with my professors."
—22-year-old gay male, senior

"I come out every day to new people all the time. It's surprising to me how positive the reaction has been on campus. Faculty, classmates and others are really open to me being how I am, talking about my girlfriend, or trying to be sensitive to how I feel. I'm really comfortable being out here at MSU."
—19-year-old anthrosexual female, sophomore

INFO

MICHIGAN STATE UNIVERSITY
250 Administration Building
East Lansing, MI 48824
Phone: 517-355-8332
Fax: 517-353-1647
E-mail: admis@msu.edu
Website: www.msu.edu

CAMPUS STATS
Type of Institution: Public university
Founding Year: 1855
Size: 35,107
Avg. Class Size: 20–29 students
Popular Majors: Communication Studies/Speech, Education, Business, Journalism
Cost: In-state tuition: $6,893
Out-of-state tuition: $17,640
Admission Application Deadline: February 15

OUTRAGEOUS FACTOID

According to Dr. Marc Breedlove, professor of neuroscience at Michigan State University, it's all in your index finger. His research has revealed that the ring-finger-to-index-finger ratio on women can be a significant indicator of the increased likelihood of lesbian identity. Testosterone causes men's ring fingers to be longer than the index fingers on their right hand. Many lesbians share this same trait.

RAINBOW RUMOR

In addition to having an openly lesbian officer, the Michigan State police force is gay-friendly, according to LGBT students. The safety on campus is also enhanced by the variety of supportive LGBT organizations, as well as the education and visibility of the LGBT Concerns Office.

THAT'S SO GAY!

ANNUAL LGBT EVENT HIGHLIGHTS

LBGT Student Reception: September

Solidarity SLAM: September (first week of September)

Fishbowl Trans Issues: Fall/Spring

National Coming Out Days Week: October

Homecoming Parade Queer Float: Mid-October

National Transgender Day of Remembrance: November 20

World AIDS Day: December 1

Show and Tell Drag Show: Mid-March

Pride Week: April

Day of Silence: April

Lavender Graduation: April

Queer March on Campus: Spring

LBGTA Dance: Spring

ACADEMIC SCENE

Top Three Supportive LGBT Academic Areas:
1. Women, Gender and Social Justice   2. College of Education   3. English

How LGBT-friendly are faculty in the classroom?

"My experiences with faculty have always been very positive. Although sometimes I feel a little burdened with having to be the 'voice of diversity' when no one else will step up and do so, faculty always seem happy to hear from me."
—21-year-old gay male, senior

"The faculty have been supportive, not only of me personally but also of my efforts to include LBGT issues in class discussions. They have let me explore LBGT topics in depth by incorporating them into my research papers and presentations. As a result, I have written papers on the rhetorical impact of the Lawrence decision, queer youth voting trends, white privilege within the LGBT community and many more." *—22-year-old gay male, senior*

SOCIAL SCENE

Top Three Things in the LGBT Social Life:
1. Dancing   2. Protests   3. LGBTA Caucus

How would you describe the social scene for LGBT students?

"There's a HUGE social scene for LGBT students at MSU. There are five separate LGBT caucuses that were specifically created to fill the social needs of on-campus LGBT students to gather with people of various sexualities. Usually, the people that you meet within the LGBT organizations are the people who become your friends and your support network." *—21-year-old gay male, senior*

What annual social event should an LGBT student not miss?

"NCOD (National Coming Out Days) Week and Pride Week."
—20-year-old lesbian, junior

BUZZ BITES *Fun Queer Stuff to Know*

THE BEST...

Party Locale: Spiral Dance Club

Hangout: Espresso Royale Café

Eating Place: Bubble Island

Place to Check Out Guys: Volleyball courts outside residence halls

Place to Check Out Ladies: South Beach Complex

LGBT-Cool Athletic Sport: Women's basketball

Non-LGBT-Specific Campus Club: Outing Club

Place for LGBT Students to Live on Campus: Mason-Abbott Residence Halls

LGBT-Accepting Religious/Spiritual Organization(s): One Spirit at St. John's Church

THE GAY POINT AVERAGE
OFFICIAL CAMPUS CHECKLIST

LGBT & ally student organization ✓

LGBT resource center/office ✓

LGBT Pride Week &/or Coming Out Week ✓

Safe Zone/Safe Space or Ally Program ✓

Significant number of LGBT social activities ✓

Significant number of LGBT educational events ✓

Variety of LGBT studies/courses ✓

Nondiscrimination statement inclusive of sexual orientation ✓

Nondiscrimination statement inclusive of gender identity/expression

Extends domestic partner benefits to same-sex couples ✓

Actively recruits LGBT students to enroll on campus

Trains campus police on LGBT sensitivity ✓

Procedure for reporting LGBT bias, harassment & hate crimes ✓

Offers LGBT housing options/themes

Offers LGBT-inclusive health services/testing ✓

Offers LGBT-inclusive counseling/support groups ✓

Offers LGBT student scholarships ✓

Conducts special LGBT graduation ceremony for LGBT & ally Students

Offers support services for process of transitioning from M to F & F to M

Active LGBT alumni group ✓

MICHIGAN STATE UNIVERSITY
GAY POINT AVERAGE
(out of 20)

15

CAMPUS QUEER
RESOURCES

Select LGBT Student Organization(s):
Alliance of LBGTA Students
Founding Date: April 27, 1970
Membership: 20
Phone: 517-353-9795
E-mail: alliance@msu.edu
Website: www.msu.edu/~alliance/

LGBT Resource Center/Office:
Office of LBGT Concerns
302 Student Services
East Lansing, MI 48824
Year Established: 1994
Number of Staff: 4 professional staff
(varied levels)
Phone: 517-353-9520
E-mail: lbgtc@msu.edu
Website: www.lbgtc.msu.edu

MIDDLEBURY COLLEGE

LGBT ACTIVISM AT Middlebury College dates back to the 1970s, when student leaders began Gay People at Middlebury, known today as the Middlebury Open Queer Alliance. Middlebury was one of the first campuses of its size to have an active LGBT student group. Since then, the student coalition has worked hard to advance many LGBT-progressive policies and practices, as recorded in the Gay Point Average. In 1990, the campus added sexual orientation to the nondiscrimination policy and then in 1993 extended benefits to same-sex partners of employees. In addition to the LGBT student group, the campus also formed the Gay and Lesbian Employees at Middlebury and an LGBT alumni group in the 1980s. And every year, the student group plans events for National Coming Out Week and a month-long celebration called "GAYpril." Both have been incredibly successful in increasing the number of visible allies on campus. One of the most popular activities among both queer students and straight allies is the annual Drag Ball.

Middlebury College remains among the most LGBT-progressive campuses for its size. Strong LGBT leadership has proven to be a forceful tide. Likewise, the campus administration has taken steps over the last few years to become more queerly in tune, as one LGBT student admits: "Administrators have learned that we want action, not just words. LGBT students are just as important as anyone else. I have found the support to be there over the last couple years—The shift has been dramatic...and an LGBT-positive one."

LGBT POLITICS
Progressive Meter

Campus Community Level

Local Community Level

State Level

INFO

MIDDLEBURY COLLEGE
The Emma Willard House
5405 Middlebury College
Middlebury, VT 05753

Phone: 802-443-3000

Fax: 802-443-2056

E-mail: admissions@middlebury.edu

Website: www.middlebury.edu

CAMPUS STATS

Type of Institution: Private college

Founding Year: 1800

Size: 2,357

Avg. Class Size: 10–19 students

Popular Majors: Economics, English Language and Literature, Psychology

Cost: Tuition: $42,120

Admission Application Deadline: January 1

OUTSPOKEN *Answers from LGBT students:*

Top Three Descriptors of the LGBT Campus Environment:
1. Changing   2. Welcoming   3. Dynamic

What makes your campus feel welcoming and safe for LGBT students?
"LGBT and ally people are present in the faculty. That means a lot, and along with the many queer events, there is a net of support and visibility for LGBT students."
—*19-year-old lesbian, junior*

How do you feel about coming out on your campus?
"You can come out on campus. If they were your friends before, they will be your friends after.... I have found Middlebury to be open and accepting of who I am." —*21-year-old gay male, junior*

ACADEMIC SCENE

Top Three Supportive LGBT Academic Areas:
1. Philosophy   2. Psychology   3. Dance

How LGBT-friendly are faculty in the classroom?
"Along with the visibility of queer students, I think the faculty are the second-best thing at Middlebury on LGBT issues. I have always found the faculty to be very friendly and outgoing when it comes to making me feel welcome in my classes." —*21-year-old bisexual female, junior*

"Yes, I have had positive experiences. I have also discovered several LGBT professors."—*20-year-old bisexual male, junior*

😊 SOCIAL SCENE

Top Three Things in the LGBT Social Life:
1. Socializing   2. Moqa events   3. Parties

How would you describe the social scene for LGBT students?
"Fabulous fun. It's great when it comes to Moqa events and activities … always bigger and better." —*21-year-old gay male, senior*

What annual social event should an LGBT student not miss?
"The Drag Ball and sleepovers…what a combo!" —*20-year-old gay male, junior*

THE BEST…

Hangout:
McCullough Student Center

Eating Place: Grille *and* Juice Bar

Place to Check Out Guys: Fitness Center *and* pool

Place to Check Out Ladies: Track *and* field

LGBT-Cool Athletic Sport: Women's rugby *and* men's crew

Non-LGBT-Specific Campus Club:
College Democrats

LGBT Course Offering: Twentieth-Century Lesbian and Gay American History

LGBT Educational Involvement Opportunity:
Coming Out Week

LGBT students rave about the Moqa sleepovers on campus.

• • • • • • • • • • • • • • • • • •

One LGBT student is quoted this way in an October 13, 2005, campus news article: "The administration…won't react with the same speed and condemnation to [negative comments about] queers as it would to comments against racial minorities."

• • • • • • • • • • • • • • • • • •

ANNUAL LGBT EVENT HIGHLIGHTS

Moqa Mixers: Fall/Spring
Moqa Sleepovers: Fall/Spring
Coming Out Week: October
Building of "The Closet": October
World AIDS Day: December
Queer Dance Party: January/February
GAYpril: The month of April
Drag Ball: March/April

CAMPUS QUEER RESOURCES

Select LGBT Student Organization(s):

Middlebury Open Queer Alliance
Founding Date: 1970s
(under different names)
Membership: 20+
E-mail: moqa@middlebury.edu
Website: www.middlebury.edu/~moqa/

Resource Center/Office Responsible for LGBT Issues:

Office of Institutional Diversity
Carr Hall 102
Middlebury, VT 05753
Number of Staff: 1 full-time professional staff
Phone: 802-443-5743
Website: www.middlebury.edu/campuslife/
multiculture/diversit/

THE GAY POINT AVERAGE
OFFICIAL CAMPUS CHECKLIST

- ✔ LGBT & ally student organization
- LGBT resource center/office
- ✔ LGBT Pride Week &/or Coming Out Week
- ✔ Safe Zone/Safe Space or Ally Program
- ✔ Significant number of LGBT social activities
- ✔ Significant number of LGBT educational events
- ✔ Variety of LGBT studies/courses
- ✔ Nondiscrimination statement inclusive of sexual orientation
- ✔ Nondiscrimination statement inclusive of gender identity/expression
- ✔ Extends domestic partner benefits to same-sex couples
- Actively recruits LGBT students to enroll on campus
- Trains campus police on LGBT sensitivity
- ✔ Procedure for reporting LGBT bias, harassment & hate crimes
- Offers LGBT housing options/themes
- ✔ Offers LGBT-inclusive health services/testing
- ✔ Offers LGBT-inclusive counseling/support groups
- Offers LGBT student scholarships
- Conducts special LGBT graduation ceremony for LGBT & ally Students
- Offers support services for process of transitioning from M to F & F to M
- ✔ Active LGBT alumni group

13 MIDDLEBURY COLLEGE
GAY POINT AVERAGE
(out of 20)

MINNESOTA STATE UNIVERSITY—MANKATO

"MAKING A DIFFERENCE"—that's how many LGBT students talk about Minnesota State University—Mankato. Located in rural Minnesota, the LGBT campus vision all started in 1977 with Jim Chalgren, a graduate student in Counseling and Student Personnel, who developed the first Alternative Lifestyles Office, planting a seed of opportunity for a safer and more supportive LGBT campus. Nearly 30 years later, the seed has sprouted.

Minnesota State University—Mankato has left a lasting positive mark on the lives of thousands of LGBT and ally students. Since its beginning, what is now called the LGBT Center has flourished into an amazing support resource as well as a visible, active LGBT network of allies. Through the LGBT Center's peer advocate panels, LGBT issues are discussed in nearly 100 classrooms a year. The visibility achieved through the LGBT programs and trainings help students who are struggling internally with issues of sexuality.

Although Minnesota State University—Mankato is located in a rural setting, students find enough queer to do. From Live-Homo Acts to Coming Out Week to the Gender Bender Annual Drag Show, LGBT students can stay actively involved in activities, as well as try their hand at various queer leadership roles in LGBT campus groups like Sexuality and Gender Equality (SAGE). Throughout the year, the LGBT Center also partners with many other queer-friendly offices, including Multicultural Affairs, the Women's Center, the International Student Office, Health Services, Student Leadership, and even Athletics. Last, but certainly not least, the campus community has strong ties to the greater Mankato LGBT community, including a partnership in which they collaborate to plan the community Pride Festival.

The LGBT Center believes strongly in the motto: Feel safe; be proud; find community; become a leader. The goal is to find that queer place on campus where every student can be supported, seek friends and create a home—regardless of the stage of coming out. One newly out LGBT student agrees: "I felt like I was finally home from the moment I set foot in the center."

OUTSPOKEN *Answers from LGBT students:*

Top Three Descriptors of the LGBT Campus Environment:
1. Empowering   2. Sense of community   3. Safe

What makes your campus feel welcoming and safe for LGBT students?
"The LGBT Center makes it like I always have a place to go and someone to turn to when I need to." —*18-year-old gay male, freshman*

How do you feel about coming out on your campus?
"College was very liberating for me, and that is what really helped me come out. I have never felt more reassured about my sexuality than I do now at MSU." —*19-year-old gay male, sophomore*

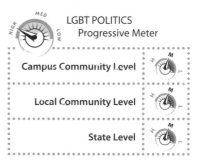

LGBT POLITICS
Progressive Meter

Campus Community Level

Local Community Level

State Level

INFO

MINNESOTA STATE UNIVERSITY—MANKATO
122 Taylor Center
Mankato, MN 56001
Phone: 507-389-1822
Fax: 507-389-1511
E-mail: admissions@mnsu.edu
Website: www.mnsu.edu

CAMPUS STATS
Type of Institution: Public university
Founding Year: 1868
Size: 12,300
Avg. Class Size: 20–29 students
Popular Majors: Computer and Information Sciences, Elementary Education and Teaching, Nursing
Cost: In-state tuition: $6,893
Out-of-state tuition: $17,640
Admission Application Deadline: February 15

OUTRAGEOUS FACTOID

In spring 2004, LGBT students staged a sit-in at the office of the president, calling for a full-time director of queer student affairs on campus. The result was the initiation of a successful search to hire someone as a full-time LGBT program coordinator.

• • • • • • • • • • • • • • • • • • • •

RAINBOW RUMOR

Students report that the *Queer as Folk* and the *L Word* DVDs in the LGBT Center are always checked out.

• • • • • • • • • • • • • • • • • • • •

THAT'S SO GAY!

ANNUAL LGBT EVENT HIGHLIGHTS

Live-Homo Acts: Fall/Spring

Coming Out Group: Biweekly, Fall/Spring

Mankato Pridefest: September

Coming Out Week: October

Gender Bender Annual Drag Show: October

World AIDS Day: December 1

LGBT Leadership Workshop: January

Squash Hate Week: First week in April

National Day of Silence: April

Peer Advocate Panel Program: Fall/Spring

SAFE ZONE Ally Training: Fall/Spring

ACADEMIC SCENE

Top Three Supportive LGBT Academic Areas:
1. Women's Studies   2. Ethnic Studies   3. Theater

How LGBT-friendly are faculty in the classroom?
"The faculty in my program are incredible! Two of the core faculty are gay themselves, and all of the faculty are sure to include LGBT issues in discussions of oppression and privilege." —*23-year-old bisexual female, graduate student*

"I do panels in classrooms all the time. Teachers are always asking us to come in and tell our coming out stories. That tells me they want to be supportive and make a difference." —*19-year-old bisexual female, sophomore*

SOCIAL SCENE

Top Three Things in the LGBT Social Life:
1. Dancing   2. Hanging out with friends   3. Laughing

How would you describe the social scene for LGBT students?
"Events are organized practically every week. If not, I can always find people at the local coffee houses. Also, being involved in SAGE and Team MSQ provides a ton of opportunity to socialize." —*18-year-old gay male, freshman*

What annual social event should an LGBT student not miss?
"Definitely the drag show. We have to turn people away every year because it's such a huge event." —*21-year-old lesbian, junior*

BUZZ BITES *Fun Queer Stuff to Know*

THE BEST...

Party Locale: House parties

Hangout: Fillin' Station

Eating Place: The Nile *and* Noodles

Place to Check Out Guys: Campus gym *and* the shopping mall

Place to Check Out Ladies: Coffee Hag *and* Coffee Klatch

LGBT-Cool Athletic Sport: Women's hockey *and* women's rugby

Non-LGBT-Specific Campus Club: Democracy Matters

Place for LGBT Students to Live on Campus: Intercultural Floor in Crawford Hall

LGBT-Accepting Religious/Spiritual Organization(s): Unitarian Universalist Fellowship, Episcopalian Church, United Church of Christ, Lutheran Campus Ministry

THE GAY POINT AVERAGE
OFFICIAL CAMPUS CHECKLIST

LGBT & ally student organization	✓
LGBT resource center/office	✓
LGBT Pride Week &/or Coming Out Week	✓
Safe Zone/Safe Space or Ally Program	✓
Significant number of LGBT social activities	✓
Significant number of LGBT educational events	✓
Variety of LGBT studies/courses	✓
Nondiscrimination statement inclusive of sexual orientation	✓
Nondiscrimination statement inclusive of gender identity/expression	✓
Extends domestic partner benefits to same-sex couples	
Actively recruits LGBT students to enroll on campus	✓
Trains campus police on LGBT sensitivity	✓
Procedure for reporting LGBT bias, harassment & hate crimes	✓
Offers LGBT housing options/themes	
Offers LGBT-inclusive health services/testing	✓
Offers LGBT-inclusive counseling/support groups	✓
Offers LGBT student scholarships	
Conducts special LGBT graduation ceremony for LGBT & ally Students	
Offers support services for process of transitioning from M to F & F to M	
Active LGBT alumni group	

MINNESOTA STATE UNIVERSITY—MANKATO GAY POINT AVERAGE
(out of 20)

14

CAMPUS QUEER RESOURCES

Select LGBT Student Organization(s):
TEAM MSQ and **Sexuality and Gender Equality (SAGE)**
Founding Date: TEAM MSQ (September 2005); SAGE (1980s)
Membership: 70+
Phone: 507-389-5131
E-mail: lgbtc@mnsu.edu; sage@mnsu.edu
Website: www.mnsu.edu/sldsl/lgbtc; rso.mnsu.edu/sage/

LGBT Resource Center/Office:
Lesbian, Gay, Bisexual, Transgender Center
Minnesota State University—Mankato
173 Centennial Student Union
Mankato, MN 56001
Year Established: 1977
Number of Staff: 1 full-time professional staff; 1 graduate assistant; several student interns
Phone: 507-389-5131
E-mail: lgbtc@mnsu.edu
Website: www.mnsu.edu/sldsl/lgbtc

NEW COLLEGE
OF FLORIDA

NEW COLLEGE OF Florida is used to being on top! *U.S. News and World Report* has ranked this campus as one of the country's leading academic institutions.

The LGBT atmosphere goes beyond acceptance: sexuality is just another part of who you are. The campus community revels in difference and is an amazingly open-minded, special place. Students at the New College of Florida enjoy thinking about life differently; they want to understand and experience things in an open and positive way.

LGBT students can easily find a place to be involved on campus—whether that is part of New College PRIDE or a non-LGBT student group. Since there are only about 700 students total, everyone knows everyone else. In addition, there are many LGBT activities, such as the Queer Ball, Kiss Your Gay Crush and the Genderf*@k Wall.

New College embraces a queer ideology that includes free thinking, artistic perspectives and activism. The campus also tends to reject one-sided, judgmental lines of thought.

No wonder the campus has received such rave reviews from LGBT students. Listen to these: "At New College, being LGBT is just another part of who you are, and what people are *really* interested in is whether or not you recycle." Another student adds: "The friends you can make here. I'm pretty picky, and I have found a handful of people who I love and with whom I have made a new kind of family."

LGBT POLITICS
Progressive Meter

Campus Community Level

Local Community Level

State Level

INFO

NEW COLLEGE OF FLORIDA
5700 North Tamiami Trail
Sarasota, FL 34243
Phone: 941-359-4269
Fax: 941-359-4435
E-mail: admissions@ncf.edu
Website: www.ncf.edu

CAMPUS STATS
Type of Institution: Public college
Founding Year: 1960
Size: 692
Avg. Class Size: 10–19 students
Popular Majors: Psychology, Political Science, Humanities
Cost: In-state tuition: $3,679
Out-of-state tuition: $19,475
Admission Application Deadline: May 1

OUTSPOKEN *Answers from LGBT students:*

Top Three Descriptors of the LGBT Campus Environment:
1. Weird   2. Free   3. Delicious

What makes your campus feel welcoming and safe for LGBT students?
"I never feel uncomfortable talking about anything related to sexual orientation here, because no one is shocked or offended—no one makes it a big deal."
—*18-year-old lesbian, freshman*

"New College students understand that everyone is different, and actually, they love it. We enjoy being different, and we enjoy seeing how other people are different. So being 'alternative' here is never made difficult."
—*19-year-old bisexual male, sophomore*

How do you feel about coming out on your campus?
"I came out my first year, and it was a lot easier here than at home. People didn't just tolerate it; they accepted it. It actually didn't really matter much to them as far as talking to me and hanging out." —*19-year-old gay male, sophomore*

⊘ ACADEMIC SCENE

Top Three Supportive LGBT Academic Areas:
1. Psychology   2. History   3. Literature

How LGBT-friendly are faculty in the classroom?

"When our professors talk about gender issues and really any issue that connects somehow to sexuality, they seem to be pretty aware of how not to offend anyone, and they seem to be pretty open and positive about the subject in general." — *18-year-old bisexual female, sophomore*

"As a literature student, a lot of my classroom experiences have been discussion-based. A number of my professors understand queer theory of literary analysis and always seem to appreciate queer readings of texts brought to the discussion. In fact, this year about fifteen students formed a multidiscipline tutorial studying queer theory. Professors (of whom a number are openly gay/lesbian/queer) also consistently identify the LGBT writers and thinkers throughout the canon and include them whenever appropriate." —*22-year-old queer male, senior*

☺ SOCIAL SCENE

Top Three Things in the LGBT Social Life:
1. Pride meetings   2. Going to the Wall (parties)   3. Dancing

How would you describe the social scene for LGBT students?

"There's no separate social scene for LGBT students as opposed to straight students here. New College is a community, and when there's a wall (what we call our parties), people go. There isn't a consideration of sexuality in things like that."—*18-year-old lesbian, freshman*

What annual social event should an LGBT student not miss?

"I really love the 'Kiss Your Gay Crush' party. This party started as a sequel to the 'Kiss Your Crush' party our campus throws annually. At 'Kiss Your Gay Crush,' New College students, regardless how they identify sexually, are encouraged to kiss at least one person of their same sex. This party is designed to help people who identify as straight to appreciate homosexual attraction and give them the opportunity to explore and expand their self-identification, while giving LGBT people a very special night full of kisses." —*22-year-old queer male, senior*

OUTRAGEOUS FACTOID Twice a month, the members of PRIDE go in drag the whole day, to classes, to eat—everywhere. They even have a whole wardrobe of second-hand clothes so students can just walk in and put together an outfit of various gender expressions. As one student states: "The campus thrives on the fluidity of sexuality and deconstruction of gender."

• •

RAINBOW RUMOR New College students love the fact that everything is different. Nobody is singled out because there is such an appreciation of diversity. The LGBT scene is one of "inactivity," according to some students. "People already accept it, so why should they do anything at all?"

• •

THAT'S SO GAY!

ANNUAL LGBT EVENT HIGHLIGHTS

National Coming Out Day: October 11

Gay Parade: November

Queer Ball: Late Fall

Kiss Your Gay Crush: March

Day of Silence: April

Genderf*@k Wall: April

Transgender Awareness Week: Spring

Love and Freedom Poetry Reading: Spring

BUZZ BITES *Fun Queer Stuff to Know*

THE BEST...

Party Locale: Palm Court

LGBT-Cool Athletic Sport: Women's soccer

Non-LGBT-Specific Campus Club: Anarchy Death Sticks Knitting Club

LGBT Course Offering: Anglo-American Feminist Theory: Conceiving Women

LGBT Educational Involvement Opportunity: Transgender Awareness Week

LGBT-Accepting Religious/Spiritual Organization(s): New College Multifaith Chapter

CAMPUS QUEER RESOURCES

Select LGBT Student Organization(s):
New College PRIDE
Founding Date: 1980s
Membership: 30+
Phone: 561-827-9509

• •

THE GAY POINT AVERAGE
OFFICIAL CAMPUS CHECKLIST

LGBT & ally student organization ✓

LGBT resource center/office

LGBT Pride Week &/or Coming Out Week ✓

Safe Zone/Safe Space or Ally Program

Significant number of LGBT social activities ✓

Significant number of LGBT educational events ✓

Variety of LGBT studies/courses

Nondiscrimination statement inclusive of sexual orientation ✓

Nondiscrimination statement inclusive of gender identity/expression ✓

Extends domestic partner benefits to same-sex couples

Actively recruits LGBT students to enroll on campus

Trains campus police on LGBT sensitivity ✓

Procedure for reporting LGBT bias, harassment & hate crimes ✓

Offers LGBT housing options/themes

Offers LGBT-inclusive health services/testing ✓

Offers LGBT-inclusive counseling/support groups ✓

Offers LGBT student scholarships

Conducts special LGBT graduation ceremony for LGBT & ally Students

Offers support services for process of transitioning from M to F & F to M ✓

Active LGBT alumni group

NEW COLLEGE OF FLORIDA
GAY POINT AVERAGE
(out of 20)

11

NEW YORK UNIVERSITY

NEW YORK UNIVERSITY encompasses arguably one of the queerest places in the United States. NYU students can learn much about LGBT life from the nearby National Museum of LGBT History. They can even visit the Stonewall Inn, the location of the 1969 Stonewall Riots.

According to current LGBT students, they "'out'number the straight students. In describing the campus climate, another LGBT student shares: "It is simply fabulous. We live in a place where 'outness' is not a factor. All support one another for who we are."

Looking at the Gay Point Average, one can easily conclude that New York University's campus has a lot to offer students with regard to LGBT-inclusive policies and practices. In the mid-1990s, the Office of LGBT Student Services was established on campus. Since then, the office has received tremendous support from the administration, more than doubling the professional staffing and financial commitment over the years. In addition, many offices and departments outside the LGBT Office sponsor LGBT-related and -inclusive programs regularly. They simply ask the LGBT Office to help advertise them. Now that's teamwork!

LGBT students receive tremendous support from the faculty, staff and students who identify as allies on campus. Several queer students state that they were attracted to NYU because of its positive and liberal reputation. Of course, being in New York City helps, too. One LGBT student puts it this way: "There can be no other university that comes close to what NYU offers for its queer student population. From the dedicated staff in the Office of LGBT Student Services to the creative and informative programming designed by students and staff alike, NYU strives to create a campus environment that is safe, inclusive, friendly, and fun for 'all' queer people and their allies."

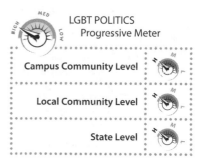

LGBT POLITICS
Progressive Meter

Campus Community Level

Local Community Level

State Level

OUTSPOKEN *Answers from LGBT students:*

Top Three Descriptors of the LGBT Campus Environment:
1. Fluid   2. Strong   3. Visible

What makes your campus feel welcome and safe for LGBT students?
"The fact that there are students who are activists and trying to change politics."
—18-year-old lesbian, freshman

How do you feel about coming out on your campus?
"As an undergrad, it is very easy. For grad students, it's dependent on the program. *—18-year-old lesbian, freshman*

"It's easy, not even an afterthought." *—21-year-old gay male, senior*

INFO

NEW YORK UNIVERSITY
22 Washington Square North
New York, NY 10011
Phone: 212-998-4500
Fax: 212-995-4902
E-mail: admissions@nyu.edu
Website: www.nyu.edu

CAMPUS STATS
Type of Institution: Private university
Founding Year: 1831
Size: 19,401
Avg. Class Size: 20–29 students
Popular Majors: Drama and Theater Arts, Finance, Liberal Arts, Sciences/ Liberal Studies
Cost: Tuition: $31,690
Admission Application Deadline: January 15

OUTRAGEOUS FACTOID

Location, location, location … NYU has it all! Not only is the campus LGBT-friendly and inclusive, but it's located in the heart of Greenwich Village and just blocks from Stonewall, the birthplace of the modern LGBT rights movement. In addition, the now-famous lesbian author Rita Mae Brown helped to start the NYU campus queer student organization—the League of Student Homophiles—while she was a student back in the late 1960s. It's now called the Queer Union.

· ·

RAINBOW RUMOR

New York University is a gateway to queer life in the city world-renowned for cultural pluralism and diversity. Nevertheless, the campus just recently added gender identity/expression to the nondiscrimination statement and antiharassment policies.

· ·

THAT'S SO GAY!

ANNUAL LGBT EVENT HIGHLIGHTS

LGBT Welcome Reception: September

Quench Lunch Series: Every week, Fall/Spring

Pride Month: October

Diva Ball: October

Transgender Awareness Week: November

La Herencia Latina Program: November

Big Gay Holiday Party: December

African Heritage Program: February

MasQueerade Dance: February

Women's HerStory Month: March

Moving Up Day Awards Ceremony and Graduation Reception: April/May

AIDS Walk New York: May

ACADEMIC SCENE

Top Three Supportive LGBT Academic Areas:
1. Center for Gender and Sexuality Studies   2. Gallatin School of Individualized Society   3. Tisch School of Arts

How LGBT-friendly are faculty in the classroom?
"I feel that most of my professors are very friendly and open. Not a lot are educated about LGBT issue—they just try to be PC."
—*18-year-old lesbian, freshman*

"My psych professor is accepting and everything—When she mentions nonstraight people, she is always very supportive."
—*19-year-old gay male, sophomore*

SOCIAL SCENE

Top Three Things in the LGBT Social Life:
1. Dancing   2. Clubs   3. Socializing at the LGBT Lounge

How would you describe the social scene for LGBT students?
"It's diverse. … The social scene is either school-oriented or socially oriented. The school has the LGBT office, events and clubs, while outside of that there's the New York City social scene." —*19-year-old queer female, sophomore*

What annual social event should an LGBT student not miss?
"Keep a look out for Diva Ball and MasQueerade!"
—*19-year-old gay male, sophomore*

BUZZ BITES *Fun Queer Stuff to Know*

THE BEST…

Party Locale: Girl Nation, Opaline *and* Slide Bar

Hangout: Chelsea Piers *and* Hell's Kitchen

Eating Place: Cafeteria *and* Diner 24

Place to Check Out Guys: Walking 8th Avenue

Place to Check Out Ladies: Starlight *and* Nation

LGBT-Cool Athletic Sport: Fencing *or* women's basketball

Non-LGBT-Specific Campus Club: Milk and Cookies

Place for LGBT Students to Live on Campus: Rubin Hall and Third North

LGBT Course Offering: Intersecting Identities of Race, Class, Gender and Sexuality

LGBT-Accepting Religious/Spiritual Organization(s): Project Menucha

THE GAY POINT AVERAGE
OFFICIAL CAMPUS CHECKLIST

- ✓ LGBT & ally student organization
- ✓ LGBT resource center/office
- ✓ LGBT Pride Week &/or Coming Out Week
- ✓ Safe Zone/Safe Space or Ally Program
- ✓ Significant number of LGBT social activities
- ✓ Significant number of LGBT educational events
- ✓ Variety of LGBT studies/courses
- ✓ Nondiscrimination statement inclusive of sexual orientation
- ✓ Nondiscrimination statement inclusive of gender identity/expression
- ✓ Extends domestic partner benefits to same sex couples
- ✓ Actively recruits LGBT students to enroll on campus
- ✓ Trains campus police on LGBT sensitivity
- ✓ Procedure for reporting LGBT bias, harassment & hate crimes
- Offers LGBT housing options/themes
- ✓ Offers LGBT-inclusive health services/testing
- ✓ Offers LGBT-inclusive counseling/support groups
- Offers LGBT student scholarships
- ✓ Conducts special LGBT graduation ceremony for LGBT & ally Students
- Offers support services for process of transitioning from M to F & F to M
- ✓ Active LGBT alumni group

17 **NEW YORK UNIVERSITY**
GAY POINT AVERAGE
(out of 20)

CAMPUS QUEER
RESOURCES

Select LGBT Student Organization(s):

Queer Union
Founding Date: 1969 (as League of Student Homophiles)
Membership: 500+
E-mail: queer.union.club@nyu.edu
Website: www.nyu.edu/clubs/queerunion/

LGBT Resource Center/Office:

Office of LGBT Student Services
60 Washington Square South, Suite 602
New York, NY 10012
Year Established: 1996
Number of Staff: 2 full-time professional staff; 2 graduate assistants; and 4–5 student workers
Phone: 212-998-4424
E-mail: lgbt.office@nyu.edu
Website: www.nyu.edu/lgbt

NORTHERN ILLINOIS UNIVERSITY

NORTHERN ILLINOIS UNIVERSITY is tucked away in farm country among miles of cornfields, situated in the town of DeKalb, where barbed wire was invented. Campus history accounts for much LGBT progress.

The story of Northern Illinois University's progress lies in the pages of Randy Shilts's 1994 chronicle, *Conduct Unbecoming*. The book details the history of lesbians and gays in the U.S. military and, more precisely, the story of a Northern Illinois University student named Danny Flaherty. In May 1965, Danny was roused from his bed, taken to the campus security office and told that the university "had reason to believe he was homosexual." It turns out he had been turned in by a fellow student for consensual sex. Danny was expelled. This was before the Stonewall Riots of 1969, when many queer students or those perceived to be queer were "flunked out" for no other cause. Flunking out of college was an immediate ticket to the Vietnam War for men like Danny. Fortunately, what happened to Danny is not the end of the story for Northern Illinois.

From 1970 to 2005, Northern Illinois fostered a thriving LGBT community and transformed itself into one of the most LGBT-friendly campuses in the Midwest. Just 5 years after Danny's expulsion, students founded the Northern Illinois University Gay Liberation Front. Then in 1971, Northern Illinois hosted 100 students from 14 Midwestern colleges at the first Midwest Regional Gay Liberation Convention. The campus celebrated its first Gay Awareness Day in 1980 and a few years later elected the campus's first openly gay student senator.

In addition, Northern Illinois University has prohibited discrimination based on sexual orientation since 1988. In the 1990s, the university president set up a campuswide LGBT task force to look at necessary campus improvements for LGBT issues. As a result, a Safe Zone program was started in 1997 and has trained hundreds of faculty and staff across campus. Then, in a sign of strong institutional LGBT commitment, the campus established a professionally staffed LGBT office and only 5 years later expanded the office into a resource center. Lastly, that same year the campus developed an academic LGBT Studies Program.

Northern Illinois now hosts some 50 LGBT events each year, offering social, educational and cultural opportunities. One LGBT student summarizes best why other queer students should give Northern Illinois a chance: "I never thought I would think of DeKalb as my home; however, the support of my fellow LGBT students and peers has made it have that warm feeling and has given me a new family."

LGBT POLITICS
Progressive Meter

Campus Community Level

Local Community Level

State Level

INFO

NORTHERN ILLINOIS UNIVERSITY
Williston Hall 101
DeKalb, IL 60115

Phone: 815-753-0446

Fax: 815-753-1783

E-mail: admissions-info@niu.edu

Website: www.niu.edu

CAMPUS STATS

Type of Institution: Public university

Founding Year: 1895

Size: 18,467

Avg. Class Size: 20–29 students

Popular Majors: Business/Marketing, Education, Art, Psychology

Cost: In-StateTuition: $5,060
Out-of-StateTuition: $10,122

Admission Application Deadline: November 15

OUTSPOKEN *Answers from LGBT students:*

Top Three Descriptors of the LGBT Campus Environment:
1. Accepting   2. Progressive   3. Inspiring

What makes your campus feel welcoming and safe for LGBT students?
"There is evidence of LGBT support all over campus. The student center has numerous posters and signs advertising upcoming events; this year there was a display featuring Allies on campus. Our school has Ally training and there are Ally placards in many offices around campus, especially in our Health Services, where feeling safe is very important." —*48-year-old bisexual F-to-M transgender, graduate student*

How do you feel about coming out on your campus?

"At first I was scared how people would treat me if they knew I was gay. I was especially worried about my roommate situation and how homophobia might affect how she treated me. But NIU has plenty of people on campus who are aware of LGBT issues. I felt very safe after finding all the resources available to me and didn't have any problem coming out." —*20-year-old lesbian, sophomore*

ACADEMIC SCENE

Top Three Supportive LGBT Academic Areas:
1. English   2. Women's Studies   3. Sociology

How LGBT-friendly are faculty in the classroom?

"To my knowledge, every teacher I have had has no problem with LGBT individuals. Some of my psychology and sociology classes have covered LGBT topics, and the teachers have been supportive."
—*24-year-old bisexual male, junior*

"Although I am not wearing a rainbow flag to class, my sexual orientation is obvious. No one treated me differently. The teachers [who] knew I am gay were very accepting and didn't really care either way. I haven't encountered any issues." —*20-year-old lesbian, sophomore*

SOCIAL SCENE

Top Three Things in the LGBT Social Life:
1. Queeraoke   2. Prism dances   3. Slam poetry

How would you describe the social scene for LGBT students?

"There are a million and a half LGBT events here on campus. Poetry nights, Queeraoke nights, community gatherings, movie nights, dances, Taboo Topics discussions, speakers, forums, Creatively Queer workshops, and a lot of other things I can't even think of!" —*20-year-old lesbian, sophomore*

What annual social event should an LGBT student not miss?

"The annual Halloween dance is a blast—but then again I'm biased towards colorful costumes and dressing up!" —*22-year-old gay male, junior*

OUTRAGEOUS FACTOID Straight hometown heroes Howard and Milly Eychaner were renowned for their business cards, which carried a pink triangle and were distributed liberally and proclaimed boldly; "Howard and Milly Eychaner: Proud of Our Gay and Non-Gay Children." In 2002, the national PFLAG organization honored them with the first-ever "Pioneer Family Award." Although Howard and Milly passed away in 2005, their legacy of leadership lives on at Northern Illinois through the annual Eychaner Awards. Each year the awards have recognized students, faculty, staff or alumni for outstanding service to the LGBT community.

RAINBOW RUMOR Plans are under way for an LGBT alumni organization, and the campus is beginning to recruit LGBT high school students as well as address the needs of transgender students.

THAT'S SO GAY!

ANNUAL LGBT EVENT HIGHLIGHTS

Rainbow Ice-Cream Social: Beginning of fall semester

LGBT History Month: October

LGBT Awareness Month: April

Ally Awards Reception: April

National Day of Silence: April

Gay Jam Drag and Variety Show: April

Taboo Topics Discussion Series: Three times per year

Creatively Queer Workshop Series: Three times per year

Prism Dances: Four times per year

Queeraoke: Every Friday night, Fall/Spring

LGBT Movie Nights: Five times per year

BUZZ BITES *Fun Queer Stuff to Know*

THE BEST...

Party Locale: Gay Night at Otto's Dance Club *and* Underground

Hangout: LGBT Resource Center *or* the House Café

Eating Place: Junction Restaurant

Place to Check Out Guys: Prism Dances *or* the Recreation Center

Place to Check Out Ladies: Wal-Mart

LGBT-Cool Athletic Sport: Women's rugby

Place for LGBT Students to Live on Campus: Neptune Hall

LGBT Course Offering: Anything in the LGBT Studies Certificate Program

LGBT Educational Involvement Opportunity: StraightTalk Speakers Bureau

LGBT-Accepting Religious/Spiritual Organization(s): United Campus Ministries Center for Spirituality and Justice

CAMPUS QUEER RESOURCES

Select LGBT Student Organization(s):

Prism of NIU
Founding Date: April 12, 1970
Membership: 40+
Phone: 815-753-0584
Website: www.niuprism.com

LGBT Resource Center/Office:

Lesbian, Gay, Bisexual, Transgender Resource Center
Holmes Student Center, 7th Floor
DeKalb, IL 60115
Year Established: 1998
Number of Staff: 2 full-time professional staff; 1 graduate assistant and 4 student employees
Phone: 815-753-5428
E-mail: lgbt@niu.edu
Website: www.niu.edu/lgbt

THE GAY POINT AVERAGE
OFFICIAL CAMPUS CHECKLIST

✓ LGBT & ally student organization

✓ LGBT resource center/office

✓ LGBT Pride Week &/or Coming Out Week

✓ Safe Zone/Safe Space or Ally Program

✓ Significant number of LGBT social activities

✓ Significant number of LGBT educational events

✓ Variety of LGBT studies/courses

✓ Nondiscrimination statement inclusive of sexual orientation

Nondiscrimination statement inclusive of gender identity/expression

✓ Extends domestic partner benefits to same-sex couples

✓ Actively recruits LGBT students to enroll on campus

✓ Trains campus police on LGBT sensitivity

✓ Procedure for reporting LGBT bias, harassment & hate crimes

Offers LGBT housing options/themes

✓ Offers LGBT-inclusive health services/testing

✓ Offers LGBT-inclusive counseling/support groups

Offers LGBT student scholarships

✓ Conducts special LGBT graduation ceremony for LGBT & ally Students

✓ Offers support services for process of transitioning from M to F & F to M

Active LGBT alumni group

16 NORTHERN ILLINOIS UNIVERSITY
GAY POINT AVERAGE
(out of 20)

NORTHWESTERN UNIVERSITY

NORTHWESTERN UNIVERSITY JUST lies north of downtown Chicago, in Cook County. The Gay Point Average highlights the top marks of queer progress on this campus—from policy to practice.

Much of the LGBT feedback from Northwestern cites the campus as a safe, affirming place for its queer students, faculty and staff alike. The university supports gay-friendly policies like domestic partnership benefits and inclusive language in its nondiscrimination policy.

LGBT students have ample opportunities for an active campus life, from the drag show to Rainbow Week to the Day of Silence. In addition, students have access to the LGBT Resource Center, multiple and diverse LGBT student groups and various educational offerings on LGBT topics. Rainbow Alliance, the undergraduate LGBT student organization, remains an active, top-tier organization with over 300 members. Additionally, there are LGBT organizations within the Graduate School, Kellogg School of Management, the Feinberg School of Medicine and Northwestern Law School. In addition, the Safe Space program offers a comprehensive support network of LGBT allies across the entire campus. It is currently the most successful LGBT program on campus to date. There's even a waiting list of over 100 people who want to complete the training!

LGBT students on campus agree that Northwestern is a supportive queer family. One LGBT student remarks: "The LGBT Community on campus is very accepting. … We are always there for each other and someone always seems to be around. Everyone is really passionate and enthusiastic, from so many different walks of life. … Newly out and newly arrived members of the community are entirely welcomed."

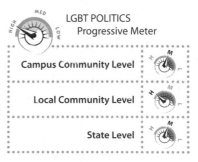

LGBT POLITICS
Progressive Meter

Campus Community Level

Local Community Level

State Level

OUTSPOKEN *Answers from LGBT students:*

Top Three Descriptors of the LGBT Campus Environment:
1. Active   2. Eclectic   3. Inclusive

What makes your campus feel welcoming and safe for LGBT students?
"There is a network of resources available from the moment you step on campus. I remember feeling so in need of some form of outreach in high school and was amazed with the resources available to me seemingly instantly on campus. The community is strong here, and their presence is felt."
—18-year-old gay male, freshman

How do you feel about coming out on your campus?
"I was a part of a Northwestern campus campaign for the admissions department and am quite visible as the president of the LGBT student group. I feel very safe and welcome on campus. The great thing about Northwestern is you have the ability to be as out as you want to be. Some people you come out to might not accept you, but many other people will."
—21-year-old bisexual female, senior

INFO

NORTHWESTERN UNIVERSITY
PO Box 3060
1801 Hinman Avenue
Evanston, IL 60208
Phone: 847-491-7271
Fax: 847-491-4333
E-mail: ug-admission@northwestern.edu
Website: www.northwestern.edu

CAMPUS STATS
Type of Institution: Private university
Founding Year: 1851
Size: 8,290
Avg. Class Size: 20–29 students
Popular Majors: Economics, Engineering, Communications/Communication Technologies, and Journalism
Cost: Tuition: $31,644
Admission Application Deadline: January 1

OUTRAGEOUS FACTOID Northwestern has a bit of glam for everyone. Even the College Republicans get a piece of the action by judging the annual drag show. To top it off, Northwestern is home to Chicago's own Tony Award–winning director, Frank Galati, and the fabulous starlet Megan Mullaly from the hit show *Will and Grace*.

• • • • • • • • • • • • • • • • • • • •

RAINBOW RUMOR Northwestern's LGBT Resource Center opened its doors in January 2004. The response tremendous growth and visibility, but the staffing of the center is still less than the LGBT community considers necessary. Because of space limitations at the Resource Center, the students have jokingly referred to it as "the closet." Although the center is a comfortable, intimate space for a handful of people, it is a tight squeeze for larger groups or events.

• • • • • • • • • • • • • • • • • • • •

THAT'S SO GAY!

ANNUAL LGBT EVENT HIGHLIGHTS

New Student Week: September

Discover Queer Chicago: September

National Coming Out Day: October

Rainbow Alliance Speaker: October/November

Drag Show: March

Day of Silence/Night of Noise: April

Rainbow Week: April

ACADEMIC SCENE

Top Three Supportive LGBT Academic Areas:
1. Gender Studies 2. Communication Studies 3. Theater

How LGBT-friendly are faculty in the classroom?
"Orgo (Organic Chemistry) is pretty strenuous…I've heard many times that Orgo at Harvard is easier than it is here. Anyway, the Orgo professor, a very well known campus figure, decided to come out, in drag and be a co-MC of our annual drag show last winter, which said so much about the level of acceptance this university really has—no matter how seriously academic." —*19-year-old lesbian, sophomore*

"Honestly, it depends on many things. Northwestern has some famous professors who have come up with research or ideas that have hurt the gay community. But we also have many more that are supportive and accepting. Plus, homophobia and discrimination in the classroom are not tolerated. So even if a professor is homophobic or unfriendly, it is unlikely to play out in a way that hurts the student." —*21-year-old bisexual female, senior*

SOCIAL SCENE

Top Three Things in the LGBT Social Life:
1. Gender-bending 2. Queer dancing 3. Andersonville and Boystown

How would you describe the social scene for LGBT students?
"The social scene around campus is pretty relegated to private parties and Rainbow Alliance bar nights/events. Everyone knows that Rainbow parties are the best. For off-campus, Boystown is only a train ride away." —*22-year-old gay male, senior*

What annual social event should an LGBT student not miss?
"Definitely Rainbow Week. With keynote speakers such as Dan Savage, Jason West and Mandy Carter, panel discussions on intersections between sexuality and race or religion, and everyone's favorite, the end-of-the-week BBQ, it's a program not to be missed." —*25-year-old gay male, graduate student*

BUZZ BITES *Fun Queer Stuff to Know*

THE BEST...

Party Locale: Boystown *or* the Co-op

Hangout: Beatnik's *or* LGBT Resource Center

Eating Place: XO *or* Nookies

Place to Check Out Guys: Musical theater

Place to Check Out Ladies: Rainbow bar nights

LGBT-Cool Athletic Sport: Rugby

Non-LGBT-Specific Campus Club: Dance Marathon

Place for LGBT Students to Live on Campus: South Campus

LGBT Course Offering: The Drama of Homosexuality

LGBT Educational Involvement Opportunity: Straight But Not Narrow Training

LGBT-Accepting Religious/Spiritual Organization(s): Hillel *or* University Christian Ministry

THE GAY POINT AVERAGE
OFFICIAL CAMPUS CHECKLIST

LGBT & ally student organization ✓

LGBT resource center/office ✓

LGBT Pride Week &/or Coming Out Week ✓

Safe Zone/Safe Space or Ally Program ✓

Significant number of LGBT social activities ✓

Significant number of LGBT educational events ✓

Variety of LGBT studies/courses ✓

Nondiscrimination statement inclusive of sexual orientation ✓

Nondiscrimination statement inclusive of gender identity/expression ✓

Extends domestic partner benefits to same-sex couples ✓

Actively recruits LGBT students to enroll on campus ✓

Trains campus police on LGBT sensitivity

Procedure for reporting LGBT bias, harassment & hate crimes ✓

Offers LGBT housing options/themes

Offers LGBT-inclusive health services/testing ✓

Offers LGBT-inclusive counseling/support groups ✓

Offers LGBT student scholarships

Conducts special LGBT graduation ceremony for LGBT & ally Students ✓

Offers support services for process of transitioning from M to F & F to M ✓

Active LGBT alumni group ✓

NORTHWESTERN UNIVERSITY
GAY POINT AVERAGE （17）
(out of 20)

**CAMPUS QUEER
RESOURCES**

Select LGBT Student Organization(s):
Rainbow Alliance
Founding Date: 1970
Membership: 350+
Website: groups.northwestern.edu/
rainbow/

LGBT Resource Center/Office:
LGBT Resource Center
Norris University Center, Office L
1999 Campus Drive
Evanston, IL 60208
Year Established: 2004
Number of Staff: 2 professional part-
time staff; 2 student staff
Phone: 847-491-1205
E-mail: lgbtcenter@northwestern.edu
Website: www.lgbtcenter.northwestern.
edu

BEST OF THE BEST **TOP 20**

OBERLIN COLLEGE

FOUNDED IN 1833, Oberlin College comprises two divisions, the College of Arts and Sciences and the Conservatory of Music. Even the campus admits that the presence of both colleges on one campus is "rare and enriching for everyone."

But perhaps the LGBT inclusiveness at Oberlin College comes from its progressive institutional stance on queer issues. First, the Multicultural Resource Center helps to facilitate a campus culture and dialogue focused on the intersectionality of sexuality with other vectors of analysis like race, class and gender. Several staff work collaboratively on LGBT issues and foster a more sophisticated discourse about the multiple identities present within LGBT communities.

Second, LGBT students have access to a large range of resources and support. There are curricular programs like Comparative American Studies— where one of the major areas of study is LGBT and Sexuality Studies. In addition, there are many LGBT-identified and allied faculty, as well as an equally impressive number of queer resources available across campus to students around LGBT issues and concerns. Finally, the LGBT-inclusive environment largely stems from the high level of visibility of LGBT issues and the involvement of LGBT students across all campus organizations. Many inclusive events are sponsored not just by LGBT groups but also by non-LGBT-specific groups. One year, for example, the South Asian Students Association incorporated LGBT concerns into its annual cultural show.

All the LGBT students are in unison about Oberlin being "a nurturing, safe environment." In the words of one LGBT student: "Oberlin's so queer that when people say something heterosexist or trans-phobic, there's usually someone— sometimes a professor or staff person—who is willing to speak up. It's nice not having to be the only one, like it was in high school."

LGBT POLITICS
Progressive Meter

Campus Community Level

Local Community Level

State Level

OUTSPOKEN *Answers from LGBT students:*

Top Three Descriptors of the LGBT Campus Environment:
1. Welcoming   2. Diverse   3. Activist

What makes your campus feel welcoming and safe for LGBT students?
"A relatively large percentage of Oberlin's students identify as LGBT, and I would say most consider themselves allies. The history of Oberlin's being a liberal, progressive-minded place remains the status quo and encourages open-minded people to come here." —*19-year-old lesbian, sophomore*

How do you feel about coming out on your campus?
"I've been out as queer since about 8th grade and genderqueer since 11th grade. The first time I talked to my freshman year roommate on the phone before coming to school at Oberlin, I was upfront about being genderqueer, and she said 'Wow, I've never really known any queer people, so I was kind of hoping to live with a lesbian, but you're even better!' I was a bit weirded out by that, but it's certainly better than a negative reaction."
—*20-year-old genderqueer, sophomore*

INFO

OBERLIN COLLEGE
101 North Professor Street
Carnegie Building
Oberlin, OH 44074

Phone: 440-775-8411

Fax: 440-775-6905

E-mail: college.admissions@oberlin.edu

Website: www.oberlin.edu

CAMPUS STATS

Type of Institution: Private college

Founding Year: 1833

Size: 2,807

Avg. Class Size: 10–19 students

Popular Majors: Biology/Biological Sciences, English Language, Literature, History

Cost: Tuition: $32,524

Admission Application Deadline: January 1

"I feel like coming out at Oberlin would be a really anticlimactic thing to do."
—23-year-old gay male, senior

ACADEMIC SCENE

Top Three Supportive LGBT Academic Areas:
1. Comparative American Studies   2. Gender and Women's Studies
3. Conservatory of Music

How LGBT-friendly are faculty in the classroom?
"There are people who are not educated or mis-educated about LGBT issues, but I would not say that I have encountered any prejudice against me or other queer students." —*20-year-old bisexual male, senior*

"I generally ask professors to refer to me as 'he' in class. Most of my professors do a pretty good job of it and only mess up occasionally. And when I've chosen to speak about the fact that I'm transgendered in class, it's pretty much always been because I felt safe enough to do so. The professor made a space where I knew it wouldn't be a big issue. I'm definitely thankful for that."
—20-year-old genderqueer, sophomore

SOCIAL SCENE

Top Three Things in the LGBT Social Life:
1. Dancing   2. Dykes vs. Fags Throw-Down Parties   3. Safer Sex Night

How would you describe the social scene for LGBT students?
"There are definitely more social options for LGBT folk at Oberlin than at most colleges. There are so many queer people here that it's not been hard to meet groups of queer and trans people to hang out with. My biggest concern right now is finding a similarly comfortable environment after I graduate."
—22-year-old genderqueer, senior

What annual social event should an LGBT student not miss?
"Drag Ball. But I guess that's not an event that only LGBT students shouldn't miss. No one should miss that—and not too many people do."
—22-year-old queer male, senior

BUZZ BITES
Fun Queer Stuff to Know

THE BEST...

Party Locale: 'Sco Bar

Eating Place: The Feve

Place to Check Out Guys: Wilder Bowl

Place to Check Out Ladies: Rugby matches

LGBT-Cool Athletic Sport: Women's rugby

Non-LGBT-Specific Campus Club: Sexual Information Center

Place for LGBT Students to Live on Campus: Third World House

LGBT Course Offering: An Ever-Present Past: The Intersection of Colonialism and Sexuality in the United States

LGBT Educational Involvement Opportunity: Queer Peers and Transgender Advocacy Group

OUTRAGEOUS FACTOID Many claim a Safe Zone program for allies is not necessary at Oberlin. The college spends concerted energy addressing the multiple identities of LGBT students and the complexities of race, class, and gender within and between LGBT communities. One queer student states: "Campus is inherently, largely queer. ... It's uncool to be pronouncing oneself gay—because duh, we are all a little gay."

• • • • • • • • • • • • • • • • • • •

RAINBOW RUMOR Queer folklore has Oberlin College's Drag Ball listed as "the biggest and wildest college queer party" in the Midwest. But when it comes to queer policy, Oberlin College still lacks gender identity/expression in its campus nondiscrimination policy. Despite this, the campus has many practices that are truly trans-inclusive.

• • • • • • • • • • • • • • • • • • •

THAT'S SO GAY!

ANNUAL LGBT EVENT HIGHLIGHTS

New LGBT Student Reception: September

Packing Heat Drag King Event: Fall

Coming Out Week: October

Trans Awareness Week: October

Intersex Awareness Day: October

Transgender Day of Remembrance: November

Oberlin Lambda Alumni Association Symposium: March

Drag Ball: April

Lavender Graduation: May

Trans 101 Training: Fall/Spring

LGBTQ Film Series: Fall/Spring

My Name Is My Own Series: Queering the Intersections of Race, Class, Gender and Sexuality: Fall/Spring

CAMPUS QUEER RESOURCES

Select LGBT Student Organization(s):

Lambda Union and Transgender Advocacy Group

Founding Date: Early 1990s

Membership: 60+

E-mail: Lambda.Union@Oberlin.edu; tag@oberlin.edu

Website: www.oberlin.edu/stuorg/lambda

LGBT Resource Center/Office:

Multicultural Resource Center

LGBT Community Services
Oberlin College
105 Wilder Hall
135 West Lorain Street
Oberlin, OH 44074

Year Established: 1995

Number of Staff: 6 full-time professional staff (which includes 1 full-time professional staff for LGBT concerns)

Phone: 440-775-8802

E-mail: mrc@oberlin.edu

Website: www.oberlin.edu/mrc

THE GAY POINT AVERAGE OFFICIAL CAMPUS CHECKLIST

- ✓ LGBT & ally student organization
- ✓ LGBT resource center/office
- ✓ LGBT Pride Week &/or Coming Out Week
- Safe Zone/Safe Space or Ally Program
- ✓ Significant number of LGBT social activities
- ✓ Significant number of LGBT educational events
- ✓ Variety of LGBT studies/courses
- ✓ Nondiscrimination statement inclusive of sexual orientation
- Nondiscrimination statement inclusive of gender identity/expression
- ✓ Extends domestic partner benefits to same-sex couples
- ✓ Actively recruits LGBT students to enroll on campus
- ✓ Trains campus police on LGBT sensitivity
- ✓ Procedure for reporting LGBT bias, harassment & hate crimes
- ✓ Offers LGBT housing options/themes
- ✓ Offers LGBT-inclusive health services/testing
- ✓ Offers LGBT-inclusive counseling/support groups
- ✓ Offers LGBT student scholarships
- ✓ Conducts special LGBT graduation ceremony for LGBT & ally Students
- ✓ Offers support services for process of transitioning from M to F & F to M
- ✓ Active LGBT alumni group

18 OBERLIN COLLEGE GAY POINT AVERAGE (out of 20)

OHIO STATE UNIVERSITY

IN ALL THE state of Ohio, the city of Columbus is probably the most queer-friendly place to be. Ohio State University is uniquely placed there. The campus has proven to be not only LGBT-progressive but also a national leader in transgender issues.

Ohio State provides plenty for LGBT leaders to see and do. The campus has a dozen LGBT student organizations, and several major LGBT events occur every month. Some of the most popular events include the Other Prom, Transgender Days of Remembrance and Action and the Valentine's Day Dance. In addition, the campus has one of the oldest campus LGBT centers in the country. The center's premier activities include the Speakers Bureau and an LGBT ally program, Homophobia Is Everyone's Responsibility to Overcome (HERO).

The campus also has a significant number of LGBT and ally faculty and staff. For example, more than 600 faculty, staff and graduate students signed a 2-page ad in the student newspaper for National Coming Out Day. In addition, the campus established a Sexuality Studies minor in 2002 and has approval to create a graduate specialization in Sexuality Studies. The gay agenda is to continue to expand LGBT-related courses, with the hope of someday establishing a national center in Sexuality Studies.

Ohio State is arguably the most trans-supportive public university in the country. Not only did the campus add gender identity and expression to its nondiscrimination policy, but also it required that all new and renovated buildings include gender-neutral bathrooms. In addition, the university implemented a policy whereby students can easily change their name and gender on all campus records without medical intervention. Every institutional form was revised to enable transgender students to self-identify if they chose to do so. Ohio State plans to create a trans health care team to provide comprehensive health services to transitioning students and investigate options for student health insurance to cover the cost of hormones.

The campus rating on the Gay Point Average puts this campus among the top colleges and universities for LGBT students. An LGBT student recommends: "Try it out. ... My experience has been wonderful. LGBT students have something to look forward to here."

OUTSPOKEN *Answers from LGBT students:*

Top Three Descriptors of the LGBT Campus Environment:
1. Diverse   2. Supportive   3. Active

What makes your campus feel welcoming and safe for LGBT students?
"Lots of residence hall staff are openly LGBT, and everyone seems to have positive experiences with gay, lesbian, bisexual and trans role models. Organizations like Allies for Diversity (a residence hall collective for multicultural groups) help make everyone feel safe and welcome."
—*20-year-old bisexual female, junior*

"For National Coming Out Day, our student newspaper published a 2-full-page ad with the names of those individuals who were members of or allies of the GBLT community. Several of the upper-level administrators had included their names, as well as teachers from nearly every department. It made me feel safe to know that those in power are so supportive." —*21-year-old gay male, junior*

LGBT POLITICS
Progressive Meter

Campus Community Level

Local Community Level

State Level

INFO

OHIO STATE UNIVERSITY
110 Enarson Hall
154 West 12th Avenue
Columbus, OH 43210
Phone: 614-292-3980
Fax: 614-292-4818
E-mail: askabuckeye@osu.edu
Website: www.osu.edu

CAMPUS STATS
Type of Institution: Public university
Founding Year: 1870
Size: 37,400
Avg. Class Size: 20–29 students
Popular Majors: Biology/Biological Sciences, English Language and Literature, Psychology
Cost: In-state tuition: $7,929
Out-of-state tuition: $19,152
Admission Application Deadline: February 1

OUTRAGEOUS FACTOID Ohio State is nationally known for football and fraternities. But even in these traditional bastions, gay people are represented and a part of campus life. Every home football game, the GLBT Alumni Society sponsors a tailgate party to support the Buckeyes! In addition, Delta Lambda Phi, the nation's oldest and largest fraternity for gay, bisexual and allied men, has a burgeoning chapter on campus.

• •

RAINBOW RUMOR This past year an out African American gay man won Homecoming King and served as chair of the campus programming board—which allocates nearly $1 million to bring big-name speakers, performers and events to campus. Plus, there are out students leading the undergraduate and graduate student government. It is not unusual at Ohio State for LGBT students to be leaders outside the LGBT community.

• •

THAT'S SO GAY!

ANNUAL LGBT EVENT HIGHLIGHTS

GLBTA Welcome Week Events: September

Coming Out Week: October

Ladyfest Ohio: October

Intersex Awareness Day: October

Transgender Days of Remembrance and Action: November

GLBTA Awareness Weeks: January

Valentine's Day Dance: February

Day of Silence: April

Other Prom: May

A Matter of Pride Conference: May

Rainbow Graduation: June

How do you feel about coming out on your campus?

"As a senior, I've never felt unsafe anywhere on Ohio State's campus, in classes, while presenting 'Guess the Straight Person' panels, or in any other situation on campus. And I've always been welcomed among peers and supported by faculty and staff." —*23-year-old lesbian, senior*

ACADEMIC SCENE

Top Three Supportive LGBT Academic Areas:
1. Education   2. Sexuality Studies   3. Women's Studies

How LGBT-friendly are faculty in the classroom?

"We have a sexuality studies minor at Ohio State. All of the professors who teach classes in the minor are sort of de facto allies (if not openly LGBT), and they always make it a point to be inclusive." —*23-year-old lesbian, senior*

SOCIAL SCENE

Top Three Things in the LGBT Social Life:
1. Hanging out with friends   2. Dancing   3. Short North

How would you describe the social scene for LGBT students?

"There is plenty to do in Columbus for GBLT persons and the Short North arts district, which is home to the gay clubs and restaurants, is only 5 minutes from campus. There are around 10 GBLT-based student organizations on campus, and there is always at least 1 on-campus event per week. There [are] plenty of GBLT social things to do." —*21-year-old gay male, junior*

What annual social event should an LGBT student not miss?

"The Other Prom will be in its 7th year in 2006. Don't miss it!" —*20-year-old bisexual female, junior*

BUZZ BITES *Fun Queer Stuff to Know*

THE BEST...

Party Locale: Wall Street *and* Axis

Hangout: Stonewall Columbus

Eating Place: Union Station

Place to Check Out Guys: Axis

Place to Check Out Ladies: Wall Street

LGBT-Cool Athletic Sport: Crew *and* hockey

Non-LGBT-Specific Campus Club: Student Alumni Council

Place for LGBT Students to Live on Campus: Baker West

LGBT Course Offering: Studies in Gay and Lesbian Language and Literature

LGBT Educational Involvement Opportunity: GLBT Student Services Speakers Bureau

LGBT-Accepting Religious/Spiritual Organization(s): King Avenue United Methodist Church, Saint Stephen's Episcopal Church, and Hillel

THE GAY POINT AVERAGE
OFFICIAL CAMPUS CHECKLIST

LGBT & ally student organization ✓

LGBT resource center/office ✓

LGBT Pride Week &/or Coming Out Week ✓

Safe Zone/Safe Space or Ally Program ✓

Significant number of LGBT social activities ✓

Significant number of LGBT educational events ✓

Variety of LGBT studies/courses ✓

Nondiscrimination statement inclusive of sexual orientation ✓

Nondiscrimination statement inclusive of gender identity/expression ✓

Extends domestic partner benefits to same-sex couples ✓

Actively recruits LGBT students to enroll on campus ✓

Trains campus police on LGBT sensitivity ✓

Procedure for reporting LGBT bias, harassment & hate crimes ✓

Offers LGBT housing options/themes ✓

Offers LGBT-inclusive health services/testing ✓

Offers LGBT-inclusive counseling/support groups ✓

Offers LGBT student scholarships ✓

Conducts special LGBT graduation ceremony for LGBT & ally Students ✓

Offers support services for process of transitioning from M to F & F to M ✓

Active LGBT alumni group ✓

OHIO STATE UNIVERSITY (19)

CAMPUS QUEER RESOURCES

Select LGBT Student Organization(s):
Fusion
Founding Date: 1971
Membership: 50+ (varies)
Phone: 614-688-8449
E-mail: Fusion@osu.edu
Website: fusion.org.ohio-state.edu

LGBT Resource Center/Office:
Gay, Lesbian, Bisexual and Transgender Student Services
Multicultural Center
Ohio State University
4th floor, Ohio Union
1739 North High Street
Columbus, OH 43210
Year Established: 1990
Number of Staff: 1 full-time professional staff, 1 half-time graduate assistant
Phone: 614-688-8449
E-mail: glbtss@osu.edu
Website: multiculturalcenter.osu.edu/glbtss

OHIO UNIVERSITY

LGBT STUDENTS CONSIDER Ohio University to be a "welcoming place." Since the early 1970s, Ohio U students have been organizing on campus. In fact, Open Doors, the LGBTIQQA Student Union, was founded in 1973 and is one of the oldest student organizations on campus today. Throughout the 1990s, there was a tremendous surge in LGBT student organizing, and, subsequently, several LGBT-inclusive polices were passed by the administration. In 1998, the campus administration created the LGBT Programs Center to support and serve the needs of LGBT students.

Today there are many opportunities for LGBT students to be involved at Ohio U. Both the LGBT student organizations and the LGBT Programs Center organize a multitude of events, including Out Week, Queer Prom and the Day of Silence. The LGBT center also offers training programs like Safe Zone and SpeakOUT! through which an LGBT student can educate others about queer issues on campus. Although there may not be any local gay bars or clubs, LGBT students at Ohio U keep busy as leaders and plan an impressive number of activities throughout the year.

Ohio U has a solid commitment to the quality of life of LGBT students. Check out its excellent score on the "Gay Point Average," and you will then understand why LGBT students consider this campus "welcoming." One queer student says: "Ohio University is great place to be LGBT. While I was almost entirely closeted before transferring here, I felt comfortable enough to be very out as queer from the very beginning of my college experience."

LGBT POLITICS
Progressive Meter

Campus Community Level 

Local Community Level 

State Level 

OUTSPOKEN *Answers from LGBT students:*

Top Three Descriptors of the LGBT Campus Environment:
1. Liberal 2. Active 3. Caring

What makes your campus feel welcome and safe for LGBT students?
"Having so many LGBTA organizations on campus and so many ways to get involved and meet people definitely made me feel welcome here at OU. Seeing professors, RAs and fellow students with Safe Zone cards was also very welcoming because I knew where I could definitely find a safe space if I needed one. I transferred from a university where no one was visibly out, so coming here where so many people can be open about their sexuality was like a breath of fresh air." *—21-year-old queer F to M, senior*

How do you feel about coming out on your campus?
"My 'coming out' emerged from Judy Shepard's 'Call to Action,' which she communicated to members of the Ohio University community upon her visit to campus. She stressed the importance of being 'out,' whether you identify as an ally or an LGBT person. She made me realize that openly communicating my full identity to others can help make homosexuality seem less mysterious and subversive. I came out to my residence hall immediately following Judy's presentation and immediately found her advice to be sound."
—20-year-old gay male, junior

INFO

OHIO UNIVERSITY
120 Chubb Hall
Athens, OH 45701
Phone: 740-593-4100
Fax: 740-593-0560
E-mail: admissions@ohio.edu
Website: www.ohio.edu

CAMPUS STATS
Type of Institution: Public university
Founding Year: 1804
Size: 16,640
Avg. Class Size: 10–19 students
Popular Majors: Human Development and Family Studies, Journalism, Kinesiology and Exercise Science
Cost: In-state tuition: $8,235
Out-of-state tuition: $17,199
Admission Application Deadline: February 1

"I came to campus having already come out. I arrived exhausted and ready to give up on LGBT advocacy. The LGBT community on campus has been a great source of energy, and it has reminded me why I wanted to come out in the first place."
—*21-year-old gay male, junior*

ACADEMIC SCENE

Top Three Supportive LGBT Academic Areas:
1. Political Science   2. English   3. Women's Studies

How LGBT-friendly are faculty in the classroom?
"The faculty at Ohio University are extremely LGBT-friendly. They handle queer issues with understanding and tact. I have always felt comfortable voicing my opinions in class, and professors welcome LGBT viewpoints in class discussion."
—*20-year-old lesbian, junior*

SOCIAL SCENE

Top Three Things in the LGBT Social Life:
1. Open Door monthly dance parties   2. Theme Week variety shows
3. Hanging out at the Union Street Diner

How would you describe the social scene for LGBT students?
"The social scene in Athens is undergoing a great deal of transformation. In the past two years, I have seen tremendous growth. I think we are finally beginning to see the convergence of a nonactivist social scene with a more traditional LGBT student activist element."- -*21-year-old gay male, junior*

What annual social event should an LGBT student not miss?
"The Queer Prom (sponsored by the ally group) in the middle of Winter Quarter is always amazingly fun. A Prom Queen, King and Court are selected by drawing names, with some interesting results. It is always a big community party."
—*21-year-old queer F to M, senior*

BUZZ BITES
Fun Queer Stuff to Know

THE BEST...

Party Locale: Casa Nueva on LGBT Dance Night

Hangout: Donkey Coffee *and* Espresso Shop

Eating Place: Casa Nueva Cantina and Restaurant

Place to Check Out Guys: Facebook.com

Place to Check Out Ladies: Library

LGBT-Cool Athletic Sport: Volleyball

Non-LGBT-Specific Campus Club: InterAct! Fetish Organization

Place for LGBT Students to Live on Campus: Read-Johnson Scholars' Complex

LGBT Course Offering: Gay and Lesbian Politics

LGBT Educational Involvement Opportunity: SpeakOUT! The Speakers Bureau and Education Project

LGBT-Accepting Religious/Spiritual Organization(s): University Campus Ministries: Center for Spiritual Growth and Social Justice

OUTRAGEOUS FACTOID Since the early 1970s, the campus has had a visible LGBT presence, due to pioneering student leaders, as well as out LGBT faculty and staff.

RAINBOW RUMOR The main area of improvement targeted by LGBT students is inclusiveness of gender identity issues. One student remarks: "Going to the restroom can be awkward and, in some instances, dangerous for transgender people. For this reason, the LGBT Programs Center has been working to get the university to add more single-stall, lockable bathrooms around campus."

THAT'S SO GAY!

ANNUAL LGBT EVENT HIGHLIGHTS

LGBTA Leaderships Council Retreat and Meetings: September

OUT Week: Week of October 11

LGBT History Month: October

Out and About: Coming OUT Discussion Group: Fall/Spring

Queer Prom: February

LGBT Health Awareness Week: March

Day of Silence: April

Mom's Weekend LGTBA Tea and Social: May

Pride Graduation and Community Celebration: May

Visibility Week: Spring

Pride Week: Spring

CAMPUS QUEER RESOURCES

Select LGBT Student Organization(s)

Open Doors: LGBTIQQA Student Union
Founding Date: 1973
Membership: 125
Phone: 740-593-0239
E-mail: opendoor@ohio.edu
Website: welcome.to/opendoors

LGBT Resource Center/Office:

Lesbian, Gay, Bisexual, Transgender Programs Center
314 Baker University Center
Athens, OH 45701
Year Established: 1998
Number of Staff: 1 full-time professional staff; 1 graduate assistant; 4 student office assistants
Phone: 740-593-0239
Fax: 740-593-0223
E-mail: lgbt@ohio.edu
Website: www.ohio.edu/lgbt

THE GAY POINT AVERAGE
OFFICIAL CAMPUS CHECKLIST

✓ LGBT & ally student organization

✓ LGBT resource center/office

✓ LGBT Pride Week &/or Coming Out Week

✓ Safe Zone/Safe Space or Ally Program

✓ Significant number of LGBT social activities

✓ Significant number of LGBT educational events

✓ Variety of LGBT studies/courses

✓ Nondiscrimination statement inclusive of sexual orientation

Nondiscrimination statement inclusive of gender identity/expression

✓ Extends domestic partner benefits to same-sex couples

✓ Actively recruits LGBT students to enroll on campus

✓ Trains campus police on LGBT sensitivity

✓ Procedure for reporting LGBT bias, harassment & hate crimes

Offers LGBT housing options/themes

✓ Offers LGBT-inclusive health services/testing

✓ Offers LGBT-inclusive counseling/support groups

Offers LGBT student scholarships

✓ Conducts special LGBT graduation ceremony for LGBT & ally Students

✓ Offers support services for process of transitioning from M to F & F to M

✓ Active LGBT alumni group

17 **OHIO UNIVERSITY GAY POINT AVERAGE**
(out of 20)

OREGON STATE UNIVERSITY

AFTER ESTABLISHING THE Pride Center for LGBT students in 2001, Oregon State University decided to build a freestanding house for the new Pride Center three years later. Totaling 900 square feet, the Pride Center is a restored Arts and Crafts bungalow located on campus.

The Pride Center is one example of the LGBT institutional commitment at Oregon State. Thousands of dollars went into the building from student government and top levels of the administration. There is even a special covenant that guarantees that the Pride Center will exist in perpetuity. Other examples of queer commitment and progressiveness can be found in the "Gay Point Average." The campus recently added gender identity/expression to the campus nondiscrimination policy and extends same-sex domestic partner benefits to employees.

The Rainbow Continuum for LGBT students was founded in the late 1970s and still remains one of the more popular student groups on campus. The organization has been pivotal to the university's progress over the years in becoming a more queer-friendly campus. The legendary Drag Show, Queer Pride Week, Lube and Jello Wrestling and even Drag Racing are a sample of LGBT events offered throughout the year.

Oregon State University scores high marks when it comes to support and institutional commitment to LGBT issues. One LGBT student shares: "From the moment I visited campus and walked into the Pride Center, I knew I was welcome. The feeling is shared among all."

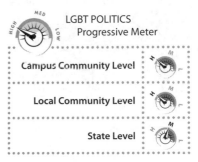

LGBT POLITICS
Progressive Meter

Campus Community Level

Local Community Level

State Level

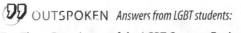 OUTSPOKEN *Answers from LGBT students:*

Top Three Descriptors of the LGBT Campus Environment:
1. Active   2. Supportive   3. Festive

What makes your campus feel welcoming and safe for LGBT students?
"The Pride Center! There seems to be a large group of people working towards making the campus feel safe for us. I also like the large acronym—LGBTQQIA [lesbian, gay, bisexual, transgender, queer, questioning, intersex, allies]. It's not just for gays and lesbians, but for everybody." —*17-year-old lesbian, freshman*

How do you feel about coming out on your campus?
"I've come out to several thousand people on campus via my work with LGBT student panels, and each time is terrifying but ultimately noneventful."
—*21-year-old gay male, senior*

ACADEMIC SCENE

Top Three Supportive LGBT Academic Areas:
1. Graphic Design   2. Humanities   3. Environmental Sciences

INFO

OREGON STATE UNIVERSITY
104 Kerr Administration Building
Corvallis, OR 97331
Phone: 541-737-4411
Fax: 541-737-2482
E-mail: osuadmit@orst.edu
Website: www.oregonstate.edu

CAMPUS STATS
Type of Institution: Public university
Founding Year: 1858
Size: 15,757
Avg. Class Size: 20–29 students
Popular Majors:
Business Administration/Management, Engineering, Liberal Arts and Sciences
Cost: In-state tuition: $5,385
Out-of-state tuition: $17,442
Admission Application Deadline: February 1

The Pride Center is the only LGBT campus resource center in the United States to have a "covenant" relationship with its university. That means that as long as there is a university, there will always be a Pride Center. The university will never attempt to close, move or defund the Pride Center without first consulting the LGBT campus community.

• • • • • • • • • • • • • • • • • • •

Originally called the Queer Resource Center, the primary venue for LGBT students began its life in the closet of the Women's Center. But today the Pride Center has moved into a chic, newly redecorated home on the south side of town, where it plans to plant a garden of pansies and roses. Next on the LGBT campus agenda is creating an LGBT academic studies department and holding monthly barbecues at the Pride Center.

• • • • • • • • • • • • • • • • • • •

THAT'S SO GAY!

ANNUAL LGBT EVENT HIGHLIGHTS

Welcome Week BBQ: Late September

"Guess the Hetero" Game Show Panel: September

Queer History Month: October

National Coming Out Day: October 11

Coming Out Week: Around October 11

Fall Drag Competition: Late October

Trans Awareness Week: Mid-November

Trans Day of Remembrance: November 20

World AIDS Day: December 1

Pride Center Birthday: March 14

Day of Silence: April 20

Drag Races on the Quad: May

Drag Show: May

Queer Pride Week: Mid-May

Lavender Graduation: May

How LGBT-friendly are faculty in the classroom?

"I feel safe sharing personal stories about my family and queer interests in the classroom." —*24-year-old queer female, graduate student*

"Hit or miss. I've shown up in drag to my engineering classes before and had professors encourage and support me. I've also heard professors make sexist and homophobic comments, so I don't think I could classify all faculty as supportive or nonsupportive." —*21-year-old gay male, senior*

☺ SOCIAL SCENE

Top Three Things in the LGBT Social Life:
1. Rainbow Continuum 2. Drag Show
3. Pride Week Lube and Jello Wrestling

How would you describe the social scene for LGBT students?

"It is very informal among friends, focused on house parties and group outings. There's also a thriving official campus social scene, mostly centered around the Rainbow Continuum student group." —*19-year-old lesbian, sophomore*

What annual social event should an LGBT student not miss?

"The Drag Competition in October or the Drag Show in May. They're amazing and always fantastically fun!" —*21-year-old gay male, senior*

BUZZ BITES *Fun Queer Stuff to Know*

THE BEST...

Party Locale: Rugby Team House

Hangout: Pride Center

Eating Place: Bombs Away *and* Interzone Café

Place to Check Out Guys: Dixon Recreation Center

Place to Check Out Ladies: Women's rugby games

LGBT-Cool Athletic Sport: Rugby

Non-LGBT-Specific Campus Club: Black Poets Society

Place for LGBT Students to Live on Campus: McNary Complex

LGBT Course Offering: Lesbian and Gay Movements in Modern America

LGBT Educational Involvement Opportunity: Pride Center Task Force

THE GAY POINT AVERAGE
OFFICIAL CAMPUS CHECKLIST

LGBT & ally student organization ✓

LGBT resource center/office ✓

LGBT Pride Week &/or Coming Out Week ✓

Safe Zone/Safe Space or Ally Program ✓

Significant number of LGBT social activities ✓

Significant number of LGBT educational events ✓

Variety of LGBT studies/courses

Nondiscrimination statement inclusive of sexual orientation ✓

Nondiscrimination statement inclusive of gender identity/expression ✓

Extends domestic partner benefits to same-sex couples ✓

Actively recruits LGBT students to enroll on campus

Trains campus police on LGBT sensitivity ✓

Procedure for reporting LGBT bias, harassment & hate crimes ✓

Offers LGBT housing options/themes ✓

Offers LGBT-inclusive health services/testing ✓

Offers LGBT-inclusive counseling/support groups ✓

Offers LGBT student scholarships ✓

Conducts special LGBT graduation ceremony for LGBT & ally Students ✓

Offers support services for process of transitioning from M to F & F to M

Active LGBT alumni group

OREGON STATE UNIVERSITY
GAY POINT AVERAGE   16
(out of 20)

CAMPUS QUEER RESOURCES

Select LGBT Student Organization(s)

Rainbow Continuum
Founding Date: 1978
Membership: 35–40
Phone: 541-737-6360
E-mail: rcosu_@_oregonstate.edu.
Website: oregonstate.edu/groups/rcosu/index.php

LGBT Resource Center/Office:

The Pride Center
1553 SW "A" Avenue
149 MU East
Corvallis, OR 97333
Year Established: 2001
Number of Staff: 8 student staff
(varying levels)
Phone: 541-737-9161
E-mail: pride.center@oregonstate.edu
Website: oregonstate.edu/pridecenter

BEST OF THE BEST TOP 20

PENNSYLVANIA STATE UNIVERSITY

PENNSYLVANIA STATE UNIVERSITY takes LGBT issues seriously and, as some LGBT students explain, with a "passion." Out in rural Pennsylvania, the university has fostered a gay-friendliness that is astounding. Polices and practices are so progressive that Penn State is merely one point away from a perfect Gay Point Average.

Penn State's LGBT and ally population enjoy all that there it is to offer. Whether it's National Coming Out Week, the One in Ten Film Festival or the drag shows, students can always find something queer on campus. The LGBT and Ally Student Resource Center runs several programs, including the LGBT Mentorship Program and the LGBT Support Network, which has over 450 members. There is even an LGBT student newsletter called OUTRider.

Penn State also boasts several campus clubs and organizations, including Allies, Undertones for LGBT Students of Color, and Shalem, the LGBT interfaith religious group. Involvement on campus is increasingly high, and queer student groups actively collaborate with other campus organizations.

Years of LGBT progress indicate this campus will soon have a perfect Gay Point Average. One LGBT student agrees: "I came out at Penn State and I have found nothing but support among my friends, the faculty … the entire campus really. We have work to do on adding gender identity/expression to campus policies, but I have high hopes that will happen soon."

LGBT POLITICS
Progressive Meter

Campus Community Level	
Local Community Level	
State Level	

INFO

PENNSYLVANIA STATE UNIVERSITY
201 Shields Building
PO Box 3000
University Park, PA 16804
Phone: 814-865-5471
Fax: 814-863-7590
E-mail: admissions@psu.edu
Website: www.psu.edu

CAMPUS STATS

Type of Institution: Public university
Founding Year: 1855
Size: 34,056
Avg. Class Size: 20–29 students
Popular Majors: Business/Marketing, Engineering, Communications
Cost: In-state tuition: $11,024
Out-of-state tuition: $21,260
Admission Application Deadline: November 1

OUTSPOKEN *Answers from LGBT students:*

Top Three Descriptors of the LGBT Campus Environment:
1. Accepting   2. Supportive   3. Safe

What makes your campus feel welcoming and safe for LGBT students?
"Penn State makes me feel safe because of the student groups and LGBTA Resource Center. There are three very active LGBTA groups on campus: Allies, Coalition of LGBT Graduate Students, and Undertones."
—*24-year-old gay male, senior*

How do you feel about coming out on your campus?
"Well, since college is a place where students typically come out, I knew that I would be able to find some accepting people. I was still very apprehensive because I was afraid of the black community not accepting me and/or stigmatizing me. I thought that I wouldn't have any black female friends. Now I'm pretty much out to a lot of people." —*20-year-old lesbian, sophomore*

ACADEMIC SCENE

Top Three Supportive LGBT Academic Areas:
1. Bio-Behavioral Health   2. Human Development and Family Studies
3. Women's Studies

How LGBT-friendly are faculty in the classroom?

"While the vast majority of professors may not be aware of their heterosexism, quite a few are members of the LGBT support network. These professors display a sticker on their office doors to signify a safe space for queer students."
—*20-year-old lesbian, sophomore*

SOCIAL SCENE

Top Three Things in the LGBT Social Life:

1. Player's Rainbow Nights   2. House parties   3. Hanging out

How would you describe the social scene for LGBT students?

"Lots of drama, gay boys and some lezzies. Facebook is huge! There are tons of hotties." —*19-year-old gay male, freshman*

What annual social event should an LGBT student not miss?

"The National Coming Out Day Rally is a very important event on campus. It affects the campus's view and perspective on LGBTA issues. Fight for your rights!" —*20-year-old gay male, junior*

"The Pride Week Prom. Ever wished for a gay prom? Your wish is granted!"
—*20-year-old gay male, sophomore*

 OUTRAGEOUS FACTOID Renowned LGBT campus climate researcher Dr. Susan R. Rankin and LGBT human development researcher Dr. Anthony R. D'Augelli are on the faculty of Penn State.

 RAINBOW RUMOR Penn State has a goal to score more allies and increase LGBT awareness with college athletes on campus. LGBT students mention the pressing need for more education to occur on homophobia and heterosexism in athletics, as well as inclusive efforts for the broader campus community to add gender identity/expression to the nondiscrimination policy.

THAT'S SO GAY! ANNUAL LGBT EVENT HIGHLIGHTS

Parent and Family Weekend Open House: September

LGBT Undergraduate Leadership Retreat: Fall

Coming Out Week: October

PFLAG Thanksgiving Dinner: November

Student Drag Show: October/November

Transgender Day of Awareness: November

One in Ten Film Festival: April

Pride Week: March April

Sex Fair, "Live Homosexual Acts": Spring

Lavender Graduation Ceremony: Late April

Friends of the Center Alumni Event: Fall/Spring

LGBTA Lecture Series: Fall/Spring Monthly

Support Network Film Series: Fall/Spring Monthly

BUZZ BITES *Fun Queer Stuff to Know*

THE BEST...

Party Locale: Rainbow Nights at Player's Dance Club

Hangout: LGBTA Student Resource Center

Eating Place: HUB *and* Panera's

Place to Check Out Guys: Chumley's *and* Facebook.com

Place to Check Out Ladies: Crow Bar concerts

LGBT-Cool Athletic Sport: Women's field hockey *and* men's gymnastics

Non-LGBT-Specific Campus Club: No Refund Theater

Place for LGBT Students to Live on Campus: MLK Floor and East View Terrace

LGBT Course Offering: Sexual Identity over the Lifespan

LGBT Educational Involvement Opportunity: "Straight Talks" Speakers Bureau

LGBT-Accepting Religious/Spiritual Organization(s): Gay-Affirming Interfaith Network (GAIN)

CAMPUS QUEER RESOURCES

Select LGBT Student Organization(s):

Allies

Membership: 150+

Phone: 814-865-0710

E-mail: allies@psu.edu

Website: www.clubs.psu.edu/up/
allies/index.htm

LGBT Resource Center/Office:

**Lesbian, Gay, Bisexual, Transgender
and Ally Student Resource Center**

101 Boucke Building
University Park, PA 16802

Year Established: 1994

Number of Staff: 3 full-time professional
staff; 1 half-time graduate assistant;
18 student interns

Phone: 814-863-1248

E-mail: lgbta@psu.edu

Website: www.sa.psu.edu/lgbt

THE GAY POINT AVERAGE
OFFICIAL CAMPUS CHECKLIST

✓ LGBT & ally student organization

✓ LGBT resource center/office

✓ LGBT Pride Week &/or Coming Out Week

✓ Safe Zone/Safe Space or Ally Program

✓ Significant number of LGBT social activities

✓ Significant number of LGBT educational events

✓ Variety of LGBT studies/courses

✓ Nondiscrimination statement inclusive of sexual orientation

Nondiscrimination statement inclusive of gender identity/expression

✓ Extends domestic partner benefits to same-sex couples

✓ Actively recruits LGBT students to enroll on campus

✓ Trains campus police on LGBT sensitivity

✓ Procedure for reporting LGBT bias, harassment & hate crimes

✓ Offers LGBT housing options/themes

✓ Offers LGBT-inclusive health services/testing

✓ Offers LGBT-inclusive counseling/support groups

✓ Offers LGBT student scholarships

✓ Conducts special LGBT graduation ceremony for LGBT & ally Students

✓ Offers support services for process of transitioning from M to F & F to M

✓ Active LGBT alumni group

19 **PENNSYLVANIA STATE UNIVERSITY
GAY POINT AVERAGE**
(out of 20)

PRINCETON UNIVERSITY

PRINCETON UNIVERSITY SHINES brightly as one of the most LGBT-progressive campuses in the United States. A short train ride away from New York City and Philadelphia, the campus is located in Princeton, New Jersey.

Princeton offers lively campus social events and educational activities. The campus even hosted the first-ever All-Ivy Drag Show Competition. In addition, the university has an LGBT Center, which plans two to three LGBT events every week, from movies and coffee houses to large lectures and lunch discussions. There are also five LGBT student coalitions and three LGBT discussion groups, which focus on such issues as outreach to allies, gay athletes, coming out and transgender issues. One of the student coalitions, called Pride Alliance, distributed over 500 "Gay? Fine by Me" t-shirts in less than 45 minutes on campus.

The campus has an impeccable Gay Point Average and a strong commitment to LGBT issues.

Princeton also boasts one of the most active and largest LGBT alumni groups in the country. The organization has over 1,000 members and an endowment of over $1 million. The alumni group hosts regular events on campus, provides scholarships, and funds an annual lecture series as well as the Lavender Graduation for LGBT students.

Princeton University represents the best when it comes to LGBT progressiveness. Even the faculty comprises the most LGBT-accomplished scholars in the country. A LGBT senior agrees: "If you want stellar academic programs from faculty who are not only LGBT-supportive but also champions [of] LGBT issues...then come to Princeton. I feel confident about how this campus has helped me grow personally."

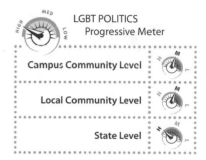

LGBT POLITICS
Progressive Meter

Campus Community Level

Local Community Level

State Level

OUTSPOKEN *Answers from LGBT students:*

Top Three Descriptors of the LGBT Campus Environment:
1. Supportive   2. Changing   3. Vibrant

What makes your campus feel welcoming and safe for LGBT students?
"Princeton University campus feels welcome and safe for LGBT students because of the abundance of introductory programming and 'welcome back' programming for LGBT students. When I first arrived on campus, there were so many large gatherings for the LGBT community to welcome new students, such as the barbeque, ice-cream social, etc. I immediately felt welcomed into the larger campus LGBT community."
—*20-year-old bisexual nongendered, sophomore*

How do you feel about coming out on your campus?
"I came out after orientation week. Every year there is an LGBT speaker, and the one when I was a freshman told a story about being out at an eating club and a huge football player coming up to him and asking 'Are you gay?' The story was great because it turned out that when the speaker responded, 'Yes, I am,' the football player said, 'Cool, I am too.' I've never had any feelings of trepidation about coming out to anyone at Princeton since then."
—*21-year-old gay male, junior*

INFO

PRINCETON UNIVERSITY
110 West College
PO Box 430
Princeton, NJ 08544
Phone: 609-258-3060
Fax: 609-258-6743
E-mail: uaoffice@princeton.edu
Website: www.princeton.edu

CAMPUS STATS
Type of Institution: Private university
Founding Year: 1746
Size: 4,710
Avg. Class Size: 10–19 students
Popular Majors: Humanities, Social Sciences, Life Sciences, Engineering
Cost: Tuition: $31,450
Admission Application Deadline: January 1

• • • • • • • • • • • • • • • •

RAINBOW RUMOR

Princeton hosted the first-ever All-Ivy League Drag Show Competition in 2005. Drag queens and kings from the nation's most elite schools fiercely competed—heel to heel—for the prestigious titles of "All-Ivy Drag Queen" and "All-Ivy Drag King." The judges included Princeton University president Shirley Tilghman.

• • • • • • • • • • • • • • • •

THAT'S SO GAY!

ANNUAL LGBT EVENT HIGHLIGHTS

LGBT Ice-Cream Social: Fall Orientation Week

Being LGBT at Princeton: First full week of classes

Welcome Back Barbeque: September

LGBT Awareness Week: October

National Coming Out Day: October 11

Gay Jeans Day: October

Drag Ball: October

National Transgender Day of Remembrance: November

"Hey Mom, I'm Gay!" Coming Out Event: December

Queer Articulations Film Festival: February

Pride Week: April

Pride Sunday in the Chapel: April

Big Gay Dance: April

National Day of Silence: April

Lavender Graduation: May

LGBT Alumni Reunions: May

Queering the Color Line: Fall/Spring

First Friday at Frist Coffee House: Monthly, Fall/Spring

ACADEMIC SCENE

Top Three Supportive LGBT Academic Areas:
1. English and Comparative Literature   2. Visual Arts
3. Women and Gender Studies

How LGBT-friendly are faculty in the classroom?
"I was really worried at Princeton that the faculty and staff would be uptight and stuffy and that I wouldn't be accepted here. Boy was I wrong. I would hazard a guess that at least 80 percent of my professors have been allies. This year alone, 3 out of 4 of my professors actively display ally pins on their bags/briefcases or ally triangles in their office. It really makes you feel like you are among friends and have so much support when you see them enter the classroom."
—20-year-old bisexual nongendered, sophomore

SOCIAL SCENE

Top Three Things in the LGBT Social Life:
1. First Fridays   2. Terrace   3. The Street

How would you describe the social scene for LGBT students?
"Princeton certainly doesn't resemble a circuit party. That said, it's also an incredibly supportive place and there are loads of activities to bring the gay people together. You'll probably find yourself having the most fun without distinguishing between a gay and a straight scene. Also, every eating club has out LGBT people in it. Ivy, Tower, and Terrace are particularly known for their high gay memberships So, in a nutshell, you can make out on the dance floor at a Princeton eating club—people might even cheer you on!"
—21-year-old gay male, junior

What annual social event should an LGBT student not miss?
"The Annual Terrace F. Club Drag Ball, hosted by the Queer Radicals. It's an amazing event where hundreds of people dress to transgress gender norms and compete to be Princeton's best drag king and drag queen. There are always a number of competitors, and many people who don't compete will dress in drag just for the fun of it." *—21-year-old gay male, sophomore*

BUZZ BITES *Fun Queer Stuff to Know*

THE BEST...

Party Locale: Terrace F. (for flaming) Club
Hangout: Café Viv
Eating Place: Frist Campus Center
Place to Check Out Guys: Ivy Club *and* D Bar
Place to Check Out Ladies: Cloister Inn
LGBT-Cool Athletic Sport: Women's rugby *and* men's wrestling

Non-LGBT-Specific Campus Club: Frist Board
LGBT Educational Involvement Opportunity: LGBT peer educators
LGBT-Accepting Religious/Spiritual Organization(s): Center for Jewish Life *and* Office of Religious Life

THE GAY POINT AVERAGE
OFFICIAL CAMPUS CHECKLIST

LGBT & ally student organization ✓

LGBT resource center/office ✓

LGBT Pride Week &/or Coming Out Week ✓

Safe Zone/Safe Space or Ally Program ✓

Significant number of LGBT social activities ✓

Significant number of LGBT educational events ✓

Variety of LGBT studies/courses ✓

Nondiscrimination statement inclusive of sexual orientation ✓

Nondiscrimination statement inclusive of gender identity/expression ✓

Extends domestic partner benefits to same-sex couples ✓

Actively recruits LGBT students to enroll on campus ✓

Trains campus police on LGBT sensitivity ✓

Procedure for reporting LGBT bias, harassment & hate crimes ✓

Offers LGBT housing options/themes

Offers LGBT-inclusive health services/testing ✓

Offers LGBT-inclusive counseling/support groups ✓

Offers LGBT student scholarships ✓

Conducts special LGBT graduation ceremony for LGBT & ally Students ✓

Offers support services for process of transitioning from M to F & F to M ✓

Active LGBT alumni group ✓

PRINCETON UNIVERSITY
GAY POINT AVERAGE
(out of 20)
19

CAMPUS QUEER RESOURCES

Select LGBT Student Organization(s):
Pride Alliance
Founding Date: 1972
Membership: 480+
Phone: 609-258-1353
E-mail: pride@princeton.edu
Website: princeton.edu/~pride

LGBT Resource Center/Office:
Lesbian, Gay, Bisexual, Transgender Center
Princeton University
246 Frist Campus Center
Princeton, NJ 08544
Year Established: 1994
Number of Staff: 2 full-time professional staff, 1 graduate intern, 3 student staff
Phone: 609-258-1353
E-mail: LGBT@princeton.edu
Website: www.princeton.edu/lgbt

ROCHESTER INSTITUTE OF TECHNOLOGY

TECHNOLOGY HAS CREATED new ways of thinking and has revolutionized the way we operate as a society today. Rochester Institute of Technology has been undergoing a similar revolution when it comes to LGBT and ally students making a positive difference on campus.

Since 1993, RIT has had a powerfully motivated group of LGBT and ally student leaders reforming the campus—step by step. The LGBT campus community, which includes the student-run Gay Alliance, has advocated for LGBT-inclusive policies on campus. As a result, the nondiscrimination policy of the campus currently covers both sexual orientation and gender identity/expression. In addition, since the mid-1990s, RIT has extended domestic partner benefits to same-sex employees. Administrators have listened to LGBT needs and have come out as queerly supportive in almost every instance. In 2005, a transgender student asked for gender-neutral bathrooms, and the campus is now taking steps to ensure trans-inclusive options in every campus building. Students are also building support in the student senate for the development of an LGBT resource center.

Every year, the Office of Residence Life sponsors Ally Week, which includes Drag Bingo and an educational film called *Queer Eye for the RIT Guy*. LGBT and ally students rave about Ally Week, and attendance continues to grow. In addition, the campus offers Safe Zone training, which is one of the most popular and successful ways to forge allies on campus. Plus, every year there are events such as National Coming Out Week, a drag show and the ImageOUT film festival. In the annual Drag Race, students rush from point A to point B and then cross-dress as fast as they can.

RIT has proven to be an open, accepting place for progress, according to LGBT students. The straight ally support across campus has left a lasting impression. One LGBT student puts it this way: "Straight allies are behind us every step of the way. RIT, from the staff to students, has phenomenal allies. … Because of this, I feel welcome and listened to. LGBT students are not alone."

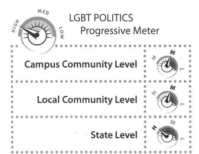

LGBT POLITICS
Progressive Meter

Campus Community Level

Local Community Level

State Level

INFO

ROCHESTER INSTITUTE OF TECHNOLOGY
1 Lomb Memorial Drive
Rochester, NY 14623
Phone: 585-475-6631
Fax: 585-475-7424
E-mail: admissions@rit.edu
Website: www.rit.edu

CAMPUS STATS
Type of Institution: Private college
Founding Year: 1829
Size: 11,750
Avg. Class Size: 20–29 students
Popular Majors: Engineering/Engineering Technologies, Business Administration Management, Information Technology, Photography
Cost: Tuition: $22,605
Admission Application Deadline: February 1

🗩 OUTSPOKEN *Answers from LGBT students:*

Top Three Descriptors of the LGBT Campus Environment:
1. United   2. Powerful   3. Inclusive

What makes your campus feel welcoming and safe for LGBT students?
"RIT has a wonderful LGBT community. Very friendly, open, warm and accepting…You can find support on campus from fellow students, faculty."
—20-year-old bisexual male, sophomore

How do you feel about coming out on your campus?
"I came out as a freshman on campus. My roommate was apprehensive at first but came along and is now a super ally. He actually helped me find my boyfriend." *—21-year-old gay male, junior*

⊘ ACADEMIC SCENE

Top Three Supportive LGBT Academic Areas:
1. Film/Animation   2. Software Engineering   3. Graphic Design

How LGBT-friendly are faculty in the classroom?
"Faculty response to LGBT issues is supportive. I have had positive experiences in class bringing queer issues into my projects. There have never been any issues that I have found." —*22-year-old bisexual female, senior*

"By my standards, I think so. I think the teachers are fabulous, and I had one come out in class. …It was great to see the reaction of fellow students."
—*19-year-old gay male, junior*

☺ SOCIAL SCENE

Top Three Things in the LGBT Social Life:
1. Hanging out with friends   2. Facebook   3. House parties

How would you describe the social scene for LGBT students?
"Variety of LGBT events and close queer community."
—*19-year-old gay male, sophomore*

What annual social event should an LGBT student not miss?
"The drag show is amazing…queens all over the place!"
—*20-year-old gay male, junior*

BUZZ BITES *Fun Queer Stuff to Know*

THE BEST…

Hangout: Spot Coffee

Eating Place: The Commons

Place to Check Out Guys: Student Life Center

Place to Check Out Ladies: Red Barn

LGBT-Cool Athletic Sport: Women's basketball

Non-LGBT-Specific Campus Club:
College Democrats

LGBT Educational Involvement Opportunity: Ally Week *or* Coming Out Week

OUTRAGEOUS FACTOID RIT has its own *Queer Eye for the RIT Guy*. The purpose of the film is to destroy LGBT stereotypes on campus and offer visibility for LGBT issues. Plus, there is "gay bingo"—where a straight line never wins, but straight friends are always welcome.

• • • • • • • • • • • • • • • • •

RAINBOW RUMOR The RIT Gay Alliance has built many bridges of understanding, and its influence continues to grow stronger as they add more allies. The student government even has an LGBT senator. The next step is to add an LGBT resource center. One LGBT student declares: "There is only so much the RIT Gay Alliance can do…especially when it comes to counseling, sensitivity trainings and other referrals."

• • • • • • • • • • • • • • • • •

THAT'S SO GAY!

ANNUAL LGBT EVENT HIGHLIGHTS

Coming Out Week: October

Ally Week: Early October

ImageOUT Film Festival:
Late October/November

World AIDS Day: December

Drag Show: February

THE GAY POINT AVERAGE
OFFICIAL CAMPUS CHECKLIST

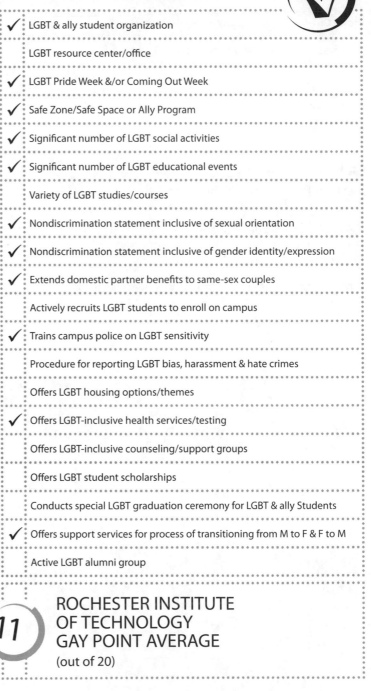

✓ LGBT & ally student organization

LGBT resource center/office

✓ LGBT Pride Week &/or Coming Out Week

✓ Safe Zone/Safe Space or Ally Program

✓ Significant number of LGBT social activities

✓ Significant number of LGBT educational events

Variety of LGBT studies/courses

✓ Nondiscrimination statement inclusive of sexual orientation

✓ Nondiscrimination statement inclusive of gender identity/expression

✓ Extends domestic partner benefits to same-sex couples

Actively recruits LGBT students to enroll on campus

✓ Trains campus police on LGBT sensitivity

Procedure for reporting LGBT bias, harassment & hate crimes

Offers LGBT housing options/themes

✓ Offers LGBT-inclusive health services/testing

Offers LGBT-inclusive counseling/support groups

Offers LGBT student scholarships

Conducts special LGBT graduation ceremony for LGBT & ally Students

✓ Offers support services for process of transitioning from M to F & F to M

Active LGBT alumni group

ROCHESTER INSTITUTE
11 OF TECHNOLOGY
GAY POINT AVERAGE
(out of 20)

RUTGERS, THE STATE UNIVERSITY OF NEW JERSEY—NEW BRUNSWICK

"LGBT HIGH-SCHOOL students come here to come out—as opposed to coming here and coming out," according to a member of the LGBT campus community. As a result, Rutgers University has created a welcoming space for LGBT students and has a proven track record of LGBT history dating back to the 1969 Stonewall riots in New York City.

It all started when an African-American Rutgers sophomore, Lionel Cuffie, founded the Rutgers Homophile League, making Rutgers one of the first campuses with a post-Stonewall college student organization and the site of some of the earliest gay liberation conferences. The purpose of the Rutgers Homophile League was to be a vocal advocate for a safe and friendly environment for LGBT students attending Rutgers. Such an LGBT foundation of activism and visibility ultimately led Rutgers, in 1981, to be among the first institutions of higher learning to include sexual orientation in its nondiscrimination policy.

Six years later, in an unprecedented move at the time, the university president charged a Select Committee on Lesbian and Gay Concerns to assess the quality of life on Rutgers's three campuses—Camden, Newark and New Brunswick. The published 1989 report was a model for other institutions that wished to assess the campus climate and make recommendations for LGBT students. The result was the establishment of the Office of Diverse Community Affairs and Lesbian Gay Concerns in 1992, which has recently been restructured and renamed the Office of Social Justice Education and LGBT Communities.

The Rutgers Homophile League evolved into the Bisexual, Gay and Lesbian Alliance of Rutgers University (BiGLARU). Both LGBT entities work hand in hand to provide support services as well as social, cultural and educational events for the queer community, including annual celebrations such as Coming Out Week and a month full of LGBT activities called "Gaypril."

The Gay Point Average highlights the queer university commitment, from policy to practice. An LGBT student agrees: "Rutgers does care. The queer scene is visibly out there … plenty to do from social to activist. … I am proud to be at a campus with a rich queer history of activism and social justice."

OUTSPOKEN *Answers from LGBT students:*

Top Three Descriptors of the LGBT Campus Environment:
1. Supportive   2. Diverse   3. Inclusive

What makes your campus feel welcoming and safe for LGBT students?
"The acceptance can be seen through the people, LGBT services and the programs that are queer. I found support easily in my first year to come out. … unlike [in] high school, I had unconditional support."
—22-year-old bisexual female, freshman

How do you feel about coming out on your campus?
"Spill it…Seriously I think the campus is an atmosphere that has a proven record of queer support." *—21-year-old gay male, junior*

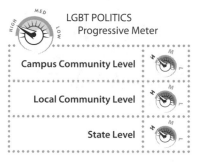

LGBT POLITICS
Progressive Meter

Campus Community Level

Local Community Level

State Level

INFO

RUTGERS, THE STATE UNIVERSITY OF NEW JERSEY—NEW BRUNSWICK
65 Davidson Road
Piscataway, NJ 08854
Phone: 732-932-4636
Fax: 732-445-0237
E-mail: admissions@rci.rutgers.edu
Website: www.rutgers.edu

CAMPUS STATS
Type of Institution: Public university
Founding Year: 1766
Size: 26,366
Avg. Class Size: 20–29 students
Popular Majors: Social Sciences and History, Psychology, Business/Marketing, Communications/Communication Technologies
Cost: In-state tuition: $7,512
Out-of-state tuition: $15,697
Admission Application Deadline: December 15

In 1990 the campus was thrust into the national spotlight when James Dale, an out Rutgers gay student and then president of BiGLARU, challenged the discriminatory values of the Boy Scouts of America—all the way up to the U.S. Supreme Court ten years later.

• • • • • • • • • • • • • • • • • • • •

The Office for Social Justice Education and LGBT Communities will organize a new task force on Transgender Student Life. The task force will recommend how to make the campus more trans-inclusive. Also, Rutgers queers should be on the lookout for an introductory course for what may eventually become a new minor in Critical Sexualities Studies.

• • • • • • • • • • • • • • • • • • • •

ANNUAL LGBT EVENT HIGHLIGHTS

Queer Student Leadership Retreat, Part 1: Fall

LGBT Community Reception: September

Coming Out Week: Week of October 11

Out on the Job: November

World AIDS Day: December 1

Queer Student Leadership Retreat, Part 2: Spring

Black History Month Queer of All Colors Film Festival: February

Gaypril Month: April

Day of Silence: April

Queer Appreciation Week: April

Lionel Cuffie Award for Activism and Excellence: May

Rainbow Graduation Dinner: May

ACADEMIC SCENE

Top Three Supportive LGBT Academic Areas:
1. Gender Studies 2. English 3. History

How LGBT-friendly are faculty in the classroom?
"It varies. … but all in all, my experiences have been LGBT-inclusive and really progressive, actually. The queer faculty are highly visible and are quite well-known in their fields, too." —*22-year-old lesbian, senior*

"Several queer faculty are out on campus. I never realized that there were so many until my sophomore year." —*21-year-old bisexual male, senior*

SOCIAL SCENE

Top Three Things in the LGBT Social Life:
1. Dancing 2. Going to bars 3. House parties

How would you describe the social scene for LGBT students?
"Outrageous…We have New York City close by and great queer events on campus, too." —*19 year-old gay male, sophomore*

What annual social event should an LGBT student not miss?
"Coming Out Week…I had the best time." —*19-year-old lesbian, sophomore*

BUZZ BITES *Fun Queer Stuff to Know*

THE BEST…

Party Locale: Off-campus house parties

Hangout: New Jersey Pride Center

Eating Place: Chelsea

Place for LGBT Students to Live on Campus: Demarest Hall on College Avenue

LGBT Course Offering: Lesbians and Gay Men in Society

LGBT Educational Involvement Opportunity: Peer Educators on Sexuality and Queer Issues

THE GAY POINT AVERAGE
OFFICIAL CAMPUS CHECKLIST

LGBT & ally student organization ✓

LGBT resource center/office ✓

LGBT Pride Week &/or Coming Out Week ✓

Safe Zone/Safe Space or Ally Program ✓

Significant number of LGBT social activities ✓

Significant number of LGBT educational events ✓

Variety of LGBT studies/courses

Nondiscrimination statement inclusive of sexual orientation ✓

Nondiscrimination statement inclusive of gender identity/expression

Extends domestic partner benefits to same-sex couples ✓

Actively recruits LGBT students to enroll on campus

Trains campus police on LGBT sensitivity

Procedure for reporting LGBT bias, harassment & hate crimes ✓

Offers LGBT housing options/themes ✓

Offers LGBT-inclusive health services/testing ✓

Offers LGBT-inclusive counseling/support groups ✓

Offers LGBT student scholarships

Conducts special LGBT graduation ceremony for LGBT & ally Students ✓

Offers support services for process of transitioning from M to F & F to M

Active LGBT alumni group ✓

CAMPUS QUEER RESOURCES

Select LGBT Student Organization(s):

Bisexual, Gay and Lesbian Alliance of Rutgers University (BiGLARU)

Founding Date: 1969 (as the Rutgers Homophile League)

Membership: 70

E-mail: biglaru@yahoogroups.com

Website: www.scils.rutgers.edu/~biglaru/

LGBT Resource Center/Office:

Office for Social Justice Education and LGBT Communities

3 Bartlett Street
New Brunswick, NJ 08901

Year Established: 1992

Number of Staff: 3 full-time professional staff and student interns

Phone: 732-932-1711

Website: www.rci.rutgers.edu/~divcoaff/

RUTGERS, THE STATE UNIVERSITY OF NEW JERSEY—NEW BRUNSWICK GAY POINT AVERAGE

14

(out of 20)

SARAH LAWRENCE COLLEGE

LOCATED JUST 15 miles north of New York City on a wooded, serene campus, the Sarah Lawrence College motto is "You are different. So are we…." The campus is a bastion of diversity and freedom of expression.

Long respected as a national leader in arts education, Sarah Lawrence has a most definitely LGBT-friendly atmosphere, from the academic experience to the social scene. Academically, the faculty are highly LGBT-engaged in responding to the needs of queer students. Even the teaching philosophy is LGBT-inclusive: "The task of the college is to teach liberalism… which draws individual human beings closer together, teaches a concern for the welfare of all social groups." There are also several out LGBT faculty as well as an academic concentration in Queer Studies.

But beyond academics, the campus also provides a dynamic social scene that consists of two LGBT organizations—the Queer Variety Coalition and ACTS UP! It's a surprising number for a small liberal arts college. Both queer groups are active in planning social activities and educational events for the campus community, including the Queer Fall Festival, Pride Month and Deb Ball. One of the most anticipated events is the three-day-long Queer Film Festival, highlighting a variety of independent films and big budget spectacles. It culminates annually in a midnight screening of *Priscilla, Queen of the Desert*. In addition, LGBT students can take full advantage of New York City, only a 25-minute train ride away.

So if you're looking for a quintessential college experience with a thought-provoking twist, Sarah Lawrence might be the college for you. The "Gay Point Average" highlights a commitment to LGBT-inclusive policies and practices from the administration. But, most important, the campus climate is extremely LGBT-friendly and "queer quirky," according to a couple of LGBT students. Another student agrees: "Sarah Lawrence is unique. It has provided me with a more intimate sense of community, a feeling of openness and a queer-friendliness that I have never encountered before. I love it here!"

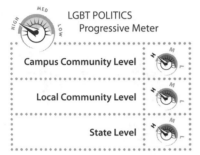

LGBT POLITICS
Progressive Meter

Campus Community Level

Local Community Level

State Level

INFO

SARAH LAWRENCE COLLEGE
1 Mead Way
Bronxville, NY 10708
Phone: 914-395-2510
Fax: 914-395-2515
E-mail: slcadmit@acs.slc.edu
Website: www.sarahlawrence.edu

CAMPUS STATS
Type of Institution: Private college
Founding Year: 1928
Size: 1,292
Avg. Class Size: Less than 10 students
Popular Majors: Liberal Arts/General Studies
Cost: Tuition: $33,270
Admission Application Deadline: January 1

OUTSPOKEN   *Answers from LGBT students:*

Top Three Descriptors of the LGBT Campus Environment:
1. Individualistic   2. Quirky   3. Passionate

What makes your campus feel welcoming and safe for LGBT students?
"I remember touring the campus when I was thinking of applying. I felt instantly at home. I was concerned that I wouldn't make friends or be accepted as gay, but the LGBT and Ally Welcome Reception changed all that."
—19-year-old lesbian, sophomore

How do you feel about coming out on your campus?
"I'm pretty out all over campus. I felt uncomfortable at first, because I was afraid people would stereotype me, but I'm fine with it now. I haven't experienced any negative reactions, and it's kind of nice to have people I meet already know that I am gay." *—21-year-old gay male, junior*

ACADEMIC SCENE

Top Three Supportive LGBT Academic Areas:
1. Sociology   2. Women's History   3. Writing and Literature

How LGBT-friendly are faculty in the classroom?
"The faculty are supportive and inclusive. If antigay stuff happened in class, some of them would address it as a teachable moment. I know a professor who did just that. … Other faculty might be too flustered to know what to do."
—*19-year-old lesbian, sophomore*

"There are excellent faculty, and I know a few out members of the faculty and staff. LGBT topics in the classroom are handled very well, and I have never felt out of place being queer in class." —*21-year-old gay male, junior*

SOCIAL SCENE

Top Three Things in the LGBT Social Life:
1. Hanging Out   2. Dancing   3. Parties

How would you describe the social scene for LGBT students?
"Passionate … I have been most surprised at the passion and closeness of the community." —*19-year-old bisexual male, freshman*

What annual social event should an LGBT student not miss?
"Queer Film Festival…It's a three-day film fest full of awesome queer movies…"
—*21-year-old gay male, junior*

OUTRAGEOUS FACTOID

L-Word lovers, listen up! Lesbian heartthrob Guinevere Turner is actually among the out famous alumni of Sarah Lawrence College. Her past queer-positive roles include movies like *Go Fish* and *Chasing Amy*. But Sarah Lawrence queer fans love catching her on the Showtime smash series *The L Word*, playing the role of bitchy Gabby!

RAINBOW RUMOR

Sarah Lawrence LGBT students often struggle with the partnership between the Queer Variety Coalition and ACTS UP! One is more social in nature, whereas the other is more activist-based in scope. Balancing programming and resources can be a challenging task.

THAT'S SO GAY!

ANNUAL LGBT EVENT HIGHLIGHTS

LGBT and Ally Welcome Reception: Fall

Queer Fall Festival: October

National Coming Out Day: October 11

Coming Out Stories Night: October

Pride Month: October

Queer Film Festival: October

AIDS Awareness Day: December

LGBT Comedy Night: April

Day of Silence: April

Deb Ball: Spring

BUZZ BITES *Fun Queer Stuff to Know*

THE BEST…

Party Locale: Manhattan

Hangout: The Pub

Eating Place: Bates

Place to Check Out Guys: Black Squirrel

Place to Check Out Ladies: Siegel Center

LGBT-Cool Athletic Sport: Crew *or* softball

LGBT Course Offering: Pretty, Witty and Gay: The Classics

Non-LGBT-Specific Campus Club: SLC Democrats

LGBT Educational Involvement Opportunity: Pride Month

THE GAY POINT AVERAGE
OFFICIAL CAMPUS CHECKLIST

✓ LGBT & ally student organization

LGBT resource center/office

✓ LGBT Pride Week &/or Coming Out Week

Safe Zone/Safe Space or Ally Program

✓ Significant number of LGBT social activities

✓ Significant number of LGBT educational events

✓ Variety of LGBT studies/courses

✓ Nondiscrimination statement inclusive of sexual orientation

✓ Nondiscrimination statement inclusive of gender identity/expression

✓ Extends domestic partner benefits to same-sex couples

✓ Actively recruits LGBT students to enroll on campus

✓ Trains campus police on LGBT sensitivity

✓ Procedure for reporting LGBT bias, harassment & hate crimes

Offers LGBT housing options/themes

✓ Offers LGBT-inclusive health services/testing

✓ Offers LGBT-inclusive counseling/support groups

✓ Offers LGBT student scholarships

Conducts special LGBT graduation ceremony for LGBT & ally Students

✓ Offers support services for process of transitioning from M to F & F to M

Active LGBT alumni group

15 SARAH LAWRENCE COLLEGE
GAY POINT AVERAGE
(out of 20)

SKIDMORE COLLEGE

EVERY YEAR, SKIDMORE College students select one man who represents the values and ideals of the campus for the coveted title of "Mr. Skidmore." This past year, for the first time ever, a young man in drag won!

Mr. Skidmore is just one sign of gay-friendliness on the Skidmore campus. In addition, the annual award for Club of the Year was recently given to the Skidmore Pride Alliance. Many on campus hail the active student coalition for its outreach efforts and phenomenal queer events. Whether it's Bisexuality Awareness Day, Queer as Prom, Date Auction or Gayme Nights, there is always something queer to do on this small campus. As a result, Pride Alliance partners with many other diversity clubs on campus, as well as academic departments, to invite speakers and cosponsor events.

The college also has a Center for Sex and Gender Relations, which works collaboratively to support LGBT students in the academic setting. There are resources to support LGBT students at just about every stage of their coming out process—from the Coming Out and Beyond Support Group to ally training throughout the year. And if that is not enough, you can also choose to live on the Gender and Orientation Safe Living Floor, especially designed as a welcoming home for queer student living.

"Being LGBT at Skidmore is not a big deal," states one queer student. And, from the sound of it, that's exactly right. The LGBT progressiveness can be seen firsthand in administration actions as well as the policies in the Gay Point Average. Even after graduation, LGBT students can continue their involvement in the LGBT Skidmore alumni organization. An LGBT student summarizes it perfectly: "To be queer at Skidmore is to be yourself. I have grown so much in my identity and comfortableness with who I am. It is a beginning, not an ending."

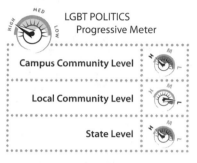

LGBT POLITICS
Progressive Meter

Campus Community Level

Local Community Level

State Level

OUTSPOKEN *Answers from LGBT students:*

Top Three Descriptors of the LGBT Campus Environment:
1. Creative   2. Supportive   3. Welcoming

What makes your campus feel welcoming and safe for LGBT students?
"The moment I came onto campus, it felt welcoming. Other LGBT students introduced themselves and did not seem afraid to be out. Their openness made me feel safe." —*18-year-old lesbian, freshman*

How do you feel about coming out on your campus?
"No big deal. There are several out straight allies, and the numbers seem to be growing as far as queer students. I think we have a unique campus to offer an LGBT student." —*21-year-old lesbian, junior*

ACADEMIC SCENE

Top Three Supportive LGBT Academic Areas:
1. Social Work   2. English   3. Neuroscience

INFO

SKIDMORE COLLEGE
815 North Broadway
Saratoga Springs, NY 12866
Phone: 518-580-5570
Fax: 518-580-5584
E-mail: admissions@skidmore.edu
Website: www.skidmore.edu

CAMPUS STATS
Type of Institution: Private college
Founding Year: 1903
Size: 2,309
Avg. Class Size: 10–19 students
Popular Majors: Business Administration/Management, English Language and Literature, Psychology
Cost: Tuition: $32,340
Admission Application Deadline: January 15

• •

• •

ANNUAL LGBT EVENT HIGHLIGHTS

Bisexuality Awareness Day: September

National Coming Out Day: October

Queer as Prom: October

Transgender Day of Remembrance: November

World AIDS Day: December 1

Day of Silence: April

Pride Week: April

Date Auction: Spring

Spectrum Dance: Spring

Ally Trainings: Fall/Spring

Gayme Nights: Fall/Spring

How LGBT-friendly are faculty in the classroom?

"Faculty are extremely LGBT-friendly. I come out all the time in my classes when I write papers or in class discussion. It is never a big deal, and fellow students are interested in my thoughts." —*19-year-old bisexual male, freshman*

"I was worried at first, but that quickly changed when I saw more students who were allies and LGBT on campus. Many of them were very out in the classroom too." —*22-year-old gay male, senior*

😀 SOCIAL SCENE

Top Three Things in the LGBT Social Life:
1. Socializing with friends   2. Movies   3. Parties

How would you describe the social scene for LGBT students?

"Appealing and down-to-earth. I enjoy hanging out and socializing with my friends—straight or gay." —*19 year-old gay male, freshman*

What annual social event should an LGBT student not miss?

"Check out Queer as Prom! The outfits that some of the guys put together are 'gender fabulous.' It is a night where everyone explores the expression of gender, and many are not afraid to show some leg!" —*20-year-old bisexual female, junior*

BUZZ BITES *Fun Queer Stuff to Know*

THE BEST...

Party Locale: Sexuality and Gender Awareness House in Scribner Village

Hangout: Gender and Orientation Safe Living Floor

Eating Place: Uncommon Grounds Coffee Shop

LGBT-Cool Athletic Sport: Women's ice hockey

Non-LGBT-Specific Campus Club: Ad-Libs Improv Comedy Troupe

Place for LGBT Students to Live on Campus: Gender and Orientation Safe Living Floor

LGBT Course Offering: Queer Fictions

LGBT-Accepting Religious/Spiritual Organization(s): Jewish Student Union

THE GAY POINT AVERAGE
OFFICIAL CAMPUS CHECKLIST

LGBT & ally student organization ✓

LGBT resource center/office ✓

LGBT Pride Week &/or Coming Out Week ✓

Safe Zone/Safe Space or Ally Program ✓

Significant number of LGBT social activities ✓

Significant number of LGBT educational events ✓

Variety of LGBT studies/courses

Nondiscrimination statement inclusive of sexual orientation ✓

Nondiscrimination statement inclusive of gender identity/expression

Extends domestic partner benefits to same-sex couples ✓

Actively recruits LGBT students to enroll on campus

Trains campus police on LGBT sensitivity

Procedure for reporting LGBT bias, harassment & hate crimes ✓

Offers LGBT housing options/themes ✓

Offers LGBT-inclusive health services/testing

Offers LGBT-inclusive counseling/support groups ✓

Offers LGBT student scholarships

Conducts special LGBT graduation ceremony for LGBT & ally Students

Offers support services for process of transitioning from M to F & F to M

Active LGBT alumni group ✓

CAMPUS QUEER RESOURCES

Select LGBT Student Organization(s)

Skidmore Pride Alliance

Membership: 100+

Website: www.skidmore.edu/
studentorgs/spa

*Resource Center/Office Responsible
for LGBT Issues:*

Center for Sex and Gender Relations
Skidmore College
815 North Broadway
Saratoga Springs, NY 12866

Year Established: 2003

Number of Staff: 1 full-time staff plus
student volunteers

Phone: 518-580-8255

E-mail: cssr@skidmore.edu

Website: www.skidmore.edu/campuslife/
center.htm

SKIDMORE COLLEGE
GAY POINT AVERAGE
(out of 20)

12

BEST
OF THE BEST
TOP 20

STANFORD UNIVERSITY

LGBT STUDENTS OFTEN have their pick of private academic institutions among many other choices to consider. One LGBT teenager was looking for a top biology research program—and at least as important, a community that would be supportive of her as a lesbian. As the story goes, she found just that when she stepped onto Stanford University's sandstone campus. "I came here and there were rainbow flags everywhere," states the now senior, who had come out her last year in high school. "It was so nice."

Stanford University is a testament to LGBT progress and has a solid institutional commitment to LGBT issues. The campus boasts a vibrant, diverse queer community—and a history of LGBT student activism dating back to gay rights pioneer Harry Hay in the 1940s. Stanford was one of the first U.S. colleges to offer domestic partner benefits to its faculty and staff and to offer same-sex-couple housing to students. Additionally, the Stanford School of Medicine houses one of the world's oldest and most highly esteemed sexual reassignment programs.

As far as LGBT student life goes, Stanford's LGBT Community Resources Center is home to over fourteen queer student organizations offering a range of programs, services and resources. The center has a popular and widely used study and meeting area, featuring a computer cluster, library, lounge and widescreen TV. The staff of the resource center put a strong emphasis on advising, counseling and advocacy for individual LGBT students, as well as for those questioning their sexual orientations and/or gender identities. The campus also specifically nurtures queer and queer-allied ethnic groups, such as La Familia, Queer and Asian and the student group Black and Queer at Stanford. Plus, Stanford has some of the queerest annual traditions and events, such as Queer Moon on the Quad and the Genderfuk Drag Ball.

Are you ready to apply yet? Well, go ahead and check out the Gay Point Average of this outstanding LGBT campus. And if you're still wondering about Stanford University, listen to this LGBT student perspective: "There's support for any student who wants to start something LGBT-related on campus. ... expand your social circle among the queer community… and party and have a good time with friends."

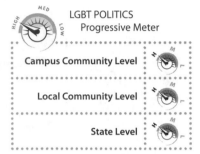

LGBT POLITICS
Progressive Meter

Campus Community Level

Local Community Level

State Level

INFO

STANFORD UNIVERSITY
Old Union 232
Stanford, CA 94305
Phone: 650-723-2091
Fax: 650-723-6050
E-mail: admissions@stanford.edu
Website: www.stanford.edu

CAMPUS STATS
Type of Institution: Private college
Founding Year: 1885
Size: 6,753
Avg. Class Size: 10–19 students
Popular Majors: Biology/Biological Sciences, Computer Science, Economics
Cost: Tuition: $29,847
Admission Application Deadline: December 15

OUTSPOKEN *Answers from LGBT students:*

Top Three Descriptors of the LGBT Campus Environment:
1. Unique   2. Progressive   3. Welcoming

What makes your campus feel welcoming and safe for LGBT students?
"I see a lot of rainbow flags hanging from buildings and dorm rooms. That makes me feel comfortable about Stanford's stance on LGBT issues."
—18-year-old lesbian, freshman

How do you feel about coming out on your campus?
"I feel that coming out at Stanford is easy for most students because they don't have to deal with pressure from home. It's like we have a clean slate and we can start anew." *—20-year-old gay male, junior*

"I don't think that coming out at Stanford is a big deal. Everyone here is a freakin' liberal! I think I'd be more concerned if I had to come out as a Republican, instead." —*19-year-old bisexual female, sophomore*

ACADEMIC SCENE

Top Three Supportive LGBT Academic Areas:
1. Cultural and Social Anthropology   2. Modern Thought and Literature
3. Feminist Studies

How LGBT-friendly are faculty in the classroom?
"The faculty here could care less if you're straight or queer. I think that they're more concerned about your performance as a Stanford student, not an LGBT student." —*21-year-old female bisexual, senior*

"If any of my teachers are LGBT-unfriendly, then I haven't noticed. I mean, are they going to give me a harder time because I am gay? That doesn't happen at Stanford." —*21-year-old gay male, senior*

SOCIAL SCENE

Top Three Things in the LGBT Social Life:
1. Parties   2. Going to bars   3. Dancing

How would you describe the social scene for LGBT students?
"The social scene is small, but it's great! I definitely enjoy the queer parties that we have on campus." —*22-year-old gay male, senior*

What annual social event should an LGBT student not miss?
"We have this Stanford tradition where on the first full moon of the year, the seniors are supposed to kiss the freshmen in the Quad. For LGBT students, we call it Queer Moon on the Quad." —*23-year-old gay male, senior*

BUZZ BITES *Fun Queer Stuff to Know*

THE BEST...

Party Locale: Terra House
Hangout: LGBT Community Resource Center
Eating Place: Moonbeans
Place to Check Out Guys: Roble Gym
Place to Check Out Ladies: *L Word* Screenings
LGBT-Cool Athletic Sport: Swimming *and* rugby
Non-LGBT-Specific Campus Club: Synergy House

Place for LGBT Students to Live on Campus: Terra House
LGBT Course Offering: Introduction to Queer Studies
LGBT Educational Involvement Opportunity: LGBT Community Resource Center
LGBT-Accepting Religious/Spiritual Organization(s): Queer Spirit

OUTRAGEOUS FACTOID *CosmoGirl!* magazine named Stanford "Best LGBT Campus" in 2004.

RAINBOW RUMOR Stanford has very few out transgender students, and the campus antidiscrimination statement does not include gender identity. Although faculty and staff are largely supportive, the campus offers little in the way of established resources and support services for trans students. Nevertheless, the university provides trans-sensitivity training to senior student affairs administrators and plans to include gender-neutral restrooms and informational materials in its newly renovated student union.

THAT'S SO GAY!

ANNUAL LGBT EVENT HIGHLIGHTS

Terra House Parties: Fall/Spring, 1 every 10 weeks

Safe and Open Spaces at Stanford Panels: Fall/Spring

Queer Moon on the Quad: Fall quarter

National Coming Out Day: October

Queer Reunion Homecoming: October

A Queer Art Affair: Winter quarter

Parents' Weekend Dinner: Winter quarter

Admit Weekend Queer Life at Stanford Panel: Spring quarter

Queer Awareness Days: Spring quarter

Genderfuk Drag Ball: Spring quarter

National Day of Silence: April

Queer Graduation: May

THE GAY POINT AVERAGE
OFFICIAL CAMPUS CHECKLIST

CAMPUS QUEER RESOURCES

Select LGBT Student Organization(s):

Queer Straight Alliance
Founding Date: 1999
Membership: 125+
E-mail: qsalliance@lists.stanford.edu

LGBT Resource Center/Office:

LGBT Community Resources Center
459 Lagunita Drive, Suite 9
Stanford, CA 94305
Year Established: 1973 (as Gay People's Union)
Number of Staff: 2 full-time professional staff, 13 part-time student employees
Phone: 650-725-4222
E-mail: lgbt-staff@lists.stanford.edu
Website: LGBT.stanford.edu

- ✓ LGBT & ally student organization
- ✓ LGBT resource center/office
- ✓ LGBT Pride Week &/or Coming Out Week
- ✓ Safe Zone/Safe Space or Ally Program
- ✓ Significant number of LGBT social activities
- ✓ Significant number of LGBT educational events
- ✓ Variety of LGBT studies/courses
- ✓ Nondiscrimination statement inclusive of sexual orientation
-   Nondiscrimination statement inclusive of gender identity/expression
- ✓ Extends domestic partner benefits to same-sex couples
- ✓ Actively recruits LGBT students to enroll on campus
- ✓ Trains campus police on LGBT sensitivity
- ✓ Procedure for reporting LGBT bias, harassment & hate crimes
- ✓ Offers LGBT housing options/themes
- ✓ Offers LGBT-inclusive health services/testing
- ✓ Offers LGBT-inclusive counseling/support groups
-   Offers LGBT student scholarships
- ✓ Conducts special LGBT graduation ceremony for LGBT & ally Students
- ✓ Offers support services for process of transitioning from M to F & F to M
- ✓ Active LGBT alumni group

18

STANFORD UNIVERSITY
GAY POINT AVERAGE
(out of 20)

STATE UNIVERSITY OF NEW YORK— PURCHASE COLLEGE

THE STATE UNIVERSITY of New York—Purchase College has always had a history of being a "gay college." Even LGBT alumni from 30 years ago would agree. But what makes it so gay?

Queer history depicts SUNY Purchase as a most LGBT-progressive campus. As early as the late 1970s, the student GLBT Union was formed to advocate for queer concerns and issues. Today the university has a nondiscrimination policy inclusive of sexual orientation and extends domestic partner benefits to same-sex couples.

Let's look closer: the queerness is truly in the campus life. The GLBT Union, along with the Leadership, Education, Advocacy and Diversity Center, plans a variety of LGBT events, from lectures to awareness weeks to the performing arts. The official kickoff to every year is the Lavender Luau to welcome new LGBT students to campus. Then throughout the year, event highlights include the Fall Ball Drag Show, Transgender Day of Remembrance, Madonnarama Dance Party, Pride Week and the Purchase Gay Prom. Keep in mind that New York City is only 30 minutes away, and the nearby city of Westchester's local LGBT center called the Loft offers more queer life, too.

When you consider SUNY Purchase as your college home, keep these words from a current LGBT student in the back of your head: "It doesn't matter being gay on campus. Purchase is absolutely queer beyond belief. I can get involved in the GLBT Union, kiss my boyfriend, dress in drag…. it's never a problem. We are a huge gay family."

OUTSPOKEN *Answers from LGBT students:*

Top Three Descriptors of the LGBT Campus Environment:
1. Diverse   2. Accepting   3. Creative

What makes your campus feel welcoming and safe for LGBT students?
"First and foremost is the healthy population of gay students. Being surrounded by your own kind carries with it an intrinsic feeling of safety. Purchase tries to foster an open and accepting environment." *—18-year-old gay male, freshman*

How do you feel about coming out on your campus?
"I felt completely comfortable and safe doing so. And coming here allowed me to come out to my own parents for Coming Out Day last month." *—20-year-old gay male, junior*

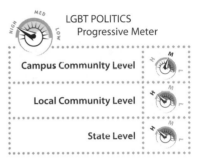

LGBT POLITICS
Progressive Meter

Campus Community Level

Local Community Level

State Level

INFO

STATE UNIVERSITY OF NEW YORK—PURCHASE COLLEGE
735 Anderson Hill Road
Purchase, NY 10577

Phone: 914-251-6300
Fax: 914-251-6314
E-mail: admissions@purchase.edu
Website: www.purchase.edu

CAMPUS STATS
Type of Institution: Public university
Founding Year: 1967
Size: 3,944
Avg. Class Size: 10–19 students
Popular Majors: Liberal Arts and Sciences/Liberal Studies, Psychology, Visual and Performing Arts
Cost: In-state tuition: $4,350
Out-of-state tuition: $10,610
Admission Application Deadline: February 1

The most famous sculpture on campus is Henry Moore's *Two Large Forms*. When you take the campus tour, students joke that "only Purchase would have a huge bronze sculpture of two vaginas—or, depending on your view, two assholes." A sight to be seen, for sure!

· ·

RAINBOW RUMOR

Famous Hollywood actor Wesley Snipes attended SUNY Purchase. It was not a campus surprise when the actor starred as a sensuous drag queen in the hit movie *To Wong Foo: Thanks for Everything, Julie Newmar*. Sadly, however, due to administrative red tape, trans students on campus still can't find gender-neutral bathrooms.

· ·

THAT'S SO GAY!

ANNUAL LGBT EVENT HIGHLIGHTS

Lavender Luau: August/September

Livetease Striptease: October

National Coming Out Day: October 11

Fall Ball Drag Show Competition: November

Transgender Day of Remembrance: November 20

World AIDS Day: December 1

Madonnarama Dance Party: January

Pride Week: April

Day of Silence: April

Purchase Gay Prom: April

ACADEMIC SCENE

Top Three Supportive LGBT Academic Areas:
1. Visual Arts   2. Drama Studies   3. Anthropology

How LGBT-friendly are faculty in the classroom?
"There are many professors who teach in areas outside of queer studies who identify as LGBT. These professors are always friendly, attend GLBT Union events, serve as role models for students and are there for support."
—*20-year-old lesbian, junior*

"I'm into the arts, so many of my classes are dominated by LGBT students or at minimum are very queer-friendly. Outside of these classes, I do not change how I act or what I share openly in the classroom. It's never been an issue for me."
—*22-year-old gay male, senior*

SOCIAL SCENE

Top Three Things in the LGBT Social Life:
1. Parties   2. Dressing in drag   3. Fall Ball

How would you describe the social scene for LGBT students?
"The LGBT social scene is there, but it's not the most prevalent one on campus. Sure, there are the 'gay parties' where 90 percent of the attendance is gay, but they don't happen every Friday and Saturday night."
—*20-year-old gay male, sophomore*

What annual social event should an LGBT student not miss?
"The Lavender Luau at the beginning of the year is amazing. It's a great chance to meet your fellow students (gay, straight, bisexual, transgender) and such."
—*20-year-old gay male, junior*

BUZZ BITES *Fun Queer Stuff to Know*

THE BEST...

Party Locale: Old Apartment Drag Queen House Parties

Hangout: Mall *and* the Hammocks

Eating Place: Terra Ve

Place to Check Out Guys: Visual Arts Building

Place to Check Out Ladies: Co-op

LGBT-Cool Athletic Sport: Women's soccer

Non-LGBT-Specific Campus Club: NYPIRG

Place for LGBT Students to Live on Campus: Old Apartments

LGBT Course Offering: Homosexuality and Religion

LGBT Educational Involvement Opportunity: Health and Peer Education Network

LGBT-Accepting Religious/Spiritual Organization(s): Hillel

THE GAY POINT AVERAGE
OFFICIAL CAMPUS CHECKLIST

LGBT & ally student organization	✓
LGBT resource center/office	
LGBT Pride Week &/or Coming Out Week	✓
Safe Zone/Safe Space or Ally Program	✓
Significant number of LGBT social activities	✓
Significant number of LGBT educational events	✓
Variety of LGBT studies/courses	✓
Nondiscrimination statement inclusive of sexual orientation	✓
Nondiscrimination statement inclusive of gender Identity/expression	
Extends domestic partner benefits to same-sex couples	✓
Actively recruits LGBT students to enroll on campus	
Trains campus police on LGBT sensitivity	✓
Procedure for reporting LGBT bias, harassment & hate crimes	✓
Offers LGBT housing options/themes	
Offers LGBT-inclusive health services/testing	✓
Offers LGBT-inclusive counseling/support groups	
Offers LGBT student scholarships	
Conducts special LGBT graduation ceremony for LGBT & ally Students	
Offers support services for process of transitioning from M to F & F to M	
Active LGBT alumni group	

CAMPUS QUEER RESOURCES

Select LGBT Student Organization(s):

Gay, Lesbian, Bisexual, Transgender Union

Founding Date: Late 1970s
Membership: 110+
Phone: 914-251-6976
E-mail: purchaseglbtu@yahoogroups.com

Resource Center/Office Responsible for LGBT Issues:

Leadership, Education, Advocacy and Diversity Center

Number of Staff: 2 full-time professional staff (varying responsibilities)
Phone: 914-251-6333
Website: www.purchase.edu/studaff/lead/

STATE UNIVERSITY OF NEW YORK—PURCHASE COLLEGE GAY POINT AVERAGE
(out of 20)

11

SUFFOLK UNIVERSITY

SUFFOLK UNIVERSITY WAS founded on the ideology of providing access to a quality education for those individuals discriminated against elsewhere. Sitting in the heart of downtown Boston, Massachusetts, the campus has a rich history of inclusion, even for LGBT students. Today Suffolk remains committed to queer issues and has proven to be among the most LGBT-friendly places for college.

The queer visibility starts each year at convocation, when the president welcomes incoming students and introduces the importance of diversity, explicitly including LGBT examples in his remarks. Queer students agree that the campus commitment goes beyond these words and shows in the actions of the president. He not only attends LGBT events on campus but also openly supports ways to make LGBT students feel more welcome. Recently, the campus formed a president's commission on LGBT issues, which was charged with exploring trans-student needs and what would be involved in adding gender identity/expression to the university's nondiscrimination policy.

In addition, many of the faculty and staff at Suffolk are visibly out and willing to take a stand on issues concerning LGBT students. Since 2001, over 300 faculty and staff have become trained as allies in the Safe Zone program. Both the faculty and the administration work collaboratively with the two LGBT student groups, the Rainbow Alliance and the Queer Law Alliance. Together, the campus queer constituencies plan social and educational LGBT events like the annual GLBT Welcome Reception, GLBT History Month, Transgender Day of Remembrance and spring Drag Show. Incoming LGBT students also have the queer frenzy of social outlets in Boston at their fingertips. One LGBT student shares: "Truly an exhilarating queer experience. …There's much to queer life on campus and in the Boston area. The campus is extremely friendly on queer issues."

Well, such LGBT inclusiveness might be expected from the first state to grant full and equal same-sex marriage in the country. Suffolk University has most certainly risen to the challenge of being LGBT-friendly. Still not convinced that Suffolk is the college choice for you? Listen closely to this LGBT student perspective: "Suffolk is awesome. I came here hoping for a place where I can be openly gay and I got much more…support of faculty, friends who are allies and pride in myself and a place to call home."

LGBT POLITICS
Progressive Meter

Campus Community Level

Local Community Level

State Level

INFO

SUFFOLK UNIVERSITY
8 Ashburton Place
Boston, MA 02108

Phone: 617-573-8460

Fax: 617-742-4291

E-mail: admission@suffolk.edu

Website: www.suffolk.edu

CAMPUS STATS

Type of Institution: Private college

Founding Year: 1906

Size: 4,617

Avg. Class Size: 20–29 students

Popular Majors: Business Administration/Management, Communications Studies/Speech Communication and Rhetoric, Sociology

Cost: Tuition: $21,140

Admission Application Deadline: March 1

OUTSPOKEN *Answers from LGBT students:*

Top Three Descriptors of the LGBT Campus Environment:
1. Accepting   2. Supportive   3. Diverse

What makes your campus feel welcome and safe for LGBT students?
"Suffolk starts making LGBT students feel comfortable right at Freshman Orientation. All incoming freshmen must attend a theatrical performance called Acting Out. …There is always a skit on coming out, and LGB characters are mixed into skits on safe sex. …it made me feel a part of the community right away."
—*22-year-old bisexual female, senior*

How do you feel about coming out on your campus?
"There are so many resources and so many people who care and support you, that most of the time being out on campus is almost a nonissue … definitely much more accepting than high school." —*21-year-old gay male, junior*

⏱ ACADEMIC SCENE

Top Three Supportive LGBT Academic Areas:
1. Psychology   2. Sociology   3. Communications

How LGBT-friendly are faculty in the classroom?
"All of my professors were very open and accepting. I remember one poly-sci professor who kept saying 'sexual preference' in class and that kind of bothered me. … it implied that being gay was a choice. … I talked to the professor after class and explained my concerns to him and asked that he say 'sexual orientation' instead. He apologized on the spot (which I hadn't asked for but appreciated), and from that point on he always said 'sexual orientation.'"
—24-year-old gay male, senior

"Generally, if there is a discussion about LGBT issues in class I come out to the entire class, and it has never been an issue. If you need to know how supportive a certain professor is, ask the Rainbow Alliance or someone else you trust. I would imagine that if anything anti-LGBT ever came before a dean, they would take it very, very seriously." *—20-year-old lesbian, junior*

😊 SOCIAL SCENE

Top Three Things in the LGBT Social Life:
1. Parties   2. Going to bars   3. Socializing with friends

How would you describe the social scene for LGBT students?
"Flirtatious and fun. … I find new queer stuff to do every year!"
—20-year-old bisexual male, junior

What annual social event should an LGBT student not miss?
"The Drag Show! Performing Arts hires drag queens from a local bar to perform at school. It gets bigger every year. It is amazing!" *—22-year-old gay male, senior*

OUTRAGEOUS FACTOID

Suffolk University has a "no-nonsense" policy toward discrimination of any kind. As the story goes, an LGBT student was the secretary of the Rainbow Alliance and also the secretary of a Christian student group on campus. When the Christian group found out that she was a lesbian, they kicked her out, saying that she was a "sinner." LGBT students went to the administration and asked that something be done. Immediately, the Christian group was forced to apologize and had to attend diversity training with a local lesbian pastor. The reprimand came with a warning that if they ever discriminated against an LGBT student again, the campus would rescind the group's recognition status. How positively affirming!

RAINBOW RUMOR

Suffolk remains committed to equity and access for all, and the campus is constantly evaluating how it can be more inclusive. The top LGBT priority on campus is addressing transgender issues.

THAT'S SO GAY!

ANNUAL LGBT EVENT HIGHLIGHTS

GLBT Welcome Reception: September
GLBT History Month: October
Transgender Day of Remembrance: November
World AIDS Day: December
Unity Week Diversity Celebration: March
Drag Show: April
Day of Silence: April
Lavender Graduation: May

BUZZ BITES
Fun Queer Stuff to Know

THE BEST…

Party Locale: Rise and Axis
Hangout: Club Café
Place to Check Out Guys: Fitness Center
Place to Check Out Ladies: Toast
LGBT-Cool Athletic Sport: Men's soccer *or* women's volleyball
Non-LGBT-Specific Campus Club: Acting Out!
LGBT Educational Involvement Opportunity: Safe Zone Program

LGBT-Accepting Religious/Spiritual Organization(s): Interfaith Campus Center, University Chaplain

CAMPUS QUEER RESOURCES

Select LGBT Student Organization(s):

Rainbow Alliance
Membership: 30+
E-mail: rainbow@suffolk.edu

Resource Center/Office Responsible for LGBT Issues:

Office of Diversity Services
41 Temple St, Donahue 209
Boston, MA 02114
Number of Staff: 2 full-time staff professionals (varying responsibilities)
Phone: 617-573-8613
E-mail: glbt@suffolk.edu
Website: www.suffolk.edu/diversity

THE GAY POINT AVERAGE
OFFICIAL CAMPUS CHECKLIST

✓ LGBT & ally student organization

LGBT resource center/office

✓ LGBT Pride Week &/or Coming Out Week

✓ Safe Zone/Safe Space or Ally Program

✓ Significant number of LGBT social activities

✓ Significant number of LGBT educational events

✓ Variety of LGBT studies/courses

✓ Nondiscrimination statement inclusive of sexual orientation

Nondiscrimination statement inclusive of gender identity/expression

✓ Extends domestic partner benefits to same-sex couples

✓ Actively recruits LGBT students to enroll on campus

✓ Trains campus police on LGBT sensitivity

Procedure for reporting LGBT bias, harassment & hate crimes

Offers LGBT housing options/themes

✓ Offers LGBT-inclusive health services/testing

✓ Offers LGBT-inclusive counseling/support groups

Offers LGBT student scholarships

✓ Conducts special LGBT graduation ceremony for LGBT & ally Students

Offers support services for process of transitioning from M to F & F to M

Active LGBT alumni group

(13) SUFFOLK UNIVERSITY GAY POINT AVERAGE
(out of 20)

SYRACUSE UNIVERSITY

NOT RURAL, NOT urban, Syracuse University has the perfect setting. Buildings range from the historic to the contemporary. And the campus has superb positioning—on a hill overlooking downtown Syracuse.

LGBT students refer to the campus as "impressive!" That is true if you consider the many LGBT social and educational activities happening throughout Syracuse University. One of the uniquely queer activities happens at Café Q every Thursday. There, funky performing arts coffee house meets queer mystery space—along with music, food and much laughter. Of course, you can also count on other annual LGBT events like Pride Week, the Totally Fabulous Drag Show and the Reel Queer Film Festival. Several queer-fabulous artists, speakers and entertainers have dropped by campus, including Kate Clinton, Dan Savage, Leslie Feinberg and even super-ally Kathy Griffin.

Syracuse University established an LGBT Resource Center in the fall of 2001, staffed by several full-time professionals. During Coming Out Week, over 100 LGBT individuals and allies form a human rainbow stretching across the campus quad. Each LGBT student and ally wears different colors of the rainbow, symbolizing diversity and strength in community.

With regard to institutional support for LGBT students and gay-friendliness, consider the campus Gay Point Average, along with this impressive timeline of queer achievements. In 2001, the campus had two recognized queer-focused student organizations: Pride Union and Open Doors. Since then, that number has increased to 6 groups, including a gay-progressive fraternity, Delta Lambda Phi, and a campus group for LGBT people of color, Fusion. Then, in the spring of 2003, same-sex domestic partner benefits were extended to students, faculty and staff on campus, and in the spring of 2005, gender identity/expression was added to the university nondiscrimination policy. An LGBT interdisciplinary minor is coming soon. And the ball keeps rolling from there.

Syracuse University has made much LGBT progress and has built strong LGBT student coalitions. An LGBT senior concurs: "There is something LGBT-related—discussion groups, meetings, programs—every day of the week, Monday through Thursday, and then there are weekend activities, too! There is a lot to do here—you just have to make time for it!"

OUTSPOKEN *Answers from LGBT students:*

Top Three Descriptors of the LGBT Campus Environment:
1. Supportive   2. Lively   3. Inclusive

What makes your campus feel welcoming and safe for LGBT students?
"The fact that there are so many LGBT resources on campus makes me feel safe and valued. When I was coming out, I went to some discussion groups and got to know other people in the same boat as me. It was nice to be able to relate to others who were going through the same thing I was. Now I've been out for a while and I'm out to everyone on campus." *—20-year-old bisexual female, junior*

How do you feel about coming out on your campus?
"Though [I was] nervous at first, coming out on campus was way easier than I expected. I was happy to see that my friends not only cared how I was doing as a result of my coming out, but that many of them also took an active role in becoming an ally and attending LGBT events with me."
—21-year-old gay male, senior

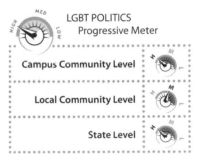

LGBT POLITICS
Progressive Meter

Campus Community Level

Local Community Level

State Level

INFO

SYRACUSE UNIVERSITY
200 Crouse-Hinds Hall
900 South Crouse Avenue
Syracuse, NY 13244
Phone: 315-443-3611
Fax: 315-443-4226
E-mail: orange@syr.edu
Website: www.syracuse.edu

CAMPUS STATS
Type of Institution: Private university
Founding Year: 1870
Size: 12,450
Avg. Class Size: 20–29 students
Popular Majors: Information Sciences/ Studies, Political Science and Government, Psychology
Cost: Tuition: $27,210
Admission Application Deadline: January 1

OUTRAGEOUS FACTOID The Boy Scouts of America is banned from renting facilities for their annual fundraiser due to their anti-LGBT policies.

● ● ● ● ● ● ● ● ● ● ● ● ● ● ● ● ● ● ● ●

RAINBOW RUMOR A proposal for an interdisciplinary minor in LGBT Studies has been submitted to the Syracuse University Senate Curriculum Committee. This proposal includes 12 newly designed LGBT courses that will be offered at least every other year. There is tremendous support for the minor, and it seems a queer bet for approval! In addition, hopeful efforts are well under way to develop an LGBT living and learning community and an LGBT alumni group. Watch out!

● ● ● ● ● ● ● ● ● ● ● ● ● ● ● ● ● ● ● ●

THAT'S SO GAY!

ANNUAL LGBT EVENT HIGHLIGHTS

LGBTQA Student Social: August

LGBTQA Community Picnic: August

Big Gay Dance: October

National Coming Out Day/Week: October

Transgender Day of Remembrance: November

Totally Fabulous Drag Show: February

Reel Queer Film Festival: April

Day of Silence—Break the Silence Rally: April

Rainbow Banquet: April

ACADEMIC SCENE

Top Three Supportive LGBT Academic Areas:
1. Women's Studies   2. Sociology   3. Writing/English Textual Studies

How LGBT-friendly are faculty in the classroom?
"About two-thirds of the professors in my department (social work) have Safe Space stickers but there's still one professor who uses gender stereotyping in his humor and makes it hard to be open in his class. Two of my three professors include LGBT material in their classes without any external pressure, and integrate it in a way that doesn't stigmatize LGBT people into a 'them'-or 'the other'-type status." —*23-year-old F-to-M pansexual, graduate student*

"Faculty and staff on this campus are extremely LGBT-friendly. I have come out to numerous faculty members, and I have always been received very warmly. The LGBT students are a growing force on this campus, and the professors know that. I think they are beginning to understand and trying to cater to us in any way possible." —*21-year-old gay male, junior*

SOCIAL SCENE

Top Three Things in the LGBT Social Life:
1. Going to Spirits   2. Café Q LGBT coffeehouse   3. Campus events

How would you describe the social scene for LGBT students?
"There is something to do for everyone. There are a number of social events like the Big Gay Dance, the Totally Fabulous Drag Show, etc. There are also meetings and group discussions which tend to be a lot of fun, especially if you are looking to meet new people. And of course there are house parties and bars and stuff like that." —*20-year-old bisexual female, junior*

What annual social event should an LGBT student not miss?
"The Totally Fabulous Drag Show is an annual event that sells out every single year with over 1,000 students. There are professional drag queens/kings, and students compete in drag as well. It is such a hilarious and fun-filled night!" —*21-year-old bisexual male, senior*

BUZZ BITES *Fun Queer Stuff to Know*

THE BEST...

Party Locale: Spirits

Hangout: LGBT Resource Center

Eating Place: Marshall Street

Place to Check Out Guys: Quad

Place to Check Out Ladies: Spirits

LGBT-Cool Athletic Sport: Women's rugby

Non-LGBT-Specific Campus Club: Danceworks

Place for LGBT Students to Live on Campus: Brewster/Boland

LGBT Educational Involvement Opportunity: Human Rainbow Bridge for Coming Out Week

LGBT-Accepting Religious/Spiritual Organization(s): Hillel Center for Jewish Life

THE GAY POINT AVERAGE
OFFICIAL CAMPUS CHECKLIST

LGBT & ally student organization	✓
LGBT resource center/office	✓
LGBT Pride Week &/or Coming Out Week	✓
Safe Zone/Safe Space or Ally Program	✓
Significant number of LGBT social activities	✓
Significant number of LGBT educational events	✓
Variety of LGBT studies/courses	✓
Nondiscrimination statement inclusive of sexual orientation	✓
Nondiscrimination statement inclusive of gender identity/expression	✓
Extends domestic partner benefits to same-sex couples	✓
Actively recruits LGBT students to enroll on campus	✓
Trains campus police on LGBT sensitivity	✓
Procedure for reporting LGBT bias, harassment & hate crimes	✓
Offers LGBT housing options/themes	
Offers LGBT-inclusive health services/testing	✓
Offers LGBT-inclusive counseling/support groups	✓
Offers LGBT student scholarships	
Conducts special LGBT graduation ceremony for LGBT & ally Students	✓
Offers support services for process of transitioning from M to F & F to M	✓
Active LGBT alumni group	

SYRACUSE UNIVERSITY
GAY POINT AVERAGE
(out of 20)
17

**CAMPUS QUEER
RESOURCES**

Select LGBT Student Organization(s):
Pride Union and Open Doors
Founding Date: Pride Union was founded in 1990 for undergraduates, and Open Doors was founded in 1985 for graduate students.
Membership: 120+
Phone: 315-443-3983
E-mail: suprideunionprez@yahoo.com; opendoorssu@yahoo.com
Website: students.syr.edu/prideunion; students.syr.edu/opendoors

LGBT Resource Center/Office:
LGBT Resource Center
750 Ostrom Avenue
Syracuse, NY 13244
Year Established: 2001
Number of Staff: 3 full-time professional staff;1 graduate assistant; 6 student assistants
Phone: 315-443-3983
E-mail: lgbt@syr.edu
Website: students.syr.edu/lgbt/index.html

TEMPLE UNIVERSITY

TEMPLE UNIVERSITY STUDENTS commonly refer to the campus as "Diversity University." Temple's strength lies in the many diverse facets of the campus population. Temple emphatically includes the LGBT community as an essential part of that diversity.

Although Temple University does not have individual centers for any minority groups, it does offer LGBT services through the Multicultural Center. The spirit of collaboration is continued through the student organizations as well. It is not uncommon to see students from Common Ground, the universal LGBT student group, working with a faith-based campus group. Some might think that is rare, but not at Temple University. Common Ground also actively supports Gatekeepers, a group for LGBT students of color, and both student coalitions work together and overlap in membership with one another. Simply put, the groups are not segregated, as you might find elsewhere.

Temple University also demonstrates LGBT-progressiveness when it comes to policy: it approved an LGBT academic minor in 2002 and became the state of Pennsylvania's first public university to offer domestic partner benefits in 2003. Of course, LGBT students who attend Temple University also benefit from the cultural life of historic Philadelphia, where the modern-day LGBT movement began in front of Independence Hall in Olde City back in 1965.

Temple offers an abundance of LGBT activities, such as Pride Week in October, held in conjunction with National Coming Out Day, and the Queer Prom in the spring. In addition, a number of academic offices sponsor educational programs to support the LGBT community. Temple was the queer choice for this African American LGBT new student, who says: "If students are looking for a campus community where they will fit in and be accepted, Temple University deserves to be looked at—come for a tour and see for yourself why so many students like it here. I took a tour myself my junior year of high school and was able to ask questions that allowed me to feel secure about my decision to attend Temple."

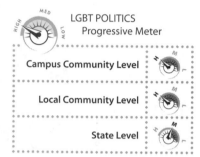

LGBT POLITICS
Progressive Meter

Campus Community Level

Local Community Level

State Level

INFO

TEMPLE UNIVERSITY
Broad Street and Montgomery
Philadelphia, PA 19122
Phone: 215-204-7200
Fax: 215-204-5694
E-mail: tuadm@temple.edu
Website: www.temple.edu

CAMPUS STATS

Type of Institution: Public university
Founding Year: 1884
Size: 22,982
Avg. Class Size: 20–29 students
Popular Majors: Elementary Education and Teaching, Journalism, Psychology
Cost: In-state tuition: $8,622
Out-of-state tuition: $15,788
Admission Application Deadline: April 1

OUTSPOKEN *Answers from LGBT students:*

Top Three Descriptors of the LGBT Campus Environment:
1. Growing   2. Embracing   3. Diverse

What makes your campus feel welcoming and safe for LGBT students?
"Temple University is a great place for LGBT students because it is in the heart of Philadelphia. One of the ways Temple University caters to LGBT students is that it acts as a launch pad to the city's LGBT life. It is also a little-known fact that Temple University is also a place where a student can pick up *Philadelphia Gay News* newspaper." —*18-year-old gay male, freshman*

"As an African American Lesbian Woman, Temple University has allowed me to bring my multiple identities to the table without compromise. I do not know if I would have found that at other institutions." —*18-year-old lesbian, freshman*

How do you feel about coming out on your campus?
"I have been out throughout the duration of my stay here, and I've been president of the LGBT student group for three years. The most common

response from students when they meet me is 'Oh yeah, you're that gay kid!' In a good way." —20-year-old gay male, senior

ACADEMIC SCENE

Top Three Supportive LGBT Academic Areas:
1. Women's Studies   2. English   3. Performing Arts

How LGBT-friendly are faculty in the classroom?
"Most are very accepting and have been openly receptive."
—20-year-old bi-curious questioning female, senior

"When topics of homosexuality come up in classroom, no one really makes a big deal out of it, except for the highly bigoted kids who come from small towns. Everyone else is pretty much accepting and even discusses homosexuality openly. Most teachers don't sidestep the issue, and most students aren't shocked by the mention of homosexuality." —18-year-old gay male, sophomore

SOCIAL SCENE

Top Three Things in the LGBT Social Life:
1. LGBT dances   2. Movie nights   3. Queer Café

How would you describe the social scene for LGBT students?
"The social scene is best in downtown Center City Philadelphia, where there are several 'Gayborhood' clubs dedicated to LGBT-themed events and interests."
— 20-year-old bi-curious questioning female, senior

What annual social event should an LGBT student not miss?
"Queer Prom, sponsored by Common Ground. Our Queer Prom last year, themed Night on the Town, was a huge success. I had a wonderful time; it was among the top three of my dance experiences." —20-year-old gay male, junior

 OUTRAGEOUS FACTOID Rabbi Rebecca Albert, author of *Like Bread on the Seder Plate: Jewish Lesbians and the Transformation of Tradition*, is a professor and coordinator of the Women's Studies program at Temple.

RAINBOW RUMOR Temple University was the first state college or university to offer domestic partner benefits in Pennsylvania. In addition, Temple granted approval in 2002 to develop a minor in LGBT studies. Nevertheless, the campus still says it does not "actively" recruit LGBT students.

THAT'S SO GAY!

ANNUAL LGBT EVENT HIGHLIGHTS

Outfest: October
National Coming Out Day: October
Coming Out Week: October
Queer Café: October
World AIDS Day: December
Winter Dance: December
Equality Forum: May
Queer Prom: Spring
Equality Forum: May/June
Philly Pride Celebration: June
Philadelphia Gay and Lesbian Film Festival: July

BUZZ BITES *Fun Queer Stuff to Know*

THE BEST...

Party Locale: 12th Air Command, Pure, The Dive

Hangout: Gayborhood shops on 12th Street

Eating Place: More Than Just Ice Cream *and* Cosi's

Place to Check Out Guys: Woody's

Place to Check Out Ladies: Sister's *and* The Dive

LGBT-Cool Athletic Sport: Male cheerleading *and* Gryphones rugby

Non-LGBT-Specific Campus Club: Football *and* Feminist Majority Leadership Alliance

Place for LGBT Students to Live on Campus: Gertrude Peabody Residence Hall

LGBT Educational Involvement Opportunity: Temple Health Empowerment Office (THEO) Programs

LGBT-Accepting Religious/Spiritual Organization(s): Hillel Jewish Student Union *and* Lutheran/Episcopal Campus Ministries

THE GAY POINT AVERAGE
OFFICIAL CAMPUS CHECKLIST

**CAMPUS QUEER
RESOURCES**

Select LGBT Student Organization(s):

Common Ground
Founding Date: late 1970s, early 1980s
Membership: 100+
Website: www.temple.edu/cg

*Resource Center/Office Responsible
for LGBT Issues:*

Multicultural Affairs
Mitten Hall, Lower Level
1913 North Broad Street
Philadelphia, PA 19122
Year Established: 2004
Number of Staff: 7 staff professionals
(varying LGBT shared responsibilities)
Phone: 215-204-7303

✓ LGBT & ally student organization

LGBT resource center/office

✓ LGBT Pride Week &/or Coming Out Week

Safe Zone/Safe Space or Ally Program

✓ Significant number of LGBT social activities

✓ Significant number of LGBT educational events

✓ Variety of LGBT studies/courses

✓ Nondiscrimination statement inclusive of sexual orientation

Nondiscrimination statement inclusive of gender identity/expression

✓ Extends domestic partner benefits to same-sex couples

Actively recruits LGBT students to enroll on campus

✓ Trains campus police on LGBT sensitivity

✓ Procedure for reporting LGBT bias, harassment & hate crimes

Offers LGBT housing options/themes

✓ Offers LGBT-inclusive health services/testing

✓ Offers LGBT-inclusive counseling/support groups

Offers LGBT student scholarships

Conducts special LGBT graduation ceremony for LGBT & ally Students

✓ Offers support services for process of transitioning from M to F & F to M

Active LGBT alumni group

12 **TEMPLE UNIVERSITY
GAY POINT AVERAGE**
(out of 20)

TUFTS UNIVERSITY

BEST
OF THE BEST
TOP 20

TUFTS UNIVERSITY CELEBRATES GAYpril, with LGBT-related flyers plastered across campus and proactive, playful LGBT chalkings everywhere. LGBT and straight ally students wear Tufts rainbow pins, and the crowds are mixed at queer events.

Located in Boston, Massachusetts, Tufts University has the look and feel of a small liberal arts college in New England. The campus is only a 10-minute walk from Davis Square, an extremely queer-friendly part of greater Boston. Students have easy access to Boston via the "T," or subway. On campus, Tufts provides a full range of resources and services to LGBT students. Students can immerse themselves almost every day of the week in LGBT activities and events planned by the Tufts Transgender, Lesbian, Gay, Bisexual Collective (TTLGBC), Queer Straight Alliance, Queer Students of Color and others on campus.

The LGBT Center is a 2-floor space where students can hang out, study, watch DVDs and use public computers. There are many weekly group discussions based on identity and interest, plus opportunities to become an LGBT-trained speaker or a peer mentor. The LGBT Center is part of what's known as the Group of Six, a division of six centers that also includes the Africana, Asian American, Latino, International and Women's Centers. Such a designation means not only that the LGBT Center works in frequent collaboration with other underrepresented, oppressed communities but also that LGBT concerns are considered integral to the institutional commitment to diversity. In addition, the LGBT Center also advises the Rainbow House, an LGBT and ally housing unit, which hosts queer parties and other social activities throughout the year.

Tufts University's Gay Point Average is equally as progressive as the political landscape of Massachusetts, the only state in which same-sex marriage is legal. An atmosphere in which students can be out, proud and at ease is something that Tufts prides itself on creating; this university might be the right queer choice for you. Just listen to this LGBT student: "The enormous presence that the queer community has on campus makes Tufts a great place. From my first day freshman year, I've felt I was a part of this huge, open community."

LGBT POLITICS
Progressive Meter

Campus Community Level

Local Community Level

State Level

OUTSPOKEN *Answers from LGBT students:*

Top Three Descriptors of the LGBT Campus Environment:
1. Comfortable   2. Well-resourced   3. Fun

What makes your campus feel welcome and safe for LGBT students?
"Queer visibility is high at Tufts. Everywhere the sheer magnitude of LGBT students and allies makes one feel welcome and safe.
I love it!" —*22-year-old lesbian, senior*

How do you feel about coming out on your campus?
"Coming out for me was really easy and relaxed. As a freshman, I joined the Queer Women's Group (a discussion group). At this group, I asked the older women for advice. Hearing other stories and different perspectives helped me understand a lot about myself, and I came out later in the year."
—*19-year-old bisexual female, sophomore*

"I never had a problem coming out at Tufts, and from the sheer number of people that come out here every week, it doesn't seem to be a problem for a lot of people." —*21-year-old gay male, senior*

INFO

TUFTS UNIVERSITY
Bendetson Hall
Medford, MA 02155
Phone: 617-627-3170
Fax: 617-627-3860
E-mail: admissions.inquiry@ase.tufts.edu
Website: www.tufts.edu

CAMPUS STATS
Type of Institution: Private university
Founding Year: 1852
Size: 4,300
Avg. Class Size: 10–19 students
Popular Majors: Economics, English Language and Literature, International Relations and Affairs
Cost: Tuition: $28,859
Admission Application Deadline: January 1

ACADEMIC SCENE

Top Three Supportive LGBT Academic Areas:
1. English   2. Women's Studies   3. American Studies

How LGBT-friendly are faculty in the classroom?
"There are many supportive faculty in every department; I haven't encountered any discomfort here. I also have some queer professors."
—*19-year-old bisexual female, sophomore*

"Queer issues have come up in a great deal of my classes, most often by the professors. Through class discussions, I've come out to many of my classes and never had any negative reactions from doing so." —*21-year-old gay male, senior*

SOCIAL SCENE

Top Three Things in the LGBT Social Life:
1. Hanging out at Rainbow House   2. Going to clubs and bars
3. LGBT discussion groups

How would you describe the social scene for LGBT students?
"The Rainbow House gives the best parties on campus, hands down, and a lot of straight people come for that reason. There are always many queer things to do each week, and you can always go into Boston if you want more."
—*21-year-old gay female, junior*

What annual social event should an LGBT student not miss?
"The Rainbow House Halloween party is always one of the year's best parties, campuswide. Lots of straight people, as well as LGBT students, come to it, and everyone has a blast." —*21-year-old gay male, senior*

BUZZ BITES *Fun Queer Stuff to Know*

THE BEST...

Party Locale: Rainbow House

Hangout: LGBT Center

Eating Place: Diesel Café in Davis Square

Place to Check Out Guys: Queer Straight Alliance

Place to Check Out Ladies: Toast *and* Tribe

LGBT-Cool Athletic Sport: Swimming *and* women's rugby

Non-LGBT-Specific Campus Club: Tufts Democrats

Place for LGBT Students to Live on Campus: Rainbow House

LGBT Course Offering: Introduction to Queer Studies

LGBT Educational Involvement Opportunity: Team Q Speakers Bureau

LGBT-Accepting Religious/Spiritual Organization(s): Hillel Center *and* J Quest

THE GAY POINT AVERAGE
OFFICIAL CAMPUS CHECKLIST

LGBT & ally student organization ✓

LGBT resource center/office ✓

LGBT Pride Week &/or Coming Out Week ✓

Safe Zone/Safe Space or Ally Program ✓

Significant number of LGBT social activities ✓

Significant number of LGBT educational events ✓

Variety of LGBT studies/courses ✓

Nondiscrimination statement inclusive of sexual orientation ✓

Nondiscrimination statement inclusive of gender identity/expression ✓

Extends domestic partner benefits to same-sex couples ✓

Actively recruits LGBT students to enroll on campus

Trains campus police on LGBT sensitivity ✓

Procedure for reporting LGBT bias, harassment & hate crimes ✓

Offers LGBT housing options/themes ✓

Offers LGBT-inclusive health services/testing ✓

Offers LGBT-inclusive counseling/support groups ✓

Offers LGBT student scholarships

Conducts special LGBT graduation ceremony for LGBT & ally Students ✓

Offers support services for process of transitioning from M to F & F to M ✓

Active LGBT alumni group ✓

TUFTS UNIVERSITY
GAY POINT AVERAGE (18)
(out of 20)

CAMPUS QUEER RESOURCES

LGBT Student Organization:

Tufts Transgender, Lesbian, Gay, Bisexual Collective (TTLGBC); the Queer Straight Alliance

Founding Date: 1973

Membership: 170+

Phone: 617-627-3770

E-mail: lgbt@tufts.edu

Website: ase.tufts.edu/ttlgbc/; ase.tufts.edu/QSA/

LGBT Resource Center/Office:

Lesbian, Gay, Bisexual, Transgender Center

Tufts University

Bolles House
226 College Avenue
Medford, MA 02155

Year Established: 1992

Number of Staff: 1 full-time staff professional, 1 part-time staff; 6 student workers

Phone: 617-627-3770

E-mail: lgbt@tufts.edu

Website: ase.tufts.edu/lgbt/

UNIVERSITY OF ARIZONA

THE UNIVERSITY OF Arizona has displayed the utmost perseverance over the years. "Understanding and improving" is how one LGBT student puts it. Another states: "I came to Arizona over other area colleges because I felt more openness, the support of allies and LGBT students. There are many on campus working hard to continue that trend."

The campus has made several LGBT improvements, and the climate is notably LGBT-friendly. Along with a nondiscrimination policy inclusive of both sexual orientation and gender identity/expression, the campus has a commendable Gay Point Average. The main policy area lacking is domestic partner benefits for same-sex employees. A recent study by the Dean of Students Office discovered that general student attitudes on campus are amazingly LGBT-supportive. Plus, 70 percent of all students believe that gays should have the same rights as straight people.

Much of the positive attitude shift on campus is likely due to the increased visibility of LGBT issues. The student-run Pride Alliance, formed in 1991, offers a variety of queer programs and services, ranging from support for students coming out to educational outreach to straight allies. Highlights of programs every year include Safe Zone workshops, Coming Out Week, the Coming Out Ball and Diva La Paz. Last year, hundreds of students attended the popular Diva La Paz celebration and panel. One LGBT student notes: "An outrageous time… educational and entertaining, the best drag show in Arizona."

Other LGBT students mention the importance of LGBT community activists. Without them, the students argue, "nothing would happen." Yet the campus has established a Social Justice Leadership Center to focus specifically on developing future educational programs of particular interest to the LGBT community and other underrepresented populations.

Although the University of Arizona may not be as progressive as neighboring campuses in California, it does represent the most LGBT-friendly campus in the state and one of the best choices in the Southwest. LGBT students do not readily disagree, but they do argue that positive queer change has been slow to come. One LGBT student shares: "More LGBT-friendly, the campus has gradually changed, not because of the upper-level administration but because of the unyielding efforts of the LGBT and ally campus community. More needs to be done, but I don't regret my college choice or the impact I have made here."

OUTSPOKEN *Answers from LGBT students:*

Top Three Descriptors of the LGBT Campus Environment:
1. Supportive   2. Progressive   3. Welcoming

What makes your campus feel welcome and safe for LGBT students?
"From the get-go, a strong presence of LGBT students and allies. … I also met another gay student online before coming to campus. He helped me know where to go, find support, and what there is to do on campus."
—*20-year-old bisexual male, junior*

How do you feel about coming out on your campus?
"Most of my friends, I've told one-on-one and they have been very supportive and interested in what it's like to be lesbian. The campus has come a long way, and it can always improve to be more supportive, like getting an LGBT center."
—*21-year-old lesbian, junior*

LGBT POLITICS
Progressive Meter

Campus Community Level

Local Community Level

State Level

INFO

UNIVERSITY OF ARIZONA
PO Box 210040
Tucson, AZ 85721
Phone: 520-621-3237
Fax: 520-621-9799
E-mail: anseweb@email.arizona.edu
Website: www.arizona.edu

CAMPUS STATS
Type of Institution: Public university
Founding Year: 1885
Size: 31,000
Avg. Class Size: 20–29 students
Popular Majors: Elementary Education and Teaching, Political Science and Government, Psychology
Cost: In-state tuition: $4,498
Out-of-state tuition: $13,682
Admission Application Deadline: December 1

ACADEMIC SCENE

Top Three Supportive LGBT Academic Areas:
1. Social and Behavioral Sciences   2. Science   3. Law

How LGBT-friendly are faculty in the classroom?
"Faculty are normally supportive of LGBT issues. There are several faculty members who are openly gay. I have never met or heard about a homophobic faculty member." —*19-year-old bisexual male, junior*

"In my interactions with faculty, most have been very accepting of my sexual orientation when it came up, which it actually has a lot. …although not all of the professors are very knowledgeable about queer issues, they seem to try." —*20-year-old queer male, junior*

SOCIAL SCENE

Top Three Things in the LGBT Social Life:
1. Dancing   2. Shopping   3. Hanging out

How would you describe the social scene for LGBT students?
"Discreet but out there. I find some LGBT students not to be as involved. We could use more queer social life and educational events to bring everyone together." —*19-year-old gay male, sophomore*

What annual social event should an LGBT student not miss?
"Pride Week or Coming Out Week. There always seems to be a lot going on… more people come out each year." —*20-year-old lesbian, junior*

OUTRAGEOUS FACTOID
LGBT students admit that public displays of affection are not readily encouraged, not even same-sex holding of hands.

• • • • • • • • • • • • • • • • • • •

RAINBOW RUMOR
Several LGBT students agree that it is time for an actual LGBT Resource Center. In answering a question as to what the campus needs, an LGBT student explains: "a complete resource center. There should be an office, service center, and a full-time staff member whose job is primarily to help promote an LGBT-aware and respectful campus."

• • • • • • • • • • • • • • • • • • •

THAT'S SO GAY!

ANNUAL LGBT EVENT HIGHLIGHTS

Safe Zone Workshops: Fall/Spring
Pride Alliance Coming Out Week: October
Coming Out Ball: October
Diva La Paz: October
Tuscon Pride OUToberfest : October
World AIDS Day: December
Pride Alliance PRIDE Week: February
LGBT Ally Recognition Ceremony: Spring

BUZZ BITES
Fun Queer Stuff to Know

THE BEST…

Party Locale: IBT's
Hangout: Eon
Eating Place: Colors
Place to Check Out Guys: Abercrombie & Fitch
Place to Check Out Ladies: The Biz
LGBT-Cool Athletic Sport: Tennis *or* women's basketball
Non-LGBT-Specific Campus Club: Alpha Phi Omega

Place for LGBT Students to Live on Campus: La Paz Hall
LGBT Educational Involvement Opportunity: Safe Zone Program
LGBT-Accepting Religious/Spiritual Organization(s): College Quakers, Water of Life Metropolitan Community Church

**CAMPUS QUEER
RESOURCES**

Select LGBT Student Organization(s):

Pride Alliance
Founding Date: 1991
Membership: 30
Phone: 520-621-7585
E-mail: pride@email.arizona.edu
Website: pride.asua.arizona.edu

• •

THE GAY POINT AVERAGE
OFFICIAL CAMPUS CHECKLIST

✓ LGBT & ally student organization

LGBT resource center/office

✓ LGBT Pride Week &/or Coming Out Week

✓ Safe Zone/Safe Space or Ally Program

✓ Significant number of LGBT social activities

✓ Significant number of LGBT educational events

✓ Variety of LGBT studies/courses

✓ Nondiscrimination statement inclusive of sexual orientation

✓ Nondiscrimination statement inclusive of gender identity/expression

Extends domestic partner benefits to same-sex couples

Actively recruits LGBT students to enroll on campus

✓ Trains campus police on LGBT sensitivity

✓ Procedure for reporting LGBT bias, harassment & hate crimes

Offers LGBT housing options/themes

✓ Offers LGBT-inclusive health services/testing

✓ Offers LGBT-inclusive counseling/support groups

✓ Offers LGBT student scholarships

Conducts special LGBT graduation ceremony for LGBT & ally Students

✓ Offers support services for process of transitioning from M to F & F to M

✓ Active LGBT alumni group

15 UNIVERSITY OF ARIZONA
GAY POINT AVERAGE
(out of 20)

UNIVERSITY OF CALIFORNIA—BERKELEY

CHARACTERIZED BY LGBT students as a "queer gateway," the University of California—Berkeley has long been a champion for LGBT inclusion and progressiveness. Near San Francisco, the campus has been leading the LGBT charge for a number of years and has created a highly progressive, LGBT-friendly campus climate.

The timeline of LGBT progress and accomplishments at UC Berkeley started in 1882 when the controversial Oscar Wilde, a literary master known for his same-sex proclivities, paid a campus visit to the UC Berkeley library, escorted by William Dallam Armes, a young student and disciple of his. The visit was tame for Wilde, but it ignited a firestorm of interest on campus and was not forgotten anytime soon. Visits by other literary greats like Willa Cather, Gertrude Stein and Thornton Wilder followed.

Almost a century later, in 1969, two student organizations were formed: the Students for Gay Power and the Gay Liberation Front. The latter was among the first gay liberation groups in the country organized in major cities. The Gay Liberation Front's goal was to create a safe space on campus where gay people could live openly. They held many protests and demonstrations, advocating for the end of discrimination against homosexuals.

Today the results show on campus. Now named the Queer Resource Center, the student coalition has been pivotal in creating a safe, welcoming campus environment for LGBT students. In 1997, the university created LGBT Programs and Services to support student-run LGBT efforts and offer administrative direction for LGBT campus life. Today, the office, along with about a dozen LGBT-themed student groups, plans numerous lectures, discussions and workshops every year. Annual event highlights include the Cal Rainbow Pride Welcome Orientation, National Coming Out Week, Gender and Sexual Identity Awareness Days and the Lavender Graduation. As one student notes: "We are fortunate to be on a campus where being queer is cool. We have the gift of abundant acceptance."

LGBT POLITICS
Progressive Meter

Campus Community Level

Local Community Level

State Level

OUTSPOKEN *Answers from LGBT students:*

Top Three Descriptors of the LGBT Campus Environment:
1. Diverse   2. Safe   3. Supportive

What makes your campus feel welcoming and safe for LGBT students?
"The whole campus is gay. Seriously, there is such an understanding of difference that nobody is the same. Queers naturally seem to just be there and fit in." —*22-year-old queer dyke, senior*

How do you feel about coming out on your campus?
"Berkeley rocks for being out and proud! Take it slow: you're away from the parents now, but that does not mean start partying, fucking and doing everything you were ever told not to. … Also, keep a close network of support, This is a big growing stage for all of us and doing it together is easier than going [it] alone." —*21-year-old gay male, junior*

INFO

UNIVERSITY OF CALIFORNIA—BERKELEY
110 Sproul Hall, Room 5800
Berkeley, CA 94720
Phone: 510-642-3175
Fax: 510-642-7333
E-mail: ouars@uclink.berkeley.edu
Website: www.berkeley.edu

CAMPUS STATS
Type of Institution: Public university
Founding Year: 1868
Size: 22,880
Avg. Class Size: 20–29 students
Popular Majors: Computer Engineering, English Language and Literature, Political Science and Government
Cost: In-state tuition: $6,730
Out-of-state tuition: $24,332
Admission Application Deadline: November 30

A graduate of UC Berkeley, Mark Bingham died on board United Airlines flight 93 in the September 11, 2001, attacks on the United States. Mark is believed to have been among the passengers who stormed the cockpit to prevent hijackers from using the plane to kill hundreds or thousands of additional victims. As an LGBT student at UC Berkeley, Mark had been president of his fraternity, Chi Psi, and was a leading champion on the college rugby team. After college, he continued playing for the local gay rugby team, the San Francisco Fog. In his honor, the International Gay Rugby Association named its biannual international rugby competition the Bingham Cup. A portion of the proceeds from every competition is donated to a campus leadership fund. The UC Berkeley graduate was also honored as *The Advocate*'s 2001 Person of the Year.

• • • • • • • • • • • • • • • • • •

RAINBOW RUMOR

UC Berkeley is by far one of the most queer-progressive of campuses; however, LGBT campus community members will say that they are only on a "steady path to understanding" with regard to trans students needs and services. Although the trans commitment has never been stronger, one member of the LGBT community states: "The welcome sign is there…but not quite polished and ready to be hung up."

• • • • • • • • • • • • • • • • • •

THAT'S SO GAY!

ANNUAL LGBT EVENT HIGHLIGHTS

LGBT Socials/Dances: Fall/Spring

Cal Rainbow Pride Welcome Orientation: September

National Coming Out Day/Week: October

Transgender/Intersex Awareness Week: November

World AIDS Day: December

Vagina Monologues: February

Queer Awareness Week: April

Gender and Sexual Identity Awareness Days: April

Lavender Graduation: May

"I talk openly about my queerness without worrying, no matter who, what, when, where and why it's in conversation. It's a natural part of me, like talking about eating, sleeping, and work."
—*20-year-old bisexual male, junior*

ACADEMIC SCENE

Top Three Supportive LGBT Academic Areas:
1. Social Welfare 2. Anthropology
3. Theater, Dance and Performance Studies

How LGBT-friendly are faculty in the classroom?
"Extremely open. There are many out and proud faculty too."
—*19-year-old bisexual female, sophomore*

"In my classes, I have come out. It is seen as a bonus to many of my profs that I am willing to talk openly and share my experience in the class discussion. I also have done several papers on faith and sexuality. Never has it hurt or been negative." —*22-year-old gay male, senior*

SOCIAL SCENE

Top Three Things in the LGBT Social Life:
1. Bars 2. Dancing 3. Coffee House

How would you describe the social scene for LGBT students?
"Well, it's Berkeley. I should not have to say more than that. But, it's better than your wildest queer dreams." —*21-year-old queer gay male, junior*

What annual social event should an LGBT student not miss?
"Queer Awareness Week… it's queer, baby!" —*20-year-old lesbian, junior*

BUZZ BITES *Fun Queer Stuff to Know*

THE BEST…

Party Locale: White Horse

Hangout: Sproul Hall

Eating Place: Bear's Lair

LGBT-Cool Athletic Sport: Intramural soccer and volleyball

Place for LGBT Students to Live on Campus: White House

LGBT Course Offering: Queer Visual and Literary Studies

LGBT Educational Involvement Opportunity: Queer Resource Center

LGBT-Accepting Religious/Spiritual Organization(s): Twice Blessed Jewish Group, BLG Catholics

THE GAY POINT AVERAGE
OFFICIAL CAMPUS CHECKLIST

LGBT & ally student organization ✓

LGBT resource center/office ✓

LGBT Pride Week &/or Coming Out Week ✓

Safe Zone/Safe Space or Ally Program ✓

Significant number of LGBT social activities ✓

Significant number of LGBT educational events ✓

Variety of LGBT studies/courses ✓

Nondiscrimination statement inclusive of sexual orientation ✓

Nondiscrimination statement inclusive of gender identity/expression ✓

Extends domestic partner benefits to same-sex couples ✓

Actively recruits LGBT students to enroll on campus

Trains campus police on LGBT sensitivity ✓

Procedure for reporting LGBT bias, harassment & hate crimes ✓

Offers LGBT housing options/themes ✓

Offers LGBT-inclusive health services/testing ✓

Offers LGBT-inclusive counseling/support groups ✓

Offers LGBT student scholarships ✓

Conducts special LGBT graduation ceremony for LGBT & ally Students ✓

Offers support services for process of transitioning from M to F & F to M ✓

Active LGBT alumni group ✓

CAMPUS QUEER RESOURCES

Select LGBT Student Organization(s):
Queer Resource Center
Founding Date: 1969 (as Gay Liberation Front)
Membership: 100+
Website: queer.berkeley.edu

LGBT Resource Center/Office:
LGBT Programs and Services
Gender Equity Resource Center, MC#2440
University of California—Berkeley
Berkeley, CA 94720-2440
Year Established: 1997
Number of Staff: 2 full-time professional staff
Phone: 510-642-4786
E-mail: lgbt@berkeley.edu
Website: geneq.berkeley.edu

UNIVERSITY OF CALIFORNIA— BERKELEY GAY POINT AVERAGE
(out of 20)
19

UNIVERSITY OF CALIFORNIA—DAVIS

UNIVERSITY OF CALIFORNIA—DAVIS sits in the heart of the Central Valley, close to the state capital and San Francisco Bay Area. The campus works hard to address all issues of oppression and to ensure that LGBT students feel welcome.

UC Davis is quite well known for the "Davis Is Burning" drag show, just one of the many LGBT activities available to queer students. In addition to the annual Pride Week, the campus features an annual Trans Action Week for transgender education and awareness, as well as an Intersex Awareness Week. UC Davis claims to be the first university in the country to host a full week of programs focused on issues that affect people with intersex conditions. Through the LGBT Resource Center, the campus also offers ongoing Safe Zone trainings and a Peer Educator Program to train students to present LGBT programs, particularly in residence halls.

If you glance at the Gay Point Average, you will find a comprehensive approach to LGBT issues that reflects a strong institutional commitment from policy to practice. A new LGBT student agrees: "I could tell from the moment I met other LGBT students on campus that UC Davis was the right choice. The campus is supportive and welcoming. I love it here!"

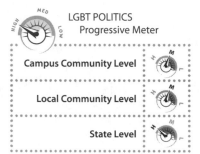

LGBT POLITICS
Progressive Meter

Campus Community Level

Local Community Level

State Level

INFO

UNIVERSITY OF CALIFORNIA—DAVIS
178 Mrak Hall
1 Shields Avenue
Davis, CA 95616
Phone: 530-752-2971
Fax: 530-752-1280
E-mail: freshmanadmissions@ucdavis.edu
Website: www.ucdavis.edu

CAMPUS STATS
Type of Institution: Public university
Founding Year: 1905
Size: 22,735
Avg. Class Size: 20–29 students
Popular Majors: Social Sciences and History, Biological/Life Sciences, Agriculture, Engineering
Cost: In-state tuition: $5,853
Out-of-state tuition: $24,777
Admission Application Deadline: November 30

OUTSPOKEN *Answers from LGBT students:*

Top Three Descriptors of the LGBT Campus Environment:
1. Curious   2. Diverse   3. Apathetic

What makes your campus feel welcoming and safe for LGBT students?
"There are an increasing number of student organizations and support groups that cater to the diverse LGBT community at UC Davis. These organizations continue to empower and educate both the LGBT and non-LGBT community. UC Davis is increasingly becoming a Safe Zone for LGBT students."
—*21-year-old gay male, senior*

How do you feel about coming out on your campus?
"In general, I feel like the campus is pretty safe. I have heard in other places people who are genderqueer get glared at; here it seems more like a curiosity. Nowhere is completely safe; there will always be people who are ignorant. The LGBT Resource Center puts on programs like Pride Week to help people learn and accept or at least tolerate." —*22-year-old genderqueer, junior*

ACADEMIC SCENE

Top Three Supportive LGBT Academic Areas:
1. Women and Gender Studies   2. English   3. Theater and Dance

How LGBT-friendly are faculty in the classroom?
"From my experiences the liberal arts classes are more queer-friendly, and the professors strive to incorporate queer writers into their courses. We have strong

Asian American Studies and Women and Gender Studies departments. We also just launched a Queer Studies minor, which will become more and more successful as time goes on."—*21-year-old gay male, senior*

"I have actually had some queer faculty. I haven't had to deal with a professor who is homophobic. However, male professors often take into consideration what males say more than females, especially in my science classes." —*21-year-old queer female, senior*

🙂 SOCIAL SCENE

Top Three Things in the LGBT Social Life:
1. Pride Week   2. Davis Is Burning Drag Show   3. Off-campus parties

How would you describe the social scene for LGBT students?
"The LGBT social scene definitely depends on the student organizations and the students themselves, because the city itself does not provide social spaces for the LGBT community." —*21-year-old gay male, senior*

What annual social event should an LGBT student not miss?
"Davis Is Burning, because it rocks!" —*20-year-old gay male, junior*

 OUTRAGEOUS FACTOID One of the hottest social events on this campus involves "flaming queens"! It's the annual "Davis Is Burning" Drag Show, hosted by the gay, bisexual and allied men's fraternity Delta Lambda Phi.

 RAINBOW RUMOR Close to Sacramento, the capital of California, UC Davis can be a hotbed of political frenzy in election years when LGBT issues get on the ballot. But, sadly, according to some students, the apathetic nature of the campus is "stifling" at other times. One student replies: "LGBT students would rather surf the Web or be hooked into PlayStation!"

 THAT'S SO GAY! **ANNUAL LGBT EVENT HIGHLIGHTS**

Rainbow Festival: September
"Davis Is Burning" Drag Show: October
Pride Week: October
Trans Action Week: November
Intersex Awareness Week: Spring
Lavender Graduation: June

BUZZ BITES *Fun Queer Stuff to Know*

THE BEST...

Party Locale: Club 21 *and* Faces
Hangout: LGBT Resource Center
Eating Place: Delta of Venus
Place to Check Out Guys: Recreation Center
Place to Check Out Ladies: Women's Center
LGBT-Cool Athletic Sport: Rugby *and* lacrosse
Non-LGBT-Specific Campus Club: Men Acting Against Rape

Place for LGBT Students to Live on Campus: Rainbow House
LGBT Course Offering: Introduction to Queer Studies
LGBT-Accepting Religious/Spiritual Organization(s): Cal Aggie Christian Association

THE GAY POINT AVERAGE
OFFICIAL CAMPUS CHECKLIST

CAMPUS QUEER RESOURCES

Select LGBT Student Organization(s):

Asian Pacific Islander Queers (APIQ); La Familia

Founding Date: 2002

Membership: 40+

E-mail: apiq@ucdavis.edu; familiajunta@ucdavis.edu

Website: www.ucdapiq.com/

LGBT Resource Center/Office:

Lesbian, Gay, Bisexual, Transgender Resource Center
University House Annex
1 Shields Avenue
Davis, CA 95616

Year Established: 1995

Number of Staff: 2 full-time staff professionals; 2 undergraduate student workers

Phone: 530-752-2452

E-mail: lgbtresourcecenter@ucdavis.edu

Website: lgbtcenter.ucdavis.edu/

- ✓ LGBT & ally student organization
- ✓ LGBT resource center/office
- ✓ LGBT Pride Week &/or Coming Out Week
- ✓ Safe Zone/Safe Space or Ally Program
- ✓ Significant number of LGBT social activities
- ✓ Significant number of LGBT educational events
- ✓ Variety of LGBT studies/courses
- ✓ Nondiscrimination statement inclusive of sexual orientation
- ✓ Nondiscrimination statement inclusive of gender identity/expression
- ✓ Extends domestic partner benefits to same-sex couples
- Actively recruits LGBT students to enroll on campus
- Trains campus police on LGBT sensitivity
- ✓ Procedure for reporting LGBT bias, harassment & hate crimes
- ✓ Offers LGBT housing options/themes
- ✓ Offers LGBT-inclusive health services/testing
- ✓ Offers LGBT-inclusive counseling/support groups
- Offers LGBT student scholarships
- ✓ Conducts special LGBT graduation ceremony for LGBT & ally Students
- ✓ Offers support services for process of transitioning from M to F & F to M
- ✓ Active LGBT alumni group

17 UNIVERSITY OF CALIFORNIA— DAVIS GAY POINT AVERAGE
(out of 20)

UNIVERSITY OF CALIFORNIA— LOS ANGELES

LOCATED ABOUT 10 minutes from West Hollywood, UCLA has one of the most LGBT-progressive campus climates in the country and provides a diverse array of queer life.

In the 1950s, the campus made important historic contributions to the LGBT movement. It first began with UCLA faculty member and research psychologist Evelyn Hooker, who studied homosexuality and published the first empirical research on the issue. Her groundbreaking work ultimately led to the declassification of homosexuality as a mental disorder and fostered a spirit of queer conviction that has been alive on campus ever since. Two decades later, shortly after the Stonewall Riots in New York City, a dozen students on campus started the first queer student organization, the Gay Student Union, in 1971. The new student coalition hosted the first-ever Gay Awareness Week 3 years later.

The Gay Student Union is now called the Queer Alliance. Thirty years later, it has been joined by over a dozen other LGBT-themed campus organizations. The LGBT Center was founded in 1995. Together, the queer campus entities plan numerous educational and social activities, including dances, films, brown bag lunch discussions, awareness weeks and more. Recently, the LGBT Center expanded its services: along with educational outreach and advocacy, it now offers a library with 3,000 titles and a cyber-center for queer students. There is even an undergraduate minor in Lesbian, Gay, Bisexual and Transgender Studies. In neighboring West Hollywood, there are literally hundreds of LGBT-owned and LGBT-friendly social and entertainment establishments.

UCLA is a frontrunner in California and across the country for the friendliest progressive LGBT campus. But what really matters is what the queer students have to say: "I am constantly impressed. … It's hard to know what's gay and what's not. UCLA offers a safe place to be queer and to learn…That's what it's all about!"

OUTSPOKEN *Answers from LGBT students:*

Top Three Descriptors of the LGBT Campus Environment:
1. Diverse   2. Supportive   3. Passionate

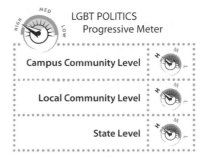

LGBT POLITICS
Progressive Meter

Campus Community Level

Local Community Level

State Level

INFO

UNIVERSITY OF CALIFORNIA— LOS ANGELES
1147 Murphy Hall
PO Box 951436
Los Angeles, CA 90095
Phone: 310-825-3101
Fax: 310-206-1206
E-mail: ugadm@saonet.ucla.edu
Website: www.ucla.edu

CAMPUS STATS
Type of Institution: Public university
Founding Year: 1919
Size: 25,715
Avg. Class Size: 20–29 students
Popular Majors: Economics, Political Science and Government, Psychology
Cost: In-state tuition: $6,504
Out-of-state tuition: $17,304
Admission Application Deadline: November 30

- - - - - - - - - - - - - - - - - - - -

- - - - - - - - - - - - - - - - - - - -

What makes your campus feel welcoming and safe for LGBT students?
"The many LGBT programs held throughout the year and the LGBT Center. There is always something queer going on." —*20-year-old gay male, junior*

How do you feel about coming out on your campus?
"Queer voices are everywhere. I was out when I got to campus, and so was everyone else, practically. I do know a couple friends who came out for the first time at UCLA. They also felt acceptance and pride to do so."
—*21-year-old lesbian, junior*

ACADEMIC SCENE

Top Three Supportive LGBT Academic Areas:
1. Women's Studies   2. Chicano/Chicana Studies   3. Music

How LGBT-friendly are faculty in the classroom?
"Not a problem at all. I am open about my sexuality. Faculty usually want to know more most of the time. A few faculty have made hetero assumptions in class, but I call them on it. … It all works out." —*22-year-old queer dyke, senior*

"Astounding acceptance. There are many out queers on faculty, too. … and some of the best allies you will ever find." —*20-year-old gay male, sophomore*

SOCIAL SCENE

Top Three Things in the LGBT Social Life:
1. Los Angeles clubs   2. Dancing   3. Queer films

How would you describe the social scene for LGBT students?
"Diverse. I can go anywhere anytime and bump into queers of all walks of life. It's wonderful…the campus is so engrained within the larger Los Angeles queer community." —*19-year-old gay male, sophomore*

What annual social event should an LGBT student not miss?
"Voices of Heroes. There is such a diversity of queer topics as part of the series and usually awesome speakers." —*20-year-old queer male, junior*

BUZZ BITES *Fun Queer Stuff to Know*

THE BEST…

Party Locale: The Abbey or Rage

Hangout: Queer Student Center

Place to Check Out Guys: Student Activities Center Pool

Place to Check Out Ladies: Library

LGBT-Cool Athletic Sport: Cheer Squad

Non-LGBT-Specific Campus Club: Feminist Majority Leaders Association

Place for LGBT Students to Live on Campus: Saxon Hall

LGBT Course Offering: Queer Hollywood

LGBT Educational Involvement Opportunity: Transgender Day of Remembrance

LGBT-Accepting Religious/Spiritual Organization(s): Jewish Center, University Catholic Center

THE GAY POINT AVERAGE
OFFICIAL CAMPUS CHECKLIST

LGBT & ally student organization ✓

LGBT resource center/office ✓

LGBT Pride Week &/or Coming Out Week ✓

Safe Zone/Safe Space or Ally Program ✓

Significant number of LGBT social activities ✓

Significant number of LGBT educational events ✓

Variety of LGBT studies/courses ✓

Nondiscrimination statement inclusive of sexual orientation ✓

Nondiscrimination statement inclusive of gender identity/expression ✓

Extends domestic partner benefits to same-sex couples ✓

Actively recruits LGBT students to enroll on campus ✓

Trains campus police on LGBT sensitivity ✓

Procedure for reporting LGBT bias, harassment & hate crimes ✓

Offers LGBT housing options/themes

Offers LGBT-inclusive health services/testing ✓

Offers LGBT-inclusive counseling/support groups ✓

Offers LGBT student scholarships ✓

Conducts special LGBT graduation ceremony for LGBT & ally Students ✓

Offers support services for process of transitioning from M to F & F to M ✓

Active LGBT alumni group ✓

UNIVERSITY OF CALIFORNIA— LOS ANGELES GAY POINT AVERAGE
(out of 20)

19

CAMPUS QUEER RESOURCES

Select LGBT Student Organizations:

Queer Alliance
Founding Date: 1971 (as the Gay Student Union)
Membership: 90+
E-mail: qa@yahoo.com

LGBT Resource Center/Office:

UCLA LGBT Center
220 Westwood Plaza, Suite B36
Los Angeles, CA 90095
Year Established: 1995
Number of Staff: 2 full-time professional staff; 2 graduate student interns; 4 student employees
Phone: 310-206-3628
E-mail: lgbt@ucla.edu
Website: www.lgbt.ucla.edu

UNIVERSITY OF CALIFORNIA—RIVERSIDE

PROGRESS AND LGBT visibility run high at the University of California—Riverside, located in Southern California. LGBT students note that the climate is "welcoming." One student notes: "I've come out to more people in four weeks at UCR than in four years in high school."

The state of California has been known for leading the nation when it comes to social justice issues. UC Riverside also has been relentless in LGBT advocacy efforts. In 1983, the campus added sexual orientation to the nondiscrimination statement and in 1998 added domestic partner benefits, including health care, for partners of same-sex employees. As recent as 2004, the campus also included gender identity/expression in its nondiscrimination policy—as would be expected of a campus in California.

But now consider these facts. UC Riverside was the first California campus to open a staffed LGBT resource center (1993), the first California campus to establish an LGBT Studies minor (1996), and the first public campus in the nation to offer gender-neutral housing to all students. Such a queer timeline of progress can also be supported by the campus's high Gay Point Average. Further queer improvements will happen in 2008, when the LGBT Resource Center moves into a new, larger locale with enough room for a library and a program for peer mentoring.

There is a wide range of LGBT groups on campus, such as the Queer Alliance, Grrrl Talk, Guy Talk, Fluidity, Leather Life, Bi Talk and Queer Asian Discussion. The LGBT Resource Center works with various student groups to promote and organize campuswide events such as Pride Week. One of the absolute favorites all year is the Dragalicious Drag Ball. LGBT students remark that it's a combination of "fashion, sass and trash."

UC Riverside might be just the LGBT climate you're looking for. The forecast is true! LGBT progress has been happening quite queerly at UC Riverside. The campus has a lot to offer that is LGBT-friendly. One LGBT student agrees: "There are tons of LGBT resources…and allies are visible everywhere. I feel safe and have found the support I needed."

LGBT POLITICS
Progressive Meter

Campus Community Level

Local Community Level

State Level

INFO

UNIVERSITY OF CALIFORNIA—RIVERSIDE
1120 Hinderaker Hall
Riverside, CA 92521
Phone: 951-827-3411
Fax: 951-827-6344
E-mail: discover@ucr.edu
Website: www.ucr.edu

CAMPUS STATS

Type of Institution: Public university
Founding Year: 1954
Size: 15,282
Avg. Class Size: 20–29 students
Popular Majors: Biology/Biological Sciences, Business Administration/ Management, Social Sciences
Cost: In-state tuition: $6,684
Out-of-state tuition: $23,640
Admission Application Deadline: November 30

OUTSPOKEN *Answers from LGBT students:*

Top Three Descriptors of the LGBT Campus Environment:
1. Friendly   2. Supportive   3. Safe

What makes your campus feel welcoming and safe for LGBT students?
"A large number of LGBT friends and the fact that there are queer resources."
—20-year-old queer female, junior

"The LGBT Resource Center has a number of queer events to choose from. … campus is visibly LGBT-friendly." *—19-year-old gay male, sophomore*

How do you feel about coming out on your campus?
"Thanks to the work of the LGBT Resource Center, the campus is a welcoming safe space. I feel more than comfortable being out."
—23-year-old queer male, senior

ACADEMIC SCENE

Top Three Supportive LGBT Academic Areas:
1. English   2. Women's Studies   3. Dance

How LGBT-friendly are faculty in the classroom?
"You can actively dialogue about queer issues in classes. I do all the time. Faculty seem receptive, open-minded, and many of mine have taken a genuine interest in my queer identity." —*21-year-old queer lesbian, junior*

"Professors welcome queer views in all kinds of classes, not just LGBT studies courses." —*19-year-old gay male, senior*

SOCIAL SCENE

Top Three Things in the LGBT Social Life:
1. Parties   2. Dressing in drag   3. Hanging out at the LGBT Center

How would you describe the social scene for LGBT students?
"Not a lot happening in Riverside; we have to leave town to find a social scene." —*23-year-old gay male, graduate student*

What annual social event should an LGBT student not miss?
"Dragalicious Drag Ball." —*20-year-old queer female, junior*

Fun Queer Stuff to Know

THE BEST...

Hangout: Back to the Grind Coffee House
LGBT-Cool Athletic Sport: Soccer or softball
Non-LGBT-Specific Campus Club: Katipunan Filipino/a American Student Group
Place for LGBT Students to Live On Campus: Stonewall Hall
LGBT Educational Involvement Opportunity: Allies Safe Zone Program

LGBT-Accepting Religious/Spiritual Organization(s): Hillel

OUTRAGEOUS FACTOID In 2001, an anonymous queer transformed the huge yellow concrete "C" on the top of the mountain overlooking campus to a big pink "Q." It's not the first time the "C" has been changed: a "C+" before finals and "C–" after finals. But this time, it was a queer signal not to be missed!

RAINBOW RUMOR Although there are institutional policies, educational events and resources to support transgender students, UC Riverside LGBT officials admit that there are few "out" trans students. One LGBT student agrees: "Transgender visibility is low as far as trans people being 'out.'" Trans issues are considered to be a work in progress.

THAT'S SO GAY!

ANNUAL LGBT EVENT HIGHLIGHTS

Q-Camp: October

LGBT Resource Center Open House: October

National Coming Out Day: October 11

LGBT History Month: October

Intersex Awareness Day: October

Transgender Day of Remembrance Display: November

World AIDS Day: December

LGBT Winter Student Retreat: January

Allies Brown-Bag Lunch Series: January/February

Pride Week: April

Dragalicious Drag Ball: April

National Day of Silence: April

Pride Prom: May

Lambda Celebration: June

CAMPUS QUEER RESOURCES

Select LGBT Student Organizations:

Queer Alliance
Founding Date: Before 1991 (as the Union of Lesbians, Gays, Bisexuals)
Membership: 40+
Phone: 951-827-2267

LGBT Resource Center/Office:

LGBT Resource Center
250 Costo Hall
Riverside, CA 92521
Year Established: 1993
Number of Staff: 3 full-time professional staff
Phone: 951-827-2267
E-mail: out@ucr.edu
Website: www.out.ucr.edu

THE GAY POINT AVERAGE
OFFICIAL CAMPUS CHECKLIST

✓ LGBT & ally student organization

✓ LGBT resource center/office

✓ LGBT Pride Week &/or Coming Out Week

✓ Safe Zone/Safe Space or Ally Program

Significant number of LGBT social activities

✓ Significant number of LGBT educational events

✓ Variety of LGBT studies/courses

✓ Nondiscrimination statement inclusive of sexual orientation

✓ Nondiscrimination statement inclusive of gender identity/expression

✓ Extends domestic partner benefits to same-sex couples

✓ Actively recruits LGBT students to enroll on campus

✓ Trains campus police on LGBT sensitivity

✓ Procedure for reporting LGBT bias, harassment & hate crimes

✓ Offers LGBT housing options/themes

✓ Offers LGBT-inclusive health services/testing

✓ Offers LGBT-inclusive counseling/support groups

✓ Offers LGBT student scholarships

✓ Conducts special LGBT graduation ceremony for LGBT & ally Students

Offers support services for process of transitioning from M to F & F to M

Active LGBT alumni group

17 UNIVERSITY OF CALIFORNIA—
RIVERSIDE GAY POINT AVERAGE
(out of 20)

UNIVERSITY OF CALIFORNIA—SAN DIEGO

"OUT LOUD AND outrageous" is how one LGBT student describes the queer scene at the University of California—San Diego. The campus offers an innovative, fresh approach when it comes to the curriculum, as well as its commitment to LGBT issues.

Nestled along the Pacific Ocean, UC San Diego has a history of ultimately getting what queers want. Since the early 1990s, concerned staff, faculty and student activists sought to establish institutional support for the LGBT campus community and its issues. The Chancellor's Advisory Committee on LGBT Issues specifically recommended a staffed resource center in a 1992 LGBT campus climate report and again in 1995 and 1997. Persistence and patience paid off! Finally, in March 1999, the chancellor appointed a steering committee to establish an LGBT Resource Center and allocated a set of rooms and budget for operations and staff.

The LGBT Resource Center provides that "out loud" visible presence on campus and enhances the sense of LGBT community. Students are encouraged to subscribe to the center's Rainbow Newsletter and get involved with the array of LGBT student groups. There are literally over a dozen social, peer support and educational LGBT student coalitions from which to choose—including Queer by Nature, for those who like to explore the wilderness, and an educational group called Queer People of Color, for LGBT students of color. Annual LGBT events include the Out and Proud Week, the Queer Kiss-In and 6 LGBT-themed dances.

UC San Diego built and moved into a brand-new LGBT Resource Center in 2006. The stand-alone building more than doubles the past square footage and features a large conference room, small group meeting room, common room, library and a wireless cyber-center funded through the David Bohnett Foundation. Large screens of queer art are featured in the floor-to-ceiling windows for all passers-by to see.

The new LGBT Resource Center is quite the queer gem and demonstrates the LGBT commitment from policy to practice. A look at UC San Diego's Gay Point Average illustrates this point further. An LGBT student responds: "You never question that UCSD is a welcoming place for LGBT issues. The resource center ensures this. …A number of queer groups also create an acceptance and lively atmosphere for queers of all kinds, beliefs."

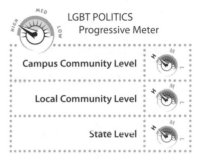

LGBT POLITICS
Progressive Meter

Campus Community Level

Local Community Level

State Level

OUTSPOKEN *Answers from LGBT students:*

Top Three Descriptors of the LGBT Campus Environment:
1. Vibrant   2. Networking   3. Active

What makes your campus feel welcoming and safe for LGBT students?
"The LGBT resource center is the heart of everything queer; it is the home everyone should have somewhere on a campus. A large part of the staff…all over campus is out…or supportive of the community. There are more people than you might expect who are accepting of being out, or allies."
—24-year-old questioning male, senior

INFO

UNIVERSITY OF CALIFORNIA—SAN DIEGO
9500 Gilman Drive, 0021
301 University Center
La Jolla, CA 92093
Phone: 858-534-4831
Fax: 858-534-5723
E-mail: admissionsinfo@ucsd.edu
Website: www.ucsd.edu

CAMPUS STATS
Type of Institution: Public university
Founding Year: 1959
Size: 20,339
Avg. Class Size: 20–29 students
Popular Majors: Social Sciences and History, Biological/Life Sciences, Engineering/Engineering Technologies, Psychology
Cost: In-state tuition: $6,020
Out-of-state tuition: $18,109
Admission Application Deadline: November 30

"Incredible." That's how one LGBT student describes the queer dances held 6 times a year. Each dance attracts 600 to 1,000 out LGBT students and allies from all over San Diego.

Queer housing options do not exist currently at UC San Diego. Because only first- and second-year students are guaranteed on-campus housing, there is definitely a queer impact. One LGBT student cites that it can be the "luck of the draw" as to whom an out LGBT student gets assigned as a roommate.

ANNUAL LGBT EVENT HIGHLIGHTS

Q Camp: September

LGBT Dances: Six times during Fall and Spring

National Coming Out Day: October 11

LGBT Alumni Breakfast: October

LGBT Resource Center Anniversary Celebration: November

World AIDS Day: December 1

Queer Kiss-In: February 14

UCLGBTIA Conference: February

Out and Proud Week: April/May

Rainbow Graduation: June

How do you feel about coming out on your campus?
"Well, I came out to my parents this year, and it was a very smooth process, thanks to the help of the community here." —*21-year-old gay male, junior*

 **ACADEMIC SCENE**

Top Three Supportive LGBT Academic Areas:
1. Critical Gender Studies 2. Sociology 3. Theater

How LGBT-friendly are faculty in the classroom?
"Faculty are amazingly friendly to LGBT students, and a number of the classes I have taken have included queer segments. One of my classes last year had an optional reading segment. … Among the books in the list was one on gay men in China.…It is rather impressive that this was part of the curriculum, optional or not. In fact, queer faculty themselves are relatively well accepted, making it easier for queer ideas to come up in a classroom setting."
—*21-year-old gay male, senior*

"All of the faculty are very concerned with the students' welfare."
—*21-year-old gay male, junior*

SOCIAL SCENE

Top Three Things in the LGBT Social Life:
1. Clubbing 2. Hanging out 3. Dancing

How would you describe the social scene for LGBT students?
"We have dances, [and] there is Hillcrest (read 'the Castro of San Diego'), so there is always something for LGBT students to do here." —*21-year-old gay male, junior*

What annual social event should an LGBT student not miss?
"Q Camp and the Drag Show are the two biggest, most amazing events on campus, but there are more." —*21-year-old gay male, senior*

BUZZ BITES *Fun Queer Stuff to Know*

THE BEST…

Party Locale: Hillcrest

Place to Check Out Guys: LGBT dances

Place to Check Out Ladies: Recreational practice

LGBT-Cool Athletic Sport: Swimming *and* women's rugby

Place for LGBT Students to Live on Campus: Eleanor Roosevelt College

LGBT Educational Involvement Opportunity: "Guess Who's LGBT" Speakers Bureau

THE GAY POINT AVERAGE
OFFICIAL CAMPUS CHECKLIST

LGBT & ally student organization ✓

LGBT resource center/office ✓

LGBT Pride Week &/or Coming Out Week ✓

Safe Zone/Safe Space or Ally Program ✓

Significant number of LGBT social activities ✓

Significant number of LGBT educational events ✓

Variety of LGBT studies/courses

Nondiscrimination statement inclusive of sexual orientation ✓

Nondiscrimination statement inclusive of gender identity/expression ✓

Extends domestic partner benefits to same-sex couples ✓

Actively recruits LGBT students to enroll on campus

Trains campus police on LGBT sensitivity ✓

Procedure for reporting LGBT bias, harassment & hate crimes ✓

Offers LGBT housing options/themes

Offers LGBT-inclusive health services/testing

Offers LGBT-inclusive counseling/support groups ✓

Offers LGBT student scholarships ✓

Conducts special LGBT graduation ceremony for LGBT & ally Students ✓

Offers support services for process of transitioning from M to F & F to M

Active LGBT alumni group ✓

UNIVERSITY OF CALIFORNIA—
SAN DIEGO GAY POINT AVERAGE (15)
(out of 20)

CAMPUS QUEER RESOURCES

Select LGBT Student Organization(s):

Lesbian, Gay, Bisexual, Transgender Queer Intersex Association

Founding Date: November 17, 1977
(as the Gay Student Union)

Membership: 160+

Phone: 858-534-GAYS (4297)

E-mail: lgbtqia@ucsd.edu

Website: acs.ucsd.edu/~lgbtqia/

LGBT Resource Center/Office:

Lesbian Gay Bisexual Transgender Resource Center

University of California—San Diego
9500 Gilman Drive, 0023
La Jolla, CA 92093-0023

Year Established: 1999

Number of Staff: 3 full-time professional staff;
1 graduate assistant, 8 student workers

Phone: 858-822-3493

E-mail: rainbow@ucsd.edu

Website: lgbt.ucsd.edu

UNIVERSITY OF CALIFORNIA— SANTA CRUZ

WANT TO KNOW about the LGBT history at the University of California—Santa Cruz? Buy the book! Yep, that's right—this most progressive campus even has its own LGBT publication, titled *Out in the Redwoods: Documenting Gay, Lesbian, Bisexual, Transgender History at the University of California, Santa Cruz, 1965–2003.* Plus, the campus has an out lesbian chancellor.

Founded in 1965, the relatively young campus had LGBT visibility practically from the beginning. The campus and local community of Santa Cruz have long been known as a "lesbian mecca," situated among the Redwood Forest on a hilltop in central California. The LGBT Resource Center was created in 1990 and renamed the Lionel Cantú GLBT Intersex Resource Center in 2004. The namesake was a tribute to a young gay professor of sociology who embodied the spirit of LGBT inclusiveness on campus and the essence of the center as a multicultural community space, where people of diverse cultures, classes, sexual orientations, gender expressions, ages and abilities come together.

The center, along with several LGBT student groups, actively engages the campus community throughout the year with activities like the National Coming Out Day Dance, Intersex Awareness Day, LGBT Health Awareness Week, Queer Fashion Show and the Oakes Drag Ball, to name a few. Not only are there plenty of queer events, but there is also a lively LGBT-identified student body.

If you're an LGBT student who prefers scenic hiking trails to an urban scene with concrete sidewalks, UC Santa Cruz deserves to be at the top of your list of queer college choices. One LGBT student agrees: "There cannot be a better place… welcoming, safe and full of queer life."

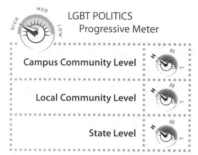

LGBT POLITICS
Progressive Meter

Campus Community Level

Local Community Level

State Level

INFO

UNIVERSITY OF CALIFORNIA—SANTA CRUZ
Cook House
1156 High Street
Santa Cruz, CA 95064
Phone: 831-459-4008
Fax: 831-459-4452
E-mail: admissions@ucsc.edu
Website: www.ucsc.edu

CAMPUS STATS

Type of Institution: Public university
Founding Year: 1965
Size: 13,647
Avg. Class Size: 20–29 students
Popular Majors: Biology/Biological Sciences, English Language and Literature, Psychology
Cost: In-state tuition: $7,603
Out-of-state tuition: $17,304
Admission Application Deadline: November 30

OUTSPOKEN *Answers from LGBT students:*

Top Three Descriptors of the LGBT Campus Environment:
1. Chill   2. Fluid   3. Supportive

What makes your campus feel welcoming and safe for LGBT students?
"I've never been in a place till now where I can free be the way that I am, discuss anything that is queer-related with ease to anyone that I speak with and table in the Quarry Plaza about queer events without receiving any kind of negative responses [from] my fellow students." —*20-year-old gay male, junior*

"I believe that 13 percent of the student body on campus is queer-identified. One study showed that number to be twice that of any other UC campus. Also, the current chancellor, Denice D. Denton, is an open lesbian woman." —*28-year-old queer female, graduate student*

How do you feel about coming out on your campus?
"Coming out has never been an issue for me. We have a widely publicized Coming Out Day, and the staff and students are incredibly supportive."
—*21-year-old queer male, junior*

ACADEMIC SCENE

Top Three Supportive LGBT Academic Areas:
1. Community Studies   2. Feminist Studies   3. Theater Arts

How LGBT-friendly are faculty in the classroom?
"I've taken several courses on queer issues—New Queer Cinema, Lesbian Gay Queer Film and Video, Sexuality and Culture and Queer Theory. Teachers in other courses have been supportive as well."
—*28-year-old queer female, graduate student*

"Attending several queer faculty social mixers, I was surprised at the large number of queer faculty and staff members here. … I have never had issues with my queer identity on campus. I would even go as far as saying that they are supportive of queer rights." —*24-year-old queer male, senior*

☺ SOCIAL SCENE

Top Three Things in the LGBT Social Life:
1. House parties   2. Dancing   3. Hanging out with queers

How would you describe the social scene for LGBT students?
"There is definitely a large queer student population. … Basically any house party is queer-friendly. If house parties aren't enough and going out clubbing is what you're looking for, we have Dakota and Club Caution and Blue Lagoon right here in downtown Santa Cruz." —*24-year-old queer male, senior*

What annual social event should an LGBT student not miss?
"Queer Fashion Show! It's an annual play where the queer students and their allies come together and do funny, loving, sexy and lesson-learning skits. …it is such a positive display of queer pride and acceptance. And, what's even better, the show is sold out each year." —*20-year-old gay male, junior*

BUZZ BITES *Fun Queer Stuff to Know*

THE BEST…

Party Locale: Dakota
Hangout: Lionel Cantú GLBT Intersex Resource Center
Eating Place: Saturn Café
Place to Check Out Guys: Porter College
Place to Check Out Ladies: Women's rugby
Non-LGBT-Specific Campus Club: Movimiento Estudiantil Chicano de Aztlan (MECHA)

Place for LGBT Students to Live on Campus: Porter College and Merril College
LGBT Course Offering: New Queer Cinema
LGBT Educational Involvement Opportunity: Lionel Cantú GLBT Intersex Resource Center
LGBT-Accepting Religious/Spiritual Organization(s): Unitarian Universalists, Hillel

OUTRAGEOUS FACTOID The campus has chosen the "queerest of all" mascots—the banana slug. The bright yellow, slimy, shell-less mollusk is found in the campus's Redwood Forest. These slugs are bisexual and intersex. The slugs can act as both males and females, inserting their penises into each other simultaneously. Sometimes after mating, the slugs will chew the penis completely off one another—a process called apophallation.

RAINBOW RUMOR Pentagon officials have an eye and an ear on queers at UC Santa Cruz. Media reports indicate that a "Don't Ask, Don't Tell" protest on campus, which included a gay kiss-in, was labeled as a "credible threat" of terrorism by federal officials. Along with LGBT students on other campuses, the queers have been subject to monitoring and surveillance for their differing views.

THAT'S SO GAY!

ANNUAL LGBT EVENT HIGHLIGHTS

Fall Mixer: October
National Coming Out Day/Dance: October 11
Intersex Awareness Day: November
Transgender Remembrance Day: November 20
Gay American Smoke OUT: November
World AIDS Day December 1
LGBT Health Awareness Week: March
National Day of Silence: April
Queer Fashion Show: April
Rainbow Club Dance: May
Oakes Drag Ball: May
Santa Cruz County PRIDE: June

CAMPUS QUEER RESOURCES

Select LGBT Student Organization(s):

Gay, Lesbian, Bisexual, Transgender, Intersex Network
Founding Date: 1989
Membership: 40+
Phone: 831-459-2468
E-mail: glbtin@ucsc.edu

LGBT Resource Center/Office:

Lionel Cantú GLBT Intersex Resource Center
1156 High Street
Santa Cruz, CA 95064
Year Established: 1990
Number of Staff: 2 full-time professional staff; several student workers
Phone: 831-459-2468
E-mail: queer@ucsc.edu
Website: queer.ucsc.edu

THE GAY POINT AVERAGE
OFFICIAL CAMPUS CHECKLIST

- ✓ LGBT & ally student organization
- ✓ LGBT resource center/office
- ✓ LGBT Pride Week &/or Coming Out Week
- ✓ Safe Zone/Safe Space or Ally Program
- ✓ Significant number of LGBT social activities
- ✓ Significant number of LGBT educational events
- ✓ Variety of LGBT studies/courses
- ✓ Nondiscrimination statement inclusive of sexual orientation
- ✓ Nondiscrimination statement inclusive of gender identity/expression
- ✓ Extends domestic partner benefits to same-sex couples
-   Actively recruits LGBT students to enroll on campus
-   Trains campus police on LGBT sensitivity
- ✓ Procedure for reporting LGBT bias, harassment & hate crimes
- ✓ Offers LGBT housing options/themes
- ✓ Offers LGBT-inclusive health services/testing
- ✓ Offers LGBT-inclusive counseling/support groups
- ✓ Offers LGBT student scholarships
- ✓ Conducts special LGBT graduation ceremony for LGBT & ally Students
- ✓ Offers support services for process of transitioning from M to F & F to M
- ✓ Active LGBT alumni group

18 UNIVERSITY OF CALIFORNIA—
SANTA CRUZ GAY POINT AVERAGE
(out of 20)

UNIVERSITY OF COLORADO—BOULDER

THE UNIVERSITY OF Colorado—Boulder is often perceived by the rest of the state as being liberally progressive, or a "hippie" institution. Even the city of Boulder is so described—despite the conservative attitudes in evidence. The facts are evident when you look at the campus score on the Gay Point Average. UC Boulder is as LGBT-progressive as they come!

According to those in the LGBT campus community, the school's liberal reputation has only supported and strengthened the progress on LGBT issues. Much of it started as a result of a former football coach who made very public homophobic comments over a dozen years ago. The campus responded by supporting LGBT issues and creating a task force to look at the overall campus climate for LGBT students. UC Boulder has since worked to be more than queer in the campus institutional commitment and support of LGBT issues. Since the early 1990s, the campus has opened a GLBT Resource Center, started a Safe Zone program, added same-sex partner benefits for LGBT employees, created an LGBT academic certificate program, launched a transgender task force, initiated a chancellor's standing committee for LGBT climate issues and fostered numerous LGBT educational partnerships across campus.

From the Welcome Back BBQ to Intersex Awareness Week, there is something queer to do regularly. Even the Gay Straight Alliance has over 200 proud student members. But perhaps this statement from a campus LGBT student makes it real: "UC Boulder is so much fun. I have been an active student leader on campus, and it doesn't matter that I am gay. You can easily be queer on this campus. There is excellent support and resources. I never have felt more welcome—and at home."

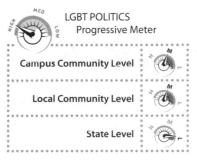

LGBT POLITICS
Progressive Meter

Campus Community Level

Local Community Level

State Level

OUTSPOKEN *Answers from LGBT students:*

Top Three Descriptors of the LGBT Campus Environment:
1. Carefree   2. Accepting   3. Open

What makes your campus feel welcoming and safe for LGBT students?
"Right off the bat at orientation, the staff tells all the students about different groups around campus like the GLBT Resource Center and the GSA. It tells me that the school thinks highly of the diversity this campus is known for."
—*19-year-old gay male, sophomore*

How do you feel about coming out on your campus?
"I feel being gay here is no different to people than being a vegetarian."
—*19-year-old gay male, freshman*

"I feel totally comfortable revealing my sexuality to anyone."
—*23-year-old bisexual male, sophomore*

INFO

UNIVERSITY OF COLORADO—BOULDER
Regent Administrative Center 125
552 UCB
Boulder, CO 80309
Phone: 303-492-6301
Fax: 303-492-7115
E-mail: apply@colorado.edu
Website: www.colorado.edu

CAMPUS STATS
Type of Institution: Public university
Founding Year: 1876
Size: 25,607
Avg. Class Size: 20–29 students
Popular Majors: English Language and Literature, Journalism, Psychology
Cost: In-state tuition: $4,451
Out-of-state tuition: $20,592
Admission Application Deadline: January 15

OUTRAGEOUS FACTOID

"Campus Crusade for Queers" often has students dress in drag as fairies to pass out condoms on campus.

RAINBOW RUMOR

The University of Colorado—Boulder is considered by many to be one of the most liberal places in Colorado. Recently, the campus had a student featured on the Sundance Channel in the popular documentary *TransGeneration*. As a result, the campus has initiated a trans-inclusive plan to improve the campus climate, which includes trans/genderqueer support groups, unisex and multistall gender-neutral bathrooms and gender-neutral housing options.

THAT'S SO GAY!

ANNUAL LGBT EVENT HIGHLIGHTS

Student Drag Show: Fall/Spring

Welcome Back BBQ: September

National Coming Out Day: October 11

World Aids Day: December 1

National Day of Silence: April

Intersex Awareness Week: Fall

Trans Film Festival: Fall

Lavender Graduation: May

Boulder Pride Event: September

End-of-Year Celebration: April

Peer Education Trainings: September/January

ACADEMIC SCENE

Top Three Supportive LGBT Academic Areas:
1. English   2. Film Studies   3. Sociology

How LGBT-friendly are faculty in the classroom?
"I have had good experiences so far with being trans. Most teachers try their best to use the correct pronouns. Some teachers even want to learn more. When LGBT issues arise in class, the professors are usually respectful and supportive and teach tolerance. I have had only one bad experience with a teaching assistant in this respect." —*20-year-old genderqueer lesbian, junior*

"Faculty are generally accepting on campus. Many go so far as to post Safe Zone signs on their office doors. I even took an American History class that presented the Stonewall Riots as an important attribute of continuing the Civil Rights movement." —*19-year-old gay male, sophomore*

SOCIAL SCENE

Top Three Things in the LGBT Social Life:
1. Parties   2. Movies   3. Dancing

How would you describe the social scene for LGBT students?
"The social scene is varied. Many GLBT students party a lot, while others prefer small gatherings, maybe to watch a movie or have coffee. Drag shows in Boulder and gay clubs are popular." —*20-year-old lesbian, junior*

What annual social event should an LGBT student not miss?
"There are too many—the big ones like Coming Out Day, the annual Welcome Back BBQ and the Delta Lambda Phi Fraternity Drag Show."
—*22-year-old gay male, sophomore*

BUZZ BITES *Fun Queer Stuff to Know*

THE BEST...

Party Locale: Tracks Dance Club

Hangout: GLBT Resource Center

Eating Place: Walnut Café

Place to Check Out Guys: Rec Center

Place to Check Out Ladies: Rugby Field

LGBT-Cool Athletic Sport: Track and Field

Non-LGBT-Specific Campus Club: Stop Hate on Campus

LGBT Course Offering: Social Construction of Sexuality

LGBT Educational Involvement Opportunity: LGBT Peer Education

LGBT-Accepting Religious/Spiritual Organization(s): Coming Out Faithful, United Ministries in Higher Education

THE GAY POINT AVERAGE
OFFICIAL CAMPUS CHECKLIST

LGBT & ally student organization ✓

LGBT resource center/office ✓

LGBT Pride Week &/or Coming Out Week ✓

Safe Zone/Safe Space or Ally Program ✓

Significant number of LGBT social activities ✓

Significant number of LGBT educational events ✓

Variety of LGBT studies/courses ✓

Nondiscrimination statement inclusive of sexual orientation ✓

Nondiscrimination statement inclusive of gender identity/expression

Extends domestic partner benefits to same-sex couples ✓

Actively recruits LGBT students to enroll on campus

Trains campus police on LGBT sensitivity

Procedure for reporting LGBT bias, harassment & hate crimes ✓

Offers LGBT housing options/themes ✓

Offers LGBT-inclusive health services/testing ✓

Offers LGBT-inclusive counseling/support groups ✓

Offers LGBT student scholarships ✓

Conducts special LGBT graduation ceremony for LGBT & ally Students ✓

Offers support services for process of transitioning from M to F & F to M ✓

Active LGBT alumni group ✓

UNIVERSITY OF COLORADO— BOULDER GAY POINT AVERAGE 17
(out of 20)

CAMPUS QUEER RESOURCES

Select LGBT Student Organization(s):
Gay Straight Alliance
Founding Date: 2001
Membership: 200
Phone: 303-735-5173
Website: www.colorado.edu/education/gsa/index.htm

LGBT Resource Center/Office:
GLBT Resource Center
227 Willard, 103 UCB
Boulder, CO 80309
Year Established: 1995
Number of Staff: 2 full-time staff; 5 part-time student staff (varying roles)
Phone: 303-492-1377
E-mail: glbtrc@colorado.edu
Website: www.colorado.edu/glbtrc

UNIVERSITY OF COLORADO— DENVER AND HEALTH SCIENCES CENTER

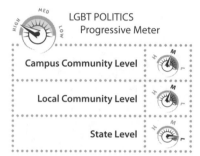

LGBT POLITICS
Progressive Meter

Campus Community Level

Local Community Level

State Level

THE UNIVERSITY OF COLORADO—DENVER is located in downtown Denver, just steps from the Denver Center for the Performing Arts and the chic LoDo District. Recently, the campus merged operations with the nearby Health Sciences Center and shares a joint urban campus with Metropolitan State College of Denver and the Community College of Denver. The campus has demonstrated past support for LGBT-friendly policies by extending domestic partner benefits to faculty, staff and students and by including sexual orientation in its nondiscrimination clause.

In 1992, when Metro State created an office of GLBT Student Services, UC Denver jumped at the opportunity to be closely involved and share the office equally between the 2 campuses. The office has been located ever since in the student union, the campus's central building, and has grown from a single "closet-sized" office to the current suite with a lounge, library and workstations for about 6 student employees.

Every year, the office plans a monthlong campaign of LGBT awareness, a National Coming Out Day celebration, a Queer Prom and a special Lavender Graduation ceremony for departing LGBT and ally seniors. Even sports teams call on the office to do LGBT-sensitivity training to make the campus athletic teams more queer-friendly. Additionally, the university has an active, involved LGBT alumni association as well as an LGBT faculty and staff association on campus. The only queer slack seems to be with the LGBT student group, which has been on an indefinite hiatus for the past year. However, LGBT student efforts are under way to revive the defunct campus organization as soon as possible.

UC Denver should be saluted for its Gay Point Average in a politically conservative, anti-LGBT part of the country. The campus has demonstrated progressive LGBT stances and historically has bucked the system to do what is queerly right. An LGBT student agrees: "If you choose this campus, you will find a home away from home for LGBT students. The support I feel…. the leadership of the campus is right on. LGBT students are a priority…and the campus deserves to be listed for not backing down…but pushing ahead."

🗩 OUTSPOKEN *Answers from LGBT students:*

Top Three Descriptors of the LGBT Campus Environment:
1. Open   2. Fabulous   3. Supportive

INFO

UNIVERSITY OF COLORADO—DENVER and HEALTH SCIENCES CENTER
1250 14th Street
CU-Annex Building
Denver, CO 80217

Phone: 303-556-2704

Fax: 303-556-4838

E-mail: admissions@cudenver.edu

Website: www.cudenver.edu

CAMPUS STATS

Type of Institution: Public university

Founding Year: 1912

Size: 12,070

Avg. Class Size: 10–19 students

Popular Majors: Biology/Biological Sciences, Business Administration/ Management, Psychology

Cost: In-state tuition: $5,952
Out-of-state tuition: $15,394

Admission Application Deadline: July 22

What makes your campus feel welcoming and safe for LGBT students?
"The large LGBT and ally faculty and staff population and the presence of LGBT student services [make] campus feel welcoming and safe for students."
—*27-year-old gay male, junior*

How do you feel about coming out on your campus?
"I have no problems with being out or coming out on campus. The majority of students are LGBT-friendly. GLBT Student Services encourages a positive LGBT presence, and I haven't experienced any negative bias with respect to being out."
—*25-year-old bisexual male, graduate student*

ACADEMIC SCENE

Top Three Supportive LGBT Academic Areas:
1. Ethnic Studies   2. Political Science   3. Counseling Education

How LGBT-friendly are faculty in the classroom?
"All faculty I have had experience with are LGBT-friendly. They have used positive LGBT examples and LGBT experiences in the course curriculum when appropriate and take a stand against negative speech in the classroom if it ever occurs." —*25-year-old bisexual male, graduate student*

"Faculty have always been understanding and receptive to LGBT issues in my classes. It makes me feel good about being here."
—*25-year-old bisexual female, junior*

SOCIAL SCENE

Top Three Things in the LGBT Social Life:
1. Parties   2. Coffee with friends   3. Movies

How would you describe the social scene for LGBT students?
"Typical. Not all over the place, but not invisible." —*27-year-old gay male, junior*

What annual social event should an LGBT student not miss?
"All GLBT students on campus should pay special attention to the month of October, when GLBTSS has its annual LGBT Awareness Month. Multiple LGBT-themed events take place every week."
—*25-year-old bisexual male, graduate student*

OUTRAGEOUS FACTOID
Queers on campus love to proclaim that the campus mascot, Ralphie the Buffalo, is gay.

RAINBOW RUMOR
The University of Colorado—Denver recently merged with the Health Sciences Center. The merger doubled the student body, but the queers still have yet to revive their LGBT student group, defunct since 2005. The GLBT Student Services and a few students are initiating discussions on what type of student group might work best on this commuter-based campus.

THAT'S SO GAY!

ANNUAL LGBT EVENT HIGHLIGHTS

Welcome Back Reception: August/September
LGBT Awareness Month: October
National Coming Out Day: October 11
Annual High Tea for Allies: October
Transgender Day of Remembrance: November
World AIDS Day: December 1
Black History Month GLBT Event: February
Women's History Month GLBT Event: March
Queer Prom: April/May
Lavender Graduation: April/May

BUZZ BITES *Fun Queer Stuff to Know*

THE BEST...

Hangout: GLBT Student Services
Eating Place: Common Grounds
Place to Check Out Guys: Flagpole area
Place to Check Out Ladies: Compound

LGBT-Cool Athletic Sport: Soccer *and* swimming
Non-LGBT-Specific Campus Club: Creative Resistance

CAMPUS QUEER RESOURCES

LGBT Resource Center/Office:

Gay, Lesbian, Bisexual, Transgender Student Services at Auraria
Tivoli Student Union
900 Auraria Parkway, Suite 213
Denver, CO 80204

Year Established: 1992

Number of Staff: 1 full-time professional staff; 4–6 student employees

Phone: 303-556-6333

E-mail: info@glbtss.org

Website: www.glbtss.org

THE GAY POINT AVERAGE
OFFICIAL CAMPUS CHECKLIST

- LGBT & ally student organization
- ✓ LGBT resource center/office
- ✓ LGBT Pride Week &/or Coming Out Week
- ✓ Safe Zone/Safe Space or Ally Program
- ✓ Significant number of LGBT social activities
- ✓ Significant number of LGBT educational events
- Variety of LGBT studies/courses
- ✓ Nondiscrimination statement inclusive of sexual orientation
- Nondiscrimination statement inclusive of gender identity/expression
- ✓ Extends domestic partner benefits to same-sex couples
- ✓ Actively recruits LGBT students to enroll on campus
- Trains campus police on LGBT sensitivity
- ✓ Procedure for reporting LGBT bias, harassment & hate crimes
- Offers LGBT housing options/themes
- ✓ Offers LGBT-inclusive health services/testing
- ✓ Offers LGBT-inclusive counseling/support groups
- ✓ Offers LGBT student scholarships
- ✓ Conducts special LGBT graduation ceremony for LGBT & ally Students
- ✓ Offers support services for process of transitioning from M to F & F to M
- ✓ Active LGBT alumni group

15 UNIVERSITY OF COLORADO— DENVER AND HEALTH SCIENCES CENTER GAY POINT AVERAGE
(out of 20)

UNIVERSITY OF CONNECTICUT

"DRASTIC POSITIVE CHANGE" is how one LGBT student describes the University of Connecticut with regard to LGBT friendliness. Although it suffered from an LGBT history of homophobic acts and inadequate campus response, UCONN has met homophobia straight on since the mid-1990s.

LGBT students no longer characterize the campus in a negative way. Since the founding of the Rainbow Center, the campus community has undergone a queer makeover of sorts. Founded in 1998, the Rainbow Center has been well-funded by the campus administration in an effort to educate on LGBT issues and, most important, provide a safe space for LGBT students on campus.

The center is located in the Student Union, the heart of the campus, and features an extensive library of LGBT resources, including books and videos. Among many educational program offerings, the center employs student leaders to conduct the Heterosexism 101 workshop and a Safe Space initiative called the Queer Resources and Response Network. In addition, some of the more popular campuswide programs include the LGBT Speakers Bureau and a lunchtime lecture series titled Out to Lunch, featuring LGBT topics for class credit.

There are also a number of LGBT student groups on campus that have fostered a more welcoming, queer-progressive attitude at UCONN in recent years. Queers United Against Discrimination is an activist group; another example is the social group Ally and Queer Undergraduate Association (AQUA). Whether it's queer bowling, a campus ban on the American Red Cross Blood Drive, the annual Drag Dance or a production of the Laramie Project, these LGBT student groups have actively engaged queer students to be a part of the campus community and to be a remedy for positive LGBT changes.

UCONN is now out of the closet and proud of the LGBT-friendly programs and policies in place on campus. The Gay Point Average shows that congratulations are in order, and LGBT students agree "UCONN has been my queer home. I have found a safe place in the Rainbow Center.... like any campus, we have areas of improvement and pockets of homophobia, but we know how to make LGBT students feel safe and welcome now.... that really matters more than anything."

LGBT POLITICS
Progressive Meter

Campus Community Level

Local Community Level

State Level

OUTSPOKEN *Answers from LGBT students:*

Top Three Descriptors of the LGBT Campus Environment:
1. Accepting 2. Exciting 3. Improving

What makes your campus feel welcoming and safe for LGBT students?
"Just having a Rainbow Center that is active in campus events says to everyone, 'Hey, we exist.'" *—20-year-old gay male, junior*

How do you feel about coming out on your campus?
"Coming out is very much a personal decision and choice, and someone will come out if they are ready to. Someone can definitely be openly gay on campus." *—19-year-old gay male, sophomore*

INFO

UNIVERSITY OF CONNECTICUT
2131 Hillside Road, Unit 3088
Storrs, CT 06269
Phone: 860-486-3137
Fax: 860-486-1476
E-mail: beahusky@uconn.edu
Website: www.uconn.edu

CAMPUS STATS
Type of Institution: Public university
Founding Year: 1881
Size: 15,700
Avg. Class Size: 20–29 students
Popular Majors: Nursing/Registered Nurse Training, Political Science and Government, Psychology
Cost: In-state tuition: $6,096
Out-of-state tuition: $18,600
Admission Application Deadline: February 1

UNIVERSITY OF CONNECTICUT **221**

• • • • • • • • • • • • • • • • • • • •

RAINBOW RUMOR

From the white Husky campus mascot to the student body, UCONN may be "too white" for some students. Although LGBT students of color regularly visit the Rainbow Center and participate in the LGBT student groups, the visibility of students of color remains weak—particularly among African American students. A student agrees: "People of color definitely aren't visible in the LGBT community. The African American community and the LGBT community especially don't mix."

• • • • • • • • • • • • • • • • • • • •

THAT'S SO GAY!

ANNUAL LGBT EVENT HIGHLIGHTS

LGBT Movie Night: Fall and Spring, Monday nights

LGBT Coffee House: Fall and Spring, Friday nights

Out to Lunch Lecture Series: Fall and Spring, Wednesdays

LGBT Awareness Month: October

National Coming Out Day Chalking: October 10

National Coming Out Day: October 11

Trans Remembrance Day: November

Red Cross Blood Ban Tabling: Fall/Spring

Homecoming Parade LGBT Entry: October

Annual Drag Dance: Halloween weekend

World AIDS Day Week: November/December

Ooze Ball Mud Volleyball: Spring

Lavender Graduation: May

ACADEMIC SCENE

Top Three Supportive LGBT Academic Areas:
1. Women's Studies   2. Fine Arts   3. Health Education Department

How LGBT-friendly are faculty in the classroom?
"In my basic Comm 100 class of like 300 students, mostly underclassmen, I feel like I have to educate the instructor and remind him to mention to the class that the so-called ways that men and women 'act' refer to straight men and straight women. The good news was that he was receptive to what I had to say."
—*20-year-old gay male, junior*

"I've actually had quite a few gay TAs, and it's great because they don't have to make a big deal out of it. Also, there are a couple female deans who are openly lesbian or bisexual and LGBT activists." —*21-year-old gay male, senior*

SOCIAL SCENE

Top Three Things in the LGBT Social Life:
1. Rainbow Center   2. AQUA   3. Clubbing

How would you describe the social scene for LGBT students?
"I met my [lesbian and bisexual] friends at the Women's Center because of their Between Women group. We hang out a lot on the weekends and have TV nights together." —*22-year-old lesbian, senior*

What annual social event should an LGBT student not miss?
"Definitely the Drag Dance." —*18-year-old gay male, sophomore*

BUZZ BITES
Fun Queer Stuff to Know

THE BEST...

Party Locale: House parties

Hangout: Rainbow Center

Place to Check Out Guys: Among Men social group

Place to Check Out Ladies: Between Women social group

LGBT-Cool Athletic Sport: Rugby

Non-LGBT-Specific Campus Club: NOW Campus Chapter

Place for LGBT Students to Live on Campus: Towers South

LGBT Course Offering: Queer Studies across the Disciplines

LGBT Educational Involvement Opportunity: Heterosexism 101 Workshop

LGBT-Accepting Religious/Spiritual Organization(s): Saint Paul's Collegiate Church, Hillel: Jewish Student Center

THE GAY POINT AVERAGE
OFFICIAL CAMPUS CHECKLIST

LGBT & ally student organization ✓

LGBT resource center/office ✓

LGBT Pride Week &/or Coming Out Week ✓

Safe Zone/Safe Space or Ally Program ✓

Significant number of LGBT social activities ✓

Significant number of LGBT educational events ✓

Variety of LGBT studies/courses ✓

Nondiscrimination statement inclusive of sexual orientation ✓

Nondiscrimination statement inclusive of gender identity/expression ✓

Extends domestic partner benefits to same-sex couples ✓

Actively recruits LGBT students to enroll on campus ✓

Trains campus police on LGBT sensitivity ✓

Procedure for reporting LGBT bias, harassment & hate crimes ✓

Offers LGBT housing options/themes

Offers LGBT-inclusive health services/testing ✓

Offers LGBT-inclusive counseling/support groups ✓

Offers LGBT student scholarships

Conducts special LGBT graduation ceremony for LGBT & ally Students ✓

Offers support services for process of transitioning from M to F & F to M

Active LGBT alumni group ✓

UNIVERSITY OF CONNECTICUT
GAY POINT AVERAGE
(out of 20)

17

CAMPUS QUEER RESOURCES

Select LGBT Student Organization(s):
Ally and Queer Undergraduate Association (AQUA)
Founding Date: 2000
Membership: 50+
Phone: 860-486-5821

LGBT Resource Center/Office:
Rainbow Center
Student Union, Fourth Floor
2110 Hillside Road, Unit 3096
Storrs, CT 06269-3096
Year Established: 1998
Number of Staff: 1 full-time professional staff; 1 administrative assistant; 10 student workers
Phone: 860-486-5821
E-mail: rnbwdir@uconn.edu
Website: www.rainbowcenter.uconn.edu

UNIVERSITY OF FLORIDA

LOOKING TO THE South for college? There are not many LGBT-progressive choices there, but the University of Florida "Gay-tors" might just be it. Located in the north-central part of the state, the campus is one of the largest in the nation and has made significant strides in becoming a more welcoming, friendly place for LGBT students.

The University of Florida created an office of LGBT Affairs in 2001 and funded a director for LGBT issues in 2004. This bold move made the University of Florida the only campus in the state with a full-time LGBT director and one of the only campuses with LGBT services in the South. Add this LGBT progress to the school's already strong Gay Point Average and the University of Florida offers a viable choice for LGBT students.

But perhaps the best LGBT review can be seen on campus in the extremely large and diverse LGBT student population and one of the nation's strongest LGBT student coalitions, the Pride Student Union. Boasting a hefty programming budget, the coalition offers excellent program choices, including the National Coming Out Day Celebration, Same-Sex Hand-Holding Day, the America's Divas competition and the Queer Ball. Plus, there is the annual Pride Awareness Month, which rivals any event on campus, having in the past attracted speakers including Ellen DeGeneres, Margaret Cho and Karamo from *The Real World*.

The "Gay-tors" agree that the LGBT student life is the best—offering a wide variety of choices, from educational events to social opportunities. Many of the LGBT students also note "tremendous strides" in the LGBT campus climate toward combating homophobia. Even academically, there are a number of LGBT course offerings to choose from.

Advice from an LGBT student: "The University of Florida is a great place to go to school, no matter what your sexual orientation. The administration is behind its LGBT community…. Whether you're a gender bender, genderqueer or just out loud and proud, University of Florida is the place to be yourself, make a difference, meet interesting minds and maybe attend a class or two."

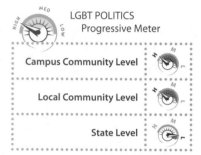

LGBT POLITICS
Progressive Meter

Campus Community Level

Local Community Level

State Level

INFO

UNIVERSITY OF FLORIDA
201 Criser Hall
Box 114000
Gainesville, FL 32611
Phone: 352-392-1365
Fax: 904-392-3987
E-mail: ourwebrequests@registrar.ufl.edu
Website: www.ufl.edu

CAMPUS STATS
Type of Institution: Public university
Founding Year: 1853
Size: 33,600
Avg. Class Size: 20–29 students
Popular Majors: Business Administration/Management, Finance, Psychology
Cost: In-state tuition: $3,094
Out-of-state tuition: $17,222
Admission Application Deadline: January 15

OUTSPOKEN *Answers from LGBT students:*

Top Three Descriptors of the LGBT Campus Environment:
1. Improving   2. Supportive   3. Diverse

What makes your campus feel welcoming and safe for LGBT students?
"There is a great community of LGBT students at UF…. I also feel safe because I believe that students here are open-minded…. It's reassuring to see students, straight and gay, who object to the protests by preachers on campus that homosexuality is an immoral choice. I feel like there are more people 'on our side' on this campus than against us." —*19-year-old bisexual female, junior*

How do you feel about coming out on your campus?
"With few exceptions, I have received a lot of positive response in doing panels, where I tell my coming out story and share the experience of being largely closeted my first year here." —*20-year-old gay male, junior*

⊘ ACADEMIC SCENE

Top Three Supportive LGBT Academic Areas:
1. English   2. Sociology   3. Women's Studies

How LGBT-friendly are faculty in the classroom?
"I was having trouble in school during the coming out process, so I confided in a few of my professors, needing their help. The few professors that I talked to were understanding and willing to help me, which gave me the strong impression that UF was in fact aware of gay issues and very open-minded."
—*21-year-old lesbian, senior*

"I have had the best experiences with professors on this campus. One professor in particular is always very careful to use gender-inclusive language, is very sensitive to LGBT issues and does not tolerate homophobic or heterosexist comments in her classroom. I know for a fact that she is not the only one who does this." —*19-year-old genderqueer homosexual, sophomore*

☺ SOCIAL SCENE

Top Three Things in the LGBT Social Life:
1. Dancing   2. Hanging out   3. Going to Pride Student Union

How would you describe the social scene for LGBT students?
"There are many places in Gainesville for LGBT students to socialize and have a good time, and UF LGBT students seem to make the most of it."
—*21-year-old lesbian, senior*

What annual social event should an LGBT student not miss?
"Queer Ball. It's so amazing. It's the gay prom that you never had. Such a great way to end the semester!" —*19-year-old genderqueer homosexual, sophomore*

BUZZ BITES *Fun Queer Stuff to Know*

THE BEST...

Party Locale: University Club
Hangout: Maude's Café
Eating Place: The Top *and* The Bistro
Place to Check Out Guys: Starbucks
Place to Check Out Ladies: Knightz *and* Maiden's Night
LGBT-Cool Athletic Sport: Women's rugby
Non-LGBT-Specific Campus Club: Feminist Knitting and Crochet Circle

Place for LGBT Students to Live on Campus: Rawlings, Broward *or* Hume Residence Halls
LGBT Educational Involvement Opportunity: Friends Ally Training Program
LGBT-Accepting Religious/Spiritual Organization(s): Presbyterian and Disciples Christ Student Center

OUTRAGEOUS FACTOID Breaking down stereotypes is what UF is all about. The campus has LGBT football fans and queer theory fans, transgender activists and gay fraternity brothers. The queer mix extends even beyond the borders of the United States, with LGBT students from Jamaica, Latin America and India. Queer students participate in everything queer and between—including a float in the annual homecoming parade. Last year, the reverend of the Presbyterian and Disciples Christ Student Center marched beside the queer float to show support for the Pride Student Union.

• • • • • • • • • • • • • • • • • •

RAINBOW RUMOR A lot has changed since Rita Mae Brown, famous lesbian and novelist best-known for her work *Rubyfruit Jungle*, was kicked out of UF in 1964 for her activism on civil rights issues. The campus has had a great "queer awakening," according to some LGBT students. The next step is to increase campus efforts for trans inclusion and to continue developing the new LGBT alumni group. But, let the truth be told, wouldn't Rita Mae and her cat "Sneaky Pie" be proud of UF today?

• • • • • • • • • • • • • • • • • •

THAT'S SO GAY!

ANNUAL LGBT EVENT HIGHLIGHTS

LGBTQ Welcome Assembly: September
National Coming Out Day Celebration: October
Pride Float at Homecoming: October
LGBT Alumni Homecoming Event: October
Transgender Remembrance Day Vigil: November
Same-Sex Hand-Holding Day: January/February
LGBT Black History Month Event: February
Lesbian, Bi and Queer Women's Leadership Events: March
Pride Awareness Month: April
Queer Ball: April
My Big Fat Gay Wedding: April
LGBT Film Festival: April
America's Divas: April
Lavender Graduation: April or May

CAMPUS QUEER RESOURCES

Select LGBT Student Organization(s):

Pride Student Union and
Gator Gay Straight Alliance

Founding Date: January 28, 2002

Membership: 100+

Phone: 352-392-1665, ext. 326

E-mail: pride@ufpride.org

Website: www.ufpride.org

LGBT Resource Center/Office:

LGBT Affairs

Dean of Students Office
202 Peabody Hall
PO Box 114075
Gainesville, FL 32611

Year Established: 2001

Number of Staff: 1 full-time professional staff; 1 student employee

Phone: 352-392-5586, ext. 224

E-mail: lgbt@dso.ufl.edu

Website: www.lgbt.ufl.edu

THE GAY POINT AVERAGE
OFFICIAL CAMPUS CHECKLIST

- ✓ LGBT & ally student organization
- ✓ LGBT resource center/office
- ✓ LGBT Pride Week &/or Coming Out Week
- ✓ Safe Zone/Safe Space or Ally Program
- ✓ Significant number of LGBT social activities
- ✓ Significant number of LGBT educational events
- ✓ Variety of LGBT studies/courses
- ✓ Nondiscrimination statement inclusive of sexual orientation
- Nondiscrimination statement inclusive of gender identity/expression
- ✓ Extends domestic partner benefits to same-sex couples
- Actively recruits LGBT students to enroll on campus
- ✓ Trains campus police on LGBT sensitivity
- ✓ Procedure for reporting LGBT bias, harassment & hate crimes
- Offers LGBT housing options/themes
- ✓ Offers LGBT-inclusive health services/testing
- ✓ Offers LGBT-inclusive counseling/support groups
- ✓ Offers LGBT student scholarships
- ✓ Conducts special LGBT graduation ceremony for LGBT & ally Students
- ✓ Offers support services for process of transitioning from M to F & F to M
- ✓ Active LGBT alumni group

17 UNIVERSITY OF FLORIDA GAY POINT AVERAGE
(out of 20)

UNIVERSITY OF ILLINOIS—CHICAGO

OUT FACULTY AND LGBT students are incredibly visible at the University of Illinois—Chicago. A close look at the campus shows a large and thriving LGBT community, possibly because of the many LGBT-progressive policies and practices. The Gay Point Average says so.

As early as the 1990s, this campus was known as progressive and gay-friendly, and it shows throughout campus life today. From student coalitions like PRIDE to the Office of GLBT Concerns, there are many LGBT services and queer-fabulous events like the Vagina Monologues, Lunch 'n' Learn Lecture Series and Love Your Body Week. In addition, this campus takes the "T" seriously. It's not just another letter in the abbreviation LGBT. The campus has written groundbreaking transgender-housing policies. They even hired Deirdre McCloskey, an internationally known economist and transgender activist, as a faculty member. In addition, the campus also boasts more faculty who are leading LGBT theorists and scholars than most colleges in the country. As a result, many of the academic departments and offices are aligned with queer progressiveness and seek the support of the Office of GLBT Concerns. The office routinely presents Safe Zone trainings and a host of other LGBT-inclusive services slated to raise awareness on gender identity and sexuality issues.

And don't forget that the campus is located in the city of Chicago! For one LGBT student, the choice was obvious: "The campus, the city of Chicago…. All of that made it easy for me. There was so much to offer a 'newbie' gay man. I could tell from the Office of GLBT Concerns that this was a safe and welcoming space. I could be myself without worry."

LGBT POLITICS
Progressive Meter

Campus Community Level

Local Community Level

State Level

OUTSPOKEN *Answers from LGBT students:*

Top Three Descriptors of the LGBT Campus Environment:
1. Supportive   2. Friendly   3. Activist-oriented

What makes your campus feel welcoming and safe for LGBT students?
"What makes our campus feel warm and safe for LGBT students is the community we have. Our school has an Office of GLBT Concerns, a Chancellor's Committee on the Status of LGBT Issues and a student-run Pride group. All of these groups are constantly working to make LGBT-friendly events available, and we also work to make a difference for all LGBT people in the community."
—21-year-old queer female, junior

How do you feel about coming out on your campus?
"I feel safe coming out on campus. I know of enough people on campus [who] support LGBT students that I know there are places to go where I can get help and feel safe." *—21-year-old gay male, junior*

INFO

UNIVERSITY OF ILLINOIS—CHICAGO
1200 West Harrison Street
PO Box 5220
Chicago, IL 60607
Phone: 312-996-4350
Fax: 312-413-7628
E-mail: uicadmit@uic.edu
Website: www.uic.edu

CAMPUS STATS

Type of Institution: Public university
Founding Year: 1982
Size: 15,828
Avg. Class Size: 20–29 students
Popular Majors: Business/Marketing, Engineering/Engineering Technologies, Psychology, Health Professions and Related Sciences
Cost: In-state tuition: $4,151
Out-of-state tuition: $10,346
Admission Application Deadline: January 1

OUTRAGEOUS FACTOID

Did you know that Chicago hosts the only known GLBT Hall of Fame in the United States? Two famous names among the many LGBT pioneers listed call University of Illinois—Chicago home: gay historian John D'Emilio and lesbian health researcher Tonda Hughes. Both are active members of the LGBT community on campus!

· · · · · · · · · · · · · · · · · · · ·

RAINBOW RUMOR

Equal is not quite equal, at least when it comes to domestic partnership benefits for same-sex couples. Although the campus does offer benefits for same-sex couples, it's far from equitable in comparison to other non-LGBT faculty and staff. Ounce for ounce, the benefits just do not match up, and according to many LGBT campus members are not "practical or viable."

· · · · · · · · · · · · · · · · · · · ·

THAT'S SO GAY!

ANNUAL LGBT EVENT HIGHLIGHTS

Rainbow Social: August

Lunch 'n' Learn Lecture Series: Fall/Spring

GLBT History Month: October

National Coming Out Day: October

Love Your Body Week: November

Transgender Memorial: November

World AIDS Day: December 1

Vagina Monologues: February/March

Chicago Collegiate Pride Fest: April

National Day of Silence: April

Pride Month: June

ACADEMIC SCENE

Top Three Supportive LGBT Academic Areas:
1. Gender and Women's Studies   2. African American Studies
3. Asian American Studies

How LGBT-friendly are faculty in the classroom?
"In my social-work classes, students who know very little about the LGBT world are eager to learn, and this is supported by faculty. My professors have also used updated definitions of cultural diversity that include LGBT individuals. In my Gender and Women's Studies classes, everyone is LGB-friendly, but there is less comfort about transgender identities and issues."
—*21-year-old queer female, junior*

SOCIAL SCENE

Top Three Things in the LGBT Social Life:
1. Parties   2. Bars and clubs   3. Dancing

How would you describe the social scene for LGBT students?
"One of the best things about UIC is that it's in Chicago. There's always a ton of stuff you can do and people to meet—whatever your scene might be. On campus, there are many social events throughout the year, such as the Pride Fest…big enough to date but small enough for a sense of community."
—*19-year-old gay male, sophomore*

What annual social event should an LGBT student not miss?
"I love Chicago Collegiate Pride Fest because it's hosted by UIC but done with other area colleges and universities. The campus also hosts quarterly Lunch 'n' Learns, which are always informative and have good food!"
—*20-year-old gay male, junior*

BUZZ BITES *Fun Queer Stuff to Know*

THE BEST…

Party Locale: House parties

Hangout: Rainbow Resource Library

Place to Check Out Guys: Boystown

Place to Check Out Ladies: Andersonville

LGBT-Cool Athletic Sport: Rugby

Non-LGBT-Specific Campus Club: Feminists United

Place for LGBT Students to Live on Campus: Courtyard

LGBT Educational Involvement Opportunity: National Coming Out Day on the Campus Quad

LGBT-Accepting Religious/Spiritual Organization(s): Agape House *and* Hillel

THE GAY POINT AVERAGE
OFFICIAL CAMPUS CHECKLIST

LGBT & ally student organization ✓

LGBT resource center/office ✓

LGBT Pride Week &/or Coming Out Week ✓

Safe Zone/Safe Space or Ally Program ✓

Significant number of LGBT social activities ✓

Significant number of LGBT educational events ✓

Variety of LGBT studies/courses ✓

Nondiscrimination statement inclusive of sexual orientation ✓

Nondiscrimination statement inclusive of gender identity/expression ✓

Extends domestic partner benefits to same-sex couples ✓

Actively recruits LGBT students to enroll on campus

Trains campus police on LGBT sensitivity ✓

Procedure for reporting LGBT bias, harassment & hate crimes ✓

Offers LGBT housing options/themes ✓

Offers LGBT-inclusive health services/testing ✓

Offers LGBT-inclusive counseling/support groups ✓

Offers LGBT student scholarships ✓

Conducts special LGBT graduation ceremony for LGBT & ally Students

Offers support services for process of transitioning from M to F & F to M ✓

Active LGBT alumni group

UNIVERSITY OF ILLINOIS—CHICAGO
GAY POINT AVERAGE
(out of 20)

17

CAMPUS QUEER RESOURCES

Select LGBT Student Organization(s):
PRIDE@UIC
Gay, Lesbian, Bisexual and Transgender People Advocating for Diversity
Founding Date: 1990
Membership: 50
Phone: 312-413-3036
E-mail: pride@uic.edu
Website: icarus.uic.edu/stud_orgs/pride/

LGBT Resource Center/Office:
Office of GLBT Concerns
UIC OGLBTC M/C 369
1007 West Harrison Street
Chicago, IL 60607
Year Established: 1995
Number of Staff: 3 full-time professional staff (varying levels)
Phone: 312-413-8619
E-mail: oglbc-1@uic.edu
Website: www.glbc.uic.edu

UNIVERSITY OF ILLINOIS— URBANA-CHAMPAIGN

UNIVERSITY OF ILLINOIS—Urbana-Champaign is located in the middle of rural Illinois. Much queer progress has been made over the years in this quaint college town. LGBT students do not disagree: in fact, many acknowledge they chose the campus because it has "transformed" into a queer-progressive place with community LGBT-related groups. New groups tend to pop up all the time. An example would be the recent formation of the Colors of Pride group for LGBT students of color or the Ladies Loving Ladies group for the specific needs of women. In addition, the campus founded the first-ever Greek Allies group for LGBT fraternity and sorority straight allies in the country. Such LGBT efforts put this campus out in front when it comes to strong, diverse student coalitions.

As far as LGBT-progressive polices and practices, you can see from the Gay Point Average that the university comes out at the top. Sexual orientation has been included in the university's nondiscrimination policy since 1993, and gender identity was recently added a year ago. Even with budget reductions across campus, the Office of LGBT Concerns received additional LGBT programming monies to pay the salary for a full-time director and an assistant director. All these LGBT achievements are possible because of amazing allies— from the chancellor to the provost to the faculty.

The Office of LGBT Concerns credits much of the LGBT progress and educational efforts over the years to successful partnerships—whether with Residence Life, the Illini Union Board, University Police or the McKinley Health Center, to name a few. As one LGBT student states: "LGBT issues are present throughout campus. The visibility is great, and I feel safe here. I also think the phenomenal LGBT-inclusive faculty make this campus a wonderful choice."

OUTSPOKEN *Answers from LGBT students:*

Top Three Descriptors of the LGBT Campus Environment:
1. Safe   2. Engaging   3. Alive

What makes your campus feel welcoming and safe for LGBT students?
"Above all, the LGBT Concerns Office is what made me feel welcome on campus. It took me almost six months after arrival on campus to work up the nerve to visit, but man am I glad that I did! By now the office almost seems like a second home. I've never had any problems being out on campus."
—19-year-old queer gay male, sophomore

How do you feel about coming out on your campus?
"I was lucky to find a campus support group for me when I came out of the closet just recently. The group gave me the opportunity to just talk about coming out to my parents at home. It seems that even though I'm still growing from this, I can at least come to a safe setting where I don't feel at all judged."
—19-year-old bisexual male, sophomore

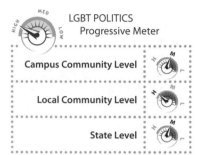

LGBT POLITICS
Progressive Meter

Campus Community Level

Local Community Level

State Level

INFO

UNIVERSITY OF ILLINOIS— URBANA-CHAMPAIGN
901 West Illinois Street
Urbana, IL 61801
Phone: 217-333-0302
Fax: 217-244-4614
E-mail: ugradadmissions@uiuc.edu
Website: www.uiuc.edu

CAMPUS STATS
Type of Institution: Public university
Founding Year: 1867
Size: 30,453
Avg. Class Size: 20–29 students
Popular Majors: Biology/Biological Sciences, Business/Marketing, Engineering/Engineering Technologies
Cost: In-state tuition: $7,042
Out-of-state tuition: $21,128
Admission Application Deadline: December 15

"Coming out for me wasn't really that hard of an experience, but it's still pretty cool that I have that sort of community on campus where I can just be who I am. I get to be the person that I want to be, and that's really the only thing that matters." —*20-year-old bisexual female, sophomore*

ACADEMIC SCENE

Top Three Supportive LGBT Academic Areas:
1. Gender and Women's Studies   2. Sociology   3. Theater

How LGBT-friendly are faculty in the classroom?
"I was having a hard time in engineering my sophomore year because there were definitely some homophobic students in some of my classes. I was pretty relieved when I went to talk to an academic adviser about my being out when she pointed out her 'ALLY' sign on her office wall. Relief was the first physical reaction, and it felt so good."—*21-year-old gay male junior*

"Professors and faculty, or at least the ones that I know, can be pretty accepting with LGBT students' concerns or issues, and they are able to challenge us like any other student as well as serve as awesome supports."
—*20-year-old bisexual female, junior*

SOCIAL SCENE

Top Three Things in the LGBT Social Life:
1. The Bar   2. Movies   3. Hanging out

How would you describe the social scene for LGBT students?
"The social scene on campus is really driven by the people you know. At this point, I spend most of my time socializing within the LGBT community."
—*19-year-old queer gay male, sophomore*

What annual social event should an LGBT student not miss?
"Definitely the Day of Silence rally here. Day of Silence is very big on this campus, and it's one of those events where people just get together and celebrate together." —*21-year-old lesbian, junior*

BUZZ BITES *Fun Queer Stuff to Know*

THE BEST...

Party Locale: Chester Street Bar
Hangout: Union
Eating Place: Steak and Shake
Place to Check Out Guys: Chester Street Bar
Place to Check Out Ladies: Canopy Club
LGBT-Cool Athletic Sport: Basketball
Non-LGBT-Specific Campus Club: Illini Union Board

Place for LGBT Students to Live on Campus: Allen Residence Hall
LGBT Course Offering: GWS 350: Intro to Queer Studies
LGBT Educational Involvement Opportunity: Lunch 'n' Learn Events
LGBT-Accepting Religious/Spiritual Organization(s): McKinley Foundation, Campus United Church of Christ

OUTRAGEOUS FACTOID The University of Illinois—Urbana-Champaign is the first campus in the country to have developed a specific Greek Allies group for members of fraternities and sororities who are LGBT allies. Greek Allies was founded in 2004 and has been going strong ever since.

RAINBOW RUMOR One African-American student explains: "We have a difficult time reaching out to the smaller, more silent groups within the community, such as trans people, queer women, and queer people of color. We need to strive for more integration and diversity within the community."

THAT'S SO GAY!
ANNUAL LGBT EVENT HIGHLIGHTS

LGBT Welcome Back Picnic: September
Coming Out Week: October
National Coming Out Day Rally: October 11
Trans Day of Remembrance: November
World AIDS Day: December
Drag Show: March
LGBT Awareness Month: April
Day of Silence Protest and Rally: April
Rainbow Graduation: May

THE GAY POINT AVERAGE
OFFICIAL CAMPUS CHECKLIST

CAMPUS QUEER RESOURCES

Select LGBT Student Organization(s):

PRIDE
Founding Date: 1975
Membership: 300+
Website: www.uiuc.edu/ro/pride

LGBT Resource Center/Office:

Office for LGBT Concerns
University of Illinois—
Urbana-Champaign
323 Illini Union
1401 West Green Street
Urbana, Illinois 61801
Year Established: 1993
Number of Staff: 2 full-time professional staff; 1 part-time graduate assistant; 2 student workers
Phone: 217-244-8863
Website: www.lgbt.uiuc.edu

✓ LGBT & ally student organization

✓ LGBT resource center/office

✓ LGBT Pride Week &/or Coming Out Week

✓ Safe Zone/Safe Space or Ally Program

✓ Significant number of LGBT social activities

✓ Significant number of LGBT educational events

✓ Variety of LGBT studies/courses

✓ Nondiscrimination statement inclusive of sexual orientation

✓ Nondiscrimination statement inclusive of gender identity/expression

✓ Extends domestic partner benefits to same-sex couples

   Actively recruits LGBT students to enroll on campus

✓ Trains campus police on LGBT sensitivity

✓ Procedure for reporting LGBT bias, harassment & hate crimes

   Offers LGBT housing options/themes

✓ Offers LGBT-inclusive health services/testing

✓ Offers LGBT-inclusive counseling/support groups

   Offers LGBT student scholarships

✓ Conducts special LGBT graduation ceremony for LGBT & ally Students

✓ Offers support services for process of transitioning from M to F & F to M

   Active LGBT alumni group

16   UNIVERSITY OF ILLINOIS— URBANA-CHAMPAIGN GAY POINT AVERAGE
(out of 20)

UNIVERSITY OF KANSAS

LAWRENCE, KANSAS, AN ultra-hip, liberal college town is home to the University of Kansas. The LGBT history of both the town and the campus are particularly progressive for the state of Kansas. Prospective students should look for a combination of LGBT-inclusive policies and a welcoming student climate when considering this campus.

The LGBT movement on campus has been in full force from 1970 on. The student group Queers and Allies has been around since then and accounts for much of the activism still going on today. In the 1990s, for example, the Kansas Board of Regents added sexual orientation to the campus nondiscrimination policy. LGBT and ally students on campus were the leading change agents advocating for that policy.

The campus is also the first and only college in Kansas to have an LGBT resource center, LGBT Programs and Services, which opened its doors in the mid-1990s. Other, more recent LGBT support comes from Douglas County, home to the city of Lawrence, was the only county in Kansas voting to reject the state constitutional amendment banning gay marriage. An important factor in that vote was the pro-gay voice of the student body. Earlier in 2005, the Student Senate took a stance on gay marriage and began campaigning actively against the amendment. The student body president was quoted as saying, "We are elected to represent students. It is very important that we protect their rights all the time."

In addition to LGBT support and advocacy, Queers and Allies also provides an excellent social outlet for the LGBT community. Annual event highlights include National Coming Out Day speakers, an LGBT Rally and Parade and a Pride Week chock full of speakers, panels and competitions. One LGBT student shares: "Queer life at KU is the best. We have an active group, a number of queer social activities, great allies and the most gay-friendly environment for Kansas." Many LGBT students agree, taking pride in at being one of the spirited "Gayhawks."

University of Kansas ranks up there among the best, most LGBT-friendly in the Midwest. Year after year, LGBT students and allies on campus have shown astounding queer progressiveness and an affirming LGBT community. One LGBT student states: "There's a place for everyone. I was not out in high school, but at KU I have been able to come out in ways unimaginable. The campus has given me the freedom to be myself, every part of who I am."

OUTSPOKEN *Answers from LGBT students:*

Top Three Descriptors of the LGBT Campus Environment:
1. Inclusive   2. Progressive   3. Fabulous

What makes your campus feel welcoming and safe for LGBT students?
"Rainbow pins on backpacks. Plus Queers and Allies had a table full of queer resources ... and the first week other LGBT students made me feel welcome and at home on campus." *—19-year-old gay male, sophomore*

How do you feel about coming out on your campus?
"I feel very safe being out on campus. When my girlfriend came to visit me, we openly held hands and hugged in public spaces on campus. Never once were we bothered or met any kind of derision for doing so. The city of Lawrence is also ultra-liberal too." *—21-year-old lesbian, junior*

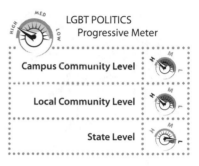

LGBT POLITICS
Progressive Meter

Campus Community Level

Local Community Level

State Level

INFO

UNIVERSITY OF KANSAS
1502 Iowa Street
Lawrence, KS 66045
Phone: 785-864-3911
Fax: 785-864-5017
E-mail: adm@ku.edu
Website: www.ku.edu

CAMPUS STATS
Type of Institution: Public university
Founding Year: 1863
Size: 20,908
Avg. Class Size: 20–29 students
Popular Majors: Business Administration/Management, Journalism, Speech and Rhetoric Studies, Psychology
Cost: In-state tuition: $5,413
Out-of-state tuition: $13,865
Admission Application Deadline: December 1

The official mascot of the University of Kansas is a fictional red-and-blue bird with a yellow beak called the "Jayhawk." The term comes from Kansas Civil War terminology for the relentless, impassioned people who made Kansas a "Free State." Today, KU queers affectionately call the mascot the "Gayhawk" to highlight the LGBT friendliness of the campus.

• •

RAINBOW RUMOR Slow but steady progress: the University of Kansas leads the way in the heartland for queers. The campus is actively implementing more resources for the LGBT resource coordinator, which is currently a part-time graduate-level staff position. With the support of Queers and Allies, the word on the street is that you may "expect a full-time professional staff for LGBT students" within the next couple of years.

• •

THAT'S SO GAY!

ANNUAL LGBT EVENT HIGHLIGHTS

National Coming Out Day: October 11

World AIDS Day: December 1

Pride Week: April

Drag Show: April

LGBT Rally and Parade: April

Queer Awards: April/May

"I feel wonderful coming out on campus. Everyone I have ever come out to has been open, loving, supportive." —*20-year-old gay male, junior*

ACADEMIC SCENE

Top Three Supportive LGBT Academic Areas:
1. Social Welfare 2. Women's Studies 3. Education

How LGBT-friendly are faculty in the classroom?
"In general, faculty perceptions are based on department. There needs to be more LGBT training done for faculty. However, a surprising amount of professors include LGBT issues in their courses, and I have only had positive experiences." —*22-year-old gay male, senior*

"Faculty for the most part are very accepting. There are a large number of allies in the faculty, and there are very, very few of my professors that I would have strong reservations about coming out to." —*21-year-old lesbian, junior*

SOCIAL SCENE

Top Three Things in the LGBT Social Life:
1. Dancing 2. House parties 3. Bars

How would you describe the social scene for LGBT students?
"Ultra-queer and liberal. Lawrence is by far the most queer place in Kansas. KU is just a big ole gay mecca." —*19-year-old gay male, freshman*

What annual social event should an LGBT student not miss?
"Anything drag-related. … straight students love to watch and it can be a hilarious time!" —*20-year-old gay male, junior*

BUZZ BITES *Fun Queer Stuff to Know*

THE BEST…

Party Locale: Limelight

Hangout: Java Break Coffee Shop

Eating Place: Milton's

Place to Check Out Guys: Fraternity Row

Place to Check Out Ladies: Rugby games

LGBT-Cool Athletic Sport: Women's basketball

Non-LGBT-Specific Campus Club: Delta Force

Place for LGBT Students to Live on Campus: Hashinger Hall

LGBT Educational Involvement Opportunity: LGBT Speakers Bureau

LGBT-Accepting Religious/Spiritual Organization(s): Ecumenical Christian Ministries

THE GAY POINT AVERAGE
OFFICIAL CAMPUS CHECKLIST

LGBT & ally student organization ✓

LGBT resource center/office ✓

LGBT Pride Week &/or Coming Out Week ✓

Safe Zone/Safe Space or Ally Program ✓

Significant number of LGBT social activities ✓

Significant number of LGBT educational events ✓

Variety of LGBT studies/courses

Nondiscrimination statement inclusive of sexual orientation ✓

Nondiscrimination statement inclusive of gender identity/expression

Extends domestic partner benefits to same-sex couples

Actively recruits LGBT students to enroll on campus

Trains campus police on LGBT sensitivity ✓

Procedure for reporting LGBT bias, harassment & hate crimes ✓

Offers LGBT housing options/themes

Offers LGBT-inclusive health services/testing ✓

Offers LGBT-inclusive counseling/support groups ✓

Offers LGBT student scholarships ✓

Conducts special LGBT graduation ceremony for LGBT & ally Students

Offers support services for process of transitioning from M to F & F to M ✓

Active LGBT alumni group

UNIVERSITY OF KANSAS
GAY POINT AVERAGE (13)
(out of 20)

CAMPUS QUEER RESOURCES

Select LGBT Student Organization(s):
Queers and Allies
Founding Date: 1970
Membership: 50
Phone: 785-864-3091
E-mail: QandA@ku.edu
Website: www.ku.edu/~qanda/

LGBT Resource Center/Office:
LGBT Programs and Services
Room 400, Kansas Union
1301 Jayhawk Boulevard
Lawrence, KS 66045
Year Established: Mid-1990s
Number of Staff: 1 graduate assistant
Phone: 785-864-4861
E-mail: lbgt@ku.edu
Website: www.silc.ku.edu/lgbt/

UNIVERSITY OF LOUISVILLE

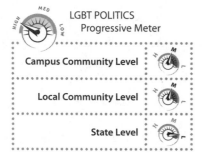

LGBT POLITICS
Progressive Meter

Campus Community Level

Local Community Level

State Level

INFO

UNIVERSITY OF LOUISVILLE
Houchens Building, Room 150
Louisville, KY 40292
Phone: 502-852-6531
Fax: 502-852-4776
E-mail: admitme@louisville.edu
Website: www.louisville.edu

CAMPUS STATS
Type of Institution: Public university
Founding Year: 1798
Size: 21,725
Avg. Class Size: 20–29 students
Popular Majors: Communication/
Communication Technologies, Social
Sciences and History, Engineering and
Engineering Technologies
Cost: In-state tuition: $5,532
Out-of-state tuition: $15,092
Admission Application Deadline: March 1

THE UNIVERSITY OF Louisville is the lone leader for LGBT students in the state of Kentucky. A queer student remarks: "It is really the only choice in Kentucky." History on campus shows signs of the most visible progress and a steady commitment to LGBT students.

Although the state of Kentucky is queerly conservative, the University of Louisville is the first campus in the state to have an LGBT resource center and to allocate financial resources for an LGBT full-time professional staff member. The Center for Lesbian, Gay, Bisexual, and Transgender Services opened in 2003.

In addition, sexual orientation was added to the nondiscrimination policy as early as 1985, and a petition drive has been conducted to show support for adding gender identity/expression. Administration officials as well as faculty have shown a noticeable dedication to LGBT issues. Most recently, the president and the provost signed off on domestic partner benefits for faculty, staff and students, which will be enacted beginning January 2007. Contracts are currently being drawn up.

Such efforts show a progressive LGBT stance by the university and an unwavering commitment to queers. Along with the LGBT and ally student group CommonGround, the university also supports numerous LGBT special events, which include favorites like National Coming Out Day, Pride Week and the annual "Pink" Drag Show Fundraiser. The campus also brings nationally renowned queer speakers to educate and show an affirmative stance for LGBT students. Another indication of the campus climate is the success of the Safe Zone training for allies, conducted year-round to an increasingly wide audience of students, faculty and staff. An LGBT student remarks: "The sheer number of allies and visible LGBT students make this campus stand out. It's continually improving."

Indeed, the campus does "stand out." The University of Louisville offers the most supportive LGBT campus climate in Kentucky. There are a number of student leaders, from student government to fraternities, who are openly gay. Together, LGBT students and allies are making a positive visible impact on the campus culture. One LGBT student agrees: "We have active LGBT leadership on campus and the opportunity to have an impact. ... I have seen the progress firsthand and know that we have something special to offer in Kentucky."

OUTSPOKEN *Answers from LGBT students:*

Top Three Descriptors of the LGBT Campus Environment:
1. Supportive   2. Welcoming   3. Improving

What makes your campus feel welcoming and safe for LGBT students?
"The campus tries to make LGBT students feel welcome through the organization known as CommonGround. I attended the meetings, and they do an excellent job of making students feel welcome and accepted on this campus." *—20-year-old bisexual female, junior*

"The volume of allies visible through the Safe Zone program."
—18-year-old gay male, sophomore

How do you feel about coming out on your campus?

"I was in the closet during my freshman year. Initially I felt isolated…as I came out one by one to my close friends and various faculty/staff, something changed. I soon realized that all of the pressure was off. From then on, I have felt 100 percent supported and comfortable being gay." —*21-year-old gay male, junior*

ACADEMIC SCENE

Top Three Supportive LGBT Academic Areas:
1. Social Work   2. Humanities   3. Law

How LGBT-friendly are faculty in the classroom?

"The acceptance of faculty toward GLBT individuals varies on a person-to-person basis. But, mostly I have found faculty in class to be courteous and interested in general about LGBT perspectives." —*22-year old gay male, senior*

"Most faculty are great. … there are a few that are overly conservative … but the student body is very vocal when a professor or the administration shows any sort of discrimination." —*20-year-old lesbian, junior*

SOCIAL SCENE

Top Three Things in the LGBT Social Life:
1. House parties   2. Bars   3. Movies

How would you describe the social scene for LGBT students?

"Remote but visibly improving. … There is more queer stuff to do than when I got here my first year. I have been surprised and happy."
—*22-year-old gay male, senior*

What annual social event should an LGBT student not miss?

"The 'Pink' drag show. It's a fundraiser and a wildly outrageous time."
—*21-year-old gay male, junior*

OUTRAGEOUS FACTOID Better than 1 billboard, 1,000 walking billboards! University of Louisville queers blanket the campus with "pro-gay" t-shirts during Pride Week. In 2005, in less than 60 minutes, the LGBT student group handed out 1,000 t-shirts free of charge. Straight students stood in long lines to make sure they got their best queer pick!

• • • • • • • • • • • • • • • • • • • •

RAINBOW RUMOR There's an LGBT agenda in the works to make the campus transgender-friendly. Such efforts include advocating for gender-neutral bathrooms and adding "gender identity and expression" to the campus nondiscrimination clause.

• • • • • • • • • • • • • • • • • • • •

THAT'S SO GAY!

ANNUAL LGBT EVENT HIGHLIGHTS

National Coming Out Day: October 11

Pride Week: October

LGBT T-shirt Campaign [AU: I missed this in the regular edit—when is it? ED]

Transgender Awareness 101: November

LGBT Showcase Speaker: February/March

"Pink" Drag Show Fundraiser: April

Safe Zone Training: Fall/Spring

BUZZ BITES
Fun Queer Stuff to Know

THE BEST…

Party Locale: Connections *and* Q

Hangout: Days Coffee Shop

Eating Place: Mitz's *and* Bearno's Pizza

Place to Check Out Guys: HSC Fitness Center

Place to Check Out Ladies: Red Barn

LGBT-Cool Athletic Sport: Women's soccer *or* softball

Non-LGBT-Specific Campus Club:
Pagan Student Union

LGBT Educational Involvement Opportunity:
Safe Zone

CAMPUS QUEER RESOURCES

Select LGBT Student Organization(s):

CommonGround
Founding Date: 1995
Membership: 200+
E-mail: commonground@louisville.edu
Website: www.louisville.edu/rso/
commonground/

LGBT Resource Center/Office:

**Center for Lesbian, Gay, Bisexual,
and Transgender Services**
University of Louisville
Houchens Building 04B
Louisville, KY 40292
Year Established: 2003
Number of Staff: 1 full-time professional staff
Phone: 502-852-0696
E-mail: clconl02@louisville.edu
Website: www.louisville.edu/provost/
diversity/LGBT_services.html

THE GAY POINT AVERAGE
OFFICIAL CAMPUS CHECKLIST

- ✓ LGBT & ally student organization
- ✓ LGBT resource center/office
- ✓ LGBT Pride Week &/or Coming Out Week
- ✓ Safe Zone/Safe Space or Ally Program
- ✓ Significant number of LGBT social activities
- ✓ Significant number of LGBT educational events
- Variety of LGBT studies/courses
- ✓ Nondiscrimination statement inclusive of sexual orientation
- Nondiscrimination statement inclusive of gender identity/expression
- Extends domestic partner benefits to same-sex couples
- Actively recruits LGBT students to enroll on campus
- ✓ Trains campus police on LGBT sensitivity
- ✓ Procedure for reporting LGBT bias, harassment & hate crimes
- Offers LGBT housing options/themes
- ✓ Offers LGBT-inclusive health services/testing
- ✓ Offers LGBT-inclusive counseling/support groups
- Offers LGBT student scholarships
- Conducts special LGBT graduation ceremony for LGBT & ally Students
- Offers support services for process of transitioning from M to F & F to M
- ✓ Active LGBT alumni group

12 UNIVERSITY OF LOUISVILLE
GAY POINT AVERAGE
(out of 20)

UNIVERSITY OF MAINE

THE UNIVERSITY OF MAINE has become one of the most accepting and affirming LGBT campuses in the country. Queer history highlights that UMaine was among the first major universities to recognize an official student group for LGBT people and to include sexual orientation in nondiscrimination policies.

Being the largest, most comprehensive university in the state, the campus attracts LGBT youth turning to higher education as a safe space to grow. Over the years, many LGBT youth have called the campus home. Campus visitors walking through the Union often comment on the diversity of sexualities and genders visible on any given day. Even such traditionally homophobic settings as the Greek system are notably LGBT-friendly. One straight fraternity brother states: "As I see it, a brother is a brother. If he brings a guy to the formal, so be it. I love him for who he is." In addition, the Rainbow Resource Center and Wilde Stein Alliance actively educate the campus community with various LGBT programs and services.

Undoubtedly, UMaine hails as one of the best, most LGBT-progressive campuses in the Northeast. The one hope all other campuses can have is that the old saying, "As goes Maine, so goes the nation," reigns true. One LGBT student wholeheartedly agrees: "UMaine has been my home. It's really special to me because I was able to come out here, for the first time in my life. I never thought that was possible. I can only hope that there are more campuses like UMaine for other LGBT college students."

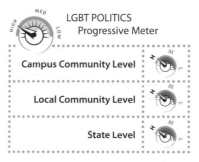

LGBT POLITICS
Progressive Meter

Campus Community Level

Local Community Level

State Level

𝟿𝟿 OUTSPOKEN *Answers from LGBT students:*

Top Three Descriptors of the LGBT Campus Environment:
1. Progressive   2. Reaffirming   3. Open

What makes your campus feel welcoming and safe for LGBT students?
"Definitely the community. People are always out here supporting and reaffirming everyone, like with the whole effort in the recent election [on the statewide gay rights measure]. So many people, gay, straight, whatever, stepped up to help out their GLBT brothers and sisters." —*21-year-old gay male, junior*

How do you feel about coming out on your campus?
"So far my experience has been that my coming out was more a concern for me than anyone else." —*37-year-old lesbian, sophomore*

⊘ ACADEMIC SCENE

Top Three Supportive LGBT Academic Areas:
1. Women's Studies   2. Sociology   3. Human Development

How LGBT-friendly are faculty in the classroom?
"I've always felt very welcome and comforted in the classroom. The majority of professors have gone out of their way to show support."
—*20-year-old bisexual female, junior*

INFO

UNIVERSITY OF MAINE
5713 Chadbourne Hall
Orono, ME 04469
Phone: 207-581-1561
Fax: 207-581-1213
E-mail: um-admit@maine.edu
Website: www.umaine.edu

CAMPUS STATS
Type of Institution: Public university
Founding Year: 1865
Size: 10,400
Avg. Class Size: 10–19 students
Popular Majors: Business Administration/ Management, Education, Engineering
Cost: In-state tuition: $6,910
Out-of-state tuition: $17,050
Admission Application Deadline: January 1

OUTRAGEOUS FACTOID

A recent statewide gay rights measure had more than 80 percent of the campus casting a vote in favor of LGBT rights. The local newspaper noted that such a voting record made Orono the "most progressive town in Maine when it comes to gay rights."

• •

RAINBOW RUMOR

Boasting one of the oldest LGBT student groups in the nation, the University of Maine is acutely aware of LGBT student needs and concerns. The most recent attention has gone toward creating an LGBT studies minor and a more trans-inclusive approach to current campus services. No longer in a basement, Wilde Stein—and its namesakes Oscar Wilde and Gertrude Stein—should be proud!

• •

THAT'S SO GAY!

ANNUAL LGBT EVENT HIGHLIGHTS

National Coming Out Day/Week: October

Day of Silence: First week of April

Rainbow Speaker Series: Fall/Spring

Pride Week: Spring

Drag Show: Spring

Lavender Graduation: April/May

"There are so many examples of support in the classroom. You just know that professors are there for you. You just know they are supportive."
—*21-year-old gay male, junior*

☺ SOCIAL SCENE

Top Three Things in the LGBT Social Life:
1. Wilde Stein   2. Pride Week   3. Parties

How would you describe the social scene for LGBT students?
"The scene is pretty active because of different organizations and gay bars downtown. You can always meet people, even in typically 'straight' settings."
—*21-year-old gay male, junior*

What annual social event should an LGBT student not miss?
"The drag show is a huge hit. Drag queens of all kinds!"
—*20-year-old lesbian, junior*

Fun Queer Stuff to Know

THE BEST...

Party Locale: Karma

Hangout: Oakes Room

Eating Place: Club Detour

Place to Check Out Guys: Carnegie Hall

Place to Check Out Ladies: Oakes Room

LGBT-Cool Athletic Sport: Swim Team

Non-LGBT-Specific Campus Club: Campus Activities Board

Place for LGBT Students to Live on Campus: Stodder Hall and Hancock Hall

LGBT Course Offering: Sociology of Gay and Lesbian Families and Relationships

LGBT Educational Involvement Opportunity: Coming Out Week (COW)

LGBT-Accepting Religious/Spiritual Organization(s): Wilson Center

THE GAY POINT AVERAGE
OFFICIAL CAMPUS CHECKLIST

LGBT & ally student organization	✓
LGBT resource center/office	✓
LGBT Pride Week &/or Coming Out Week	✓
Safe Zone/Safe Space or Ally Program	✓
Significant number of LGBT social activities	✓
Significant number of LGBT educational events	✓
Variety of LGBT studies/courses	✓
Nondiscrimination statement inclusive of sexual orientation	✓
Nondiscrimination statement inclusive of gender identity/expression	✓
Extends domestic partner benefits to same-sex couples	✓
Actively recruits LGBT students to enroll on campus	✓
Trains campus police on LGBT sensitivity	✓
Procedure for reporting LGBT bias, harassment & hate crimes	✓
Offers LGBT housing options/themes	✓
Offers LGBT-inclusive health services/testing	✓
Offers LGBT-inclusive counseling/support groups	✓
Offers LGBT student scholarships	
Conducts special LGBT graduation ceremony for LGBT & ally Students	✓
Offers support services for process of transitioning from M to F & F to M	
Active LGBT alumni group	

UNIVERSITY OF MAINE
GAY POINT AVERAGE
17
(out of 20)

CAMPUS QUEER RESOURCES

Select LGBT Student Organization(s):
Wilde Stein Alliance
Founding Date: 1973
Membership: 200+
Phone: 207-581-1596
E-mail: Wilde.Stein@umit.maine.edu
Website: www.ume.maine.edu/~wstein/

LGBT Resource Center/Office:
Rainbow Resource Center
5748 Memorial Union, Room 162
Orono, ME 04469
Year Established: 2002
Number of Staff: 2 staff (varying levels of responsibility)
Phone: 207-581-1439
Website: www.umaine.edu/glbt

UNIVERSITY OF MARYLAND

THE SPORTS MASCOT for the University of Maryland is Testudo—a terrapin, which is a particular turtle native to the Chesapeake Bay. Typically, at a sports game you see slogans or hear chants: "Fear the Turtle." But now, with more LGBT progress, and particularly in 2002, with the addition of the Program in LGBT Studies, University of Maryland LGBT students have proclaimed: "Queer the Turtle!"

The turtle symbolizes the steady and relentless queer progress at the University of Maryland. Historically, the campus has struggled with LGBT issues with the politically appointed statewide Board of Regents.

In full anticipation of the Board of Regents's negative response, the campus president has made it clear that the entire university will observe this new trans-inclusive policy. In addition, the campus Gay Point Average shows high marks in all other LGBT-progressive areas.

The campus has much to offer LGBT students, such as the Office of LGBT Equity, the Program in LGBT Studies and the President's Commission on LGBT Issues. In addition, an LGBT student can find specific services in many individual units, such as a coordinator for LGBT Student Involvement, the Rainbow Walk-In Hour at the Counseling Center and an LGBT liaison career counselor in the Career Center. The list really does go on and on.

LGBT activities and events include All-Nighter Drag Karaoke, Pride Days and Quick and Dirty: Queer Studies Symposium. LGBT students can also choose from a variety of queer coalitions and involvement opportunities, including the Pride Alliance, Bisexuals at Maryland and Safe Zone. If that's not enough, Washington, DC, is accessible via the Metro subway system.

Winning the race is the ultimate game plan of the University of Maryland when it comes to LGBT progressiveness and being gay-friendly. This campus has the LGBT-dedicated resources to place among the top heat of contenders in the U.S. mid-Atlantic region. One LGBT senior shares: "I have seen this campus grow tremendously on LGBT issues. I never doubted the campus commitment to LGBT students because you can see it in everyday actions. Even the faculty are gay-friendly…I have always felt welcome on campus."

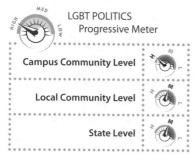

LGBT POLITICS
Progressive Meter

Campus Community Level

Local Community Level

State Level

OUTSPOKEN *Answers from LGBT students:*

Top Three Descriptors of the LGBT Campus Environment:
1. Diverse   2. Supportive   3. Progressive

What makes your campus feel welcoming and safe for LGBT students?
"There's such a large diversity of people on campus that at some point, you have to interact with people from tons of different cultures. This large diversity helps to create a campus that is much more understanding and supporting of people's differences." *—20-year-old gay male sophomore*

How do you feel about coming out on your campus?
"I've never had a problem coming out on campus—everyone I know is very open to and accepting of sexual diversity. I remember coming out to a future roommate as we were trying to navigate the room-selection process. I told him I was bisexual and asked if it was going to be an issue if we ended up sharing a room. He replied, 'I don't care who you sleep with—I just want us to get a good room!'" *—21-year-old queer bisexual male, senior*

INFO

UNIVERSITY OF MARYLAND
Mitchell Building
College Park, MD 20742
Phone: 301-314-8385
Fax: 301-314-9693
E-mail: um-admit@uga.umd.edu
Website: www.umd.edu

CAMPUS STATS
Type of Institution: Public university
Founding Year: 1856
Size: 25,442
Avg. Class Size: 20–29 students
Popular Majors: Computer Science, Criminology, Political Science and Government
Cost: In-state tuition: $7,821
Out-of-state tuition: $20,145
Admission Application Deadline: January 20

⊘ ACADEMIC SCENE

Top Three Supportive LGBT Academic Areas:
1. American Studies   2. English   3. Women's Studies

How LGBT-friendly are faculty in the classroom?
"I have never experienced an LGBT-unfriendly faculty member. It has never been an issue for me or any of my professors." —*23-year-old queer male, senior*

"I've always enjoyed the fact that not only do I know almost two dozen openly LGBT professors, staff, and faculty on campus (in a variety of disciplines) but that I've had multiple teachers (many who are not LGBT themselves) who display Safe Person, Safe Space cards on their office doors or other visible locations. In class, I have felt most of the time that my professors make an effort for their classes to be open and accepting spaces." —*23-year-old queer bisexual female, junior*

☺ SOCIAL SCENE

Top Three Things in the LGBT Social Life:
1. Clubs and bars   2. Drag Karaoke   3. Movies

How would you describe the social scene for LGBT students?
"Maryland's queer social scene is very friendly and open but can be insular at times. The social scene at Maryland also blurs into the DC queer social scene to some extent, given the campus' proximity to DC's vibrant queer community." —*21-year-old queer bisexual male, senior*

What annual social event should an LGBT student not miss?
"At the campus All-Nighter they have Drag Karaoke. It's an event that definitely should not be missed." —*23-year-old queer male, senior*

BUZZ BITES *Fun Queer Stuff to Know*

THE BEST...

Party Locale: Nation *or* Apex

Hangout: Pride Alliance Office

Eating Place: Food Co-op *and* Ten Ren

Place to Check Out Guys: The Mall *and* the Quad on Frat Row

Place to Check Out Ladies: Campus Rec Center

LGBT-Cool Athletic Sport: Soccer *or* women's rugby

Non-LGBT-Specific Campus Club: Gymkanna

Place for LGBT Students to Live on Campus: The Commons

LGBT Course Offering: Special Topics in Lesbian, Gay, Bisexual and Transgender Literatures: Love and Sex in Nineteenth-Century Poetry

LGBT Educational Involvement Opportunity: LGBT Speakers Bureau

LGBT-Accepting Religious/Spiritual Organization(s): Unitarian Universalists, Jewish Student Organization, Reform Judaism, Anglican/Episcopal Ministry

OUTRAGEOUS FACTOID The University of Maryland had a hand in creating one of America's first ambiguously gay couples for kids. Didn't you wonder about Bert and Ernie? *Sesame Street* creator Jim Henson is a Maryland alum.

RAINBOW RUMOR La, la, la…sing along! The University of Maryland woefully acknowledges that it has some hurdles to overcome related to inclusive policies for gender identity and expression. Recently, the University Senate unanimously passed a resolution to include gender identity/expression in the Human Relations Code nondiscrimination policy, and the campus president immediately signed the proposal. However, the statewide Board of Regents strongly resisted. Nevertheless, the campus has pushed ahead with being more inclusive of transgender students. The University of Maryland Office of Legal Affairs observed, "We may not have the words, but we have the music. And some day we will have the words."

THAT'S SO GAY! **ANNUAL LGBT EVENT HIGHLIGHTS**

LGBT Welcome Reception: September

All-Nighter Drag Karaoke: September

National Coming Out Day: October 11

Transgender Day of Remembrance: November 20

Pride Days: March/April

Quick and Dirty: Queer Studies Symposium: March/April

Lavender Graduation: May

CAMPUS QUEER RESOURCES

Select LGBT Student Organization(s):

Pride Alliance

Founding Date: 1969 to 1971

Membership: 300+

Phone: 301-314-8497

E-mail: adviser.pride@umd.edu

Website: www.pridealliance.umd.edu

LGBT Resource Center/Office:

Office of Lesbian, Gay, Bisexual, and Transgender Equity

0119 Cole Student Activities Building
University of Maryland
College Park, MD 20742

Year Established: 1998

Number of Staff: 1 full-time professional staff member; 2 part-time professional staff member, 2 student workers

Phone: 301-405-8720

E-mail: lgbt@umd.edu

Website: www.umd.edu/lgbt

THE GAY POINT AVERAGE
OFFICIAL CAMPUS CHECKLIST

- ✓ LGBT & ally student organization
- ✓ LGBT resource center/office
- ✓ LGBT Pride Week &/or Coming Out Week
- ✓ Safe Zone/Safe Space or Ally Program
- ✓ Significant number of LGBT social activities
- ✓ Significant number of LGBT educational events
- ✓ Variety of LGBT studies/courses
- ✓ Nondiscrimination statement inclusive of sexual orientation
- Nondiscrimination statement inclusive of gender identity/expression
- Extends domestic partner benefits to same-sex couples
- ✓ Actively recruits LGBT students to enroll on campus
- ✓ Trains campus police on LGBT sensitivity
- ✓ Procedure for reporting LGBT bias, harassment & hate crimes
- Offers LGBT housing options/themes
- ✓ Offers LGBT-inclusive health services/testing
- ✓ Offers LGBT-inclusive counseling/support groups
- ✓ Offers LGBT student scholarships
- ✓ Conducts special LGBT graduation ceremony for LGBT & ally Students
- ✓ Offers support services for process of transitioning from M to F & F to M
- ✓ Active LGBT alumni group

17

UNIVERSITY OF MARYLAND
GAY POINT AVERAGE
(out of 20)

UNIVERSITY OF MASSACHUSETTS— AMHERST

THE UNIVERSITY OF Massachusetts—Amherst campus is situated in the only state in the country to allow gay marriage. In addition, the campus is located in the LGBT-progressive Pioneer Valley of Amherst, near a mecca of queer clubs, bookstores, coffee shops and bars.

UMass has long been known as a campus that fosters and appreciates diversity, especially on LGBT issues. Campus history provides a glimpse of UMass as one of the oldest, leading, queer-progressive campuses. In 1985, UMass had the first "Hug a Homosexual" booth and opened the doors to the Program for Gay, Lesbian and Bisexual Concerns, now called the Stonewall Center. The center was one of the first professionally staffed centers in the country established to serve the needs of the LGBT community and create a positive environment for LGBT students through education and advocacy. The campus was also among the first to have a living community specifically to house LGBT students and allies, called "2 in 20." The campus Gay Point Average ranks UMass at the top when it comes to LGBT-progressive policies and practices. The only remaining area of improvement would be trans inclusion, and reportedly it's already under way.

Out LGBT faculty and administrators contribute to queer visibility. Campus queers participate in everything from student government to religious groups and even fraternities and sororities. The most popular annual events on campus include the Drag Ball and QueerFest.

If you want to help plan any of them, you can easily become involved as a leader in the Pride Alliance. That student coalition is one of the largest on campus and works hand in hand with other organizations to bring LGBT speakers and entertainers to campus. In the words of one LGBT student: "It's very easy to be out! And you can get involved in so many ways on campus, from the Stonewall Center to events planned by Pride Alliance. I could not have asked for a more gay-friendly, inclusive campus. It's everything I thought of UMass and more."

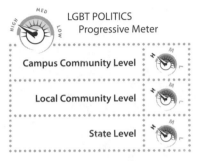

LGBT POLITICS
Progressive Meter

Campus Community Level

Local Community Level

State Level

OUTSPOKEN *Answers from LGBT students:*

Top Three Descriptors of the LGBT Campus Environment:
1. Accepting   2. Inclusive   3. Supportive

What makes your campus feel welcoming and safe for LGBT students?
"The existence of the Stonewall Center is key, as well as the large amount of activism that is inclusive of more than 'gay' issues."
—26-year-old genderqueer lesbian, senior

How do you feel about coming out on your campus?
"I feel that it is relatively safe, and people will question, but they won't violently attack. I have encountered ignorance rather than violence. I also find that a lot of the time when coming out, the other person either comes out in return or that they feel compelled to explore their identity further than they have before. This is a pleasant outcome." *—19-year-old genderqueer pansexual, freshman*

INFO

UNIVERSITY OF MASSACHUSETTS—AMHERST
University Admissions Center
Mather Building
37 Mather Drive
Amherst, MA 01003

Phone: 413-545-0222

Fax: 413-545-4312

E-mail: mail@admissions.umass.edu

Website: www.umass.edu

CAMPUS STATS

Type of Institution: Public university

Founding Year: 1863

Size: 18,966

Avg. Class Size: 20–29 students

Popular Majors: Biology/Biological/Life Sciences, Communication Studies/ Speech Communication and Rhetoric, Psychology

Cost: In-state tuition: $1,714
Out-of-state tuition: $9,937

Admission Application Deadline: January 15

OUTRAGEOUS FACTOID

The 2 in 20 learning community for LGBT and ally students to live on campus was actually one of the first in the United States.

RAINBOW RUMOR

Liberals love UMass! The campus is a gem of progressiveness on LGBT issues. One of the main objectives remaining is the development of an academic department for Queer Studies and/or Gender Studies.

THAT'S SO GAY!

ANNUAL LGBT EVENT HIGHLIGHTS

Movie Night: Weekly, Fall/Spring

Café Outings: Every month, Fall/Spring

Film Festival: Spring

Concerts: Fall/Spring

Poetry Slams: Fall/Spring

Gay and Lesbian History Month: October

Trans Awareness Month: November

Drag Ball: November and April

Day of Silence: April

QueerFest: Late April

ACADEMIC SCENE

Top Three Supportive LGBT Academic Areas:
1. Women's Studies   2. English   3. Arts and Humanities

How LGBT-friendly are faculty in the classroom?
"Overall, faculty really try to be inclusive. Lately the marriage issue has brought up a lot of debate and discussion."
—*26-year-old genderqueer lesbian, senior*

"LGBT issues have come up from time to time. Many professors are very liberal. Most have personally been approachable and understanding."
—*19-year-old gay male sophomore*

SOCIAL SCENE

Top Three Things in the LGBT Social Life:
1. Dancing   2. Socializing at 2 in 20 floor   3. Activism

How would you describe the social scene for LGBT students?
"The words *vibrant* and *friendly* come to mind. The 2 in 20 floor for LGBT students and straight allies is a learning community. Many LGBT students live there, and I find that to be a wonderful way to be social and get involved."
—*20-year-old gay male, sophomore*

What annual social event should an LGBT student not miss?
"The Drag Ball! There's a DJ, performers, and everyone has a lot of fun. QueerFest in the spring is good too." —*20-year-old lesbian, junior*

BUZZ BITES *Fun Queer Stuff to Know*

THE BEST...

Party Locale: Diva's Nightclub

Hangout: 2 in 20 Floor *or* Rainbow Resource Center

Eating Place: Earthfood's Café

Place to Check Out Guys: ROTC drills

Place to Check Out Ladies: Women's lacrosse

Non-LGBT-Specific Campus Club: Ballroom Dancing Club

Place for LGBT Students to Live on Campus: 2 in 20 residence hall floor

LGBT Educational Involvement Opportunity: "Guess the Straight Person" Panel

LGBT-Accepting Religious/Spiritual Organization(s): Hillel House

THE GAY POINT AVERAGE
OFFICIAL CAMPUS CHECKLIST

LGBT & ally student organization ✓

LGBT resource center/office ✓

LGBT Pride Week &/or Coming Out Week ✓

Safe Zone/Safe Space or Ally Program ✓

Significant number of LGBT social activities ✓

Significant number of LGBT educational events ✓

Variety of LGBT studies/courses ✓

Nondiscrimination statement inclusive of sexual orientation ✓

Nondiscrimination statement inclusive of gender identity/expression

Extends domestic partner benefits to same-sex couples ✓

Actively recruits LGBT students to enroll on campus ✓

Trains campus police on LGBT sensitivity ✓

Procedure for reporting LGBT bias, harassment & hate crimes ✓

Offers LGBT housing options/themes ✓

Offers LGBT-inclusive health services/testing ✓

Offers LGBT-inclusive counseling/support groups ✓

Offers LGBT student scholarships ✓

Conducts special LGBT graduation ceremony for LGBT & ally Students ✓

Offers support services for process of transitioning from M to F & F to M

Active LGBT alumni group

UNIVERSITY OF MASSACHUSETTS —AMHERST GAY POINT AVERAGE
(out of 20)

17

CAMPUS QUEER RESOURCES

Select LGBT Student Organization(s):

Pride Alliance
Founding Date: 1980s
Membership: 130+
Phone: 413-545-0154
E-mail: pride@stuaf.umass.edu
Website: www.umass.edu/rso/pride

LGBT Resource Center/Office:

Stonewall Center
256 Sunset Avenue Office
Crampton House SW
Amherst, MA 01003
Year Established: 1985
Number of Staff: 1 full-time professional staff; 1 full-time office manager; 1 graduate assistant, several undergraduate student workers
Phone: 413-545-4824
E-mail: stonewall@stuaf.umass.edu
Website: www.umass.edu/stonewall

UNIVERSITY OF MICHIGAN

THE UNIVERSITY OF Michigan boasts the oldest LGBT campus resource center in the country. In 1971, the campus proved itself a leader by being the first major university to offer support services to lesbian and gay students. Over the span of three decades, the Office of LGBT Affairs has also been at the forefront of extending services to bisexual, transgender, queer and ally students. With a Speakers Bureau of 100-plus members, the LGBT education programs reach over 5,000 people each semester.

The campus is also home to 16 student organizations that focus specifically on LGBT-related issues, as well as numerous other student groups that incorporate LGBT advocacy into their overall mission. The Gay Point Average score reflects this 34-year commitment and drive to lead the way on LGBT issues. One senior sets the record straight: "The University of Michigan has got to be among the best schools for LGBT students. There are so many opportunities available to students, academic and otherwise—social groups, spiritual groups, and athletic groups geared toward LGBT students. There are so many gay students, and so many queer opportunities…. Ann Arbor is not New York City, Berkeley or New Haven, but it offers just as much—something for everyone."

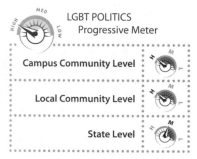

LGBT POLITICS
Progressive Meter

Campus Community Level

Local Community Level

State Level

🗩 OUTSPOKEN *Answers from LGBT students:*

Top Three Descriptors of the LGBT Campus Environment:
1. Passionate   2. Open Minds and Hearts   3. Aware

What makes your campus feel welcoming and safe for LGBT students?
"There are always so many events happening all around campus, especially for LGBT and ally students…. Everyone can feel welcome and be able to have a good time. Not only that, but the Office of LGBT Affairs is like a second home for me." —*20-year-old bisexual male, junior*

How do you feel about coming out on your campus?
"I didn't come out until I reached U of M. From the first moment on campus, I felt alright—not just from my support network of friends, but from all the resources available to me. National Coming Out Week showcased how friendly and nonintimidating the LGBT community was on campus. Plus, the Office of LGBT Affairs has a closed, confidential LGBT group for people still working through the personal stages of coming out and questioning." —*20-year-old lesbian, junior*

✎ ACADEMIC SCENE

Top Three Supportive LGBT Academic Areas:
1. Social Work   2. Public Health   3. Education

How LGBT-friendly are faculty in the classroom?
"I have never had a negative reaction in any class. In fact, my professor for computer programming (a subject where you might not expect to find allies)

INFO

UNIVERSITY OF MICHIGAN
1220 Student Activities Building
Ann Arbor, MI 48109

Phone: 734-764-7433

Fax: 734-936-0740

E-mail: ugadmiss@umich.edu

Website: www.umich.edu

CAMPUS STATS

Type of Institution: Public university

Founding Year: 1817

Size: 24,677

Avg. Class Size: 20–29 students

Popular Majors: Engineering, Law, Medicine, Liberal Arts

Cost: In-state tuition: $8,294 approx.
Out of State Tuition: $25,460 approx.

Admission Application Deadline: February 1

was my strongest supporter. My current math professor is comfortable using masculine pronouns with me (I use both masculine and feminine pronouns to describe myself)." —*19-year-old genderqueer, sophomore*

"This is such a liberal university that it is unacceptable to be politically incorrect. I would dare to say that most, if not all faculty are LGBT-friendly, and a good deal of them are LGBT anyhow." —*21-year-old gay male, senior*

☺ SOCIAL SCENE

Top Three Things in the LGBT Social Life:
1. Concerts at the Blind Pig   2. ColorSplash Social for LGBTA Students, Staff, and Faculty of Color   3. Coffee shops

How would you describe the social scene for LGBT students?
"There are plenty of ways for students to meet. One nightclub near campus has Pride Night every Friday night, which many students enjoy. Last year I co-founded Queers in Residence, a social/support group for LGBTA and questioning students in the residence halls, which provides a more relaxed environment where students can relax. My favorite, however, is gender-free dancing (swing, salsa, and hip-hop) put on by Dance Revolution, a queer locally owned and operated dance studio just off campus." —*20-year-old bisexual male, junior*

What annual social event should an LGBT student not miss?
"An LGBT student should not miss Gayz Craze. It happens at the beginning of every school year as a part of Welcome Week. It is the first time in the year when all the queer students, new and continuing, unite, meet one another and build lasting friendships. You find out about all the different LGBT and LGBT-friendly groups on campus and just have a great time making tie-dye t-shirts, playing football and tug-o-war…. I think this event is more important than going to clubs. When was the last time you met a best friend at the club? At Gayz Craze, it is your time to meet new people!" —*21-year-old gay male, senior*

THE BEST…

Party Locale: Friday nights at Necto

Eating Place: New York Pizza Depot, Seva or the Aut Bar

Place to Check Out Guys: Coffee shops are the best, *or* perhaps the campus gym, for those who secretly fantasize about Michigan athletes.

Place to Check Out Ladies: The Diag

LGBT-Cool Athletic Sport: Gymnastics, fencing

Place for LGBT Students to Live on Campus: East Quad

Place for LGBT Students to Live off Campus: Any of the 18 cooperative houses in the Inter Co-operative Council

LGBT Course Offering: How to Be Gay: Male Homosexuality and Initiation

LGBT Educational Involvement Opportunity: LGBTA Speakers

THAT'S SO GAY!

ANNUAL LGBT EVENT HIGHLIGHTS

Camp Trans: August

Gayz Craze: First week of fall classes

OutFest: September

Speakers Bureau Panels: Ongoing, all year

National Coming Out Week: Second week of October

Transgender Day of Remembrance: November

ColorSplash for LGBT Students, Staff and Faculty of Color: Once per semester

Flaming Menorah Party: Hanukkah

Queer Soiree: February 14

Visibility Week (includes Flames on Ice, Kiss-In Rally): March

Lavender Graduation: April

THE GAY POINT AVERAGE
OFFICIAL CAMPUS CHECKLIST

Select LGBT Student Organization(s):

LGBT Commission, Gender Explorers and Lambda Grads

Membership: 500+

Phone: 734-763-4186

E-mail: lgbta@umich.edu

Website: www.umich.edu/~lgbta

LGBT Resource Center/Office:

Lesbian Gay Bisexual Transgender Affairs

3200 Michigan Union
530 S. State Street
Ann Arbor, MI 48103

Year Established: 1971

Number of Staff: 4 full-time professional staff, 6 graduate/undergraduate staff

Phone: 734-763-4186

E-mail: lgbta@umich.edu

Website: www.umich.edu/~lgbta

- ✓ LGBT & ally student organization
- ✓ LGBT resource center/office
- ✓ LGBT Pride Week &/or Coming Out Week
- ✓ Safe Zone/Safe Space or Ally Program
- ✓ Significant number of LGBT social activities
- ✓ Significant number of LGBT educational events
- ✓ Variety of LGBT studies/courses
- ✓ Nondiscrimination statement inclusive of sexual orientation
- ✓ Nondiscrimination statement inclusive of gender identity/expression
- ✓ Extends domestic partner benefits to same-sex couples
- ✓ Actively recruits LGBT students to enroll on campus
- ✓ Trains campus police on LGBT sensitivity
- ✓ Procedure for reporting LGBT bias, harassment & hate crimes
- Offers LGBT housing options/themes
- ✓ Offers LGBT-inclusive health services/testing
- ✓ Offers LGBT-inclusive counseling/support groups
- Offers LGBT student scholarships
- ✓ Conducts special LGBT graduation ceremony for LGBT & ally Students
- ✓ Offers support services for process of transitioning from M to F & F to M
- ✓ Active LGBT alumni group

18 UNIVERSITY OF MICHIGAN GAY POINT AVERAGE
(out of 20)

UNIVERSITY OF MINNESOTA—DULUTH

LGBT STUDENTS ACKNOWLEDGE that "diverse allies" are the reason the University of Minnesota stands out as gay-friendly.

The Queer Students' Union and GLBT Services have worked hard over the years to create an inclusive approach to developing allies. The UM Duluth philosophy is to have all multicultural organizations working side by side with other neighboring organizations: African American, Asian/Pacific Islander, Latino/Chicana students, international students, students with disabilities—and the list continues. As a result, the queer campus environment is not nearly as segregated as it is on other campuses, and there are more diverse allies. LGBT students with intersecting identities can also feel a level of affirmation for all aspects of themselves. Such an approach sets UM Duluth apart when it comes to ally outreach and is a credit to the university's success.

This campus is unusual in that it provides LGBT-specific endowments for scholarships, leadership and activities. These monies are supported by the LGBT alumni organization, as well as the LGBT faculty and staff organization. Such efforts are beyond the scope of most campuses, showing how UM Duluth is out there for queer progress. The campus has even started to recruit LGBT students.

Scan the Gay Point Average and you will quickly see that this campus is most LGBT-progressive. One LGBT student summarizes: "I think the campus is a wonderful place.... LGBT Services alongside the Multicultural Center adds an environment that is very open to all kinds of diversity. It's also very nice that the Queer Students' Union can be so close to the other student groups, because we can work together to make the campus and community more accepting."

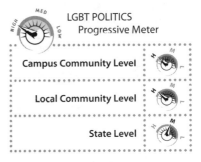

LGBT POLITICS
Progressive Meter

Campus Community Level

Local Community Level

State Level

💬 OUTSPOKEN *Answers from LGBT students:*

Top Three Descriptors of the LGBT Campus Environment:
1. Energetic   2. Supportive   3. Welcoming

What makes your campus feel welcoming and safe for LGBT students?
"I feel it is a very welcoming climate. The Queer Students Union and GLBT Services office are very visible. You see people walking around with 'Gay? Fine by Me' t-shirts and rainbow pins, [and that] shows that the GLBT community is out there and that the allies are in full force." —*19-year-old bisexual male, junior*

How do you feel about coming out on your campus?
"UMD is a great place to come out; the people are very open and affirming. I came out on campus and felt very safe and supported throughout the whole process." —*19-year-old lesbian, sophomore*

🖋 ACADEMIC SCENE

Top Three Supportive LGBT Academic Areas:
1. Women's Studies   2. Geography   3. Social Sciences

INFO

UNIVERSITY OF MINNESOTA—DULUTH
23 Solon Campus Center
1117 University Drive
Duluth, MN 55812
Phone: 218-726-7171
Fax: 218-726-7040
E-mail: umdadmis@d.umn.edu
Website: www.d.umn.edu

CAMPUS STATS
Type of Institution: Public university
Founding Year: 1947
Size: 8,931
Avg. Class Size: 20–29 students
Popular Majors: Biological/Life Sciences, Business, Administration/Management, Elementary Education and Teaching
Cost: In-state tuition: $8,428
Out-of-state tuition: $18,794
Admission Application Deadline: February 1

OUTRAGEOUS FACTOID The mayor of Duluth was on the front cover of the statewide LGBT magazine, featured as "queerly amazing," with an A+ rating on LGBT issues. He said his favorite group on campus was the Queer Student Union. Not shocking to Duluth, however: the city was also recently voted by *Out* magazine to have the "Hottest Smalltown Pride Event" in the nation.

• • • • • • • • • • • • • • • • • • •

RAINBOW RUMOR Despite an inclusive LGBT nondiscrimination statement, several queer students point out that more advocacy and education efforts are necessary in regard to transgender individuals.

• • • • • • • • • • • • • • • • • • •

THAT'S SO GAY!

ANNUAL LGBT EVENT HIGHLIGHTS

GLBT Orientation: September

National Coming Out Day Week/Coming Out Week: October

Hate Crimes Vigil: October

Fall Drag Show: October

Transgender Awareness Month: November

World AIDS Day observance: December

Rainbow Days Pride Week: April

Spring Drag Show: April

Fabulous Farewell Lavender Graduation: April

How LGBT-friendly are faculty in the classroom?

"Faculty have been incredible here at UMD. One psychology professor in particular has been a very vocal ally and has been a role model for me. She teaches a class called Gender in Society and makes it very clear that she will not tolerate any kind of intolerance regarding LGBT persons. This was great to hear from day one of class." —*20-year-old lesbian, junior*

"From what I can see, the faculty are extremely friendly. I once sat in a class during the first day and heard a professor say, 'This class is going to discuss, at length, human sexuality. I'm not asking you to be accepting or change your views, but if you can't learn to be respectful, there's the door.' It was awesome!" —*22-year-old gay male, senior*

😃 SOCIAL SCENE

Top Three Things in the LGBT Social Life:
1. Drag Show   2. Queer Student Union   3. Dancing

How would you describe the social scene for LGBT students?
"The social scene is awesome! The GLBT community and their allies are phenomenal. Even for those under 21, the social scene is still very alive with LGBT student groups providing a whole range of opportunities." —*20-year-old lesbian, junior*

What annual social event should an LGBT student not miss?
"The Drag Show. It is awesome whether you perform in it or just go to watch it. Everyone there is an ally, and it is great to see the support we have on campus!" —*19-year-old bisexual male, junior*

BUZZ BITES *Fun Queer Stuff to Know*

THE BEST...

Party Locale: The Main
Hangout: Jitters Coffee House
Eating Place: Grandma's Restaurant
Place to Check Out Guys: Miller Hill Mall
Place to Check Out Ladies: Queer Student Union
LGBT-Cool Athletic Sport: Women's hockey
Non-LGBT-Specific Campus Club: Feminists Advocating for Change

LGBT Educational Involvement Opportunity: LGBT Speakers Bureau
LGBT-Accepting Religious/Spiritual Organization(s): Peace UCC, Unitarian Church

THE GAY POINT AVERAGE
OFFICIAL CAMPUS CHECKLIST

LGBT & ally student organization ✓

LGBT resource center/office ✓

LGBT Pride Week &/or Coming Out Week ✓

Safe Zone/Safe Space or Ally Program ✓

Significant number of LGBT social activities ✓

Significant number of LGBT educational events ✓

Variety of LGBT studies/courses

Nondiscrimination statement inclusive of sexual orientation ✓

Nondiscrimination statement inclusive of gender identity/expression ✓

Extends domestic partner benefits to same-sex couples ✓

Actively recruits LGBT students to enroll on campus ✓

Trains campus police on LGBT sensitivity ✓

Procedure for reporting LGBT bias, harassment & hate crimes ✓

Offers LGBT housing options/themes

Offers LGBT-inclusive health services/testing ✓

Offers LGBT-inclusive counseling/support groups ✓

Offers LGBT student scholarships ✓

Conducts special LGBT graduation ceremony for LGBT & ally Students ✓

Offers support services for process of transitioning from M to F & F to M

Active LGBT alumni group ✓

CAMPUS QUEER RESOURCES

Select LGBT Student Organization(s):
Queer Students' Union
Founding Date: 1983
Membership: 25
Phone: 218-726-7041
E-mail: qsu@d.umn.edu
Website: www.d.umn.edu/~qsu/

LGBT Resource Center/Office:
GLBT Services
Kirby 236
1120 Kirby Drive
Duluth, MN 55812
Year Established: 2000
Number of Staff: 1 full-time professional staff member, 1 graduate assistant, 1 part-time student employee
Phone: 218-726-7300
Website: www.d.umn.edu/mlrc/glbt

UNIVERSITY OF MINNESOTA—DULUTH GAY POINT AVERAGE
(out of 20)

17

BEST
OF THE BEST
TOP 20

UNIVERSITY OF MINNESOTA—TWIN CITIES

LOCATED IN THE metropolis of Minneapolis, Minnesota, the university has been a champion of LGBT inclusiveness and progress.

Early LGBT campus history dates back to 1969, with the creation of the first LGBT student coalition, now named the Queer Student Cultural Center. It was one of the first in the nation. But in a true test of LGBT inclusiveness, only one year later the campus elected an openly gay man as student body president. Such a move was definitely a queer first in the United States and demonstrates an LGBT-progressive past.

In the early 1990s, the university president established a committee to explore the LGBT campus climate. Among five recommendations was the establishment of the GLBT Programs Office. The office opened in 1993 and has since grown by leaps and bounds, developing many worthwhile LGBT programs and services. One of the most phenomenal is the annual Stand with Us campaign, in which out LGBT students are pictured on posters with captions that foster inclusion. Students love to participate, and the campus raves about the effective visibility. "I was part of the campaign. You can't miss it. I had so many positive remarks, and I felt like the campus was truly accepting," states one LGBT student. In addition, there are over 100 LGBT student organizations on campus, and each has several annual events and activities. Some of the most popular are Coming Out Week and Pride Week, when many queer students and allies come together to listen to guest speakers and attend panels and social gatherings.

The University of Minnesota—Twin Cities campus has been a leader in LGBT progress and has fostered a positive experience for its queer students. One LGBT student shares: "I am at home here. The GLBT Programs Office staff gives support and creates a welcoming space to be who you are. I have learned a great deal…grown as a leader, and my queer identity is still very much intact."

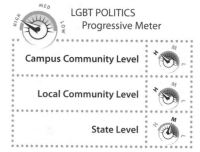

LGBT POLITICS
Progressive Meter

Campus Community Level

Local Community Level

State Level

OUTSPOKEN *Answers from LGBT students:*

Top Three Descriptors of the LGBT Campus Environment:
1. Support   2. Welcoming   3. Active

What makes your campus feel welcoming and safe for LGBT students?
"The amount of awareness on campus and the number of allies. … Every year in April there is a LGBT campaign that has huge photos of different LGBT people on campus. Captions under the photos say things like 'I am a Republican,' 'I am your roommate' and 'I am a parent.' It's really cool and makes me proud to be gay." —*20-year-old gay male, junior*

How do you feel about coming out on your campus?
"Every building that I have been to, there has been a LGBT support sign or sticker, at least somewhere. I can come out anywhere and feel safe."
—*19-year-old queer male, sophomore*

INFO

UNIVERSITY OF MINNESOTA—TWIN CITIES
240 Williamson Hall
231 Pillsbury Drive SE
Minneapolis, MN 55455

Phone: 612-625-2008
Fax: 612-626-1693
E-mail: admissions@tc.umn.edu
Website: www.umn.edu

CAMPUS STATS
Type of Institution: Public university
Founding Year: 1851
Size: 28,103
Avg. Class Size: 10–19 students
Popular Majors: Social Sciences and History, Business/Marketing, Engineering/Engineering Technologies
Cost: In-state tuition: $5,420
Out-of-state tuition: $15,994
Admission Application Deadline: January 15

"I feel comfortable and safe for those who I know. I came out to one of my friends, and she said, 'I already knew and it's cool. I love you.' It was a good feeling." —*20-year-old lesbian, sophomore*

ACADEMIC SCENE

Top Three Supportive LGBT Academic Areas:
1. Education and Human Development 2. History 3. Dance

How LGBT-friendly are faculty in the classroom?
"Great for the most part. I am out in pretty much all of my classes. Some of the faculty bring up LGBT issues just to make other students view the topics differently…It's awesome!" —*20-year-old bisexual female, junior*

"Definitely queer-supportive. I am sure there are some that are less than LGBT-friendly, but I don't know of any myself. I have found a vast amount of acceptance for queer ideas in my classes."
—*22-year-old genderqueer, senior*

SOCIAL SCENE

Top Three Things in the LGBT Social Life:
1. Shopping 2. Dancing 3. Hanging out

How would you describe the social scene for LGBT students?
"Exciting and active mostly…. but you have to really put yourself out there. The best times in college are not going to come from sitting in front of your computer." —*21 year old gay male, senior*

What annual social event should an LGBT student not miss?
"National Coming Out Week. One of the best times I have each year, so much queer to do." —*20-year-old bisexual female, junior*

BUZZ BITES *Fun Queer Stuff to Know*

THE BEST…

Party Locale: Gay 90s
Hangout: GLBT Programs Office
Eating Place: Blue Moon Coffee Café
Place to Check Out Guys: University Recreation Center
Place to Check Out Ladies: Cowle Stadium
LGBT-Cool Athletic Sport: Volleyball

LGBT Course Offering: Theory, Knowledge and Power, Transgender Studies
LGBT Educational Involvement Opportunity: Stand with Us ad campaign

OUTRAGEOUS FACTOID Delta Lambda Phi, the nation's oldest and largest fraternity for gay, bisexual and straight ally men, has its largest fraternity chapter at the University of Minnesota—Twin Cities.

RAINBOW RUMOR The University of Minnesota—Twin Cities was among the first universities in 2004 to settle out of court in a challenge to its campus nondiscrimination statement. Outside Christian legal groups had sued the campus on behalf of a complaint by a student organization called the Maranatha Christian Fellowship. The student group did not want to abide by the campus nondiscrimination policy which included membership being open to all members, regardless of race, religion, national origin, sexual orientation and so on. The university administration responded that the settlement was only a clarification of language and that the final decision respects the "community of ideas."

THAT's SO GAY!

ANNUAL LGBT EVENT HIGHLIGHTS

National Coming Out Day Luncheon: October 11

Coming Out Week: October

LGBT Film Festival: January

Pride Week: Spring

Day of Silence: First week of April

Lavender Graduation and Awards Ceremony: April/May

Drag Show: Fall and Spring

LGBT Health Series: Fall/Spring

Schochet Distinguished Lecture Series: Fall/Spring

Stand with Us Ad Campaign: Fall/Spring

CAMPUS QUEER RESOURCES

Select LGBT Student Organization(s):

Queer Student Cultural Center
Founding Date: 1969
Membership: 660+
Phone: 612-626-2344
E-mail: qscc@umn.edu
Website: www.qscc.org

LGBT Resource Center/Office:

GLBT Programs Office
University of Minnesota
138 Klaeber Court
320 16th Avenue SE
Minneapolis, MN 55455
Year Established: 1993
Number of Staff: 2 full-time professional staff, 1 graduate assistant
Phone: 612-625-0537
E-mail: glbt@umn.edu
Website: www.umn.edu/glbt

THE GAY POINT AVERAGE
OFFICIAL CAMPUS CHECKLIST

✓ LGBT & ally student organization

✓ LGBT resource center/office

✓ LGBT Pride Week &/or Coming Out Week

Safe Zone/Safe Space or Ally Program

✓ Significant number of LGBT social activities

✓ Significant number of LGBT educational events

✓ Variety of LGBT studies/courses

✓ Nondiscrimination statement inclusive of sexual orientation

✓ Nondiscrimination statement inclusive of gender identity/expression

✓ Extends domestic partner benefits to same-sex couples

✓ Actively recruits LGBT students to enroll on campus

✓ Trains campus police on LGBT sensitivity

✓ Procedure for reporting LGBT bias, harassment & hate crimes

✓ Offers LGBT housing options/themes

✓ Offers LGBT-inclusive health services/testing

✓ Offers LGBT-inclusive counseling/support groups

✓ Offers LGBT student scholarships

✓ Conducts special LGBT graduation ceremony for LGBT & ally Students

✓ Offers support services for process of transitioning from M to F & F to M

✓ Active LGBT alumni group

19 UNIVERSITY OF MINNESOTA— TWIN CITIES GAY POINT AVERAGE
(out of 20)

UNIVERSITY OF MISSOURI—KANSAS CITY

IN 1978, GAY students at the University of Missouri—Kansas City filed suit against the university for their right to assemble and be recognized as a student organization on campus. In a landmark case, the U.S. Supreme Court ruled in favor of the Gay Student Union. LGBT-friendly history has been moving forward ever since.

UMKC has made major strides, and the momentum has been building. Most significantly, the campus made a substantial stride in creating the LGBT Programs and Services office in 2003. What started out as an idea by a concerned group of LGBT individuals on campus has become a widely known campus resource today.

There is a variety of LGBT services available to queer students, including educational and social programs offered four times per month. The office also provides Safe Space diversity training, where faculty and staff learn how to be sensitive to and supportive of LGBT students. Additionally, the LGBT office works closely with the student coalition Queers and Allies. One of the biggest, a drag show planned by both the LGBT office and Queers and Allies, brings together the LGBT and ally community twice a year along with other queer events including Gay Pride Week, Day of Silence and World AIDS Day.

UMKC may still be a "queer newbie" when it comes to LGBT progressiveness, but the campus stands out proudly. As one LGBT student explains: "Campus support for LGBT issues is growing. I finally feel like we are being heard. The LGBT actions are speaking louder than the words…I feel more proud than ever."

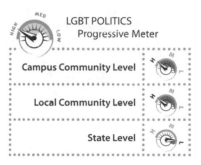

LGBT POLITICS
Progressive Meter

Campus Community Level

Local Community Level

State Level

OUTSPOKEN *Answers from LGBT students:*

Top Three Descriptors of the LGBT Campus Environment:
1. Accepting   2. Eventful   3. Friendly

What makes your campus feel welcoming and safe for LGBT students?
"Everywhere you look there seems to be something for gay and lesbian students to do. Whether it is a social event put on in the residence halls or a drag show put on by queers and allies…There is always something for students to do."
—18-year-old gay male, freshman

How do you feel about coming out on your campus?
"At first I wasn't out at school, but after seeing so many allies on campus, I felt comfortable enough to tell my closest friend and then come out to everyone on National Coming Out Day." *—21-year-old gay male, junior*

ACADEMIC SCENE

Top Three Supportive LGBT Academic Areas:
1. English   2. History   3. Women and Gender Studies

INFO

UNIVERSITY OF MISSOURI— KANSAS CITY
5100 Rockhill Road
101 Administrative Center Building, Room 120
Kansas City, MO 64110
Phone: 816-235-1111
Fax: 816-235-5544
E-mail: admit@umkc.edu
Website: www.umkc.edu

CAMPUS STATS
Type of Institution: Public university
Founding Year: 1929
Size: 12,151
Avg. Class Size: 20–29 students
Popular Majors: Business Administration/ Management, Liberal Arts and Sciences/Liberal Studies, Psychology
Cost: In-state tuition: $7,031
Out-of-state tuition: $17,102
Admission Application Deadline: March 1

Lea Hopkins, the first African American *Playboy* bunny and first out lesbian to appear in *Essence* magazine, served as adviser for the UMKC Gay Student Union (now called Queers and Allies). Hopkins also organized the first Gay Pride Parade in Kansas City, Missouri, in 1979. She recently came back to UMKC to serve as a special keynote speaker for the first Lavender Graduation Ceremony in May 2005.

RAINBOW RUMOR

Some LGBT students wish that there was more to show when it comes to programming specifically geared toward women and people of color in the LGBT community. One LGBT student says: "As a woman of color, I sometimes feel that some of the issues I deal with aren't addressed as well as they could be."

THAT'S SO GAY!

ANNUAL LGBT EVENT HIGHLIGHTS

Q&A Drag Show: Fall and Spring

Annual Scholarship Benefit: Fall

Gay Straight Youth Empowerment Summit: Fall

Welcome Week Social: First week of fall classes

Foam Dance: Fall

Gay Pride Week: October

Coming Out Day Picnic: October 11

KC Gay History Tour: October

Transgender Day of Remembrance: November 20

World AIDS Day: December 1

Diversity Week: February

Boxes and Walls: February

Day of Silence/Break the Silence: April

Lavender Graduation: May

How LGBT-friendly are faculty in the classroom?

"In my sociology class my professor includes sexual orientation in the majority of his lectures. It really gives the gay and lesbian community visibility to those students in class that may not even consider LGBT issues, not because they're not accepting, it's just that they have never thought about it."
—*18-year-old gay male, freshman*

"Oh, they're all friendly. I've never had a professor that isn't gay-friendly here at UMKC." —*19-year-old gay male, sophomore*

😊 SOCIAL SCENE

Top Three Things in the LGBT Social Life:
1. Parties   2. Bars   3. Dancing

How would you describe the social scene for LGBT students?
"The social scene is really open and welcoming. There are frequent events for LGBT students to go to that are positive and fun."
—*19-year-old gay male, sophomore*

What annual social event should an LGBT student not miss?
"Oh, the Foam Dance! It is so much fun. It's a great place to meet new people at the beginning of the year. A lot of my friends that I have now, I met at the Foam Dance." —*18-year-old gay male, freshman*

BUZZ BITES *Fun Queer Stuff to Know*

THE BEST...

Party Locale: Club NV

Hangout: LGBT Programs and Services

Eating Place: Chubby's

Place to Check Out Guys: Grant Hall Music and Theater Building

Place to Check Out Ladies: Coffee Girls

LGBT-Cool Athletic Sport: KC Waves Swim Team

Non-LGBT-Specific Campus Club: Campus Greens

Place for LGBT Students to Live on Campus: Oak Street Residence Hall

LGBT Educational Involvement Opportunity: Queers and Allies

LGBT-Accepting Religious/Spiritual Organization(s): United Campus Ministries

THE GAY POINT AVERAGE
OFFICIAL CAMPUS CHECKLIST

LGBT & ally student organization	✓
LGBT resource center/office	✓
LGBT Pride Week &/or Coming Out Week	✓
Safe Zone/Safe Space or Ally Program	✓
Significant number of LGBT social activities	✓
Significant number of LGBT educational events	✓
Variety of LGBT studies/courses	
Nondiscrimination statement inclusive of sexual orientation	✓
Nondiscrimination statement inclusive of gender identity/expression	
Extends domestic partner benefits to same-sex couples	
Actively recruits LGBT students to enroll on campus	
Trains campus police on LGBT sensitivity	
Procedure for reporting LGBT bias, harassment & hate crimes	✓
Offers LGBT housing options/themes	✓
Offers LGBT-inclusive health services/testing	✓
Offers LGBT-inclusive counseling/support groups	✓
Offers LGBT student scholarships	
Conducts special LGBT graduation ceremony for LGBT & ally Students	✓
Offers support services for process of transitioning from M to F & F to M	✓
Active LGBT alumni group	

UNIVERSITY OF MISSOURI—KANSAS CITY GAY POINT AVERAGE
(out of 20)

13

CAMPUS QUEER RESOURCES

Select LGBT Student Organization(s):
Queers and Allies
Founding Date: 1978 (as Gay Student Union)
Membership: 120+
Phone: 816-235-1407
E-mail: qa@umkc.edu
Website: studo.umkc.edu/qa/

LGBT Resource Center/Office:
LGBT Programs and Services
G-6 University Center
5100 Rockhill Road
Kansas City, Missouri 64110
Year Established: 2003
Number of Staff: 1 full-time professional staff, 2 part-time student staff
Phone: 816-235-1639
E-mail: lgbtoffice@umkc.edu
Website: www.umkc.edu/lgbt

UNIVERSITY OF NORTH CAROLINA—CHAPEL HILL

THE UNIVERSITY OF North Carolina—Chapel Hill is located in the most LGBT-progressive area of North Carolina, suitably named the "Triangle."

The University of North Carolina strives to offer a welcoming and safe place for all students. To meet the growing interest in and pressing needs of LGBT students, the university created the LGBTQ Office in 2003, staffing it with one full-time employee. Today the office offers a variety of support services and educational programs to foster a more positive LGBT campus climate. An LGBT student comments: "Having the LGBTQ Office here has helped me tremendously. I could not imagine making it through my four years without its support."

The most noticeably visible program that the LGBTQ Office offers is the Safe Zone program. There are currently over 600 trained and active Safe Zone allies within the campus community, including a broad range of staff and faculty. In 2006, the LGBTQ office will be expanding into a larger physical space, and the campus will be adding a new academic minor in sexuality studies. As on most campuses, this LGBT progress would not have been possible without major efforts by past and current students. The campus has an exemplary LGBT Straight Alliance, which is known regionally for its leadership dating from the 1970s.

Every year since 2001, the alliance has sponsored the Unity Conference, an annual gathering of progressive LGBT people and allies in the Southeast. The conference focuses on the intersections of gender and sexuality with other multiple identities, such as ability, race/ethnicity, age, class and faith. In addition, the coalition touts that it has one of nation's oldest student-run LGBT campus publications, LAMBDA, founded in 1976 as the "voice of UNC's gay and lesbian community." The most extravagant queer affair on campus seems to be the annual drag show campus fundraiser. The show has sold out for almost the entire last decade, with over 500 attendees.

UNC—Chapel Hill has performed remarkably, making impressive progress in its efforts to create a welcoming campus for LGBT students. An LGBT student states: "I loved every minute of my four years at UNC—Chapel Hill and would whole-heartedly recommend the university to any LGBTQ-identified student."

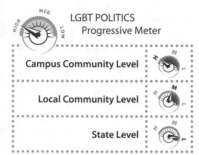

LGBT POLITICS
Progressive Meter

Campus Community Level

Local Community Level

State Level

INFO

UNIVERSITY OF NORTH CAROLINA—CHAPEL HILL

Jackson Hall 153A

Campus Box 2200

Chapel Hill, NC 27599

Phone: 919-966-3621

Fax: 919-962-3045

E-mail: uadm@email.unc.edu

Website: www.unc.edu

CAMPUS STATS

Type of Institution: Public university

Founding Year: 1789

Size: 16,800

Avg. Class Size: 10–19 students

Popular Majors: Biology/Biological Sciences, Mass Communications/Communication Studies, Psychology

Cost: In-state tuition: $4,400

Out-of-state tuition: $17,500

Admission Application Deadline: January 15

OUTSPOKEN *Answers from LGBT students:*

Top Three Descriptors of the LGBT Campus Environment:
1. Activist   2. Supportive   3. Friendly

What makes your campus feel welcoming and safe for LGBT students?
"Perhaps what makes UNC feel welcoming and safe for LGBT students are the many resources available to first-year students. After coming out during my second semester, I received a lot of information from the LGBTQ office about health issues, faith, and politics. The fact that the office addressed those very important topics made me feel more comfortable with being gay on campus."
—*19-year-old gay male, junior*

How do you feel about coming out on your campus?

"I have been out on campus ever since I moved into a campus dorm…and I never thought twice about it. Without question, the staff and faculty are extremely supportive…. for the most part, the student body is equally welcoming." —*21-year-old gay male, senior*

✏️ ACADEMIC SCENE

Top Three Supportive LGBT Academic Areas:
1. Sexuality Studies   2. Women's Studies   3. Political Science

How LGBT-friendly are faculty in the classroom?
"I find faculty to be super-supportive and gay-friendly. I even had one come out to me after I wrote about being lesbian and coming out for an assignment." —*20-year-old lesbian, junior*

"The faculty is amazingly supportive and surprisingly conscious of LGBT issues while in the classroom. The university actually has an ally-training program in which many faculty members already have or are highly encouraged to participate. In addition, a contingent of LGBT faculty can often be looked upon to help LGBT students." —*21-year-old gay male, senior*

😊 SOCIAL SCENE

Top Three Things in the LGBT Social Life:
1. Socials   2. Bars   3. Drag shows

How would you describe the social scene for LGBT students?
"Limited, but it depends how creative you are. … I always find something to get into." —*19-year-old gay male, sophomore*

What annual social event should an LGBT student not miss?
"The Drag Show is a fantastic event put on every semester at Carolina. LGBTSA does a great job of inviting professional drag persons to perform at the Great Hall each year." —*19-year-old gay male, junior*

RAINBOW RUMOR The campus has made LGBT progress in many areas but seems to be having difficulty reaching out to ethnic minorities in the LGBT community. According to one student: "When I first arrived at Carolina I thought it was fantastic to be surrounded by gay people but was disheartened by the fact that they were mostly white."

THAT'S SO GAY!

ANNUAL LGBT EVENT HIGHLIGHTS

NC Gay and Lesbian Film Festival: August

Coming Out Week Celebration: October

Drag Show: October and March

Q-Ball Dance: November

Transgender Awareness Week: November

Ally Week: February

Black History LGBT Awareness Month: February

Pride Celebration Week: March

Unity Conference: April

National Day of Silence: April

Lavender Graduation Celebration: May

BUZZ BITES
Fun Queer Stuff to Know

THE BEST…

Hangout: Café Driade

Eating Place: Spotted Dog

Place to Check Out Guys: Legends

Place to Check Out Ladies: Vision

Non-LGBT-Specific Campus Club: Campus Y

Place for LGBT Students to Live on Campus: UNITAS Multicultural Theme House

LGBT Course Offering: Politics of Sexuality and Progression of LGBT Rights in the United States

LGBT Educational Involvement Opportunity: Safe Zone

LGBT-Accepting Religious/Spiritual Organization(s): Wesley Foundation and Catholic Newman Center

CAMPUS QUEER
RESOURCES

Select LGBT Student Organization(s):

Gay, Lesbian, Bisexual Transgender Straight Alliance Founding Date: 1970 (under a different name)

Membership: 500+

Phone: 919-962-3191

E-mail: glbtsa@unc.edu

Website: www.unc.edu/glbtsa/

LGBT Resource Center/Office:

LGBTQ Office

10 Steele Building, Campus Box 5100
Chapel Hill, NC 27599-5100

Year Established: 2003

Number of Staff: 1 full-time professional staff, 1 half-time graduate student, 2 quarter-time student employees

Phone: 919-843-5376

E-mail: lgbt@unc.edu

Website: lgbt.unc.edu

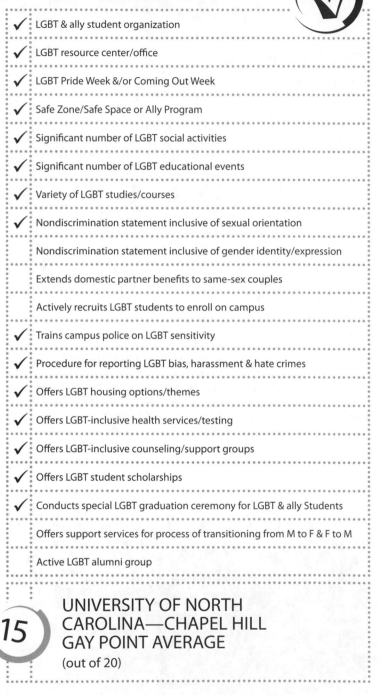

THE GAY POINT AVERAGE
OFFICIAL CAMPUS CHECKLIST

✔ LGBT & ally student organization

✔ LGBT resource center/office

✔ LGBT Pride Week &/or Coming Out Week

✔ Safe Zone/Safe Space or Ally Program

✔ Significant number of LGBT social activities

✔ Significant number of LGBT educational events

✔ Variety of LGBT studies/courses

✔ Nondiscrimination statement inclusive of sexual orientation

Nondiscrimination statement inclusive of gender identity/expression

Extends domestic partner benefits to same-sex couples

Actively recruits LGBT students to enroll on campus

✔ Trains campus police on LGBT sensitivity

✔ Procedure for reporting LGBT bias, harassment & hate crimes

✔ Offers LGBT housing options/themes

✔ Offers LGBT-inclusive health services/testing

✔ Offers LGBT-inclusive counseling/support groups

✔ Offers LGBT student scholarships

✔ Conducts special LGBT graduation ceremony for LGBT & ally Students

Offers support services for process of transitioning from M to F & F to M

Active LGBT alumni group

15 UNIVERSITY OF NORTH CAROLINA—CHAPEL HILL GAY POINT AVERAGE
(out of 20)

UNIVERSITY OF NORTH TEXAS

DESPITE THE FACT that Texas is a conservative state, the University of North Texas in Denton, Texas, prides itself on offering a friendly, safe and inclusive environment—even for queers.

Located 35 miles north of Dallas and Fort Worth, the campus has had a history of LGBT progress for a number of years. Sexual orientation was included in nondiscrimination policies in the early 1990s. The Gay and Lesbian Association of Denton was founded in 1988, and, most recently, the Ally Program within the Diversity and Equity Office was created in 1998. LGBT students mention the Ally Program as one of the most effective support services on campus. The program was developed to create a more inclusive, welcoming and supportive environment. In addition, there are many LGBT events, including Day of Silence, National Coming Out Day and Transgender Day of Remembrance. The campus also invites major LGBT artists, musicians and speakers to come to campus throughout the year.

The Gay Point Average shows that this southern university is on top when it comes to LGBT-inclusive policies and practices. An LGBT student agrees: "The Ally Program on campus makes me feel safe. I came out on campus and the support was there….from friends, from staff and others. It is an extremely friendly place to be gay."

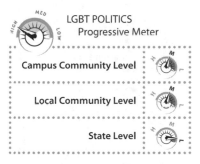

LGBT POLITICS
Progressive Meter

Campus Community Level

Local Community Level

State Level

OUTSPOKEN *Answers from LGBT students:*

Top Three Descriptors of the LGBT Campus Environment:
1. Comfortable   2. Diverse   3. Open

What makes your campus feel welcoming and safe for LGBT students?
"I've never been concerned about violence on campus."
—17-year-old bisexual female, freshman

"I acknowledge this is Texas, the home state of George W. But, the campus has a sincere commitment to LGBT students, and that in itself makes a difference to me." *—20-year-old gay male, junior*

How do you feel about coming out on your campus?
"I think it's probably easier as a gay or lesbian student and a little more difficult for trans-people. But the people I've told, especially faculty in the anthropology department, have been really cool." *—20-year-old gay F to M, senior*

ACADEMIC SCENE

Top Three Supportive LGBT Academic Areas:
1. Women's Studies   2. Anthropology   3. Sociology

How LGBT-friendly are faculty in the classroom?
"I find my interactions with faculty to be comfortable. I am a lesbian, and I contribute openly, but I question the level of comfort on the trans issue in

INFO

UNIVERSITY OF NORTH TEXAS
PO Box 311277
Denton, TX 76203
Phone: 940-565-2681
Fax: 940-565-2408
E-mail: undergrad@unt.edu
Website: www.unt.edu

CAMPUS STATS
Type of Institution: Public university
Founding Year: 1890
Size: 32,181
Avg. Class Size: 20–29 students
Popular Majors: Computer Science, Elementary Education and Teaching, Psychology
Cost: In-state tuition: $4,685
Out-of-state tuition: $14,652
Admission Application Deadline: December 1

They're nuts for squirrels and one squirrel in particular: the UNT albino squirrel, the unofficial mascot, is said to symbolize inclusion and diversity on campus. One UNT person shares: "The albino squirrel is a perfect example of how we can embrace diversity. Something different can be something good." The tree where the albino squirrel lives on campus is clearly marked with a sign as well as "Squirrel Xing" marks on the sidewalk below. Although the gender identity and sexual orientation of the squirrel are unknown, the squirrel does have a fuzzy tail and revels in posing for snapshots. The squirrel is even featured on campus Valentine's Day cards. How queer and fabulous!

· · · · · · · · · · · · · · · · · · · ·

RAINBOW RUMOR

Even Texan George W. had at one point supported the notion that states may grant same-sex couples domestic partner benefits…or was that just to get reelected? Either way, UNT faculty and staff lack any domestic partner benefits in the Lone Star State. And as far as trans-inclusive policies go, don't hold your breath!

· · · · · · · · · · · · · · · · · · · ·

THAT'S SO GAY!
ANNUAL LGBT EVENT HIGHLIGHTS

Ally Training: Fall/Spring

Dallas Pride Parade: September

Gay Day at Six Flags: September

National Coming Out Activities: October

Halloween Block Party on Cedar Springs: October

Transgender Day of Remembrance: November

World AIDS Day: December

Day of Silence: April

---

the classroom. Not many people have an understanding of the differences and concerns that trans students face." —*22-year-old lesbian, senior*

"Not a problem for me at all. I was pleasantly surprised when I wrote a paper for my English class that mentioned my boyfriend at the time. I got an A+, and the teacher was always very accepting in class. I always felt welcome." —*22-year-old gay male, senior*

😃 SOCIAL SCENE

Top Three Things in the LGBT Social Life:
1. Movies   2. Coffee shops   3. Clubs and bars in Dallas

How would you describe the social scene for LGBT students?
"It's pretty laid-back. Pretty much everyone just meets up at the coffee shop or at Mable's to hang out." —*37-year-old lesbian, senior*

What annual social event should an LGBT student not miss?
"Coming Out Week—it has the most events going on." —*20-year-old gay F to M, senior*

BUZZ BITES *Fun Queer Stuff to Know*

THE BEST…

Party Locale: Chainsaw Repair Shop

Hangout: Mable Peabody's Beauty Parlor

Eating Place: Banter

Place to Check Out Guys: Jupiter House Coffee Shop

Place to Check Out Ladies: Texas Woman's University

LGBT-Cool Athletic Sport: Women's basketball

Non-LGBT-Specific Campus Club: Feminist Majority Leadership Alliance

Place for LGBT Students to Live on Campus: Bruce Hall

LGBT Educational Involvement Opportunity: Ally Training

LGBT-Accepting Religious/Spiritual Organization(s): Circle of the Three Trees and Harvest Metropolitan Community Church

THE GAY POINT AVERAGE
OFFICIAL CAMPUS CHECKLIST

LGBT & ally student organization ✓

LGBT resource center/office ✓

LGBT Pride Week &/or Coming Out Week ✓

Safe Zone/Safe Space or Ally Program ✓

Significant number of LGBT social activities ✓

Significant number of LGBT educational events ✓

Variety of LGBT studies/courses ✓

Nondiscrimination statement inclusive of sexual orientation ✓

Nondiscrimination statement inclusive of gender identity/expression

Extends domestic partner benefits to same-sex couples

Actively recruits LGBT students to enroll on campus ✓

Trains campus police on LGBT sensitivity

Procedure for reporting LGBT bias, harassment & hate crimes ✓

Offers LGBT housing options/themes

Offers LGBT-inclusive health services/testing ✓

Offers LGBT-inclusive counseling/support groups ✓

Offers LGBT student scholarships ✓

Conducts special LGBT graduation ceremony for LGBT & ally Students

Offers support services for process of transitioning from M to F & F to M ✓

Active LGBT alumni group

UNIVERSITY OF NORTH TEXAS
GAY POINT AVERAGE (14)
(out of 20)

**CAMPUS QUEER
RESOURCES**

Select LGBT Student Organization(s):
Gay and Lesbian Association of Denton (GLAD); Transcending Gender Denton (TGD)
Founding Date: GLAD (1988); TGD (2004)
Membership: 70+
E-mail: glad@unt.edu; tgd@unt.edu
Website: orgs.unt.edu/GLAD; orgs.unt.edu/tgd/

LGBT Resource Center/Office:
Division of Equity and Diversity, Ally Program
Administration Building, Room 175
Denton, Texas 76203
Year Established: 1998
Number of Staff: 3 full-time professional staff (varying responsibilities)
Phone: 940-565-2456
Website: www.unt.edu/ally

UNIVERSITY OF OREGON

AS POSTED ON its Website, University of Oregon states that it is an activist community "energized by students and faculty members who live out the university motto: *Mens agitat molem*—Minds move mountains."

Since the 1960s, the University of Oregon has had a history of student activism, including the fight for LGBT equality. Many LGBT and ally students admit that they chose the university because they wanted to make a positive difference in life. Eugene, Oregon, the city where the campus is located, is well known for a thriving "hippie" culture that values independence, freedom and fairness.

As early as 1967, the student coalition now called the Lesbian, Gay, Bisexual, Transgender, Queer Alliance was organizing under a different name on campus. The queer student coalition was among the first of its kind in the nation to form prior to the time of the Stonewall Riots in New York City. The coalition's pioneering LGBT work, along with the support of dedicated LGBT and ally campus staff and faculty, laid a progressive foundation. Subsequently, the campus put LGBT-inclusive policies and practices in place, including a comprehensive LGBT nondiscrimination statement and trans-inclusive health services.

Such LGBT efforts also paved the way for the development in 1991 of the Lesbian, Gay, Bisexual, and Transgender Education and Support Services Program. Adding to the thriving queer activism, the LGBT Education & Support Services Program plans more than 50 LGBT educational, social and cultural events a year, including Pride Week, the Queer Prom and the Queer Film Festival. Plus, there are almost 40 LGBT panels each year that feature LGBT members of the campus community who work to break down barriers and offer LGBT education firsthand.

An activist campus, the University of Oregon has already "moved mountains" and has left an ever-lasting mark of progress for many LGBT students. That University of Oregon cares wholeheartedly about LGBT issues is confirmed by its excellent Gay Point Average. As one LGBT student states: "You get to know everyone here and recognize other LGBT students in your classes and at events. I feel like if something were to happen, I would know there were allies there…. I don't think I would feel that way at a big campus like NYU, or UCLA. It's like *Cheers*; sometimes you want to go where everyone knows your name."

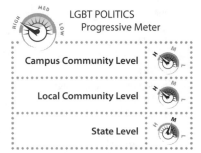

LGBT POLITICS
Progressive Meter

Campus Community Level

Local Community Level

State Level

INFO

UNIVERSITY OF OREGON
1217 University of Oregon
Eugene, OR 97403

Phone: 541-346-3201

Fax: 541-346-5815

E-mail: uoadmit@oregon.uoregon.edu

Website: www.uoregon.edu

CAMPUS STATS

Type of Institution: Public university

Founding Year: 1876

Size: 14,326

Avg. Class Size: 20–29 students

Popular Majors: Business Administration/ Management, Journalism, Psychology

Cost: In-state tuition: $5,568
Out-of-state tuition: $17,424

Admission Application Deadline: January 15

OUTSPOKEN *Answers from LGBT students:*

Top Three Descriptors of the LGBT Campus Environment:
1. Proactive   2. Diverse   3. Progressive

What makes your campus feel welcoming and safe for LGBT students?
"The university supports, financially and otherwise, an LGBT advocate out of Student Life…. I am sure it is difficult to balance the needs of the diverse student body. Knowing that the administration supports the advancement of queer students and staff makes me feel very welcomed and safe here."
—26-year-old genderqueer, junior

How do you feel about coming out on your campus?
"Coming out on campus was easy; I am out in all of my classes and on-campus workplaces. My girlfriend and I are comfortable being affectionate and out wherever we go, and we see plenty of other same-sex couples doing the same."
—21-year-old lesbian, senior

⊘ ACADEMIC SCENE

Top Three Supportive LGBT Academic Areas:
1. Women and Gender Studies   2. Arts and Administration   3. English

How LGBT-friendly are faculty in the classroom?
"Most profs that I've had have been very LGBT-friendly."
—*20-year-old bisexual female, sophomore*

"Very…Several of my professors have worn buttons showing their support for the gay community as well as sponsored a supportive ad in the *Emerald* for National Coming Out Day." —*27-year-old gay male, graduate student*

☺ SOCIAL SCENE

Top Three Things in the LGBT Social Life:
1. Parties   2. Hanging out with friends   3. Getting involved as a leader

How would you describe the social scene for LGBT students?
"There always seems to be something going on for queers on campus, either through the LGBTQA or another queer program on campus… As a queer student, I have been able to enjoy all the aspects of college, academic and otherwise." —*26-year-old genderqueer, junior*

What annual social event should an LGBT student not miss?
"National Coming Out Week and the Big Drag Show."
—*19-year-old lesbian, sophomore*

OUTRAGEOUS FACTOID Lesbian and preeminent polar explorer Ann Bancroft graduated in 1981 from University of Oregon. Among many accomplishments, she was the first woman to reach the North Pole on foot and by sled and the first woman to ski across Greenland. In 1992 and 1993 Bancroft also led an all-women expedition to the South Pole on skis, making her the first lesbian to reach both poles.

• • • • • • • • • • • • • • • • • • •

RAINBOW RUMOR The campus has no limits when it comes to being supportive of the LGBT community. One LGBT student states: "All of the minorities on this campus stick together; if there is a queer issue being dealt with the Black Student Union is there, and so are the Latin Americans, Asian Americans, and Hillel, and the LGBT does the same if the issue is reversed. There is just a sense of community that I have never felt anywhere else. I know whatever comes up, there will be others there to help take care of it."

• • • • • • • • • • • • • • • • • • •

BUZZ ⊕ BITES   *Fun Queer Stuff to Know*

THE BEST…

Party Locale: Neighbor's Bar
Hangout: LGBTQA Office
Eating Place: Café Roma
Place to Check Out Guys: Third Floor Music Library
Place to Check Out Ladies: Sam's Place
LGBT-Cool Athletic Sport: Lacrosse, fencing
LGBT Course Offering: Queer Literature

LGBT Educational Involvement Opportunity: Bridges Program
LGBT-Accepting Religious/Spiritual Organization(s): Unitarian Universalist Church, Two Rivers Metropolitan Community Church, Hillel

THAT'S SO GAY! ANNUAL LGBT EVENT HIGHLIGHTS

Emperors Drag Show: Fall/Spring
Week of Welcome: August
Coming Out Day Celebration: October
Guess the Straight RA: Fall
World AIDS Day: December 1
Queer Film Festival: February
Pride Week: April
Lavender Graduation: April/May
Day of Silence/Night of Noise: Spring
InterSEXtions: Spring
LGBTQA Drag Show: Spring
Queer Prom: Spring

CAMPUS QUEER RESOURCES

Select LGBT Student Organization(s):

Lesbian, Gay, Bisexual, Transgender, Queer Alliance (LGBTQA)

Founding Date: 1967 to 1970

Membership: 140

Phone: 541-346-3360

E-mail: lgbtqa@uoregon.edu

Website: gladstone.uoregon.edu/~lgbtqa

LGBT Resource Center/Office:

Lesbian, Gay, Bisexual, and Transgender Education and Support Services Program (LGBTESSP)

University of Oregon
164 Oregon Hall
Eugene, Oregon 97403

Year Established: 1991

Number of Staff: 1 full-time professional staff, 6 student workers

Phone: 541-346-1134

E-mail: program@uoregon.edu

Website: lgbt.uoregon.edu

THE GAY POINT AVERAGE OFFICIAL CAMPUS CHECKLIST

- ✓ LGBT & ally student organization
- ✓ LGBT resource center/office
- ✓ LGBT Pride Week &/or Coming Out Week
- ✓ Safe Zone/Safe Space or Ally Program
- ✓ Significant number of LGBT social activities
- ✓ Significant number of LGBT educational events
- ✓ Variety of LGBT studies/courses
- ✓ Nondiscrimination statement inclusive of sexual orientation
- ✓ Nondiscrimination statement inclusive of gender identity/expression
- ✓ Extends domestic partner benefits to same-sex couples
- ✓ Actively recruits LGBT students to enroll on campus
- ✓ Trains campus police on LGBT sensitivity
- ✓ Procedure for reporting LGBT bias, harassment & hate crimes
-   Offers LGBT housing options/themes
- ✓ Offers LGBT-inclusive health services/testing
- ✓ Offers LGBT-inclusive counseling/support groups
- ✓ Offers LGBT student scholarships
- ✓ Conducts special LGBT graduation ceremony for LGBT & ally Students
- ✓ Offers support services for process of transitioning from M to F & F to M
- ✓ Active LGBT alumni group

19 UNIVERSITY OF OREGON GAY POINT AVERAGE
(out of 20)

UNIVERSITY OF PENNSYLVANIA

THE UNIVERSITY OF Pennsylvania has been in the forefront of Ivy League institutions since its beginning in 1740 as "America's first university" (Harvard being "America's first college"). Located in downtown Philadelphia, it has a vibrant LGBT community and municipal protection against discrimination on the basis of sexual orientation and gender identity/expression.

Penn is an accepting place for LGBT students, staff and faculty. As early as 1967, the campus had queer students organizing pre-Stonewall under the auspice of a campus gay liberation organization. Then, in 1979, the campus passed a policy of nondiscrimination based on sexual orientation, which was expanded in 2002 to include gender identity. Penn also offers completely equitable domestic partner benefits to its lesbian and gay employees and was recently recognized by the Human Rights Campaign Workplace Project as an exemplary employer.

There are more than a dozen LGBT and ally student organizations on campus. Some, such as the Queer Student Alliance and Allies, are university-wide whereas others are specific to one of Penn's twelve schools, such as the Wharton Alliance for the School of Business and Lambda Law for the Law School. Qpenn, a campuswide week of LGBT celebration and education, takes place on campus every March. The events are promoted in a 32- to 40-page supplement to the campus newspaper, *The Daily Pennsylvanian*. Qpenn events include lectures, workshops, academic roundtables and the biggest queer party of the year, the QBall.

The state-of-the-art LGBT Center at Penn is located in the Carriage House, a beautifully renovated historical landmark constructed in the 1870s. The center features 5,500 square feet of meeting rooms and a reading room with a large circulating collection of books, videotapes and DVDs. In addition, the center is fully staffed with three full-time professionals and a host of graduate and undergraduate employees.

Penn scored a perfect Gay Point Average. Such positive LGBT-inclusive efforts put Penn in the forefront once again. One LGBT student surmises: "There has been an increasingly strong desire of the Penn community at all levels—administration, faculty, staff, students and alumni—to make the campus comfortable for students who identify as LGBT….This is very encouraging and impressive."

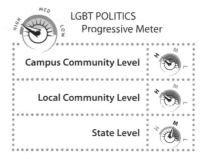

LGBT POLITICS
Progressive Meter

Campus Community Level

Local Community Level

State Level

OUTSPOKEN *Answers from LGBT students:*

Top Three Descriptors of the LGBT Campus Environment:
1. Active   2. Multifaceted   3. Accepting

What makes your campus feel welcoming and safe for LGBT students?
"There is an incredible LGBT center that is centrally located on campus, which does a lot of outreach to the Penn community. Student groups are visible on Locust Walk, advertising events and giving out educational materials. Many

INFO

UNIVERSITY OF PENNSYLVANIA
1 College Hall
Philadelphia, PA 19104
Phone: 215-898-7507
Fax: 215-898-9670
E-mail: info@admissions.ugao.upenn.edu
Website: www.upenn.edu

CAMPUS STATS
Type of Institution: Private university
Founding Year: 1740
Size: 10,047
Avg. Class Size: 20–29 students
Popular Majors: Business Administration/Management, Economics, Finance, History
Cost: Tuition: $32,364
Admission Application Deadline: January 1

OUTRAGEOUS FACTOID
Olivia Cruises and Resorts founder and Chief Executive Officer, Amy Errett, is a proud Penn alumnus. The lesbian entrepreneur has created a home and a community for lesbian women around the world.

• • • • • • • • • • • • • • • • • • •

RAINBOW RUMOR
Without any pressure from the LGBT community, the president and legal counsel decided to file an amicus brief in the U.S. Supreme Court regarding the Solomon Amendment, which denies federal funding to institutions that prohibit ROTC or military recruitment on campus. Like many campuses, Penn continues to debate and struggle with the presence of ROTC and military recruiters on campus. Their antigay stances are contradictory to the campus nondiscrimination policy including sexual orientation. The LGBT community was thrilled by the decision to file the amicus brief against the Solomon Amendment. Penn stands to lose hundreds of millions of dollars.

• • • • • • • • • • • • • • • • • • •

THAT'S SO GAY!

ANNUAL LGBT EVENT HIGHLIGHTS

Queer Social: October

OutFest/Sunday OUT: October

World AIDS Day: December 1

Freedom to Marry Day: Mid-February

Q Ball: March

Qpenn Week: March

Equality Forum: April/May

LGBT Commencement Reception: May

PhillyPRIDE: June

---

resident advisers have Safe Zone stickers on their doors and thus the college houses feel very safe." *—20-year-old gay male, junior*

How do you feel about coming out on your campus?
"For me, coming out has always been easy. Especially on Penn's campus it is easy due to the level of openness, visibility, and involvement that the LGBTQ community has at Penn." *—19-year-old lesbian, sophomore*

ACADEMIC SCENE

Top Three Supportive LGBT Academic Areas:
1. Sociology   2. Women's Studies   3. English

How LGBT-friendly are faculty in the classroom?
"On Penn's campus I have never had a problem with a homophobic teacher. I think they know that once the gays turn, it'll get ugly."
—19-year-old lesbian, sophomore

"During Penn's LGBT awareness week, we had a number of high-profile and popular professors speak about LGBT issues at brown-bag lunches and at our rally on College Green. It was great to see faculty make public statements in support of the community and raise important issues that affect the LGBT community." *—20-year-old gay male, junior*

SOCIAL SCENE

Top Three Things in the LGBT Social Life:
1. Gay Fridays at Cliff's   2. Gayborhood in Philly   3. Allies Coffeehouse

How would you describe the social scene for LGBT students?
"The social scene is amazing. There are biweekly parties on campus that attract upwards of 200 students each ("Gay Fridays at Cliff's"). There are big LGBT club dances. And there are tons of LGBT student groups, so those social avenues are open as well." *—20-year-old gay male, senior*

What annual social event should an LGBT student not miss?
"Q-Ball, the dance in the spring, is an incredible event. Last year, many allies attended and it was a safe and welcoming environment for me and my straight friends to have fun together." *—20-year-old gay male, junior*

BUZZ BITES *Fun Queer Stuff to Know*

THE BEST...

Party Locale: Shampoo on Friday nights
Hangout: LGBT Center
Eating Place: Hamburger Mary's
Place to Check Out Guys: Pottruck Gym on campus
Place to Check Out Ladies: Locust Walk
LGBT-Cool Athletic Sport: Women's basketball
Non-LGBT-Specific Campus Club: Penn Democrats

Place for LGBT Students to Live on Campus: Harrison College House
LGBT Course Offering: Theories of Gender and Sexuality
LGBT Educational Involvement Opportunity: LGBT Speakers Bureau
LGBT-Accepting Religious/Spiritual Organization(s): Queer Christian Fellowship, Hillel

THE GAY POINT AVERAGE
OFFICIAL CAMPUS CHECKLIST

LGBT & ally student organization ✓

LGBT resource center/office ✓

LGBT Pride Week &/or Coming Out Week ✓

Safe Zone/Safe Space or Ally Program ✓

Significant number of LGBT social activities ✓

Significant number of LGBT educational events ✓

Variety of LGBT studies/courses ✓

Nondiscrimination statement inclusive of sexual orientation ✓

Nondiscrimination statement inclusive of gender identity/expression ✓

Extends domestic partner benefits to same-sex couples ✓

Actively recruits LGBT students to enroll on campus ✓

Trains campus police on LGBT sensitivity ✓

Procedure for reporting LGBT bias, harassment & hate crimes ✓

Offers LGBT housing options/themes ✓

Offers LGBT-inclusive health services/testing ✓

Offers LGBT-inclusive counseling/support groups ✓

Offers LGBT student scholarships ✓

Conducts special LGBT graduation ceremony for LGBT & ally Students ✓

Offers support services for process of transitioning from M to F & F to M ✓

Active LGBT alumni group ✓

UNIVERSITY OF PENNSYLVANIA
GAY POINT AVERAGE (20)
(out of 20)

CAMPUS QUEER RESOURCES

Select LGBT Student Organization(s):
Queer Student Alliance
Founding Date: 1967
Membership: 100+
Phone: 215-898-5044
E-mail: qsa@dolphin.upenn.edu
Website: dolphin.upenn.edu/~qsa

LGBT Resource Center/Office:
Lesbian Gay Bisexual Transgender Center
University of Pennsylvania
3907 Spruce Street
Philadelphia, PA 19104
Year Established: 1982
Number of Staff: 3 full-time professional staff; 8 part-time student employees and interns
Phone: 215-898-5044
E-mail: center@dolphin.upenn.edu
Website: www.vpul.upenn.edu/lgbtc/

UNIVERSITY OF PUGET SOUND

LOCATED IN TACOMA, Washington, in close proximity to Seattle, the University of Puget Sound campus has an amazing history of LGBT progress and an outstanding LGBT institutional commitment.

Puget Sound was among the first colleges in the Pacific Northwest to have inclusive nondiscrimination policies, not only of sexual orientation but also gender identity/expression. The campus was also among the first in the area to grant same-sex domestic partner benefits. In addition, the student coalition Bisexuals, Gays, Lesbians and Allies for Diversity (BGLAD) is the largest, most active, most visible group on campus and provides several queer activities. Of course, the most popular is the annual drag show, but other queer favorites include the Coming Out Dance, the Queer 101 Forum, Intersex Awareness Day and the Masquerade Ball. And for those LGBT leaders who get involved on campus, there is even an LGBT-alumni-endowed leadership scholarship for queers.

Puget Sound is unabashedly supportive and proactive with regard to LGBT issues and has high marks on its Gay Point Average to prove it. Even admissions staff, publications and forms are queer-friendly. As one student states: "On the campus Website for prospective students, there's a page describing what it might be like for a student to be LGBT on campus. That definitely made me feel welcomed before I set foot on the campus. When I visited, I saw gay couples walking around hand in hand, and I'd certainly feel safe doing that too."

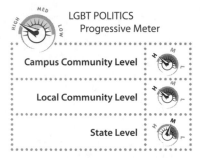

LGBT POLITICS
Progressive Meter

Campus Community Level

Local Community Level

State Level

OUTSPOKEN *Answers from LGBT students:*

Top Three Descriptors of the LGBT Campus Environment:
1. Queer-affirming   2. Proactive   3. Engaging

What makes your campus feel welcoming and safe for LGBT students?
"BGLAD, the queer student group, almost always has a large turnout, usually with standing room only. You can always see fellow BGLAD members around campus. I've not yet had an antigay sentiment aimed my way. Come to think of it, I haven't noticed other students using 'gay' or 'fag' to insult one another."
—19-year-old lesbian, sophomore

How do you feel about coming out on your campus?
"I feel very encouraged to come out, because it seems like such a safe and open environment. I feel like I'm in very good company when I'm open about my sexuality." *—22-year-old gay male, senior*

"Extremely safe. It was really a matter of deciding 'when' rather than 'if' for me."
—19-year-old gay male, sophomore

INFO

UNIVERSITY OF PUGET SOUND
1500 North Warner Street
CMB 1062
Tacoma, WA 98416
Phone: 253-879-3100
Fax: 253-879-3993
E-mail: admission@ups.edu
Website: www.ups.edu

CAMPUS STATS
Type of Institution: Private university
Founding Year: 1888
Size: 2,595
Avg. Class Size: 10–19 students
Popular Majors: Business Administration/ Management, Psychology, English Language and Literature
Cost: Tuition: $28,270
Admission Application Deadline: February 1

ACADEMIC SCENE

Top Three Supportive LGBT Academic Areas:

1. Gender Studies   2. Humanities   3. Arts

How LGBT-friendly are faculty in the classroom?

"I feel they are very friendly and willing to discuss LGBT issues in the classroom. My U.S. history class uses a textbook that fully integrates the gay experience in the course of U.S. history, and in my Colonial Latin America class, we talked about homosexuality among Native Americans."
—*19-year-old lesbian, sophomore*

"I've never heard anything homophobic from any of my professors, and they even take steps to include same-sex partnerships when discussing relationships."
—*24-year-old bisexual female, graduate student*

SOCIAL SCENE

Top Three Things in the LGBT Social Life:

1. BGLAD   2. Drag queens   3. House parties

How would you describe the social scene for LGBT students?

"It seems like one of those places where everyone you meet is queer—I think there's a strong social scene on campus, and I know many people head up to Seattle as well." —*19-year-old gay male, freshman*

"Apparently, there's an underground lesbian network, but I'm far too out for it. Mostly, I hang out with my nerdy friends who are mostly queer—they get my *Lord of the Rings*, *Star Trek*, and *Buffy the Vampire Slayer* jokes."
—*21-year-old bisexual female, senior*

What annual social event should an LGBT student not miss?

"Queer 101 and the numerous drag shows." —*22-year-old gay male, senior*

OUTRAGEOUS FACTOID BGLAD, the LGBT student organization, remains the largest, most active, and most visible club on campus. They have virtually outgrown the Student Diversity Center. Plus the Lavender Loggers, the Queer Puget Sound alumni group, single handedly raised $30,000 in less than one year to endow the LGBT Leadership Scholarship. Donors included alumni from the 1960s, 1970s, 1980s, and 1990s!

RAINBOW RUMOR Fraternities and sororities constitute 25 percent of the student population. Although there are some Greeks who are LGBT and out, there are relatively few Greek allies who are equally as visible. Next year, the campus plans on being more proactive and on doing more outreach for allies within fraternities and sororities.

THAT'S SO GAY!

ANNUAL LGBT EVENT HIGHLIGHTS

Queer History Month: October

National Coming Out Day: October 11

Queer 101 Forum: October 11

Coming Out Dance: October 11

Drag 101: October

Intersex Awareness Day: October

Masquerade Ball: October 28

Transgender Day of Remembrance: November

World AIDS Day: December 1

Conspiracy of Hope Marriage Booth: February

Day of Silence: April

Annual Drag Show: April

Take Back the Night: April

BUZZ BITES *Fun Queer Stuff to Know*

THE BEST...

Party Locale: Theater parties

Hangout: Diversions Café

Eating Place: Wild Orchid

Place to Check Out Guys: Silver Stones

Place to Check Out Ladies: Gym

LGBT-Cool Athletic Sport: Crew or women's basketball

Non-LGBT-Specific Campus Club: Repertory Dance Group

Place for LGBT Students to Live on Campus: Regester All Women Hall

LGBT Course Offering: Gender Matters

LGBT Educational Involvement Opportunity: Queer 101 Panel

LGBT-Accepting Religious/Spiritual Organization(s): Jewish Student Organization, Pagan Student Alliance

CAMPUS QUEER RESOURCES

Select LGBT Student Organization(s)

Bisexuals, Gays, Lesbians and Allies for Diversity (BGLAD)

Founding Date: 1985

Membership: 60

Phone: 253-879-4044

E-mail: b-glad@ups.edu

Website: asups.ups.edu/clubs/bglad/Website/default.htm

Resource Center/Office Responsible for LGBT Issues:

Student Diversity Center

3211 North 15th Street
Tacoma, WA 98416

Year Established: 1996

Number of Staff: 1 full-time professional employee; 4 student employees

Phone: 253-879-4044

E-mail: diversitycenter@ups.edu

Website: www.ups.edu/x639.xml

THE GAY POINT AVERAGE
OFFICIAL CAMPUS CHECKLIST

- ✓ LGBT & ally student organization
- LGBT resource center/office
- ✓ LGBT Pride Week &/or Coming Out Week
- ✓ Safe Zone/Safe Space or Ally Program
- ✓ Significant number of LGBT social activities
- ✓ Significant number of LGBT educational events
- ✓ Variety of LGBT studies/courses
- ✓ Nondiscrimination statement inclusive of sexual orientation
- ✓ Nondiscrimination statement inclusive of gender identity/expression
- ✓ Extends domestic partner benefits to same-sex couples
- ✓ Actively recruits LGBT students to enroll on campus
- ✓ Trains campus police on LGBT sensitivity
- ✓ Procedure for reporting LGBT bias, harassment & hate crimes
- ✓ Offers LGBT housing options/themes
- ✓ Offers LGBT-inclusive health services/testing
- ✓ Offers LGBT-inclusive counseling/support groups
- ✓ Offers LGBT student scholarships
- ✓ Conducts special LGBT graduation ceremony for LGBT & ally Students
- ✓ Offers support services for process of transitioning from M to F & F to M
- ✓ Active LGBT alumni group

19 UNIVERSITY OF PUGET SOUND GAY POINT AVERAGE
(out of 20)

UNIVERSITY OF RHODE ISLAND

THIS COASTAL CAMPUS, located near beautiful ocean beaches, has been burdened by a past reputation of lackluster LGBT friendliness. But the last five years have been LGBT progressive. One LGBT student states: "The veil of ignorance has been ruthlessly ripped off....Despite obstacles in our way, students, staff and administrators are investing a lot of hard work to make the campus more affirming and open for all."

The Gay Point Average is further proof of progress. In 2001, the campus set up an official GLBT Center, creating a positive, more welcoming LGBT campus climate. The center provides an array of LGBT programs and services, including themed discussion groups, the Welcome Project and the Out and Proud Queer Film Series. The center also works with the student group OutURI to engage the campus community in LGBT awareness and educational activities like National Coming Out Week, Gay Bingo and World AIDS Day.

By 2003, the campus had also included gender identity/expression into nondiscrimination policies. "There are no reservations," states a LGBT student. "The administration understands and supports LGBT issues." There is even the recently added Rainbow Diversity House, a learning community sitting in the heart of Fraternity Circle. The house is a welcoming place for students interested in social justice and social service. Although Rainbow House is not themed solely around queer issues, LGBT students and allies naturally gravitate to this housing option.

One tradition since 1993 has been the annual LGBT Symposium. Past programs have ranged from artistic to literary to theatrical and social presentations. Participants and presenters have come from around the world to share in this contemporary queer academic endeavor.

LGBT students should take note of progress being made at the University of Rhode Island. One LGBT student notes: "URI is an up-and-coming campus. Take it from me, the LGBT support is there along with a growing, strong visible presence from faculty and students. I have found that and more coming out on campus."

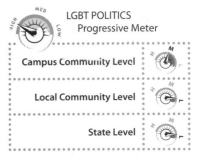

LGBT POLITICS
Progressive Meter

Campus Community Level

Local Community Level

State Level

𝄽 OUTSPOKEN *Answers from LGBT students:*

Top Three Descriptors of the LGBT Campus Environment:
1. Improving   2. Coming Out   3. Strong

What makes your campus feel welcoming and safe for LGBT students?
"A small but strong community of LGBT support and visibility...You see the 'Welcome Project' stickers everywhere, and allies are out in force with the 'Gay? Fine by Me' T-shirts too! The GLBT Center sends a clear welcome from the beginning." —*20-year-old gay male, junior*

How do you feel about coming out on your campus?
"I believe the campus is a safe place to come out. I do it all the time. At first, I was concerned with a couple lame reactions, but I think the impact was positive overall. I encourage others to come out when they are ready."
—*21-year-old bisexual female, senior*

INFO

UNIVERSITY OF RHODE ISLAND
Newman Hall
14 Upper College Road
Kingston, RI 02881

Phone: 401-874-7000
Fax: 401-874-5523
E-mail: admissions@uri.edu
Website: www.uri.edu

CAMPUS STATS
Type of Institution: Public university
Founding Year: 1892
Size: 11,957
Avg. Class Size: 20–29 students
Popular Majors: Political Science, Communications Studies, Speech Communication and Rhetoric, Nursing/ Registered Nurse Training, Psychology
Cost: In-state tuition: $5,258
Out-of-state tuition: $17,900
Admission Application Deadline: February 1

OUTRAGEOUS FACTOID A couple of LGBT students commented that there is a tradition of "sheer nakedness" on nearby Rhode Island beaches.

RAINBOW RUMOR As a result of a gay-bashing assault in 2001, the university established a GLBT Center and appointed the first assistant to the vice president of student affairs responsible for gay, lesbian, bisexual and transgender programs and services. The center's mission is to create a more welcoming and inclusive campus, and it has been doing just that with newfound LGBT support from campus officials.

ANNUAL LGBT EVENT HIGHLIGHTS

Out and Proud Queer Film Series: Fall/Spring

Gay Bingo: Monthly, Fall/Spring

LGBT Dance: Fall/Spring

LGBT Annual Welcome Night: September

National Coming Out Week: October

World AIDS Day: December

Annual LGBT Symposium: April

Annual Diversity Awards: April

ACADEMIC SCENE

Top Three Supportive LGBT Academic Areas:
1. Sociology   2. Psychology   3. English

How LGBT-friendly are faculty in the classroom?
"I know an out LGBT faculty member who is wonderful. Other faculty are inclusive of queer stuff when it is appropriate. I give faculty on this campus a straight 'A' for trying." —*19-year-old lesbian, sophomore*

"Quite friendly for sexual orientation issues. Some faculty have a problem understanding trans issues, and there are many stereotypes often shared that are not always sensitive. There needs to be greater campus awareness in general on this topic." —*22-year-old queer male, senior*

SOCIAL SCENE

Top Three Things in the LGBT Social Life:
1. Movies   2. Hanging out with friends   3. Dancing

How would you describe the social scene for LGBT students?
"There are a lot of LGBT activities on campus…film series, dance, the annual symposium….There are options close-by for partying too!"
—*22-year-old gay male, senior*

What annual social event should an LGBT student not miss?
"National Coming Out Week…gotta love it, full of gay stuff!"
—*19-year-old gay male, junior*

BUZZ BITES *Fun Queer Stuff to Know*

THE BEST...

Eating Place: Bagels Inc.

Place to Check Out Guys: Mackal Fitness Center

Place to Check Out Ladies: Memorial Union

LGBT-Cool Athletic Sport: Women's rugby

Non-LGBT-Specific Campus Club: Students for Social Change

LGBT Educational Involvement Opportunity: "Welcome Project" Campaign

LGBT-Accepting Religious/Spiritual Organization(s): Hillel: The Center for Jewish Life on Campus

THE GAY POINT AVERAGE
OFFICIAL CAMPUS CHECKLIST

LGBT & ally student organization ✓

LGBT resource center/office ✓

LGBT Pride Week &/or Coming Out Week ✓

Safe Zone/Safe Space or Ally Program ✓

Significant number of LGBT social activities ✓

Significant number of LGBT educational events ✓

Variety of LGBT studies/courses

Nondiscrimination statement Inclusive of sexual orientation ✓

Nondiscrimination statement inclusive of gender identity/expression ✓

Extends domestic partner benefits to same-sex couples ✓

Actively recruits LGBT students to enroll on campus ✓

Trains campus police on LGBT sensitivity ✓

Procedure for reporting LGBT bias, harassment & hate crimes ✓

Offers LGBT housing options/themes

Offers LGBT-inclusive health services/testing ✓

Offers LGBT-inclusive counseling/support groups ✓

Offers LGBT student scholarships

Conducts special LGBT graduation ceremony for LGBT & ally Students

Offers support services for process of transitioning from M to F & F to M

Active LGBT alumni group

UNIVERSITY OF RHODE ISLAND
GAY POINT AVERAGE (14)
(out of 20)

CAMPUS QUEER RESOURCES

Select LGBT Student Organization(s)

OutURI
Founding Date: 1973
Membership: 30+
E-mail: OutURI@gmail.com
Website: www.outri.org/

LGBT Resource Center/Office:

GLBT Center
Adams Hall, Room 111
112 Roger Williams Building
Kingston, RI 02881
Year Established: 2001
Number of Staff: 2 full-time professional staff, 1 student employee
Phone: 401-874-2894
Website: www.uri.edu/glbt/

UNIVERSITY OF SOUTHERN CALIFORNIA

LOCATED IN THE heart of downtown Los Angeles, the University of Southern California has a perfect Gay Point Average. The campus has tremendous institutional support for LGBT issues and the most LGBT-progressive polices and practices possible.

In 1995, the LGBT Resource Center was opened to foster a more inclusive LGBT community on campus. Before that, in 1970, the GLBT Assembly started as a program board of the Undergraduate Student Senate. It now serves as the umbrella coalition for several queer student organizations, including QUEERS, Ally Alliance and OutREACH. Annual events include National Coming Out Week, Pridefest, and World AIDS Day.

The campus also has seven active LGBT graduate student organizations that are discipline-specific in areas such as social work, business, medicine and law. Queer students have more than ample opportunities for LGBT involvement, including a new Safe Zone program for outreach to allies. In addition, LGBT students can request a living space on the Rainbow Floor, reserved only for LGBT and ally students. There is even an LGBT alumni association with a primary goal to raise scholarship money for LGBT students.

As one LGBT student explains: "I am out and proud….I love it here. I could not possibly imagine a more gay place than my campus. After all, we have a naked Trojan man nicknamed Tommy. He's on the LGBT center Website."

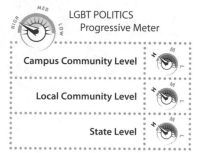

LGBT POLITICS
Progressive Meter

Campus Community Level

Local Community Level

State Level

𝄇 OUTSPOKEN *Answers from LGBT students:*

Top Three Descriptors of the LGBT Campus Environment:
1. Spirited   2. Trendy   3. Accepting

What makes your campus feel welcoming and safe for LGBT students?
"Not only [do] the diversity and availability of LGBT activities and resources make students feel welcome, but the proactive stance they take in advertising, reaching out and including all students into the already-strong LGBT community show that they go the extra mile." *—18-year-old gay male, freshman*

How do you feel about coming out on your campus?
"I always felt pretty comfortable with coming out on campus. My roommate was straight, but I told him early on in our freshman year, and it was never a problem. He remains one of my closest friends at USC, and we are actually planning on living together again next semester. In fact, the overwhelming majority of my friends and the people that I spend time with are heterosexual, and they are all fully aware that I am not. I have honestly never felt threatened or even left out on campus because of the fact that I am gay." *—20-year-old gay male, junior*

⌖ ACADEMIC SCENE

Top Three Supportive LGBT Academic Areas:
1. Gender Studies   2. Theater   3. Anthropology

INFO

UNIVERSITY OF SOUTHERN CALIFORNIA
Administrative Services
John Hubbard Hall
700 Childs Way
Los Angeles, CA 90089
Phone: 213-740-1111
Fax: 213-740-6364
E-mail: admitusc@usc.edu
Website: www.usc.edu

CAMPUS STATS

Type of Institution: Private university
Founding Year: 1880
Size: 16,271
Avg. Class Size: 20–29 students
Popular Majors: Business Administration/ Management, Communications Studies/Speech Communication and Rhetoric, Psychology
Cost: Tuition: $32,008
Admission Application Deadline: January 10

How LGBT-friendly are faculty in the classroom?

"I've had really great experiences with my professors in regards to LGBT issues. I wrote a term paper on bisexuality and television last semester, and my professors and TAs were really interested in the topic. They knew a lot of LGBT resources for research and were very aware."
—*19-year-old bisexual female, sophomore*

"I would say that most professors at USC are supportive of queer rights. I have never had an experience where I felt that a professor at USC was even mildly homophobic. There are also several queer professors and staff members at USC; this helps make the campus feel like it is a place where being queer is not only tolerated, but accepted and even welcomed." —*21-year-old gay male, senior*

SOCIAL SCENE

Top Three Things in the LGBT Social Life:
1. Off-campus theme parties   2. Film soirees   3. WeHO (West Hollywood)

How would you describe the social scene for LGBT students?

"The social scene for LGBT students at USC is one of the most welcoming environments ever and not just from the LGBT perspective. Never before have I felt like I was being welcomed not just into a group, but more so into a family."
—*20-year-old lesbian female, junior*

What annual social event should an LGBT student not miss?

"You can't miss the dance during National Coming Out Week. Each year the whole week has a specific theme. This year we had a dance with a 'Hoedown' theme. Everyone came dressed as cowboys, and it was pretty hot. The best part? Because the event was school-sponsored and couldn't serve alcohol—there was plenty of Red Bull instead." —*18-year-old gay male, freshman*

BUZZ BITES *Fun Queer Stuff to Know*

THE BEST...

Party Locale: Big Gay House

Hangout: Rainbow Floor

Eating Place: Parkside

Place to Check Out Guys: McDonald Swim Stadium during dive practice

Place to Check Out Ladies: Big Gay House

LGBT-Cool Athletic Sport: Dance Company

Non-LGBT-Specific Campus Club: Women's Student Assembly

Place for LGBT Students to Live on Campus: Rainbow Floor

LGBT Course Offering: Social Issues in Gender

LGBT Educational Involvement Opportunity: LGBT Resource Center

LGBT-Accepting Religious/Spiritual Organization(s): United University Church

OUTRAGEOUS FACTOID The University of Southern California paid tribute to its fiftieth birthday celebration by erecting a life-size bronze statue of a Trojan warrior, which was quickly nicknamed "Tommy Trojan." Sculpted by Roger Noble Burnham, Tommy Trojan was modeled after different campus football players and comes fully equipped with a shield and sword. On the bronze statue's granite pedestal are inscribed the qualities of the ideal Trojan: "faithful, scholarly, skillful, courageous, and ambitious." Built to last, Tommy Trojan leaves a lot of men envious, gay or straight....He was last seen on the main page of the LGBT Center Website!

RAINBOW RUMOR One student candidly reveals: "Gay boys at USC have a bizarre cosmopolitanism about them—they know everything about anything, they come from wealthy, upper-crust families, but they listen to Britney Spears and read books titled *Bergdorf Blondes*." Another student chimes in: "It's like an episode of the OC every day, but 'gayer'!"

THAT'S SO GAY! **ANNUAL LGBT EVENT HIGHLIGHTS**

Welcome Back Picnic: August

Safe Zone/Allies Orientation: September and January

Coming Out Week: October

LGBT Parents' Tailgate for Parents' Weekend: October

Queer Studies Conference: November

World AIDS Day: December

Speak Out: February

Pridefest: March

Gender and Sexuality Week: March

Gen-Q Retreat: April

Lavender Commencement: May

CAMPUS QUEER RESOURCES

Select LGBT Student Organization(s):

Gay Lesbian Bisexual Transgender Assembly
Founding Date: 1970
Membership: 20
Phone: 213-740-5656
E-mail: glbta@usc.edu
Website: www.glbta.org

LGBT Resource Center/Office:

LGBT Resource Center
3601 Trousdale Parkway
Student Union 202 B
Los Angeles, CA 90089-0890
Year Established: 1995
Number of Staff: 1 full-time professional staff; 4 part-time student workers
Phone: 213-740-7619
E-mail: lgbt@usc.edu
Website: www.usc.edu/lgbt

THE GAY POINT AVERAGE
OFFICIAL CAMPUS CHECKLIST

✓ LGBT & ally student organization

✓ LGBT resource center/office

✓ LGBT Pride Week &/or Coming Out Week

✓ Safe Zone/Safe Space or Ally Program

✓ Significant number of LGBT social activities

✓ Significant number of LGBT educational events

✓ Variety of LGBT studies/courses

✓ Nondiscrimination statement inclusive of sexual orientation

✓ Nondiscrimination statement inclusive of gender identity/expression

✓ Extends domestic partner benefits to same-sex couples

✓ Actively recruits LGBT students to enroll on campus

✓ Trains campus police on LGBT sensitivity

✓ Procedure for reporting LGBT bias, harassment & hate crimes

✓ Offers LGBT housing options/themes

✓ Offers LGBT-inclusive health services/testing

✓ Offers LGBT-inclusive counseling/support groups

✓ Offers LGBT student scholarships

✓ Conducts special LGBT graduation ceremony for LGBT & ally Students

✓ Offers support services for process of transitioning from M to F & F to M

✓ Active LGBT alumni group

20 UNIVERSITY OF SOUTHERN CALIFORNIA GAY POINT AVERAGE
(out of 20)

UNIVERSITY OF SOUTHERN MAINE

FIFTEEN YEARS AGO, a straight student who was a member of the board of trustees cast one of two votes that gave all Maine campuses systemwide a nondiscrimination clause inclusive of sexual orientation. The other person was an African American.

Both spoke adamantly in support to convince the board of traditionally conservative men and women who did not want the clause. Without those two allies, the policy would have been defeated. Eight years later, domestic partner benefits were extended to same-sex employees too.

But besides queer inclusive policies, why does Southern Maine deserve to be listed among the best? The measure of progress can be found in the campus's continued support for LGBT life. The commitment is obvious over the years—from the beginnings of LGBT student activism in the 1990s to the founding of the Center for Sexualities and Gender Diversity in 2001. Support has also come from the top down, with unparalleled responses from the university president and the vice president for student and university life. Residential Life created gender-neutral housing in 2004, and the Intercultural Development Office and Leadership Office are implementing in 2006 an annual Social Justice Retreat titled "Voices of Change" to prepare future LGBT leaders. According to LGBT members of the campus community, Southern Maine is the kind of institution "that sees change and the role that diversity serves as integral to the success of its students."

Most important, Southern Maine stands out because of the large number of LGBT students and the surprising number of straight allies on campus. As a result, the overwhelming level of public awareness of the Safe Zone program has created a welcoming campus openness to queer issues. What better learning community for LGBT students? One LGBT student answers: "There are many out LGBT and ally students and staff/faculty on campus…visible in every way possible. My favorite aspect of the campus is that I feel comfortable being who I am. I can learn without fear….the campus stands behind me…and for people like me."

OUTSPOKEN *Answers from LGBT students:*

Top Three Descriptors of the LGBT Campus Environment:
1. Open-minded   2. Flamboyant   3. Responsive

What makes your campus feel welcoming and safe for LGBT students?
"We have a really diverse student population and support from the GLBTQA center…We also have great LGBT inclusive faculty and staff."
—23-year-old lesbian, senior

How do you feel about coming out on your campus?
"I am totally out on campus and feel comfortable discussing my experiences as a queer person on campus and in classes, holding my partner's hand in public."
—22-year-old lesbian, senior

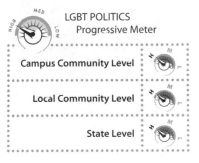

LGBT POLITICS
Progressive Meter

Campus Community Level

Local Community Level

State Level

INFO

UNIVERSITY OF SOUTHERN MAINE
37 College Avenue
Gorham, ME 04038
Phone: 207-780-5670
Fax: 207-780-5640
E-mail: usmadm@usm.maine.edu
Website: www.usm.maine.edu

CAMPUS STATS
Type of Institution: Public university
Founding Year: 1878
Size: 6,842
Avg. Class Size: 20–29 students
Popular Majors: Business/Commerce, Surgical Nurse/Nursing, Psychology
Cost: In-state tuition: $4,980
Out-of-state tuition: $12,780
Admission Application Deadline: January 1

Whether it's *Carrie, The Shining* or *The Shawshank Redemption,* acclaimed horror writer Stephen King frightens the jeepers out of queers and straights alike. A native of the state of Maine, his daughter Naomi Rachel is a Women's Studies major who graduated from the University of Southern Maine, and she's an LGBT ally.

• • • • • • • • • • • • • • • • • • •

 RAINBOW RUMOR

The Center for Sexualities and Gender Diversity was founded in 2001 and received funding to hire an LGBT coordinator. Unfortunately, because of resignations and budget cuts, the campus has not always been able to fill the position. Hopes are high that with a new restructuring of campus staff, the LGBT coordinator position will be filled in a speedy manner.

• • • • • • • • • • • • • • • • • • •

THAT'S SO GAY!

ANNUAL LGBT EVENT HIGHLIGHTS

National Coming Out Day: October 11

Coming Out Week: October

Transgender Day of Remembrance: November

Drag Show: November

World AIDS Day: December 1

Pride Week: April

Day of Silence: April

Pier Dance: June

"When I came out on campus, there was a very visible and affirming queer presence that made me feel welcomed and safe." —*22-year-old gay male, senior*

ACADEMIC SCENE

Top Three Supportive LGBT Academic Areas:
1. Women's Studies   2. Sociology   3. Human Resource Development

How LGBT-friendly are faculty in the classroom?
"I've always had good experiences with faculty in terms of LGBT inclusion in various topics and in general have found faculty to be open-minded on LGBT issues." —*25-year-old lesbian, graduate student*

"I am a major in Women's Studies which has great progressive faculty. My experiences with faculty have been excellent, and I love that queer faculty are out to students." —*22-year-old lesbian, senior*

SOCIAL SCENE

Top Three Things in the LGBT Social Life:
1. Hanging out   2. Movies   3. Parties

How would you describe the social scene for LGBT students?
"Queer students seem to facilitate the social scene here. Many students are involved in high-profile student activities." —*22-year-old gay male, senior*

What annual social event should an LGBT student not miss?
"The Drag Show is the big event at USM. Also political activism…" —*23-year-old lesbian, senior*

BUZZ BITES *Fun Queer Stuff to Know*

THE BEST…

Party Locale: Styxx-Bar

Hangout: Casco Bay Books

Eating Place: Granny's Burritos

Place to Check Out Guys: Spring Street

Place to Check Out Ladies: Brooks Student Center

LGBT-Cool Athletic Sport: Women's ice hockey and basketball

Place for LGBT Students to Live on Campus: Portland Hall

LGBT Course Offering: Lesbian Fiction

LGBT Educational Involvement Opportunity: Safe Zone Project

THE GAY POINT AVERAGE
OFFICIAL CAMPUS CHECKLIST

LGBT & ally student organization	✓
LGBT resource center/office	✓
LGBT Pride Week &/or Coming Out Week	✓
Safe Zone/Safe Space or Ally Program	✓
Significant number of LGBT social activities	✓
Significant number of LGBT educational events	✓
Variety of LGBT studies/courses	✓
Nondiscrimination statement inclusive of sexual orientation	✓
Nondiscrimination statement inclusive of gender identity/expression	✓
Extends domestic partner benefits to same-sex couples	✓
Actively recruits LGBT students to enroll on campus	
Trains campus police on LGBT sensitivity	✓
Procedure for reporting LGBT bias, harassment & hate crimes	✓
Offers LGBT housing options/themes	
Offers LGBT-inclusive health services/testing	✓
Offers LGBT-inclusive counseling/support groups	✓
Offers LGBT student scholarships	
Conducts special LGBT graduation ceremony for LGBT & ally Students	
Offers support services for process of transitioning from M to F & F to M	✓
Active LGBT alumni group	

UNIVERSITY OF SOUTHERN MAINE
GAY POINT AVERAGE
(out of 20)

15

CAMPUS QUEER
RESOURCES

Select LGBT Student Organization(s):
Queer Insurgency
Founding Date: September 2005
Membership: 20+
Phone: 207-228-8235

LGBT Resource Center/Office:
Center for Sexualities and Gender Diversity
University of Southern Maine
132 Woodbury Campus Center
PO Box 9300
Gorham, ME 04104
Year Established: 2001
Number of Staff: 1 full-time professional staff; 5 student employees
Phone: 207-228-8235
E-mail: glbtiqa@usm.maine.edu
Website: www.usm.maine.edu/glbtiqa

UNIVERSITY OF TEXAS—AUSTIN

AUSTIN IS UNDOUBTEDLY one of the most highly progressive areas in Texas, with huge queer visibility. The University of Texas—Austin campus is known to be a "safe haven" in the Lone Star State for LGBT students. There is a large campus queer population, and there are more than 10 queer-identified student coalitions. As early as 1990, the campus included sexual orientation in the campus nondiscrimination policy. And just as recently as 2004, the campus started the Gender and Sexuality Center to address the needs and concerns of LGBT students. The center, along with the various queer student coalitions, plans social and educational programs on campus like the Pride Rally, the XYX Experience, National Coming Out Week and, of course, the drag shows.

In addition, the queer student coalitions also advocate political awareness and recently mobilized hundreds of students against the anti–gay marriage amendment Proposition 2. Travis County, where UT Austin is located, bucked the state trend and was the only county to reject the anti–gay marriage amendment. The voting record on campus was 9 to 1 against the amendment. Such results show the LGBT openness in public support for LGBT issues on campus.

Although it's deep in the heart of Texas, UT Austin is one of the most LGBT-progressive Southern campuses out there. It has definitely set an example in the South. One LGBT student agrees: "LGBT students should give UT Austin a chance. As a Texan, I did not have many queer choices. This campus was my only hope…. it is most definitely queer for Texas. I am out and have never felt more welcome."

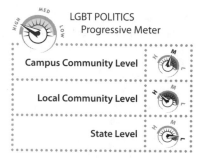

LGBT POLITICS
Progressive Meter

Campus Community Level

Local Community Level

State Level

INFO

UNIVERSITY OF TEXAS—AUSTIN

PO Box 8058
Austin, TX 78713
Phone: 512-475-7440
Fax: 512-475-7475
E-mail: frmn@uts.cc.utexas.edu
Website: www.utexas.edu

CAMPUS STATS

Type of Institution: Public university
Founding Year: 1883
Size: 36,473
Avg. Class Size: 10–19 students
Popular Majors: Biology/Biological Sciences, Economics, Political Science and Government
Cost: In-state tuition: $7,000
Out-of-state tuition: $15,000
Admission Application Deadline: December 1

OUTSPOKEN Answers from LGBT students:

Top Three Descriptors of the LGBT Campus Environment:
1. Integrated   2. Open   3. Accepting

What makes your campus feel welcoming and safe for LGBT students?
"There is a wide variety of student organizations in which I can become an active member. It is also located inside the liberal city of Austin."
—*21-year-old gay male, junior*

How do you feel about coming out on your campus?
"I feel okay coming out; I have no problem doing it. I actually came out to an entire class the other day. All of the people at UT seem to be very accepting and tolerant toward those who are different." —*21-year-old gay male, senior*

ACADEMIC SCENE

Top Three Supportive LGBT Academic Areas:
1. Women and Gender Studies   2. Radio, Television and Film   3. Sociology

How LGBT-friendly are faculty in the classroom?

"I wouldn't be surprised if I saw mine wearing Pride shirts outside of the classroom." —*21-year-old gay male, senior*

"The professors are sensitive to LGBT issues generally. I have never had a problem. In fact, I believe the faculty are some of the best allies on campus." —*22-year-old lesbian, senior*

☺ SOCIAL SCENE

Top Three Things in the LGBT Social Life:

1. Parties   2. Sharing with friends   3. Dances

How would you describe the social scene for LGBT students?

"Country chic! After all, it's Texas and everything is bigger and better!" —*19-year-old gay male, freshman*

What annual social event should an LGBT student not miss?

"Pride Week always has the best to offer. I think every year the activities get better, gayer than ever!"—*20-year-old bisexual female, junior*

OUTRAGEOUS FACTOID Deep in the heart of Texas, the UT—Austin student body elected an out lesbian as student government president in the 1990s. That's probably why UT—Austin is sometimes not-so-affectionately known as a place for "queers and steers."

RAINBOW RUMOR UT Austin stands out in a state known for anti-LGBT politics. The LGBT students on campus continue to forge a path of understanding and recently have initiated efforts to identify and include gender-neutral bathrooms on campus.

THAT'S SO GAY!

ANNUAL LGBT EVENT HIGHLIGHTS

Sex Workers Art Show: Fall/Spring

Safe Space Training: Fall/Spring

The XYX Experience: Monthly, Fall/Spring

To Be a Man Series on Masculinity: Fall/Spring

Gay Movie Night: Fall/Spring

Drag Queen/Drag King Shows: Fall/Spring

LGBT Welcome Picnic: August

Coming Out Week/Pride Week: October

Pride Rally: October

Transgender Day of Remembrance: November

LGBT Awareness Week: April

National Day of Silence: April

BUZZ BITES
Fun Queer Stuff to Know

THE BEST...

Party Locale: Clubs on 4th Street

Hangout: Little City

Non-LGBT-Specific Campus Club:
University Democrats

LGBT Educational Involvement Opportunity:
Safe Space

LGBT-Accepting Religious/Spiritual Organization(s):
University Baptist Center, University Lutherans

CAMPUS QUEER RESOURCES

Select LGBT Student Organization(s):

Queer Student Alliance; Hang Out

Founding Date: Queer Student Alliance (1999, as GLBTA Affairs Agency); Hang Out (2000)

Membership: 70+

Website: www.queertx.org; www.comehangout.net

LGBT Resource Center/Office:

Gender and Sexuality Center
Student Services Building
100 West Dean Keeton Street
Austin, TX 78705

Year Established: 2004

Number of Staff: 1 full-time professional staff; 2 graduate assistant staff, 3 student assistants

Phone: 512-232-1831

E-mail: gsc@uts.cc.utexas.edu

Website: deanofstudents.utexas.edu/gsc/

THE GAY POINT AVERAGE
OFFICIAL CAMPUS CHECKLIST

- ✓ LGBT & ally student organization
- ✓ LGBT resource center/office
- ✓ LGBT Pride Week &/or Coming Out Week
- ✓ Safe Zone/Safe Space or Ally Program
- ✓ Significant number of LGBT social activities
- ✓ Significant number of LGBT educational events
- Variety of LGBT studies/courses
- ✓ Nondiscrimination statement inclusive of sexual orientation
- Nondiscrimination statement inclusive of gender identity/expression
- Extends domestic partner benefits to same-sex couples
- Actively recruits LGBT students to enroll on campus
- Trains campus police on LGBT sensitivity
- ✓ Procedure for reporting LGBT bias, harassment & hate crimes
- Offers LGBT housing options/themes
- ✓ Offers LGBT-inclusive health services/testing
- ✓ Offers LGBT-inclusive counseling/support groups
- Offers LGBT student scholarships
- Conducts special LGBT graduation ceremony for LGBT & ally Students
- Offers support services for process of transitioning from M to F & F to M
- Active LGBT alumni group

10 UNIVERSITY OF TEXAS—AUSTIN GAY POINT AVERAGE
(out of 20)

UNIVERSITY OF UTAH

SURPRISE! THE UNIVERSITY of Utah made the list! Credit might be given to the liberal impression left behind from the 2002 Winter Olympics or the fact that the area elected an openly gay woman in 1998 as a representative to the Utah State legislature. But the real truth lies in the campus history of LGBT mobilization and activism.

In 1974, the Lesbian Gay Student Union, the first of its kind in the state of Utah, was founded on campus. The student coalition grew strong early on out of a need to confront religious conservatism of the Mormon Church. The Lesbian Gay Student Union was actually one of the first places in Utah for openly gay and lesbian individuals to meet in public. Such a queer start met with divisive reactions from Mormons on campus. But LGBT and ally campus community members stuck together and ultimately prevailed. Today, one LGBT student remarks: "It is comforting to see Mormon students openly ally themselves with LGBT people; it helps bridge that very wide gap." Indeed, the bridge of LGBT understanding has been built.

In 1998, the campus added sexual orientation to the nondiscrimination statement, and in 2002 it became the only institution of higher education in the state with an LGBT resource center. The university is also the only campus with domestic partner benefits, an LGBT faculty/staff association and an annual Pride celebration. As recently as 2003, the university president even released a legal memo defining gender identity/expression as protected under the "gender" category of the campus nondiscrimination policy. Quite LGBT-progressive for the state of Utah.

Queer campus life also gets highly favorable marks. Annual LGBT events include Pride Week, National Transgender Day of Remembrance and National Day of Silence. The annual concert for Pride Week has featured national music and comedy acts like the Indigo Girls, Ani DiFranco and Margaret Cho. In addition, the LGBT Resource Center offers popular educational programs and services such as Queer Peers, the LGBT Speakers Bureau and Safe Zone trainings for allies.

The University of Utah has definitely been a leading institution statewide for LGBT change. One LGBT student affirms: "The University of Utah and the LGBT Resource Center help to create a comfortable climate on campus: it's nice to know that there are safe places for everyone."

OUTSPOKEN *Answers from LGBT students:*

Top Three Descriptors of the LGBT Campus Environment:
1. Tolerant   2. Inviting   3. Friendly

What makes your campus feel welcoming and safe for LGBT students?
"The number of out LGBT students and the fact that there are so many LGBT activities throughout the year. We also have excellent allies who are faculty and staff." *--21-year-old gay male, junior*

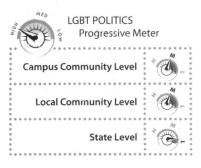

LGBT POLITICS
Progressive Meter

Campus Community Level

Local Community Level

State Level

INFO

UNIVERSITY OF UTAH
201 South 1460 East, Room 250S
Salt Lake City, UT 84112
Phone: 801-581-7281
Fax: 801-585-7864
E-mail: admissions@sa.utah.edu
Website: www.utah.edu

CAMPUS STATS
Type of Institution: Public university
Founding Year: 1850
Size: 22,661
Avg. Class Size: 20–29 students
Popular Majors: Business Administration/Management, Elementary Education and Teaching, Psychology
Cost: In-state tuition: $4,298
Out-of-state tuition: $13,371
Admission Application Deadline: August 1

OUTRAGEOUS FACTOID

A little-known fact is that the campus actually has a large number of LGBT students. One LGBT student admits: "Many of them just aren't necessarily out completely or don't participate in LGBT university events."

RAINBOW RUMOR

Overwhelmingly—62 percent—University of Utah students hold accepting attitudes toward LGBT students, according to a recent campus climate study. Unfortunately, campus staff don't necessarily share those perspectives, and Safe Zone trainings are not required for campus staff.

THAT'S SO GAY!

ANNUAL LGBT EVENT HIGHLIGHTS

Out at Lunch Series: Bimonthly, Fall/Spring

Pride Week: Second week of October

Pride Concert: October

National Transgender Day of Remembrance: November

Coming Out 101 Support Group: Weekly, Fall/Spring

L-Word Lounge: Biweekly, Fall/Spring

National Day of Silence: April

Safe Zone Trainings: Biweekly, Fall/Spring

Lavender Graduation: May

How do you feel about coming out on your campus?
"I think it depends greatly. It is not the easiest thing to do, and you have to choose the time and place. But, all in all, I come out to those on campus who need to know and who I think will be open-minded… even Mormons are gay-friendly." —*20-year-old gay male, sophomore*

ACADEMIC SCENE

Top Three Supportive LGBT Academic Areas:
1. Humanities   2. Fine Arts   3. Social and Behavioral Sciences

How LGBT-friendly are faculty in the classroom?
"We may be in Utah, but still discrimination toward gays in the classroom is not tolerated on this campus. Many faculty are supportive…All faculty give me respect for my views and who I am." —*21-year-old bisexual female, junior*

"We have an openly transgender professor in our geology department. The university and the department chair were very supportive from when 'she' was still a 'he' all the way up until now; she is now tenured and very visible as a transgender individual. I think that's a good sign."
—*22-year-old bisexual male, graduate student*

SOCIAL SCENE

Top Three Things in the LGBT Social Life:
1. Hanging out with friends   2. Coffeehouses   3. LGSU meetings

How would you describe the social scene for LGBT students?
"The social scene is pretty large. There are a number of opportunities to meet a wide variety of LGBT students." —*20 year-old gay male, junior*

What annual social event should an LGBT student not miss?
"The LGBT Resource Center's Gala Dinner Fundraiser. I look forward to this event every October and have attended it every school year. It's always a great opportunity to dress up and meet a lot of people." —*20-year-old gay male, junior*

BUZZ BITES *Fun Queer Stuff to Know*

THE BEST…

Hangout: Coffee Garden

Eating Place: Trio Restaurant

Place to Check Out Guys: Rec Center

Place to Check Out Ladies: Paper Moon

LGBT-Cool Athletic Sport: Softball

Place for LGBT Students to Live on Campus: Officer's Circle

LGBT Educational Involvement Opportunity: LGBT Speakers Bureau

LGBT-Accepting Religious/Spiritual Organization(s): Episcopal Church

THE GAY POINT AVERAGE
OFFICIAL CAMPUS CHECKLIST

LGBT & ally student organization ✓

LGBT resource center/office ✓

LGBT Pride Week &/or Coming Out Week ✓

Safe Zone/Safe Space or Ally Program ✓

Significant number of LGBT social activities ✓

Significant number of LGBT educational events ✓

Variety of LGBT studies/courses ✓

Nondiscrimination statement inclusive of sexual orientation ✓

Nondiscrimination statement inclusive of gender identity/expression ✓

Extends domestic partner benefits to same-sex couples

Actively recruits LGBT students to enroll on campus ✓

Trains campus police on LGBT sensitivity ✓

Procedure for reporting LGBT bias, harassment & hate crimes

Offers LGBT housing options/themes

Offers LGBT-inclusive health services/testing ✓

Offers LGBT-inclusive counseling/support groups ✓

Offers LGBT student scholarships ✓

Conducts special LGBT graduation ceremony for LGBT & ally Students ✓

Offers support services for process of transitioning from M to F & F to M ✓

Active LGBT alumni group

UNIVERSITY OF UTAH
GAY POINT AVERAGE
(out of 20)

16

CAMPUS QUEER RESOURCES

Select LGBT Student Organization(s):
Lesbian Gay Student Union
Founding Date: September 1974
Membership: 50+
Phone: 801-587-7973
E-mail: lgsu0506@gmail.com
Website: www.utah.edu/lgsu

LGBT Resource Center/Office:
LGBT Resource Center
University of Utah
200 South Central Campus Drive,
Room 317
Salt Lake City, UT 84112
Year Established: 2002
Number of Staff: 1 full-time professional
staff; 5 student employees
Phone: 801-587-7973
E-mail: lgbtrc@sa.utah.edu
Website: www.sa.utah.edu/lgbt/

UNIVERSITY OF VERMONT

DON'T LET THE ice fishing on Lake Champlain fool you! The University of Vermont is red-hot for LGBT progress and is situated in one of the state's most liberal and progressive areas.

The University of Vermont has been resolute in advancing LGBT-inclusive policies and practices. As early as 1987, the campus included sexual orientation in nondiscrimination policies and, in 2005, added gender identity/expression. Even in the mid-1990s, before there were state-sanctioned civil unions, the campus was ahead of the curve, granting full domestic partner benefits for same-sex employees.

One LGBT student explains: "The LGBT campus community works very hard to create a welcoming environment. They have been more than successful, and it shows." Indeed, many queer students echo similar sentiments of praise. Founded in 1999, LGBTQA Services is responsible for most of the LGBT campus life, along with the queer student organization aptly named Free to Be. The Welcome Back Picnic is where it all starts every September for incoming and returning queer students.

Other events, like Cupcakes and Condoms, National Coming Out Week and Twister and Lube, fill out the calendar. Plus the campus is home to the Translating Identity Conference, the region's largest conference on gender and trans issues and their relevance to other sexual identities. Last year, the conference drew a record attendance of over 500 people; almost double expectations. An LGBT student proclaims: "The best conference ever…. UVM LGBT life has become a leader for trans issues in the area. I learned invaluable ideas, got inspired and created friends." Signs of queer life only seem to increase. The campus even brought Ellen Degeneres for National Coming Out Week and had over 2,000 students there. Yep, it's gay!

Like many universities, the University of Vermont has had to fight hard for LGBT progress and has come a long way since the 1990s. Most important, the LGBT campus community has had a proud knockout record of success. This LGBT student says: "I am a part of UVM, and it has been there for me as I came out on campus. Faculty, staff and fellow LGBT students have made this campus a more supportive queer place. I am thankful."

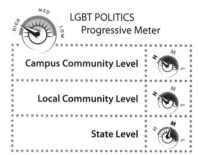

LGBT POLITICS
Progressive Meter

Campus Community Level

Local Community Level

State Level

🗩🗩 OUTSPOKEN *Answers from LGBT students:*

Top Three Descriptors of the LGBT Campus Environment:
1. Friendly   2. Active   3. Supportive

What makes your campus feel welcoming and safe for LGBT students?
"The queer attitude is great. I found LGBT friends immediately at the Welcome Back Picnic. I also learned about the LGBT services available. I felt support … and the friendships only continue to grow." —*20-year-old queer female, junior*

How do you feel about coming out on your campus?
"Just be open about it. If I feel like someone needs to know I will tell them. To date, I have not had a negative reaction from fellow students."
—*21-year-old gay male, junior*

INFO

UNIVERSITY OF VERMONT
194 South Prospect Street
Burlington, VT 05401

Phone: 802-656-3370

Fax: 802-656-8611

E-mail: admissions@uvm.edu

Website: www.uvm.edu

CAMPUS STATS

Type of Institution: Public university

Founding Year: 1791

Size: 8,143

Avg. Class Size: 10–19 students

Popular Majors: Biology/Biological Sciences, Business Administration/ Management, Psychology

Cost: In-state tuition: $9,452
Out-of-state tuition: $22,638

Admission Application Deadline: January 15

ⓘ ACADEMIC SCENE

Top Three Supportive LGBT Academic Areas:
1. Sexuality and Gender Identity Studies   2. Social Work
3. Human Development and Family Studies

How LGBT-friendly are faculty in the classroom?
"Extremely supportive, caring…. that has been my experience in my classes. I have never had a fellow student or faculty say anything derogatory about LGBT issues. Instead, I have heard several positive things said."
—21-year-old bisexual female, junior

"Language can be an issue, but it is always confronted to my knowledge. Homophobia is not tolerated. Instructors always keep students under control."
—22-year-old gay male, senior

☺ SOCIAL SCENE

Top Three Things in the LGBT Social Life:
1. Hanging out   2. Parties   3. Going to coffeehouses

How would you describe the social scene for LGBT students?
"Bustling…we all keep busy with LGBT activism and planning…but you have to get involved." *—19-year-old bisexual male, sophomore*

What annual social event should an LGBT student not miss?
"The Translating Identity Conference has been the most worthwhile…have always gained a lot." *—20-year-old bisexual female, junior*

BUZZ BITES
Fun Queer Stuff to Know

THE BEST...

Party Locale: 185 Pearl
Hangout: Uncommon Ground
Eating Place: Sweetwaters
Place to Check Out Guys: Border's Bookstore
Place to Check Out Ladies: Soccer field
LGBT-Cool Athletic Sport: Women's basketball
Non-LGBT-Specific Campus Club: College Democrats

LGBT Course Offering: Sexual Dissidence and American Culture
LGBT Educational Involvement Opportunity: Trans Remembrance Day Vigil

OUTRAGEOUS FACTOID Back in the late 1960s, faculty members in the psychology department were rumored to have been using a form of aversion therapy on gay men in clinics. Now the American Psychological Association denounces such practices. And today, the LGBT visibility at the University of Vermont shows that it obviously did not work.

RAINBOW RUMOR What's your grade? In November 2002, Assistant Professor Val Rohy initiated plans with other students and faculty members to create a minor in Sexuality and Gender Identity Studies. Now, the program is going strong, and significant growth in course offerings is expected in the years to come!

THAT'S SO GAY!

ANNUAL LGBT EVENT HIGHLIGHTS

Welcome Back Picnic: September
Cupcake and Condoms: September
Coming Out Week: October
SpeakOUT Rally: October
Trans Remembrance Day Vigil: November
Twister and Lube: January
Translating Identity Conference: February
LGBTQ Week: April
National Day of Silence: April
Rainbow Graduation and Awards: May

CAMPUS QUEER RESOURCES

Select LGBT Student Organization(s):

Free to Be
Founding Date: 1983
Membership: 30+
E-mail: free2b@uvm.edu
Phone: 802-656-0699
Website: www.uvm.edu/~free2b

LGBT Resource Center/Office:

LGBTQA Services
University of Vermont
461 Main Street
Burlington, VT 05405
Year Established: 1999
Number of Staff: 2 full-time professional staff
Phone: 802-656-8637
E-mail: lgbtqa@uvm.edu
Website: www.uvm.edu/~lgbtqa

THE GAY POINT AVERAGE
OFFICIAL CAMPUS CHECKLIST

✓ LGBT & ally student organization

✓ LGBT resource center/office

✓ LGBT Pride Week &/or Coming Out Week

✓ Safe Zone/Safe Space or Ally Program

✓ Significant number of LGBT social activities

✓ Significant number of LGBT educational events

✓ Variety of LGBT studies/courses

✓ Nondiscrimination statement inclusive of sexual orientation

✓ Nondiscrimination statement inclusive of gender identity/expression

✓ Extends domestic partner benefits to same-sex couples

  Actively recruits LGBT students to enroll on campus

✓ Trains campus police on LGBT sensitivity

✓ Procedure for reporting LGBT bias, harassment & hate crimes

✓ Offers LGBT housing options/themes

✓ Offers LGBT-inclusive health services/testing

✓ Offers LGBT-inclusive counseling/support groups

  Offers LGBT student scholarships

✓ Conducts special LGBT graduation ceremony for LGBT & ally Students

  Offers support services for process of transitioning from M to F & F to M

  Active LGBT alumni group

16 UNIVERSITY OF VERMONT
GAY POINT AVERAGE
(out of 20)

UNIVERSITY OF WASHINGTON

PROGRESS HAS BLOSSOMED for LGBT students at University of Washington. Located along the shores of Lake Washington, the campus is 5 minutes from downtown Seattle. The picturesque campus is described by some as having "a laid-back atmosphere." At any given moment, a student is no less than an hour away from either the mountains or the ocean.

Unlike other campuses that are still fighting for administrative support for LGBT equality, the University of Washington touts support at the top levels of the administration, with the Vice President's Office of Student Affairs and the Vice President's Office of Minority Affairs financially sponsoring the Q Center for LGBT student issues. The campus also has active and dedicated LGBT students, faculty and staff. Since 2000, there has been a burst of social and political activity on campus, with the creation of new LGBT student groups, such as Queer Women and Trans Individual Interest Group; the Working for Equality Project; Delta Lambda Phi (a gay, bisexual and progressive men's fraternity); Queers and Disability; and the continued strengthening of the Gay, Bisexual, Lesbian, and Trans Commission. In addition, there is a large and ever-growing Safe Zone project. To more directly serve and support queer communities of color on campus, Qolors, a task force of students, faculty, and staff of color, was formed.

The bottom queer line is this: "LGBT work is being done in a creative, challenging and progressive manner at University of Washington." The campus is a powerful change agent on LGBT issues. The campus even held a Mother's Day brunch for LGBT students and their families hosted by a national drag queen. One LGBT student shares from the heart: "I have never felt a greater sense of family. My LGBT and ally friends are my lifeblood. My self-esteem has grown with my identity.... I never had this opportunity at home or in high school.... I would not be who I am today if it were not for this campus. I love this place."

🗩 OUTSPOKEN *Answers from LGBT students:*

Top Three Descriptors of the LGBT Campus Environment:
1. Progressive   2. Gender-bending   3. Husky queer

What makes your campus feel welcoming and safe for LGBT students?
"The Q Center! It is safe and warm, and fun people work there."
—19-year-old gay male, sophomore

"The Safe Zone project and the signs I see all over campus."
—19-year-old queer female, sophomore

How do you feel about coming out on your campus?
"Coming out on the UW campus was a gradual process for me. As a gay person of color, I felt that the recognition for diversity within the gay community on campus was lacking. Until the Q Center came around to really begin to address this issue, coming out on the UW campus was very Euro-centric; if you were to come out, you do it the 'white/right way.' "*—21-year-old gay male, senior*

LGBT POLITICS
Progressive Meter

Campus Community Level

Local Community Level

State Level

INFO

UNIVERSITY OF WASHINGTON
320 Schmitz Hall
1410 NE Campus Parkway
PO Box 355852
Seattle, WA 98195
Phone: 206-543-9686
Fax: 206-685-3655
E-mail: askuwadm@u.washington.edu
Website: www.washington.edu

CAMPUS STATS
Type of Institution: Public university
Founding Year: 1861
Size: 25,469
Avg. Class Size: 20–29 students
Popular Majors: Economics, Political Science and Government, Psychology
Cost: In-state tuition: $5,710
Out-of-state tuition: $19,908
Admission Application Deadline: January 15

OUTRAGEOUS FACTOID

Touchdown! UW alumnus Dave Kopay was the first professional football player to come out of the closet back in 1975. He played professionally for San Francisco, Green Bay, Washington, Detroit and New Orleans. He's been fighting the good fight, and to those who think that queers have not made LGBT progress, Dave states: "Are you kidding me? We've made huge progress."

• •

RAINBOW RUMOR

UW has several health insurance plans that cover its students, faculty and staff. Currently, the campus health plans restrict coverage for transgender individuals who are transitioning. Such a limit on health coverage can create problems for trans individuals in accessing health care for services both related and unrelated to the transition process. Queers are united and are currently working to remove these health care restrictions.

• • • • • • • • • • • • • • • • • • • •

THAT'S SO GAY!

ANNUAL LGBT EVENT HIGHLIGHTS

Welcome Week: Last week of September

Coming Out Day: October 11

World AIDS Day: December 1

Drag Show: February

Ally Week: February

Q Center Birthday: February

Mother's Day Celebration: May

Pride Week: May

Lavender Graduation: June

ACADEMIC SCENE

Top Three Supportive LGBT Academic Areas:
1. Comparative History of Ideas Program   2. Nursing   3. English

How LGBT-friendly are faculty in the classroom?
"Some people are radically supportive and nurturing while others aren't quite sure what to do with you."
—*21-year-old queer female, senior*

"Some instructors totally get it and others don't…but I think the Safe Zone program is changing things." —*19-year-old queer female, sophomore*

SOCIAL SCENE

Top Three Things in the LGBT Social Life:
1. Q Center   2. Activism   3. Going out for coffee

How would you describe the social scene for LGBT students?
"My social scene consists of activism and meetings…with a daily visit to Trabant Chai Lounge." —*24-year-old bisexual female, senior*

What annual social event should an LGBT student not miss?
"Drag Show: Gender Bender!!!! Youth from all over western Washington come… Last year, they turned away 100 people, and it is totally gender bending."
—*22-year-old gay male, senior*

BUZZ BITES *Fun Queer Stuff to Know*

THE BEST…

Party Locale: Capital Hill, house parties

Hangout: Q Center

Eating Place: Wasabi Bistro

Place to Check Out Guys: IMA Campus Gym

Place to Check Out Ladies: Trabant Chai Lounge

LGBT-Cool Athletic Sport: Ultimate frisbee

Non-LGBT-Specific Campus Club: Disability Advocacy Student Alliance

Place for LGBT Students to Live on Campus: Delta Lambda Phi Gay Fraternity Apartment Cluster

LGBT Course Offering: Queer Performance Poetry

LGBT Educational Involvement Opportunity: Safe Zone

LGBT-Accepting Religious/Spiritual Organization(s): Hillel

THE GAY POINT AVERAGE
OFFICIAL CAMPUS CHECKLIST

LGBT & ally student organization ✓

LGBT resource center/office ✓

LGBT Pride Week &/or Coming Out Week ✓

Safe Zone/Safe Space or Ally Program ✓

Significant number of LGBT social activities ✓

Significant number of LGBT educational events ✓

Variety of LGBT studies/courses ✓

Nondiscrimination statement inclusive of sexual orientation ✓

Nondiscrimination statement inclusive of gender identity/expression ✓

Extends domestic partner benefits to same-sex couples ✓

Actively recruits LGBT students to enroll on campus

Trains campus police on LGBT sensitivity

Procedure for reporting LGBT bias, harassment & hate crimes ✓

Offers LGBT housing options/themes

Offers LGBT-inclusive health services/testing ✓

Offers LGBT-inclusive counseling/support groups ✓

Offers LGBT student scholarships ✓

Conducts special LGBT graduation ceremony for LGBT & ally Students ✓

Offers support services for process of transitioning from M to F & F to M

Active LGBT alumni group

UNIVERSITY OF WASHINGTON
GAY POINT AVERAGE (15)
(out of 20)

CAMPUS QUEER RESOURCES

Select LGBT Student Organization(s)
Gay, Lesbian, Bisexual, Trans Student Commission
Founding Date: 1991
Membership: 190+
Phone: 206-685-4232
E-mail: asuwgblc@u.washington.edu
Website: gbltc.asuw.org

LGBT Resource Center/Office:
Q Center
450 Schmitz Hall
PO Box 355838
Seattle, WA 98195
Year Established: 2004
Number of Staff: 1 full-time professional staff; 5 student workers
Phone: 206-897-1430
E-mail: qcenter@u.washington.edu
Website: www.qcenter.washington.edu/

UNIVERSITY OF WISCONSIN—LA CROSSE

SINCE THE MID-1980S, the University of Wisconsin—La Crosse has demonstrated conviction on LGBT issues and has fostered a welcoming, affirming LGBT campus community. UW La Crosse boasts that it was the first school in the statewide campus system to have an office dedicated to supporting gay, lesbian and bisexual students and their allies. The office was originally called the Diversity Resource Center and provided education and support for all diversity issues. During a demonstration for National Day of Silence in 2002, students voiced strongly the need to change the name to something more recognizable and to have the priority be solely with queer issues. The name was subsequently changed to the current Pride Center, services and programs to address LGBT student concerns only. Today the campus has one of only three LGBT support centers in the state of Wisconsin.

In addition, one attribute not noted on the Gay Point Average is that the campus offers "soft" domestic partner benefits for same-sex employees, which allows a partner and family members to use limited, campus-based services such as child care, the library and recreation facilities. Nearby UW Madison followed this lead, adopting similar "soft" benefits. Such queer leadership and vision are largely due to the number of LGBT faculty and staff dedicated to positive queer change, along with the LGBT student group Rainbow Unity. Queer activism has been a hallmark of the La Crosse campus experience, making the student voice queerly heard. One LGBT campus member lovingly calls the LGBT community a "family of choice." And according to recent LGBT outreach efforts, this family is looking to grow. The campus participates in the LGBT College Fair in Washington, D.C., and has done outreach to high school youth at area Pride events.

The campus has a nurturing, lively family of queer activists and has demonstrated an LGBT commitment to progress. One LGBT student adds: "I am part of a queer family here…that is welcoming, affirming and committed to change. I feel a part of something bigger….We are making a difference for future students."

LGBT POLITICS
Progressive Meter

Campus Community Level

Local Community Level

State Level

🗣 OUTSPOKEN *Answers from LGBT students:*

Top Three Descriptors of the LGBT Campus Environment:
1. Family   2. Queer   3. Political

What makes your campus feel welcome and safe for LGBT students?
"Faculty and staff have SAFE SPACE signs on their doors. The signs mean it's okay if you're LGBT…. It's a pretty neat way to signify that you are an ally. You'll also notice in class, from how comfortably teachers talk about gay issues."
—19-year-old lesbian, sophomore

How do you feel about coming out on your campus?
If you want to come out to people, just tell them right off the bat. Don't let them assume you're straight….Someone might ask you if you have a boyfriend or girlfriend. Just tell them, 'I'm gay and I'm looking for a boyfriend.' It's much easier to be straight up….Students here are awesome and understanding. I've never, ever, had a problem coming out to anyone."
—21-year-old gay male, senior

INFO

UNIVERSITY OF WISCONSIN— LA CROSSE
1725 State Street
115 Graff Main Hall
La Crosse, WI 54601
Phone: 608-785-8939
Fax: 608-785-8940
E-mail: admissions@uwlax.edu
Website: www.uwlax.edu

CAMPUS STATS
Type of Institution: Public university
Founding Year: 1909
Size: 7,900
Avg. Class Size: 20–29 students
Popular Majors: Marketing/Marketing Management, Parks, Recreation and Leisure Studies, Social Sciences
Cost: In-state tuition: $9,465
Out-of-state tuition: $19,511
Admission Application Deadline: December 15

"The campus is fine. You can snuggle with your sweety or kiss in the quad and you won't get more than a look or two. It's nice that way."
—*22-year-old bisexual female, graduate student*

ACADEMIC SCENE

Top Three Supportive LGBT Academic Areas:
1. College of Liberal Studies   2. Sexuality, Gender and Women's Studies   3. Philosophy

How LGBT-friendly are faculty in the classroom?
"One of the psych teachers participates in the Drag Show every year. Students tease him terribly, and he loves it!" —*20-year-old gay male, junior*

"Faculty are very friendly. Wherever you go on campus and whatever department or building, [there are] going to be a lot of allies there."
—*21-year-old lesbian, senior*

SOCIAL SCENE

Top Three Things in the LGBT Social Life:
1. House parties   2. Dancing   3. Hanging out

How would you describe the social scene for LGBT students?
"Humorous and active…We know how to keep ourselves busy with LGBT stuff, and it's like a big family." —*21-year-old bisexual female, junior*

What annual social event should an LGBT student not miss?
"Drag Show we do every April…Drag queens and kings come from all over the surrounding states and perform for a blissful three or four hours. It draws the biggest crowd of any campus event all year!" —*20-year-old gay male, junior*

BUZZ BITES
Fun Queer Stuff to Know

THE BEST…

Party Locale: Players
Hangout: Safe Space in Cartwright
Eating Place: Menucci's Pizzeria
Place to Check Out Guys: Sitting by the clock tower
Place to Check Out Ladies: Rainbow's End
LGBT-Cool Athletic Sport: Volleyball
Non-LGBT-Specific Campus Club: Black Student Unity

Place for LGBT Students to Live on Campus: Trowbridge Hall or Baird Hall
LGBT Course Offering: Lesbian Studies
LGBT Educational Involvement Opportunity: Ally trainings
LGBT-Accepting Religious/Spiritual Organization(s): Unitarian Church of Christ

OUTRAGEOUS FACTOID In 2003 the University of Wisconsin—La Crosse held its first Queer Carnival. Publicity included the phrase: "Come Watch Real Live Queer Acts." Once inside the big tent, people saw students folding their laundry, eating dinner, studying, going out on a date and other typical stuff. The Lesbian Studies Class created the event to help the campus understand that LGBT people are not "circus acts, but everyday people."

RAINBOW RUMOR If you're going to live on campus, more LGBT improvements are in the works. Campus officials are looking to develop an ally living community and/or a process to allow LGBT students on campus to check a box to ask for a queer-sensitive roommate.

THAT'S SO GAY!

ANNUAL LGBT EVENT HIGHLIGHTS

Welcome Social for LGBTIAQQ Students, Faculty and Staff: Fall
LGBT Films: Fall/Spring
Ally Trainings: Fall/Spring
LGBT Speakers: Fall/Spring
National Coming Out Day: October 11
Trans Remembrance Week: November
Queer Carnival: Spring
GAYLA Month: April
Day of Silence: April
Drag Show: April
Rainbow Graduation: December and May

CAMPUS QUEER RESOURCES

Select LGBT Student Organization(s):

Rainbow Unity: People Advocating for Unity and Love

Founding Date: Mid-1980s (as Straights and Gays for Equality)

Membership: 30

Phone: 608-785-8870

Website: www.uwlax.edu/rainbowunity/

LGBT Resource Center/Office:

Pride Center
University of Wisconsin—La Crosse
1725 State Street
La Crosse, WI 54601

Year Established: Mid-1980s (as Diversity Resource Center)

Number of Staff: 1 full-time professional staff; 1 graduate assistant; 2 student workers

Phone: 608-785-8870

E-mail: pridecenter@uwlax.edu

Website: www.uwlax.edu/pridecenter/

THE GAY POINT AVERAGE
OFFICIAL CAMPUS CHECKLIST

✓ LGBT & ally student organization

✓ LGBT resource center/office

✓ LGBT Pride Week &/or Coming Out Week

✓ Safe Zone/Safe Space or Ally Program

✓ Significant number of LGBT social activities

✓ Significant number of LGBT educational events

Variety of LGBT studies/courses

✓ Nondiscrimination statement inclusive of sexual orientation

✓ Nondiscrimination statement inclusive of gender identity/expression

Extends domestic partner benefits to same-sex couples

Actively recruits LGBT students to enroll on campus

Trains campus police on LGBT sensitivity

✓ Procedure for reporting LGBT bias, harassment & hate crimes

Offers LGBT housing options/themes

✓ Offers LGBT-inclusive health services/testing

✓ Offers LGBT-inclusive counseling/support groups

Offers LGBT student scholarships

✓ Conducts special LGBT graduation ceremony for LGBT & ally Students

Offers support services for process of transitioning from M to F & F to M

✓ Active LGBT alumni group

(13) UNIVERSITY OF WISCONSIN— LA CROSSE GAY POINT AVERAGE
(out of 20)

UNIVERSITY OF WISCONSIN—MADISON

THE UNIVERSITY OF Wisconsin—Madison was founded on the "Wisconsin idea." The premise that the campus would "never be content until the beneficent influence of the university [is] available to every home in the state." For over a century, this concept has guided the actions of the campus and has forged partnerships as well as a greater sense of community. But what about LGBT progressiveness and being gay-friendly?

The Gay Point Average illustrates that UW Madison has several LGBT-inclusive policies and practices. It has both sexual orientation and gender identity/expression as part of campus nondiscrimination policies, but it is the only Big 10 institution to not offer same-sex domestic partner benefits.

The campus founded the LGBT Campus Center in 1991. It serves as an open meeting place for all queer students and works to create an LGBT-inclusive campus community. In addition, the oldest queer student coalition on campus is the Ten Percent Society, founded in 1983. Together, both the center and the LGBT student groups on campus plan a host of activities, from movie nights to guest speakers to awareness weeks such as Coming Out Week.

The "Wisconsin idea" holds true for the LGBT community, too. A UW Madison education must not only be available to every home in the state, but the university must also create a home for everyone on campus—including LGBT students. A queer student agrees: "The size of the campus intimidated me, coming from a farm community, plus the fact that I was gay. The LGBT Campus Center made it much easier—to be accepted, to be out, to feel safe and to find a place to call home on campus."

OUTSPOKEN *Answers from LGBT students:*

Top Three Descriptors of the LGBT Campus Environment:
1. Innovative   2. Fierce   3. Loving

What makes your campus feel welcoming and safe for LGBT students?
"This campus feels welcome and safe because there are many LGBT resources for students, and one can walk down the street and recognize friends."
—20-year-old lesbian, junior

How do you feel about coming out on your campus?
"With so many students on campus and the general liberal ideology, coming out on campus was relatively easy compared to coming out in high school."
—19-year-old gay genderqueer, sophomore

ACADEMIC SCENE

Top Three Supportive LGBT Academic Areas:
1. Sociology   2. Women's Studies   3. Psychology

INFO

UNIVERSITY OF WISCONSIN—MADISON
Armory and Gymnasium
716 Langdon Street
Madison, WI 53706
Phone: 608-262-3961
Fax: 608-262-7706
E-mail: onwisconsin@admissions.wisc.edu
Website: www.wisc.edu

CAMPUS STATS
Type of Institution: Public university
Founding Year: 1848
Size: 28,217
Avg. Class Size: 20–29 students
Popular Majors: History, Political Science and Government, Psychology
Cost: In-state tuition: $5,800
Out-of-state tuition: $21,000
Admission Application Deadline: February 1

OUTRAGEOUS FACTOID Did you know Camp Randall on campus was the site of a Civil War training camp? It now houses a 77,000-seat stadium and a memorial arch.

. . . .

RAINBOW RUMOR There were rumors that the LGBT Campus Center would be restructured as part of the Multicultural Student Center, leaving queer issues with less funding and visibility. LGBT faculty and alumni came to the rescue and stopped it from happening.

. . . .

THAT'S SO GAY!

ANNUAL LGBT EVENT HIGHLIGHTS

LGBT Movie Night: Fall/Spring, Weekly

LGBT Resource Fair: September

Coming Out Week: October

Transgender Day of Remembrance: November

LGBT Research Symposium: November

World AIDS Day: December

Pink Party, New Year's Eve: December

Out and About Month: April

LGBT Film Festival: April

Day of Silence: April

LGBT Graduation Reception: April/May

How LGBT-friendly are faculty in the classroom?
"I have only had wonderful experiences with both faculty and teaching assistants. Faculty are very inclusive and strive to infuse the curricula with LGBT issues wherever possible. The union for the teaching assistants has worked very hard for many years to get full domestic partner benefits."
—29-year-old queer male, senior

"Faculty are understanding and open, with true allies spread throughout the campus." *—24-year-old metasexual, senior*

😊 SOCIAL SCENE

Top Three Things in the LGBT Social Life:
1. Dances   2. Coffee shops   3. Hanging out with friends

How would you describe the social scene for LGBT students?
"The social scene is rather minimal for LGBT students. Aside from a few dances and Tuesday nights [18+] at Club 5, there is not a lot offered."
—19-year-old gay genderqueer, sophomore

What annual social event should an LGBT student not miss?
"Coming Out Week and Out and About Month events are wonderful—including Day of Silence." *—20-year-old female, junior*

BUZZ BITES *Fun Queer Stuff to Know*

THE BEST...

Party Locale: Café Montmartre

Hangout: LGBT Campus Center

Eating Place: Expresso Royale Café

Place to Check Out Guys: Club 5

Place to Check Out Ladies: A Room of One's Own Feminist Bookstore

LGBT-Cool Athletic Sport: Women's hockey

Place for LGBT Students to Live on Campus: Chadbourne Residence Hall

LGBT Course Offering: Sexual Discourses, Cultural Contexts

LGBT Educational Involvement Opportunity: LGBT Education Outreach Bureau

LGBT-Accepting Religious/Spiritual Organization(s): Unitarian Universalist Fellowship

THE GAY POINT AVERAGE
OFFICIAL CAMPUS CHECKLIST

LGBT & ally student organization ✓

LGBT resource center/office ✓

LGBT Pride Week &/or Coming Out Week ✓

Safe Zone/Safe Space or Ally Program ✓

Significant number of LGBT social activities ✓

Significant number of LGBT educational events ✓

Variety of LGBT studies/courses ✓

Nondiscrimination statement inclusive of sexual orientation ✓

Nondiscrimination statement inclusive of gender identity/expression ✓

Extends domestic partner benefits to same-sex couples

Actively recruits LGBT students to enroll on campus

Trains campus police on LGBT sensitivity ✓

Procedure for reporting LGBT bias, harassment & hate crimes ✓

Offers LGBT housing options/themes

Offers LGBT-inclusive health services/testing ✓

Offers LGBT-inclusive counseling/support groups ✓

Offers LGBT student scholarships ✓

Conducts special LGBT graduation ceremony for LGBT & ally Students ✓

Offers support services for process of transitioning from M to F & F to M ✓

Active LGBT alumni group ✓

UNIVERSITY OF WISCONSIN—
MADISON GAY POINT AVERAGE
(out of 20)

17

CAMPUS QUEER RESOURCES

Name of LGBT Student Organization(s):
Ten Percent Society
Founding Date: 19823
Membership: 45+
Phone: 608-262-7365
E-mail: co-presidents@tps.studentorg.wisc.edu
Website: tps.stdorg.wisc.edu

LGBT Resource Center/Office:
LGBT Campus Center
2nd Floor, Memorial Union
800 Langdon Street
Madison, WI 53706
Year Established: 1991
Number of Staff: 2 professional full-time staff; 8 part-time student staff
Phone: 608-265-3344
E mail: lghtcc@rso.wisc.edu
Website: lgbtcc.studentorg.wisc.edu

UNIVERSITY OF WISCONSIN—MILWAUKEE

"A PILLAR OF support" is how one LGBT student describes the environment at University of Wisconsin—Milwaukee. Other LGBT students echo similar queer-positive words, such as "welcoming, open and accepting."

Known for "building bridges" on campus, the LGBT Resource Center founded in 2001 has forged many alliances to develop a more inclusive LGBT campus community. The center offers a safe space for LGBT students and allies to meet, support one another and network. It houses a library of over 600 books, videos, tapes, pamphlets, magazines and research materials. If you want virtually any queer resource or service, you can find it in the center or at least get a referral.

UW Milwaukee is home to student-initiated support/social groups like Lucky Lady, Spiffy New Bi-Thing, Knit and Bitch, MISFIT and Trans Folk and Allies, to name a sampling. In collaboration with student coalitions like the Rainbow Alliance, the center also offers programs and events like Speed Meet, National Coming Out Week and Transgender Week of Remembrance. The goal is always to bring together different facets of the LGBT community while meeting a variety of LGBT perspectives and needs.

UW Milwaukee does a lot right. The LGBT Resource Center plays a pivotal role, along with active student coalitions and LGBT faculty representation. There is even an academic certificate program in LGBT studies. Learn why LGBT students consider UW Milwaukee to be a supportive place. One LGBT student explains: "Coming out on campus was easy. In college it's almost expected that there are going to be a lot of gay students. At UW Milwaukee, it's almost as if you're not cool unless you have a gay friend. It's nice to feel accepted everywhere, even in classes."

LGBT POLITICS
Progressive Meter

Campus Community Level	
Local Community Level	
State Level	

INFO

UNIVERSITY OF WISCONSIN—MILWAUKEE
PO Box 749
Milwaukee, WI 53201
Phone: 414-229-3800
Fax: 414-229-6940
E-mail: uwmlook@des.uwm.edu
Website: www.uwm.edu

CAMPUS STATS
Type of Institution: Public university
Founding Year: 1956
Size: 23,388
Avg. Class Size: 20–29 students
Popular Majors: Business/Marketing, Visual and Performing Arts, Social Sciences and History
Cost: In-state tuition: $6,246
Out-of-state tuition: $18,988
Admission Application Deadline: August 1

🗨️ OUTSPOKEN *Answers from LGBT students:*

Top Three Descriptors of the LGBT Campus Environment:
1. Welcoming   2. Inspirational   3. Fun

What makes your campus feel welcoming and safe for LGBT students?
"Aside from the LGBT Center on campus, which really makes me feel very safe, there is also a group called Rainbow Alliance. Also, our campus does a very good job of making sure that all voices are heard and heard fairly, so we always hold events that celebrate LGBTQ-ness."
—*18-year-old lesbian, freshman*

How do you feel about coming out on your campus?
"I think it's pretty safe to come out. I've never felt threatened or unsafe. However, I've also used my judgment in knowing when it is safe to be open and honest, and when it might not be." —*21-year-old queer female, senior*

ⓐ ACADEMIC SCENE

Top Three Supportive LGBT Academic Areas:
1. Sociology   2. Psychology   3. Film Department

How LGBT-friendly are faculty in the classroom?
"The classroom settings are totally accepting. In my Geography 390 class, for example, there was a whole section on gay and lesbian spaces within communities. And being gay in a classroom has never been an uncomfortable setting for me." —*20-year-old gay male, senior*

"I have come out to at least five of my professors from a variety of disciplines, either directly or indirectly in conversation. Regardless of whether they have a "safe space" sticker on their door, they have all been openly supportive and affirming." —*21-year-old bisexual female, senior*

☺ SOCIAL SCENE

Top Three Things in the LGBT Social Life:
1. Independent theaters   2. Bars and cafés   3. Gay district

How would you describe the social scene for LGBT students?
"There are so many queer students that it's really easy to find something queer to do. From going to the video store to rent a gay movie, to going to the gay club/bar, there are lots of options." —*21-year-old queer female, senior*

What annual social event should an LGBT student not miss?
"The Drag Ball, hands down. The performances are always amazing, and the audience is wonderfully supportive. As a bonus, it raises a ton of money for the Milwaukee LGBT Community Center." —*21-year old bisexual female, senior*

OUTRAGEOUS FACTOID Wonder Woman, Batman, Aqua Man, Green Lantern, Cat Woman … you name it! These superheroes are just a sample of the costumes worn during Coming Out Week.

• •

RAINBOW RUMOR The LGBT Resource Center is known for building bridges and forging alliances. A conservative campus group brought a "former homosexual" to talk about how to cure LGBT people. Most of the audience members were said to be LGBT students and allies protesting the lecture.

• •

THAT's SO GAY!

ANNUAL LGBT EVENT HIGHLIGHTS

Speed Meet: September

LGBT Film Festival: September/October

Coming Out Week: October

Transgender Week of Remembrance: November

World AIDS Day: December

Drag Ball: February

SHADE/Day of Silence: April

Pride Fest Milwaukee: June

BUZZ BITES *Fun Queer Stuff to Know*

THE BEST...

Hangout: Outwords Bookstore and LGBT Center

Eating Place: Bella Café

Place to Check Out Guys: Student Union

Place to Check Out Ladies: Women's Resource Center

LGBT-Cool Athletic Sport: Women's rugby or men's swimming

Non-LGBT-Specific Campus Club: Amnesty International

Place for LGBT Students to Live on Campus: Sandburg Halls

LGBT Course Offering: Sociology of Sexuality and Homosexuality in History

LGBT-Accepting Religious/Spiritual Organization(s): United Church of Christ, University Christian Ministries

CAMPUS QUEER RESOURCES

Select LGBT Student Organization(s)

Rainbow Alliance
Founding Date: 1970s
Membership: 300+
Phone: 414-229-6555
E-mail: glbc@uwm.edu
Website: www.uwm.edu/StudentOrg/GLBC/

LGBT Resource Center/Office:

LGBT Resource Center
UWM Union WG89
2200 East Kenwood Boulevard
Milwaukee, WI, 53211
Year Established: 2001
Number of Staff: 2 full-time professional staff
Phone: 414-229-4116
Website: www.uwm.edu/Dept/OSL/LGBT/

THE GAY POINT AVERAGE
OFFICIAL CAMPUS CHECKLIST

- ✓ LGBT & ally student organization
- ✓ LGBT resource center/office
- ✓ LGBT Pride Week &/or Coming Out Week
- ✓ Safe Zone/Safe Space or Ally Program
- ✓ Significant number of LGBT social activities
- ✓ Significant number of LGBT educational events
- ✓ Variety of LGBT studies/courses
- ✓ Nondiscrimination statement inclusive of sexual orientation
- ✓ Nondiscrimination statement inclusive of gender identity/expression
- Extends domestic partner benefits to same-sex couples
- Actively recruits LGBT students to enroll on campus
- ✓ Trains campus police on LGBT sensitivity
- ✓ Procedure for reporting LGBT bias, harassment & hate crimes
- Offers LGBT housing options/themes
- Offers LGBT-inclusive health services/testing
- Offers LGBT-inclusive counseling/support groups
- Offers LGBT student scholarships
- Conducts special LGBT graduation ceremony for LGBT & ally Students
- Offers support services for process of transitioning from M to F & F to M
- Active LGBT alumni group

(11) UNIVERSITY OF WISCONSON—MILWAUKEE GAY POINT AVERAGE
(out of 20)

VASSAR COLLEGE

IN THE SCENIC Hudson Valley, 90 minutes from the frenzy of New York City, sits Vassar College. Queer experiences at Vassar have been documented as early as 1930; in *Wolf Girls at Vassar: Lesbian and Gay Experiences 1930–1990*, alumnus Anne MacKay recounts the college's long history of acknowledging the possibility of love between women.

A reluctant acceptance of LGBT people began in 1969 shortly after the school went co-ed. Today Vassar and its current president are fully committed to equality for LGBT students, staff and faculty. Along with LGBT-inclusive policies, several services and resources are available to LGBT students through the student government's Queer Coalition of Vassar College and different programs offered by Blegen House, a campus resource center that is a branch of the Campus Life Office. Both are formally supported by the administration and seamlessly collaborate with other offices and student groups on campus.

LGBT activities run the gamut—from the political to the educational to the social—and there is a strong commitment to progressive queer discourse. In addition, the campus boasts of innovative LGBT outreach efforts, including Circles, a support group for local high school students. Academic departments also offer LGBT-based courses, such as a freshman course called Queer Alphabets. Queer Theory courses are taught in both the Women's Studies program and the philosophy department. Even the athletics department conducts sessions for coaches and trainers on how to make sure their sporting teams are LGBT-inclusive.

An LGBT beacon of progress, Vassar College has zero tolerance for anti-LGBT behavior and is alma mater to many LGBT groundbreakers, from legendary lesbian poets like Elizabeth Bishop, Muriel Rukeyser and Edna St. Vincent Millay to contemporary activists like Urvashi Vaid, Eric Marcus and Ann Northrop. Vassar expects to be the home to many more LGBT leaders. One LGBT student reiterates her choice: "I have created many lasting relationships and have had amazing opportunities for queer leadership. If I had to pick a college again, I would choose Vassar."

OUTSPOKEN *Answers from LGBT students:*

Top Three Descriptors of the LGBT Campus Environment:
1. Respectful   2. Private   3. Safe

What makes your campus feel welcoming and safe for LGBT students?
"I think organizations and safe places such as the queer coalition [QCVC]or Blegen House make it feel safe. Also, alternative sexualities are openly discussed in student conversation, classroom discussions and lectures."
—19-year-old queer female, sophomore

How do you feel about coming out on your campus?
"I came out when I was 16 years old. I wanted to make sure to be able to attend a college where I did not have to feel ashamed of my homosexuality. Vassar was definitely the place to be. I have not had any problems being out at Vassar."
—22-year-old gay male, senior

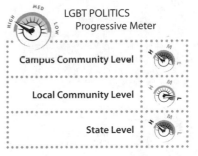

LGBT POLITICS
Progressive Meter

Campus Community Level

Local Community Level

State Level

INFO

VASSAR COLLEGE
124 Raymond Avenue, Box 10
Poughkeepsie, NY 12604
Phone: 845-437-7300
Fax: 845-437-7063
E-mail: admissions@vassar.edu
Website: www.vassar.edu

CAMPUS STATS
Type of Institution: Private college
Founding Year: 1861
Size: 2,428
Avg. Class Size: 10–19 students
Popular Majors: English Language and Literature, Political Science and Government, Psychology
Cost: Tuition: $41,700
Admission Application Deadline: January 1

OUTRAGEOUS FACTOID For several decades, the biggest social event of the year was the Homo Hop, attended by virtually everyone on campus, straight and gay. The dance party was created by a drag queen named "Jackie St. James" (a.k.a. "Sheldon Weiss"). The drag queen actually served as the president of the senior class ('74).

• • • • • • • • • • • • • • • •

RAINBOW RUMOR According to one LGBT student: "The Vassar gay community seems to be white-dominated, and in turn exclusionary. Whose fault is it? Who knows, but the fact is that it does exist."

• • • • • • • • • • • • • • • •

THAT'S SO GAY!

ANNUAL LGBT EVENT HIGHLIGHTS

"Gays of Our Lives" Quiz Show for Freshmen Orientation: August

Blegen House Gala BBQ and Vegan Picnic: September

Queer Alphabets Class: October

Queer History Month: October

Sexpo Health Fair: December

V-Day Dance Party: February

Vagina Monologues: February

All Campus SpeakOut: March

Queer Prom: Spring

LGBT Movie Nights: Fall/Spring

LGBT Lectures: Fall/Spring

ACADEMIC SCENE

Top Three Supportive LGBT Academic Areas:
1. Africana Studies   2. English   3. Women's Studies

How LGBT-friendly are faculty in the classroom?
"I have never encountered any negative attitudes toward the QLGBT community within a classroom setting. Any discussion of sexuality, just as any other topic in the classroom, has been academically discussed and respected."
—*20-year-old gay male, junior*

"The faculty with whom I am acquainted are very open-minded as far as sexuality is concerned. I have been comfortable enough to talk about my sexuality with professors during their office hours and even in class. Having an opportunity like this is rare." —*22-year-old gay male, senior*

SOCIAL SCENE

Top Three Things in the LGBT Social Life:
1. Movie nights   2. Parties   3. Socializing

How would you describe the social scene for LGBT students?
"The social scene widely varies for different LGBT students. I don't think it's removed from the general social scene, but there is somewhat a separation of lesbian, gay, and genderqueer cliques, although never malicious or explicit."
—*20-year-old queer female, junior*

What annual social event should an LGBT student not miss?
"Gays of Our Lives. It's a panel discussion at the beginning of the year where freshmen ask a panel of people of different sexualities questions to try and guess each panel member's sexuality." —*19-year-old queer female, sophomore*

BUZZ BITES *Fun Queer Stuff to Know*

THE BEST...

Party Locale: Friday's Bar

Hangout: Blegen House

Place to Check Out Guys: The Mug

Place to Check Out Ladies: The Cubby Hole

LGBT-Cool Athletic Sport: Men's tennis and women's rugby

Non-LGBT-Specific Campus Club: Twat Chat

LGBT Course Offering: Queer Theory

LGBT Educational Involvement Opportunity: Queer Coalition of Vassar College

THE GAY POINT AVERAGE
OFFICIAL CAMPUS CHECKLIST

LGBT & ally student organization ✓

LGBT resource center/office ✓

LGBT Pride Week &/or Coming Out Week ✓

Safe Zone/Safe Space or Ally Program

Significant number of LGBT social activities ✓

Significant number of LGBT educational events ✓

Variety of LGBT studies/courses ✓

Nondiscrimination statement inclusive of sexual orientation ✓

Nondiscrimination statement inclusive of gender identity/expression ✓

Extends domestic partner benefits to same-sex couples ✓

Actively recruits LGBT students to enroll on campus

Trains campus police on LGBT sensitivity ✓

Procedure for reporting LGBT bias, harassment & hate crimes ✓

Offers LGBT housing options/themes

Offers LGBT-inclusive health services/testing ✓

Offers LGBT-inclusive counseling/support groups ✓

Offers LGBT student scholarships

Conducts special LGBT graduation ceremony for LGBT & ally Students

Offers support services for process of transitioning from M to F & F to M

Active LGBT alumni group ✓

VASSAR COLLEGE
GAY POINT AVERAGE
(out of 20)

14

CAMPUS QUEER
RESOURCES

Select LGBT Student Organization(s):
Queer Coalition of Vassar College (QCVC)
Founding Date: 1980s (under a different name)
Membership: 50+
E-mail: queer@vsa.vassar.edu
Website: vsa.vassar.edu/~qcvc

LGBT Resource Center/Office:
Blegen House
37 Collegeview Avenue
Poughkeepsie, NY 12604
Year Established: 1991
Number of Staff: 1 full-time professional staff, 5 student employees
Phone: 845-451-3521
E-mail: blegen@vassar.edu
Website: blegenhouse.vassar.edu

WASHINGTON STATE UNIVERSITY

OVER THE YEARS, Washington State University has done several things to further LGBT progress and to foster a gay-friendly campus. In 1994, the Gender Identity/ Expression and Sexual Orientation Resource Center was created as a result of advocacy by LGBT campus members and allies. Take a look at the Gay Point Average, and you will notice that a great deal of LGBT-inclusive policies and practices have been enacted since then.

Most recently, as of 2005, a presidential commission worked to make the nondiscrimination statement inclusive of transgender and gender-variant individuals. But when it comes to everyday queerness, the campus life only gets better. One LGBT student jokes: "Gay life is like an addiction that keeps coming back. I love it here." There are annual events like the Welcome Back BBQ, Pride Week, the "Family" Thanksgiving and World AIDS Day. Each provides a sense of queer spirit to keep LGBT students engaged and, most importantly, feeling welcomed on campus.

In 2005, for World AIDS Day, LGBT students displayed three panels of the Names Project AIDS Memorial Quilt and staged a "die-in." How queer-radical is that? It definitely stirred up attention, according to some LGBT students. Even when the issue pertains to LGBT student leadership, the campus has a background of being a queer educator for the area. In 1998 and 2004, the campus served as a host for the regional queer student conference that drew participants from neighboring colleges and universities. An LGBT student remarks: "There are many ways to get involved as a leader on campus.... whether it's gay or not, you fit right in."

Washington State has created a welcoming place for LGBT students among the vast wheat fields and farmlands of greater Washington state. One LGBT student shares: "A surprise to me, but this campus is most welcoming.... Who would have expected it, really? A gay friend once told me it was in the water, [and] now I believe him ... without a question, an accepting place to create change and be yourself."

OUTSPOKEN *Answers from LGBT students:*

Top Three Descriptors of the LGBT Campus Environment:
1. Accepting   2. Supportive   3. Welcoming

What makes your campus feel welcoming and safe for LGBT students?
"My first week on campus, I met someone else who was also gay. We both discovered quickly that we could be out on campus without it being a problem. There were other visible LGBT students.... the support was undeniable."
—20-year-old gay male, junior

How do you feel about coming out on your campus?
"I came out to my roommate my freshman year. She and I have become best friends.... I have also found acceptance across campus. It's fun to be queer!"
—21-year-old queer female, senior

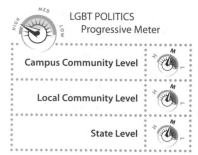

LGBT POLITICS
Progressive Meter

Campus Community Level

Local Community Level

State Level

INFO

WASHINGTON STATE UNIVERSITY
370 Lighty Student Services
PO Box 641067
Pullman, WA 99164
Phone: 509-335-5586
Fax: 509-335-4902
E-mail: admiss2@wsu.edu
Website: www.wsu.edu

CAMPUS STATS
Type of Institution: Public university
Founding Year: 1890
Size: 18,690
Avg. Class Size: 10–19 students
Popular Majors: Business Administration/ Management, History Teacher Education, Social Sciences
Cost: In-state tuition: $5,506
Out-of-state tuition: $14,514
Admission Application Deadline: January 31

ⓘ ACADEMIC SCENE

Top Three Supportive LGBT Academic Areas:
1. Women's Studies   2. Educational Administration
3. Comparative Ethnic Studies

How LGBT-friendly are faculty in the classroom?
"Faculty have encouraged me to participate openly in class discussions. Remarks are kept respectful, and often class members and faculty express support for LGBT issues before I do." —*20-year-old lesbian, junior*

"In my classes I have been the gay guy. It is always exciting to have a dialogue about queer issues…. it's safe and understanding." —*22-year-old gay male, senior*

☺ SOCIAL SCENE

Top Three Things in the LGBT Social Life:
1. Parties   2. Socializing with friends   3. Dancing

How would you describe the social scene for LGBT students?
"Socially it's a close community where you support one another. I have never been at a loss for a good time." —*19-year-old lesbian, freshman*

What annual social event should an LGBT student not miss?
"The 'Family' Thanksgiving has been my ultimate favorite … it's a great time to be thankful for your LGBT allies." —*20-year-old gay male, junior*

BUZZ BITES *Fun Queer Stuff to Know*

THE BEST…

Party Locale: The Beach
Hangout: Daily Grind
Place to Check Out Guys: The Beach
Place to Check Out Ladies: Women's soccer
Non-LGBT-Specific Campus Club: Anti-Hate Coalition
LGBT Course Offering: Lesbian and Gay Studies

LGBT Educational Involvement Opportunity: LGBT Speakers Bureau

OUTRAGEOUS FACTOID If you need to catch up on some sleep, the LGBT resource center has the most comfy couches around.

RAINBOW RUMOR Residence life is the most LGBT-friendly office on campus, and there are future plans to create application and room-assignment processes that are more supportive of the specific needs and concerns of trans and gender-variant residents. Other trans happenings are also planned on campus, such as gender-neutral bathroom facilities in all-new and renovated buildings and the option to change your name with the registrar's office.

THAT'S SO GAY!

ANNUAL LGBT EVENT HIGHLIGHTS

LGBT Brown Bag Discussions: Monthly, Fall/Spring

LGBT Knitting Circle: Monthly, Fall/Spring

Drag Shows: Monthly, Fall/Spring

Welcome Back BBQ: August

Pride Week: October

National Coming Out Day: October 11

National Day of Transgender Remembrance: November

"Family" Thanksgiving: November

World AIDS Day: December 1

National Freedom to Marry Day: February

National Day of Silence: March/April

Week of Dignity: March/April

Lavender Graduation: April

CAMPUS QUEER
RESOURCES

Select LGBT Student Organization(s):

Gay, Lesbian, Bisexual, Transgender and Allies Committee

Founding Date: 1998

Membership: 50

Phone: 509-335-4311

E-mail: wsuglbta@hotmail.com

Website: www.wsu.edu/~glbta/

LGBT Resource Center/Office:

Gender Identity/Expression and Sexual Orientation Resource Center

PO Box 641430
Smith Gym 303
Pullman, Washington 99164

Year Established: 1994

Number of Staff: 1 full-time professional staff; 1 part-time staff

Phone: 509-335-6388

E-mail: hstanton@wsu.edu

Website: www.thecenter.wsu.edu/

THE GAY POINT AVERAGE
OFFICIAL CAMPUS CHECKLIST

✓ LGBT & ally student organization

✓ LGBT resource center/office

✓ LGBT Pride Week &/or Coming Out Week

✓ Safe Zone/Safe Space or Ally Program

✓ Significant number of LGBT social activities

✓ Significant number of LGBT educational events

✓ Variety of LGBT studies/courses

✓ Nondiscrimination statement inclusive of sexual orientation

✓ Nondiscrimination statement inclusive of gender identity/expression

✓ Extends domestic partner benefits to same-sex couples

Actively recruits LGBT students to enroll on campus

✓ Trains campus police on LGBT sensitivity

✓ Procedure for reporting LGBT bias, harassment & hate crimes

✓ Offers LGBT housing options/themes

✓ Offers LGBT-inclusive health services/testing

✓ Offers LGBT-inclusive counseling/support groups

✓ Offers LGBT student scholarships

✓ Conducts special LGBT graduation ceremony for LGBT & ally Students

✓ Offers support services for process of transitioning from M to F & F to M

Active LGBT alumni group

18 WASHINGTON STATE UNIVERSITY GAY POINT AVERAGE
(out of 20)

WELLESLEY COLLEGE

A LIBERAL ARTS COLLEGE located west of Boston, Massachusetts, Wellesley College offers much for women. Queer thinking is engrained in the learning philosophy of the institution, so it is no wonder that the campus is queer-progressive. Just like other students, LGBT women are leaders and role models in every aspect of Wellesley College life. There are out LGBT members of the faculty and staff too. Such visibility allows for a sense of pride and safety, as well as freedom to be who you are—without any fears. One out lesbian senior notes: "I have never, ever in my time at Wellesley felt closeted or silenced or uncomfortable about my sexuality."

Multiple LGBT programs and activities are planned throughout the year to support the queer student experience. Wellesley's annual LesBiTrans Week, organized by the student-run Spectrum, features speeches, films, panels and performances that celebrate the LGBT experience. Traditionally, one of the week's highlights is a large dance party, where students from Wellesley and area campuses dress in creative black tie and are free to express themselves, their sexuality and their gender. One of the most successful events that week is Straight Talks, a panel discussion organized and presented by students who openly discuss LGBT issues, their own coming-out stories and the realities—positive and negative—of their lives. There are even supportive messages on the campuswide electronic bulletin board for queer events like National Coming Out Day. The thread begins: "Support your queer siblings because…" Queer students often say that reading the hundreds of posted comments of LGBT support is one of the most powerful experiences they have ever had.

Building a community where everyone feels welcome can be a tall order anywhere. But Wellesley College seems to have done it. The campus integrates LGBT support at all levels. One lesbian junior states: "The queer spirit is high among everyone. Wellesley is a supportive place for lesbian and bisexual women…. [where you are] free to be yourself and celebrate individuality."

OUTSPOKEN *Answers from LGBT students:*

Top Three Descriptors of the LGBT Campus Environment:
1. Allied   2. Safe   3. Inclusive

What makes your campus feel welcoming and safe for LGBT students?
"Spectrum for LGBT students and allies works hard to create an inclusive feeling for all queers on campus. I have been impressed at the number of allies who continually come out in support of LGBT issues." —*19-year-old lesbian, junior*

How do you feel about coming out on your campus?
"I most definitely tell people that I am gay. It's really a nonissue for me and for them. I see it as my duty to be open and honest with others. Wellesley makes it easy." —*20-year-old queer female, senior*

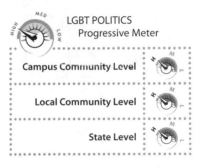

LGBT POLITICS
Progressive Meter

Campus Community Level

Local Community Level

State Level

INFO

WELLESLEY COLLEGE
106 Central Street
Wellesley, MA 02481
Phone: 781-283-2270
Fax: 781-283-3678
E-mail: admission@wellesley.edu
Website: www.wellesley.edu

CAMPUS STATS
Type of Institution: Private college for women
Founding Year: 1870
Size: 2,229
Avg. Class Size: 10–19 students
Popular Majors: Economics, Psychology, English Language and Literature
Cost: Tuition: $31,348
Admission Application Deadline: January 15

OUTRAGEOUS FACTOID At this all-women's college, you never have to wait for a dance partner. Everybody dances with everybody.

RAINBOW RUMOR Wellesley is about making a difference by honoring difference. Diversity within the LGBT community at Wellesley, particularly at the leadership and programmatic levels, is an issue that the campus is working on. Over the past few years, more students of color have been elected to leadership positions within Spectrum. Programs specific to the intersection of race and sexuality, as well as religion and sexuality, are now being offered. One student makes clear: "There are lots of 'queer' women of color at Wellesley. You might have to look for us, but we are here and getting louder and prouder every day."

THAT'S SO GAY! ANNUAL LGBT EVENT HIGHLIGHTS

Dyke Ball: Fall/Spring

Straight Talks: September/October

National Coming Out Day/Coming Out Week: October

Trans Day of Remembrance: November

Global AIDS Day: December 1

Pride Lights Boston Tree-Lighting Ceremony: December

LesBiTrans Week: March

National Day of Silence: April

Equal Marriage Day: May

✐ ACADEMIC SCENE

Top Three Supportive LGBT Academic Areas:
1. Women's Studies   2. English   3. History

How LGBT-friendly are faculty in the classroom?
"Wellesley's faculty is incredibly queer-loving. We have an awesome women's studies department, which focuses on queer theory and the queer perspective. Additionally all of our religious departments are accepting and welcome the queer community to service." —*19-year-old lesbian, junior*

"In terms of the classroom, I have not had many encounters regarding queer issues. While some courses have been openly friendly (i.e., courses in Women's Studies and English), other professors have not been so LGBT-savvy or open-minded." —*20-year-old queer female, senior*

☺ SOCIAL SCENE

Top Three Things in the LGBT Social Life:
1. Spectrum   2. Hanging out with friends   3. Dancing

How would you describe the social scene for LGBT students?
"I would not say that Wellesley is a 'party school,' but I was surprised to see so many dances, theater presentations, organizations and social meeting areas that are either queer or queer-friendly. It is pretty easy to meet people (queer or straight) to do things." —*18-year-old lesbian, freshman*

What annual social event should an LGBT student not miss?
"No one should miss Dyke Ball; despite all the media attention the dance is truly a lot of fun, and a great time." —*19-year-old lesbian, junior*

BUZZ BITES *Fun Queer Stuff to Know*

THE BEST...

Party Locale: Punch's Alley
Hangout: The Hoop
Place to Check Out Ladies: Sports practice
LGBT-Cool Athletic Sport: Lacrosse and rugby
Non-LGBT-Specific Campus Club: The Hoop
Place for LGBT Students to Live on Campus: Shafer
LGBT Course Offering: History of Sexuality

LGBT-Accepting Religious/Spiritual Organization(s): Hillel, Protestant chaplaincy

THE GAY POINT AVERAGE
OFFICIAL CAMPUS CHECKLIST

LGBT & ally student organization ✓

LGBT resource center/office ✓

LGBT Pride Week &/or Coming Out Week ✓

Safe Zone/Safe Space or Ally Program ✓

Significant number of LGBT social activities ✓

Significant number of LGBT educational events ✓

Variety of LGBT studies/courses ✓

Nondiscrimination statement inclusive of sexual orientation ✓

Nondiscrimination statement inclusive of gender identity/expression

Extends domestic partner benefits to same-sex couples ✓

Actively recruits LGBT students to enroll on campus ✓

Trains campus police on LGBT sensitivity ✓

Procedure for reporting LGBT bias, harassment & hate crimes ✓

Offers LGBT housing options/themes ✓

Offers LGBT-inclusive health services/testing ✓

Offers LGBT-inclusive counseling/support groups ✓

Offers LGBT student scholarships

Conducts special LGBT graduation ceremony for LGBT & ally Students

Offers support services for process of transitioning from M to F & F to M ✓

Active LGBT alumni group

WELLESLEY COLLEGE
GAY POINT AVERAGE
(out of 20)

16

CAMPUS QUEER RESOURCES

Select LGBT Student Organization(s):
Spectrum Wellesley Lesbians, Bisexuals, Transgenders and Friends
Founding Date: 1967
Membership: 250+
Phone: 781-283-1000
E-mail: spectrumexec@wellesley.edu
Website: www.wellesley.edu/Activities/ homepage/spectrum/

LGBT Resource Center/Office:
Office of Programs and Services for LGBTQA Students, Faculty and Staff
Wellesley College
Schneider Center
106 Central Street
Wellesley, MA 02481
Year Established: 2002
Number of Staff: 1 full-time professional staff
Phone: 781-283-2682

WHITMAN COLLEGE

HOME TO WHITMAN College, Walla Walla, a small, remote and rural area of Washington, boasts immaculate lawns, beautiful green rolling hills and spring foliage. The quaint town of Walla Walla is four to five hours away from any large metropolitan area. The culture of the local community is progressive and open-minded and embraces the LGBT community. The whole place is like a gay-friendly village. The LGBT progressiveness is the result of years of work by the LGBT campus community.

For instance, Residence Life staff have received LGBT training every year for over 20 years. The counseling center has supported countless queer students coming out and dealing with their identity and family issues. Faculty members have also built into the curriculum courses on gender studies in all major disciplines. Today, Gender Studies is offered as an academic major on campus.

Last, LGBT and ally alumni have donated time and financial resources over the years to support the LGBT community on campus. Most notably, there is the "David Nord Award," named after a gay alum who passed away from AIDS. Annually, the award funds LGBT-themed academic projects for students. One particularly noteworthy project resulted in a docudrama titled *In One Room*. The LGBT-themed play is now used as a part of fall orientation activities for incoming students.

LGBT students on campus are not ever considered weird—rather, "to be queer is to be cool." Plus, the campus community shares a solid, unwavering devotion to one another. Consider this perspective from one LGBT student: "Whitman College is a special place to be gay. I truly feel at home on campus being out…. If you're looking for a small campus with a lot of LGBT support, then come try us on for size."

OUTSPOKEN *Answers from LGBT students:*

Top Three Descriptors of the LGBT Campus Environment:
1. Vibrant   2. Passionate   3. Accepting

What makes your campus feel welcome and safe for LGBT students?
"There is a strong and open population of GLBTQ students on campus. The administration is understanding, and provides resources for any problems that you might have. The overall student body does not have negative reactions to gay students in LGBT relationships on campus. Same-sex cuddling and hand-holding are not censored."
—20-year-old queer female, sophomore

How do you feel about coming out on your campus?
"I came out to my friends here after only a week or two—just enough time for me to realize how open and accepting the campus truly is. Since that time I have never regretted coming out here and have been made to feel loved and respected. … Universally among LGBT students the sentiments are the same."
—22-year-old queer male, senior

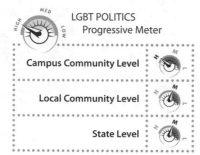

LGBT POLITICS
Progressive Meter

Campus Community Level

Local Community Level

State Level

INFO

WHITMAN COLLEGE
515 Boyer Avenue
Walla Walla, WA 99362
Phone: 509-527-5176
Fax: 509-527-4967
E-mail: admission@whitman.edu
Website: www.whitman.edu

CAMPUS STATS
Type of Institution: Private college
Founding Year: 1882
Size: 1,452
Avg. Class Size: 10–19 students
Popular Majors: Sociology, Psychology, English Language and Literature
Cost: Tuition: $28,400
Admission Application Deadline: January 15

⊘ ACADEMIC SCENE

Top Three Supportive LGBT Academic Areas:
1. Social Sciences   2. Religion   3. Foreign Languages

How LGBT-friendly are faculty in the classroom?
"I have never had a teacher be outwardly against the LGBT community, but I have had several who are all for it. Many of my teachers did their Ph.D. work on LGBT issues." —*20-year-old gay male, sophomore*

"The professors are very friendly, and seem sensitive to LGBT issues in class discussions. Certain professors, gay and straight, have really stood out in their willingness to listen to my personal feelings and concerns. They are more than friendly; they are true friends and allies." —*20-year-old queer female, sophomore*

☺ SOCIAL SCENE

Top Three Things in the LGBT Social Life:
1. Dragfest   2. Hanging out   3. LGBTQ socials

How would you describe the social scene for LGBT students?
"Considering that we're a small campus in a small town, it's not so bad. You kinda have to carve out your own social space, but once you find the confidence to do that you're in good shape." —*24-year-old gay male, senior*

What annual social event should an LGBT student not miss?
"Definitely do not miss Dragfest! It is so much fun seeing everyone cross-dress … and [it] makes everyone more open to gender-bending and same-sex relationships." —*20-year-old queer female, sophomore*

OUTRAGEOUS FACTOID Whitman is known for its large population of mallards, often seen waddling around the campus. One LGBT student recalls: "The ratio of male to female ducks is abnormally high. You can often see male ducks paired up together."

RAINBOW RUMOR Too much Greek? The Whitman College social scene revolves around sororities and fraternities. Although there are many out LGBT Greek members, campus involvement in these organizations may limit the ability of some students to seek out a queer community. At least that's the opinion of one LGBT senior upperclassman, but then he continues: "Many colleges have entire resource centers for LGBT students—that might be the real answer to creating greater visibility."

THAT'S SO GAY!

ANNUAL LGBT EVENT HIGHLIGHTS

Homecoming Celebration with LGBT Alumni: Fall

Same-Sex Hand-Holding Day: Fall

Bisexuality Awareness Day: October

National Coming Out Day: October

Queer Prom/Rainbow Rage: October

World AIDS Day: December

Dragweek and Dragfest: April

National Day of Silence Observance: April

Matthew Shepard Lecture Series: Fall/Spring

David Nord Award for Gay and Lesbian Studies: Spring

BUZZ BITES
Fun Queer Stuff to Know

THE BEST...

Party Locale: Beta Fraternity House

Hangout: Women's Resource Center

Eating Place: Creek Town Café

Place to Check Out Guys: Akeny Field

Place to Check Out Ladies: Basketball practice

LGBT-Cool Athletic Sport: Ultimate frisbee *or* intramural football

Non-LGBT-Specific Campus Club: Feminists Advocating Change and Empowerment

Place for LGBT Students to Live on Campus: Lyman House

LGBT Course Offering: Queer Religiosities *or* Sexuality and Textuality

LGBT Educational Involvement Opportunity: National Day of Silence

LGBT-Accepting Religious/Spiritual Organization(s): Shalom, First Congregational Church

CAMPUS QUEER RESOURCES

Select LGBT Student Organization(s):

Gay, Lesbian, Bisexual, Transgender and Questioning Student Organization (GLBTQ); Coalition Against Homophobia (CAH)

Founding Date: GLBTQ (1982); CAH (1990)

Membership: 120+

E-mail: glbtq@whitman.edu; queer_whitman@yahoo.com

Website: www.whitman.edu/glbtq/

Resource Center/Office Responsible for LGBT Issues:

Intercultural Center
Whitman College
345 Boyer Avenue
Walla Walla, WA 99362

Year Established: 1979

Number of Staff: 3 full-time professional staff (varying responsibilities)

Phone: 509-527-5596

Website: www.whitman.edu/intercultural_center

THE GAY POINT AVERAGE OFFICIAL CAMPUS CHECKLIST

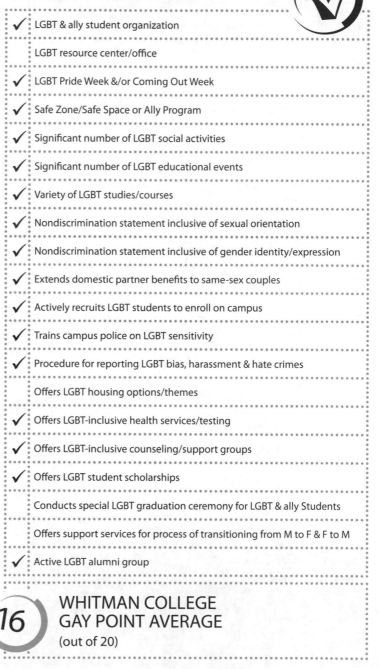

- ✓ LGBT & ally student organization
-   LGBT resource center/office
- ✓ LGBT Pride Week &/or Coming Out Week
- ✓ Safe Zone/Safe Space or Ally Program
- ✓ Significant number of LGBT social activities
- ✓ Significant number of LGBT educational events
- ✓ Variety of LGBT studies/courses
- ✓ Nondiscrimination statement inclusive of sexual orientation
- ✓ Nondiscrimination statement inclusive of gender identity/expression
- ✓ Extends domestic partner benefits to same-sex couples
- ✓ Actively recruits LGBT students to enroll on campus
- ✓ Trains campus police on LGBT sensitivity
- ✓ Procedure for reporting LGBT bias, harassment & hate crimes
-   Offers LGBT housing options/themes
- ✓ Offers LGBT-inclusive health services/testing
- ✓ Offers LGBT-inclusive counseling/support groups
- ✓ Offers LGBT student scholarships
-   Conducts special LGBT graduation ceremony for LGBT & ally Students
-   Offers support services for process of transitioning from M to F & F to M
- ✓ Active LGBT alumni group

16 WHITMAN COLLEGE GAY POINT AVERAGE
(out of 20)

WILLIAMS COLLEGE

LOCATED AT THE base of Mount Greylock in the bucolic Berkshire Mountains of northwestern Massachusetts, Williams College has proven to be a progressive place for LGBT policies and practices. In 2000, the campus started the Queer Life Office, housed in the Multicultural Center, to address the needs and concerns of LGBT students. In just a short period of time, the campus has moved from tolerance into acceptance. The campus Gay Point Average illustrates the several LGBT achievements and the firm queer commitment on campus. The main area of future improvement would be gender identity/expression issues, but there are currently ongoing efforts to address that issue.

In addition, the campus has had an active student coalition—the Queer Student Union—since 1985. Campus LGBT activities include the Queer Bash, which is the largest party of the year for the entire campus community. As far as educational efforts, the Queer Life Office conducts several ally trainings and does outreach on LGBT issues in the classroom. But most important, one of the hottest events of the year is the Rainbow Graduation for graduating LGBT students—standing room only.

An LGBT student describes Williams: "I have found the campus to be very welcoming and supportive … the faculty and fellow students. My straight friends love me for being gay and think it's cool. There is great pride being gay on campus. I would call that gay-friendly."

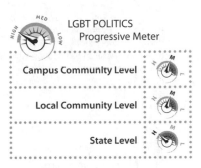

LGBT POLITICS
Progressive Meter

Campus Community Level

Local Community Level

State Level

𝄢 OUTSPOKEN *Answers from LGBT students:*

Top Three Descriptors of the LGBT Campus Environment:
1. Accepting   2. Nurturing   3. Intimate

What makes your campus feel welcoming and safe for LGBT students?
"I was really impressed with how the campus welcomes us. The Queer Welcome Reception really made me feel like I was embraced and made me want to become part of the Queer Student Union. The invitations were fabulous."
—*17-year-old gay male, freshman*

How do you feel about coming out on your campus?
"I was really nervous because I'm an athlete, and everyone just assumes we're all dykes. I didn't want to be thought of as just that, so I waited. I didn't need to, though. The crew team was great, and they include me in everything. The other teams pretty much seem to accept lesbians too, so it's not as big a deal as it seems to be in other schools." —*19-year-old lesbian, sophomore*

✒ ACADEMIC SCENE

Top Three Supportive LGBT Academic Areas:
1. History   2. Women and Gender Studies   3. English

How LGBT-friendly are faculty in the classroom?
"Queer topics have never come up in my classes, but I'm friends with all my profs, so I don't think it would be a problem." —*21-year-old queer male, senior*

INFO

WILLIAMS COLLEGE
33 Stetson Court
Williamstown, MA 01267
Phone: 413-597-2211
Fax: 413-597-4052
E-mail: admission@williams.edu
Web site: www.williams.edu

CAMPUS STATS
Type of Institution: Private college
Founding Year: 1793
Size: 1,931
Avg. Class Size: 10–19 students
Popular Majors: Art/Art Studies, Economics, Political Science and Government
Cost: Tuition: $29,786
Admission Application Deadline: January 1

OUTRAGEOUS FACTOID Queer Bash is the largest party of the year. All the students rave about the parties during Coming Out Days and Queer Pride Days. And if you want to go grocery shopping with Gwyneth Paltrow, stick around for the summer Williamstown Theatre Festival.

RAINBOW RUMOR A new tradition at Williams College is Rainbow Graduation; a special time to recognize all the graduating LGBT students. Honors include a certificate of "queerness," mortarboard with rainbow tassel and a fabulous light-up rainbow feather boa. Last year was standing room only.

ANNUAL LGBT EVENT HIGHLIGHTS

Welcome Reception for Queer Students: September

LGBT Lunchtable Series: Monthly Fall/Spring

Transgender Remembrance Day: November

Coming Out Days: Week of October 11

Queer Bash: October and April

Queer Pride Days: April

Rainbow Graduation: May

"I was amazed at how many allies and out faculty and staff there are on such a small campus. I couldn't get over how many were at the Queer Welcome Reception when I came." —*17-year-old gay male, freshman*

😊 SOCIAL SCENE

Top Three Things in the LGBT Social Life:
1. Hardy parties   2. Movie nights   3. Queer Bash

How would you describe the social scene for LGBT students?
"I don't see a lot of difference between the straight social scene and gay social scene. It's hard to date here because it's such a small group of people and we all seem to know each other." —*17-year-old gay male, freshman*

What annual social event should an LGBT student not miss?
"Queer Bash. It's legendary." —*19-year-old lesbian, sophomore*

BUZZ BITES *Fun Queer Stuff to Know*

THE BEST...

Party Locale: Mezze

Hangout: Queer Life Office

Eating Place: Hardy House

Place to Check Out Guys: Pool

Place to Check Out Ladies: Library

LGBT-Cool Athletic Sport: Crew and swimming

Non-LGBT-Specific Campus Club: Nothin' But Cuties Hip-Hop Dance Group

LGBT Course Offering: Sex, Gender and Political Theory

LGBT Educational Involvement Opportunity: Queer Pride Days

LGBT-Accepting Religious/Spiritual Organization(s): Chaplain's Office, First Congregational Church and Lehman Council

THE GAY POINT AVERAGE
OFFICIAL CAMPUS CHECKLIST

LGBT & ally student organization ✓

LGBT resource center/office ✓

LGBT Pride Week &/or Coming Out Week ✓

Safe Zone/Safe Space or Ally Program ✓

Significant number of LGBT social activities ✓

Significant number of LGBT educational events ✓

Variety of LGBT studies/courses ✓

Nondiscrimination statement inclusive of sexual orientation ✓

Nondiscrimination statement inclusive of gender identity/expression

Extends domestic partner benefits to same-sex couples ✓

Actively recruits LGBT students to enroll on campus ✓

Trains campus police on LGBT sensitivity ✓

Procedure for reporting LGBT bias, harassment & hate crimes ✓

Offers LGBT housing options/themes

Offers LGBT-inclusive health services/testing ✓

Offers LGBT-inclusive counseling/support groups ✓

Offers LGBT student scholarships

Conducts special LGBT graduation ceremony for LGBT & ally Students ✓

Offers support services for process of transitioning from M to F & F to M

Active LGBT alumni group ✓

WILLIAMS COLLEGE
GAY POINT AVERAGE
(out of 20)

16

CAMPUS QUEER RESOURCES

LGBT Student Organization:
Queer Student Union
Founding Date: 1985
Membership: 60
Phone: 413-597-3353

LGBT Resource Center/Office:
Queer Life Office
Multicultural Center
10 Morley Drive
Williamstown, MA 01267
Year Established: 2000
Number of Staff: 1 full-time staff professional
Phone: 413-597-3353
Website: www.williams.edu/MCC/

YALE UNIVERSITY

YALE UNIVERSITY HAS been affectionately termed the Gay Ivy. Located in New Haven, Connecticut, the campus has a strong history of student involvement and activism to change the queer tides on campus.

Unlike the other Ivy League campuses listed, Yale University relies solely on out LGBT student leaders to push for the advancement of queer issues and to create a welcoming LGBT campus climate. Yale's LGBT students take a tremendous amount of pride in their self-reliance and admit that the Yale LGBT experience is what you make of it. The LGBT Cooperative, founded in 1981, is the leading student-run umbrella group that supports the work of a number of student LGBT coalitions. These groups include an active Queer Political Action Committee, a peer-run group for freshmen called Not So Straight Frosh, and social groups called Queer Women/Ya!Lesbians and GaYalies.

Each group, under the umbrella of the LGBT Co-op, generates all kinds of queer activities during the semester. The most notorious of these is the Co-op Dance—a scandalous schoolwide queer dance that serves as the largest LGBT fundraiser on campus. Other LGBT activities include study breaks, dance parties, protests, guest speakers, workshops, movie nights, performances and art projects—to name a few. LGBT life at Yale is constantly changing with the flow of student organizers and leaders within the LGBT Co-op. The result is a dynamic, ever-changing queer scene and ample opportunities for leadership on campus.

Students at Yale should be commended for the steady LGBT progress over the years. A careful look at Yale's Gay Point Average shows positive queer achievements, along with notable areas for further attention such as trans-inclusive policies. But, regardless, LGBT students on campus remark that Yale is "one of the most accepting places." In the fight for the title of "Most Gay Ivy," who is the winner? One LGBT student declares: "It's easy to be queer here. Yale is very accepting and supportive of alternative sexuality. Even with the extreme diversity of thought on campus, most students have at the least a live-and-let-live attitude towards students."

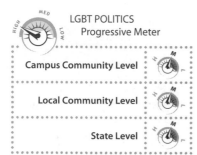

LGBT POLITICS
Progressive Meter

Campus Community Level

Local Community Level

State Level

INFO

YALE UNIVERSITY
PO Box 208234
38 Hillhouse Avenue
New Haven, CT 06520

Phone: 203-432-9300

Fax: 203-432-9392

E-mail: undergraduate.admissions@yale.edu

Website: www.yale.edu

CAMPUS STATS

Type of Institution: Private university

Founding Year: 1701

Size: 5,294

Avg. Class Size: 10–19 students

Popular Majors: Social Sciences and History, English, Biological/Life Sciences, Psychology

Cost: Tuition: $43,700

Admission Application Deadline: December 31

🗨 OUTSPOKEN *Answers from LGBT students:*

Top Three Descriptors of the LGBT Campus Environment:
1. Visible   2. Fluid   3. Comfortable

What makes your campus feel welcoming and safe for LGBT students?
"There are a lot of events and meetings that create a space for queer people to organize, interact and make friends." —*18-year-old lesbian, freshman*

How do you feel about coming out on your campus?
"The anticipation is always worse than what actually happens. I was afraid my roommates would get really freaked out that I was gay, but their response was pretty anticlimactic." —*21-year-old gay male, junior*

✍ ACADEMIC SCENE

Top Three Supportive LGBT Academic Areas:
1. Women's, Gender, and Sexuality Studies   2. English   3. Theater/Studio Art

How LGBT-friendly are faculty in the classroom?

"I've written most of my papers on things relating to homosexuality. All my professors are always excited that I'm studying something so close to my heart."
—*20-year-old queer female, junior*

"Most professors, especially social science professors, really reach out to queer students. They are always talking about gender and sexuality in a way that benefits the entire community." —*22-year-old gay male, senior*

☺ SOCIAL SCENE

Top Three Things in the LGBT Social Life:

1. Dancing   2. Eating with friends   3. LGBT Co-op

How would you describe the social scene for LGBT students?

"The lesbian population leaves much to be desired, but the Ya!Lesbian parties are legendary." —*19-year-old lesbian, freshman*

What annual social event should an LGBT student not miss?

"The Glam Jam is one of the most fun, raucous performances I've ever seen! The drag queens' mouths are incredibly dirty, and the student drag competitors are amazing! It's awesome to see friends shake it, Sir-Mix-a-Lot style—proper."
—*20-year-old gay male, junior*

BUZZ BITES *Fun Queer Stuff to Know*

THE BEST...

Hangout: Queer Resource Center

Eating Place: Brunch at 168 York Street Café

Place to Check Out Guys: LGBT Co-op

Place to Check Out Ladies: Queer Women wine and cheese nights

LGBT-Cool Athletic Sport: Women's rugby

LGBT Course Offering: Sexuality and Popular Culture

LGBT Educational Involvement Opportunity: Queer Peer Counseling Program

LGBT-Accepting Religious/Spiritual Organization(s): Slifka Center for Jewish Life

OUTRAGEOUS FACTOID

Yale has an old rhyme about the extent of the queer population on campus. It goes: "One in four, maybe more; one in three, maybe me; one in two, maybe you?"

• • • • • • • • • • • • • • • • • • • •

RAINBOW RUMOR

Yale takes pride in being called the "Gay Ivy." But is it exactly true? A quick glance at the history would show that LGBT students have had to fend for themselves. Other Ivy League schools have LGBT staff, a resource center and other established institutional commitments to support queer student life. One LGBT student states: "We are looking to join our peer institutions in having an LGBTQ Student Center as well as an LGBTQ administrator to ensure the quality of queer life at Yale."

• • • • • • • • • • • • • • • • • • • •

THAT'S SO GAY!

ANNUAL LGBT EVENT HIGHLIGHTS

LGBT Co-op Meeting: Monthly, starting in September

Fall LGBT Co-op Dance: October

Queer Alumni Dinner: November

Queer Superbowl Party: January

Trans Week: February

Pride Week: First Week in April

Glam Jam Drag Competition: Spring

Spring LGBT Co-op Dance: April

CAMPUS QUEER RESOURCES

Select LGBT Student Organization(s):

LGBT Cooperative at Yale
PO Box 202031
New Haven, CT 06520-2031
Founding Date: 1981
Membership: 50+
Phone: 203-436-4868
E-mail: lgbt@yale.edu
Website: www.yale.edu/lgbt

THE GAY POINT AVERAGE
OFFICIAL CAMPUS CHECKLIST

- ✓ LGBT & ally student organization
- LGBT resource center/office
- ✓ LGBT Pride Week &/or Coming Out Week
- ✓ Safe Zone/Safe Space or Ally Program
- ✓ Significant number of LGBT social activities
- ✓ Significant number of LGBT educational events
- ✓ Variety of LGBT studies/courses
- ✓ Nondiscrimination statement inclusive of sexual orientation
- Nondiscrimination statement inclusive of gender identity/expression
- ✓ Extends domestic partner benefits to same-sex couples
- Actively recruits LGBT students to enroll on campus
- Trains campus police on LGBT sensitivity
- Procedure for reporting LGBT bias, harassment & hate crimes
- Offers LGBT housing options/themes
- ✓ Offers LGBT-inclusive health services/testing
- ✓ Offers LGBT-inclusive counseling/support groups
- ✓ Offers LGBT student scholarships
- Conducts special LGBT graduation ceremony for LGBT & ally Students
- Offers support services for process of transitioning from M to F & F to M
- ✓ Active LGBT alumni group

12 YALE UNIVERSITY
GAY POINT AVERAGE
(out of 20)

YOUR LGBT CAMPUS CHOICE INDEX

By Gay Point Average

Perfect Score of 20
University of Pennsylvania
University of Southern California

Score of 19
American University
Ohio State University
Pennsylvania State University
Princeton University
University of California—Berkeley
University of California—Los Angeles
University of Minnesota—Twin Cities
University of Oregon
University of Puget Sound

Score of 18
Duke University
Eastern Michigan University
Indiana University
Ithaca College
Massachusetts Institute of Technology
Oberlin College
Stanford University
Tufts University
University of California—Santa Cruz
University of Michigan
Washington State University

Score of 17
California State Polytechnic
    University—Pomona
Central Washington University
Colorado State University
Cornell University
New York University
Northwestern University
Ohio University
Syracuse University
University of California—Davis
University of California—Riverside
University of Colorado—Boulder
University of Connecticut
University of Florida
University of Illinois—Chicago
University of Maine
University of Maryland
University of Massachusetts—Amherst

University of Minnesota—Duluth
University of Wisconsin—Madison

Score of 16
Carleton College
Colby College
Colgate University
Dartmouth College
Macalester College
Northern Illinois University
Oregon State University
University of Illinois—
    Urbana-Champaign
University of Utah
University of Vermont
Wellesley College
Whitman College
Williams College

Score of 15
Grinnell College
Haverford College
Iowa State University
Knox College
Michigan State University
Sarah Lawrence College
University of Arizona
University of California—San Diego
University of Colorado—Denver and
    Health Sciences Center
University of North Carolina—
    Chapel Hill
University of Southern Maine
University of Washington

Score of 14
DePauw University
Emory University
Minnesota State University—Mankato
Rutgers, The State University of
    New Jersey—New Brunswick
University of North Texas
University of Rhode Island
Vassar College

Score of 13
Antioch College

Carnegie Mellon University
George Mason University
Lawrence University
Marlboro College
Metropolitan State College of Denver
Middlebury College
Suffolk University
University of Kansas
University of Missouri—Kansas City
University of Wisconsin—La Crosse

Score of 12
Central Michigan University
DePaul University
Skidmore College
Temple University
University of Louisville
Yale University

Score of 11
Bowling Green State University
Bryn Mawr College
New College of Florida
Rochester Institute of Technology
State University of New York—
    Purchase College
University of Wisconsin—Milwaukee

Score of 10
Case Western Reserve University
Columbia College—Chicago
Kalamazoo College
University of Texas—Austin

By Those Offering Same-Sex Domestic Partner Benefits

American University
Antioch College
Bryn Mawr College
California State Polytechnic
    University—Pomona
Carleton College
Carnegie Mellon University
Case Western Reserve University
Central Michigan University
Central Washington University
Colby College
Colgate University
Columbia College—Chicago
Cornell University
Dartmouth College
DePauw University
Duke University
Eastern Michigan University
Emory University
Grinnell College
Haverford College
Indiana University
Iowa State University
Ithaca College
Knox College
Lawrence University
Macalester College
Marlboro College
Massachusetts Institute of Technology

Michigan State University
Middlebury College
New York University
Northern Illinois University
Northwestern University
Oberlin College
Ohio State University
Ohio University
Oregon State University
Pennsylvania State University
Princeton University
Rochester Institute of Technology
Rutgers, The State University of
    New Jersey—New Brunswick
Sarah Lawrence College
Skidmore College
Stanford University
State University of New York—
    Purchase College
Suffolk University
Syracuse University
Temple University
Tufts University
University of California—Berkeley
University of California—Davis
University of California—Los Angeles
University of California—Riverside
University of California—San Diego
University of California—Santa Cruz

University of Colorado—Boulder
University of Colorado—Denver and
    Health Sciences Center
University of Connecticut
University of Florida
University of Illinois—Chicago
University of Illinois—
    Urbana-Champaign
University of Maine
University of Massachusetts—Amherst
University of Michigan
University of Minnesota—Duluth
University of Minnesota—Twin Cities
University of Oregon
University of Pennsylvania
University of Puget Sound
University of Rhode Island
University of Southern California
University of Southern Maine
University of Vermont
University of Washington
Vassar College
Washington State University
Wellesley College
Whitman College
Williams College
Yale University

By Those Including Gender Identity and/or Expression in Nondiscrimination Policy

American University
Antioch College
California State Polytechnic
    University—Pomona*
Carnegie Mellon University
Central Washington University
Colby College
Colorado State University
Cornell University
DePauw University
Iowa State University
Kalamazoo College
Knox College
Massachusetts Institute
    of Technology
Middlebury College
Minnesota State
    University—Mankato*
New College of Florida
New York University
Northwestern University*
Ohio State University
Oregon State University
Princeton University
Rochester Institute of Technology
Sarah Lawrence College
Syracuse University
Tufts University
University of Arizona

University of California—Berkeley
University of California—Davis
University of California—Los Angeles
University of California—Riverside
University of California—San Diego
University of California—Santa Cruz
University of Connecticut*
University of Illinois—Chicago
University of Illinois—
    Urbana-Champaign
University of Maine*
University of Michigan*
University of Minnesota— Duluth*
University of Minnesota—Twin Cities*
University of Oregon
University of Pennsylvania
University of Puget Sound
University of Rhode Island
University of Southern California
University of Southern Maine*
University of Utah*
University of Vermont
University of Washington
University of Wisconsin—La Crosse
University of Wisconsin—Madison
University of Wisconsin—Milwaukee
Vassar College
Washington State University
Whitman College

Notes:

An asterisk* indicates a college or university that does not explicitly have the words "gender identity and/or expression" in its nondiscrimination policy. Instead, the campus has a state law, legal opinion/ruling, or other administrative determination that it believes covers "gender identity and/or expression" under other categories, such as "sex," "gender," and/or "sexual orientation." This distinction is important to note, because laws, court decisions, and administrative rulings are subject to change and because the explicit inclusion in policies sends the message that transgender people are valued and included on the campus. All 100 colleges and universities listed in *The Advocate College Guide for LGBT Students* include the term "sexual orientation" in campus nondiscrimination policies.

By Those with Religious Affiliation

DePaul University (Catholic)
DePauw University (Methodist)
Duke University (Methodist)
Emory University (Methodist)
Macalester College (Presbyterian)

By Women's Colleges

Bryn Mawr College
Wellesley College

By Region

New England Region

Includes Connecticut, Maine, Massachusetts, New Hampshire, Rhode Island, and Vermont.

Connecticut
University of Connecticut
Yale University
Maine
Colby College
University of Maine
University of Southern Maine
Massachusetts
Massachusetts Institute of Technology
Suffolk University
Tufts University
University of Massachusetts—Amherst
Wellesley College
Williams College
New Hampshire
Dartmouth College
Rhode Island
University of Rhode Island
Vermont
Marlboro College
Middlebury College
University of Vermont

Mid-Atlantic Region

Includes Delaware, District of Columbia, Maryland, New Jersey, New York, and Pennsylvania.

District of Columbia
American University
Maryland
University of Maryland
New Jersey
Princeton University
Rutgers, The State University of New Jersey—New Brunswick
New York
Colgate University
Cornell University

Ithaca College
New York University
Rochester Institute of Technology
Sarah Lawrence College
Skidmore College
State University of New York—Purchase College
Syracuse University
Vassar College
Pennsylvania
Bryn Mawr College
Carnegie Mellon University
Haverford College
Pennsylvania State University
Temple University
University of Pennsylvania

Midwest Region

Includes Illinois, Indiana, Iowa, Kansas, Michigan, Minnesota, Missouri, Nebraska, North Dakota, Ohio, South Dakota, and Wisconsin.

Illinois
Columbia College—Chicago
DePaul University
Knox College
Northern Illinois University
Northwestern University
University of Illinois—Chicago
University of Illinois—Urbana-Champaign
Indiana
DePauw University
Indiana University
Iowa
Grinnell College
Iowa State University
Kansas
University of Kansas
Michigan
Central Michigan University
Eastern Michigan University
Kalamazoo College

Michigan State University
University of Michigan
Minnesota
Carleton College
Macalester College
Minnesota State University—Mankato
University of Minnesota—Duluth
University of Minnesota—Twin Cities
Missouri
University of Missouri—Kansas City
Ohio
Antioch College
Bowling Green State University
Case Western Reserve University
Oberlin College
Ohio State University
Ohio University
Wisconsin
Lawrence University
University of Wisconsin—La Crosse
University of Wisconsin—Madison
University of Wisconsin—Milwaukee

South Region

Includes Alabama, Arkansas, Florida, Georgia, Kentucky, Louisiana, Mississippi, North Carolina, South Carolina, Tennessee, Virginia, and West Virginia,

Florida
New College of Florida
University of Florida
Georgia
Emory University
Kentucky
University of Louisville
North Carolina
Duke University
University of North Carolina—Chapel Hill
Virginia
George Mason University

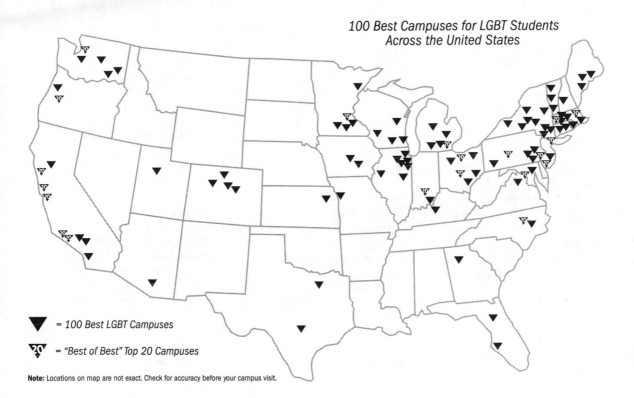

100 Best Campuses for LGBT Students Across the United States

▼ = 100 Best LGBT Campuses

▼20 = "Best of Best" Top 20 Campuses

Note: Locations on map are not exact. Check for accuracy before your campus visit.

Southwest Region
Includes Arizona, New Mexico, Oklahoma, and Texas.

Arizona
University of Arizona

Texas
University of North Texas
University of Texas—Austin

West Region
Includes Alaska, California, Colorado, Hawaii, Idaho, Montana, Nevada, Oregon, Utah, Washington, and Wyoming.

California
California State Polytechnic
    University—Pomona
Stanford University

University of California—Berkeley
University of California—Davis
University of California—Los Angeles
University of California—Riverside
University of California—San Diego
University of California—Santa Cruz
University of Southern California

Colorado
Colorado State University
Metropolitan State College of Denver
University of Colorado—Boulder
University of Colorado—Denver and
Health Sciences Center

Oregon
Oregon State University
University of Oregon

Utah
University of Utah

Washington
Central Washington University
University of Puget Sound
University of Washington
Washington State University
Whitman College

By State

Arizona
University of Arizona

California
California State Polytechnic
        University—Pomona
Stanford University
University of California—Berkeley
University of California—Davis
University of California—Los Angeles
University of California—Riverside
University of California—San Diego
University of California—Santa Cruz
University of Southern California

Colorado
Colorado State University
Metropolitan State College of Denver
University of Colorado—Boulder
University of Colorado—Denver
        and Health Sciences Center

Connecticut
University of Connecticut
Yale University

District of Columbia
American University

Florida
New College of Florida
University of Florida

Georgia
Emory University

Illinois
Columbia College—Chicago
DePaul University
Knox College
Northern Illinois University
Northwestern University
University of Illinois—Chicago
University of Illinois—
        Urbana-Champaign

Indiana
DePauw University
Indiana University

Iowa
Grinnell College
Iowa State University

Kansas
University of Kansas

Kentucky
University of Louisville

Maine
Colby College
University of Maine
University of Southern Maine

Maryland
University of Maryland

Massachusetts
Massachusetts Institute of Technology
Suffolk University
Tufts University
University of Massachusetts—Amherst
Wellesley College
Williams College

Michigan
Central Michigan University
Eastern Michigan University
Kalamazoo College
Michigan State University
University of Michigan

Minnesota
Carleton College
Macalester College
Minnesota State University—Mankato
University of Minnesota—Duluth
University of Minnesota—Twin Cities

Missouri
University of Missouri—Kansas City

New Hampshire
Dartmouth College

New Jersey
Princeton University
Rutgers, The State University of
        New Jersey—New Brunswick

New York
Colgate University
Cornell University
Ithaca College
New York University
Rochester Institute of Technology
Sarah Lawrence College
Skidmore College
State University of New York—
        Purchase College
Syracuse University
Vassar College

North Carolina
Duke University
University of North Carolina—
        Chapel Hill

Ohio
Antioch College
Bowling Green State University
Case Western Reserve University
Oberlin College
Ohio State University
Ohio University

Oregon
Oregon State University
University of Oregon

Pennsylvania
Bryn Mawr College
Carnegie Mellon University
Haverford College
Pennsylvania State University
Temple University
University of Pennsylvania

Rhode Island
University of Rhode Island

Texas
University of North Texas
University of Texas—Austin

Utah
University of Utah

Vermont
Marlboro College
Middlebury College
University of Vermont

Virginia
George Mason University

Washington
Central Washington University
University of Puget Sound
University of Washington
Washington State University
Whitman College

Wisconsin
Lawrence University
University of Wisconsin—La Crosse
University of Wisconsin—Madison
University of Wisconsin—Milwaukee

By Type of Institution

Private Colleges and Universities
American University
Antioch College
Bryn Mawr College
Carleton College
Carnegie Mellon University
Case Western Reserve University
Colby College
Colgate University
Columbia College—Chicago
Cornell University
Dartmouth College
DePaul University
DePauw University
Duke University
Emory University
Grinnell College
Haverford College
Ithaca College
Kalamazoo College
Knox College
Lawrence University
Macalester College
Marlboro College
Massachusetts Institute of Technology
Middlebury College
New York University
Northwestern University
Oberlin College
Princeton University
Rochester Institute of Technology
Sarah Lawrence College
Skidmore College
Stanford University
Suffolk University
Syracuse University

Tufts University
University of Pennsylvania
University of Puget Sound
University of Southern California
Vassar College
Wellesley College
Whitman College
Williams College
Yale University

Public Colleges and Universities
Bowling Green State University
California State Polytechnic
    University—Pomona
Central Michigan University
Central Washington University
Colorado State University
Eastern Michigan University
George Mason University
Indiana University
Iowa State University
Metropolitan State College of Denver
Michigan State University
Minnesota State University—Mankato
New College of Florida
Northern Illinois University
Ohio State University
Ohio University
Oregon State University
Pennsylvania State University
Rutgers, The State University of
    New Jersey—New Brunswick
State University of New York—
    Purchase College
Temple University
University of Arizona
University of California—Berkeley

University of California—Davis
University of California—Los Angeles
University of California—Riverside
University of California—San Diego
University of California—Santa Cruz
University of Colorado—Boulder
University of Colorado—Denver and
    Health Sciences Center
University of Connecticut
University of Florida
University of Illinois—Chicago
University of Illinois—
    Urbana-Champaign
University of Kansas
University of Louisville
University of Maine
University of Maryland
University of Massachusetts—Amherst
University of Michigan
University of Minnesota—Duluth
University of Minnesota—Twin Cities
University of Missouri—Kansas City
University of North Carolina—Chapel Hill
University of North Texas
University of Oregon
University of Rhode Island
University of Southern Maine
University of Texas—Austin
University of Utah
University of Vermont
University of Washington
University of Wisconsin—La Crosse
University of Wisconsin—Madison
University of Wisconsin—Milwaukee
Washington State University

By Size

Under 1,000 students
Antioch College
Marlboro College
New College of Florida

1,001 to 2,500 students
Bryn Mawr College
Carleton College
Colby College
DePauw University
Grinnell College
Haverford College
Kalamazoo College
Knox College
Lawrence University
Macalester College
Middlebury College
Sarah Lawrence College
Skidmore College
Vassar College
Wellesley College
Whitman College
Williams College

2,501 to 5,000 students
Case Western Reserve University
Colgate University
Dartmouth College
Massachusetts Institute of Technology
Oberlin College
Princeton University
State University of New York—
    Purchase College
Suffolk University
Tufts University
University of Puget Sound

5,001 to 10,000 students
American University
Carnegie Mellon University

Central Washington University
Columbia College—Chicago
Duke University
Emory University
Ithaca College
Northwestern University
Stanford University
University of Minnesota—Duluth
University of Southern Maine
University of Vermont
University of Wisconsin—La Crosse
Yale University

10,001 to 20,000 students
Bowling Green State University
California State Polytechnic
    University—Pomona
Cornell University
DePaul University
Eastern Michigan University
George Mason University
Minnesota State University—Mankato
New York University
Northern Illinois University
Ohio University
Oregon State University
Rochester Institute of Technology
Syracuse University
University of California—Riverside
University of California—Santa Cruz
University of Colorado—Denver and
    Health Sciences Center
University of Connecticut
University of Illinois—Chicago
University of Maine
University of Massachusetts—Amherst
University of Missouri—Kansas City
University of North Carolina—Chapel Hill
University of Oregon
University of Pennsylvania

University of Rhode Island
University of Southern California
Washington State University

20,001 to 30,000 students
Central Michigan University
Colorado State University
Indiana University
Iowa State University
Metropolitan State College of Denver
Rutgers, The State University of
    New Jersey—New Brunswick
Temple University
University of California—Berkeley
University of California—Davis
University of California—Los Angeles
University of California—San Diego
University of Colorado—Boulder
University of Kansas
University of Louisville
University of Maryland
University of Michigan
University of Minnesota—Twin Cities
University of Utah
University of Washington
University of Wisconsin—Madison
University of Wisconsin—Milwaukee

Over 30,000 students
Michigan State University
Ohio State University
Pennsylvania State University
University of Arizona
University of Florida
University of Illinois—Urbana-
Champaign
University of North Texas
University of Texas—Austin

By In-state Tuition

Under $3,500

California State Polytechnic University—Pomona

Metropolitan State College of Denver

University of Florida

University of Massachusetts—Amherst

Between $3,501 and $5,000

Central Michigan University

Central Washington University

Colorado State University

Eastern Michigan University

Indiana University

Iowa State University

New College of Florida

State University of New York—Purchase College

University of Arizona

University of Colorado—Boulder

University of Illinois—Chicago

University of North Carolina—Chapel Hill

University of North Texas

University of Southern Maine

University of Utah

Between $5,001 and $7,500

Bowling Green State University

George Mason University

Michigan State University

Minnesota State University—Mankato

Northern Illinois University

Oregon State University

University of California—Berkeley

University of California—Davis

University of California—Los Angeles

University of California—Riverside

University of California—San Diego

University of Colorado—Denver and Health Sciences Center

University of Connecticut

University of Illinois—Urbana-Champaign

University of Kansas

University of Louisville

University of Maine

University of Minnesota—Twin Cities

University of Missouri—Kansas City

University of Oregon

University of Rhode Island

University of Texas—Austin

University of Washington

University of Wisconsin—Madison

University of Wisconsin—Milwaukee

Washington State University

Between $7,501 and $10,000

Rutgers, The State University of New Jersey—New Brunswick

Ohio State University

Ohio University

Temple University

University of California—Santa Cruz

University of Maryland

University of Michigan

University of Minnesota—Duluth

University of Vermont

University of Wisconsin—La Crosse

Between $10,001 and $20,000

Columbia College—Chicago

DePaul University

Pennsylvania State University

Between $20,001 and $30,000

American University

Antioch College

Bryn Mawr College

Case Western Reserve University

Ithaca College

Knox College

Lawrence University

Macalester College

Marlboro College

Rochester Institute of Technology

Stanford University

Suffolk University

Syracuse University

Tufts University

University of Puget Sound

Whitman College

Williams College

Between $30,001 and $35,000

Carleton College

Carnegie Mellon University

Colgate University

Cornell University

Dartmouth College

DePauw University

Duke University

Emory University

Grinnell College

Haverford College

Kalamazoo College

Massachusetts Institute of Technology

New York University

Northwestern University

Oberlin College

Princeton University

Sarah Lawrence College

Skidmore College

University of Pennsylvania

University of Southern California

Wellesley College

Over $35,000

Colby College

Middlebury College

Vassar College

Yale University

Note:

Private institutions have only one tuition rate for both in-state and out-of-state students. As a result, the private institution tuition amounts are the same on both the in-state and out-of-state tuition listings.

By Out-of-state Tuition

Under $10,000
Metropolitan State College of Denver
University of Massachusetts—Amherst

Between $10,001 and $15,000
Bowling Green State University
California State Polytechnic
University—Pomona
Central Michigan University
Central Washington University
Colorado State University
Eastern Michigan University
Iowa State University
Northern Illinois University
State University of New York—
Purchase College
University of Arizona
University of Illinois—Chicago
University of Kansas
University of North Texas
University of Southern Maine
University of Texas—Austin
University of Utah
Washington State University

Between $15,001 and $20,000
Columbia College—Chicago
DePaul University
George Mason University
Indiana University
Michigan State University
Minnesota State University—Mankato
New College of Florida
Ohio State University
Ohio University
Oregon State University
Rutgers, The State University of
New Jersey—New Brunswick
Temple University
University of California—Los Angeles
University of California—San Diego
University of California—Santa Cruz
University of Colorado—Denver and
Health Sciences Center

University of Connecticut
University of Florida
University of Louisville
University of Maine
University of Minnesota—Duluth
University of Minnesota—Twin Cities
University of Missouri—Kansas City
University of North Carolina—Chapel Hill
University of Oregon
University of Rhode Island
University of Washington
University of Wisconsin—La Crosse
University of Wisconsin—Milwaukee

Between $20,001 and $25,000
Pennsylvania State University
Rochester Institute of Technology
Suffolk University
University of California—Berkeley
University of California—Davis
University of California—Riverside
University of Colorado—Boulder
University of Illinois—
Urbana-Champaign
University of Maryland
University of Vermont
University of Wisconsin—Madison

Between $25,001 and $30,000
American University
Antioch College
Bryn Mawr College
Case Western Reserve University
Ithaca College
Knox College
Lawrence University
Macalester College
Marlboro College
Stanford University
Syracuse University
Tufts University
University of Michigan
University of Puget Sound
Whitman College

Williams College

Between $30,001 and $35,000
Carleton College
Carnegie Mellon University
Colgate University
Cornell University
Dartmouth College
DePauw University
Duke University
Emory University
Grinnell College
Haverford College
Kalamazoo College
Massachusetts Institute of Technology
New York University
Northwestern University
Oberlin College
Princeton University
Sarah Lawrence College
Skidmore College
University of Pennsylvania
University of Southern California
Wellesley College

Over $35,000
Colby College
Middlebury College
Vassar College
Yale University

Note: Private institutions have only one tuition rate for both in-state and out-of-state students. As a result, the private institution tuition amounts are the same on both the in-state and out-of-state tuition listings.

TOOLS FOR MAKING YOUR LGBT CAMPUS CHOICE

Minding Your P's and Q's to Choose Your Perfect LGBT Campus

WHAT DO P'S and Q's have to do with determining the perfect LGBT campus for you? P's and Q's will help steer you in the right direction until you find what you're looking for.

PICTURE: Envision Yourself on Campus
It may sound silly, but there is a lot of truth to picturing what you want and making it happen. Step back for a moment and imagine yourself on your ideal campus. What does the campus look like? What kind of buildings, trees, and physical environment do you see? Think of yourself in classes, involved in campus life, or going out on the town. Take mental notes of what the campus looks like. Believe it or not, if you have an ideal place in your head, it might be the best fit for you. Don't give up, do your research, and try to find it!

PASSION: Find Your Passion
The secret to finding that perfect campus is understanding your passion. What makes you tick? This is true for anyone regardless of sexual orientation or gender identity or expression. Think hard about what you enjoy the most in life and what drives you. Do you like helping children or the elderly? Do you find math or science to be your calling? Or maybe your passion lies in artistic expression? There are so many people who are not doing what they truly love in life because they never searched for their passion early on or were not willing to take the necessary risks to pursue it. Of course, it's okay if you do not know your passion right off the bat or if it changes in college. But right now, dig deep inside and discover what you love most in life. It will help guide your actions to choose a campus where that passion can come alive.

QUESTIONS: Ask Plenty of Questions
Call the campus and speak to the various staff or faculty who are responsible for LGBT issues. When you visit the campus, plan to meet out students or attend LGBT functions where you can discuss openly your thoughts and concerns with other out members of the LGBT campus community. There is no such thing as a bad question, especially if it helps you make your decision.

PATIENCE: Be Patient
It may be a long process full of many challenges. As an LGBT student, you may be faced with some difficult or even awkward situations. Always listen to what is being said and be respectful, even if it is not what you want to hear. It is better to learn the truth about the campus now, than to have the wrong impression later. Plus, your goal is to find a campus where you can be queer in all aspects of your life. Remember, some students pick one campus and find what they want while others have to visit five campuses before they make up their mind. Take your time and plan ahead!

PREPARE: Be Prepared
Preparation can be the answer to tackling the bureaucracy of the college search. Learn the application deadlines, review financial aid procedures, and

plan a campus visit with plenty of time for visiting other campuses, too. The best route is to create a plan of action with a timeline for choosing your college or university. The plan will help make sure you are on task and don't forget something important. The college search can be easier if you're organized and efficient in your preparation.

PROBE: Learn about the Environment

Depending on where you live or where you grew up, this may not be as significant to you. Some of you may have been in conservative parts of the country all your life while others have been accustomed to more LGBT-progressive ways of thinking. Probe the local community and the campus community while on your campus visit or do an online search beforehand. Also consider the state where the campus resides. Many campuses are much more progressive and have stood out when compared to their area of the country. It's okay to choose a campus in a region where there are still many challenges politically and socially. Just remember this and the fact that you will be spending four or more years there.

QUIRKY and FUN: Have a Sense of Humor

A good sense of humor can break the ice and relieve stress along the way. LGBT life can be notoriously clique-oriented depending on the scene. Find out how much fun the campus life is for LGBT students. Are there plenty of LGBT social outlets and entertainment choices? Does the campus let its hair down now and then? Are there places to make friendships? Think about what you want and have a sense of humor getting there.

PRIORITIES: Don't Forget the Reason for College

Why do you go to college? Academics, of course. It can be addictive getting caught up in the process of choosing a campus and forgetting about the academic studies that the campus offers. If you're not interested in LGBT studies, you do not have to include this in your criteria. But, do remember to consider the academic standards, the job placement of graduates, and the faculty in choosing your perfect campus. Also, ask about the degree to which the academic world is LGBT-inclusive. Believe it or not, they sometimes operate on separate tracks and can be much different than the student life world. Oh, and don't forget to keep your grades up during the last couple of years in high school. It could determine whether or not you get an awesome scholarship!

PRIDE: Celebrate Who You Are

No matter how you choose to identify, envision yourself living happily on this campus. You want a place where you feel welcome, safe, and comfortable being who you are; where you can feel challenged academically and thrive holistically in the pursuit of bettering yourself. For some, this may mean discovering for the first time who they are. And, for others, this could be the opportunity to explore interests away from home. In both cases, your perfect campus should be a place where you are encouraged daily to be yourself and show pride in being queer. Look for that campus where you can celebrate who you are and be part of future progress.

Personal Campus Inventory Quiz

INSTRUCTIONS: Learn more about yourself and what you are looking for when picking the best LGBT campus. Utilize the worksheet as a preplanning step to answer key questions about what you desire. Then go on the search to find it!

• • • • • • • • • • • • • • • • • • • •

1. What do you identify as your passion or academic pursuits? What would be your dream job after college? Please describe.

2. Describe your ideal campus environment. What academic disciplines are offered? What is the campus community like? How does the campus look and feel? What does the visible commitment to LGBT students look like? Be as specific as possible.

3. What extracurricular activities interest you? Which of these involvement opportunities relate to or could relate to being LGBT? List all examples.

4. How much money do you want to spend per year going to a college or university? What's your overall budget for living expenses, books, and tuition?

5. In what region of the country do you want to go to college? Do you have limitations imposed by costs that are keeping you close to home?

6. What about the type of institution, the campus size, and the diversity? Do you prefer a private or a public institution? How large or small do you want the campus population to be?

LGBT-INCLUSIVE FACTORS IN CONSIDERING YOUR CAMPUS PRIORITIES

LGBT and Ally Student Groups	1	2	3	4	5
LGBT resource center/office	1	2	3	4	5
LGBT Social Activities	1	2	3	4	5
LGBT Educational Events	1	2	3	4	5
LGBT Studies/Courses	1	2	3	4	5
Nondiscrimination Policy Inclusive of Sexual Orientation	1	2	3	4	5
Nondiscrimination Policy Inclusive of Gender Identity or Expression	1	2	3	4	5
High Number of Out Faculty and Staff	1	2	3	4	5
High Number of Out LGBT Students	1	2	3	4	5
High Number of LGBT Allies Who Are Faculty and Staff	1	2	3	4	5
High Number of LGBT Allies Who Are Students	1	2	3	4	5
Visible LGBT Students of Color	1	2	3	4	5
Visible Trans-Identified Individuals	1	2	3	4	5
LGBT Student of Color Organization(s)	1	2	3	4	5
Safe Space/Safe Zone or Ally Training Program	1	2	3	4	5
LGBT-Sensitive Fraternities and Sororities	1	2	3	4	5
LGBT-Sensitive Religious and Spiritual Opportunities	1	2	3	4	5
LGBT-Sensitive Campus Police	1	2	3	4	5
LGBT-Sensitive Health Services	1	2	3	4	5
Gender-Neutral Bathrooms	1	2	3	4	5
LGBT Student Scholarship Opportunities	1	2	3	4	5
Support Services for Transitioning from M to F & F to M	1	2	3	4	5
LGBT Dating Options	1	2	3	4	5
LGBT Dance Clubs/Bars	1	2	3	4	5

Please determine where the following LGBT-inclusive factors rank to determine what's important in choosing your best fit for an LGBT college/university. Ask yourself the question: How important is it to have _____ on my future campus? Use these responses to prioritize your interests and figure out your top campus choices. Compare this to the Gay Point Average ranking and to what you look for on your campus visit.

LGBT FACTORS:

5   Most Important

4   Very Important

3   Important

2   Relatively Important

1   Not Important

Individual Action Plan
for LGBT College Seeker

INSTRUCTIONS: An action plan for an LGBT college seeker comprises many of the same aspects as it does for other prospective college students. However, there are certain LGBT considerations to keep in mind. Please complete the planning worksheet based on the considerations and priorities from your Personal Campus Inventory Quiz. The result will be a list of deadlines with an action plan that you can use to keep on track during your quest as an LGBT college seeker.

1. Overall Approach

Describe your overall approach to choosing a college or university based on the responses from your Personal Campus Inventory Quiz. What are your needs and priorities? These can be LGBT-specific or more broadly oriented to your self-identity.

2. Identify Your Top Five LGBT Campus Choices

Limit yourself to no more than five top choices. Any more than five potentially dilutes your ability to research each and apply yourself fully.

Name of College/University: _____

Particular Reason(s) for Selecting This Campus:

Application Deadline:
Application Requirements:
Testing Requirements:
Possible Dates for Campus Visit:

Name of College/University: _____

Particular Reason(s) for Selecting This Campus:

Application Deadline:
Application Requirements:
Testing Requirements:
Possible Dates for Campus Visit:

Name of College/University: _____

Particular Reason(s) for Selecting This Campus:

Application Deadline:
Application Requirements:
Testing Requirements:
Possible Dates for Campus Visit:

Name of College/University: _____

Particular Reason(s) for Selecting This Campus:

Application Deadline:

Application Requirements:

Testing Requirements:

Possible Dates for Campus Visit:

Name of College/University: _____

Particular Reason(s) for Selecting This Campus:

Application Deadline:

Application Requirements:

Testing Requirements:

Possible Dates for Campus Visit:

3. Determine the most significant LGBT-inclusive factors that you want to learn more about in order to compare your top campus choices. These can be from the Personal Campus Inventory Quiz or other factors you have determined. *e.g., high number of LGBT students, LGBT sensitive health services, LGBT social events, etcetera.*

4. Describe any challenge(s) that you might face in researching the LGBT-friendliness of these selected campuses. Please create a list of these concerns.

5. List resources, people, and/or organizations that can help you overcome any challenges or assist in learning more about your final LGBT campus choice.

The Campus Visit Scorecard for LGBT Students and Their Parents/Family Members

The time has come for the ultimate test—the campus visit. It's time to discover for yourself just how LGBT-friendly and progressive your top campus choices are. Whether or not your campus is listed in this book, you must still put the campus through your own personal test and ask all your questions. To make your campus visit easier, you can easily grade and compare campuses with this nifty LGBT-friendly scorecard. Simply be sure to collect the necessary information during the campus visit to completely answer the questions. Then after all your campus visits, you can tally up your scorecards and see what campus ends up on top.

Fill-in the * with five of your LGBT-friendly questions to look for on campus. Decide what's most important to ask for your perfect campus choice to measure up. Such questions might include the following:

• Visible LGBT students of color?
• Visible trans-identified individuals?
• LGBT student of color organizations?
• LGBT-sensitive fraternities and sororities?
• LGBT-sensitive religious and spiritual organizations?
• M to F and F to M support services for trans students?

NAME OF COLLEGE/UNIVERSITY:	✔ YES
1. High number of out LGBT students?	
2. High number of out LGBT faculty/staff?	
3. High number of visible LGBT allies?	
4. Significant number of LGBT social events?	
5. Significant number of LGBT educational events?	
6. Visible signs/symbols of LGBT support on campus?	
7. LGBT and ally student organization?	
8. LGBT resource center/office funded by campus?	
9. LGBT Pride Week/Coming Out Week?	
10. Variety of LGBT studies/courses?	
11. Safe Zone/Safe Space or Ally Program?	
12. LGBT student scholarships available?	
13. Nondiscrimination policy inclusive of sexual orientation?	
14. Nondiscrimination policy inclusive of gender identity/expression?	
15. Same-sex domestic partner benefits available?	
16. LGBT-inclusive housing options/themes?	
17. LGBT-inclusive health services/testing?	
18. LGBT-inclusive counseling/support groups?	
19. Procedure for reporting LGBT bias, harassment, and hate crimes?	
20. First-Year experience/orientation program inclusive of LGBT issues?	
21. *	
22.. *	
23. *	
24. *	
25. *	

SCORING RESULTS

Once you've finished, it's time to score. Tally up the number of Yes responses and learn the results of your campus visit.

19+ Yes responses:
Most LGBT-friendly campus; definitely a worthy contender.

10–18 Yes responses:
More than likely LGBT-friendly or at least on the path to being LGBT-friendly, but has apparent areas for improvement; still worthy of further consideration.

1–9 Yes responses:
Lacks LGBT-friendly criteria and warrants more research before consideration.

FRIENDLY REMINDER:

Here are some "Not So Queer" questions to ask:
- Learn more about the application process and deadlines. Is an essay or interview necessary?
- Are there testing requirements, such as ACT/SAT?
- Find out about financial aid processes and deadlines.

FINAL QUEER TIP:

Choose if and how you want to come out as LGBT. Some students may want to do this in the application process in response to the essay question, or during the campus visit. Keep in mind that you never know if the individual(s) involved with these processes are LGBT-friendly. But, if that is a concern or becomes an issue, you may want to think twice about going there anyway. It's always your choice!

ADVICE FOR INCOMING
LGBT COLLEGE STUDENTS

How to Come Out on Campus

Debbie Bazarsky and Allison Subasic

THINKING ABOUT COMING out in college? Did you come out in high school and are wondering what being openly LGBT in college is like? Many students arrive to campus already out. However, being in a new community, there is a first-time coming out process to roommates, classmates, faculty, and friends. Other students specifically wait until they leave for college to come out of the closet or even begin to question their sexual orientation. The following are some things to think about as you are choosing whether or not to come out at your college or university.

Coming Out as a Process

Coming out is a personal journey. For most of us, it is something that happens over and over again, as you meet new people or move to new places. It is also a process that happens gradually. First, you might come out to yourself, tell a friend or family member, and over time, you become more and more comfortable telling others. For some, this process may take a semester or even years. Questioning your sexuality and coming out need to be done on your terms and happen when you are ready.

Coming Out in College

Universities and colleges are vibrant and exciting places to come out. There are often many resources available, and people to support you. The vast majority of schools have LGBT student organizations, coming out resources, and safe and confidential people for you to talk with about your feelings and experiences. Some campuses may not have LGBT-specific support services, especially religious institutions that may have objections to "homosexuality." When choosing a school to attend, you might want to keep this in mind and search for a campus with LGBT resources—like the ones listed in this guidebook.

Things to Look For When Coming Out:

1. Look for a safe person with whom you can talk. This can be a resident assistant, staff, faculty member, or friend. Some campuses have LGBT peer educators or mentorship programs with students who can speak one-on-one with you about coming out issues and resources.

2. If your school has an Ally or Safe Space/Zone program, an easy way to identify who participates is by the official sign on their door or button they may be wearing. Also, some staff and faculty may display small signs or symbols, such as rainbow flags or gay and lesbian books, in their office to convey that they are supportive people with whom you can talk.

3. A great place to go, if you are really struggling with coming out or having concerns with relationships or family members, is the counseling center on your campus. Many also run coming-out support and discussion groups for the LGBT community. These groups are an excellent place to explore many of the questions you may have. Plus, you can meet other students who are also in the process of coming out.

4. Check out the LGBT student organizations and/or LGBT center on your college campus. They are often able to offer support, and this can also be a great way to become involved on campus. Some schools and their surrounding communities have LGBT groups beyond the primary undergraduate or graduate organizations—LGBT religious groups (such as LGBT Jews), LGBT racial and ethnic organizations (such as Queer Chicanas, or QPOC—Queer People of Color), transgender and bi groups, or LGBT groups by academic profession (such as OutLaw). If your campus does not have the type of group you are looking for, there are often wonderful online community groups and chat rooms as well.

5. Look online for a variety of resources about coming out and for ways to address your specific campus. Some schools sponsor LGBT chat rooms, or many students use Facebook.com to connect with other LGBT students on their respective campuses. Another worthwhile source for coming out support online is the Human Rights Campaign's National Coming Out Project (www.hrc.org/comingout) and Parents, Families and Friends of Lesbians and Gays (www.pflag.org).

6. Don't underestimate books. Most LGBT centers have a wide selection of books and magazines. Your school library and local book store will also have an LGBT section with books about coming out and a variety of topics about sexual identity. There is also a whole host of LGBT magazines that cover social and political topics, which you might find interesting and helpful.

Choosing a Campus Where You Can Come Out

There are resources on most campuses for LGBT students, certainly the ones listed in this guidebook. Before you choose a campus, check out its Website to get a taste of LGBT life and whether you might feel comfortable coming out at that school. When visiting the campus, if comfortable, ask about people's experiences with LGBT students to get a better sense of what your new home may feel like. If you are not comfortable asking people, then research online and look for indicators. Type in words, such as "lesbian, gay, bisexual, transgender, queer" in the campus search engine and see what comes up. Find out the name of the primary LGBT student organization and check out their Website to see what the group is all about and if they have any coming out support groups/ resources. Every school uses different acronyms and words to describe the LGBT community, so try more than just "gay and lesbian" when doing a search.

Remember on your campus visit to look for visible signals that may show support for coming out. Are there any Safe Space/Zone or Ally stickers up on office doors? Are there LGBT support groups offered in the counseling center or LGBT center? What, if any, posters are around campus advertising LGBT events? Are LGBT options included in the campus visit or outlined in future orientation/welcome week activities? Again, the easiest thing to do is ask around, but looking for visual cues can be another useful way to find out about LGBT support on campus. If your potential campus has an LGBT center, give the staff a call to set up a visit, or better yet, just drop by. They can tell you what the campus climate is like, share coming out resources and/or introduce you to other LGBT students.

Coming out for some is easy and for others it is often challenging, with obstacles to overcome. There is no one way to come out, and there certainly is no right way or wrong way. Everybody's process is different, so take your time and do what is most comfortable for you. Most important, find at least one individual on campus who can support you. Someone from the Ally or Safe

Space/Zone program, a counselor, a friend…and, even more important, remember you are not alone. Enjoy this exciting new time in your life and make the most of your college experience as an "out" student.

Debbie Bazarsky *is director of the LGBT Center at Princeton University. She was previously the LGBT Resource Center coordinator at the University of California, Santa Barbara. She serves on the board and youth advisory council for National Conference for Community and Justice—NJ and co-directs their summer camp for multicultural education.*

Allison Subasic *is currently the LGBTA Student Resource Center director at the Pennsylvania State University. Previously, she coordinated of the LGBT Resource Center at the University of California, Davis. Allison has been a member of the National Consortium of Directors of LGBT Resources in Higher Education since its founding in 1997.*

Suggestions for LGBT Students of Color

Andrea "Dre" Domingue and Gwendolyn Alden Dean

MANY LGBT COMMUNITIES of color are flourishing across the United States in local communities and college campuses. Nevertheless, as LGBT students of color, we often encounter campuses that do not support us holistically as complex individuals with multiple identity groups. We are often pressured to choose between our race or ethnicity and our sexual orientation or gender identity/expression. We must do so for either our entire undergraduate career, through or for every event, program, group, political action, and the list goes on.

Typically, LGBT students of color experience the racism of both the mainstream white community and the racism of white members of the LGBT community. We also experience the heterosexism of the mainstream straight community and the LGBT prejudice of straight members of communities of color. LGBT students of color have even less visibility than their white counterparts. As a result, we are often rendered invisible within the very communities we look to for support and recognition. Such can be the truth of campus life for many LGBT students of color. Campuses must recognize these needs outright in creating a place for everyone.

Here are important suggestions to help us find a supportive college or university, for coping cope with a less than ideal environment, and for strategies to improve the campus climate for the future.

Choosing a College or University That Supports LGBT Students of Color

IDENTIFY AVAILABLE RESOURCES   Much of this information can be found on the campus Website or discovered on your campus visit. Look for and ask about everything: student group(s) for LGBT people of color; multicultural center(s); ethnic studies programs; multicultural living-learning program(s); organization(s) for alumni/ae of color; diversity advisers in various departments; training programs or organizations for white allies; and a campuswide diversity council, task force, or presidential advisory group.

FIND A GROUP FOR LGBT STUDENTS OF COLOR   Since names vary widely among LGBT of color student groups and often don't explain the group's purpose, finding an organization may be challenging. Examples of LGBT student of color groups are Queer Students of Color Alliance (Q-SOCA), Young Queers United for Empowerment (Y Que), LLEGO, Mosaic, Colors of Pride, and Shades. Many campuses in this guidebook are indicated as having groups specifically for LGBT students of color. In addition, communities of color may use terms other than lesbian, gay, bisexual, queer, and transgender to describe themselves. For example, Same Gender Loving (SGL) is a term originating in the African American community that describes individuals who are attracted to individuals of the same gender. Some people who prefer this term may feel that terms such as gay, lesbian, bisexual, and queer are Eurocentric terms that do not historically represent communities of color. Two Spirit is an American Indian/First Nation term for people who blend traditionally polar gender identities. It was used historically to describe individuals who crossed gender boundaries and were accepted by American Indian/First Nation cultures. It is used today by some transgender and sometimes gay, lesbian, and bisexual American Indians to describe themselves.[1]

If a school doesn't have a group for LGBT students of color, check to see if another local institution has an LGBT student of color group. Some campuses allow other nonaffiliated students and community members to attend group meetings or events. Once you find a group in your community, ask if you can participate.

EVALUATE THE COLLEGE STATEMENT ON DIVERSITY   Look at how the campus envisions "diversity" and what aspects of diversity are included in the statement. Typically, this information is located on the campus admissions Website along with a list of resources available that relate to diversity.

ASK QUESTIONS   When you've determined which resources are available at a given campus, e-mail or telephone to ask some of the following questions: What kind of programs and resources are there for LGBT students of color; for educating white students about antiracism; and for educating straight students of color about antiheterosexism? What is your understanding of the needs of LGBT students of color and the campus climate for LGBT students of color? How does the LGBT center/adviser/group collaborate with the multicultural center(s)/adviser(s)/group(s) and vice versa? Are there local resources for LGBT people of color? Are there LGBT students of color I could contact to discuss these issues?

TALK TO CURRENT LGBT STUDENTS OF COLOR   Some LGBT students of color feel strongly that if a campus has a healthy LGBT person of color community, then a prospective student should be able to get in contact with an LGBT student of color. If you have an opportunity to discuss campus climate with one or more current LGBT students of color, this will be your best source of information about what you can expect at that particular campus. Crucial questions include: What have your personal experiences been as an LGBT person of color? Do you think your experience is representative of others? How do you meet LGBT students of color? If an LGBT student of color group exists, ask about the group's membership, activities, goals, and mission. If an LGBT of color group doesn't exist, ask why not and if there has ever been any effort to form one.

Thriving as an LGBT Student of Color at Your Chosen College or University

TAKE GOOD CARE OF YOURSELF   While creating an inclusive campus community is vital to the success of LGBT students of color, you do not need to hold the burden on your shoulders. Usually only a few individuals, typically LGBT students of color themselves, take responsibility for creating an environment inclusive of LGBT students of color. While some students are eager to take on leadership roles to help improve their campus climate, this is a personal choice, not an obligation. It is important to remember to think about your individual needs and what you can do to take care of yourself during your college years.

BUILD A SUPPORT NETWORK   To establish a means of support for yourself, connect with LGBT students, faculty, and staff of color. It is important to find a safe space where you can talk about your experiences and interact with others who share your identity. In addition to social and emotional benefits, these individuals are vital links to LGBT people of color resources on campus and locally in your community. Also, consider technology as a means for meeting others, through such resources as listservs, discussion forums, and e-communities (e.g., Facebook, Friendster, etcetera). Also, be sure to identify white allies on campus who will not only advocate for LGBT student of color concerns but also be people with whom you can share openly without feeling pressure to educate someone on racism and heterosexism.

CHANGE THE CAMPUS CLIMATE   Strategies LGBT students of color and their allies can use to make a campus more inclusive include: advocating for LGBT-focused programming in multicultural offices/groups; supporting multicultural programming among LGBT offices/groups; collaborating with local LGBT of color organizations through campus programming; working with student affairs professionals to incorporate antiracist and antiheterosexist themes in student staff and leadership trainings; offering continual dialogue on the intersection of multiple identities with peers or within student activities; becoming a campus leader; establishing an LGBT student, faculty, and staff of color support network; and creating a webpage or print resource to welcome incoming LGBT students of color.

LGBT students of color present wonderful opportunities for a progressive dialogue and experience on campus. But, the campus needs to take ownership in fostering an inclusive climate for these students. We still have a long way to go in defeating racism and heterosexism both on campus and within society at large. Nevertheless, resources and support for LGBT students of color has increased substantially in the last few years. More and more administrators and student services staff are cognizant of and concerned about the needs of LGBT students of color. Awareness has also increased among white LGBT students and straight students of color as well. The key to handling the complex challenges of multiple marginalizations is to identify and utilize appropriate resources as well as prioritize self-care and your personal well-being. This approach can help you, as an LGBT student of color, make the most out of your college experience.

Notes:

1. Beemyn, Brett Genny. 2005. "Transgender Terminology." http://multiculturalcenter. osu.edu/posts/documents/115_2.pdf, accessed December 15, 2005.

Andrea "Dre" Domingue *is the program adviser for New York University's Office of LGBT Student Services. She earned her M.A. in higher education administration from NYU in 2005. She also serves as an executive board member for the National Consortium of LGBT Directors in Higher Education.*

Gwendolyn Alden Dean *is the coordinator of the LGBT Resource Center at Cornell University. She is a past chair of the National Consortium of Directors of LGBT Resources in Higher Education and hopes that if she works very hard, she'll make her job obsolete.*

The Out Student Leader's Agenda

Greg Varnum and Chad Grandy

OPPONENTS OF LGBT civil rights have always said that LGBT people have an agenda. And we do: it's an agenda of equality for everyone—regardless of gender/identity expression or sexual orientation. But, as an LGBT student on campus, what is your agenda as an LGBT leader? A leader, regardless of who he or she is, must have a vision and a plan to make that vision a reality. So an agenda is a necessary tool for any leader. Remember that there is no one agenda that best applies to everyone; it's up to you to write your agenda as a leader on campus. This resource will help you get started.

Writing Your Agenda

LOOK AT YOURSELF   Before you can truly excel at helping others, you have to be sure that you're able to help yourself. Consider looking at what type of leadership style works best for you. Ask yourself if you are having fun, and if not, why? You should be enjoying yourself and getting the most out of your leadership experience.

BE PASSIONATE   Think about what matters most to you, and what issues and ideas really drive you. If you're passionate about what you're doing, not only will you produce greater results yourself, but your passion will be contagious and inspire others.

EDUCATE YOURSELF   What does your local community really need? Talk to people and find out what's been done already, whether it was successful, and what should be done next. Take the time to understand the climate, politically and socially, both in the local community and at your college. Be sure you understand all sides of an issue, including the historical side. You'll be able to plan better if you understand better. No one is ever criticized for knowing too much about something they're advocating for.

BE REALISTIC   Some things may not be timely, the most effective next step, or something you can effectively work on given the time you have to give. Remember that as a student, you'll only be on campus for four or five (or in some cases ten) years. That shouldn't stop you from doing something, but it should impact how you plan. Figure out how you can involve other students who will continue the work after you leave. Also be on the lookout for faculty and staff who are passionate about these issues and make sure to involve them for a greater impact.

CONSIDER ALL OF THE ISSUES   Passion is important, but so is acknowledging the greater good. True equality means equal rights for everyone, not just you and those like you. You'll sound hypocritical if you ignore the oppression of other people and fail to help them in their time of need. Plus, it will only help you, if others succeed, as they'll be more apt to do the same for your cause.

Suggested Agenda Items

1. ESTABLISH STRATEGIC ALLIANCES AND COMMUNICATION WITH ADMINISTRATION   If you have an open dialogue with your college's admini-stration and allies in strategic places, it helps a great deal with getting the right information, with specific objectives, to the right people. Taking the time to

build these relationships and strengthening them is well worth it. Make sure they are receiving thorough and accurate information from everyone. Ignoring an obvious problem or presenting misleading or inaccurate information only hurts your credibility and hinders progress. It's better to be patient—not to be confused with complacent—and honest rather than forceful and deceiving.

2. ENSURE POLICIES OFFER PROTECTIONS AGAINST DISCRIMINATION   Without inclusive LGBT policies in place, statements of support from the college are just talk. The administration and staff may have good intentions, but it will be hard for them to enforce their statements without policies to back them up. Review your college's current policies. Does housing have accommodations for trans-gender students? Would students with same-sex partners get the same treat-ment as legally married students if their partner's health required them to miss an exam?

Policies help create a climate where the message is clear—discrimination is *never* okay. Be sure that they include the words "sexual orientation" and "gender identity or expression." Also consider what other populations are excluded. Working strategically with other campus and local community groups can help. Utilize the communication with your administration and strategic allies to determine who has the final say on writing these policies, and strategize how to get them updated.

3. DEVELOP EFFECTIVE TRAINING OPPORTUNITIES FOR FACULTY/STAFF/STUDENTS   Work with your administration to enforce mandatory diversity training—such as an Ally or Safe Space/Zone program for faculty and staff (including student staff)—that includes information on sexual orientation and gender identity and expression. Consider what areas might need specific training. Is the housing staff trained on how to handle homophobia, biphobia, or transphobia? Are admissions counselors able to answer potential LGBT students' questions? Does the police force know how to handle same-sex domestic abuse? Are health officials trained on lesbian or transgender health issues? Consider making similar trainings available for students; after all, they make up the largest population at your college and can help to convince others that the training is necessary.

4. CREATE FINANCIAL AID RESOURCES FOR LGBT STUDENTS   LGBT students are more likely to be in need of financial assistance. Some may no longer have contact with their parents or guardians and as a result face challenges applying for financial aid. Others may have faced discrimination in the workplace, and with no legal retribution available to them, now face a financial shortfall. Consider what can be done at your college to offer scholarships or other financial assistance specifically to LGBT students in need.

5. EXTEND DOMESTIC PARTNERSHIP BENEFITS   Without these benefits, many LGBT people are unable to provide basic health care for their families. That makes them less interested in working for your college and sends them looking elsewhere. Not only does this impede the college's ability to recruit the best faculty and staff possible, it also decreases the number of positive LGBT role models and mentors on campus to work with LGBT students. Consider looking at whether these benefits extend to students as well. Does a student's opposite-sex partner get treated the same way as a same-gender student's partner on campus? If a same-gender couple receives a discount to a college facility or event, then so should an opposite-sex couple.

Regardless of what you decide to undertake as your personal agenda, one thing is for sure: you're choosing to get involved during one of the most revolutionary times of the modern LGBT rights movement. Your generation will no doubt extend true equality to LGBT people. Be proud of your out student leader agenda and share your vision to inspire others. Most certainly know that you will make an impact in someone's life, some way, somehow. By so doing, you bring all of us one step closer to true equality. Good luck, and remember, have fun!

Chad Grandy *is a Triangle Foundation trustee and Youth Committee chair. He has worked successfully on campus, local, state, and national LGBT issues.*

Greg Varnum *is executive assistant and youth initiatives coordinator at Triangle Foundation. He is a national presenter on LGBT youth topics and has worked extensively on campus LGBT issues.*

Triangle Foundation *is Michigan's statewide civil rights, advocacy, and antiviolence organization serving the gay, lesbian, bisexual, transgender, and allied communities. For more information visit us online: www.tri.org.*

10 Steps for Planning LGBT Events

Regina Young Hyatt, M.S., Ed.

ONE OF THE WAYS LGBT students find success on campus is by involvement with LGBT student organizations. These organizations have a number of purposes: to help LGBT students interact with one another socially; to bring education and awareness about LGBT concerns to campus; or to get students involved actively in politics. Almost all student organizations use campuswide events and activities as a way to meet these goals. It is important as a leader to be able to plan the best LGBT events to garner active participation, no matter what the need or concern. The following are ten tips on how to plan a successful event, as well as suggested ideas for spreading the word. Completing these steps will ensure your LGBT efforts are the most successful possible.

1. THE BIG IDEA   Every event starts with an idea, concept, or brainstorm. Get your group together to discuss ways it wants to reach out to the campus community, educate, and/or entertain. Many minds together are more creative than one, so together actively brainstorm ideas for events and activities. Once you have your idea in place, think about the goals for the program. Is your purpose to educate, to entertain, to provide a social opportunity for LGBT students, to bring about political awareness of LGBT issues, or a combination of several of these things? Your goals will guide how you ultimately move forward!

2. WORKING WITH YOUR ADVISER   Talk with your adviser about your idea to get his or her feedback. An adviser can share with you any potential obstacles as well as the best way to make your idea a success. If you don't have an adviser, go to the student activities office or multicultural resource center for support and guidance.

3. GETTING OUTSIDE HELP   Contact the speaker, agency, disc jockey, movie company, or whatever outside person or persons you may need to have your event. If you are having a speaker, call and see if he or she is available to come to campus and do the talk, and find out what the logistics are and how much he or she will charge. Your adviser may have to do this step in case a contract for payment is required. But investigate your choices, rather than reinvent the wheel or waste your time if it is not possible due to budget, time, or availability.

4. IT'S ALL IN THE DETAILS   You've got your idea and your event goal(s), now comes the down and dirty part! The details. Choose a date, time, and place that you think will best serve the audience you are reaching out to. Then make a reservation for the space. If you don't know how to do this, go to your student activities or student affairs office and ask someone. Decide if you need any technical equipment for the event before you make your reservation. If you are having a speaker, reserve a podium, microphone, etcetera. Decide on the set up of the room—do you want the chairs in a large circle or classroom style with tables and chairs? The atmosphere you create with your event can be a significant component to the quality and mood of the event.

5. USE AN EVENT COMMITTEE   A true team works together. So involve your committee in the planning and execution of the event. Order food, prizes, and giveaways well in advance. These are wonderful tasks to delegate to other

members of the group to help everyone feel like they have contributed to the success of the event. Go ahead and create your programs and an event evaluation form in advance, too. Don't forget to arrange volunteers to work before, during, and after the event by passing out flyers, setting up the space, taking tickets, serving as ushers, or picking up and/or dropping off the speaker or entertainer.

6. PUBLICITY 101   Now for the fun part—publicity. This is the most critical part of creating a worthwhile event that students will remember. The next set of tips will give you some specific ideas on how to promote your queer event. Just understand, the early bird gets the worm, so start early spreading the word about your event. Be creative with your flyers and posters. Everyone is used to seeing 8 1/2 by 11 flyers around campus; consider making your flyers stand out by cutting them into a shape. Triangle anyone? Or make it a bright color or bigger in size. Use your organization's logo on every piece of publicity that goes out. The flyers, posters, invitations, Website, and e-mail should have your logo. Consistency is important; so be sure to include the date, time, place, event title, and short event description on every piece of publicity.

7. ONE DAY TO GO   If you are bringing in someone from outside campus, contact the entertainer, agent, or movie company the day before the event to be sure everything is in order. This will ensure that you prevent any unnecessary problems caused by misinformation or lack of communication. Also, remember that fellow students have busy schedules, so they may forget your publicity efforts from a week ago. Do a last minute publicity blitz with small flyers and sidewalk chalk.

8. IT'S SHOW TIME   On the day of the event, make sure the room is set up properly and your volunteers are reminded when to be there. Practice your introduction or welcome speech before you go in front of the group. Add some special touches to the room with decorations or fun posters. Everyone likes a festive look!

9. FUN! FUN! FUN   Have fun! You have done all this work; be sure to enjoy and remember the event. Acknowledge the work of your fellow committee members. You have created something special and should feel proud. Sit back and enjoy the feeling of success.

10. EVALUATE FOR IMPROVEMENT   After the event is over, pass out a short evaluation form to all participants to get their feedback. At the next meeting of your group, take time to get feedback from group members as well. Be sure to write everything down and pass it on to the next person who may be planning an LGBT event. Feedback guarantees future improvement and success.

Regina Young Hyatt, M.S., Ed., *is the director of student life at the University of South Florida—St. Petersburg. She was formerly associate director of student activities at the University of North Carolina—Charlotte. Regina serves on the board of directors of the National Association for Campus Activities and has published several articles in their* Programming *magazine.*

ADVICE FOR CAMPUS OFFICIALS
TO IMPROVE LGBT EFFORTS

10 Academic Strategies for a More Inclusive LGBT Classroom

Saralyn Chesnut, Ph.D., and Angela C. Nichols, M.S., Ed.

OFTEN, WHEN CONSIDERING options to improve a campus climate for LGBT students, the focus is on what happens outside the classroom—having active LGBT student organizations, making sure residence halls and public spaces are safe and welcoming, offering LGBT-specific co-curricular events and programs, and educating staff and administrators about the needs and concerns of LGBT students. However, on a college or university campus what happens in the classroom often carries more weight than anything else. LGBT students can feel strongly validated, or have their existence further marginalized. This all depends on how LGBT-inclusive the course and the professors are in teaching the subject matter. The following resource offers ten strategies for creating LGBT-inclusive classrooms; they range from simple suggestions that individual faculty members can pursue, to measures that require a significant commitment on behalf of faculty and administrators.

LGBT Strategies for Individual Faculty Members

1. INCLUSIVE LANGUAGE AND EXAMPLES   Always assume that there is at least one LGBT student in every class. Use language that reflects that assumption; for example, use gender-neutral pronouns, and terms like "partner" instead of "wife" or "husband" or even "spouse." When you use examples to illustrate a point, avoid using examples that are exclusively drawn from the heterosexual world, and throw in a specifically LGBT one from time to time.

2. ADDRESS DEROGATORY COMMENTS   Decide ahead of time how you will handle off-hand or off-topic derogatory comments about LGBT people made by students in your classes. Do not just let them go unchallenged. You might simply remind your students that there are likely to be LGBT students in each class they're in, and make clear that in your classroom, you expect people to respect one another despite differences of race, gender, religion, nationality, sexual orientation, gender identity/expression, etcetera.

3. ESTABLISH GROUND RULES FOR DIALOGUE   Carefully prepare each class for difficult discussions, especially in courses in which LGBT issues are on the syllabus (e.g., a religion course that will include material about what the Bible does/does not say about "homosexuality"). The intent is not to stifle speech or the free expression of (informed) opinions, but to create an atmosphere in which everyone's personhood will be respected. Before any discussion takes place, establish ground rules that will ensure this, and during discussions, enforce the ground rules.

4. INCORPORATE SPECIFIC CONTENT INTO CURRICULUM   Incorporate LGBT content into your courses whenever possible. For example, a course on social movements would include the LGBT rights movement; a literature course in which Walt Whitman is read would include mention of Whitman's sexual orientation; a course on feminist theory would include lesbian feminist theory; and so on.

5. LEARN MORE AND INVOLVE YOURSELF   To prepare yourself, take advantage of opportunities your campus provides to learn more about LGBT people, as well as about LGBT/queer studies. Seek opportunities to develop your knowledge of the contributions of LGBT/queer studies scholars in your discipline. If your campus has a Safe Space/Zone or Ally program, participate in it. Attend LGBT events, and get to know LGBT students on a one on one basis.

LGBT Strategies for Faculty Groups and Administrators

Underlying these suggested strategies is the assumption that in order to equip both faculty and administrators to create LGBT-inclusive classrooms, a campus must commit resources to the LGBT academic experience. Campus administrators should seek ways to make available the knowledge, theories, and insights developed by scholars in the burgeoning, interdisciplinary field of LGBT/queer studies. As faculty and administrators develop knowledge in this area of inquiry, they will be better informed for LGBT inclusion efforts. Specifically, faculty can gain knowledge that will enable them to incorporate LGBT content into courses they are already teaching.

6. DEVELOP BROWN-BAG LUNCH DISCUSSIONS   Hold a series of brown-bag lunch discussions on topics in LGBT/queer studies, where interested faculty, staff, and students can come together to read and comment on each other's work, or read and discuss a book or article, in LGBT/queer studies.

7. ENCOURAGE AND RECOGNIZE OUTSTANDING WORK   Offer prizes for outstanding student work in LGBT/queer studies topics, on both the graduate and undergraduate levels if possible. This will encourage student work in LGBT/queer studies and increase the visibility of LGBT students and pursuit of scholarship. Publicize the awards extensively, including ads in student and faculty/staff campus newspapers. The work eligible for a prize should include papers written for courses at the institution, papers presented at conferences, and chapters of dissertations and theses. A faculty committee can evaluate the work and select the graduate and undergraduate winners. Ideally, the awards will be presented at a public event by a top-level administrator.

8. PLAN ANNUAL EVENTS FOR ACADEMIC LEARNING   Go one step beyond a brown-bag lunch series by establishing a lecture series in LGBT/queer studies: Each year, bring to campus several scholars in LGBT/queer studies to give formal lectures, offer colloquia, and meet informally with interested faculty. Funding can come from academic departments as well as potentially from student groups. A committee made up of faculty, relevant staff, and students could meet regularly to plan and publicize the specific lectures and other topical events.

9. CREATE ONGOING DEVELOPMENT SEMINAR FOR FACULTY   To go even further with the goal of preparing faculty to include LGBT content in non-LGBT studies courses, offer a faculty development seminar that would meet over the course of a semester or even a year. The seminar could be taught by a faculty member who has expertise in the field of LGBT/queer studies, or by a visiting professor or series of professors, brought to campus for just this purpose.

10. BUILD AND INSTITUTIONALIZE COURSE OFFERINGS   Offer as many courses as possible specifically in LGBT/queer studies. The courses may initially be taught by existing faculty and teaching assistants with some expertise in an area of LGBT/queer studies. Once a number of courses are being offered, and student

interest has been documented, departments that are hiring can be urged to consider hiring someone with a specialty in LGBT/queer studies; for example, an English department might look for someone with a specialty in queer literature or queer theory.

Saralyn Chesnut, Ph.D., *is director of the Office of LGBT Life and adjunct assistant professor of Women's Studies and American Studies at Emory University in Atlanta, Georgia. She received her Ph.D. in liberal arts from Emory, and regularly teaches courses in LGBT studies, focusing on LGBT identities and politics in twentieth-century America.*

Angela C. Nichols, M.S., Ed., *is the LGBT services director at the University of Minnesota—Duluth (UMD). She holds her M.S. in Education, with a concentration in college student personnel. She is the founding director of the UMD LGBT Office and has been there since August 2000.*

8 Steps to Improve Campus Housing for LGBT Students

Kaaren M. Williamsen-Garvey and Steve Wisener

WHERE ONE LIVES is among the biggest areas of concern for LGBT college and university students. The basic need for safety and security in student housing is particularly intense for LGBT students. Because of the vast diversity in the LGBT student community, it can be tricky for those who oversee campus housing to address the myriad concerns and needs from LGBT students. The following list of eight steps provides practical guidance to help you begin to improve or reevaluate your campus housing for LGBT students.

1. HOUSING STAFF   The foundation for any good housing program is its staff. From front line student staff to the people in the central office who make the decisions, these people have direct impact on the overall climate for LGBT students living in campus housing. Because of this, it's imperative that you are intentional in your recruiting, hiring, and training to ensure that staff at all levels are willing and able to deal with issues of sexual orientation and gender identity/expression.

When recruiting and hiring staff, it is important to make an effort to have a staff that consists of visible role models for all of your student populations, including LGBT students. To be able to do this effectively, you must have an open and accepting LGBT climate in your housing department so that these potential staff members want to work for you and can be comfortable being out on the job.

There should be significant training that addresses the needs of LGBT students and the available resources in and around your community. Staff need to be comfortable with the issues surrounding LGBT students before such students move into their buildings and onto their floors. Ongoing training that focuses on issues such as coming out, heterosexism and homophobia, gender diversity, and current social and legal issues, also helps to keep your staff up-to-date with LGBT concerns. This also sends a message that you are serious about your support for LGBT students.

Nevertheless, you should also work to make sure that live-in graduate and professional LGBT staff have the same rights and domestic partner benefits (including health coverage for a partner, allowing a partner to live with them, and allowing a partner to be on the meal plan) that straight employees have access to and are allowed for their loved ones. Having visible same-sex couples who are on staff is just one more way to role model to all of your students.

2. HOUSING POLICIES   Housing policies should include clear language that communicates to LGBT students that their needs can and will be addressed by your staff. LGBT students need to know that if they have issues surrounding their identity, it's okay to talk to housing staff and that there are policies and procedures in place to address those needs. These policies should be clearly published in all of your publications so that a student never has to wonder if they exist. Examples of such policies that are often LGBT applicable include changing roommates, requesting single rooms, and how to get a housing requirement exemption if appropriate campus housing is not available.

A noteworthy caution in writing policies that address LGBT students' needs is finding the balance between having good policies that address the needs, but also flexible enough policies to allow for the diversity of needs that can be present in the LGBT community. You don't want to write a policy that is so firm and specific that it will not allow for exceptions and actually works against the students it's written to support.

3. HOUSING OPTIONS   The needs of LGBT students can be as diverse as the students themselves. Because of this, it's important to have as many campus housing options as possible for LGBT students, including:

- Single room availability for students who don't feel safe or comfortable living with a member of the same gender.
- Housing options that specifically address the needs of LGBT students, such as an LGBT floor or house.
- Gender-neutral housing options. Having housing options where students don't have to be housed according to gender restrictions on rooms and roommates can address concerns for transgender students and LGBT students. The more options you have, the more students you can accommodate.
- Private or coed bathroom availability for safety and privacy.

LGBT students and other campus populations often find it difficult, if not impossible, for whatever reason, to return home over breaks. If your college offers campus housing over these breaks, make sure there is the possibility for LGBT students to access this housing if needed.

4. VISIBLE SYMBOLS OF SUPPORT   LGBT students will not know that they are supported unless it is clearly communicated. Early on this can be accomplished through simple steps such as inclusive forms (with gender identity options beyond male and female) and clear information about community standards and LGBT support on the housing Website and in general brochures. Throughout the year support can be made visible in a number of possible ways including:

- Displaying LGBT resource or event posters or Ally or Safe Space/Zone stickers.
- Placing LGBT programming in the halls or planning a floor activity to go to an LGBT event together.
- Providing surveys and other assessment tools inclusive of climate questions for LGBT issues.

Students will be watching to see if housing staff are supportive and whether it is safe to come out. Other students will also be watching to see what kind of behavior is expected and appropriate in this regard. Visible symbols of support can go a long way in creating an LGBT-welcoming living environment.

5. COMMUNITY STANDARDS   Most housing programs have a list of community standards that they expect their communities and residents to support and uphold. Another way to ensure this support for LGBT students is to make sure that sexual orientation and gender identity/expression are included in any standard or language addressing the acceptance and/or appreciation of diversity and freedom from harassment.

6. NETWORK   As housing professionals it can be very easy to be all consumed by the hustle and bustle of residential life. But to best support all students, it is very important to create a positive collegial network on campus. This means knowing who works where and making it a priority to attend other events. Students notice who shows up where, and housing staff will be able to communicate support very clearly just by showing up to an LGBT event.

7. DOCUMENTATION AND FOLLOW-UP   No one wants discrimination or harassment on their campus. But ignoring these instances doesn't make them

disappear. When housing staff document and respond to graffiti, hate speech, or other instances of discrimination, it helps to create an environment where this behavior is not tolerated. An effective response is also a way to prevent future bias from happening.

Procedures for reporting incidents should be clear and easily accessed by all students. Students, especially LGBT, should know what and how to report bias and discrimination in all its forms. Housing staff should also receive training in responding to these reports and on supporting individuals who are affected by the harassment. Appropriate follow-up may also include a facilitated community discussion on the effects of the harassment. Helping students communicate to each other—including how the harassment has affected them can be very educational. Housing staff, as a result of their role on campus, can be the best resource for helping students interrupt anti-LGBT behavior and actions.

8. BE THE CAMPUS ROLE MODEL   When students feel comfortable in their home they are better prepared to succeed academically and elsewhere on campus. Campus housing offices have a major impact on the lives of LGBT students, and have the opportunity to serve as positive role models for other campus offices in offering support to this population of students.

Kaaren M. Williamsen-Garvey *is the founding director of the Gender and Sexuality Center at Carleton College where she started as a hall director and LGBT adviser. She completed her undergraduate degree at Gustavus Adolphus College, her M.S. in women's studies at Minnesota State University—Mankato, and her M.A. in counseling and student personnel at the University of Minnesota.*

Steve Wisener *is the associate director of residential life at Carleton College. He has worked in housing at Iowa State University and Macalester College. He has an M.Ed. in student personnel administration from Western Washington University.*

10 Physical and Emotional Health Concerns of LGBT Students

Ric Chollar, LCSW

LGBT STUDENTS FACE unique challenges related to physical and emotional health care. College counselors and health care providers need to be aware of these concerns. Many of the issues are interrelated, impacting one another, with a common theme of coping in a potentially hostile, homophobic, anti-LGBT world. Keep in mind that the vast majority of queer students arrive and thrive at college as extremely healthy, confident, strong, and resilient young adults. Thus not all LGBT students will experience these physical and emotional health problems, but a number of students might (and some with life-threatening severity). The following resource identifies ten areas of concern regarding the health care and counseling of LGBT students. By actively being aware of these concerns, a campus can be better prepared to offer support and possibly prevent escalation of a particular issue or concern.

1. ACCESS, COMFORT, AND TRUST IN PROVIDERS   For campus health and counseling centers, creating a welcoming environment for LGBT students includes outreach, visual cues in office space, language and questions on intake forms, policies for nondiscrimination and confidentiality, and provider's verbal and nonverbal communication.

Because of negative past experiences with counselors and health providers, the power imbalance between provider/counselor and student, and the student's history and fear of anti-LGBT oppression—many LGBT students will not disclose their orientation, same-sex behavior, or gender variance in initial counseling or health care sessions. Others avoid seeking health care altogether.

It is up to the provider to demonstrate an atmosphere of openness, inclusion, and affirmation with students of all genders and sexual orientations. Ways providers can contribute to a trusting relationship include: using open questions in their assessment interviews (e.g., "Are you attracted to men, women, or both?"); being explicit about protecting privacy and confidentiality; and learning about LGBT campus/community resources.

2. COMING OUT   The "coming out process" speaks to the experiences of many, but not all, LGBT students as they discover, accept, explore, and disclose to others their sexual orientation or gender identity. Understanding sexual and gender identity development is a step in gaining knowledge and perspective about the unique health and counseling issues young LGBT people may face.

There is no one correct way or single process of coming out—in fact, some LGBT people do not come out at all. The process is unique for each individual, and every coming-out-related decision is a personal choice.

Many queer youth come out long before they get to college. Research on sexual orientation currently suggests that the average age of initial awareness of same-sex attraction is between 10 or 11 years, while the average for self-identifying is ages 13–15.[1] Many transgender students report having experienced conflict over the gender assigned to them, throughout childhood and puberty. Additionally, many transsexual youth report extreme discomfort with the sex of their bodies, starting in early childhood.[2]

But LGBT students experience much of their identity exploration and development in college years, and even for those who first came out much earlier, their coming out process continues through college life. Students face whether or not to out themselves to their family, friends, roommates, classmates, teammates, faculty, and staff. Over time, students realize that coming out is an ongoing process of decision-making, with a situation-by-situation assessment of risks versus benefits of publicly identifying oneself.

These decisions are even more complicated for some subgroups of LGBT students: students who reject labels and/or experience their identities as fluid; students who are exploring both sexual orientation and gender variance; and/or youth who hold additional marginalized identities, such as students of color, international students, and students with cultural and religious backgrounds outside of middle–upper class, Western–European, Christian traditions.

3. HEALING FROM OPPRESSION (HOMO-, BI- OR, TRANS-PHOBIA)

The experience of anti-LGBT discrimination, violence, and hate can lead to problems in physical and mental health. Victimization can take away an LGBT survivor's sense of trust, safety, and security in the world; with potential after-effects of sleeping difficulties, headaches, digestive problems, agitation, substance abuse, posttraumatic stress disorder, hyper-vigilance, and expectations of future rejection and discrimination.[3]

Even in the absence of external or overt experiences of violence, discrimination, or hate, LGBT people are also at risk of directing negative social attitudes toward themselves. This internalized oppression—homo-, bi- or trans-phobia—can contribute to a devaluing of one's self and poor self-regard. Although it is often most strongly felt early in one's coming out process, it is unlikely that internalized oppression completely disappears even if the LGBT person has accepted his or her sexual orientation or gender identity.

Because of the strength of early socialization and continued exposure to anti-LGBT attitudes, internalized oppression can remain a factor in the LGBT student's adjustment throughout college.

4. COPING WITH STRESS, ANXIETY, AND DEPRESSION

As previously mentioned, coming out (or not) strategies and dealing with oppression can add tremendous stress to an LGBT student's already stressful college life. Research suggests that queer people may literally embody these stresses, leading to higher rates of anxiety and depression.

One study found that gay and bisexual men were three times more likely to have had major depression, and four times more likely to have a panic disorder than heterosexual men. Lesbian and bisexual women showed greater prevalence (four times more likely) of generalized anxiety disorder than heterosexual women. Researchers suggested potential reasons for these differences: (a) social stigma of homosexuality, (b) ways that LGBT lives differ from heterosexuals, (c) experiences of discrimination, and (d) lack of social support.[4]

Through coming out, accepting themselves, and reaching out for support from family, peers, and professionals, LGBT students can learn to cope effectively with stress. Studies have shown that family support and self-acceptance reduce the impact of anti-LGBT abuse on anxiety and depression; and that LGBT people counteract stress by establishing alternative structures and values that enhance their community.[5] Thus, the presence of active LGBT student organizations, resource centers, and affirmative counseling and health centers all play crucial roles in countering stress, anxiety, and depression in LGBT college students.

5. SURVIVING SUICIDAL THOUGHTS, PLANS, OR ATTEMPTS

Decades of research have consistently documented a link between LGBT young people and suicide (thoughts, plans, and/or attempts).[6]

In a Massachusetts survey of high school students, students who described themselves as gay, lesbian, or bisexual were over five times more likely to have attempted suicide in the past year, and over eight times as likely to have required medical attention as a result of a suicide attempt.[7]

One potential factor in higher suicide rates in LGBT youth may be gender identity and/or expression. In one study, college students who reported "cross gender roles"—having gender traits or expression more often associated with the other sex—were at higher risk for suicidal symptoms, regardless of their sexual orientation.[8] And among self-identified transgender youth, some experts estimate that as many as 50 to 88 percent have seriously considered or attempted suicide.[9]

6. SEXUAL HEALTH CONCERNS   Sexually transmitted infections (STIs) are a consequence of specific risk-taking behaviors, not sexual orientation or gender identity themselves. Regardless of how a student self-identifies, providers should inquire about a range of sexual behaviors, number and gender of sexual partners, and safer sex practices.

Health care providers should be aware of the STIs for which LGBT college students are at risk and the necessary screening, testing, and treatment. However, while it is vital to recognize that LGBT students are at risk for STIs, it is also important not to view the youth restrictively within this narrow perspective.

Many of today's LGBT students understand the importance of condom use (although do not always practice it) during vaginal and anal sex; however, they seldom use barrier protection (condoms, gloves, or dams) in sexual contact involving mouths, fingers, hands, and toys used in penetration.

In a recent Internet survey, 89 percent of U.S. LGBT college students reported having sex with someone of the same sex and 45 percent had six or more sex partners during their lifetime. Most reported using a condom consistently during penile-vaginal (61 percent) and anal sex (63 percent). However, only 4 percent used a condom or other barrier consistently during oral sex[10]

While epidemiological rates of gonorrhea, chlamydia, and syphilis have generally decreased in adolescents over the past fifteen years, the rates for all three of these STIs have increased in the populations of young men who have sex with men (MSM).[11]

Many women who partner with women believe they are not at risk of STI transmission. Yet sex between women can transmit herpes (HSV), chlamydia, gonorrhea, hepatitis A and B, trichomonas, and human papilloma virus (HPV). Sexual health education of lesbian and bi women should correct the assumptions that sex between women carries no risk.[12]

Most cervical cancers are linked to the presence of HPV. Yearly pap smears are the best defense against cervical cancer because they reveal HPV and other precancerous changes that can be stopped and they can detect cancer at its earliest stages, when it is much easier to treat—and defeat. Yet many women are not properly screened for HPV, and health care providers don't always tell women that they need pap tests. Regular gynecological exams (including pap, pelvic, and breast exams) are important for queer women because they can detect many kinds of abnormalities which, if undetected, could lead to serious health problems. [13]

A student's gender presentation does not necessarily equate with the sexual and reproductive organs in his or her body. For example, not all sexual organs from birth may have been surgically removed in postoperative transsexual individuals, and there may be consequent screening exams that need to be performed. Students of all genders who have female genitalia require regular pap tests. Also, it would be appropriate to conduct prostate exams for students born male who have prostate glands (including post-operative M-to-Fs). Respectfully ask the student what sex they were born with, and which surgeries, if any, they have undergone. [14]

7. HIV/AIDS   In the United States, the rates of new HIV infection among men who have sex with men have recently begun to increase (up 8 percent in 2004) after over thirteen years of decreasing and stable infection rates. Center for Disease Control (CDC) data showed that 61 percent of new male diagnoses came from men who had sex with other men, compared to 17 percent of transmissions from heterosexual sex and 16 percent from intravenous drug use. The survey found the rate of infection was eight times higher for black men than white men, and black men make up more than half of all HIV diagnoses.[15]

Transgender youth, particularly M-to-F transsexuals, are at extremely high risk for HIV infection. Studies of urban transgender populations have found HIV seroprevalence rates ranging from 14 to 70 percent, and once again, people of color are disproportionately affected (in the Washington, D.C. area, the rate is four times higher than white trans youth).[16]

In queer communities in the United States, not using a condom during anal inter-course continues to represent the greatest risk of HIV transmission. Research points to the following possible factors for increases in unprotected anal sex: improvements in HIV treatment, substance abuse, complex sexual decision making, seeking sex partners on the Internet, and failure to maintain prevention practices.[17]

The rates of risky behaviors are higher among queer youth than older LGBT people. Not having seen firsthand the toll of AIDS, young people may be less motivated to practice safer sex. Almost twenty-five years into the HIV epidemic, today's generation of queer youth seem to underestimate their risk, have trouble maintaining safer sexual practices, and require new and creative HIV prevention efforts.[18] Given the disproportionate rate of HIV infection within young MSM and M-to-F transsexuals of color, culturally competent prevention and education services are crucial.

8. SMOKING   The effects of smoking kill more LGBT people than HIV/AIDS, hate crimes, suicide, and breast cancer combined.[19] In the first statewide survey in the United States to assess tobacco use in the LGBT population, the California Department of Health Services found that over 43 percent of young gay men and lesbians (aged 18–24 years-old) smoke, compared with approximately 17 percent of the general population of 18–24 year-olds (2.5 times higher).[20]

Researchers suggest several possible factors for the high smoking rates in LGBT youth: (1) The tobacco industry has targeted initiatives and advertising directly at LGBT communities, (2) many queer youth spend significant time in the clubs where cigarettes are a social connection, (3) smoking may be used to medicate stress and feelings of loneliness and alienation, and to alleviate depression (nicotine affects the same neurotransmitters as many anti-depressants).[21]

Suggestions for successful tobacco cessation programming for LGBT college students include: (1) involve LGBT students in program design and implementation, (2) address positive LGBT identity development and coming out issues, (3) be entertaining, supportive, and interactive, (4) address the LGBT-related psychosocial and cultural underpinnings of tobacco use, (5) offer practical nonsmoking alternatives and tools, and (6) include options of pharmacological smoking cessation aids.[22]

9. DRINKING AND OTHER DRUG USE   Studies indicate that, when compared with the general population, LGBT people are more likely to use alcohol and other drugs, have higher rates of substance abuse, and are less likely to abstain from use. Studies that compared gay men and lesbians with heterosexuals have found that from 20 to 25 percent of gay men and lesbians are heavy alcohol users, compared with 3 to 10 percent of the heterosexuals studied.[23] Within the transgender community, one urban study found that 34 percent reported alcohol problems.[24]

Risk factors for abusing alcohol include relying on clubs for socializing and peer support; the negative effects of homophobia, heterosexism, biphobia, transphobia, and/or internalized oppression; additional stress related to coming out or hiding/concealing one's identity; and the effects of trauma from history of violence or abuse.[25]

Some drugs seem to be more popular in the LGBT communities than in majority populations. Greater marijuana and cocaine use has been found among lesbians than among heterosexual women. Studies have also found that gay and bisexual men, and other MSM are more likely to have used marijuana, psychedelics, hallucinogens, stimulants, sedatives, cocaine, barbiturates, MDMA (methylenedioxymethamphetamine, also known as ecstasy, XTC, or X), Special K (ketamine), and GHB (gamma hydroxybutyrate) than are heterosexual men. Party or club drugs (including ecstasy, Special K, GHB, and crystal meth (methamphetamine)—often used during raves and circuit parties—decrease inhibition, impair judgment, and increase risky sexual behavior. [26]

10. BODY IMAGE   Bi and lesbian women's experience of body image and what they expect of themselves can be complicated, as they are socialized as women, but also influenced by their LGBT communities. They are exposed to conflicting ideals of beauty espoused by both mainstream and queer communities. Women in the queer community may reject traditional standards of beauty for women, while embracing alternative ideals. Some queer women may feel pressure from their community to reject concerns about weight, or to believe that wanting to lose weight is wrong—potentially at the expense of physical health and well-being.

While queer women may fight with conflicting ideals about body image and femininity, queer men may struggle to achieve an exaggerated sense of male attractiveness. Gay and bisexual men are expected (by both mainstream and gay cultures) to be fit, muscular, well-dressed, and into trends and fashion. Some queer men report fearing that being too fat, too thin, too unattractive, or too old will prevent them from finding partners and/or achieving loving relationships. Others describe feeling that working out and being physically fit will help them regain control of their own lives and bodies, which are all too often taken over by discussions of what men should or should not look like.

Notes:

1. Smith, S. D., Dermer, S. B., & Astramovich, R. L. (2005). Working with nonheterosexual youth to understand sexual identity development, at-risk behaviors, and implications for health care professionals. *Psychological Reports*, Vol. 96(3 Pt 1), pp. 651–4.

2. Israel, G. E., & Tarver, D. E. (1997). *Transgender Care: Recommended guidelines, practical information and personal accounts*. Philadelphia, Temple University Press, pp. 7–20.

3. Meyer, I. H. (2003). Prejudice, social stress, and mental health in lesbian, gay, and bisexual populations: Conceptual issues and research evidence. *Psychological Bulletin*, Vol. 129(5), pp. 674–97.

4. Cochran, S. D., Greer Sullivan, J., Mays, V. M. (2003). Prevalence of mental disorders, psychological distress, and mental health services use among lesbian, gay, and bisexual adults in the United States. *Journal of Consulting and Clinical Psychology*, 0022006X.

5. Meyer.

6. Russell, S. T. (2003). Sexual minority youth and suicide risk. *American Behavioral Scientist*, Vol 46. (9), Special issue: Suicide in Youth, pp. 1241–1257.

7. Massachusetts High School Students and Sexual Orientation: Results of the 2003 Youth Risk Behavior Survey. Massachusetts Department of Education.

8. Fitzpatrick, K. K., Euton, S. J., Jones, J. N., Schmidt, N. B. (2005). Gender role, sexual orientation and suicide risk. *Journal of Affective Disorders*, Vol. 87(1), pp. 35–42.

9. Israel.

10. Lindley, L. L., Nicholson, T. J., Kerby, M. B., Lu, N. (2003). HIV/STI-associated risk behaviors among self-identified lesbian, gay, bisexual, and transgender college students in the United States. *AIDS Education and Prevention*, Vol. 15(5), pp. 413–29.

11. Benson, P. A., & Hergenroeder, A. C. (2005). Bacterial sexually transmitted infections in gay, lesbian, and bisexual adolescents: Medical and public health perspectives. *Seminars in Pediatric Infectious Diseases*, Vol. 16(3), pp. 181–91.

12. Marrazzo, J. M., Coffey, P., Elliott, M. N. (2005, March). Sexual practices, risk perception and knowledge of sexually transmitted disease risk among lesbian and bisexual women. *Perspectives on Sexual and Reproductive Health*, Vol. 37(1), pp. 6–12.

13. Marrazzo.

14. Israel.

15. Centers for Disease Control and Prevention (CDC), 2005. HIV/AIDS Among Men Who Have Sex with Men. Fact Sheet. National Center for HIV, STD and TB Prevention, Divisions of HIV/AIDS Prevention. http://www.cdc.gov/hiv/pubs/facts/msm.htm, accessed January 11, 2006.

16. Xavier, J. M. (2000). Final Report of the Washington Transgender Needs Assessment Survey. Washington, D.C.: Administration for HIV and AIDS, District of Columbia Department of Health.

17. CDC.

18. CDC.

19. Remafedi, G, & Carol, H. (2005). Preventing tobacco use among lesbian, gay, bisexual, and transgender youths. *Nicotine and Tobacco Research*, Vol. 7(2), pp. 249–56.

20. California Department of Health Services, 2005. New Data Show California Military, Korean Men and LGBT Populations Smoke Much More than Others in the State. Press Release #05-60. http://www.dhs.ca.gov/ps/cdic/tcs/documents/press/PressReleaseSept6_05.pdf, accessed January 11, 2006.

21. Remafedi.

22. Remafedi.

23. Center for Substance Abuse Treatment (CSAT) (2001). *A Provider's Introduction to substance abuse treatment for lesbian, gay, bisexual, and transgender individuals.* DHHS Publication No. 01- 3498, Rockville, MD: CSAT.

24. Xavier.

25. CSAT.

26. CSAT.

Ric Chollar, LCSW, *is the assistant director with the Office of Diversity Programs and Services for LGBT Resources at George Mason University, where he has also taught for over ten years. Ric earned his M.S.W. from the University of Michigan, interning with their human sexuality office, the nation's first university resource center for gay and lesbian students.*

7 Ways for Campus Safety to Support LGBT Students

Eric W. Trekell

IN OCTOBER OF 2005, the Gay, Lesbian, and Straight Education Network (GLSEN) issued a survey on U.S. secondary school climate, indicating that 65 percent of teens reported being harassed in the past year, with perceived or actual sexual orientation the second most commonly cited (33 percent) reason for harassment. Moreover, a majority of students (57 percent) indicated never reporting harassment they experienced, and 27 percent of LGBT students believed staff and faculty in their schools would take no action if harassment were reported.[1]

These statistics provide an indication of the culture many high school students have when transitioning to college: experiences of LGBT students being harassed and straight students engaging in harassment or, at best, not intervening when witnessing it. Most disconcerting, these statistics illustrate a culture of nonreporting among LGBT students. Thus, colleges need to work actively at overcoming that culture.

On campus, student affairs offices commonly have some staff committed to supporting LGBT students and encouraging LGBT students to report harassment. Indeed, many campuses have the appropriate processes and policies in place. But it can be particularly difficult for campus law enforcement to be seen as playing an equally supportive role.

That shouldn't be a surprise: a history of distrustful relationships between the LGBT community and law enforcement has been well documented, and the 1969 Stonewall Riots in New York City, celebrated as the birthplace of the modern gay rights movement, was a direct response to police harassment. Certainly, efforts to end distrust are occurring, but Amnesty International (AI) USA has detailed how problems persist: in a recent study on how law enforcement agencies throughout the United States interact with LGBT individuals, the AI report "confirms that in the United States, LGBT people continue to be targeted for human rights abuses by the police based on their real or perceived sexual orientation or gender identity."[2]

So, with all this information in mind, what can campus safety officials do to be supportive of LGBT students? Every student is entitled to a safe academic learning environment; one where students can learn and be themselves. Campus safety provides the mechanism for this to happen by being visible and enforcing campus policies and laws. The following list represents seven suggestions for campus safety officials to do their part—creating an LGBT supportive campus climate unobstructed by harassment, violence, or other negative behaviors.

1. CREATE AN LGBT LIAISON OFFICER   Establishing an LGBT liaison officer is justifiable for two reasons: because of the history of police violence against LGBT people, and because the LGBT community is not always visible. For both reasons, it's not always easy for law enforcement to engage in dialogue with the LGBT community. Giving an openly LGBT officer responsibility for developing contacts with the LGBT campus community will help to overcome both of those challenges and encourage the community to collaborate with and trust campus safety.

2. ACTIVELY RECRUIT LGBT OFFICERS   Even though it may be challenging to hire LGBT officers, taking steps to illustrate openness to hiring LGBT people can have a positive impact. One simple step may be wording on job advertisements like "women, minorities, and LGBT people encouraged to apply."

3. BE VISIBLE AT LGBT EVENTS AND STUDENT ORGANIZATION MEETINGS
This can be a particularly valuable use of time for a LGBT liaison officer. However, *all* members of the security force should be able to interact comfortably with LGBT campus members, and feel comfortable in "gay" spaces. Examples: assign the LGBT liaison officer to security detail at LGBT student social events (if necessary); straight officers can provide workshops to LGBT student groups on "personal safety."

4. APPOINT AN LGBT PERSON TO THE CAMPUS SAFETY ADVISORY BOARD   If your campus safety/police department doesn't have an advisory board comprised of students, faculty, staff, and alumni, it probably should. And at least one visible "out" LGBT student (as well as representatives of other underrepresented groups) should be on that board. The purpose of the advisory board: to review policies and practices; to provide advice on how to deal with potentially challenging issues; and to work as liaisons between campus safety and the campus community.

5. INSTITUTE AN LGBT ISSUES TRAINING COMPONENT FOR CAMPUS SAFETY STAFF   Certainly, personal anti-LGBT prejudices of officers can be an issue, but one of the most common reasons for difficulties between police and members of the LGBT community is a lack of training. Often, officers don't know what questions to ask, how to ask them, and what to do with the information once they have it.[3] Basic training can provide officers with the most common, appropriate language used to describe the LGBT community, discuss myths and misconceptions, and begin to work on an understanding of homophobia, biphobia, transphobia, heterosexism, and the barriers they create to reporting, investigating, and prosecuting violence against LGBT people.

6. HARASSMENT REPORTING POLICIES AND PROCEDURES   Policies should be clear, widely distributed, and explicit in encouraging LGBT students to report harassment. Procedures should be easily accessible, via Websites and multiple offices; they should offer anonymity, and a student advocate should be with the student during face-to-face meetings. Accurate figures of LGBT harassment incidents on campus should be public knowledge, discussed, and not downplayed because of concerns over campus image.

7. TRANSGENDER ISSUES NEED SPECIAL ATTENTION   Transgender members of the campus community have unique issues, of which campus safety officers need to be aware, largely because of issues nontrans people may manifest. For example, the presence of a male-to-female (M-to-F) trans person in a female restroom or other sex-segregated facility does not inherently prove harassment of another female co-occupying that space. Thus, in responding, campus security officers should focus on the actual *behavior* of the trans person. Another important issue for transpeople includes how officers may react when responding to reported violence against a trans person, and assisting with medical care—in such situations, campus security forces need to be advocates for victims, not part of the problem.

Additional Resources

BOOKS

Stewart, Chuck (1999). *Sexually Stigmatized communities: Reducing heterosexism and homophobia*. Thousand Oaks, CA: Sage Publications, Inc.

An awareness training manual developed specifically for law enforcement trainings, but contains exercises that can be applied to other groups.

WEBSITES

The following police organizations are recognized for their excellence in LGBT training and community liaison work:

Gay Officers Action League of New England
http://goalne.org/

Washington D.C. Metropolitan Police Department Gay and Lesbian Liaison Unit
http://www.gaydc.net/gllu/

Notes:

1. Harris Interactive and GLSEN. (2005). *From teasing to torment: School climate in America, a survey of students and teachers.* New York: GLSEN.

2. Amnesty International USA. (2005). *Stonewalled. Police abuse and misconduct against lesbian, gay, bisexual and transgender people in the U.S.* New York: Amnesty International Publications. 2005, p. 2.

3. On the streets. (2003, Winter). Intelligence Report, Southern Poverty Law Center. http://www.splcenter.org/intel/intelreport/article.jsp?pid=281, accessed December 12, 2005.

Eric W. Trekell *is director of the LGBT Campus Center at the University of Wisconsin— Madison. He has a B.A. in government from Adams State College and an M.S. in educational administration from Texas A&M University, where he taught student success courses and was an assistant director of the Texas A&M campus in Koriyama, Japan.*

10 Recommendations to Improve Trans Inclusiveness on Campus

Brett Genny Beemyn, Ph.D.

MORE AND MORE students are coming out as transgender at colleges and universities across the United States. But most institutions have been slow to recognize their specific needs, much less to take steps to create a more trans-supportive campus environment. As a result, transgender and other gender-diverse students often encounter hostile classmates, uneducated faculty and student affairs staff, insensitive campus health care providers, and campus policies and practices that are based on binary gender categories.[1,2,3] Much can be done by colleges and universities to create a more welcoming campus climate for transgender people. The following ten recommendations represent significant ways that students, staff, and faculty can make their campuses more trans-inclusive.

1. ADD "GENDER IDENTITY OR EXPRESSION" TO THE CAMPUS NONDISCRIMI-NATION POLICY   Recognizing that the inclusion of "sex" and "sexual orientation" in nondiscrimination policies does not necessarily cover transgender and other gender-diverse people, who experience discrimination based on their gender identity and/or expression, nearly fifty colleges and college systems have added "gender identity or expression" to their policies in the last decade.

2. ADVOCATE FOR THE CAMPUS HEALTH CENTER TO PROVIDE DIRECT INSURANCE COVERAGE FOR HORMONES AND GENDER CONFIRMATION SURGERIES FOR TRANSITIONING STUDENTS.   Although more students are coming out as transsexual and seeking to transition during their college years, colleges have been slow to address their health care needs by including hormones and gender confirmation surgeries in health insurance plans.

3. WORK WITH RESIDENCE LIFE STAFF TO CREATE TRANSGENDER-INCLUSIVE HOUSING OPTIONS, INCLUDING GENDER-NEUTRAL ROOMS OR FLOORS. Because many residence halls are designated as "single-sex" by building and/or room, transgender students often have few safe, comfortable on-campus housing options. To address this situation, colleges should offer gender-neutral housing options, in which students are assigned a roommate regardless of gender.

4. CONVERT EXISTING SINGLE-OCCUPANCY MEN'S AND WOMEN'S RESTROOMS INTO GENDER-NEUTRAL BATHROOMS AND CREATE GENDER-NEUTRAL BATHROOMS IN NEW AND RENOVATED BUILDINGS   Because students who are perceived as violating traditional gender boundaries are vulnerable to harassment and violence when using campus restrooms designated for "women" and "men," a growing number of colleges are changing male/female restrooms into gender-neutral ones (typically single-stall, lockable restrooms available to people of all genders), publicizing the locations of these facilities, and making sure that new and renovated buildings include gender-neutral bathroom options.

5. WORK WITH STUDENT ACTIVITIES, GREEK LIFE, ATHLETICS, AND OTHER CAMPUS DEPARTMENTS TO DEVELOP POLICIES THAT ENSURE THAT TRANSGENDER STUDENTS CAN BE PART OF GENDER-SPECIFIC STUDENT GROUPS, FRATERNITIES AND SORORITIES, AND SPORTS TEAMS   Student should be able to participate in campus activities in keeping with how they identify and express their gender identities.

6. WORK WITH THE REGISTRAR'S OFFICE TO ESTABLISH A SIMPLE, ONE-STOP PROCEDURE FOR STUDENTS TO CHANGE THE NAME AND/OR GENDER ON ALL OF THEIR CAMPUS RECORDS AND DOCUMENTS Students who do not identify as the gender assigned to them at birth should be able to have their appropriate gender reflected on college documents, including identification cards, transcripts, financial aid and employment forms, and enrollment records. Besides being a matter of fairness and respect, an accurate gender designation in college files is critical to avoid outing transgender students and to help protect them from discrimination when they apply for jobs, seek admission to graduate and professional schools, and at any other time that they must show a college document. An institution should never insist that individuals complete gender confirmation surgeries before changing their records, as many younger transgender people are deciding not to transition entirely, and even students who desire the surgeries have limited access to health care and often cannot afford the procedures, which are almost never covered by insurance.

7. ADVOCATE FOR STUDENT AFFAIRS OFFICES TO CHANGE THE GENDER CATEGORY ON THEIR STANDARDIZED FORMS TO ENABLE TRANSGENDER STUDENTS TO SELF-IDENTIFY, IF THEY WISH. College forms that ask students to indicate whether they are female or male, and brochures and Websites that use "he/she" ignore the complexities of gender and signal to transgender students that they do not belong at the institution. Offering more inclusive language would not only be supportive of trans-identified people, but also help educate the campus community about gender diversity.

8. SPONSOR REGULAR TRANSGENDER-SPECIFIC PROGRAMS AND INCLUDE TRANSGENDER-RELATED EVENTS DURING LGBT PRIDE WEEKS AND AWARENESS MONTHS Some student groups participate in the national Transgender Day of Remembrance, an annual event that honors individuals killed because of their actual or perceived gender identity/expression. Campus organizations should not only sponsor activities that recognize the deaths of transgender people, but also hold events that speak to and celebrate their lives.

9. INCLUDE EXTENSIVE TRANSGENDER INFORMATION AND RESOURCES AS PART OF AN ALLY OR SAFE SPACE/ZONE PROGRAM   Many colleges offer an Ally or Safe Space/Zone program to raise awareness and understanding of the experiences of LGBT people and to create visible allies among staff, faculty, and administrators. But many of these programs include little, if any, trans-specific content, even though transgender issues are invariably much less understood than lesbian or gay concerns. Using "LGBT" when the circumstances being described are not applicable to transgender people is an insult, not inclusion.

10. WIDELY PUBLICIZE THE CAMPUS TRANS-INCLUSIVE POLICIES   Developing transgender-supportive policies will have a limited effect if people are unaware of the changes. The most effective way to publicize the policies to students would be to create an online transgender resource guide. For staff and faculty,

utilize the institutionalized methods of information sharing and communication (e.g., department head meetings, presidential memo, newsletters).

Notes:

1. Beemyn, Brett Genny. (2005.) Trans on campus: Measuring and improving the climate for transgender students. *On campus with women* 34: n.p. Available at http://www.ocww.org.

2. Beemyn, Brett, Curtis, Billy, Davis, Masen, and Tubbs, Nancy Jean. (2005.) Transgender issues on college campuses. In *Gender identity and sexual orientation: Research, policy, and personal perspectives: New directions for student services*, Ronni Sanlo (ed.), San Francisco: Jossey-Bass; pp. 49--60.

3. McKinney, Jeff. (2005.) On the margins: A study of the experiences of transgender college students. *Journal of Gay and Lesbian Issues in Education*, 3(1) , pp. 63–75.

Brett Genny Beemyn, Ph.D. *is the director of the Stonewall Center at the University of Massachusetts—Amherst, co-chair of the National Consortium of Directors of LGBT Resources in Higher Education, and a board member of the Transgender Law and Policy Institute. Brett Genny has published and spoken extensively on transgender college students and trans-inclusive campus policies and, along with Sue Rankin, is currently conducting a national study of transgender identity development.*

Reaching Out to LGBT Youth through College Admissions

W. Houston Dougharty

THE VIBE ONE gets from a college campus is critical. One of the most important places where that vibe is felt is the admissions office—the publications they produce, the staff that represent the campus, the opportunities they provide for incoming prospective students. Now more than ever, as the first generation of "out" LGBT students are graduating from high school, the admissions office needs to consider LGBT students as a vital recruitment population and prepare accordingly. Since admission offices and staffs represent their campuses' values and attitudes, their response to LGBT questions and issues can be significant to a prospective LGBT student determining the LGBT friendliness of the campus. The following list shares ten ways for an admissions office to be visibly LGBT friendly and reach out to LGBT prospective students.

1. CAMPUS POLICIES   Campus policies say a lot about campus values. LGBT prospective students pay close attention to policies and want to know this information. The admissions office should visibly publish their campus nondiscrimination policy in print publications and on the Internet. If a campus fails to include the words "sexual orientation" and "gender identity or expression" in their policy this raises a red flag for a prospective LGBT student. Admissions staff should be prepared to answer questions about the campus position on LGBT issues, especially the nondiscrimination policy. Another telling issue for LGBT students is the domestic partnership policy for same-sex couples (which relates to health insurance, housing, and educational benefits).

Possible Questions: Are sexual orientation and gender identity/expression included in your campus nondiscrimination policies? Are there same-sex domestic partnership benefits for your students, staff, and faculty?

2. THE APPLICATION ITSELF   How can a college application be queer friendly? One place is in the "Family" section where applicants are asked to list family members. Does it assume the heterosexist norm and ask about "Father" and "Mother" or is language used that allows for other families (like "Parent" and "Parent")? Many students come from families that do not include a father and mother and it's meaningful if an application is sensitive to that reality. Applications for admission should also consider being trans and gender variant-inclusive by offering a broader gender identification, rather than just female and male.

Possible Questions: Does your application allow LGBT families and students to be openly represented? Can I change my name and gender identification easily in the campus registrar's office?

3. ACADEMIC COURSES AND PROGRAMS   Many LGBT students gain the queer sense of a college by perusing the lists of classes that are offered. Many campuses offer courses that are LGBT related, like *Studies in Lesbian and Gay Literature* at Puget Sound (WA), *Sociology of Lesbian and Gay Communities* at University of California—Santa Barbara, *Music and Queer Identity* at Cornell University (NY), and *Human Sexual Identities* at Allegheny College (PA). Colleges

also offer concentrations, minors, and even majors in LGBT, queer, or gender studies, like San Francisco State, SUNY—Purchase, Bowdoin College (ME), and Western Washington University. Admissions office staff should not only be aware of these courses but also be able to articulate openly without hesitation about such opportunities.

Possible Questions: What queer-related courses do you offer? Who teaches them? Are the classes open to all students or are they discipline-specific to students majoring in certain areas?

4. PUBLICATIONS, WEBSITES, PHOTOS, AND LANGUAGE   Much information is conveyed through the print and web media that colleges produce (and bombard prospects with daily!). The admissions office should pay close attention to these important publications and Websites—particularly noting the images and language that are used. Are all the glossy photos of straight couples holding hands and sitting by fountains? Are there images that are LGBT-friendly or at least orientation-neutral? Colleges that are sensitive to LGBT prospective students try not to use heterosexist images and language. Are all the LGBT campus organizations listed where other campus involvement and activities are touted? Treat LGBT students like you might other targeted recruitment populations (e.g., student athletes, international students, students of color). The admissions office should create materials to target LGBT students specifically and make sure all admission materials are LGBT sensitive and inclusive.

Possible Questions: In which publications can I find your LGBT resources? Where can I find online LGBT campus and local community resources?

5. STAFF ATTITUDE AND LANGUAGE   When admissions staff give presentations and conduct interviews, their attitude and language should make LGBT prospective students feel welcomed and affirmed. For instance, when admissions officers describe their campus climate and diversity, they should go out of their way to talk about LGBT policies, organizations, events, and/or courses. The same holds true for campus tour guides and hosts. Every staff member should feel comfortable with the language as well as competent in the subject matter.

Possible Questions: How is diversity defined on your campus? How long has "diversity" included sexual orientation and gender identity/expression?

6. SCHOLARSHIPS AND FINANCIAL AID   Financing college is often a challenge and admissions officers are excellent resources about how a campus approaches financial assistance. Many colleges offer scholarships that are specifically designed for LGBT students, such as those at Rice (TX), Utah State, Puget Sound (WA), Hofstra (NY), Duke (NC), University of the Pacific (CA), Iowa State, and Southern California. Some colleges, like Bridgewater State (MA), also have financial aid programs for LGBT students who need more funding because their families are nonsupportive. Admissions officers need to understand the needs and possible financial circumstances of LGBT students. Some may not have any financial support at all due to negative reactions of their family. Each LGBT student will be different, but be sensitive to such issues and be prepared to offer specific LGBT financial resources from your campus community.

Possible Questions: How can I take advantage of all possible financial aid opportunities at your campus? Are there any LGBT scholarships at your campus?

7. STUDENT LIFE SUPPORT   Campuses have student services staff who are responsible for areas like housing, medical and counseling services, activities, community service, and support for subpopulations of students. Colleges that are eager to enroll LGBT students work hard at making sure that queer students are comfortable and supported on campus—in the residence halls, in student government and clubs, and with staff. In many cases, campuses have established LGBT centers—like at Grinnell (IA), American (DC), Cal Poly-Pomona, Emory (GA), Colorado State, UCLA, and Stanford (CA). A growing number of campuses also have LGBT centers as well as various LGBT student organizations and student activities. Be knowledgeable about what your campus offers and showcase such offerings visibly for LGBT students. These programs and services are all bonuses to attract LGBT students to your campus and say a lot about LGBT friendliness.

Possible Questions: How does your student affairs staff support LGBT students? Do you have any LGBT theme floors in the residence halls? What are the LGBT organizations on campus and their annual events?

8. OUT FACULTY, STAFF, AND STUDENTS   Every college has an LGBT population—every last one of them (even those colleges that are actively anti-LGBT). The question is are people out on campus? It makes sense for LGBT students to want to be on a campus where they can be themselves, be welcomed, be supported, and be part of a community. LGBT-affirming admissions officers will know who is out on campus. They should be willing to connect prospective students with out students, staff, faculty, and alumni who will be resources to prospects as they try to find a good college "fit."

Possible Questions: How easy is it to be out on your campus? Are there out members of your campus community who would tell me about LGBT life on campus?

9. COLLEGE FAIRS AND CAMPUS VISITS   Two popular ways of learning about colleges are college fairs and campus visits. While nearly every town has a college fair where many different campuses are represented, there are currently only a few college fairs designed just for LGBT prospective students. These events have met with great success in the Twin Cities (MN) and the Boston area. It is predicted that such LGBT-specific college fairs will only continue to grow in frequency and numbers over the next few years. Also, campus visits may be individually arranged (during which prospects can visit classes, tour campus, stay overnight, meet and interview with an admissions officer) or there may be larger events for prospects or those who have been accepted. In either case, admissions staff members should provide opportunities for LGBT students to explore campus and talk to LGBT members of the campus community—from current students to faculty to alumni.

Possible Questions: Can I meet with LGBT students, staff, or faculty on your campus? Are there special days to visit where I can attend an event that is LGBT-related?

10. CAMPUS EVENTS AND CULTURE   Campuses that are LGBT-affirming are proactive about sponsoring LGBT-related activities. There are many lecturers, comedians, artists, and musicians who are out and often incorporate queer issues into their presentations and performances. At many colleges these events have become a natural part of cultural and academic programming, which is an excellent sign that the campus is LGBT-friendly. Some campuses have established LGBT-specific programming and traditions (like Lavender

Graduation at Michigan, UCLA, and Puget Sound; Small Victories at Iowa State; LGBT Film Series at Bucknell; and Ally or Safe Space/Zone programs on hundreds of campuses, in addition to celebrating shared events like National Coming Out Day, Pride Month, World AIDS Day, Blue Jeans Day, and Freedom to Marry Day. As admissions staff, know as much as possible about these campus events and LGBT culture, including their past success as well as any future plans for more LGBT events.

Possible Questions: What events or programs does your campus sponsor for LGBT students? How does your campus community recognize national LGBT events and celebrations? Are there any upcoming LGBT lecturers, comedians, or musicians coming to campus?

The first generation of "out" college students stand ready at the front gates to the campus. These students are outstanding scholars, leaders, athletes, and artists. Admissions offices are finally realizing that LGBT-prospective students are valuable to target with recruitment efforts to their campuses. As admissions staff, it is important to know what LGBT policies, services, and programs your campus offers as well as be able to respond openly to any questions with LGBT-friendly answers. Remember the first impression by the admissions office may determine whether or not your college or university is the queer choice.

W. Houston Dougharty *is dean of students at Lewis & Clark College in Portland, Oregon. He earned degrees at the University of Puget Sound, Western Washington University, and UC—Santa Barbara and has been associate dean at Puget Sound and Iowa State University. He was a college admissions officer for over ten years and has led and worked in the following areas in student affairs: LGBT student services, women's center, legal services, registrar, advising, counseling and health services, multicultural student services, service learning, student union, residence life, learning skills, career services, parent programs, orientation, judicial affairs, crisis management, off-campus and adult services, and financial aid.*

OUT AND ONLINE:
LGBT LEADERSHIP, FINANCIAL AID,
AND SUPPORT RESOURCES

PREPARING FOR COLLEGE can be a daunting task. Along with finding the best LGBT choice for college, there are other pressing issues such as financial aid and scholarship opportunities to investigate and consider. These processes can often be complicated with a maze of obstacles. It can also be difficult to know where to begin to find the best, most specific LGBT college information. The following list of online resources are meant to highlight national organizations with a particular or sole focus on LGBT campus issues. Remember, you are not alone as you successfully navigate the queer waters of colleges and universities. These online resources will only make it easier before and after you step foot on campus.

Campus PrideNet
http://www.campuspride.net

Campus PrideNet represents the only national organization for student leaders and campus groups working to create a safer college environment for LGBT students. The online site contains helpful articles on preparing for college, Gay Point Average rankings for campuses, an updated, exhaustive list of scholarship and financial assistance information and a dean's list to meet other LGBT students across the country. In addition, the site also offers channels and resources for various LGBT and ally advocacy, support and leadership issues.

National Consortium of Directors of Lesbian Gay
Bisexual and Transgender Resources in Higher Education
http://www.lgbtcampus.org

The National Consortium of LGBT Resources in Higher Education works to achieve higher education environments in which lesbian, gay, bisexual, and transgender students, faculty, staff, administrators, and alumni have equity in every respect. The organization supports professional staff of LGBT office/centers and advocates for policy change, program development, and establishment of LGBT office/centers. Online there are valuable Frequently Asked Questions (FAQs) as well as a listing of all the campuses with professionally staffed LGBT office/centers.

The Point Foundation
http://www.thepointfoundation.org

The Point Foundation provides financial support, mentoring, and hope to meritorious students who are marginalized due to sexual orientation, gender expression, or gender identity. The application process is open to all LGBT students nationwide regardless of level of education. Students may apply online to a variety of scholarships including the mtvU and the Matthew Shepard Foundation awards. Application period traditionally starts January 1. All applications must be received by March 1. Decisions are made by May 1.

The Matthew Shepard Foundation
http://www.matthewshepard.org

The Matthew Shepard Foundation provides support for diversity programs in education and helps youth organizations establish environments where young people can feel safe and be themselves. Online resources include reading materials, videos, educational materials, and regional events. There are also links to LGBT-sensitive homeless shelters, drop-in centers, local PFLAG organizations, and LGBT counselors.

The Trevor Project
http://www.thetrevorproject.org
Help Line: 866-488-7386
The Trevor Helpline is the only national 24-hour, toll-free suicide prevention hot line aimed at gay and questioning youth. The Trevor Helpline is geared toward helping those in crisis, or those wanting information on how to help someone in crisis. Managed by partners at San Francisco Suicide Prevention, the Trevor Helpline calls are handled by highly trained counselors and are free and confidential.

Stop The Hate!
http://www.stophate.org
Stop The Hate! works nationally to prevent and respond to bias and hate crimes on college campuses. Along with valuable online resources and links, the organization also provides the only train-the-trainer curriculum for colleges and universities to prepare faculty, staff, and students to fight bias and hate on campus.

National Coming Out Project
http://www.hrc.org/ncop
The National Coming Out Project is part of the Human Rights Campaign Foundation. The project provides both printed and online resources and information to support gay, lesbian, bisexual, and transgender people including a *Resource Guide to Coming Out* and an online resource for *Coming Out in Communities of Color*. The project is an extension of National Coming Out Day, which is celebrated every October 11. The National Coming Out Project helps to facilitate those events by offering information about how to put on an event and materials such as posters, stickers, and literature.

Parents, Families and Friends of Lesbians and Gays
http://www.pflag.org
Parents, Families and Friends of Lesbians and Gays (PFLAG) provides support to families and friends of LGBT people. PFLAG also advocates on behalf of LGBT people, and offers educational programs to improve the general populations understanding of LGBT people. Online resources from PFLAG include support for LGBT individuals coming out as well as tools for outreach to build LGBT allies. In addition, there is also financial assistance available through the PFLAG National Scholarships Program. Scholarships are available at the national level and are awarded by many of the local chapters. Youth can receive both awards if eligible.

The Lambda 10 Project
National Clearinghouse for GLBT Fraternity and Sorority Issues
http://www.gaygreeks.org
The Lambda 10 Project provides LGBT and ally resources nationally to college fraternities and sororities in an effort to create visibility and education for LGBT issues. Online the Website shares valuable resources geared to LGBT students wanting to participate in Greek life—from rushing openly gay to coming out in the fraternity closet. The site also offers a list of current LGBT-sensitive fraternal organizations and a Who's Out List to contact men and women who are openly LGBT in Greek life.

Transgender Law and Policy Institute
http://www.transgenderlaw.org
The Transgender Law and Policy Institute engages in effective advocacy for transgender people and works on law and policy initiatives designed to advance transgender equality. Online the organization maintains a list of colleges and universities with "gender identity or expression" in their nondiscrimination policies.

National Gay & Lesbian Task Force
http://www.ngltf.org
The National Gay and Lesbian Task Force was the first national LGBT civil rights and advocacy organization in the country. The organization has tremendous grass-roots political resources and hosts the annual Creating Change Conference for LGBT and ally activists. In 2003, NGLTF published a national campus climate study, which documents experiences and perceptions of anti-LGBT bias and harassment, along with levels of institutional support for LGBT people.

Gay, Lesbian & Straight Education Network (GLSEN)
http://www.glsen.org
The Gay, Lesbian & Straight Education Network focuses its educational efforts on K-12 schools and supporting teachers and students in regards to issues surrounding sexual orientation and gender identity/expression. GLSEN also offers an array of online resources for pre-college LGBT and ally youth as well and co-organizes the annual National Day of Silence event, which is also planned on several hundred colleges every year. The National Day of Silence is a student-led day of actions where those who support making anti-LGBT bias unacceptable in schools take a day-long vow of silence to recognize and protest the discrimination and harassment—in effect, the silencing—experienced by LGBT students and their allies.

Lambda Legal Defense & Education Fund
http://www.lambdalegal.org
Lambda Legal Defense & Education Fund engages in litigation, education and public policy work to achieve full recognition of the civil rights of LGBT people. Lambda Legal supports colleges and universities with legal issues and educational outreach efforts such as advocacy for campus policies inclusive of sexual orientation and gender identity/expression.

Gay & Lesbian Alliance Against Defamation
http://www.glaad.org
The Gay & Lesbian Alliance Against Defamation ensures media images of LGBT people are fair, accurate, and inclusive. This includes news coverage, television series, and even portrayals of gay characters on the silver screen. GLAAD launches various public awareness campaigns in the media, such as the "Be an Ally & a Friend" series of televisions commercials for outreach to LGBT youth and straight allies.

ACKNOWLEDGMENTS

OH MY! WHERE does one begin? I owe a huge debt of thanks to so many people and organizations for their support of this college guide. I called in every favor I had, really. Many individuals were undoubtedly tired of my correspondence and requests for further assistance. Thank you all for hanging in there with me. It was an immense undertaking—the first of its kind—and we did it!

Not only does this book offer an informed, hopeful perspective of LGBT progress, but it also serves as a testament to the tenacity of "campus queers" everywhere. Such "campus queers" defy conventional labels and represent all sexual orientations, gender identities/expressions, ethnic and cultural backgrounds, and ages, as well as LGBT perspectives—that is what makes each of them powerful and transformational in their own right. These LGBT advocates and pioneers have lent the passion necessary for this book and for the work of Campus PrideNet since the beginning. They include the following: Sarah Holmes, Chad Wilson, Shaun Travers, Andrea "Dre" Domingue, Mike Esposito, Greg Varnum, Chad Grandy, Allison Subasic, Kaaren M. Williamsen-Garvey, Steve Wisener, Angela C. Nichols, Brett Genny Beemyn, Ric Chollar, Susan Rankin, Charlie Syms, Ronni Sanlo, Doug Bauder, Bob Schoenberg, Debbie Bazarsky, Gwendolyn Dean, Saralyn Chesnut, Eric Trekell, Houston Dougherty, Curtis Shepard, Anita Broccolino, Cheryl Ann Welsh, Dave Barnett, Jim Sears, Sally Green Heaven, Carrie Evans, Daryl Herrschaft, Candace Gingrich, Judy Shepard, Joe Solmonese, Kevin Jennings, Jorge Valencia, Jody Huckaby, Bruce Steele, Kathleen Debold, Kevin Hauswirth, Rueben Perez, Judy Riggs, Brandon Braud, Mitchell Gold, Pamela W. Freeman, Samir Luther, Damon Romine, Savannah Pacer, Kerry Pacer, Neil Giuliano, John Caldwell, Mark Shropshire, Chris Chen, Sue Hyde, Ron Schlittler, Nick Pavlick, Judy Hoff, Jon Moore, Nancy Evans, Jake Reitab, Vernon Wall, Dale Masterson, Joni Madison, Mitchell Gold, Elizabeth Birch, Jessica Pettitt, Todd Smith, Bryan Jackson, Leslie Webb, Jeannette Johnson-Licon, Kerry John Poynter, Carol Fischer, Nita Allgood, Margie Cook, Mickey Hart, Benjamin Davidson, Jeremy Hayes, Adrea Jaehnig, Billy Curtis, Nancy Tubbs, Curt McKay, Michael Franklin, Kyle Webster, Luke Jensen, Felice Yeskel, Chicora Martin, Charles Milne, Katie Van Roosenbeek, Heidi Stanton, Brian Protheroe, Roger Heineken, George Miller, Graeheme Hespe, Doug Case, Dan Maxwell, Jennifer Holladay, Steve Wessler, Debbie Stogel, Gary Levin, Brandon Wilson, Nicole Manganelli, Kelvin Datcher, Tafeni English, Brian Willoughby, Tony D'Angelo, and Jim Johnson.

A special thanks also goes out to those hundreds of campuses and thousands of individuals who participated throughout the "Call for Nominations," the online interviews, and final evaluations for this college guide. I want to personally express my deepest appreciation for all their continued LGBT campus efforts. Even though not every campus is featured in this book, many campuses are forging ahead to make a better LGBT campus climate—a safer place to live, learn, and grow in the future. Kudos!

There is also one particular organization that deserves special recognition and has ultimately laid the bricks and mortar for college campuses nationwide on LGBT issues. The National Consortium of Directors of LBGT Resources in Higher Education is the best collective of "campus queers" out there leading the way. As a member of this organization, I have been inspired personally and professionally by many of these "campus queers." Without their support, this book and Campus PrideNet would not have been possible. Several other businesses and organizations also deserve recognition: Patrick Davis Partners,

Tyvola Design, Lambda 10 Project, Stop The Hate!, mtvU, The Trevor Project, Gay, Lesbian and Straight Education Network, Human Rights Campaign, National Gay and Lesbian Taskforce, Transgender Law & Policy Institute, Association of College Unions International, Association of Fraternity Advisers, National Association of Student Personnel Administrators, American College Personnel Association, Gay and Lesbian Alliance Against Defamation, The Matthew Shepard Foundation, the Triangle Foundation, and Parents, Families and Friends of Lesbians and Gays (PFLAG).

Next at the top of my list of appreciation goes a shout out to the staff of Alyson Books and *The Advocate* national gay and lesbian newsmagazine. Over the years both Alyson Books and *The Advocate* staff have stood by my side, making my LGBT campus efforts and books like this one a reality. A specific thanks to the new Alyson team including my editor, Shannon Berning, the publisher, Dale Cunningham, managing editor, Richard Fumosa, and publicist, Jeffrey Theis, who have worked relentlessly to get this book into your hands. Together we are making a positive difference and have helped thousands of LGBT and ally youth. This book is yet another example.

And, of course, behind the scenes I have had my own "Shane L. Windmeyer" pep squad cheering me on. They're an eclectic group of sorts, with or without pom-poms. Each serves as a catalyst for motivation and love. My personal cheerleaders are Diann Windmeyer (my mom), Fred Windmeyer (my dad, who was killed in 2003 by a drunk driver but still cheers me on every day of my life), Jennifer Windmeyer (my sister), Paula Podell (my aunt), David Podell (my uncle), Jeremy Podell, Laura Podell, Bryan Podell, Brian Bradley, Jon Moore, Michelle Moore, Nick Geimer, Elizabeth Couch, Bert Woodward, Doug Bauder, Pamela W. Freeman, Christine Shaw, Neil Shaw, Nga Holt, Jennifer Garner, Phil Wells, Jay Biles, Regina Young Hyatt, Janis Singletary, Paul Fincher, Rodney Tucker, Rodney Hines, Greg Shackelford, Hal Ivey, and Tyvola (my shih tzu). Oh, and I can't forget my fellow ruggers on the Charlotte Royals Rugby team. Ruck on!

Last but certainly not least, I want to thank two extremely amazing individuals who are a part of my life. The first is a newfound friend by the name of Patrick Davis. He does not like a lot of attention but he truly is a champion in many ways for LGBT equality. He and his staff, Lisa Bigazzi Tilt and Lisa A. Sommer (aptly nicknamed Lisa Lisa & Cult Jam), and Emily S. MacDonald at Patrick Davis Partners have assisted in numerous ways to make this book a success. But most important, his friendship is a source of support for what I am doing with Campus PrideNet. He has been a true friend and a treasure.

The second person is my partner in life, Thomas Feldman. When we met over ten years ago, he inspired me to do what I do today. Together we are unstoppable and he is my "head cheerleader" as well as my personal miracle worker. He makes all my dreams come true and I love him beyond words.

As you can tell, I have been fortunate to have so many wonderful people and organizations that have been a part of my life, this book, and the success of Campus PrideNet over the years. To all of you, I send a heartfelt thank you. But, this book does not symbolize the end; rather, it is just the beginning. Campus PrideNet has much more in store. Not only does this book pay tribute to past and present "campus queers" but it also serves as a benchmark for further LGBT progress today. The bar has been set high for campuses and the expectations are now "quite queer." Together, we can indeed change colleges and universities, one campus at a time. Let us start with yours!

ABOUT THE AUTHOR

Shane L. Windmeyer M.S., Ed., recalls his "coming out" on a small rural campus in Kansas as difficult, frightening, lonely, emotionally complex, and yet liberating—all at the same time. His commitment to LGBT issues comes from this inner strength and passion to help others coming out today, and his desire to motivate college students, gay and straight, to stand up against prejudice, bigotry, and hate against all people.

Windmeyer is co-founder and coordinator of Campus PrideNet, an online community dedicated to student leaders and campus organizations. He is often best known for his pioneering work with the Lambda 10 Project—National Clearinghouse for GLBT Fraternity and Sorority Issues. His leadership with Lambda 10 led to the publishing of his first book, Alyson Books' best-seller *Out on Fraternity Row: Personal Accounts of Being Gay in a College Fraternity*. Subsequent publications by the author have been *Secret Sisters: Stories of Being Lesbian and Bisexual in a College Sorority*; *Brotherhood: Gay Life in College Fraternities*; and he was a contributing co-author of *Inspiration for LGBT Students and Their Allies*.

Windmeyer has been featured on IN THE LIFE TV and his work has received national attention from the *New York Times*, *Rolling Stone*, and *TIME* magazine. His educational efforts also have been noted by national press such as *OUT* magazine, *The Advocate* national gay newsmagazine, *Fort Worth Star-Telegram*, *Indianapolis Star, Salon* magazine, *HERO* magazine, *U.* magazine, and the *Chronicle of Higher Education*.

Windmeyer graduated from Emporia State University with a bachelor's degree in communication and received his master's degree in higher education and student affairs administration from Indiana University. He lives in Charlotte, North Carolina. www.ShaneWindmeyer.com.